Frederick Lowell Houghton

Holstein-Friesian cattle

A history of the breed and its development in America

Frederick Lowell Houghton

Holstein-Friesian cattle
A history of the breed and its development in America

ISBN/EAN: 9783743323988

Manufactured in Europe, USA, Canada, Australia, Japa

Cover: Foto ©ninafisch / pixelio.de

Manufactured and distributed by brebook publishing software (www.brebook.com)

Frederick Lowell Houghton

Holstein-Friesian cattle

Holstein-Friesian Cattle.

A HISTORY OF THE BREED

AND ITS

DEVELOPMENT IN AMERICA.

A COMPLETE LIST OF ALL PRIVATE AND AUTHENTICATED
MILK AND BUTTER YIELDS; METHODS OF BREED-
ING, HANDLING, FEEDING AND SHOWING.

*OVER ONE HUNDRED ILLUSTRATIONS OF FAMOUS CATTLE AND
BIOGRAPHIES OF LEADING BREEDERS, ETC., ETC.*

BY

FREDERICK L. HOUGHTON,

Editor of the Holstein-Friesian Register; Secretary and Editor of the Holstein-Friesian Association of America.

BRATTLEBORO, VT.:
PRESS OF THE HOLSTEIN-FRIESIAN REGISTER.
1897.

PREFACE.

IN PREPARING this work free use has been made of all available writings, including among other works the HOLSTEIN-FRIESIAN REGISTER and the Holstein and Dutch-Friesian Herd Books, to which due acknowledgment is made.

Grateful acknowledgment is made of the very valuable assistance of that profound dairy student and originator of the Advanced Registry system, Mr. Solomon Hoxie, and to those enterprising owners of Holstein-Friesian cattle upon whose advance subscription of over fourteen hundred copies this work is published.

CONTENTS.

CHAPTER.	PAGE.
I—Historical—Holland, a Cow's Paradise,	9
II—Ancestry of the Breed—System of Dairying—As a Race Stock—Earliest American Importations.	14
III—Prof. Roberts' Observations—J. H. Klippart's Description,	18
IV—Holland—Dutch Farm Houses and Stables—Methods of Handling—Hay Making—Stabling in Holland,	22
V—How Breed was Developed—Spread of the Breed in Europe,	31
VI—Milk—Quantity Yielded—Prof. Hengerveld—Prof. Stewart—King of Wirtemberg's Records—Klippart's Reports of Records—Average Yield in Holland,	37
VII—The Breed in America—Records at Shadeland—Some Remarkable Instances—Piertertje 2d, etc.—Largest Yearly Records—Actual Results,	41
VIII—Quality of Milk — Microscopic Appearance — Butter Exports from Holland—Comparison with Other Breeds—Cheese Production—Analyses of Milk—J. Van der Breggen's Statistics,	51
IX—Acclimation—Flexibility,	59
X—As a Butter Breed—Friesland's Production—American Experiences: Wells, Dudley, Yeomans, Wales, Smiths & Powell Co., Powell Bros., M. E. Moore, Dutcher, W. S. Morse, Gillett & Son—Clothilde 2d—Parthenea's Record—Natsey—Smiths & Powell's Heifers—Pauline Paul—Iowa Station—Smiths & Powell,	61
XI—Dairy Yields—Grade Holsteins,	78
XII—Michigan Agricultural College,	84
XIII—In Public Competition,	89
XIV—Tests at Experiment Stations,	115
XV—Holstein-Friesian Advanced Registry,	121
XVI—Scale of Points of the Holstein-Friesian Association,	130
XVII—Value of Holstein-Friesian Cattle for Beef and Veal,	135
XVIII—As a General Purpose Cattle,	153
XIX—Feeding for Butter Fat and Milk,	159
XX—Feeding,	163
XXI—Balanced Rations, for Calf, for Milk and Growing Weanlings and Yearlings—For Heifers—For Cows Due in the Spring—For Milk, Butter and Development—For Large Cows,	169
XXII—Families of the Breed: Aaggie, Netherland, Clothilde, Artis, Aegis, Johanna, Wayne, Mutual Friend, Pauline Paul,	178
XXIII—Care of the Cow at Calving,	197
XXIV—Rearing of Calves for the Dairy,	205
XXV—The Selection of a Sire,	223
XXVI—Preparing for the Show Ring,	231
XXVII—Some American Breeders, illustrated with 27 Portraits,	241
XXVIII—Milk and Butter Records,	305

LIST OF ILLUSTRATIONS.

	PAGE		PAGE
Pauline Paul,	*frontispiece*	Johanna 5th,	146
Aaggie Family,	12	Koningin Van Friesland 5th,	147
Aaggie 2d,	16	Koningin Van Friesland Pietertje,	149
Aegis,	19	Lady De Vries,	150
Aegis' Netherland Prince,	23	Lady of Broek 2d,	152
Amleto,	26	Lakeside Clarissa,	154
America,	29	Lutscke,	155
Avery's Oxen,	32	Maid of Vernon,	156
Billy Boelyn,	36	Maude D.,	158
Bowen,	40	Margaret Lincoln 2d's De Kol,	160
Burly,	44	Mechtchilde,	162
Boonstra,	46	Mercedes,	164
Calamity Jane,	48	Mercedes 2d,	166
Carlotta and Calf,	52	Mercedes 3d,	168
Clothilde 5th's Netherland,	56	Mink,	170
Castine,	59	Mooie,	172
Clothilde Family,	63	Netherland Alban,	173
Clothilde,	68	Netherland Baroness,	175
Count Clothilde,	71	Netherland Consul and Ideal's Lena,	177
Constantyn,	76	Netherland Dowager,	178
Chief of Maple Hill 4th,	79	Netherland Duchess,	179
Count Aaggie Clothilde,	82	Netherland Family,	180
Howtje D.,	84	Netherland Queen,	182
Belle Sarcastic,	85	Netherland Statesman's Cornelius,	184
Rosa Bonheur 5th,	88	Netherland Prince,	185
Copia,	91	Oakland Chief,	187
Colantha,	94	Ononis,	187
De Kol 2d,	97	Parthenea's 2d Sir Henry,	189
De Brave Hendrik,	100	Parana Abbekerk 2d,	191
De Ruiter,	103	Paul Alban De Kol,	193
De Schott and Twin Calves,	105	Pietertje 2d's Koningin,	194
De Vries,	108	Prince of Altidjwerk,	196
Ethelka,	110	Prince of Edam,	198
Ethelzeda,	113	Princess of Wayne and Calf,	200
Eunice Clay,	115	Princess of Wayne 3d,	202
Genesta 2d,	117	Queen of Wayne and Calf,	204
Gerben,	120	Royal Aaggie,	206
Hykolina,	122	Netherland Hengerveld,	208
Inka 4th,	124	Rhoda,	210
Iolena Fairmount,	125	Rijaneta,	211
Jaap 4th,	127	Schuiling,	212
Jacoba Hartog,	129	Shadeland Boon,	214
Jamaica and Calf,	131	Sir Jewel Echo Mechtchilde,	216
Jepma 2d,	133	De Kol 2d's Pauline,	217
Jacob 2d,	136	Sir Netherland Clothilde,	218
Jewel,	138	Sir Newton of Aaggie,	219
Jewel 2d,	140	Sjoerd,	220
Jewel Echo,	142	Soldene 2d's Netherland,	221
Johanna,	144	Soldene 2d's Clothilde,	222
Tietje 2d,	224	Vaseline,	236
Tettje Janzen,	226	Violet,	237
Texelaar,	228	Violet V. Boelyn,	239

LIST OF ILLUSTRATIONS.

	PAGE		PAGE
Third Unadilla Twisk,	230	Violet Family,	313
Tritomia,	232	Vreda,	313
Tirania's Sir Mechthilde.	233	Yuinne,	322
Tirannia,	234	Zozo,	322
Uncle Tom,	235		

SOME AMERICAN BREEDERS.

	PAGE		PAGE
Ayers Augustine R.,	240	Hoxie Solomon,	280
Bedell E. T.,	242	Huidekoper Edgar,	282
Benninger W. M.,	244	Judd Leroy F.,	284
Breuer H. F. W.,	246	Krueger C. H.,	286
Burchard S.,	248	Langdon S. A.,	288
Burke Frank H.,	250	La Grange J. W.,	290
Chenery Winthrop W...	252	Moore M. E.,	292
Coley J. W.,	254	Nauman B.,	294
Dodge Thomas H.,	256	Powell E. A.,	296
Downer L. A.,	258	Roe Frank,	298
Du Bois Solomon,	260	Smith E. F.,	300
Gardner Malcolm H.,	262	Stevens Henry,	302
Gillett W. J.,	264	Stone J. L,	304
Hallman A. C.,	266	Trexler E. W.,	306
Ham J. M.,	268	Wood Don J.,	308
Harp John D.,	270	Woodyard J. F.,	310
Harriman Fred E.,	272	Wright S. N.,	312
Haviland Joseph,	274	Whitcomb J. H. D ,	314
Holdemann H. N.,	276	Yeomans T. G.,	316
Houghton Charles,	278		

PAULINE PAUL, 21999 H. H. B., A. R. 852.

Butter record, 1153 lbs. 15½ oz. in 365 consecutive days. This record stands unequalled by a cow of any breed.

HOLSTEIN-FRIESIAN CATTLE.

CHAPTER I.

HISTORICAL—HOLLAND, A COW'S PARADISE.

The first importation to America of cattle from Holland was undoubtedly made by the early Dutch settlers. The history of the Holstein-Friesian breed in America, probably, begins with the importation sent out to John Lincklaen, agent of the Holland Land Company at Cazenovia, Madison Co., New York, in 1795. These early importations had but little permanent effect upon the cattle of the country, and the first really practical work of introducing the great Dutch Dairy breed began with the importations of Winthrop W. Chenery, of Belmont, Mass., in 1861. There is so much of interest in this wonderful breed that you turn to ancient history for details of its origin, but with meagre satisfaction, however The historian Motley said, in speaking of Holland in the seventeenth century: "On that scrap of solid ground rescued by human energy from the ocean, were the most fertile pastures in the world, an ox often weighed 2,000 lbs., the cows produced two and three calves at a time, and the sheep four and five lambs. In a single village 4,000 kine were counted. Butter and cheese were exported to the annual value of one million dollars, salted provisions to an incredible extent. The farmers were industrious, thriving and independent."

A French historian, writing in 1350, says : "At a certain siege the besieged could only receive their supply of butter from Holland, which had been famous for its dairy products for five hundred years."

Along the western shores of the European continent, between the 51st and 54th parallels, the small kingdom of the Netherlands stretches its sandy dunes and mighty dikes, whereby this low and level country is guarded against the ravages of the North Sea. As a nation its inhabitants have made their mark in the history of the world. As a colonial power it still ranks only second to England, and as a dairy country it attracts the attention of breeders of dairy cattle in all parts of the world. The wonderful adaptability of the soil and climate has brought about the rearing and breeding of cattle, from the very moment that the low lands of Northwestern Europe became inhabited by the Friesians and Batavians.

From the earliest accounts of the Friesian people they have dwelt upon the shores of the North Sea and possessed herds of cattle, from which they derived their chief means of support. Their history commences about three hundred years before the Christian era. They then inhabited a country between the river Ems and the middle arm of the Rhine. From whence they came is a matter of conjecture. There is a tradition that their progenitors came out of India and that the mother of the race was as white as snow. They appear, even at that early date, to have been a peaceable people, loving pastoral pursuits. If it is true that they came from Central Asia it is probable that they brought their cattle with them and that they journeyed westward to the shores of the North Sea in search of pasturage. Two hundred years later a German tribe came out of Hesse, a district on the upper Rhine, where they were living in hostility with their neighbors, and settled on the shores of the North Sea near the Friesians. They first occupied an island formed by the rivers Rhine, Maas and Waal, to which they gave the name of Batavia. They were also breeders of cattle, but whether they brought their herds with them or obtained them from the Friesians is unknown. It has been conjectured that they brought their cattle with them and that their cattle were black ; that the Friesian cattle at this time were a pure white and from the cross of the two the foundation of the present Holstein-Friesian breed was laid. Whatever may have been the fact, the cattle of these two tribes henceforth appear identical in history. The Roman historians, who wrote at the beginning of the Christian era, speak of these tribes as owning many cattle. Cæsar says, "they used them in traffic with one another and gave them as dowry to their children." Tacitus repeats the information, but says that "their cattle did not excel in beauty." Very little is said of their appearance and characteristics. We learn, however, that some of them were white and that cattle of this color were held in religious veneration. From this we naturally infer that white cattle were not common and that the great majority were then piebald as at the present day. The conditions under which they were kept must have rendered them rough and uncouth in appearance. The system of diking and draining that has made the provinces of North Holland and Friesland one of the best grass producing sections of the earth was then scarcely begun and the whole country must have been largely a succession of lakes, marshes, sand-hills and fertile strips along the water courses, subject to frequent inundation. Grasses poor in quality, dwarf on the sand hills and rank in the marshes, must have prevailed and constituted their only food, both in summer and in winter. The limited forests that may have existed in some sections may have afforded them partial shelter from the terrible storms that swept over the country from the North Sea. Yet we conclude that their owners, from the earliest times, were compelled to share their own rude dwellings with them in the severest weather. About the beginning of the Christian era these two tribes came virtually under the Roman yoke, although in the form of an alliance with the Roman power. The Friesians from this time forward, to the close of the Roman power, paid an annual tax of ox hides and ox horns to the Roman government. In lieu of this tax the Batavians furnished a contingent of soldiers to the Roman army, commanded by their own officers, which became especially distinguished in the various Roman wars. In this contrast of action the two tribes are illustrated very plainly in character. The Friesians in their love of pastoral pursuits preferred the breeding of cattle to the honors of war. The love which has always characterized them has bound them together and kept them a distinct people for more than two thousand years. It has also made them most conservative and has kept them breeding the same strain of cattle unadulterated, except from accidental circumstances, from the earliest knowledge of them to the present time. Rich river bottoms were protected from the flood, lakes and bays reclaimed and the well-known Polders appeared, whose inexhaustible fruitfulness still makes the meadows of the Netherlands unsurpassed in the production of grass, cattle and dairy products. During the thirteenth, fourteenth, fifteenth and sixteenth centuries, the production of butter and cheese, especially in the provinces of North and South Holland, was simply enormous, and history tells, also, of remarkably heavy meat cattle, weighing from twenty-six hundred to three thousand pounds, and presented to princes and warriors in these turbulent times.

With the Roman dominion came Roman improvements in the system of cattle raising, but no mixture of blood in the people or in the cattle. Diking and draining were systematized and greatly extended. Many of the great alluvial meadows, which distinguished this lowland country, were then produced. Improved methods of feeding and management of cattle followed. The dwellings became immense structures, designed as much for the protection of cattle as for the comfort of the family. Larger estates were occupied. Prof. Hengerveld describes one of these ancient estates, several of which remain at the present time: "The Manor House, with its various stables, was surrounded by kitchen gardens, parks, meadows, duck ponds, dikes, canals and ditches; by peasant cottages, with their cow stables and granaries, while the whole was enclosed in the encircling of some river formation." He continues: "It is true from that time to the present many changes have been effected, and the estates are less extensive, but in the main everything shows imitation of the ancient Roman villa." He says, in substance, that the method and purpose for which they have continued breeding cattle to the present time have essentially remained unchanged. The preservation of the Friesian people and their continued adhesion to cattle breeding for more than two thousand years is one of the marvels of history. Always few in number, the conflicts of war and commerce have raged over and around them, yet they have remained in or near their original home, continuously following their original pursuits. Their farm houses are fashioned after the same general model; such a farm house resembles a great castle and is still surrounded by a broad deep ditch, impassable, except by some artificial means. Over this are thrown one or more bridges, guarded by strong gates and heavy bolts. The immense roof of this farm house covers everything that requires protection. Here the cattle find shelter during the long and rigorous winter months. Here they are fed and watched for months without being turned from the door. Here the family are also sheltered, sometimes with only a single partition between the cattle stalls and the kitchen. Everything is kept with a degree of neatness marvelous to those not accustomed to such system.

The cattle become the pets of the household. At the opening of spring, when the grass is sufficiently grown, they are taken to the fields and cared for in the most quiet manner. They are never worried by dogs and are required to move about only to gather their food. The grasses upon which they feed are very rich and luxuriant. On the first appearance of winter they are returned to the stable and the simple round of the year is completed. This round is repeated year after year until they are six or seven years of age, when they are driven to the shambles. Their object is always to produce as much milk and beef as possible from the same animal. With this two-fold object in view, selection, breeding and feeding have been continued for ages by a whole race of farmers. They have had few men of remarkable genius that have risen far above their fellows in the work of improvement, but each breeder has contributed his share without special recognition. They have never tolerated in-and-in breeding, and have never produced (distinct) families of marked superiority, although differences in soil in different localities have produced different classes, varying in size and slightly in other characteristics. On the richest soils the finest cattle are produced.

The Hollanders have been specialists, in fact, for many generations. A visitor among them in the summer time is struck by the number of cattle that occupy their fields. Herds of cows are on every hand. The land seems wholly given up to them.

There is no fruit growing, very little grain raising, and nothing similar to what they call mixed husbandry. The care of cows, the gathering of food for them, the manufacture and disposal of their products, occupy the attention of the people to an extent that it is difficult to comprehend by one who has not been among them. These dairy men are mostly tenant farmers, the fee simple of the soil, as in England and many other parts of Europe long under the ancient feudal system, is in the hands of large land holders, who, as a rule, do not reside among them.

To Americans the rents paid by these dairymen seem enormous. Upon the best lands an annual rent of from fifteen to twenty dollars per acre is paid. The soil is fertile, yet it is no better than the superior dairy land of America. Their abilities to pay such rents depend largely upon the economy and skill with which they handle their herds and the character of the cattle.

A lady traveler, Eleanor H. Patterson, recently returned from Holland, writes of it as a cow's paradise. She says: "Washed, combed, groomed, petted and luxuriantly stabled in winter, like the finest of our race horses, and put to graze in flowery, well-watered green fields in summer, the cows of Holland can envy no animal the world over.

"The two lions represented upon the heraldic shield of the Netherlands might well be replaced by two great black and white Holstein-Friesian cows, for the masses of the people worship cows. Cows they watch sometimes with more care than they give their own children, cows they nurse through sickness, cows they save their money to buy, and of cows they talk while awake and dream while asleep!

"Children are brought up with the parental reverence for cows, and no member of the human family is thought too good to sleep under the same roof with the beloved kine. The traveler landing in Holland during the springtime will see vast herds of fine cattle in every stretch of green meadows, and green meadows are everywhere in this flat and almost treeless country. Every shadeless field is defined by a stream of pure water flowing between trim, flowery banks, which serve instead of fences to keep the cattle within bounds.

"A grotesque sight to people from countries where cows are not of the first importance is the spectacle of the most delicate and valuable cows enveloped

AAGGIE FAMILY.

in canvas covering. The costly creatures, lately freed from their warm winter quarters, are apt to take cold from the inclemencies of the early spring, hence their blankets are not removed until the weather becomes safely warm. The cattle remain under the blue vault of heaven day and night from the first of May until the first of November, then they are taken into the cow-houses to remain through the cold Holland winter. During the summer the cows are milked twice a day in the field.

"Cow stable is to us a name for an humble and unclean edifice, but a cow stable in Holland has another meaning. No parlor is purer nor more carefully tended than the habitation of the much loved kine. The busy Dutch farmer does not usually care to give any of his time to curiosity seekers, and it is not always easy for the stranger to gain admission to his household, but we secured a letter to a farmer near Broek, in North Holland, which admitted us to his cow-house and to his residence at the same time. Both were under one roof. Cow stable and parlor adjoined, and one was quite as clean as the other. We were conducted to the stable first, which in reality was a wide hall with a strip of oilcloth down the centre. Rows of tiny square windows, high up on both sides, were curtained with spotless lace or thin white net tied back with ribbon; pots of blooming flowers were set on the sills of the windows looking south. Beneath each curtained window was a cow-stall, there were twenty-six in all—such luxuriant and dainty little places! On the floors, which were of porcelain, a thick layer of clean white sawdust had been placed, and this was stamped into patterns of stars and wheels and various geometrical designs. Of course the return of the cows from the fields to their winter quarters breaks these pretty sawdust designs into a confused mass, but during the summer they are carefully preserved thus. Before and behind each row of stalls runs a trough of clear water—the first for the cow to drink from, the second to wash away all impurities. In the ceiling behind every stall is fixed a kind of iron hook, whose strange and ludicrous office is to hold high in the air the cow's tail that she may not soil that carefully combed member. One wonders that the cows' tails after many generations of this tying up process do not grow straight up. One extravagant book of travels tries to make us believe that the tails are often tied with blue ribbon, but this we found to be an exaggeration.

"It is not, however, an exaggeration that the cattle every day during the winter are washed off with warm soap suds, dried, rubbed, coddled and talked to as if they were children, that the air of the stable is as pure as the atmosphere outside, and that no pains are spared to keep them healthy and comfortable. Under such kind treatment they become such plump, glossy and gentle animals that they repay their owners by an enormous quantity of milk.

"Leading us from the cow stable into an adjoining apartment, the farmer's wife showed us long rows of cheese presses containing round, firm Edam cheeses which would be ready to remove from their moulds after thirty-six hours of pressure. Every press, every bowl, every churn, every linen cloth, every pot and pan used in the making of this cheese spoke of the most absolute cleanliness and told of the hours of washing and scrubbing and rubbing. After seeing the sweetness of the cheese-making process in Holland, I made a vow to eat Dutch cheese whenever I could get it. In cleanliness and purity it can be excelled by no manufactured article of food in the world. 'Clean, clean, clean,' we repeated again and again, and the rosy little farmer's wife smiled with pleasure. Clean was only the one English word she could understand. She invited us into the living-room, just in front of the cows' apartment, and offered us milk. As we drank we looked around the room and sniffed the air suspiciously, but although the stable was adjoining, not the slightest odor of cows could we detect in that clean little room.

"The one elegant piece of furniture here was a tall, carved Dutch chest. Our hostess opened the doors of this and displayed piles of white linen therein— enough to start a shop. Opening another door, which we had supposed led into another room, we saw it was simply the door to the bed, which was just a shelf in the wall piled high with feathers and linen. Whether the Hollanders shut themselves in entirely in these curious beds, or leave the doors ajar while asleep, I could not learn. 'Perhaps they are the cows' beds,' suggested the giddy one of our number: 'ask her.' The smiling little woman shook her head in reply to the question, though after what we had just seen we should hardly have been surprised if she had told us that on cold winter nights the cows curled themselves in these downy niches in the wall."

CHAPTER II.

ANCESTRY OF THE BREED—SYSTEM OF DAIRYING—AS A RACE STOCK—EARLIEST AMERICAN IMPORTATIONS.

The ancestry of these cattle may be traced unalloyed for more than two thousand years. The history of the Netherlands goes back three hundred years before the commencement of the Christian era. At that time that portion of the country bordering on the North Sea was called Fresia. It extended over the present provinces of North Holland, Friesland and Groningen, and over the German border to the river Ems. Its inhabitants were classed by the Romans with the Northern barbarians. They differed from their neighbors in their love of peaceful pursuits, especially the care and breeding of cattle.

In 1282 came the decisive inundation that produced the Zuyder Zee, a broad and permanent channel from the sea far inland, separating these cattle breeders into two groups—the western occupying a stretch of country that was for a long time called West Friesland, now constituting the major part of North Holland; the eastern, the present provinces of Friesland and Groningen. In the western division, the influence of Batavian and Celtic blood has rendered the inhabitants less conservative, and changed the language to modern Hollandish. In both divisions the cattle are of the same blood; they are kept in the same manner, and used for the same purpose. The farmers are all dairymen, and all combine the production of butter, cheese, veal and beef in their pursuits.

"The system of dairying pursued differs slightly in the two divisions," says Mr. S. Hoxie. "In Friesland butter making takes precedence. From the skim-milk cheese is made; the whey is fed to calves or older cattle, with an allowance of oil cake. Their cattle are always kept in what American farmers would call a superior condition. In North Holland the only material variation from this system is in making cheese from the milk immediately as it comes from the herd. The noted Edam cheese is thus produced.

"It will be noticed that these systems involve the utilization of every cattle product—milk, butter, cheese, veal and beef. They thus draw profits from both the leading tendencies of bovine nature—milk giving and flesh making. They give no credit to the theory that the functions of the one antagonize those of the other. On the contrary, they have demonstrated on the largest possible scale that when intense activity of the functions of one ceases, if an animal is normally developed, healthy and well fed, intense activity of the functions of the other begins.

"In looking on their herds there is a strong impression that these peasant farmers are correct in their views. The broad loins and wide rumps of their cattle seem just the place for the finest quality of beef, and equally the proper support of capacious udders.

"At two years of age, with rare exceptions, they commence giving milk, and at six or seven years old they uniformly go loaded with flesh to the butcher. These dairymen do not lose their dairy plant at the end of every eight or ten years in a lot of old and worthless cows. They sell their cows well fattened at an age when their flesh is of the best quality. The price obtained pays for extra food that may have been used, and replaces them at a profit with younger animals."

As a race stock, these cattle have become widely noted. They have sent off-shoots to all the richer grass sections of Northern and Central Europe. In some instances these have been established so long that, prevailing over the native cattle and slightly changed by environment, they have taken names corresponding to their location. Some of the most renowned breeds of Europe are of such origin. Among these are the Flanders breed of Belgium and France, the Brittenburg and Oldenburg breeds of Germany, and the Kolmogorian breed of Russia.

Our Secretary of State in 1883 procured reports from our consuls upon the breeds and products of cattle throughout the world. From Belgium such reports call special attention to the Hollandaise, or Dutch cow, and the

Flamande, or Belgium cow. In one of these reports the consul says, "The breeds to which I allude present, in outward appearance and in results both for dairy and for beef cattle that cannot be surpassed in the world."

The reports from France are confirmatory of those from Belgium. The origin of the Flemish cattle, the pure Flamande breed and the sub-breeds that have taken the names Boulonaise and Artesienne, are credited to importations from the shore of the North Sea. "Whence," says one of the writers, "came the breeds of Holland Schleswig Holstein and Jutland, all remarkable for their milking qualities." Similar reports also come from Germany. The consul of the province of Silesia selected four hundred of the largest herds of cattle in his district, with the view of ascertaining the favorite breed; two hundred and seventy-two handled exclusively pure Dutch cattle, the balance was occupied by a dozen or more of other breeds and their grades. The most interesting of all was that from Consul General Stanton of St. Petersburg. He found on the fertile lands at the river Dwina, within two and one half degrees of the Arctic circle, an off-shoot of this race named after the locality, the Kolmogorian breed. It was originally a cross between this breed and the native cattle of Archangel, and dated from the time of Peter the Great. It is remarkable for its yield of milk, and the fine quality of veal which it produces.

It is the favorite breed of St. Petersburg, and it is used to improve other Russian breeds. In the seventeenth and eighteenth centuries, the Holland cattle appeared to have been largely imported into the British Isles, and became most influential in the formation of some of the most renowned breeds of England and Scotland. Prof. Low, whose writings are regarded as eminent authority on the British breeds, says: "The Dutch breed was especially established in the district of Holderness, on the north side of the Humber, whence it extended northward through the plains of Yorkshire, and the cattle of Holderness still retain the distinct traces (in 1840) of their Dutch origin, and were long regarded as the finest dairy cows of England. Further to the north in the first fertile district of the Tees, importations likewise took place of the cattle of the opposite countries, sometimes from Holland, from Holstein or the countries on the Elbe." He adds: "Of the precise extent of these early importations we are imperfectly informed, but that they exercised a great influence on the native stock appears from this circumstance, that the breed formed by the mixture became familiarly known as the Dutch or Holstein breed, under which name it extended northward through Northumberland, and became naturalized in the south of Scotland. It was also known as the Teeswater or Shorthorn breed," from whence our modern improved Shorthorn breed originated.

Sanford Howard, an equally eminent authority, in writing of the Ayrshire breed, says. "It is nothing improbable that the chief nucleus of the improved breed was the Dunlop stock so-called, which appears to have been possessed by a distinguished family by the name of Dunlop, in the Cunningham district of Ayrshire as early as 1780. This stock was derived at least in part from animals imported from Holland."

The attention of American breeders has never been called to Holstein-Friesian cattle to any extent until within the last twenty years. The fact of our using a common language with our English cousins, and the assumption of English breeders that they alone possessed breeds of cattle worthy of our attention, have been a bar to our study of the Continental breeds, one that even now is difficult for many to break over.

Yet it is inferred that a strain of these cattle was introduced into this country at an early date from 1021 to 1664. The eastern part of the State of New York was the Dutch colony of New Netherlands. During this period many Holland farmers settled along the Hudson river and in the rich valley of the Mohawk. They probably brought cattle with them from their native land and crossed them with cattle purchased from the other colony. One thing there is a certainty, for many years after the cattle of the Mohawk valley were called Dutch cattle and were especially esteemed for their milking qualities.

The first importation of which we have any knowledge was made more than one hundred years later. It consisted of six cows and two bulls and was sent in 1795 by the Holland Land Company, which then owned large tracts in the State of New York, to their agent, Mr. John Lincklaen of Cazenovia. As described by one of the early settlers of that village, "the cows were of the size of oxen, their colors clear black and white in large patches; very handsome

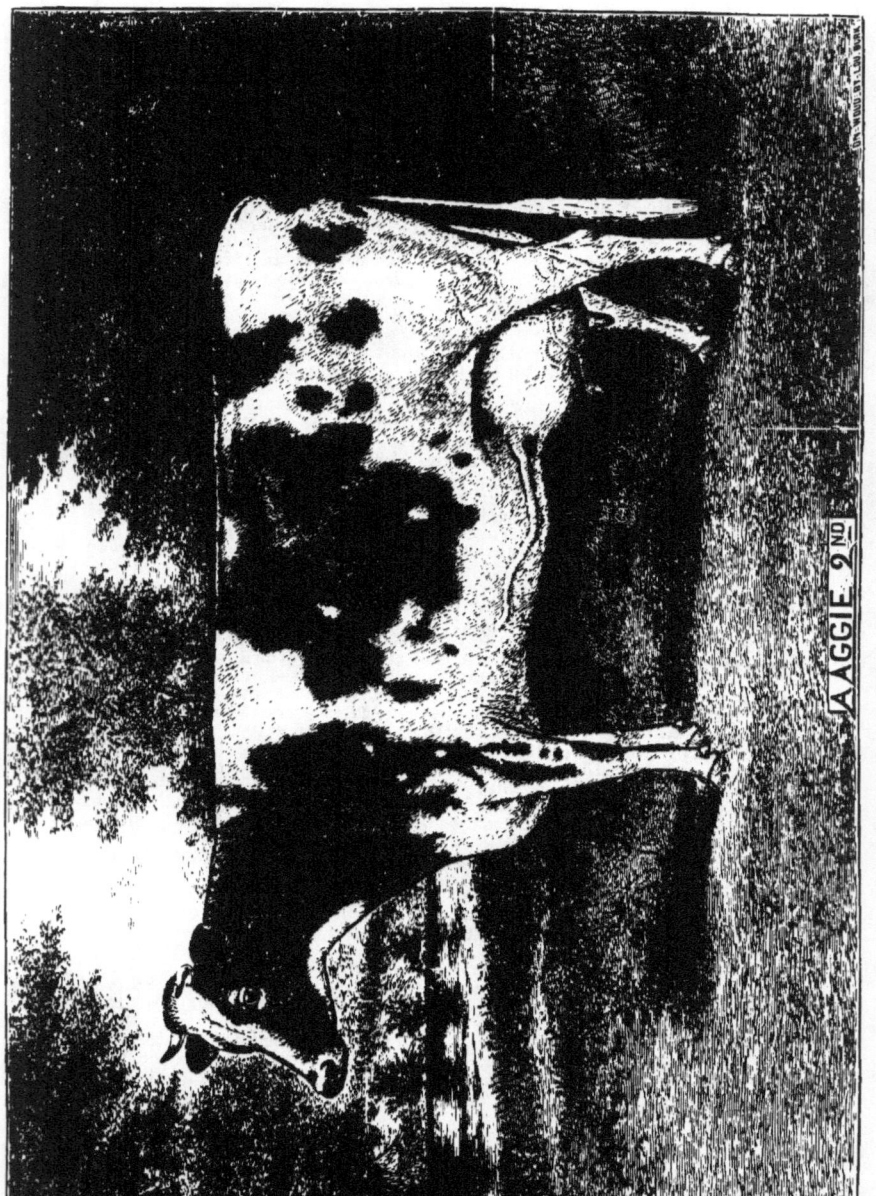

AAGGIE 2D, No. 1280 H. H. B.; Advanced Registry, No. 3.

EARLY IMPORTATIONS.

bodies and straight-limbed horns middling in size but gracefully set; their necks were seemingly too slender to carry their heads."

In 1810 a bull and two cows were imported by the Hon. William Jarvis and placed on his farm at Wethersfield, Vt. About the year 1825 another importation was made by Herman Le Roy, a part of which were sent into the valley of the Genesee. The rest were kept near New York City. Still later an importation was made into the State of Delaware. No records were kept of the descendants of these cattle. Their blood was mingled and lost in that of the native cattle, yet its impress was long recognized in the various localities to which these importations went.

The first permanent introduction of this breed was due to the perseverance of Hon. Winthrop W. Cheney of Belmont, Mass. His first two importations and their increase with the exception of a single animal were destroyed by the government in Massachusetts in consequence of a contagious disease by which they were unfortunately attacked. He made a third importation in 1861. This was followed in 1867 by an importation for the Hon. Gerrit S. Miller, of Peterboro, N. Y., made by his brother, Dudley Miller, who had been attending the noted agricultural schools at Eldena, Prussia, where this breed was regarded with great favor. These two importations with an Oldenburg cow owned by Hon. William A. Russell, of Lawrence, Mass., and three animals from East Friesland, imported by Gen. William S. Tilton of the National Military Asylum, Togus, Me., formed the nucleus of the Holstein Herd Book, the first volume of which was published in 1872.

The time was propitious for the introduction of a breed with the characteristics of these cattle. Dairying had become an important industry in the Northern States, and was extending to the prairie land of the West, where especially large cattle were demanded. No breed ever spread with such rapidity. Its progress was opposed by strong prejudice, yet it seemed to gather new force from every public manifestation of such opposition, until now, twenty-five years from the publication of that apparently insignificant volume, it has become one of the largest and most popular breeds in our country.

Notwithstanding the antiquity of this breed its first herd book was that issued by American breeders in 1872 [The Association of Breeders of Thoroughbred Holstein Cattle]. This was followed in 1875 by one in the Netherlands, its original home. Five years later another was published in America by an association of breeders who objected to the name Holstein by which they were generally known in this country and against which there was strong protest from the breeders in Europe. In view of their origin and the source from whence they were imported this association adopted the name Dutch-Friesian. In the same year another herd book was issued in and for the province of Friesland, where the breed has been especially guarded for ages.

Since then herd books of these cattle have been published both in Belgium and Germany. In 1885 the two American associations compromised on the name Holstein-Friesian and united their records. In their native country none but select cattle are admitted to the herd book. It is not enough that they are pure bred, they must also be superior. This requirement is of the highest importance. Being the "common cattle" of the Netherlands, and handled by all classes of breeders some of whom are indifferent to their standing, in whose hands they degenerate as in other hands they improve, there are great diversities in their build, quality and capacity.

To the credit of American importers they have generally sought for the best, yet it is beginning to be felt that continued selection is the basis for continued success. This is true not only of the breeders of these cattle, but also of those handling other leading breeds. In consequence of this a system of Advanced Registry has been commenced for this breed in this country, conditioned on the superior build and quality, and especially on capacity for milk or butter production. This system will be found fully detailed in another chapter of this work.

CHAPTER III.

OBSERVATIONS OF PROF. ROBERTS—AND OF J. H. KLIPPART.

American skill and enterprise find in this breed peculiar material on which to work. It is as hardy as the American scrub, it has no hereditary tendencies to disease of any kind, and it is peculiarly plastic in its adaptations, as may be seen by its perfect acclimation in the rigorous climate of Archangel, as well as in the sunny climate of France.

And as an object of pleasure and beauty no cattle respond more generously or appear more picturesque on a background of green fields and none are more emblematic of rural wealth and content.

"I had the good fortune," said Prof. I. P. Roberts of Cornell University, N. Y., in an address before the New York Dairymen's Association, "to spend some time in North Holland and Friesland, a country usually ignored by the tourist though full of instructive sights and quaint old customs. Here in ancient grass bottomed lakes, snatched from the inroads of the sea by the greatest skill and labor the world has ever known, I found the ideal milk producer. Situated in a level, rich, moist country, well adapted to the production of forage grasses, with the climate cool but equable in summer, but raw, windy and cold in winter; here favored, yet unfavored by nature, these clean, plain, intelligent Dutch have reduced to a science the economical production of milk. Of course this could not be done without a good cow and if anywhere on the face of the globe there exists a race of uniformly good milkers, the Dutch have them. I care not what a man's prejudices may be, whether an admirer of the fawn-eyed Jersey or (like myself), of that grand old breed the Shorthorn, the stately Hereford or of the piebald Ayrshire, if he really admire a good cow he cannot help falling in love with the picturesque Holstein as seen in its native pastures in the north country. He may return to his American home and conclude that his circumstances are better adapted to some other breed, but he will ever after speak of them only with praise.

"I have said they were a race of good milkers and I think I have not put it too strong when I say truthfully, that neither from Beemster Polder northward, nor in Friesland did I see what might be called a poor cow or an old cow, though I saw many hundreds. Here are people occupying lands which are seldom sold for less than five hundred dollars per acre, more frequently for a thousand and upwards, producing butter and cheese and placing it upon the European market in successful competition with that produced on lands less than a tenth of their value.

"With these facts staring us in the face it looks quite possible that we might learn something of more economical production from these mis-called dumb Dutch, notwithstanding they still cut their grass by hand, have no tongues or thills to their farm wagons, and wear wooden shoes. Without a herd book until quite recently and without any great leaders or improvers in cattle breeding as found in Bakewell, Colling, Bates and Booth in England, these quiet people, having no common-sense and universal method, long since formed a distinct breed of cattle that surpasses in their locality all others so far as tried. Jerseys have been introduced but cannot secure a footing. Here and there at long intervals we find an effort has been made to improve by a cross of the English bull, but so far as I could learn deterioration in milking qualities has resulted with but slight compensating improvement in beef quality.

"The details of ancient breeding and management of the Holsteins have not been handed down to us as that of the Shorthorn, but from the location and habits of the people, we may fairly infer that they differed but slightly, if at all, from those of modern times. Having unusually fine facilities I tried to study carefully their present methods and also their results.

"In the first place but few bulls are kept and these but two or three years at most, when they are sold to the market for beef. These bulls are selected with the utmost care, invariably being the calves of the choicest milkers. But little attention is paid to fancy points or color, though dark spotted is preferred to light spotted, though more attention is now being paid to color in order to suit

American customers. All other bull calves with scarce an exception are sold as veal, bringing about one and one-half times as much as with us. In like manner the heifer calves are sold except about twenty per cent, which are also selected with care and raised on skim milk. The age of the cow is usually denoted by the number of her calves, and in no case did I find a cow that had more than six calves, usually only four or five. Their rule is to breed so that the cow's first calf is dropped in the stable before the dam is two years old, in order that extra care and attention may be given. There are other objects gained by this method; for should the heifer fall below their high standard she goes to the butcher's market before another wintering, and though she brought little profit to the dairy, she will more than pay for her keeping at the block.

"Here we find a three-fold method of selection. First, in the sire; second, in the young calf, judged largely by the milking qualities of the dam; and lastly is applied the greatest of all tests, performance at pail; and not till she answers this satisfactorily is she accorded a permanent place in the dairy.

"The cows, no matter how good, are seldom kept till they become 'old worn-out shells,' valueless for beef, and not fit to propagate their kind, but are

AEGIS, No. 60 H. H.-B.
Milk record, 82 lbs. 12 oz. in one day; 16,823 lbs. 10 oz. in one year. Butter record, 18 lbs. 2 oz. in one week.

sold for beef while they are vigorous enough to put on flesh, profitable alike to producer and consumer and of no mean quality. I ate it for three weeks and the English beef for two, and while not so fat as the Shorthorn it was to my taste superior.

"My experience is not extended enough to justify me in saying they are the best breed for us, all things considered; but I believe them to be, and I hope they will not lose any of their valuable qualities in our hands by injudicious breeding and careless selection, or what is still worse and has been practiced by us in nearly all other breeds, no selection at all."

Within the last ten years, a degree of interest has been awakened in several parts of the Netherlands, with a view to the formation of such an improved breed. Two associations of breeders have been established, and a class of superior cattle selected and registered as foundation stock. At the present time (1884) this class numbers about four thousand animals, about equally divided between the Netherlands and the Friesian Associations. In the beginning neither association made any distinction in the colors, regarding all as equally pure, and worthy of entering into the formation of the improved breed. The Friesian Association has advanced to the classification of colors, and to the breeding of the variegated black and white as a distinct and separate class. This class very largely predominates. At the present time, at least nine-tenths of the registry of both herd books are of these black and white variegated cattle. Several volumes of the Friesian Herd-Book are exclusively of this class, and it requires but little foresight to discover that the time will shortly come when the other colors will be entirely dropped. In this description this class will be taken as the only rightful representatives of the breed.

This class of cattle are of very nearly uniform build, size and quality. Full grown cows will weigh from 1,000 to 1,500 pounds, in moderate flesh. The great majority, would, however, be included in a range from 1,100 to 1,300 pounds, and the mean of 1,200 pounds may be regarded as the live weight of the average Friesian cow. In the fifth volume of the Friesian Herd-Book, 198 cows are registered, ranging in age from two and one-half to seven years. The average height of these cows at the shoulders is 53.71 inches, and at the hips 54.29 inches. The average girth at the smallest circumference of the chest is 76.10 inches, and the average length of body, including shoulders and rump, is 66.24 inches. The average width across the hips, from one hook bone to the other, is 22.35 inches. These averages are made from measurements taken with much carefulness at the time the animals were offered for registry by the inspector. These cows were of the following ages: Forty-five between two and a half and three years, 85 between three and four years; 43 between four and five years, and 25 above five years. In the main register of the Dutch-Friesian Herd-Book two other measurements are found, the length from the hook bone to the outward point of the pelvic bone, and the width of the animal through at the thurl bone. (The latter measurement is taken by an instrument made in the form of a shoemaker's measure.) Measurements of 35 cows, very nearly averaging in other respects with the measurements given in the Friesian Herd-Book, are reported. The average length of these animals, from hips to rump, is 20.87 inches, and the average width at the thurl, 19.50 inches.

From these various measurements it is not difficult to construct the outline of the average Friesian cow with mathematical accuracy. There is no possible danger of exaggeration, except in the minute points. It will be seen at once that there is great capacity of chest; the girth at the smallest circumference is nearly six and a half feet. Here is room for the vital organs, and an assurance of a strong and vigorous constitution. The brisket is not generally low, but the chest is round and full, carrying the shoulders well out. This roundness is continued backward in the spread of the ribs and the girth of the abdomen. There is a rapid increase in circumference, giving the wedge form, but the belly does not sag, although of great dimensions. The animal appears trim and symmetrical in body. By further studying these measurements, the great capacity of the pelvic region will also be seen. The average width at the hips is 22.35 inches; at the thurl, 19.50 inches, while the length from hips to rump is 20.87 inches. These measurements include a surface of at least four hundred square inches immediately over the reproductive and milk secreting organs. Thus it will be seen that in the three great departments of the animal structure, the chest, abdomen and pelvic region, there is extraordinary development. Now if the bones are fine, we may expect superiority in milk and beef production. In the living animal this fineness is especially noticeable in the tail and in the limbs below the hocks and knees. The bones of the head and horns are also fine. The skin, though of good thickness, is soft and mellow, and the hair of a texture indicative of fineness of organization.

In filling up this outline, we fortunately have the description of Mr. John H. Klippart, late Secretary of the Ohio State Board of Agriculture. No one can question his impartiality. He had no interest in the breed, except to fairly report it, with many others, to his constituents. He says: "The most celebrated of the Holland cattle are the Friesians, which are regarded as the original stock of all. They belong to what may with propriety be called the heavy breeds, and are remarkable for their very fine bones, fine and mellow hide, and peculiar coloring. The head is long, rather narrow, with fine, light bones, but has rather a broad or wide mouth. The horns are short and fine, curving inward and downward. The neck is long and fine, somewhat curved downward on the top: the brisket well set, which is always characteristic of the lowland race. The withers and the back are broad, and as nearly level as the Shorthorn, as well as the peculiarly broad and projecting hips; the tail well set, long and fine; the chest broad and deep, and in good proportion to the belly. The limbs are fine, rather longer than in the Shorthorn, but equally fine; the bag in the cows well developed." He further adds: "The Holland bull is as large, as broad and level on the back, has the same shaped head, neck, horns, nostrils and muzzle as the Shorthorn, but lacks in development of brisket. The head, neck and horns of the Holland cow are finer than that of the Shorthorn cow, the carcass equally square, broad and deep."

There is no doubt Mr. Klippart saw and described the best representatives of the breed of thirty years ago, a class of cattle that would equal, if not lead, the present registered class of the European herd-books. He also closely and carefully discriminated between the various breeds of the lowland race, which very few writers have done. He says: "It is a very common practice to speak of Holland cattle as though they were as distinct a breed as the Shorthorn or Devon breed; and I must confess for a time 1 was misled by this generic term. In Holland there are several breeds of cattle, almost all of which owe their origin to the Holland proper breed, and it was the manifest disparity in the several animals shown me as Hollanders that led me to make a closer examination of the matter. The Oldenburgers, West Friesian, East Friesian, Groningen and Beemster are all Holland breeds, and I am assured may be traced back to one original breed, but by culture and care, careful selection in breeding and management, together with the influence of the climate, soil and food, these several distinct breeds have been produced."

In our observations we find the forehead only moderately dishing, and the orbits of the eyes not especially prominent; the eyes full; the nose straight, without flesh; upon the sides of the nose the form of the veins showing distinctly through the skin; the nostrils large and well open; the jaws light and free from flesh; the throat clean, and the head set lightly to the neck; the ears large, light, active in movement, the inside of an oily texture and yellowish brown in color, and a small dewlap extending from the brisket upward to about half the length of the neck. The only point of difference with the description of Mr. Klippart, is in the loin and rump. We find these parts more rounded than he describes, and the huckle rising in many instances, giving a slightly sloping form to the rump.

As this breed has been used from time immemorial, especially for dairy purposes, we should naturally expect large development in all those parts that relate to milk production. The udder is often of enormous size, measuring in many instances fifty to sixty inches in circumference: it extends well forward, where it has a squareness of form, and is very broad; it also fills the space between the hocks, and is well up behind, and the texture of the whole soft and pliable. The teats are cylindrical in form, not cone-shaped, and are usually from two and a half to three and a half inches in length. The milk veins are generally long and crooked, often of extraordinary size. Every variety of escutcheon is found, yet the prevalence of the Flanders, in its various orders and forms, is especially noticeable. We have often thought, while examining these cattle, that there was a wider divergence of character between the males and females than in any other breed with which we are acquainted, or in other words, a greater contrast of masculineness and feminality of appearance; and in the absence of any other discoverable cause, have ascribed it to the effects of early maturity, and the constant requirement of milk production of the cows continued for many generations.

Passing from the registered cattle, which we have taken as the proper representatives of the breed, to the unregistered, we find a great diversity of size, build and quality. Some of these unregistered cattle are very large and fine, and need only the application of their owners to be received into the registered class. There is a great diversity in size and quality caused by the soil in different localities. Upon the sandy soil they are of poorer quality and smaller size. One of the most favorable positions to observe the general appearance of the unregistered cattle, is at the spring markets at Leeuwarden, Hoorn or Alkmaar. At such markets, hundreds, and sometimes thousands of cows fresh in milk are offered for sale. They are fastened in the market places in long lines, side by side, as closely as they can conveniently stand. Passing along these lines in the rear, observing their broad rumps, finely formed limbs and immense udders, then along in front, noticing their beautiful heads and necks, and their wedge-shaped bodies, an admirer of fine cattle can scarcely repress constant exclamations of surprise and admiration. We believe no breed in any other country can make a show under similar circumstances of equal merit.

CHAPTER IV.

HOLLAND—DUTCH FARM HOUSES AND STABLES—METHODS OF HANDLING—HAY MAKING—STABLING IN HOLLAND.

The Dutch farmhouses are immense structures, usually inclosing from 8,000 to 20,000 square feet of ground under a single roof. Their outside walls are built of brick, and are from six to seven feet high. On these walls the rafters rest, and rise steeply to the ridgepoles. They are covered with brick tiles, or with heavy thatch made of coarse grass reeds from the marshes. On approaching them they are invariably found surrounded with deep ditches often from 15 to 20 feet wide. These are partially filled with water so dark in color that the bottom cannot be seen. Over them bridges are thrown, usually traversed with strong gates heavily bolted. Some of the houses recently built have an ell, or wing, thrown out from one side or end, for the exclusive use of the family. In looking upon them from a distance, they appear like great brick-colored tents scattered over the landscape.

On entering these structures, you find on one side the cattle stalls; on another side the family and dairy rooms; in the center, without flooring, the haymows; and in other parts, horse stalls, calf pens, granaries and spaces for farm machinery. Sometimes there is stationary machinery for churning, pumping water, etc., by horse power. The side occupied by the family has windows and doors like dwelling houses in America. The side occupied by the cattle stalls is pierced with smaller windows in front of each stall. On the side leading to the haymow large double doors are found, and far up in the roof the ridgepole is seen pierced with ventilators. Entering the family rooms, you find them kept neatly, and some of them furnished with beautiful carpets and ornamental furniture. Your reception is very hospitable, perhaps more courteous and dignified than among American farmers. There seems to be a peculiar calmness and restfulness pervading everything. There is, perhaps, no country in the world, and no vocation, that is loved with the depth of feeling that these dairymen have for their land and their calling. Their children are nurtured in the same love, and rarely marry with any one not of the same calling. Thus, from father to son, and from mother to daughter, from generation to generation, descend the aptitudes and characteristics of these people that have done so much to make this breed what it is today.

In Holland cattle are kept in these farmhouses, at the present time, only in winter. They never enter them in summer. They are kept with marvelous neatness. The peculiar construction of the stables, and especially the method of fastening that prevails, greatly facilitates thus keeping them. Each stall is designed for two cows, one fastened to the right, the other to the left; one milked, while in the stable, on the left side, the other on the right. They stand with their heads toward the outside wall. A small window in this wall between each stall lets in the air and light as needed. There are no mangers or permanent feeding troughs before them. Their food is all carried in from behind, between them, and laid on the floor on which they stand, within easy reach of their heads. Sometimes a narrow trough extends along the outside wall a few inches from the floor into which water is pumped for watering them by means of power located in another part of the building; otherwise, they are watered in pails also carried in between them from behind. The windows between them are usually draped neatly with cheap curtains, showing woman's care and taste in their arrangement.

A row of such stalls upon a platform raised about two feet from the ground, extending along the side of the building, and partitioned from the rest of the farmhouse, constitutes the stable. The stall partitions extend back from the outside wall to near the hips of the cows as they naturally stand in their stalls. From two to two and a half feet farther back a deep trench runs along behind the cows at right angles with these partitions the whole length of the stable. This is usually about two feet broad, and of the same depth. It slightly descends the whole length, and at the lower end opens outwardly to the manure,

AEGIS' NETHERLAND PRINCE, No. 4585 H.-F H.-B.

or compost bed, by a door, the bottom of which is on a level with the bottom of the trench. Back of this trench, on the opposite side from the cows, is the platform for the attendants. This is usually about six inches lower than the platform on which the cows stand, and about eighteen inches above the bottom of the trench. It is necessarily made wide and roomy, for from it all food is carried to the cows. Along the side of this platform, running its whole length, is the partition that separates the stable from the rest of the farmhouse. Through this partition doors open to the granary, haymow, milkroom, and sometimes to the kitchen.

There are no means for putting cows into such a stable except across this platform and trench. This would be a very serious objection to it if the cows were turned out daily for air and exercise. This is never done. Their cows are put into their stables once a year, about the middle of October, and turned out once a year, about the middle of May. Thus they remain in them, without going outside into the open air of the fields for a moment during the whole of the six months that constitutes the inclement season. They have no exercise except what they obtain in moving about within the limits of their stalls. They appear more healthy in such confinement than does the average American dairy cow that gets a taste of outside wintry weather. Their hair, almost always, looks smooth and right, not rough and staring, and there is no uneasiness manifest in their appearance. In the even temperature of such stables, with plenty of food and gentle attendance, they seem to pass the winter in the height of bovine enjoyment. In putting them in and taking them from such a stable, a small wooden bridge is used spanning the trench and wide enough for a single cow to walk on with her attendant. This moves from stall to stall. When the work is completed it is put aside until the time comes for again using it.

There are two fastenings for each cow. One, a rope passed around the head under the horns and tied to a ring in the cross partition, beside which she stands; the other a peculiar instrument that needs description to be understood by an American reader. It consists of a yoke fitting the neck like the hames of a harness, to which is added a small trace chain from five to six feet long. The yoke opens at the bottom, at the middle of which the chain is attached. In the platform at the rear of the cross partition to which the cow is tied an iron hook is placed over which the links of this chain can be firmly hooked. The object of the deep trench hitherto described, as the reader no doubt recognizes, is to receive the droppings. The object of this instrument is to keep the cow so closely to the trench that her droppings will go nowhere else. With this yoke and chain she may be drawn back or allowed to go forward at the pleasure of the attendant. The size or length of the animal would make no difference with the distance at which she may be made to stand or lie from the trench. When cattle are thus fastened there is some danger of their hind feet slipping into this trench. And it is so deep a cow is liable to be more or less bruised in the struggle to recover. This is probably the reason why permanent feeding boxes are not used. Food placed on the floor is readily kept within reach of the cow by the attendant. To further guard against slipping into the trench, a ledge about an inch and a half wide and of the same depth, drops from the floor on which they stand into the side and top. This catches her foot when the cow slips and warns her to recover. If the warning is not heeded and her feet go to the bottom she remembers the lesson for a long time, and such an accident rarely happens to her again. The stable is visited by the attendant much more frequently than in America. Very rarely an hour passes night or day that an attendant or some other member of the household does not look after the cows to cleanse the trench and adjust their fastenings.

It will be seen that the ventilation of these stables can be easily regulated. The windows in the outside wall between every two animals, the air spaces in the high roofs to which access from the stables can be easily gained, and the ventilators above, provide the most ample means, yet they are often kept very close and in the judgment of Americans altogether too warm from animal heat. But no evidence of discomfiture is shown by the cows. They seem to especially enjoy an atmosphere that is almost suffocation to a person who is habituated to the outside air. Undoubtedly they consume much less food in such an atmosphere and if they give as much milk and are as healthy, we must defer to the wisdom of these dairymen in thus keeping them.

As you enter one of these stables for the first time in winter and walk down the long line of cows that occupy it, all apparently as smooth coated and as free from filth or stain as in summer in the fields, you will perhaps think that such is not their usual state; that they have been cleansed and groomed and the white switches of their tails washed and combed for some special event. Go tomorrow, or any other day, and you find them in the same condition. You will find them yielding their milk almost as liberally as when in the fields. They have had no drying-up season as cows in this country have in early winter.

Before dropping another calf each one will have a few weeks' respite from giving milk, then she will enter again with renewed impulse on the chief object of her existence. What wonder that generations of such people should have produced a dairy cow that can be profitably kept even in the winter and in so doing adding to her owner's wealth through every season of her existence!

During the winter they are fed on hay and oil cake. The oil cake ration is usually from one to four pounds a day. To those that may be milking heavily or are reduced in strength from some other cause, the refuse skim milk is usually fed. The oil cake is the ordinary commercial cake produced from the various seeds after the expression of their oils; that from linseed is the chief, much of which is imported from America. As it comes into Holland it is hard and difficult to be broken, but it is there re-ground and re-pressed into much softer and smaller cakes, easily broken in the hand, and thus fed to the cows. The refuse of bakeries is also made into cakes and fed in this way. Cotton seed meal is slowly coming into use. Indian corn meal is sometimes fed in the scarcity of other food, but is not generally regarded with favor.

In the quality of their hay lies much of the secret of their success in maintaining a liberal flow of milk through the winter months. As it is taken from the mow it appears much like American rowen, very much bleached in curing. And it does not strike an observer from this country as being very nutritive or palatable. Before the cows every blade is eaten and they always seem desirous for more. There is no waste for bedding. While the climate of Holland is so cold that it would not mature the earliest variety of Indian corn, yet it is so tempered by the sea that grass grows throughout nine months of the year. These dairymen usually pasture their fields one season and mow them the next, and so alternate from year to year. The sod thus becomes exceedingly dense. The grass for mowing is never allowed to mature or blossom or even head. The first cutting is taken from the fields in May or early in June. A second cutting is taken in August or the fore part of September, and a third in October or November.

When the mowing begins it proceeds without interruption until the cutting for that period is completed. The mowers do not stop as in America because of cloudy or rainy weather, or to assist in gathering. On a farm of ordinary size, keeping from twenty to forty cows, two mowers are usually employed during the haying, who camp out in the meadows and furnish their own implements and board. Mowing machines have not come into general use, the majority of farmers thinking it less expensive to have their grass cut by hand, that it is cut more closely, and the sod less injured during the slow process. When partially dry the hay is put up in small cocks. As the curing goes on two or more of these cocks are put together. Often they are again redoubled and this process repeated until the hay is sufficiently dried for the mow. These cocks frequently become saturated with rain and have to be spread and re-spread to dry. In consequence the hay does not reach the mow in the farmhouse until it is quite thoroughly bleached and a large share of its fragrance gone.

All the members of the family join in the gathering. It is this scene in the hay field on which poets and painters love to dwell. The wife and daughters raking the hay, the younger children on the loaded wains, the husband and sons lifting the heavy forkfuls. It is indeed a scene of much rural enjoyment. There is little of that burning heat in the climate that characterizes haying time in America. The air is pure and invigorating, the fields are fragrant, and there is a peculiar happiness in all countries and among all people in the gathering of the harvest.

The first and second cuttings are thus cured and stowed in the mow. The last cutting is drawn to the farmhouse and fed without curing, as the cows are all ready there in the stables for the winter. This lasts for several weeks during which they are virtually soiled. This is the only period in which they receive any soiling crops. As this decreases dry hay from the mow and oil cake take its place as we have described. There is no sudden change from green to dry food as in American dairies, and consequently no special drying up time at this season of the year. Their calves have taken the skim milk up to this period. But now all that are not needed to replenish the herd are driven to the market and sold and the skim milk comes as extra food to the cows. This also helps to maintain the flow of milk at this period. Thus they pass into the winter season and summer dairying passes into winter dairying without any change in their production of milk except what naturally results from a nearer approach to the time for dropping their calves.

The method of feeding after the cows leave the stables in spring and return in autumn needs little description. They simply crop the grass of their pastures. During this period they have no other food. They frequently change pastures. The system of drainage makes small fields. Ditches impossible to cattle cross each other as fences cross in this country. It is rare to find a continuous field of more than fifteen acres. The fields communicate by bridges upon which bars or gates are erected. Thus their cows may be easily limited in range and passed

AMLETO, No. 8351 H. H.-B.
Prize cow, World's Exposition, Amsterdam, in 1884. Milk record, 79½ lbs. in one day; 13,810¼ lbs. in 277 days. Butchered in 1887; dressed 66 per cent of live weight.

from field to field as pasturage is renewed in them in growth and freshness. This is undoubtedly an advantage in keeping up a steady flow and producing the most milk possible for the acreage. It will be seen that this system of feeding from one end of the year to the other is free from violent changes; that the grasses are cut when most nutritious and least liable to injury from exposure, and that extra rations are provided at the season when most needed for keeping up the flow of milk. How far it conforms to science we leave for others to decide.

A very interesting account of the method of stabling cows in Friesland is given below, by a correspondent who was a close observer:

"To begin with, let me say that Holland, or, more properly speaking, the Netherlands, though but a small country, is not all a country of dikes and windmills, and but a small part of it is an exclusive dairy country. The different sections differ radically, as do the people who live in them. Each section has its own customs, industries, language, and own breeds of domestic animals. So I will confine myself to describing to you that with which I am best acquainted, to wit, how cattle are treated in the dairy section of the province of Friesland, the original home of the Holstein-Friesian cattle.

"There, grass is king, and plows are never seen—yes, almost unknown to many of the inhabitants. How long ago it is since those fields were sown down to grass, if grass was ever sown, I do not know; but it must be, at least, a couple of hundred years ago. But those dairymen are very careful about their grass, and if the summer is rainy and the land wet, you'll hear remarks about cows eating with five mouths, and will find many cows stabled in July or August, to be kept in till next spring if the weather does not improve. This is commonly the case, and, as a rule, cows are not stabled till about November 1, when the grass begins to fail. If the grass fails before, they are promptly stabled; if the grass is plenty and the weather not too rough, they may stay out a little longer, each cow provided with an 'overcoat' in the shape of a heavy, coarse blanket, which she keeps on all the time. But the first snowstorm or heavy frost drives the last ones to the stable, which they will not leave again 'till the lark sings high in the sky, and the grass is tall enough to hide the plover.'

"Their stalls have been ready for them for some time, the chains have all been fixed, the stalls bedded, the curtains have been taken off the windows, the mats and carpets taken up, and the floor heavily sprinkled with sand instead. Along the ceiling, the whole length of the stable, right over the gutter, a line is stretched from which dangle a number of small lines, each ending in a small leather strap by which the tails will be fastened and kept out of the filth. Hay is temptingly displayed in the mangers, and across the gutter at the first stall to be filled lies the bridge, well covered with straw. The gutter also is half filled with straw. (Right here let me say that it is only for this important occasion that the farmer appears to be so liberal with straw and sand, both of which are usually sparingly used, as they are scarce articles, and have to be shipped in from other parts of the country.)

"In the yard where the cows are gathered together will be seen the farmer with a couple of helpers, sizing up his cows with a critical eye. He is actually measuring and comparing them, for he wants to have a good-looking herd of cows this winter, and this cannot be accomplished if you put them in haphazard. The tallest cow stands in the middle of the stable, the two next in size on either side, and so down to the two smallest cows at the ends. But then the cows stand two in a stall, and width and breadth, as well as matching in color and individual cows' likes and dislikes, have to be considered. So you see it is quite a complicated job, not to be done too hastily, for it may mean money a few months afterwards, when the foreign dealer comes to buy cows, if they are stabled effectively. But before putting in the cows, maybe it would be as well to have a look at the stable first. The average farmer stables about forty head of cattle, twenty head of milch cows, ten two-year-olds, that will drop their first calves this winter, and ten yearlings—that is, they will be a year old some time between now and spring. There is always a yearling bull and sometimes an 'old bull' that is two or three years old.

"The cow stable, though under the same roof as the barn, is wholly separated from the hay by a brick wall upon which rests the ceiling. The ceiling, over the cows, is tight, but over the walk the boards are loose, so that they can be raised for ventilating purposes. The stalls (for two cows) are about five feet square, the gutter is about one foot deep and two feet wide; the walk five feet wide. The cow stalls, however, are about two feet above the walk, so the cows stand three feet higher than the bottom of the gutter, and the ceiling, which is about seven feet above the walk, is but five feet above the floor of the cow stalls. Each stall is lighted by a little window, about a foot square in the wall the cows are facing. Besides from these, the stable receives light through two long windows, one on each side of the outside stable door. The bottom stall, as a rule, is a single one, and is reserved for the bull. The partitions between each stall are three feet high, and reach back from the wall about three feet. The stalls are level, except for about a foot from the wall, which is paved with brick and slightly higher than the rest and does service as feeding floor. Sometimes in, but usually above this feeding floor mostly, is a watering trough, running the whole length of the stable. The two feet behind this feeding floor usually is clay, though sometimes flat tile, while the two-foot space next to the gutter, though still called the footboard, is seldom wood, but hard brick, laid in cement. The gutter, of course, is built of brick, also with glazed tiles in the bottom: the wall is laid in brick and cement. The stalls for yearlings and two-year-olds are on the same plan, but each a size smaller. I don't think that even the most prejudiced of Dutch farmers claim that these high stalls are an advantage, but they help to make the cows show up well, a great point with them, and besides they prevent the cows ever standing with hind feet in the gutter and thus dirty the stable, platform, and eventually themselves, another important point. Probably somebody will think that the cows, slipping on the stall, would fall in the gutter and thus get hung, or seriously injured, but experience has taught them to be careful, and they seldom slip. When they do slip serious consequences are avoided by the 'mis-step.' The gutter wall upon which the 'footboard' rests sticks out half a brick's length from under the 'footboard' thus giving a foothold to the slipping cow, of which she quickly avails herself to regain a safe position.

"Our farmer by this time has got his stable nearly filled, and you notice now as he slides the bridge along to the next stall that the one end of it rests on this mis-step, and the other on the stable floor, and that cleats, nailed on the bottom and resting against the sides of the gutter, effectually prevent its slipping. Here are the next two cows, and as we are very much in the road, we'll step on one of the stalls already filled and look at the mode of tying. Each cow carries on her neck a sort of iron yoke, with open clasp. On this are strung two chains, one of which is fastened to the partition about a foot from the wall, and the other to the post at the end of the partition, two feet from the gutter. If the cow develops a tendency to stand too far forward, the latter chain is shortened and the former lengthened, which compels her to stand nearer the gutter. If the reverse is desired, the second is lengthened and the first shortened. It is, however, of course, desirable to have the cows stand as far back as possible, and the slooping roof in front has also a tendency to throw them back when standing.

"The last cow is stabled, the bridge is taken outside to be scrubbed off and put away for further use, the farmer gets his scissors and starts to trim the tails, the cows, which did not get much to eat to-day, have devoured the hay and are bawling restlessly, and the farmer orders them fed from the grass piled up outside the barn, or, if he is a progressive man, maybe from the preserved grass. (Preserved grass is simply grass piled up into a big pile, often on top of the ground, sometimes partly in the ground, the top covered with a few feet of earth; grass ensilage without a silo.) That done, the floor is swept and the farmer left alone with his cows, save maybe for the boy who washes the tails. Winter has commenced. Before leaving we'll take a look at the tail the farmer has just finished. He has cut away all the hair on the upper part of the tail, reaching even the long hair at the root of the tail. Only the switch is left, and where it commences he has wrapped around the tail some long straws; then taking a bunch of hair of the switch, he has plaited it and the long ends of the straw together till the plait was long enough to be knotted. Over this knot he has slipped the leather strap of the tail line, fastened it, the knot preventing its slipping off again. The cow, although she has the free use of her tail, cannot drag it through the dirt when lying down, as the tail line reaches only from ceiling to within a few inches of the platform.

"In order to see the dairy in good running order and to be able to note all the small details of its management, we'll rise about 4 o'clock, one morning in April or March, and leave the village with one of the laborers, who work on the farm. After arriving there, after a five or ten minutes' walk, we arouse the still sleeping farmer, and on being let in, our guide lights his lantern and we proceed straightway to the stables. While our man takes off several coats or wrappers, for the weather is cold and raw, and puts on in their place light overalls and jackets, for the temperature here is somewhere between 60 and 70 deg., Fahr. The cows, too, wake up, rise and lazily stretch themselves. Our man has picked up an old broom and with it proceeds to clean such footboards as need it and the mis-step. Then he picks up a small can with sand, hanging on the wall, scattering a handful on every slippery stall. This done, he goes to the lower end of the stable, takes a stick with a small board nailed to the bottom, and with it shoves up the manure toward the stalls, thus allowing the urine to pass off through a drain to a cistern outside. This done he goes outside, but reappears immediately with a huge wheel-barrow and large, long-handled, wooden shovel and begins to clean out the gutter.

"Meanwhile the farmer and a couple of sons or hired hands, have made their appearance. The farmer himself opens one of the doors leading to the hay bins, and taking enough hay on his fork for two cows starts to feed. Having fed all, and carefully, with a new broom swept up all the hay he may have

AMERICA, No. 8683 H. H. B.; ADVANCED REGISTRY No. 23.

dropped, he joins the two boys, and probably a girl who has just arrived, milking.

"Meanwhile our first man has finished cleaning out the main stable, and now takes down the big wooden buckets, that have been hung up during the night on slats nailed to the ceiling, and gets ready for the first watering. In the niche behind the pump are setting three or four tubs filled with buttermilk (the whole milk is churned during the winter months, which accounts for the large amount of buttermilk) and one with oil meal gruel, and out of these he partly fills the buckets, the heaviest milkers, of course, receiving the heaviest share. One of the boys fills the pails under the pump. Dry cows get pure water. Thus with two buckets filled with 'half and half' or 'straight' as the case may be, our man jumps on the stalls. No light work as you will readily see, when you know that each bucket holds about five gallons. As soon as all have been watered the farmer starts feeding again, the man finishes cleaning out the small stables and the boys the milking.

"This all done they get ready for the second watering, for I forgot to say that the cows only got one pailful apiece, the young stock none at all. If there are troughs the second watering is very much easier, these only have to be pumped full and the young stock to be watered. Yearlings never get pure water at all, only the mixture described before and never more than from one-half to a whole pailful, according to size and season, however much they seem to desire more. By the time all have been watered the farmer has also fed them all for the third time. Leaving the cows to eat this, all proceed to breakfast. When this meal is finished the cows have also finished their hay, but as soon as the men reappear, indicate by their expectant looks and restless movements, that more is coming. This most usually consists of linseed cake, fed in cake shape, but sometimes it is cottonseed cake, corn meal, bean meal, pea meal, peanut meal cake, etc. Whatever it is, it is always fed in cake shape, corn, pea or bean meal being often baked into bread. Bean—*Faba vulgaris*.

"While the farmer is feeding them, the boys get their curry combs and brushes, and give each cow a thorough grooming. As this has been done every day since last fall, however, it does not take much time, and half an hour later all of the stalls have been swept up, and one after the other the cows lie down grumbling over their distended stomachs. The tails get washed now, the floor is carefully swept, sand is sprinkled, the watering buckets are carried out to get washed and aired, and quiet reigns. Looking at the watch we find it to be about 8 o'clock. Everybody goes to his day's work, only the farmer or one of the boys stays behind. He throws down the hay for tonight's and tomorrow morning's feeding, grinds the oil cake and mixes the gruel, cleans the stalls whenever the cows dirty them, brushes such ones as need it with a new broom occasionally, and untangles and spreads the hair of the switches, beds and brushes the young calves, which you usually will find in one of the empty hay bins, and which, though they get nothing since they were a week old but buttermilk and hay, look sleek and healthy. If a cow calves he will put the bridge behind her, put the calf in the calf pen, tie it, slip out the cow a little several times a day, and, if she is a good cow, milk her three or four times a day afterwards for several days. Besides, if she is older than three years, he'll blanket her immediately after calving, and keep her blanketed for a week or ten days. Thus he is usually kept busy till 11 o'clock, when the men arrive. They go in to their coffee, followed at 12 o'clock by dinner, after which he usually, after cleaning up, closes the blinds and leaves the cows to their dreams and cuds. Some farmers give a feed of hay at noon, but the majority object to that practice, claiming that it makes the cows restless. Half-past three he reappears; after carefully cleaning each feeding floor, slightly sprinkling each stall, all hands go in for their 4 o'clock tea, after which the performances of the morning are repeated in exactly the same succession, except the currying. Immediately after supper, however, a trip is made through the stables, all filth removed from the platforms, and this is repeated at least once more before retiring.

"Taking a view of the herd, we notice the following things: 1st, that cows older than eight years are scarce; if there be such a one, she is some exceptional milker that for some reason or other never could be sold for her full value, and by whose longer keeping nothing is lost, for cows are sold before their eighth year because a greater age unfits them for export, which fact, of course, has a depreciating effect on their market value: 2d, that two-year-olds all drop their calves early in the season—January and February; and 3d, that three-year-olds calve in April and May."

CHAPTER V.

HOW BREED WAS DEVELOPED—SPREAD OF THE BREED IN EUROPE.

This breed has been developed in the hands of these Holland dairymen, not only through the general influences of care and feeding, such as we have described, but also through appeals to the bovine instincts and provisions for the comfort of their cows, that may seem to some insignificant or valueless.

All of their milch cows are provided with blankets to be worn in the fields in damp, stormy, chilling weather. They have many days of such weather in spring and autumn. These blankets are made of heavy hempen cloth. They are made to cover the upper parts of the animal from the forward parts of the shoulder tops to nearly the extremities of their rumps. They are held in place by cords, also made of hemp, about an eighth of an inch in diameter, fastened to eyelet holes in the borders of the blankets. There are seven of these cords and fourteen eyelet holes. One of these cords passes under each forearm, one under each thigh, one around the rump and another forward of the chest at the points of the shoulders. Thus they sometimes wear them night and day for weeks at a time.

If their cows are distant in the fields they go to them to milk them rather than subject them to the fatigue of being driven to the milking yard near the farmhouse. At such times the milkers are seen going and coming with large pails suspended by yokes from their shoulders or drawing carts loaded with cans. Their milch cows are never driven by dogs. They are rarely beaten or subjected to other rough treatment. Not that these Holland dairymen are marvelously good tempered, but they recognize the fact that such treatment is poor economy; that tired or bruised muscles invariably result in loss, both of quality and quantity of milk. They have also learned that all nervous excitement of whatever nature lessens milk production. Hence not only in management but in breeding they seek to perpetuate quietness of disposition. The uneasy, fighting temperament that a class of American dairymen are trying to exalt into a bovine virtue they regard as a great vice in a milch cow. Their cows are rarely seen uneasily ranging their fields. They seldom have conflicts with one another or display a disposition for mastery. They approach strange cows with apparent desire to form a friendly acquaintance. They display strong social tendencies. They love to be petted. Children caress them without fear. And a strange person entering a herd is regarded with friendly curiosity rather than with terror or belligerency.

The practice of removing calves from the sight and hearing of their dams immediately on being dropped is universal. It has been objected to as unnatural, yet it is the kindest treatment possible in dairy husbandry. The calves learn to drink with very little trouble, and the nervous strain on the cows, the moaning and lowing that comes from parting after being together a few hours or a few days, is avoided. There is another feature in such practice that is deserving of our attention. When the calves are thus removed the instinctive affection that cows have for their offspring is often largely transferred to their milkers. How far this may affect milk production is a subject of much interest. Within certain physical limits the will of the cow has much to do with milk giving. She gives freely to an object of her attachment, less freely to an object of her indifference, and sometimes largely withholds from an object of her fear or hatred. It is possible that here lies one of the strongest influences that has operated to make the cows of this breed such extraordinary milkers. There is another fact connected with this subject. Other things being equal, the cow gives milk according to the demands made on her. Such demands are made known to her instincts by the frequency, rapidity and completeness with which her milk is drawn. These Holland dairymen often milk their cows three times a day, for a period of several weeks after dropping their calves. Their milkers, men and women, generally have large, strong hands and milk with rapidity and thoroughness. Thus the conditions for favorable appeal to the maternal instincts are maintained.

These breeders keep but few bulls. These are selected from their choicest and most vigorous milkers. They commence using them at about fourteen months old. They are rarely kept beyond three years of age. Many are turned to the butcher at the close of their first year's service. They are invariably kept in fine condition and as a rule are not allowed to run with their herds. So far as discovered no unfavorable results have followed from the use of young bulls. All classes of their cattle mature young. Probably the cattle of no other breed show such rapid growth the first year. At two years of age their heifers drop their first calves, and they are generally kept breeding as long as

AVERY'S OXEN. Weight, 6,000 lbs. Champion Draft Oxen of United States, 1895-96.

they live. Few of them milk less than ten months a year and many of them exceed this period.

The value of a breed of cattle may be judged somewhat by its aggressiveness, or in other words by the extent of territory over which it spreads in competition with other breeds. Especially is this true of dairy breeds, found,

HOW BREED WAS DEVELOPED.   33

as such breeds are, only in civilized countries and on valuable lands. Thus viewed, this breed will be found entitled to the appellation we have assumed for it. It is found in more countries than any other breed, occupying more territory, and is probably producing more milk, cheese and butter than all others combined. These facts are brought forcibly to our attention by the reports of American consuls in the commercial centers of Europe, in answer to inquiries made by our Department of State in 1883. Going south from the two Netherland provinces, North Holland and Friesland, where this breed originated, and from whence it is mainly sought, it has spread over the provinces of Utrecht and South Holland, almost exclusively occupying them. Farther south is the kingdom of Belgium, the most densely populated state in Europe. Three of its provinces are largely devoted to dairying, Antwerp and East and West Flanders. We quote from these reports, as impartially giving the position it occupies in this country.

Says Consul Stewart of Antwerp: "Antwerp prefers to improve her stock by the introduction of the Dutch race, because the dairy is the result aimed at and but little attention is paid to other products. The cow is valued only by her milk-giving qualities and for this purpose the Dutch are much the best."

Says Consul Wilson of Brussels: "In the province of Antwerp the production of milk and butter and the raising of vegetables for London and Antwerp markets are found so much more profitable than the growing of beef cattle that the farmers of that district will have nothing to do with any but such cattle as produce the largest amount of milk upon the smallest amount of food, and for this they prefer the pure Dutch cow or her crosses with the Flemish animal."

Says Consul Tanner of Liege: "So far as the different breeds of cattle in Belgium are concerned they are as numerous as there are localities of different names and there has not been that general and universal effort to retain purity of breed in Belgium, such as has been the case in England. There has been effort, however, to this end in a few cases of families of rank, who have been very particular about the pedigrees of their cattle, and therefore in this way there are several breeds that have retained their untarnished pedigrees most faithfully. The breeds to which I allude present now in outward appearance and in results for both the dairy and for beef cattle that cannot be surpassed in the world. This is more particularly true of the breeds known here as the Hollandais or Dutch cow and the Flamande or Belgium cow. There is a strong likeness between these two breeds that suggests unmistakably to a judge of cattle, a common origin.... The Hollandais or Dutch cattle, on the whole, I think, are generally more esteemed than any other."

This consul adds a table of weights, measurements, prices and numbers. We quote the last two items as follows:

Name of Breed	Price per Head (average), Cow.	No. in Belgium.
Hollandais, Dutch or Holstein,	$118 to $180	160,000
Flamande or Belgian—three types,		
Boulonnais,	105 to 232.50	210,000
Bourbonne,	118 to 148.50	210,000
Picardy,	118 to 148.50	210,000
Danois,	110 to 135	80,000
Flechet,	60 to 100	10,000
Charlerol,	60 to 90	80,000
Contentine (Norman),	60 to 90	80,000
L'Oldenbourg,	55 to 70	122,000
Durham,	65 to 85	50,000
Ayrshire,	65 to 80	15,000
Jersey,	60 to 75	10,000

Consul Wilson also gives the prices at which cattle of these two leading breeds are generally sold, as follows, viz.:

Flemish or Belgian (Flamande) bulls, $120 to $140   Holland three-year-old bulls, $100 to $120
" " cows, 200 to 240   " " cows, 160 to 200

These extracts are from the reports of all the consuls. The full force of them cannot be seen without taking into consideration the peculiar situation of Belgium. It is but a short distance from England, North Holland and the Islands of Jersey and Guernsey. Cattle from these points can be imported very cheaply. The government has granted subsidies for the importation of foreign breeds to improve the stock of the country. No country is so well situated to pass judgment on the various breeds. The dairymen of this country have been acting the part of a great jury. Their suffrages are shown in the reports from which we have quoted. The Flamande or Belgian breed is of the same race as the Holland breed, virtually originating from it. Consul Tanner says of it: "This breed of cows ranks almost equally with the Dutch, even in North Holland, and in France, Germany and Switzerland are esteemed above any English breeds by all those who know cattle. That which this breed lacks in quantity of milk it makes up in quality, and that which it lacks in size for beef is compensated for in the same way. These two breeds (Hollandais and Flamande) are as gentle and kind in disposition as it is possible for cattle to be." Consul Wilson says of them: "The color of the Belgian cattle (Flamande breed) is most frequently black and white, while the Hollanders are the same, but sometimes with a sprinkle of corn or tan color, something like that of the Alderneys. Sometimes this gets to be almost red like the Durhams; but in both the dominant colors are black and white placed in large spots over the body."

There is no doubt these two breeds, so called, are of the same blood and might be as properly ranked together as one and the same breed, as are the various colored animals of the Ayrshire breed, or indeed the various colored animals of the Jersey and Guernsey breeds. If they are thus considered, what an overwhelming verdict in its favor are the statistics that we have quoted. No one can question this verdict. From it there can be no appeal. It is from the highest possible source of authority. The trial was not of superior animals selected out of thousands to represent the breeds, but of the breeds themselves, each as a whole. It does not follow that a similar verdict would be rendered by dairymen in mountainous districts on comparatively unfertile soils, with widely different markets; but it does follow that on fertile soils and level lands, in densely populated countries, no breed or race can successfully compete with this. If, however, they are considered distinct and separate, it leaves them about equally matched: two branches from the same parent stock, each superior to the other breed. We have no animals in this country of the Flamande branch; we have only the Hollandais or Holstein-Friesian, and hence the verdict of the dairymen of Belgium goes alone to its credit.

Eastward from its place of origin, this race has spread even more extensively than southward. It has come to occupy whole provinces of the German Empire, notably, East Friesland and Oldenburg, in both of which it has been so long and so universally kept that it has become modified by the peculiarities of climate and use, and is regarded as indigenous. In East Friesland it has come to be taller and more rangy in build; in Oldenburg more nearly resembling the English Shorthorn.

In 1865 John H. Klippart, then one of the most prominent students of agriculture and secretary of the Ohio state board, was commissioned by that body to make a tour of observation upon the agricultural progress of Europe. His first attention was given to the International Fair held at Stettin, Prussia. Here he found 255 cattle classed as belonging to the milch breeds. Of these 129 were entered as Hollanders and 39 as East Friesians. The entries of no other breed exceeded ten animals. The Ayrshires were represented by six animals and the Jerseys by one. In his report he says: "The Oldenburgers do not differ materially from their progenitors, the Friesian or Holland race," but adds, "they are more rounded, plump and shorter in the body and legs." Of the East Friesian or Breitenburg race he says, "It might with great propriety be classed as a branch of the great Friesian or Holland race." Speaking further of the families or branches of the Holland race he says, "all these are celebrated milkers. the yield ranging from 22 to 38 quarts per day per cow."

In his report on the different provinces of the German Empire he says of Pomerania, "Holland cows are very popular here as milkers;" of Posen, "Imported animals on the manors consist chiefly of Holland, Oldenburg, Schwitz and Allgan races, but recently Shorthorns have been added;" of Westphalia, "In Westphalia the Holland race is very popular and extensive importations are made of this race. From forty to a hundred cows of this race are frequently found on manors;" of Brandenburg and Saxony, "In Halberstadt district there are annually a large number of calves, heifers in calf, and cows in calf imported from Holland."

These quotations show the tendency of this breed towards occupying the dairy sections of the German Empire in 1865. Since then herd book associations have been formed and herd books commenced in that country, one for registering cattle of the East Friesland branch or breed, another for the

Oldenburg branch or breed and still another for Holland cattle more recently introduced and their descendants. The effect of the associations is to further stimulate the breeding and spread of this race. Its strongest competitors are the Angeln, the Allgauer and the Schwytzer races, each of which has a herd book in Germany for their special registry.

The reports of American consuls in answer to questions from our Department of State in 1883 give us a view of the present situation. Consul Schoeule of Barmen says: "The Dutch and East Friesland breeds, which are driven into almost every German district, may be considered the predominant pure breeds of Germany." Commercial Agent Warner of Dusseldorf says: "The Dutch breed is very largely cultivated in the districts of Cleve and Rees." Consul General Brewer of Berlin says: "The cows of East Friesia are especially remarkable for the abundance of milk which they give. These cattle in form and build are heavier even than the Dutch cattle and stronger in the bone. A great many of them are sent to Mecklenburg and Pomerania, where with ordinary good treatment good results are obtained." Consul Mason of Dresden reports that in 1880 there was kept in the province of Saxony for service 2162 bulls of the Oldenburg breed, 813 of the Dutch breed and 17 of the Breitenburg (East Friesian) breed. A total of 3992 pure bred bulls of the Holstein-Friesian race. In the same year there were but 95 bulls of all the English breeds and races kept for such use in that province. The whole number of bulls of all classes was 10,128.

One of the most remarkable reports on this subject was that of Consul Ditmar for the province of Silesia. This province is situated in the extreme southeast part of the empire. He says: Taking at random 400 of the larger estates in various parts of the province in order to ascertain which is the most favorite breed I find that on the estates the following cattle are kept:

Breeds of Cattle.	Estates.	Breeds of Cattle.	Estates.
Dutch cattle of more or less pure blood,	141	Silesian and Shorthorn cross,	3
Dutch and Silesian cross,	85	Silesian, Highland and Swiss,	2
Dutch and Oldenburg cross,	20	Silesian and Friesian cross,	1
Dutch and Swiss cross,	10	Oldenburg,	15
Dutch and Shorthorn cross,	9	Oldenburg and Shorthorn cross,	8
Dutch, English and Shorthorn cross,	6	Oldenburg and Wilstermarsh cross,	3
Dutch and Zillerthat cross,	1	Oldenburg and Swiss cross,	1
Dutch and Wilstermarsh cross,	12	East Friesian,	9
Dutch and English cross,	1	East Friesian and Wilstermarsh cross,	2
Dutch and German cross,	7	Wilstermarsh,	7
Dutch, Oldenburg and Swiss cross,	2	Wilstermarsh, Montafun and Swiss cross,	1
Dutch and Murzthal (Styrian) cross,	1	Wilstermarsh and Holsteins,	2
Dutch and East Friesian cross,	1	Wilstermarsh and mixed breeds,	2
Dutch, Swiss and Wilstermarsh cross,	1	Cows of various breeds and Wilstermarsh bulls,	1
Dutch and Algan (Bavarian) cross,	3	Shorthorns,	4
Dutch and Dantzig cross,	4	Shorthorns and Ayrshires,	1
Dutch and Tondern (Schleswig-Holstein) cross,	1	Shorthorns and mixed breeds,	2
Dutch, Silesian and Wilstermarsh cross,	1	Ayrshires,	3
Dutch, Oldenburg and Wilstermarsh cross,	1	Swiss,	5
Dutch and Ayrshire cross,	1	Swiss with various crosses,	3
Mixed Dutch and other races,	14	Dantzig,	1
Silesian Lowland,	27	Murzthal,	1
Silesian Highland,	1	Algan,	3
Silesian and Oldenburg cross,	12	Old German,	1
Silesian and Swiss cross,	1	Tondern,	1
Silesian and Schleswig cross,	1	Mixed breeds of various races,	9

A report thus in detail is more significant than anything that can be given in general terms. It seems to us that this report demonstrates the conquering nature of Dutch cattle.

Silesia lies between the parallels of 49 and 52 degrees, and contains 15,500 square miles. The southern parts of Middle and Lower Silesia are mountainous. The rest of the province is level.

The grasses are timothy, rye grass, red clover, white clover, esparsette, serradella and lucerne. Indian corn is raised for fodder, but does not ripen. Much care has been bestowed on the treatment of dairy products. A dairy school is established in Upper Silesia. It is said that the reputation of Silesian butter dates from the Middle Ages. It is considered equal to Danish butter. This province is really a fine field for competition among the dairy breeds. Originally the advantages could not have been greatly in favor of the Dutch breed. The Angeln, the Allgauer and the Schytzer, all are nearer at hand. The breeds of the Channel Islands, the Jersey and Guernsey, are but little far-

BILLY BOELYN, No. 189 H.H.-B.

ther away. It is not a cheese making province, nor a beef raising province. It is a butter making province. Again we repeat that the conditions and the circumstances all seem to demonstrate the conquering character of the Holstein-Friesian as a dairy breed.

CHAPTER VI.

MILK—QUANTITY YIELDED—PROF. HENGERVELD—PROF. STEWART—KING OF WIRTEMBERG'S RECORDS—KLIPPART'S REPORTS OF RECORDS—AVERAGE YIELD IN HOLLAND.

Prof. G. J. Hengerveld of the Royal Veterinary Institute, Utrecht, Netherlands, speaking in relation to the quantity of milk yielded by this breed, says: "Much pains have been taken in foreign countries to keep an account of the quantity of milk yielded by [Holstein-] Friesian cows, and to compare it with the yield of the most productive of other races. In the yearly quantity of milk yielded by the Bern, Simmenthal, Allgan, Limborg and Ayrshire cattle, in some instances the result has been in favor of the Bern, Simmenthal, Allgan and Ayrshire cattle; but generally the superiority has been with the Holstein-Friesian. The Limburg and English breeds, in which we include the Ayrshire, cannot be compared with them.

"The quantity of milk depends much on the locality from whence the Dutch cattle are collected, whether from clayey, loamy, peaty or sandy soil. If we compare the cattle bought by the Germans on the eastern borders of our country with the cattle bred on our rich pastures, we find that the yield of the latter is far superior to the former.

"In order to obtain a correct comparison of the yield of milk of different breeds, the large, medium-sized and small animals of each breed should only be compared together. In my description of the South Holland cattle, the large and medium-sized cows, under which we may also range those of Groningen and Friesland, bred on clayey and loamy soil, thirty-five hundred litres (the litre is identical with our wine quart) a year I have given as the average yield. It is stated by many a land owner or farmer their productiveness from time to time amounts to five or six thousand litres. Cows yielding those quantities are not at all rare."

We therefore conclude, first, the yield thirty-five hundred litres a year is but a medium quantity, and cannot be accepted as the yield on the clayey, loamy and peaty soils of North Holland and Friesland. Second, though portions of North Holland are sandy and dry, yet the cattle belong to to the large variety, and these larger cattle are very superior to the best Swiss and Allgan, and even to that exquisite milk breed known under the name of Rosenstein and Wirtemburg.

The following, from a work by Prof. Stewart, illustrates the value of these cattle in comparison with others for the production of milk: "As I omitted to give the German mode of feeding in its proper place, I will give Dr. Rhode's milk ration at Eldena, in Pomerania. This is one of the most celebrated agricultural colleges in Prussia. He details those experiments in his chapter 'On the Breeds of Cattle in the Kingdom of Holland.' I do not propose to go into the characteristics of the breed he describes, but merely to consider the ration, and the result upon large and small cows."

	Aggregate Yield per Year.	Yield per Cow per Year.	Per Cow per Day.	Per Cow Per Year.
Small Cows.	Qts.	Qts.	Qts.	Lbs.
3 Ayrshire cows,	5,386	1,795	5.00	4,485
4 Tondern cows.	9,337	2,334	6.30	5,835
Large Cows.				
3 Breitenburg cows,	8,594	2,865	8.00	7,161
22 Holland cows (Dutch-Friesian),	78,100	3,550	9.85	8,875

The highest yield of the Ayrshires was 5,582 lbs., and the lowest 3,537 lbs. The highest yield of the Tondern cows was 7,012 lbs., and lowest 4,640 lbs.

The highest yield of the Breitenburg cows was 7,365 lbs., and lowest 7,050 lbs.

The highest yield of the Holland (Holstein-Freisian) cows was 15,355 lbs. and the lowest 6,315 lbs.

The average winter ration was composed of 10 lbs. of straw of summer grain, 2 1-2 lbs. of oat and wheat chaff, 25 lbs. of turnips, 10 lbs. of hay, 8 lbs. of brewers grains, wet, and 3 lbs. of rye bran. This contained of digestible nutriment 3.28 lbs. of albuminoids, and 14.3 lbs. of carbo-hydrates, having a nutritive ratio of 1: 4.2—equal in nutritive value to 42 lbs. of hay.

The average ration in summer is 135 lbs. of green clover and 8 lbs. of dry day. The hay is to modify the succulence of the clover. Dr. Rhode says this ration is equal to 45 lbs. of hay, and contains of digestible albuminoids 5.7 lbs. and of carbo-hydrates 14.91 lbs.—nutritive ratio 1: 2-5.

He says the small cows did not eat as much as the large Holland cows, though the food of each was not weighed; yet when the same amount of food was placed in two racks, it was found that nine large cows ate as much as ten small cows per day, and he thus counted them as 9 to 10, in proportion of food or the small cows consumed 45 lbs. of hay, or its equivalent, while the large consume 50 lbs.

According to the specific yield, they severally require of food for the production of one quart of milk.

Holland cows (Holstein-Friesian), little more than 5.00 lbs. hay value
Breitenburg . . . . 6.25 " " "
Tondern . . . . 7.00 " " "
Ayrshire . . . . 9.00 " " "

The Holland cows weigh from 1200 to 1400 lbs.
" Breitenburg " 1100 to 1300 lbs.
" Tondern " 900 to 1000 lbs.
" Ayrshire " 800 to 900 lbs.

Here it appears that the large cows were the more economical milk producers. Here Dr. Rhode, at the head of the Eldena Agricultural School, found a pretty wide difference between the Hollanders and Ayrshires; and we are quite inclined to think, if the food of each separate class of animals had been accurately kept through the year, the difference could not have been so large as he makes the production from the same food—80 per cent—in favor of the Holland cows. Dr. Rhode remarks on this:

"It cannot be questioned. from these results, to which race belongs the advantage. They value none in Eldena for milk but the Holland cows."

Another experiment, conducted by Villeroy, between the Hollanders and the Devons, resulted in producing 28.92 quarts of milk for 100 pounds of hay from the Hollanders, and 19.13 quarts of milk for 100 lbs. of hay from the Devons. Baron Ockle, in Frankenfelde, made a comparative experiment, between Ayrshires averaging 806 lbs. in weight, and Hollanders averaging 1,016 lbs. in weight. The smaller breed consumed 33.10 of hay to 100 lbs. of live weight, while the larger breed consumed 28.10 lbs. of hay to 100 lbs. of live weight.

Every breed of cattle that lays any claim to public recognition as a dairy breed, has had its phenomenal cows with marvelous milk or butter records; every breed has also had its worthless cows, that may have come to public notice through the reports of impartial experimenters. Manifestly, it would be unjust to take the latter class as the true exponents of a breed. Equally improper would it be to seek to impress the public mind with the idea that such phenomenal cows are its true representatives. It is for the interests of the majority of the breeders of any valuable breed, as well as for the public interest, that data be given upon which a correct average production may be safely estimated, under the varying conditions of climate, care and feed. Such records may not startle and attract like those of phenomenal cows, yet they are the best foundation upon which a valuable reputation can be built.

Perhaps the most extensive and important records that were ever reported, are those that were made upon the estates of the King of Wirtemburg, between 1833 and 1865. It is to be regretted that a full report is not within our reach. The following is either directly taken or calculated from the report of Mr. Klippart, to which we have often referred: Fifteen breeds were thoroughly tested under the same or similar circumstances. They were not fed and cared for with a view to producing extremely large records, but with a view to profitable yields under the circumstances of agriculture and markets of Wirtemburg. All are given in this table with the exception of the Zebu from East India, which is reported as having no milking qualities. The headings have been slightly changed and columns relating to acclimatization in Wirtemburg, adaption to the yoke, etc., left out, as not specially relating to the subject under consideration:

SUMMARY OF EXPERIMENTS IN CATTLE FEEDING AND MILKING ON THE ESTATES OF THE KING OF WIRTEMBURG, BETWEEN 1833 AND 1865.

NAME OF BREED.	COLOR OF BREED.	ORIGIN OF BREED.	Average Weight of Cows.	Average Annual Milk Yield.	Amount of Milk produced from 100 lbs. hay or its equivalent.	Comparative Quality for Butter Making.	Comparative Quality for Cheese Making.
North Holland, or Friesian.	Usually black-and-white, variegated	North Holland and Friesland	1,200 lbs	6,549 lbs	54 lbs	18	19
Swiss	Dark brown, with a light stripe down back	Switzerland	1,225 "	5,764 "	53 "	20½	20
Durham*	Red, or red-roan	England	1,140 "	5,000 "	46 "	18½	19
Polled Yorkshire	Reddish brown and white	"	1,100 "	5,150 "	51 "	18½	19
Polled Suffolk	Reddish brown	"	935 "	4,208 "	42 "	18½	19
Devon	Reddish brown	"	850 "	2,816 "	36 "	22	20
Hereford	Reddish brown, with white face	"	950 "	2,316 "	26 "	22	20
Canvass Cattle	Black, with white sheet around body	Appenzell, Switzerland	950 "	5,056 "	50 "	21	20
Murzthaler	White and red gray, and dark shades	Styria, Austria	985 "	3,220 "	36 "	21	19½
Limburger	Yellow dun	Wirtemburg, Ger.	850 "	4,024 "	50 "	23	21
Allgauer	Blackish brown, white mouth	Upper Swabia	800 "	4,082 "	52 "	20	20
Alderney or Jersey†	Yellow dun, or light red- and-white	Channel Islands	705 "	3,800 "	46 "	25½	?
Unnamed breed	Blackish brown, and white stripes	Uri, Switzerland	765 "	4,732 "	54 "	20	20
Hungarian	Whitish gray	Hungary	935 "	1,524 "	18 "	22	20

* The Short-horn herd consisted of four cows, selected, upon the recommendation of Sir Robert Peel, from the estate of Sir James Graham, two of which were reputed to be famous milkers. These were purchased in 1847. Ten years afterwards five cows were added, from the Model Farm of Prince Albert, at Windsor.

† These consisted of six cows, imported direct from the island of Jersey, and nine imported from England, called thoroughbred Alderneys. It is probable that the latter were not pure Jerseys, but of pure or mixed Guernsey extraction.

Mr. Klippart also reports a series of milk records made in Saxony during a period of eight years, beginning with 1852, and closing with 1859. The government, for several years, had been encouraging the importation of the best milch breeds. From 1844 to 1851, a bonus of fifty thalers had been given for an importation of ten cows or ten heifers in calf of the foreign breeds named in the second table below. Mr Klippart does not state how, or by what authority these records were made, but the presumption is that they were kept by the owners of the various herds, and reported under certain governmental regulations. The two tables that follow are made up from his report.

MILK RECORD OF HOLLAND, OR FRIESIAN, COWS IN SAXONY.

Year.	No. of cows.	Average yield per cow in quarts.	Average yield per cow in pounds.	Maximum yield of a single cow in quarts.	Maximum yield of a single cow in pounds.
1852	—	4,162	8,948	8,484	18,241
1853	55	4,156	8,935	7,034	15,012
1854	51	3,806	8,183	6,679	14,860
1855	65	3,404	7,318	5,032	10,819
1856	61	3,985	8,568	6,578	14,142
1857	55	4,031	8,667	5,947	12,873
1858	42	3,992	8,582	5,947	12,873
1859	57	4,072	8,754	7,930	17,068

The want of space forbids the giving of full reports of the other breeds; but the following table is a correct summary of the average yields of all the breeds reported. Without doubt, to produce the maximum yields, very high and skillful feeding must have been practiced.

MILK RECORDS OF THE VARIOUS BREEDS TESTED IN SAXONY BETWEEN 1852 AND 1859.

Name of Breed.	No. of years tested.	No. of cows calculated at 1 year.	Average yield per cow in quarts.	Average yield per cow in pounds.	Average of highest yields in quarts.	Average of highest yields in pounds.
Hollander or Friesian,	8	386	3,950 8-10	8,494	6,338 8-10	14,703
Allgauer,	8	1,823	3,733 3-10	8,027	6,361 2-10	13,677
Oldenburger,	7	311	3,903	8,391	6,040 5-10	12,987
Simmenthaler,	1	571	2,957 4-10	6,358	—	—
Natives of Saxony,	8	225	3,154 5-10	6,782	3,789 6-10	8,148
Walzthaler,	4	87	3,479 8-10	7,481	5,554 5-10	11,942

The milk records given in these tables appear to have been impartially made. They extend over a period of several years, and include results from a large number of cows. Many records have been made in this country within the last fifteen years. To give them all would be too great a task; to discriminate would be to show partiality. It would seem that those which have been given would be sufficient to establish the conclusion that this breed excels all others in quantity of milk production.

It appears that upon the continent of Europe quantity of production has for many years reached a point unlooked for by English and American dairymen. Hence such records have been received by them with much incredulity. The

BOWEN, No. 12041, H.-F. H.-B.
First Prize Cow at Madison Square Garden, N. Y., 1896.

introduction of this breed into this country, and the competition among its importers and breeders, is working a great change in public opinion in regard to the capacity of the dairy cow. One extreme is likely to be followed by another. From doubting moderate records, the public are being educated to expect marvelous records, and to really overestimate the average capacity of this breed. Disappointment must follow such a state of facts. Hence it becomes important to fix upon a fair average yield that each individual owner may understand where his cows rank.

The average yield per cow of the North Holland or Friesian breed, as represented by these tables, is 7,972¼ lbs. This average closely accords with the estimate of Prof. Hengerveld, in his Introduction to the Netherlands Herd-Book. It is there given as 3,500 litres, which, being reduced, is 7,952 lbs. The climate in this country is warmer and dryer during the summer season, than in the countries from which these averages are calculated. This, no doubt, will result in producing a diminished quantity, with an increased quality of product. Hence we estimate that a well-kept herd in this country should produce from 7,000 to 7,500 lbs. per cow annually. It must be borne in mind that not every cow can reach the average product. There is a wide diversity in the yield of cows in all breeds. At least as many must fall below the average as rise above it. If the range below is narrower, the proportionate number that occupy this range must be increased. This may seem to some to be underrating the breed. A moment's reflection will convince to the contrary. The average of 7,000 to 7,500 lbs. is more than double the product of the average dairy cow throughout the United States. New York state is probably as good a dairy state as there is in the Union. Especially superior are those sections devoted to the manufacture of cheese. The statistics of the cheese factories of this state in 1875 show an average product of milk per cow of 3,082 lbs.; the noted county of Herkimer leading the other sections at the average product of 3,498 lbs. The average we have given this breed is considerably more than double these amounts. If this breed is not overestimated in these reports and tests, all of which seem to have been impartially made, a great general increase of wealth would result from its universal introduction into those sections of our country to which it is adapted.

CHAPTER VII.

THE BREED IN AMERICA—RECORDS AT SHADELAND—SOME REMARKABLE INSTANCES —PIETERTJE 2D, ETC.—LARGEST YEARLY RECORDS—ACTUAL RESULTS.

In the language of Mr. S. Hoxie, the introduction of the Holstein-Friesian breed in America has greatly enlarged the possibilities of milk and butter productions throughout our rich dairy sections. Our dairymen have been awakened and have changed in regard to the capacity to which they may raise their herds. Thirty pounds of milk a day, 5000 pounds a year, and 7 pounds of butter a week were considered twenty-five years ago as large yields, and even now are above the capacity of unimproved cows. The progress of such change of views may be traced in the progress of records that have been made by cows of this breed and publicly credited. The cow Crown Princess owned by Hon. Gerrit S. Miller of Peterboro, N. Y., in six years from 1870 to 1876 made a record of 61,112 pounds of milk, an average of 10,185 lbs. per year. This was followed by the record of Lady Clifden owned by Hon. Wm. A. Russell of Lawrence, Mass. In 1875 she gave in three hundred and sixty-two days 10,274 pounds; in 1876 in two hundred and eighty-two days 12,243 pounds; and commencing May 1st, 1877, in three hundred and ninety-six days 13,232 pounds. The Maid of Twisk, owned by the Unadilla Valley Association, a company of dairy farmers in Trenton, N. Y., followed this by a record for three hundred and three days in 1876 of 12,563 pounds; for three hundred and twenty-five days in 1877 of 14,312 pounds; and for three hundred and thirty-six days in 1878 of 15,960¼ lbs. Next came the records of the noted cows Aegis and Aaggie owned by Smiths & Powell Co. of Syracuse, N. Y. In 1880, three hundred and sixty-five days, the former gave 16,823⅔ lbs. and the latter 18,004 4⁄6 pounds. With the exception of Aegis these were all imported cows and it began to be questioned whether such cows could be produced in this country. The answer came in a test of the cow Echo, bred by Mr. Miller and owned by Mr. F. C. Stevens, Attica, N. Y. It was for two successive years, beginning March 9th, 1882, and closing May 28th, 1884. During the first year she gave 18,120¼ lbs. and during the second year, after a brief rest for about ten weeks, she produced 23,775¼ lbs. These records aroused the attention of dairy writers, especially in England. They were pronounced impossible. Plausible arguments were made to show the inconsistency of such records with the amount of material for making milk that a cow could digest. Public confidence in them was shaken for a brief period.

At this stage of public sentiment a test was begun of the cow Clothilde (see page 68) by Smiths & Powell Co. They offered to pay the expenses of some of the most prominent scientists to come and thoroughly investigate this test. A number of gentlemen availed themselves of this offer. It was also placed in the official charge of the Superintendent of the Holstein-Friesian Advanced Registry, who from time to time sent official inspectors to watch the milkings, to test the scales on which they were weighed, to examine into the accuracy of the account that was being kept, and into every other detail in which there might be a possibility of error. None was discovered and the accuracy of the record was put beyond all reasonable doubt. The result was the production of 26,021¼ pounds in three hundred and sixty-five consecutive days, a record of more than 2,000 lbs. above any that had been previously made. It seemed at that time that the extreme capacity of milk production by a single cow had been reached, but later the cow Pietertje 2d owned by Mr. Dallas B. Whipple of Cuba, N. Y., in August, 1888, reached a year's record of 30,318¼. The production of this had also been closely watched by disinterested parties and the proof is so convincing, that it was received by the public with much less doubt than were the early records of half this amount. Since 1880 many other cows have exceeded Aaggie's noted record.

Among these are Ethelka at 18,131$\frac{7}{8}$ lbs., and Jamaica at 19,547 lbs., both owned by John Mitchell, Vails Gate, N. Y.; Violet at 18,677¼ lbs., by Edgar Huidekoper, Meadville, Penn.; Lady De Vries at 18,848¼ lbs., by L. H. Payne, Garrettsville, O.; Empress at 19,714¼ lbs., by Hon. G. S. Miller, Peterboro, N. Y.; Glenburine at 20.138¼ lbs. by B. B. Lord & Son, Sinclairville, N. Y.; Rhoda at 21,309 lbs. by F. C. Stevens, Attica, N. Y.; Princess of Wayne at 20,469$\frac{9}{16}$ lbs. and Aaggie 2d at 20,763$\frac{7}{8}$ lbs., both by T. G. Yeomans & Sons, Walworth, N. Y.; Boukje at 21,679¼ lbs., by Stone & Carpenter, Waverly, Penn.; Koningen Van Friesland 5th at 19,700¼ lbs. by A. Bradley and H. D. Warner, Lanesville, Conn.; Koningen Van Friesland 3d at 23,617¼ lbs., by H. O. Warner, New Milford, Conn.; Sultana at 22,043¼ lbs., by H. C. Jewett & Co., Buffalo, N. Y.; and Albino 2d at 18,484¼⅛ lbs. in two-year form, Netherland Belle at 19,516¼ lbs., Aaggie Rosa at 20,227$\frac{7}{8}$ lbs., Lady Fay at 20,602$\frac{7}{16}$ lbs., and Clothilde 2d at 23,602¼ lbs., by Smiths & Powell Co.

Such records have been of so much interest in this country that the breeders have given much more attention to the production of quantity than quality of milk. They have fed and cared for their cattle to produce quantity. In consequence, many have inferred that this breed is an excellent one for the production of milk and cheese, but that it is not adapted to the production of butter. Notwithstanding this impression, it has now been engaged for some time in a contest for the highest place as a butter breed, and the rapidity with which it is gaining such a position is a public surprise. The first step toward this was the winning of the challenge cup offered by the "Breeders' Gazette," of Chicago for the largest thirty-days butter record. The contest for this cup was open to the world, and to all breeds, until July 1st, 1882. It was won by Mercedes, a cow of this breed owned by Thomas B. Wales, then of Iowa City, Iowa. Her record was 99 lbs., 6½ ounces. This result awakened much controversy. Several competitions took place in the three years following at cattle shows in the Western states, uniformly resulting in the success of this breed ; yet they were not considered conclusive, as the best cows of other breeds were not put in competition. At this stage of public opinion, the New York Dairy Show of 1887 was conceived. Long before its opening, it was widely known that one of its most important features would be a contest for the championship in butter production. This was to be decided by a twenty-four hours' trial in the hands of an impartial committee. It was entered upon for the purpose of testing the claims of the different breeds. Cattle clubs and breeders' associations were deeply interested in it, and gave every possible encouragement to the bringing forward of the best representatives of the breed they maintained. Probably no similar contest was ever arranged and conducted on more even terms. No criticisms were made against the management up to the hour of announcing the results.

The championship was won for this breed, the cow Clothilde receiving the first prize, and the three-year-old heifer Clothilde 4th, the second prize, both owned by Smiths & Powell Co. In other departments there were contests for quality of butter where the breeds were indirectly pitted against one another. In these contests this breed also won more than its appropriate proportionate share of the prizes.

It is only within the last few years that breeders of this cattle have been specially testing the butter capacity of their cows. Messrs. T. G. Yeomans & Sons were pioneers in this work. In tests made of their herd of less than 40 cows, 29 were found to average a seven days' production of 17 lbs. 7¼ oz. Aaggie 2d made 26 lbs. 7 oz. in this length of time, 105 lbs. 10½ oz. in thirty days, and 304 lbs. 5¼ oz. in ninety days. This was followed by tests of other breeders. Mr. Thos. B. Wales also found 29 cows owned by him that made an average of 17 lbs. 2.67 oz. One of these. Tritomia, at four years of age made 25 lbs. 3½ oz. Messrs. Smiths & Powell Co. find 100 cows owned by them that average 18 lbs. $\frac{7}{100}$ oz. in tests of the same length of time. Among these Netherland Princess 4th, at 28 months old, made 21 lbs. 10¾ oz.; Albino 2d at three years old 25 lbs. 14¼ oz., while in 30 days she produced 106 lbs. 14 oz. Their cow Clothilde at full age made in seven days 28 lbs. 2¼ oz. In the small herd of Mr. Eugene Smith, Nashville, Tenn., seven cows were reported with an average of 17 lbs. 6.57 oz. in seven days. Among other noted tests is that of Florence Herbert, owned by Home Farm Co., Hampton, Ia., at 27 lbs. 13½ oz. in seven days, and that of Nieltje Korndyke, the property of E. J. Burrell, Little Falls, N. Y., at 93 lbs. 12 oz in thirty days.

The following facts and figures concerning some remarkable milk records made in 1889 by the Shadeland herd of Holsteins, will be of interest. The figures will no doubt seem large to the farmer who thinks a cow which gives 20 quarts of milk a day an unusually good one. Probably one-half the cows in Crawford county, Penn., do not give as much milk in a whole year as some of these Shadeland Holsteins give in a month. No one pretends that these great milkers keep up such a flow throughout the milking year, but the probability is that the average of the whole Shadeland herd is three times that of the best herd of crosses, or native cattle in this county or any other county in the United States. While other cows of their herd nearly equalled the records given below the following are the most remarkable, viz.:

Shadeland Daisy, No. 3181 H. H.-B.—In one day, 103 lbs. 6 oz.; in one week, 684 lbs. ½ oz.; average per day of 97 lbs. 11½ oz.

Shadeland Winnie, No. 10700 H.-F. H.-B., when only about 28 months old— In one day, 84 lbs.; in two consecutive days, 164 lbs. 12 oz.; in one week, 512 lbs. 12 oz.; average per day of 73 lbs. 4 oz.; June 17 to July 17, inclusive, 1,968 lbs. 8 oz.

Shadeland Bloom 4th, No. 6067 H.-F. H.-B., while less than thirty-six months old, which would be in her two-year old form, and with only her first calf—In one day, 107 lbs. 4 oz.; in four days, 415 lbs. 8 oz., an average per day of 103 lbs. 14 oz.; in one week, 700 lbs. 8 oz., an average per day of 100 lbs. 1¼ oz.; from July 5 to August 4, inclusive, 2,767 lbs. 10 oz.

Celeste 3d, No. 2896 H.-F. H.-B., in her three-year-old form—In one day, 107 lbs. 8 oz.; in five days, 522 lbs. 8 oz., an average per day of 104 lbs. 8 oz.; in one week, 716 lbs. 4 oz., an average per day of 102 lbs. 5¼ oz.; July 4 to August 3, inclusive, 2,878 lbs. 4 oz.

Shadeland Boon 2d, No. 5892 H. H.-B., in her five-year-old form—In one day, 122 lbs. 8 oz.; in four consecutive days, 476 lbs. 12 oz., an average per day of 119 lbs. 3 oz.; in one week, 801 lbs. 8 oz., an average per day of 114 lbs. 8 oz.; in fifteen days, one-half month, 1,641 lbs., an average per day of 109 lbs. 6⅜ oz.; during the month of July, 3,170 lbs., 4 oz.; and this after milking in six different days in June, 625 lbs. 12 oz., an average per day of 104 lbs. 4¾ oz.

It is interesting to know that these records are not mere accidents. The Advanced Register of the Holstein-Friesian Association shows that Shadeland Daisy, as a three-year old, milked 77 lbs. 11 oz. in one day (the highest record for that age up to that time), and that she has made several large records since; that Shadeland Bloom, the dam of Shadeland Bloom 4th, milked as a two-year-old 69 lbs. in one day (the highest record to that date of a two-year-old),

and since then other higher records; also that Shadeland Boon, the dam of Shadeland Boon 2d, has made various milk records, and last year made the largest monthly butter record of any cow of any breed in the world, producing 125 lbs. 12 oz. of butter in thirty-one consecutive days, and her milk being so rich it required only 14.09 lbs. of milk for a pound of butter for the whole time, and for a portion of the time it took only 11.18 lbs. of milk for one pound of butter. In 1889 she milked nearly 100 pounds per day.

To better appreciate these records it should be known that the highest record for any two-year-old previous to the above by Shadeland Winnie and Shadeland Bloom 4th, is 76 lbs. 6 oz. and that Shadeland Boon 2d has averaged considerably more for several consecutive days than the highest single day by any other cow.

If some of our readers who may feel inclined to disparage the merits of blooded animals, and who think they have a world beater of a cow of common stock, will take the trouble to weigh the milk for a few days, then would they better appreciate the cow that is able to produce 122 lbs. 8 oz. in one day. Two and one-sixth pounds is the estimated weight of one quart of milk, which would make for Shadeland Boon 2d, over 56 quarts, or more than 1¾ bushels of milk in one day. During these tests the Messrs. Powell thought it prudent in order to avoid injury to her udder to have her milked three to five times a day.

These records were all carefully made, were witnessed from time to time by disinterested parties and have been duly attested, sworn to and authenticated.

Of the great value of the Holstein-Friesian cow for milk there is most abundant evidence. Our quotations from Hengerveld, Klippart, Hoxie and others, in addition to many tests cited, amply demonstrate that no other breed approaches this in ability to produce milk.

American breeders for many years have demonstrated what the Holstein cow can do, and the list of 7,000 public and private records in another part of this work is cumulative testimony. Plain it is that the enterprise and energy of American breeders have enabled them to exceed all foreign records, and it is probable that the average production of the Holstein cow in America is in advance of that reached in Holland.

As an instance of consecutive performance extending over a period of ten years the following experience of Messrs. T. G. Yeomans & Son, Walworth, N. Y., with the famous cow, Princess of Wayne, is given in their own language and as appeared in the Holstein-Friesian Register in March, 1891: "We will give our experience with our Holstein-Friesian cow Princess of Wayne 954, A. R. 2, extending over a period of ten years since the birth of her first calf in 1881, during which time she has given us nice, vigorous healthy calves, and made five very large yearly records. She was born May 14, 1878, and selected with her dam, Queen of Wayne, in Holland by the senior member of the firm, as the best representatives he could find of his idea of perfect dairy animals. She is such a typical cow of this breed, and from the first has shown such remarkable qualities that we think a brief narrative of her performances will be of interest to many of our readers.

"She dropped her first calf when two years and ten months old, and gave 57 lbs. of milk in a day, 14,008 lbs. 9 oz. in ten months and twenty days, and dropped her next calf within one year. When ten months in milk she made 8¼ lbs. of thoroughly worked butter in a week. In her five-year-old form she made an average of 3 lbs. 9 oz. of thoroughly worked butter per day for three consecutive days; 22 lbs. ¼ oz. in a week, and 91 lbs. ⅞ oz. in thirty days, placing her at the time in the front as the greatest Holstein-Friesian butter cow of her age; her milk record at this time was 80 lbs. per day, 20,469 lbs. 9 oz. in a year, which has been excelled only by one cow, Echo. In her eight-year-old form Princess gave in 11 months and 13 days, 20,561½ lbs. of milk, and dropped her next calf 13½ months after the birth of her last one. In the next 11 months she gave 21,104 lbs. 7 oz. of milk and dropped another calf in 12½ months. From the birth of this first calf to that of the third was 800 days, during 682 days of which time she gave 41,665 lbs. 15 oz., an average of over 52 lbs. of milk per day for the entire 800 days, or an average of 61 lbs. 1½ oz. for 682 days, the actual time of the record. During these two seasons she was fed, milked and cared for the same as the whole herd with which she ran, being milked three times per day, not at equal intervals, and no effort was in any way made to crowd or force her to make a large record. In fact no one was more surprised at the record than ourselves, as we had not even footed up her record after the first four months of the first year until its close, and not even for thirty days of the second year until its close, owing to the illness and absence of the member of our firm to whom this work was allotted.

"She has given during the past year 113 lbs. 1 oz. of milk in a day, an average of 110 lbs. 11 oz. for six consecutive days; 3,182 lbs. 2 oz. in thirty days, and 29,008 lbs. 11 oz. in one year, excelling by nearly three thousand pounds all other records except that of Pietertje 2d. We did not expect to test her especially for a large record till she had been in milk twenty-eight days, which makes a difference of several hundred pounds loss in her record of the year. Her butter record is 24 lbs. 14 oz. thoroughly worked, salted butter in a week. Since the birth of her first calf in 1881 she has given by actual weight of each milking 164,310¼ lbs. of milk in ten years and twenty-five days, which is an average of 16,319 lbs. per year or $44\frac{7}{10}$ lbs. per day for the entire time including

BOONSTRA, 2D, No. 732 H. H.-B.
Imported. Milk record, 78 lbs. in one day; 2,100 lbs. in thirty days.

all the time she was dry. Princess after these ten years of hard work is in fine condition, and to all appearances equal to another trial."

The history of the wonderful record of the Holstein-Friesian cow, Pietertje 2d, is thus given by Mr. D. B. Whipple:

"On visiting several herds of Holsteins in the New England states in September, 1884, I came across Pietertje 2d in Elizur Smith's herd at Lee, Mass., he having purchased her soon after she was imported. After examining her and seeing her milked, I was fully satisfied that she was capable of milking more than any cow that I had ever seen milked, so I purchased her, together with twelve others, and shipped them home to Cuba, Allegany Co., N. Y., where she has remained ever since. With her persistent milking, and the low condition she was in, I did not think it advisable to undertake to make a year's record, although she milked 103½ lbs. after dropping her next calf. I then delayed breeding her, so there were twenty months elapsed between the births of her two last calves. This was preparatory to her making this record, although she was milked sixteen out of the twenty months before we could dry her off. I am informed that this is the only time she has ever been dry since first coming in milk. The statement made by Alfred Jencks in relation to an accident happening to Pietertje 2d on September 1st, 1887, and again on January 24th, 1888, when she was sick, is correct, and without a doubt, if nothing had happened to Pietertje 2d, her record would have been nearer 31,000 lbs. than 30,000 lbs. But as it turned out the results are quite gratifying, 30,318½ lbs. beats all previous efforts by 4,297 lbs. 6 oz. Pietertje 2d was nearly three months in calf when this record closed, being further in advance in calf than either Clothilde or Echo were, as they were not bred until their records were nearly closed. Pietertje 2d has one son and three daughters. The son is Pietertje 2d's Holland King, four years old; the first daughter is Pietertje 3d, formerly Milla; the second daughter is Pietertje 4th, formerly Pietertje 2d's Netherland, and the third daughter is Pietertje 5th, formerly Netherland Duke's Pietertje. This is all the family, no others in existence, and all owned by me.

"Pietertje 2d dropped her last calf February 19th, 1887. She commenced her record February 24th, 1887 and closed the same February 23d, 1888, and has made the following record for each month and year:

February 24th, 1887, to March 23d, 1887, inclusive,					2,454 lbs. 7 oz.
March " " " April " "					2,818 " 6 "
April " " " May " "					2,939 " 14 "
May " " " June " "					3,280 " 10 "
June " " " July " "					2,897 " 4 "
July " " " August " "					2,836 " 10 "
August " " " Sept. " "					2,586 " 14 "
September " " " Oct. " "					2,546 " 7 "
October " " " Nov. " "					2,363 " 11 "
November " " " Dec. " "					2,004 " 4 "
December " " " Jan. " 1888, "					1,804 " 12 "
January " 1888, " Feb. " " "					1,776 " 5 "
				Total,	30,318 lbs. 8 oz.

Average per day for the whole year,	83 lbs. 1 11-365 oz.
Highest day's yield, third month in milk,	112 " 7 "
Smallest day's yield, Jan. 13th 1888, when sick,	41 " 5 "
Last day of the year's record, witnessed,	60 " 13 "

Average yield per day for each month:

1st month, 87 lbs. 10½ oz.		7th month, 83 lbs. 0 27-31 oz.
2d month, 90 " 14¾ "		8th month, 84 " 14 "
3d month, 97 " 15 "		9th month, 76 " 4 "
4th month, 106 " 1⅞ "		10th month, 66 " 13 "
5th month, 96 " 9 1-5 "		11th month, 58 " 3 15-31 "
6th month, 91 " 3 "		12th month, 57 " 4 25-31 "

"It will be seen that these last months were on dry feed and in mid-winter; also cow in calf. Pietertje 2d was only milked three times per day during this record.

"The analysis of Pietertje 2d's milk was made by New York Agricultural Experiment Station, Geneva, N. Y., and Cornell University, Ithaca, N. Y., both at the same time, and from samples from the same milking. The analyses agree very closely and are as follows:

Specific Gravity	1.0284	Average Standard	1.032	
Total Solids	11.20 per cent	" "	.12	per cent.
Fat	3.16 " "	" "	3 to 3½ "	"
Solids minus fat	8.04 " "	" "	.9	"
Caseine n x	2.72 " "			
Ash	.70 " "			
Sugar (by difference)	4.52 " "			

"This is a wonderful showing considering the feed that Pietertje 2d has had. The richness of the milk would show that she is a great butter cow as well as a great milker. Her milk has been taken to the cheese factory and accepted as good milk, although no factory in this section of the country will allow patrons to feed potatoes to their cows, on account of hurting the quality of milk. Notwithstanding these facts, Pietertje 2d's milk is fully up to the standard in butter fats, and is only off a small fraction on solids. One can readily see that her food has been to stimulate quantity instead of quality, and therefore, must say that the analysis of this milk is highly gratifying to me.

CALAMITY JANE, No. 26282 H.-F. H. B.

First prize for butter at Canadian Fat Stock and Dairy Show. Record, 69.18 lbs. milk, showing 3.16 per cent. fat, yielding 2.09 lbs. butter. Age, four years.

"In summer during the warm weather she was kept in the barn daytimes and turned to pasture at night. Was fed three times per day during the entire year. The feed consisted of equal parts in measurement of ground oats and bran, ranging from 20 to 28 pounds per day, if any left it was ordinarily taken away from her. Also during the season for turnips she had about one-half bushel per day and some potatoes, the amount of both ranging from one-half to one and one-half bushel. The potatoes were fed during the whole year, and I should say would average from one-half to three-quarters of a bushel per day for the whole year. Whenever anything was refused it was usually taken away. In the day time during the summer she was fed grass and during the winter her fodder consisted of timothy hay and corn stalk, neither of them cut. During cold weather she had water to drink three times per day at a temperature of 60 degrees. No drink of any kind during this record but good water. She was also fed one pound of Blatchford's Royal Stock Food, also a small quantity of Thorley's Horse and Cattle Food. These foods were fed with the ground oats and bran, this feed being moistened with water. Her stall in which she ran loose was 13x15 feet and screened to keep flies out during the summer.

"Pietertje 2d's milk record has been kept accurately, and each milking weighed and recorded at the time. The greatest care has been taken to have this record made as publicly as possible. No record ever before was given to the public before completed for the purpose of giving the public an opportunity to come and test and examine records, and investigate parties that had made tests and sworn to the same. I say that no record was ever made by any cow where the breeders and public had the full knowledge of what was going on as they have had during the making of this record. The gentlemen that have witnessed these tests are honorable and honest men, and occupy high standing in society, and are holding high and honorable positions. The affidavits will now be referred to in their regular order.

"The affidavit of Dallas B. Whipple, of Cuba, Allegany county, N. Y., the owner of Pietertje 2d, states that Pietertje 2d dropped her calf February 19th, 1887, and commenced her record February 24th, 1887, and closed the same February 23d, 1888, just one year from the time she commenced it; and at the close of this record Pietertje 2d was nearly three months in calf. My affidavit also corroborates Rev. W. W. Rafter's statement and affidavit. I witnessed the same test that he did, and saw Pietertje 2d milk May 21st, 1887, 107 lbs. 8 oz. I also saw two milkings of the same test of Geo. H. Brooks of May 18th, in which he testifies that Pietertje 2d milked 112 lbs. 7 oz. Being called away on business, I was prevented from seeing the third milking.

"Affidavit of Geo. H. Brooks, merchant, Cuba, N. Y., testifies that on the evening of May 17th, he saw Pietertje 2d milked clean, and in just twenty-four hours thereafter closed the twenty-four hour test, and in the meantime he had seen her milk 112 lbs. 7 oz. in three milkings.

"Affidavit of Rev. W. W. Rafter, rector of Christ Church, Cuba, N. Y., testifies that within twenty-four hours after seeing Pietertje 2d milked clean, she had milked 107 lbs. 8 oz. in three milkings, May 21st, 1887.

"Prof. J. E. Dewey of Limestone Academy, Limestone, N. Y., testifies that on July 19th, after seeing Pietertje 2d milked clean, he saw her milk 94 lbs. 1 oz., within the following twenty-four hours, just five months from the date of her calving.

"Affidavit of Frank H. Robinson, the district attorney of Steuben county, N. Y., testifies that on July 24th, he visited Cuba for the purpose of witnessing a milk test of Pietertje 2d. He testifies that on that date he saw her milked clean, and saw her milk within the next twenty-four hours, at three milkings, 92 lbs. 10 oz., five months after calving.

"Affidavit of Wm. Ormiston, of the firm of Ormiston Bros., Valley Point Farm, Cuba, N. Y.—breeders of Ayrshire cattle and owners of the noted prize herd that was exhibited so successfully in the West and Southwest for two years in succession—testifies that after seeing Pietertje 2d milked dry February 6th, 1888, he saw her milk in the next twenty-four hours 59 lbs. 11 oz., 11¼ months after calving, and in middle of the winter.

"Affidavit of Solomon Hoxie of Whitestown, N. Y., superintendent of the Advanced Registry of the Holstein-Friesian Association, testifies that on February 16th, 1888, he saw Pietertje 2d milked dry, and on the 17th, just twenty-four hours from that time, he had seen milked from Pietertje 2d, 57 lbs. 9

oz., this being the last week of the year's test or record and in middle of winter with temperature 10 degrees below zero, and cow said to be nearly three months in calf.

"Affidavit of Dudley Miller of Oswego, N. Y., secretary of Board of Trade of Oswego, N. Y., testifies that after seeing Pietertje 2d milked dry the evening of February 16th, 1888, that on February 17 he saw her milk 60 lbs. 4 oz. This, the last week in the year's record and nearly three months in calf.

"Affidavit of Samuel C. Drew, Cuba, N. Y., breeder of Jerseys, testifies that he saw Pietertje 2d milked dry the evening of February 22d, 1888, and morning, noon and night milking of February 23d, 1888, making just twenty-four hours production, in which time she gave 60 lbs. 13 oz. This being the last milking of the year's record.

"Affidavit of Geo. D. Whipple, Cuba, N. Y., testifies that on February 22d, 1888, at evening milking of Pietertje 2d he saw her milked clean, and on February 23d he saw her milked in the morning, at noon and at evening, and in the twenty-four hours she milked 60 lbs.13 oz. This completed the year's record, which foots up to 30,318¼ lbs.

"Affidavit of Alfred Jencks, Cuba, N. Y., testifies that he has had full care of Pietertje 2d both in feeding and milking. He testifies that Pietertje 2d milked in exactly one year, 30,318¼ lbs., and that all the different tests are true and correct in every particular, also that Pietertje 2d was milked only three times per day during this record, and that she was nearly three months in calf when she closed her record. He also testifies in relation to Pietertje 3d, formerly Milla, a daughter of Pietertje 2d.

"Affidavits of Henry C. Morgan, cashier of First National Bank, Cuba, N.Y., and Chas. S. Davis, cashier of Cuba National Bank, Cuba, N. Y., both testify as to seeing Pietertje 2d milked, and the milk poured from pail to pail till thoroughly mixed and cooled; then that they took the same and expressed two packages—one to Cornell University, Ithica, N. Y., and the other to New York Experimental Station at Geneva, N. Y.

"Pietertje 2d's record is supported in its different forms by nearly twice as many affidavits as any other milk record ever before made."

Mr. Henry C. Jewett of Buffalo, N. Y., stated in a paper read before the Farmers' Club in Buffalo in 1886 that the milk of his herd was marketed in glass bottles in Buffalo at nine cents per quart; the gross annual income per cow exceeding $300. For five years, since the herd was established in 1880, each and all the mature cows in it, averaged over 11,200 lbs. of milk per annum with but two milkings per day and ordinary good feeding.

The following excerpt from the article of C. W. Jennings of Belleville, N. Y., in an issue of *Hoard's Dairyman*, affords a fine opportunity to recommend a practical cow to farmers. The earnings of the grade Holstein herd stand at $81 per cow as against $29.75 for the grade Jersey herd, $28.41 per cow of the mixed Jersey herd, $42.69 per cow, average of the " natives." Below is the excerpt:

"The *Jersey Bulletin* is of course an 'organ.' Its chief business seems to be the publishing of tests of high-toned Jersey cows, and belittling and misrepresenting all other breeds. It is careful to 'keep dark,' however, the *poor* Jersey's tests. Probably they are 'crowded out.' Last week in referring to the 'cow census' of this town, it dubbed the entire number of cows—5,507—as 'regular old natives that have impoverished the farmer in so many localities.' For the editor's especial benefit I subjoin the statements from two high-grade Jersey herds, one Holstein herd, and a couple of the 'regular old natives,' all of them taken from that same 'cow census' returns. They may not prove what Horace Greeley termed 'mighty entertaining reading' for the *Bulletin* of big tests, but they will do for a change.

STATEMENTS.

Cows, 22 high grade Jerseys.
Value of calves sold and raised, . . $178.94
Value of cheese, ... 472.51
Value of deacon skins, ... 3.00
No butter.
Total earnings, ... 654.45
Earnings per cow, ... 29.75

No. 54.
Cows, 11 Jerseys and Jersey grades.
Value of calves raised and sold, . . 42.00
Value of butter, ... 56.00

Value of cheese, . . . $214.55
Total earnings, . . . 312.55
Earnings per cow, . . . 28.41

No. 17.
Cows, 7 natives.
Value of calves sold and raised, . $45.00
Value of butter, ... 36.00
Value of cheese, ... 200.00
Total earnings, ... 281.00
Earnings per cow, ... 45.21

No. 198. Cows, 7 natives.		No. 302. Cows, 5 Holstein grades.	
Value of calves,	$25.00	Value of calves raised and sold,	$70.00
Value of deacon skins,	.80	Value of butter,	335.00
Value of butter,	35.00	No cheese.	
Value of cheese,	255.72	Total earnings,	405.00
Total earnings,	316.52	Earnings per cow,	81.00
Earnings per cow,	40.14		

"From the above statements it appears that the average earnings per cow of the Jersey grade herds were $29.36; of the two native herds, $42.68, or $13.38 more each cow; while those of the Holstein herd were $51.70 more per cow. There were several other herds that were part Jerseys, with no better records, and several natives with nearly as good records as those quoted. So far as the 'regular old natives' are concerned, I will say that not more than one-fourth of the 5,507 cows were of that class.

"From the above one can see how far out of the way an organ of 'breeds' can get concerning real facts."

Beginning with 1870, the greatest annual milk records of Holstein-Friesian cows, with dates when completed, are as follows:

	Month.	Name.	Lbs. oz.
1871	March 15,	Dowager, 7 H. H.-B.,	12,68 8
1876	January 29,	Lady Clifden, 150 H. H.-B.,	16,274 0
1881	February 21,	Aegis, 69 H. H.-B.,	16,822 10
1881	March 27,	Aaggie, 901 H. H.-B.,	18,063 15
1883	March 19,	Echo, 121 H. H.-B.,	18,129 8
1884	March 20,	Lady De Vries, 680 F. H.-B.,	18,846 4
1884	April 16,	Empress, 530 H. H.-B.,	19,714 4
1884	May 28,	Echo, 121 H. H.-B. ,	23,775 8
1886	August 17,	Clothilde, 1808 H. H.-B.,	26,022 2
1888	February 23,	Pietertje 2d, 3273 H. H.-B.,	30,318 8

CHAPTER VIII.

QUALITY OF MILK—MICROSCOPIC APPEARANCE—BUTTER EXPORTS FROM HOLLAND—COMPARISON WITH OTHER BREEDS—CHEESE PRODUCTION—ANALYSIS OF MILK—J. VAN DER BREGGEN'S STATISTICS.

Examinations of the milk of this breed under the microscope made by Dr. Sturtevant, Prof. Arnold and others reveal a peculiar structure. The fat globules are numerous, very uniform in size, but small. In consequence of such a structure, the cream rises slowly. Set side by side with milk of no richer quality, but of larger fat globules, in a given time less depth of cream will appear. Hence, a comparison by the cream gauge with milk of other breeds is often unfavorable. Prof. Hengerveld gives the depth of cream from 8 to 16 per cent. Mr. Amersfort, of Haarlemameer, in a weekly test of his herd, continued for years, found the average to be from 12 to 13 per cent. The peculiar structure of this milk renders it especially valuable for cheese making, as the fat globules are more readily retained in the curd. It also adds to its value for marketing. Early and late-served customers receive a more uniform quality. Such customers may not find so much cream upon the surface as in milk of larger fat globules, but a better quality throughout the measure; and they should not judge its quality by its color, but rather by its opaqueness.

The chief business of the Friesian dairymen, the originators of this breed, is butter making. It is difficult to go back and ascertain when this was not their chief occupation, so long and so continuously have they pursued it. It is of so much importance to their country that other kinds of business prosper or fail with the rise or fall of price, or the increase or decrease of the single product, butter. London is their principal export market, where it has been the standard butter from time immemorial. The color of the butter is a lemon-yellow rather than orange; its flavor light, sweet and clean; its keeping qualities are unexcelled. It is marketed in what is called by them quarter, eighth and sixteenth casks, a quarter holding forty kilos, or eighty-nine pounds avoirdupois. These casks are very neat and substantial in appearance, every one

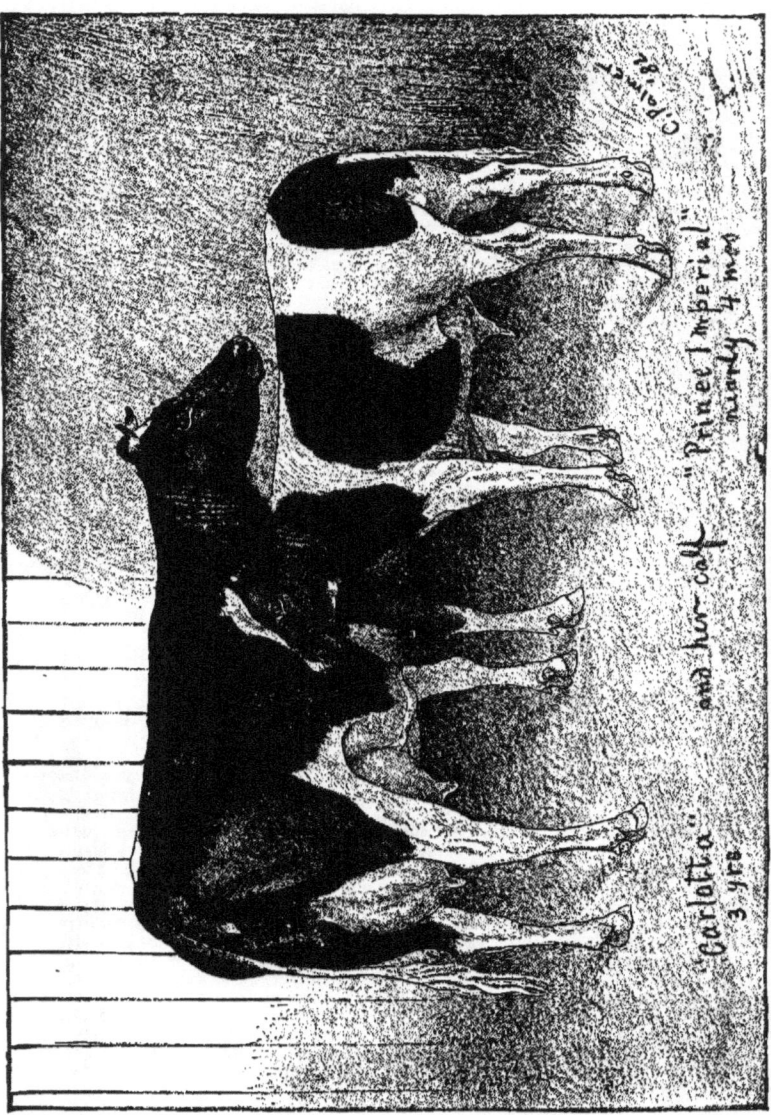

CARLOTTA AND CALF, No. 1266 H.-F. H.-B.; ADVANCED REGISTRY, No. 86.

Imported. Milk record, 70 lbs. 3 oz. in one day; 12,603 lbs. 4 oz. in one year. Butter record, 22 lbs. 11.4 oz. in one week; 18.28 lbs. of milk making one pound of butter.

bound with twelve hoops of willow, put on by threes. There are several public market places in the province of Friesland. That at Leeuwarden is one of the finest in the world. Upon this single market upwards of 9,000,000 of pounds are annually sold. This province is about equal in size to Herkimer county in Central New York.

According to Chambers' Encyclopedia, the amount of butter exported from this province to England in 1874 was 266,041 cwt., or 29,796,592 lbs. This was an average of 117¼ lbs. for every acre of grass land in the whole country. The number of cows for that year is not reported, but we find from other authorities that the number in 1879 was 144,802. Assuming an equal number in 1874, the average export per cow was 205¾ lbs. We have no data of the home consumption, but the population was 321,445. The bearing and force of these statistics will be better understood by a comparison. The number of milch cows in the state of New York in the same year was 1,301,879. The milk of 396,772 was carried to factories, and mainly manufactured into cheese. The milk of the remainder, 905,107 cows, produced 107,873,361 lbs. of butter, an average of 119¼ lbs. per cow. It will be seen by these statements that the Friesian is one of the most important butter making breeds, yet it does not hold this position by the superior richness of its milk, but rather by exceeding productiveness in quantity.

The quality for butter production as determined by the Wirtemberg tests was found to rank closely to that of other breeds of large dairy cattle. In these exhaustive trials made under the auspices of the king, its quality, determined from actual butter making, was one thirty-seventh below the Shorthorn, the Yorkshire and the Suffolk, the leading dairy breeds of England. In other words, a given quantity of milk that would make 37 lbs. from these breeds, from the Friesian breed would make 36 lbs.

As compared with the Devon, Hungarian and Hereford breeds, it was two-elevenths below, with the Allgauer and the unnamed breed from Uri, Switzerland, one-tenth below, with Limburger five-twenty-thirds below, with the Jersey breed a little less than three-tenths below, and with the Swiss breed a little less than one-eighth below. But when quantity of milk was also taken into consideration it excelled all the other breeds in butter production, excepting the Swiss. Allowing to the Jersey breed the standard yield of 200 lbs. of butter per annum, the Friesian and Swiss cows would produce 239 lbs. (dropping fractional pounds) and the Canvass cows 216 lbs. The others would fall below the standard in the following order: Yorkshires, 193 lbs.; unnamed breed from Uri, Switzerland, 192 lbs.; Allgauers, 189 lbs.; Limburgers, 188 lbs.; Durhams, 187 lbs.; Suffolks, 158 lbs.; Murzthalers, 138 lbs.; Devons, 126 lbs.; Herefords, 104 lbs., and Hungarians, 68 lbs.

For cheese production it was found equal in quality to the Durham, the Polled Yorkshire and the Polled Suffolk; it was one-twentieth below the Swiss, the Devon, the Hereford, the Canvass, the Allgauer, the Hungarian and unnamed breed from Uri, Switzerland; one-seventh below the Limburger, and one-thirty-ninth below the Murzthaler. But, as in butter making, when quality of milk was also taken into consideration, it excelled all other breeds. Allowing to the Durham breed the standard yield of 500 lbs., four breeds would go above this standard, led by the Friesians in the following order (dropping fractional pounds): Friesians, 554 lbs.; Swiss, 600 lbs.; Canvass, 532 lbs.; Yorkshires, 515 lbs. Below the standard the order would be as follows: Unnamed breed from Uri, Switzerland, 498 lbs.; Allgauers, 489 lbs.; Limburgers, 445 lbs.; Suffolks, 421 lbs.; Murzthalers, 331 lbs.; Devons, 295 lbs.; Herefords, 254 lbs., and Hungarians, 162 lbs.

According to Professor Hengerveld the milk of this breed contains from 8 to 16 per cent solids, of which from 2¼ to 4¼ per cent is fat. Much higher analyses have been published in this counry, some of which cannot be regarded as reliable. A few years ago Mr. R. F. McKedzie, assistant chemist of Michigan Agricultural College, published a table of averages of analyses of the different breeds. In this table the average per cent of fat in the milk of this breed is given at 6.84. This is undoubtedly much too high. The table was no doubt correctly calculated, but the analyses must have been obtained from unreliable sources.

The kind, quality and quantity of food, the state of the weather, the health of the animal and many other things greatly modify the quality of milk produced by any given breed, increasing or decreasing the total solids, as the circumstances are favorable or unfavorable. We give the following analyses of milk of this breed with the attendant conditions. The authorities of the city of Leeuwarden, Friesland, caused the analyses of the milk of four cows to be made on the 15th of May, 1879, for the purpose of determining the quality of milk that might be sold in the market as pure. The cows were then kept in the open fields without stabling, night or day, in a climate very cold and damp at this season. Their food was only the watery grasses of spring time.

Age of Cow.	No. Days from Calving.	Specific Gravity of Milk.	Total Solids.	Fat.
9 years.	20	1.0322	12.65	3 35
7 "	86	1.0306	11.84	3.10
4 "	25	1.0323	12.23	2.67
3 "	127	1.0324	12.72	2.96
		1.0314	12.36	3.02

On the 31st of March, 1879, the milk of four other cows was taken. These were kept in the stables on the ordinary hay of that country:

Age of Cow.	No. Days from Calving.	Specific Gravity of Milk.	Total Solids.	Fat.
4 years.	11	1.0335	13.52	3.04
6 "	43	1.0300	11.64	3.48
5 "	245	1.0306	12.00	3.54
2 "	194	1.0320	12.68	3.43
		1.0315	12.57	3.43

In an address before the Netherlands Agricultural Society in 1881, Mr. T. J. vd Pesch says that analyses of milk of this breed show a variation of constituents as follows:

In per cent. of water, ... from 84 to 88 per cent.
" " butter, ... " 2.50 " 4.50 "
" " caseine, ... " 2.50 " 5 "
" " milk sugar, ... " 3 " 6 "
" " albumen, ... " .33 " .55 "
" " other solids, ... " .07 " .08 "

As I have given facts concerning the butter of Holstein-Friesians in America, and England and Friesland, I will add the average analysis of milk taken from various races of cows at the Paris International Exposition of 1878:

No. Cows.	Races or Breeds.	Butter.	True lactic acid.	Milk Sugar.	Proteine matters—caseine, albumen.	Salts.	Water.	Total.
2	Ayrshire,	35.98	1.20	52.93	23.83	7.62	911.61	1,033.15
5	Shortborn,	35.51	1.54	51.48	25.67	7.81	911.35	1,033.36
5	Flemish,	34.18	1.86	51.18	23.45	7.93	913.86	1,032.54
5	Holland,	38.99	2.64	50.70	23.14	7.84	909.39	1,031.70
6	Norman,	38.95	1.93	51.07	26.81	8.06	906.94	1,033.75
5	Switz,	37.81	1.42	54.19	24.04	8.05	908.47	1,033.86

From this table it will be seen that the analysis does not show Holstein-Friesian milk lacking in butter, as it stands at the head of the list.

The following statistics in regard to quality were compiled by J. Van der Breggen Az, of Waddingveen, South Holland, one of the largest land owners and cheese makers in Europe.

It has often been said, but never proved, that Dutch cows give a large quantity of milk, but that the milk is poor.

I believe the milk of our Dutch cows is as rich in butter and cheese as that of other breeds, and I am glad to find that the learned Prof. Sanson is of the same opinion.

The following lists will prove the truth of my assertion. I must only observe that, as cheese making is my chief occupation, my accounts will be more detailed than those for butter making.

As for cheese making, I have, however, only a few comparing figures at my service. We have obtained the following results in six years:

	Kilograms* of Milk.	Kilograms of milk required for 1 kilogram of cheese+
1875	410,612	9.96
1876	487,801	10.48
1877	509,586	10.36
1878	525,722	10.46
1879	475.640	10.97
1880	404.914	10.88
	Av of 6 yrs.	10.5 kil., or 10.2 litres.‡

* Edam cheese requires more milk for a pound than American.
† A kilogram is 2,2085 avoirdupois.
‡ A litre is 2,113 pints.

So we required in six years, 10.2 litres of milk to make a kilogram of new cheese. On an average, there is a loss in weight of 7½ per cent when the cheese is fit for delivery. Edam cheese requires more milk for a pound than American. A kilogram is 2,2085 avoirdupois. A litre is 2,113 pints.

At Longford (a very fertile district on the river Shannon, in Ireland) they made 93,415 kilograms of new cheese from 1,000,675 litres of milk, so that they required then 10.70 litres of milk for one kilogram of fresh cheese. They found a loss in weight of 9 per cent when the cheese was delivered.

At Baron Wolff's, in Livonia (a fertile district in Western Russia, on the Gulf of Riga), they needed 14.3 litres of milk from Ayrshire-Angler cows to make one kilogram of fat cheese.

At Aas, in Norway, one kilogram of Cheddar cheese was made from 12.1 litres of milk, and the average of 100 cheese manufacturers in America is 9.82 kilograms of milk to make one kilogram of cheese.

I have not been able to find more trustworthy reports, but the foregoing list shows that they wanted more milk of English cattle of Longford, and in Russia and Norway, to make one kilogram of cheese than they do here (in Holland); the accounts from America show rather less. We may thus conclude that the milk of Dutch cows contains at least as much caseine as that from other stock.

The following list will serve as a criterion of the quality of the milk during the various months of the year:

KILOGRAMS OF MILK NEEDED TO MAKE ONE KILOGRAM OF CHEESE IN—

	Mar.	April.	May	June.	July.	Aug.	Sept.	Oct.	Nov.	Dec.
1875	....	....	9.34	9.65	10.60	10.75	10.50	9.18	9.00	....
1876	....	....	10.26	10.80	10.36	11.06	10.05	10.20	9.05	9.37
1877	10.52	11.00	10.11	10.77	11.12	10.98	10.00	9.40	9.00	9.30
1878	10.35	11.06	10.40	10.70	10.92	10.80	9.90	9.00	9.15	8.80
1879	11.10	11.30	10.60	11.00	11.10	11.20	10.70	9.50	....	9.95
1880	11.70	10.39	10.80	11.10	11.16	11.03	10.42	9.30	....	....
Av.	10.92	11.24	10.25	10.67	11.04	10.97	10.26	9.44	9.05	9.24

When we consider the results of these stastistics, it appears that in March, when the cows have newly calved, less milk is required to make one kilogram of cheese than in April; that in May, the milk grows richer, when the cows are turned upon the new grass, and gradually deteriorates in quality in the months of June and July. In August the milk again grows richer; but the richer it grows, the less it produces, and I have often remarked that the milk is poorer in warm weather and richer when the weather is cool.

Now I have still to compare the produce of butter. Butter making is not my chief business, as I have already remarked, but I think the following list

CLOTHILDE 5TH'S NETHERLAND, No. 13,105 H.-F. H. B.

will give a clear view of the production of butter from Dutch cows. The butter was weighed on delivery.

Time of Butter Making.	Litres of Milk Churned.	Kilograms of Butter Produced.	Litres of Milk per Kilogram of Butter.
Feb., 1877	1,409	51.0	27.6
March, 1877	2,341	76.5	30.6
March, 1878	518	17.0	30.5
Nov., 1880	1,943	70.2	27.7
Dec., 1880	4,977	196.0	25.4
Feb., 1881	3,772	138.7	28.2
March, 1881	8,217	204.7	27.9
April, 1881	6,178	204.8	30.1
May, 1881	5,066	137.2	36.5
June, 1881	3,210	95.0	33.
July, 1881	3,104	93.3	33.3

The following list may serve as a comparison: At Mrs. Beckhusen's at Rastede, Oldenburg (Oldenburg is in the northwest part of the German Empire). In 1874, 447.5 kilograms of butter were made from 12,609 litres of milk; so they required 28.2 litres of milk to produce one kilogram of butter. From November 1, 1874, till October 30, 1875, 34.4 litres of milk were required at the same farm to produce one kilogram of butter.

Gustaf Schwartz, at the farm of Hofgaarden (Sweden), the inventor of the ice method, required, in 1874, 30.75 litres of milk for one kilogram of butter.

Staatsrath Tesdorf used in the ten summer weeks from June 20 till August 14, in 1873, 33,743 kilograms of milk, or 32.46 litres; in 1875, 28,719 kilograms of milk, or 27.99 litres, and produced in 1873, 22,904 kilograms of butter from 661,972 litres of milk (28.9 litres for one kilogram of butter); in 1874, 21,751 kilograms of butter from 637,217 litres of milk (29.3 litres for one kilogram of butter); in 1875, 20,701 kilograms of butter from 581,241 litres of milk (28.1 litres of milk for one kilogram of butter).

The latter states that the difference in weight between new butter and that which was delivered, amounted in 1873, to 4.7 per cent; in 1874, to 6.6 per cent, and 1875, to 7.4 per cent. From this we see that to deliver one kilogram of butter in 1873, 30.32 litres of milk were required; in 1874, 31.37 litres, and in 1875, 30.34 litres.

At Rosvang, Denmark, in 1873-4, 30 litres and more were required for one kilogram of butter, weighed as soon as it was churned, and 33.6 litres on delivery.

At Count Schlieffen's, at Baden in Mecklenburg (a fertile province between the Elbe and the Baltic, noted as being the place of origin of the celebrated Rosenstein breed) in September and October, 29.1 litres of milk (from 122 cows) were required to produce one kilogram of butter.

O. Petersen, at Windhausen, required from thirty cows:

1861-2	At skimming, in	34.44 litres.	1865-6	At churning, in	31.52 litres.
1862-3	"	35.64 "	1866-7	"	28.52 "
1863-4	"	36.04 "	1867-8	"	29.00 "
1864-5	"	35.82 "	1868-9	"	28.92 "
			1869-70	"	27.72 "

At the farm Lampspringe, near Hildesheim (in the southern part of Hanover), 37 kilograms, or 35.9 litres, were required from sixty cows, from May 1, 1877, to March 1, 1878.

Hofmeester, in Ingolstadt (on the river Danube in Bavaria). The milk was probably from one of the South German or one of the Swiss breeds. In 1871 was stated to require for one kilogram of butter 28.48 litres of milk from 123 cows, and churned after the Holstein skimming system.

Holst, near Svenstrup (Schonen), requires, on the average, 27.86 litres of milk from sixty-three cows.

At Aas (Norway), 32.75 litres are required.

Loepen, at Menzlin, produced from October to February, from 49,616 litres of milk, 1,916 kilograms of newly churned butter, or 1,782 kilograms on delivery; so 25.5 litres, or on delivery 27.8 litres of milk were required.

At the farm Lillyrup, Jutland (Jutland cows are often very small, valuable and hardy), 29.94 litres of milk were required for one kilogram of new butter, or 30.97 litres for one kilogram on delivery.

Van Sanson, at Kemsta (Livonia), who has Angler and crossed Angler cows (90), and who uses Schwartz method, made 4,013 kilograms of butter from 149,158 litres of milk; so he needed 37 litres of milk for one kilogram of butter.

A cheese-making society at Obervellach (Steirermark), made from June to October, 1875, on the Alps (no doubt one of the breeds of Swiss cattle, all of which are regarded as rich milkers), 588 kilograms of butter from 18,614 litres of milk (31.17 for one kilogram of butter); and from October 1, 1875, to May, 1876, 903 kilograms of butter from 37,343 litres of milk (41.35 litres for one kilogram of butter).

A dairy society in Tyrol (this is also one of the Alpine districts) made 1,018 kilograms of butter from 34,066 litres of milk, after Schwartz' method. They required 33.46 litres for one kilogram of butter.

At Golmas, near Dutte-Bull, 83,170 litres of milk of thirty-seven Angler cows were churned, and from this quantity they obtained 2,954 kilograms of new butter, or 2,867 kilograms on delivery.

The Dairy Society at Zenten (Prussia) used, from December 1, 1876, to October 1, 1877, 1,007,788 kilograms of milk; and for one kilogram of butter they required 32.4 kilograms of milk, or 31.45 litres. From October 1, 1879, to September 30, 1880, they made 68,420.5 kilograms of butter on delivery, 32.7 kilograms of milk, or one kilogram of new butter from 33.6 kilograms, or 32.62 litres of milk, and one kilogram of butter on delivery from 34.4 kilograms, or 33.4 litres of milk.

P. Meheust, in Brittany (cattle of small size belonging to the same race as the Jerseys), makes 9,407 kilograms of butter from 222,862 litres of milk; i. e. one kilogram from 23.7 litres.

These results show clearly enough that the milk of Dutch cows is in no way inferior to that of other breeds, with regard to the produce of butter. It is remarkable that of several of these reports the produce of butter is given twice—weighed a short time after it is churned, and then when it is delivered. It is not necessary to say that only the latter report may be reckoned, and it is most probable that some accounts refer to newly churned butter, for which reason the quality of milk must, of course, be augmented.

Giving the accounts of my produce of cheese, I stated that in cool weather milk contains more caseine than in warm weather. A very remarkable list has been given by Dr. Fleishman for the produce of butter, stating the same. Until the 18th of October it was very warm, and after that day it grew cool, with an east wind. The produce of butter was as follows:

Oct. 10....37.93 kils. of milk were required for 1 kil. of butter.
" 12....37.85 " " " 1 "
" 14....35.59 " " " 1 "
" 15....36.50 " " " 1 "
" 16....35.76 " " " 1 "
" 18....31.08 " " " 1 "
" 20....31.92 " " " 1 "
" 21....32.60 " " " 1 "

I have reckoned for 1,000 litres of milk a weight of 1,030 kilograms, which is, perhaps, a little too much, but will not be far from the truth.

Before concluding, I think it remarkable enough to mention an essay in the Agricultural Review (*Tyetschrift voor Landbouwkunde*), from the pen of Mr. Brockema, teacher at Wageningen.

This essay has in view to show the necessity of milking the cows quite dry. The following list clearly proves of how much importance this is, and shows the considerable quantity of butter to be found in the last milk drawn from the udder, compared with the butter of the first milk. The figures in the first column refer to the subsequent quantities, p. 1 being the first, and p. 5 being the last milk.

Page.	Quantity in litres.	Specific weight of the milk (15 per cent).	Cream.
1	2	1.034	8 per cent.
2	1½	1.032	13 "
3	2½	1.030	15 "
4	3	1.0285	18 "
5	½	1.0225	33 "

This list clearly proves how disadvantageous it is if we do not quite milk out our cows, the last milk producing four times as much cream as the first. The column for the specific weight, too, is very remarkable, because we see from it that the first milk is the heaviest, and the last the lightest. The last is even so light, by the large quantity of fat, that in some places this milk would be considered as mixed with water, for it is known that there are towns where the milk of a specific weight less than 1.028 is rejected. It is, therefore, advisable not only to judge the milk at that weight, but also to take the quantity of fat into consideration. I think the great specific weight of the first milk is caused by its richness in caseine, while the last is, most probably, poor in this respect.

Arrived at the end of the task I laid upon myself, I may have given little that is unknown to our agriculturists (all statistics having been taken from reviews), yet I hope to have contributed a little to attack the prejudice by which the reputation of our stock is injured.

CHAPTER IX.

ACCLIMATION—FLEXIBILITY.

Undoubtedly every breed of cattle has its special adaptations and its special field in which it is most profitable. There is no other breed, however, that has such an extensive territory in which it is, or may be, especially profitable as the Holstein-Friesian. This is shown by the spread and distribution of breeds in Europe where there has been no artificial barriers against the spread of breeds and no artificial attempts to stimulate distribution. The Ayrshire breed is scarcely known outside the British Islands where it originated, the Guernsey and the Jersey breeds are not found to any extent on the continent although the island of Jersey lies in sight of the shore, and the Shorthorn breed is limited to a few localities in Belgium. France, Germany and perhaps some other states where it has been introduced by the government or the nobility to test it. On the other hand the Holstein-Friesian breed, with its offshoots under different names, is found everywhere the prevailing breed in

CASTINE, No. 3795 H. H. B.

Milk record, 74 lbs. 8 oz. in one day; 2,808 lbs. in thirty days. Butter record, 21 lbs. in seven days as three-year-old; 83 lbs. 10 oz. in thirty days as four-year-old.

the rich lowlands of France, Belgium, Holland and the western provinces of Germany. It has not become established in Great Britain, nor has it invaded the island of Jersey or of Guernsey, for the simple reason that laws have existed for many years against importations for breeding purposes from the continent. In Jersey and Guernsey such laws have been rigidly enforced for a hundred years or more. While on the other hand no laws have ever existed to prevent the unlimited importation of Jersey and Guernsey cattle or of any other breed to the continent. We refer to these facts simply for the purpose of saying that the same natural laws in relation to soils, climates and markets exist in this country that govern in Europe, and if left to work out the fate of breeds of cattle in this country without artificial influences and barriers the results must eventually be the same.

Coleman's Rural World of St. Louis, Mo., in April, 1886, states: "The Holstein-Friesian cattle have found one of their best homes in Texas and Mexico. The Texas people are especially clamorous for them. So well are they pleased with the manner in which they run the gauntlet of the acclimating fever, and supply them with big pails of milk, that they cannot get enough of them. They make a splendid cross on the native cows and in a few years their grades will be found there by thousands."

No imported stock has been found to do so well in southern Texas.

Mr. Harwood of Gonzales, Texas, reports that he imported Holstein-Friesian cattle from Lakeside Herd, Syracuse, in 1884, and that they passed the hot season without any appearance of fever. "Similar reports," says the Holstein-Friesian Register of August 1, 1886, "have reached us from South Carolina, Georgia, Mississippi and California. Our breeders in the North are making continued shipments southward and have favorable reports from all quarters. It is safe to assert that among the many desirable qualities of the Holstein, not the least is its hardy nature and easy adaptability to every climate."

A Mississippi correspondent of the Live Stock Journal wrote, November 15, 1886:

Shorthorns were our first experiment, but they could not be acclimated south of 35 degrees of parallel of latitude, even when brought from Kentucky and Tennessee, just a few degrees north of the line. Of the hundred of various ages that have been introduced it would be almost impossible to find a thoroughbred animal to-day in our section or south of us. We don't like Herefords because they are not milk producers; for beef they are splendid, and do well among the granaries of the middle states, and owing to their superior qualities as "mottlers" they give satisfaction on the prairies of the West, from the warm climate of the Rio Grande to the Platte on the north. For Dakota, Wyoming and Minnesota, we think, the cold-blooded, coarse, shaggy Galloway of North Scotland is peculiarly adapted.

But for the South we want an all-purpose animal, beef, butter, milk and cheese; animals that are docile and hardy, and in our opinion the Holstein-Friesian is the breed. No other cattle are as easily acclimated, unless perhaps it is the Jersey. Introduce a Holstein under one year old and he will stand the climate of even Florida and Louisiana without a day's sickness. Old cattle occasionally die, but the percentage is indeed small, especially if treated a few days with aconite and quinine. The more we see this grand breed the more we like them, and we predict the day is not far distant when they will be decided the cattle for the farms and plantations, and of the entire South.

A correspondent of the Reporter, Holly Springs, Miss., writing in 1887, said: "It is only about two years since the first Holstein cow was introduced into our county. . . . Their adaptability to our section has been proven beyond question."

The well-known breeder, S. N. Wright, of Elgin, Ill., writing in 1888 on this subject, said: "I have had some little experience in sending the Holstein-Friesian cattle south, as far as Leon, Old Mexico, also near the city of Mexico. In the fall of 1886 a man from Leon came to my place, after examining different herds and breeds of cattle, concluded to place his order with me for a carload of Holstein-Friesian cattle both grades, and I shipped him seventeen head on the 25th of December. In due time they arrived at their new home, all right and in fine condition. In 1887, the following spring, he sent me another order for twenty head, stating that the first lot had done so well and he was so well pleased with them, that he wanted more. On the 23d of June I shipped him another carload. They arrived at their destination about the 10th of July in good shape; they too have done well, not one single animal has been reported to me as having died from the effects of the climate."

Mr. S. B. Howard, of Bonham, Texas, writes: "I bought, in 1887, a small herd from B. B. Lord & Son, of New York, and at the same time Mr. Lord shipped a few head for me to sell, numbering in all twenty-four head. Have not lost one in acclimation nor has one failed to thrive. I also shipped, last March, one year ago, two bulls which were bred to common Texas grade Shorthorns, grade Jerseys and full-blood Shorthorns, ninety-six cows in all.

"The calves dropped by these cows from the Holsteins give better satisfaction, so far, than from any other breed that was ever shipped to this state. I have a three-year-old cow, Sir Archibald's Orphe. No. 2603, H. F. H. B., that commenced her milk record March 27; her largest day's yield is 66 lbs.; her yield for thirty days is 1,824½ lbs. This is on dry feed, Texas prarie hay, cotton seed, bran, corn and oats ground together."

Mr. Jos. E. Miller, Belleville. Ill., writes: "I have perhaps shipped as many cattle south as any other western breeder, and my shipments have been scattered al the way from Georgia to the Rio Grande, not to speak of Mexico, as cattle run no risk in acclimating on the highlands of that country. The bulk of my shipments however have been to Texas. Have also traveled considerably in that state, and met with many experienced cattlemen, and also dealers who handle all breeds, and there seems to be a general unanimity of opinion that the Holsteins acclimate there with less risk than any other breed ever brought there. I have sent many there that did not take the fever at all. In taking young animals and at the proper time of the year, the risk is very slight indeed. To illustrate the faith that is in me, I will take down one or two carloads of young things next fall to acclimate at my own risk. Of young animals, have so far, as far as I have been able to learn, lost only three head, and some of them, as I have been told, more through the carelessness of the owners than from any other cause. Last fall I shipped for another party, thirteen head of Jerseys to Arkansas, nine of which succumbed to the climate in a very short time."

Mr. R. Howes Crump, of Masonville, Ont., in address before the Canadian Holstein-Friesian Assn., delivered February 23, 1892, said: "The Holsteins thrive as well and furnish equal milk records in Canada as they do in Holland."

CHAPTER X.

AS A BUTTER BREED—FRIESLAND'S PRODUCTION—AMERICAN EXPERIENCES: WELLS, DUDLEY, YEOMANS, WALES, SMITHS & POWELL CO., POWELL BROS., M. E. MOORE. DUTCHER, W. S. MORSE, GILLETT & SON—CLOTHILDE 2D—PARTHENEA'S RECORD—NATSEY—SMITHS & POWELL'S HEIFERS—PAULINE PAUL—IOWA STATION—SMITHS & POWELL.

A butter breed according to the views of our Jersey friends, necessarily gives a small quantity of milk. According to common sense views it is a breed that produces a large quantity of butter. A Jersey cow gives 15 lbs. of milk from which one pound of butter is made, at the same time a Holstein-Friesian cow gives 50 lbs. of milk from which two pounds of equally good butter is made. Which is entitled to the pre-eminence of being called a butter cow? Common sense would decide that it is the latter. A Jersey breeder would lead one to infer that butter is not made to any great extent in Holland from the Holstein-Friesian breed of cattle. It is an impression that many of our journals under the dictation of Jersey breeders have labored to inculcate, and many honest men have obtained. We do not have statistics of the total production of butter in Holland, but we have of the amount of Holland butter imported into Great Britain.

In 1884, 124,924,128 lbs. of butter from Holland was received at British ports; from all other countries including France at 57,126,008 lbs., Denmark at 37,527,504 lbs., Germany at 16,177,288 lbs., Sweden at 11,404,064 lbs., United States at 11,231,472 lbs., there was received 152,325,028 lbs. In 1874 the province of Friesland, where our breed of cattle are exclusively used, exported 29,796,-592 lbs. of butter, which was 23,782 lbs. to every square mile of that province including lands occupied by lakes, canals, rivers, cities, marshes, as well as that cultivated for other than grass crops.

The number of square miles included within the bounds of Friesland is 1253. Probably not over half of its territory is in grass. Large quantities of cheese are also made, and great numbers of young cattle are raised for export. In view of these facts the record seems more marvelous than any produced in this country. It is a record of thousands of cows kept under ordinary conditions. We challenge the friends of any other breed to bring forward a record of their cattle that approaches it.

In 1884 the Channel Islands, where the Jersey and Guernsey breeds are exclusively kept, exported 100,464 lbs., or 1,647 lbs. to every square mile. A perusal of these figures may enlighten those that have obtained the impression that the Holstein-Friesian is not a butter breeed. The facts are that the Holstein-Friesian breed has been producing for generations more butter than any other breed in the world, more per cow, more per acre of land occupied and more in the aggregate. We have no statistics as to the number of cows either in Jersey or in Friesland in the years named. But the number varies but little from year to year. In 1879 Friesland had 144,802 cows. If the same number were kept in 1874 the average export per cow to England was 205¾ lbs. [Not a pound of oleomargarine was made in Friesland in 1874.]

The dairy is the great farming interest in Holland, and hence the conclusion that its dairymen have sought for the best possible dairy breed during the more than five hundred years that it has been the greatest butter and cheese producing country of the world.

There is not a reasonable doubt that the Holstein-Friesian is the foremost butter breed in the world. A single herd in this country has 100 cows that average 19 lbs. of butter in seven consecutive days; another herd has 32 cows that average 19¼ lbs., another has 20 cows that average over 21 lbs., and so we might continue the list, showing their enormous production by herds.

In our opinion the proportion of territory applied to butter production is not much if any larger in Friesland than in Jersey, and yet the proportion of export per square mile is as 14½ to 1. We have no data by which to determine the home consumption in these countries. But we know that the Friesian people are great butter consumers, eating melted butter almost exclusively for gravies as well as eating butter in the form in which it is consumed in Jersey and in this country.

The truth is that the Jersey was never bred as a great butter producing breed until after it was introduced in America. We do not say this to detract from the Jerseys. But in such a discussion the facts must be given. They were bred for a lawn cow. The color and style and everything about them was bred to meet the tastes of the English aristocracy for a deer-like appearing cow upon the green lawns that surround their mansions. On the other hand the Holstein-Friesian cow has been bred for untold generations as a dairy cow, a butter producing breed. And further, this breed is and has been par excellence the butter breed of Europe throughout these generations.

There are many most valuable and interesting records of tests of Holstein-Friesian cows in existence. From a large number of these we present a selection which well demonstrates the abilities of the breed as butter producers. Great care has been exercised to chronicle only those tests which are absolutely reliable, and which have been most carefully conducted, and can at any time be verified by many witnesses.

The first butter record of a Holstein-Friesian, of which we have any knowledge, was made in New York Mills, N. Y., by Mr. Solomon Hoxie, then secretary of the Dutch-Friesian Association. He tested one of his cows, using the old-fashioned four-quart pans and a small stone churn, churning each day's cream by itself. We doubt not that a large per cent of fat was left in the buttermilk. The test was made with considerable misgiving as to the result, and rather sub rosa, but the writer was permitted to know the facts, which were to be used if favorable, but never made public if unfavorable. He thinks he betrays no confidence now. The record began March 6, 1881, and continued for twenty-eight days, with the following result:

	Lbs.	Oz.
Milk of 28 days,	1757	8
Average per day,	62	12
Butter of 28 days,	73	1
Seven days' yield,	18	1
Average per day,	2.61	
Milk for pound of butter,	24	

CLOTHILDE FAMILY.

This was not a big, but a fair, record, and showed the cow Sjoerd to be valuable as a butter producer. The record was afterward published, with this comment: "It is true that individuals of breeds may be better or worse than the average, but we have no reason to think that Sjoerd is either. We believe she is a fair average." Since that date, selecting, breeding, and testing for butter has received a very strong impetus; and it is not strange that better Holstein-Friesian butter cows have come to the front.

Messrs. Wells & Sons of Wethersfield, Conn., write: "Below we give you the average record of butter made by fourteen of our herd for the past year, 1882.

"We have milked and set in creamers, the past season, the milk from two two-year-old, nine three-year-old, and three six-year-old Holstein-Friesian cows. We have just footed up the number of spaces sent to the creamery and the number of spaces it took each month to make a pound of butter, and find they have made in all 5649 lbs. of butter, equivalent to 403 8-16 lbs. for each cow.

"These cows dropped their calves in the months of January, February, March and April. They were milked on the average 270 days, many of them being due to drop their next calves inside of eleven months from their last.

"The cows were fed after dropping their calves till put in pasture daily all the good hay they would eat, and in addition one-half bushel of mangel wurtzel, four quarts wheat bran, two quarts corn meal, and two quarts cotton seed meal mixed.

"When put in pasture they were fed (owing to short pasturing) hay morning and night with four quarts of meal and bran mixed.

"This herd was not fed with any expectation of reporting a butter record."

All conversant with the subject will concede that 300 lbs. of butter from a mature cow in a year is unusually large, even from butter-bred cows.

When we consider that Messrs. Wells & Sons' herd included two-year-olds, and that the entire lot averaged but a little over three years old, and that their average product of butter per cow per year was 403¼ lbs., we are compelled to say that the Messrs. Wells' Holsteins are far above the herds of specially bred butter cows.

In 1891 Messrs. Wells further reported the butter yield of their herd as follows: "We give below the records made in our herd, and all but three have been made since January 1, 1887. In our butter tests the butter is thoroughly washed with water in a churn, then taken out and well worked over with one ounce of salt to the pound and then made into one solid mass and weighed.

"Four of these heifers, classed as three years old, were nearly four when making this record. As thirteen of these cows did not average more than three years and eight months in age, we think this is a very handsome butter showing for our herd. It took on the average a fraction over 22 lbs. of milk for one pound of butter.

COWS.		LBS.	OZ.	DAYS.
Sieberen,	4 years	14	8	7
Proserpine,	6 "	17	10	7
Janna,	6 "	19	7	7
Jaapje,	18 months	45	8	30
Jaapje,	3 years	19	7	7
Sieberen 3d,	4 "	17	8	7
Kashman,	3 "	19	0	7
Kashman,	3 "	105	9	60
Kooy,	3 "	18	5	7
Lady Social,	3 "	17	10	7
Mame Stone,	3 "	17	8	7
Lovicin,	3 "	17	8	7
Pantje,	2 "	16	7	7
Hubbard,	3 "	14	6	7
Cotter, just,	3 "	14		7
Lady Pansy,	3 "	14	8	7
Sal Watson,	3 "	10	8	7

"Considering that we have but twenty breeding animals in all, and four of them have not been tested yet, but we know they will do fairly well, we think we may justly claim our herd as among the best butter herds in this country."

Hon. N. B. Dudley, Oakville, Ky., writes under date of July 6, 1887: "My Holstein-Friesian cow Nymph, No. 2844, Vol. VI, has averaged for two months, during the flush of the milk flow, 80 lbs. of milk per day, and has made 18 lbs. of unsalted butter per week. She is five years old; had good pasture to run in both day and night. She was milked three times every day, and had for a twenty-four hours' ration 12 lbs. of ground food, being equal parts of oats, corn, meal, wheat bran and N. P. oil cake meal fed dry."

The Holstein-Friesian herd of Messrs. T. G. Yeomans & Sons, in May, 1888, included five cows that averaged 23 lbs. 7 oz., twelve cows that averaged 21 lbs. 6¾ oz., and twenty-nine cows (nine two-year-olds) that averaged 17 lbs. 7½ oz. well-worked unsalted butter in a week. To this herd belongs Aaggie 2d, that has made a butter record of 11 lbs. 12 oz. in three days, 15 lbs. 6 oz. in four days, 26 lbs. 7 oz. in seven days, 105 lbs. 10½ oz. in thirty days, 207 lbs. 3½ oz. in sixty days, and 304 lbs. 5¼ oz. in ninety days. Aaggie 2d's milk record is 20,763 lbs. 3 oz. in one year.

The herd of Thos. B. Wales, then secretary of the Holstein-Friesian Association, had to its credit twenty cows that have averaged 20 lbs. 6$\frac{8}{16}$ oz. of butter in seven days. This noted herd was headed by Mercedes Prince, whose six daughters at the average age of twenty-six months and ten days, averaged 16 lbs. 5 oz. of butter in a week. The six averaged a pound of butter from 16.32 lbs. of milk. The dam of the bull was Mercedes, that won the butter championship of the world with her butter record of 99 lbs. 6¼ oz. in thirty days. His grandam Lady Walworth's record is 19 lbs. in seven days. Tritomia is another famous butter cow of this herd that made a four-year-old butter record of 25 lbs. 8¼ oz. in seven days. Among the first honors awarded her in competition with all others was at the Minnesota State Fair in 1886; and in 1887 at the American Fat Stock and Dairy Show in Chicago her butter was awarded sweepstakes prize over all others, and scored higher than any other butter in the show.

Among other noted Holstein-Friesian herds of butter cows is that of Messrs. Smiths & Powell Co., with two cows that have records of over 100 pounds of butter in thirty days, viz.: Ægis, 100 lbs. 6 oz., and Albino 2d, 106 lbs. 14 oz. —made in her three-year-old form. Her seven-day record was 25 lbs. 14¼ oz., an average of a pound of butter to 18.69 lbs. of milk. As a two-year-old this heifer exceeded the greatest milk record for one year with her record of 18,484 lbs. 13 oz. The great Clothilde, that led the world's annual milk record with 26,021 lbs. 2 oz. in one year at the New York Dairy Show in May, 1887, won first honor as a butter cow, defeating all competitors, including Jerseys and Guernseys, with 2 lbs. 7½ oz. in twenty-four hours, her daughter, Clothilde 4th, making the next highest record with 2 lbs. ⅞ oz. Clothilde's record for seven days is 28 lbs. 2¼ oz., and Clothilde 4th's at three years, 23 lbs. 10¼ oz., averaging a pound of butter to 18.44 lbs. of milk. Ægis 2d's butter record for thirty days is 96 lbs. 5¼ oz., and Netherland Dorinda's 96 lbs. 2¼ oz. Nine cows in the herd have records for thirty days of over 90 lbs. and average over 95 lbs. The following average butter records for a week have been made in the same herd: Fifteen cows averaged 24 lbs. ¼ oz.; twenty-four cows averaged 23 lbs.; thirty-five cows averaged 22 lbs. 1 oz.; forty-seven cows averaged 21 lbs. $\frac{14}{16}$ oz.; sixty-two cows averaged 20 lbs. $\frac{13}{16}$ oz., and 100 cows averaged 18 lbs. $\frac{7}{100}$ oz. These records include those made by heifers.

Prof. Alvord, after having tested the milk record of Clothilde said, regarding this herd and its management: "Everything convinces me that there was no improper practice or deceit, but that all the conduct of the Lakeside herd was accurate and honorable, and the records thoroughly reliable."

The record of Powell Bros. great cow is thus reported: "Shadeland Boon, 8887, from June 6, to July 6, 1888, inclusive, thirty-one days, produced 125 lbs. 12 oz. of unsalted butter. This butter was made from 1,772 1-2 lbs. of milk, which she gave during that period. For this remarkable record it took only 14.09 lbs. of milk for a pound of butter. The average for the whole time was over four pounds per day. For seven consecutive days she produced 31 lbs. 15 1-2 oz., or an average of 4 lbs. 9 1-4 oz. per day; and during that week she gave 400 1-4 lbs. of milk, and it took only 12.51 lbs. of milk for a pound of butter; and for four consecutive days her milk made 19 lbs. 1 oz. of butter, and it lacked only 3 3-4 oz. per day of making 5 lbs. per day for that time. The 19 lbs. 1 oz. of butter were made from 219 lbs. of milk, which shows that it took only 11.18 lbs. of milk for a pound of butter, while for two days she lacked only 2 oz. of butter per day of averaging 5 lbs. for each day. The above remarkable record would have been beaten by several pounds had it not been for the fact that twice within the time mentioned the cow was not in first-class condition. In one case she fell off about two pounds of butter per day. Another that worked against this cow's record was the fact that her milk was taken several miles to the Albion Creamery, where the cream was separated and churned and the butter weighed. Messrs. Powell Bros. so well knew that they had a wonderful cow in Shadeland Boon before the test was made, that they issued a general invitation for any one to see her milked and the milk weighed and put under lock and key. when it was sent to the creamery, where it was separated and churned by itself. The milking. transporting, separating, churning, working and weighing of the milk and butter respectively were wholly done by disinterested and responsible persons who stand ready to make affidavit to all of the facts."

M. E. Moore of Cameron, Mo., in February, 1889, reported at that date the best showing for one week of any Holstein-Friesian cow. He had just completed a butter test with Gerben 4th. She calved October 31, 1888, and commenced the test under favorable circumstances, cow in good condition, weather fine.

DATE.	MILK.	BUTTER.
Dec. 31, 1888.	72 lbs. 3 oz.	4 lbs. 6 oz.
Jan. 1, 1889.	75 lbs. 12 oz.	4 lbs. 5 oz.
" 2, "	75 lbs. 1 oz.	4 lbs. 15 oz.
" 3, "	76 lbs. 11 oz.	4 lbs. 15 oz.
" 4, "	75 lbs. 4 oz.	4 lbs. 9 oz.
" 5, "	77 lbs. 14 oz.	4 lbs. 7 oz.
" 6, "	74 lbs. 12 oz.	4 lbs. 13 oz.
Total.	527 lbs. 9 oz.	32 lbs.

It will be noticed that her largest day's yield of milk produced the least butter, which was caused by churning the milk too warm. The loss was proven by the oil test of the buttermilk. Following are the affidavits of those handling the cow:

State of Missouri, County of Clinton, ss.

Now comes L. C. Goodale, of Cameron, Mo., and being duly sworn on his oath, says: I did feed and milk Gerben 4th, preparatory to and during said test as given in the statement hereto attached and marked "A." That I milked from said cow during the seven days test 527 9/16 lbs. of milk as above stated in said statement as aforesaid, and helped to churn said milk and saw the butter well worked and that the butter so churned from said milk weighed 32 lbs.
L. C. GOODALE.

Subscribed and sworn to before me on this 17th day of January, 1889, by said L. C. Goodale, well known to me to be the person he represents himself to be.   A. W. FREDERICK, Notary Public for Clinton Co., Mo.

State of Missouri, County of Clinton, ss.

Now comes J. B. Grover, of Cameron, Mo., and being duly sworn on his oath says: I saw a part of the milk from Gerben 4th weighed during the seven days' test (in the statement hereto attached and marked "A") referred to; that I churned nearly all of said milk and saw the butter weighed, and it did weigh 32 lbs.   J. B. GROVER.

Subscribed and sworn to before me this 17th day of January, 1889, and I further certify that I am well acquainted with J. B Grover, who has subscribed and sworn to this statement, and know him to be a gentleman entitled to credit as an honorable and truthful gentleman.
A. W. FREDERICK, Notary Public for Clinton Co., Mo.

State of Missouri, County of Clinton, ss.

Now comes M. E. Moore, of Cameron, Clinton County, Missouri, and being duly sworn, says: I am the owner of Gerben 4th, No. 1080, D.-F. H. B., recorded as Gerben No. 5562, H. H. B., and that I saw said cow fed, some of the milking done, most of the milk weighed, as set forth in the statement hereto attached and marked "A," of the seven days' test in said statement set forth. I assisted in the churning of said milk and worked all the butter churned from said milk dry as it is done at my creamery, and weighed said butter, which weighed 32 lbs.   M. E. MOORE.

Subscribed and sworn to before me, a notary public within and for Clinton County, Missouri, by M. E. Moore, to me well known and is entitled to full credit.   A. W. FREDERICK, Notary Public.

The feed consumed by Gerben 4th each day while making the test was 40 lbs. corn meal, ground fine, 15 lbs. wheat bran, all the sugar beets, clover and timothy she wanted, with a little Northwestern Condition Powder each day, and never refused to eat preparatory to or during said test; is now producing between 60 and 70 lbs. of milk daily.

Gerben 4th, 1080, D.-F. H. B., recorded as Gerben No. 5562, H. H. B., was selected in Friesland by Mr. C. Baldwin, of Nelson, Ohio, the noted "cattle expert;" was bred by A. S. Heeg, Osterend; calved May 3, 1882. Dam, Gerben 3d, No. 250, F. H. B., Europe. Grandam on both dam and sire's side, Gerben, No. 86, F. H. B., Europe.

She is large (weight before calving, 1,684 lbs.), very straight and level, remarkably broad across the hips, flanders escutcheon, udder large (measured five feet, seven and three-fourths inches), mammary veins double extension and branched. Chest vein, very thin neck, horns drooping and remarkably fine, eyes very full and prominent, mellow skin, hair silky, dandruff sections oily.

Since above test, with feed reduced, and the weather much colder, three parties saw Gerben 4th milked, weighed the milk—morning, 26 3-16 lbs.; noon, 18 3-16 lbs.; evening, 14 15-16 lbs. Total, 59 5-16 lbs., from which was churned and well worked 3 3-4 lbs. of butter.

The above butter record we believe was the largest ever made for one week by any Holstein-Friesian cow at this date.

Prof. W. A. Henry, of the Wisconsin Experiment Station, writes of this record: "From Mr. Moore we solicited a sample of milk of this cow, giving explicit directions how it should be taken. Our request was promptly acceded to, and a sample of the milk was received February 8, 1889, which analyzed: Specific gravity, 1.0314; total solids, 13.70; fat, 5.13.

"Mr. Moore reported the yield of milk on the day the sample was taken to be 63 lbs. Granting that the milk was as rich in fat as the sample received, there would be a little over 3.2 lbs. of pure butter fat in the day's milk, which if all was recovered in the butter, would make fully four pounds of butter containing 80 per cent of butter fat. Mr. Moore states that the sample was taken exactly according to directions.

"At first we thought to let the matter rest at this point, but, believing that we should get still nearer the cow, I sent Mr. F. G. Short, a chemist of this station, to Cameron to secure samples. Mr. Moore had no knowledge whatever of Mr. Short's intended visit, but received him cordially, and allowed him every privilege. Mr. Short took every precaution to secure samples of Gerben 4th's milk. attending the weighing himself and sealing the samples as soon as drawn. Three samples were taken, the first on February 17, at noon; the second in the evening, and the third the following morning. Mr. Short attended personally to seeing that the cow was milked dry in the morning of the day the first sample was taken.

"Every condition for a large milk flow and butter yield was against the cow at this date: she had been bred a few days previous, her grain feed had been changed and reduced from what it had been during the large test reported by Mr. Moore. February 16 it had rained all day, and that night had turned to zero weather; the cow was not blanketed, nor given any special attention, and went with the herd, as usual, out into a field for the water she drank. As shown by the table, she gave nearly 49 lbs. of milk in three milkings, from which samples were secured. The samples taken on February 17 and 18 were received February 22, and at once analyzed, the milk being still sweet. The following tables give the results of the analysis:

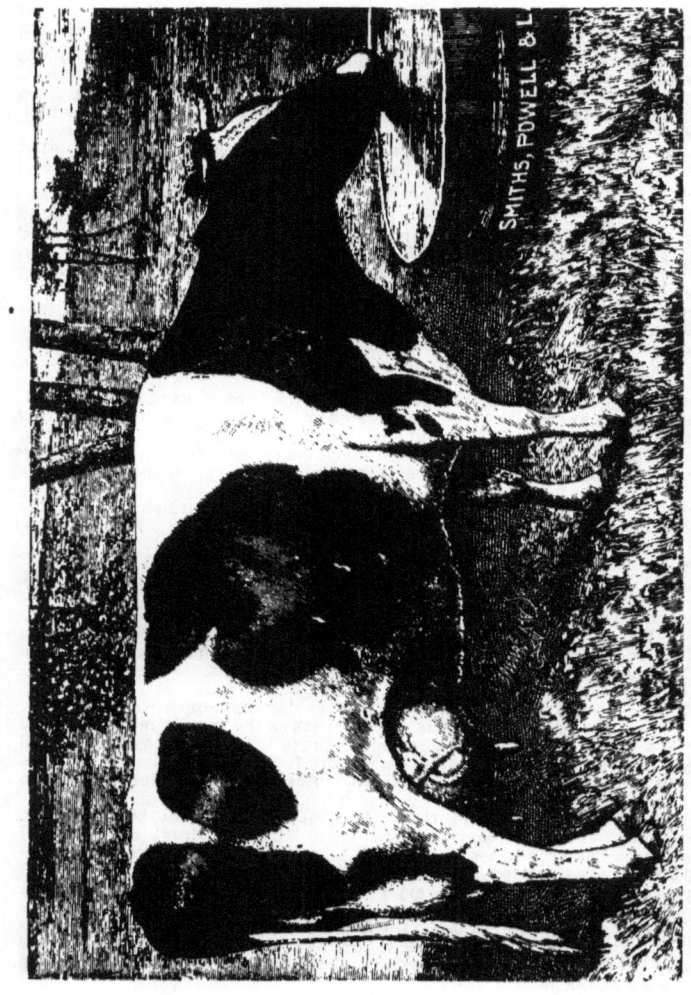

CLOTHILDE, No. 1308 H. H. B.: Advanced Registry.

Imported. Milk record, 26,021 lbs. 2 oz. in one year; average per day for whole year, 71 lbs. 4 2-3 oz.: Advanced Registry butter record, 28 lbs. 2 1-4 oz. in seven days.

Time of Milking.	Lbs. of milk.	Total solids per ct.	Fat per ct.	Solids not fat per ct.	Caseine per ct.	Ash per ct.	Sugar by differ'nce per ct.	Specific gravity.
Feb. 17, noon.	12.69	13.96	4.91	9.05	3.32	.75	4.99	1.035
Evening.	17.5	13.10	3.84	9.26	3.37	.78	5.01	1.036
Feb. 18, morning.	24.69	12.69	3.53	9.16	3.43	.70	4.95	1.036

Multiplying the milk product by the percentages of fat, we get the following:

Time of Milking.	Yield.	Per cent fat.	Amount fat.
Noon.	12.69 lbs	4.9	.623 lbs.
Evening.	11.5 lbs	3.84	.442 lbs.
Morning.	24.69 lbs	3.53	.881 lbs.
Totals.	48.88 lbs.	....	1.946 lbs.

"We have, then, a yield of over 1.9 lbs. of pure butter fat for a day of 24 hours. Granting all is recovered in the butter, at 80 per cent pure oil to the pound, it would give 2.43 lbs. of butter. At the same rate, when giving 527 lbs. 9 oz., the yield of butter would be 26.29 lbs. While this is less by 5.7 lbs. than the claim of Mr. Moore, I am more than willing to concede that the conditions under which the samples were taken amply account for such a discrepancy. After listening to Mr. Short's report of his examination of the milk record of the herd, kept by Mr. Moore, of the condition of the weather, and of the manner in which the cow was managed, I am free to state that I believe that the claim of 32 lbs. of butter in one week from Gerben 4th is entirely possible and probable."

M. E. Moore of Cameron, Mo., under date of April 29, 1889. writes: I have just completed a seven-days' butter test with my imported Holstein-Friesian cow, Empress Josephine, 429 D.-F. H. B., beginning April 2, closing April 8:

	MILK.	BUTTER.
April 2,	78 lbs.	3 lbs. 7 oz.
April 3,	79 lbs. 5 oz.	3 lbs. 0 oz.
April 4,	76 lbs.	3 lbs. 9 oz.
April 5,	80 lbs. 12 oz.	3 lbs. 12 oz.
April 6,	79 lbs. 6 oz.	3 lbs. 12 oz.
April 7,	79 lbs. 15 oz.	3 lbs. 14 oz.
April 8,	80 lbs. 2 oz.	3 lbs. 15 oz.
Total.	553 lbs. 8 oz.	25 lbs. 14 oz.

The following is the analysis of Empress Josephine's milk, samples of which were taken at the farm in February (zero weather) by Mr. Short, sent by Prof. W. A. Henry, of the Agricultural Experiment Station, Madison, Wis.:

	TOTAL SOLIDS.	FAT.	CASEINE.	ASH.
Noon.	12.89	4.00	3.28	72
6 P. M.,	12.78	3.67	3.57	77
6 A. M.,	12.27	3.01	3.50	88

Empress Josephine is now milking daily from 80 to 85 lbs.

Messrs. J. B. Dutcher & Son, Pawling, N. Y., thus report the famous record of DeKol 2d:

The Holstein-Friesian cow, De Kol 2d, 734 H. F. H. B., 412 Advanced Registry, dropped the bull calf, De Kol 2d's Netherland, 11,584 H. F. H. B., January 16, 1889, at the age of 4 years, 9 months and 27 days. From March 16 to March 22 (both inclusive), De Kol 2d gave 420 lbs. 1 oz. of milk which churned 33 lbs. 6 oz. of unsalted butter, 12.58 lbs. of milk making 1 lb. of butter; and on March 20 she gave 49 lbs. 8 oz. of milk which churned 61 lbs. 6½ oz. of unsalted butter, 9.29 lbs. of milk making 1 lb. of butter. This record has never been equalled by any Holstein-Friesian cow, of the same age, to our knowledge, while the one-day record of 6 lbs. 6½ oz. we do not believe has ever been equalled by a cow of any breed.

The food given this cow daily during her test consisted of 18 lbs. of hominy chop, 7¼ lbs. of wheat bran, 3¼ lbs. of cottonseed meal and all the good hay she would eat.

The Cooley creamer, the Davis swing churn and the Howe table scales were used during the test.

The following is the result of the seven days' test with a correct copy of all affidavits relating thereto:

DATE.	MILK.	BUTTER.
March 16, 1889.	61 lbs. 1 oz.	4 lbs. 10 oz.
" 17, "	58 lbs. 13 oz.	4 lbs. 13 oz.
" 18, "	61 lbs. 4 oz.	5 lbs. 1 oz.
" 19, "	57 lbs. 14 oz.	4 lbs. 10½ oz.
" 20, "	59 lbs. 8 oz.	6 lbs. 6½ oz.
" 21, "	62 lbs. 12 oz.	4 lbs. 4 oz.
" 22, "	58 lbs. 13 oz.	3 lbs. 9 oz.
Total, 7 days.	420 lbs. 1 oz.	33 lbs. 6 oz.

AFFIDAVITS.

1. Nelson A. Stall, superintendent Maplecroft Stock Farm, Pawling, N. Y.
State of New York, County of Duchess.

Nelson A. Stall, being duly sworn, says that he is the superintendent of the Maplecroft Farm at Pawling, N. Y. That for the seven consecutive days, from March 16 to March 22, 1889 (both inclusive), the Holstein cow, De Kol 2d, 734 H. F. H. B., 412 Advanced Registry, gave 420 lbs. 1 oz. of milk which churned 33 lbs. 6 oz. of unsalted butter. That the said cow, during said test, viz., on March 20, 1889, gave on that day 59 lbs. 8 oz. of milk which churned 6 lbs. 6½ oz. of unsalted butter.

Deponent further says that he knows of his own knowledge that the foregoing statements are true and correct in every particular.
                    (Signed)   NELSON A. STALL.
Subscribed and sworn to before me April 6, 1889.
            (Signed)   WILLIAM GEORGE TICE, Notary Public.

2. George Vail, herdsman at Maplecroft Stock Farm, Pawling, N. Y.
State of New York, County of Duchess.

George Vail, of the town of Pawling, N. Y., being duly sworn, says that for the seven consecutive days from March 16 to March 22, 1889 (both inclusive), he milked the cow, De Kol 2d, 734 H. F. H. B., 412 Advanced Registry, and that during said seven days said cow gave 420 lbs. 1 oz. milk as weighed by this deponent.   (Signed)   GEORGE VAIL.
Subscribed and sworn to before me this 6th day of April, 1889.
            (Signed)   WILLIAM GEORGE TICE, Notary Public.

3. Miss Hattie L. Stall, who had charge of the milk and the churning of the same.
State of New York, County of Duchess.

Hattie L. Stall, being duly sworn, says that she had charge of the milk given by the Holstein cow, De Kol 2d, 734 H. F. H. B., 412 Advanced Registry, and that she further had charge of the churning of the milk given in the seven consecutive days from March 16 to March 22, 1889 (both inclusive), and saw the butter so churned weighed, and that the said milk given during the said seven days, to the knowledge of this deponent, churned 33 lbs. 6 oz. of unsalted butter, and further that the milk given March 20, 1889, did churn 6 lbs. 6¼ oz. of unsalted butter.

                        (Signed)   HATTIE L. STALL.

Subscribed and sworn to before me this 6th day of April, 1889.
          (Signed)   WILLIAM GEORGE TICE, Notary Public.

4. Messrs. William J. Merwin, John J. Arnold, and George S. Holmes, all of Pawling, N. Y., were present by Mr. Nelson A. Stall's request to witness the weighing of the butter that was churned from the milk given by De Kol 2d March 20, 1889.

State of New York, County of Duchess.

William J. Merwin, John J. Arnold, and George S. Holmes, being duly sworn, says each for himself, that he did weigh the butter said to have been churned from the milk given by the Holstein cow, De Kol 2d, 734 H. F. H. B., 412 Advanced Registry, on March 20, 1889, and that the same weighed by him was of the actual weight of 6 lbs. 6¼ oz. of unsalted butter.

                                    { W. J. MERWIN.
                  Signed   { JOHN J. ARNOLD.
                                      { GEORGE S. HOLMES.

Subscribed and sworn to before me this 6th day of April, 1889.
          (Signed)   WILLIAM GEORGE TICE, Notary Public.

Mr. Willard Morse, one of the proprietors of the Windsor Dairy, Denver, Col., writes: "I wish to take up some of your valuable space to give an account of a butter test made on the Windsor farm of the Holstein-Friesian heifer, Hilda Spaanz, 2533. This heifer was calved January 1, 1886, and dropped her last calf July 31, 1889; she was consequently three years and seven months old at time of calving. I purchased this heifer in Illinois in June, shipped her to Colorado and dehorned her in the month of July. She was only in fair

COUNT CLOTHILDE, No. 9915 H. F. H. B.

condition when I purchased her and the change of altitude together with the fact that the months of July and August of this year have been very hot and dry, have operated against her and today the heifer is not in the condition she should be to do her best, and I confidently believe that another year, in the four-year-old form, this heifer will make a better record comparatively than she has this year as a three-year-old. I witnessed the weighing of several of the milkings, the churning and weighing of several days' butter product and will state of my own knowledge that the weights in the following table are correct and that the butter was well worked and of good odor and quality." The table below shows the weights of milk and of butter, all of which are attested to under oath, to comply with the rules of Advanced Registry of the Holstein-Friesian Association.

DATE.	MILK.	BUTTER.
Sept. 11, 1889.	61½ lbs.	3 lbs. 3 oz.
" 12, "	61 lbs.	2 lbs. 14 oz.
" 13, "	59 lbs.	2 lbs. 7 oz.
" 14, "	61¼ lbs.	2 lbs. 13 oz.
" 15, "	63 lbs.	2 lbs. 15 oz.
" 16, "	61½ lbs.	3 lbs.
" 17, "	63 lbs.	3 lbs. 3 oz.
Total production.	430¼ lbs.	20 lbs. 7 oz.

Accompanying the above statement is affidavit of the manager of the dairy, the herdsman and the man who did the milking.

Gillett & Son, of Rosendale, Wis., reported December 1, 1889, in detail, butter records recently made by three two-year-old heifers, Bessie Lœman, Johanna Nig and Johanna 5th, whose seven days' production stands 11 lbs. 1 oz., 11 lbs. 3 oz., and 14 lbs. 2 oz., respectively.

	BESSIE LŒMAN.			JOHANNA NIG.			JOHANNA 5TH.	
Oct.	Lbs. Milk.	Lbs. Butter.	Oct.	Lbs. Milk.	Lbs. Butter.	Sept.	Lbs. Milk.	Lbs. Butter.
7	32.13		21	33.13 1-2		29	42.8	
8	32.3 1-2	3.1	22	34.9	3.1	30	39.12	4 1-2
9	33.12 1-2		23	33.5 1-2		Oct. 1	3×1	
10	32.5	3.1 1-2	24	33.12	3.2	2	40.1	3.11
11	34.8		25	34.9		3	40.11	
12	34.14	4.1434	26	35.7	3.6	4	41.4	6.6 1-2
13	34.15		27	33.4	1.10	5	42.4	

Bessie Lœman—Total week's milk, 234.7. Butter, 11.1. Pounds of milk to one pound butter, 21 19-100.
Johanna Nig—Total week's milk, 238.12. Butter, 11.3. Pounds milk to one pound butter, 21 34-100.
Johanna 5th—Total week's milk, 284.9. Butter, 14.2. Pounds milk to one pound butter, 20 14-100. Oct. 1 and Sept. 30 rained, which reduced her milk a trifle.

The ration fed these heifers was made up as follows: One-fifth corn meal, ¼ ground oats, ⅛ oil meal, and ⅝ wheat bran, with all the timothy hay they would eat, and all the spring water they would drink. They were kept in stables during the day, and allowed to run with the herd at night; were milked at 5.45 a. m., 12.30 and 7.30 p. m. Their milk was set in pans and skimmed every 48 hours. The butter was churned at 62 degrees, washed, salted and worked before weighing.

We put no particular stress upon these records for great flow of milk, as they were tested for butter, and good quality was desired rather than great quantity; hence we say, had we fed desirous of obtaining a great daily milk record, we believe any one of these heifers would have increased in quantity several pounds per day.

We feel quite encouraged from the results of these tests, first, because all these heifers were bred by us; second, because Bessie Lœman and Johanna 5th were sired by our bull Oakland Chief, and are the first of his daughters we have ever tested; and third, because we bred the sires of them all, and that the average of the three of 12 lbs. 2 oz. speaks for itself of the merits of these youngsters as dairy cows. Johanna Nig was sired by a near descendant of the great Billy Boelyn.

CLOTHILDE 2D'S RECORD.

Clothilde 2d, at Lakeside Stock Farm, Syracuse, N. Y., completed on December 18, 1889, a week's butter record of 30 lbs. 8 oz., and it is thus reported by Smiths & Powell Co., in January, 1890. Her butter was of fine quality. She gave for the week 569 lbs. 14 oz. of milk, which shows that she averaged 1 lb. of butter from 18.68 lbs. of milk. This shows that quality and quantity can be combined in the same cow.

She was fed per day during the test, 19 lbs. of grain feed, composed of one part wheat bran, one part ground oats, one part corn meal, and one-eighth of one part linseed meal. Of coarse feed she was fed 50 lbs. corn ensilage, 22 lbs. of carrots and 3 lbs. of hay.

She dropped her last calf October 29, 1889, and up to time of commencing test had very little grain feed.

When the production of both milk and butter is considered, Clothilde 2d now stands at the head. We know of no other cow with equal records of both these products.

This cow is now eight years old, and has averaged over 19,500 lbs. of milk per year, counting the whole time in milk, commencing in her two-year-old form.

As a four-year-old she gave 23,602 lbs. 10 oz. of milk in a year. Last year, after dropping her calf, she was given a butter test of thirty days, making 25 lbs. 6¼ oz. in a week, and 104 lbs. 3¼ oz. in thirty days. All grain feed was then dropped, and during the summer she had only the pasture and soiling crops, and during the winter only corn ensilage, hay and roots, until a few weeks before the close of the year, when 6 lbs. of grain per day was added to her ration. With this feed she closed her year's milk record, at 20,487 lbs. 13 oz. This record, considering the feed consumed, has no equal.

Next to this cow in the production of milk and butter, stands her dam, Clothilde, with a milk record at six years of age, of 26,021 lbs. 2 oz. in a year, and a butter record of 28 lbs. 2¼ oz. in a week. She averaged for the whole time in milk during her life, commencing before she was two years old, 18,579 lbs. per year.

The butter records of Clothilde and her five daughters in Lakeside herd, three of them tested at three years of age, average for the six head, 22 lbs. 13 ⅝ oz., averaging for the whole number a pound of butter from 19.54 lbs. of milk.

The whole number, although three of them were but three years old at the time of making records, and one with only one-half an udder, averaged 16,065 lbs. 6¼ oz. of milk in a year.

The seven-day record was broken on June 17, 1890, by Parthenea. Mr. E. T. Gay thus reports the test: The seven-day milk and butter record recently made by Parthenea, 9592 H. H. B., a member of Maplewood herd, is, I believe, the largest ever made for that period.

Commencing June 11, her production was as follows:

DATE.	MILK.	BUTTER.
June 11, 1890,	80 lbs. 8 oz.	5 lbs. 12½ oz.
" 12, "	77 lbs. 6 oz.	4 lbs. 15½ oz.
" 13, "	75 lbs. 7 oz.	5 lbs. 11½ oz.
" 14, "	76 lbs. 3 oz.	5 lbs. 13 oz.
" 15, "	81 lbs.	5 lbs.
" 16, "	79 lbs. 3 oz.	5 lbs. 8 oz.
" 17, "	75 lbs. 9 oz.	5 lbs. 12 oz.
Total.	584 lbs. 3 oz.	38 lbs. 8½ oz.

Average number pounds of milk per day 78 and 5 oz.
Average number pounds butter per day, 5 and 8 1-14 oz.
Average number pounds milk required for one pound of butter, 14.23.
The butter was of very good grain and quality.

Parthenea is six years old and dropped her last calf April 21, 1890, and on May 15 we began increasing her feed.

During the test she received on an average 27 lbs. of ground feed, consisting of oats, bran, linseed oil meal and corn. She was allowed to run in pasture during the day with other members of the herd and kept in stall nights.

This is not Parthenea's first appearance before the public. She was imported by Mr. F. C. Stevens in 1884 as a calf, and has been a member of his show herds nearly every season since that date. She was a member of the First Prize herd at the Madison Square Garden Cattle Show in 1887 and gave over 70 lbs. of milk daily during the ten days of the great exhibition, in public, and was but three years old at that time.

Parthenea was entered in the public butter tests of 1889 and won first premium at Detroit Exposition last September for largest yield of butter in twenty-four hours—and the fact that she did so more than six months after calving speaks well for her great staying qualities.

Her last record is, we think, without exception the largest ever made and again calls attention to the superior qualities of Holstein-Friesian cattle and to members of Maplewood herd which contains many animals closely related to this noted cow.

It will be remembered that the Holstein-Friesian Association's national prize of gold medals and cash for largest milk record made at any fair or exposition during 1889 was won by Lutskè, a member of Maplewood herd, also both first and second prizes offered for largest butter record went to Tirannia and Alberta Abbekerk, also members of Maplewood herd—Alberta Abbekerk is a half sister to Parthenea and the quantities made by these cows are the largest ever made in a public test. All of the best and leading breeds were well represented in the competition and the number of contestants numbered hundreds in the different states.

In high altitudes the Holstein-Friesian appears able to produce as abundantly as on her native land. Messrs. Ehrich & White, of the Colorado Springs Gardens Company, made the following report in July, 1890, of the performance of their cow Natsey. They state the cow Natsey, 2265 H. H. B., has made an undoubted record of 34 lbs. 9 oz. of unsalted butter in seven days, which beats Lady Baker's record of last year by 3 oz., and which, we believe, is the greatest seven days' butter record ever made by a Holstein-Friesian cow.

The following table gives the weight of each day's production of milk. The cream was churned in two separate lots :

June 28,	1890,	81 1-2 lbs.	
" 29,	"	79 "	
" 30,	"	80 "	
July 1,	"	79 "	
		319	18 lbs. 13 oz. unsalted butter.
July 2,	1890,	79	
" 3,	"	79 4-16	
" 4,	"	71	
		229 4-16	15 lbs. 12 oz. unsalted butter.

Total, 548 lbs. 12 oz. milk made 34 lbs. 9 oz. butter ; 15¾ lbs. milk to 1 lb. butter.

The test was unsatisfactory in one respect. Through an unavoidable accident in handling the cream of the first four days, about one quart of it was spilled and lost. This would have added at least 7 or 8 oz. of butter to the record. This, however, is our misfortune, and we only claim the actual product of butter.

The cow was fed ground corn and oats, wheat bran, cotton seed meal, oil meal, alfalfa and green clover, all the alfalfa and clover she would eat. She had no drink except what she obtained from the water troughs in the yard. We will not take the space here to publish all the affidavits of those who had the cow in charge. Suffice it to say, that we have them in due form in our possession, and copies may be had by any one desiring them.

Natsey, 2265 H. H. B., was bred by M. S. Veeman, Marssum, Friesland, and was calved March 5, 1881, and was imported by Thomas B. Wales, July 21, 1882. She was sold to H. A. Morse, of Genoa Bluffs, Ia., who sold her to H. A. Brown of Marengo, Ia. And then Mr. Wales bought her again, and sold her to Messrs. Ehrich & White at the Chicago sale, November 14, 1889.

In June, 1889, Mr. Wales tested her, and she made 30 lbs. 9 oz. butter from 473 lbs. 15 oz. milk.

He says that the circumstances of the test were unfavorable, and was quite positive that she could surpass Lady Baker under equal conditions. Her Advanced Registry number is 646. She is a magnificent animal, and one of the strongest and heartiest cows we have ever seen.

The Smiths & Powell Co., of Syracuse, N. Y., in the spring of 1894, made a most interesting and valuable report of the yield of some herds of their own breeding. They state: "As is our custom, we have recently been testing some of our young heifers for butter, and as several of them have pedigrees which show that the ten to twenty nearest female ancestors have records which average from 18 to 20 lbs. of butter in a week, and 15,000 to 16,000 lbs. of milk in a year, we have watched with no small degree of interest the results of these tests, and they show conclusively that if you wish superior butter cows, you must breed with this purpose constantly in view.

"We recently tested a heifer which was two years old November 30. last, and had her first calf when about twenty-five months old. She made 14 lbs. 7 oz. of very choice butter, salted an ounce to a pound, and well worked.

"As this is a good showing, it will be of interest to know what her ancestors have done. Her sire was Sir Netherland Clothilde, whose thirteen nearest female ancestors, including every one in America, average 16,052 lbs. 3 oz. of milk in a year, and 19 lbs. 15 oz. of butter in a week.

"Her dam, Aegis 10th, as a two-year-old, made 14 lbs. of butter in a week, and as a three-year-old, 21 lbs. 7 oz. of butter in a week, and she gave 14,000 lbs. of milk in ten months.

"Her grandam, Aegis, was the first cow that was ever known to give 16,823 lbs. of milk in a year, and when thirteen years old she made 25 lbs. of butter in a week and over 100 lbs. in thirty days.

"Aegis 10th was by Netherland Prince, whose dam gave 13,875 lbs. of milk in a year and made 21 lbs. 3 oz. of butter in a week.

"Another heifer which is making a very fine showing is Netherland Monk's Aaggie Constance, three years old. She gave, as a two-year-old, 11,201 lbs. 7 oz. of milk in a year, and made at that age, on winter feed, 15 lbs. 8½ oz. of butter in a week. She had her second calf in December, and has recently made 20 lbs. ½ oz. of butter in a week. Her sire was Netherland Monk, whose dam, Albino 2d, was probably the greatest cow of the entire breed when age is considered. She gave as a two-year-old, 18,484 lbs. of milk in a year, and made, the fourteenth month after having her calf, as a two-year-old, 13 lbs. 14½ oz. of butter in a week. As a three-year-old, when fresh, she made about 26 lbs. and 106 lbs. in thirty days. Netherland Monk was by Netherland Prince, as given above.

"The dam of this young cow, Aaggie Constance, as a two-year-old, commencing at twenty-six months of age, gave 26,761 lbs. of milk in a year, and as a mature cow made 19 lbs. 14½ oz. of butter in a week.

"The grandam, Kappijne, gave 15,227 lbs. 7 oz. of milk in a year, and made 19 lbs. 12¾ oz. of butter in a week.

"Another promising three-year old, equally as well bred as the last two, is Countess Clothilde. She had her first calf when just past two years old, and made, on winter feed, 15 lbs. 2 oz. of butter in a week, and gave 9,251 lbs. 10 oz. of milk in a year. She had her second calf about two weeks ago, and closed a week's test for butter yesterday, making 16 lbs. 3 oz. in a week, and averaging 1 lb. of butter from less than 15 lbs. of milk, for the whole time.

"This heifer is not yet in full flow, and we are confident will make a very much higher record. We have a son of this heifer, now a little over one year old, a prize winner at the last New York State Fair, whose thirty nearest female ancestors, counting this heifer as a two-year-old, have butter records which average for the whole number 20 lbs. 4 oz. in a week, and milk records which average over 16,000 lbs. in a year. This is including every animal that has ever been imported to or bred in America.

"And now, just one word to show the importance of having animals whose ancestors on both sides, and for the entire number, are highly bred for the products desired. We will mention that we tested, a short time since, three heifers which we bought some time ago. They were sired by one of our best bred bulls—equally as well bred as those named above—but the ancestors on the dam's side had never been tested for butter, and consequently their qualities for this product were not known.

"These three heifers, tested under the same conditions as the two-year-old named above, made as follows: One of them, 7 lbs. 3½ oz. of butter in a week; another, 6 lbs. 15 oz. of butter in a week, and another, 7 lbs. 14½ oz of butter in a week.

"It will be seen that while they are as well bred for butter on one side,

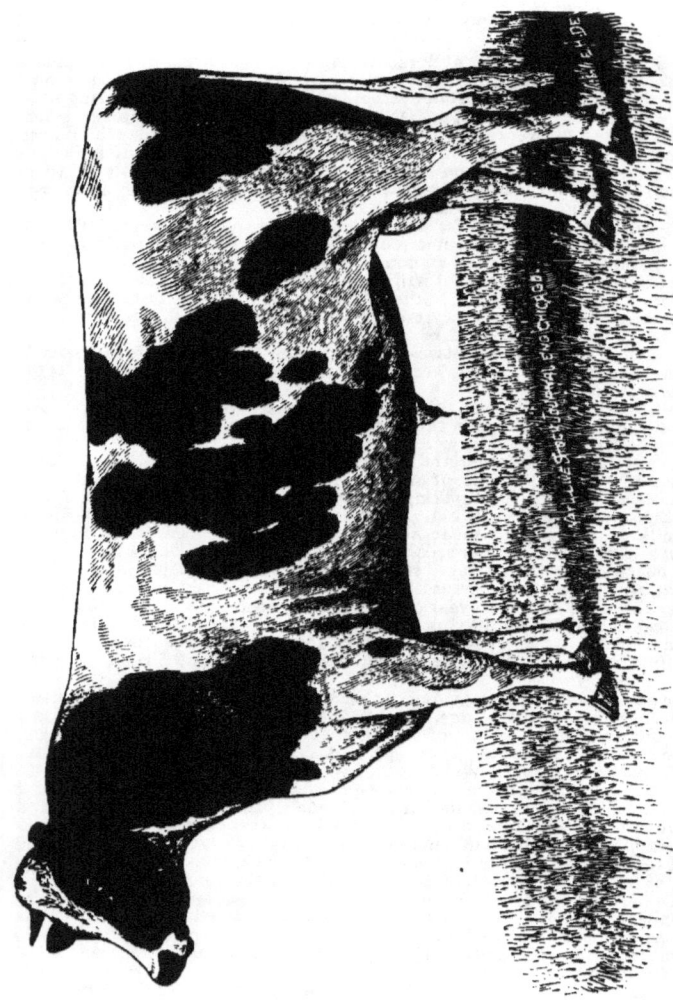

CONSTANTYN, No. 2040 H. F. H. B. 248 N. H. B.

Imported. Weight at maturity, 2,715 lbs. First prize in 1885 at Ohio, Tri-State, Illinois, North Indiana, South Michigan and Great St. Louis Fairs. In 1887 headed first prize herd at Madison Square Garden Dairy Show, New York City.

and have no breeding for butter on the other side, the product by actual test, at the same age, is just about one-half as much as the two-year-old named above, which had been bred for many generations on both sides to the highest butter strains.

"These facts, it seems to us, demonstrate most fully the importance of breeding from animals whose ancestors for many generations have proven superior in the lines desired."

The famous year's test of Pauline Paul, which is the world's record in butter production, is an example of the marvelous capacity of a Holstein-Friesian. She has been appropriately conferred with a title:

"THE QUEEN OF THE DAIRY."

And still thy record leads the world—
The greatest ever seen—
And still amid all dairy farms,
Thou hold'st thy name as queen.

Pauline Paul, 2190 H. H. B., 857 Advanced Registry, was dropped January 19, 1892. Her sire is Climax, 203 H. H. B., and her dam is Johanna Paul, 677 H. H. B.

Climax is by 2d Consul, 339 H. H. B., he by Dictator, 82, and out of Lavina, 168 H. H. B. Dam of Climax, Zuider Zee 9th, 65; she by Van Tromp, 50, and out of Zuider Zee, 62. Johanna Paul, 677. Imported.

Pauline Paul has a butter record of 1,153 lbs. 15¼ oz. in 365 consecutive days, or one year, which record stands unequalled by a cow of any breed.

She is the dam of Zozo, 10260 H. H. B.; butter record, 25 lbs. 10¼ oz. in seven days; 104 lbs. 12 oz. in thirty days; and also the dam of Pauline Paul 2d, awarded first prize as best heifer calf at Buffalo, Elmira, Syracuse, Albany and Oneonta, N. Y., 1892.

The butter record of Pauline Paul for 365 consecutive days, commencing February 8, 1890, is as below:

BUTTER.

DAYS.	LBS.	OZ.	DAYS.	LBS.	OZ.
7	31	1¾	210	795	15½
30	128	13½	240	892	7¼
60	256	11	270	963	15¾
90	382	14½	300	1031	1½
120	508	12½	330	1091	15¼
150	610	14¼	365	1153	15¾
180	700	13½			

Largest day's record of milk, March 25, 1890, 69 lbs. 10 oz.; largest day's yield of butter, 4 lbs. 9½ oz.; largest seven days' yield of milk, 449 lbs. 7 oz.; largest seven days' yield of butter, 31 lbs. 1¾ oz.; total amount of milk given through the year, 18,669 lbs. 9 oz.

The butter was worked thoroughly and salted one ounce to the pound, and prepared fit for market before weighing. During the whole period of the test an invitation, through the press and otherwise, was extended to the public to personally witness the record that Pauline Paul was making, and many took advantage of it to satisfy themselves.

The grain ration fed during the test consisted of three parts bran, two parts of ground oats, one part of corn meal by measure. She did not consume over 30 lbs. of grain per day, including the 3 lbs. of cottonseed fed daily until December 1. She had no slop food of any kind, or ensilage. The last churning of butter made from her weighed 1 lb. 9½ oz.

She came through the test in good condition without experiencing a drawback of any kind, or refusing a feed. Her robust constitution, no doubt, has been an important factor in accomplishing such remarkable results. She has been a regular breeder ever since.

Pauline Paul is now the property of Crumhorn Stock Farm, Paterson, N. J.

There are almost numberless examples of the success of the Holstein-Friesian in the hands of practical dairymen as well as breeders, in all sections of the

United States and Canada. Public institutions, experiment stations, and individuals who have used Holstein-Friesian cattle, whether grades or pure-breds, have found them uniformly the most economical producers.

The director of the Iowa Agricultural College Experiment Station, Prof. Wilson, is making excellent progress in his experiments with the Holstein-Friesian breed of cattle and others, testing them for the Advanced Registry. The director keeps some thirty head of Holstein-Friesians on the college farm, and says they are not excelled in amount of butter fat by any other breeds kept there.

The Smiths & Powell Company, Syracuse, N. Y., writes: "We have just received a letter from Mr. W. J. Hayes, of Ravenna, O., who, some years ago, bought some choice representatives of the Clothilde and Netherland families as foundation animals for a choice herd of Holstein-Friesians.

"He has been breeding but a few years, and writes us under date of January 10, 1896, as follows: 'During the year 1895, we milked from twenty-nine cows and nine heifers 387,555 lbs. of milk, averaging for each cow and heifer 10,200 lbs., and made 14,136 lbs. of butter. For this we received $4,029.30, an average price per pound of 28¼ cents.'

"From this statement it will be seen that the average returns from the whole thirty-eight cows in milk, nine of which were heifers, were $106.30, and that the whole number averaged 372 lbs. of butter per cow.

"If the heifers were counted as half cows, which is quite common among dairymen, it would show an average of over 421 lbs. of butter per cow for the year.

"Such a showing as this, it seems to us, must be very gratifying to Holstein-Friesian breeders, and it is certainly very gratifying to us, as his herd is very largely made up of the Clothilde and Netherland families."

CHAPTER XI.

DAIRY YIELDS—GRADE HOLSTEINS.

M. S. Nye, of Homer, N. Y., writes: "The past year my dairy of twenty-two Holstein-Friesian cows gave an average of 8,048 lbs. of milk per cow. Ten of the cows were four years and under. I have in the past two years made twelve tests with the scales and churn for butter in the months of May, June and July. The average amount of milk for one pound of butter was 22 lbs. Taking that for an average for the year, the dairy has produced 365 lbs. of butter per cow in one year.

"I have drawn my milk to milk depots for the past six years, and they have been well pleased with the quality of milk."

Charles Mimrich, North Heidelberg, Pa., April 1, 1895, writes: "I find my Holsteins far superior to either the Jersey or Swiss breeds of cattle which I have been breeding the past ten years."

W. A. Halsey, Port Byron, N. Y., April 1, 1895: "I am decidedly of the opinion that the Holsteins have no superior for milk, butter and beef."

W. M. Benninger, Walnutport, Pa.: "I am convinced by actual experience that good Holsteins are decidedly the best general purpose cattle. I am getting from two to five cents per pound more for my butter than the other creameries near here, which is due to the milk being from a pure-bred herd of Holsteins."

E. S. Allen, Baxter, Iowa: "I have twenty-five head of the favorite black-and-white cattle. We milked eight cows and three heifers last season. They averaged me one pound of butter a day for ten months in the year. In the winter they were fed dry corn in the ear and timothy hay, and in summer I soaked the corn and fed them ten ears night and morning. The weather was so dry that the pasture all dried up. In the fall, until cold weather, they were fed what pumpkins they would eat. I raised seven calves, feeding milk direct from the cow until they were from 15 to 20 days old, then put them on skim milk, and oil cake meal and salt and the milk poured over it, with what hay and corn they would eat, but no grass until they were weaned.

"The milk was sold to creamery and run through a separator, we getting 80 per cent in skim milk to bring home. My test ran from 4 1-5 to 3 1-4 fat or butter. The best month was May, when they averaged 42 lbs. of butter per head. Most of the skim milk was fed to pigs, and the pigs and calves I still have on hand. I have had high grade Shorthorns and common stock, but find the Holsteins much more profitable than any of the others. This winter I am feeding shredded corn fodder and corn and cobmeal, and like it very much."

Mr. Peter Hammen, Beechwood, Wis., writes: The following is the result in one year at the Beechwood Valley Herd of Holsteins. Having bought a cream separator and commenced the first day of March, 1893, with nineteen cows in the herd, until March 1, 1894, cream was received by the Kewaskum creamery, which is run entirely under the gathering system. Cream was taken from the farm twice a week which is eleven miles from the creamery. The following is the number of inches of cream and number of pounds of butter derived from the cream in one year and prices per pound. Payments are made once a month:

Months.	No. of in.	No. of lbs.	Price per lb.	Months.	No. of in.	No. of lbs.	Price per lb.
March, 1893,	185.5	196.94	24 cts.	Sept. 1893.		151.24	22 cts.
April, "	387	462.16	24 "	" "		158.65	23 "
May, "	538.3	241.28	20 "	Oct. "	396	285.38	24 "
" "		404	18 "	" "		96.84	23 "
June, "	649.7	450.78	14 "	" "		98.17	22 "
" "		355.59	15 "	Nov. "	342.9	185.22	21 "
July, "	532.7	658.82	15 "	" "		223.30	20 "
August, "	630.6	424.67	16 "	Dec. "	313.2	308.37	22 "
" "		351.67	18 "	Jan. 1894.	330.1	372.61	17 "
Sept., "	504.4	406.87	20 "	Feb. "	305.5	375.48	18 "

Total number of inches, 5,185. Total number of pounds 6,267½. Average price per pound, 19 cents. Average number of pounds per cow, 329½ lbs. Average in money per cow, $62.55.

CHIEF OF MAPLE HILL 4TH, No. 17224 H. F. H. B.

First prize and sweepstakes, Iowa and Nebraska State Fairs; first prize at St. Louis, 1894; first prize and sweepstakes, Minnesota, St. Louis and Illinois in 1895.

Frank Roe, Augusta, N. J., writes: "Our dairy for the past year, 1895, has numbered thirty in milk. Their milk was sold to a dealer in Brooklyn, N. Y., who has had it for the past five years. From the thirty we have received $3,668.38, an average from each cow of $122.27. The same number last year from January, '94, to January, '95, averaged $120.96. The present year they have given more milk, but prices were lower for one month, which reduced the average about two dollars for each cow. The dairy is composed of twenty-three pure bred Holstein-Friesians, five pure Guernseys and two grade Holsteins. If we could sell the Guernseys and fill their places with pure-bred Holstein-Friesians we would materially increase the average, as the Holsteins give us nearly double the quantity of milk. Our Holstein milk shows from 4 to 4.4 per cent butterfat while the Guernsey milk is about 1 per cent richer. We have tested both frequently, both separately and also the mixed milk from both. The individual Guernseys show from 4 to 6 per cent, while the Holsteins show from 3.5 to 5 per cent. For our business the Holstein is very much the better cow as we can produce a quart of milk from them cheaper than from the Guernsey. All milk that will show 12 per cent solids brings the same price in our market. The milk from our Holsteins will show better than 13 per cent solids.

"During the past year we have been testing all our pure-bred cows that became fresh and were in condition with the result given below. All were examined and accepted by Mr. Hoxie and duly entered in Advanced Registry. Only one cow failed that we tested, Jane, No. 14,328, who had only two good quarters. She only lacked 92-100 of an oz. of butter. Her milk during the week averaged 4.2 per cent of fat."

	AGE. YRS. MOS.		LBS.	OZ.	NO. LBS. MILK TO 1 LB. OF BUTTER.
Dorinda, 776 D.·F.	7		15	3	26 00
Dorinda Wayne, 25,206	3		16	2 87-100	18.92
Dorinda's Roxie, 14,331	5		20	11 71-100	20.22
Roxie Wayne, 25,207	3		18	3 97 100	20 47
Roxie Wayne, 25,207	4		21	1 60 100	19.30
Lilith's Beauty, 8866	3		15	10	23.50
Lilith Aaggie Wayne, 25,205	3		16	1 26-100	23.88
Brookside Lilith, 34,025	1	9	10	1 6-100	20.59
Brookside Lilith, 34,025	2	10	14	8 2-100	20.53
Aaggie Cornucopia, 21,127	6		21	8	18.31
Aaggie Cornucopia 2d, 30,597	3		16	12 22-100	20.04
Aaggie Cornucopia 3d, 34,026	2		14	1 81-100	24.06
Jetske Roe, 14,329	6		15	15 25-100	22.90
Jetske Wayne, 25,203	3		16	7 97-100	21.59
Jeike 2d, 1389 D.-F.	6		19		20.25
Mulvie, 10,701	7		21	7 103-200	18 07
Miss Tutts, 7161	8		16	8 93-100	21.35
Zanca, 10,703	6		18	15 43-100	19.50
May Hartog of Brookside, 36,420	2		13	3	23.38
May Hartog of Brookside, 36,420	3		18	4 39-100	18.80
Dorothy Ondine Wayne, 25,209	3		21	5 11-200	18.07
Celeste 3d, 2896	10		20	4 56-100	17.91
Brookside Maggie, 33,216	5		19	15 75-100	20.89
Jolie 4th, 10,537	7		16	11 9-100	22.49
Ondine's Model 2d's Empress, 11,080	3		15	1	28.00
Jaire, from two quarters, 14,328	7		14	14 8-100	

F. M. Bauman, Fremont, Ohio, writes: "I am still breeding the white and black cattle, and find them more profitable than any other breed that I ever handled.

"As they give a large flow of milk, make a large amount of butter, and excellent beef, with these three great producing elements combined in one, it cannot help but make them the best general purpose cattle at the present time.

"My herd is small, eleven head; eight full bloods and three grades. I find the better the blood, the better the cow.

"Have five cows now; three full blood and two grades. My method of handling is pasture in the summer and stable in winter, with a little exercise in the yard in pleasant weather.

"Winter feed consists of clover hay, corn fodder, roots, corn meal and bran.

"Butter is my object. The skim milk goes to calves and pigs. Last year from three cows made 980 lbs of butter; average per cow 326¼ lbs; cost of keep per cow, $82.

"Veals sold at four weeks old, hog dressed, weighed from 128 lbs. to 145 lbs. Price received, six and seven cents per pound. Steers live weight, two years old, 1000 lbs.; price three cents. So I find the Holstein cow more profitable than any other breed.

"Average per cow on butter the past year, $67.90, without calf."

Mr. Edward A. Powell, of Syracuse, N. Y., writes the following practical and interesting article on grade Holsteins: "The annual report of Dairy Commissioner Brown, of this state, for 1888, and the 'cow census' of a portion of Jefferson county, both seem to show that the dairy cows of the state average only about 3,000 pounds of milk per year.

"Those reports present such a dark picture to all dairymen—the cows of this state being, doubtless, equal to those of any other—that every enterprising party in the business will at once ask himself, is there no remedy? Is there no brighter future for the dairy business of this country?

"I have given the subject some attention, and am convinced that there is a remedy within the reach of every dairyman. By breeding better, by selecting bulls from breeds and from families which have been proven by careful test, extending through several generations, to be superior for both milk and butter—bulls in which these tendencies have become so thoroughly established that they will transmit these qualities to their offspring, and, by crossing them upon the best cows in any dairy, a herd can very soon be built up that will produce double the present average product.

"Pure-bloods are, of course, superior to grades, but it is not practical for every dairyman to have pure-bred cows.

"He can, however, at small expense compared with the result to be attained, secure bulls of the highest quality and best breeding.

"These bulls should not only be pure-bloods, and recorded, but, which is of far greater consequence, they should come from families whose superiority has been established beyond all question, by actual and well-established records.

"It is not enough that the dam alone has a good record. Every female in every line for several generations should be proven, showing that there are no blanks.

"Every ancestor should be superior, not only for milk, but for butter; for the dairy that can be used with profit for the production of either product is much more valuable, and is a safer investment, than if it must be confined to one.

"The farmer who converts his milk into butter this year may find it much more profitable to make cheese, or sell milk, next. He will also find a larger field for the sale of his surplus stock.

"The following statements will convey some idea of what can be accomplished by breeding from superior bulls:

"Messrs. Wood & Son, of West Exeter, N. Y., only a few years ago bought a thoroughbred bull and a few heifers, at an outlay of only a few hundred dollars. They now have thirty cows, pure bloods and high grades, nine of them only three years old.

"They sold at the factory this last year over 183,117 lbs. of milk. They sold 1,535 lbs. of butter, which, at 25 lbs. of milk to a pound of butter, would require 38,375 lbs.; 570 lbs. from skimmings. at an average of 4½ lbs., equal to 2,500 lbs. They raised on new milk thirty-six calves, which they estimate at 500 lbs. each, equal to 8,000; 90 quarts of milk sold, equal to 180 lbs.

"The milk, cream and butter for a family of six were also furnished from the dairy, which, at the low estimate of 12 quarts per day, would require 8,700 lbs. for the year.

"This makes a total of 240,990 lbs. for the thirty cows, about one-third of which were three-year-olds, making an average of over 8,000 lbs. per cow.

"Messrs. Henry Jerome & Son, intelligent, enterprising farmers living near Syracuse, commenced a few years ago to improve their herd by selecting the best cows in the country, and grading up from this foundation by the use of a fine Holstein-Friesian bull About two-thirds to three-fourths of the herd are now fine grades. They feed liberally and well, but only in such quantity as they deem most profitable.

"Their herd consisted this year of eighteen cows, including three two-year-old heifers.

"They sold their milk to the Onondaga County Milk Association, of Syracuse, and received their pay a few days since for 8,839$\frac{55}{100}$ lbs. of milk for each cow. The herd averaged them $105.55 per cow. This was the amount sold, and cash received. Besides this, the tables for two families for the year, and another for three months, were supplied from the dairy, and three calves were raised.

"During the year four cows which were not satisfactory were replaced by better ones, which were fresh, but the total number of cows was kept at eighteen. Had the milk used in the three families, and that fed to the calves, been weighed, it would doubtless have shown an average of three times the amount Commissioner Brown reports as the average yield for the cows of the state.

"P. J. Schuyler, Esq., a neighbor who sold his milk to the same association, has ten cows, eight of which are of the same breed, and nearly all representing one family, which averaged for 1888 10,449 lbs. of milk, for which he was paid $127 per cow, or $90 per cow above the average of the cows of the state, according to the report of Commissioner Brown.

"I recently called at the farm of G. L. Merril to see a fine grade Holstein-Friesian cow, of which I had heard very favorable reports.

COUNT AAGGIE CLOTHILDE, No. 10209 H. F. H. B.

"His foreman informed me that she had dropped her calf about six weeks ago, and had given since that date from 56 to 71 lbs. of milk a day, the former being the smallest, and the latter the largest daily yields. He also assured me that by actual tests she was making over 2 lbs. of butter per day. His wife with pride brought out for our inspection a churning for one day, which she had just finished working. It was as yellow as could be desired, without artificial coloring, the grain was good, and the flavor superior.

"Another neighbor recently had a grade cow, which, by actual weight, gave in the months of January and February over 3,800 lbs. of milk.

"By the use of the very best class of bulls, and rearing only the calves from our best cows, the production of our herds can be doubled in a very few years.

"The greatest hindrance to success is the fact that the poorest class of bulls, merely because they are a little cheaper, are used by most dairymen."

A comparison of Holstein grades, Jerseys, Guernseys and their grades will be of interest.

While at the annual meeting of the New York State Dairymen's Association at Ithaca in December, 1889, I was quite interested in Secretary Shull's description of the results of a dairy conference held at Cedarsburg, N. Y., writes Mr. Dudley Miller in February, 1890.

At these conferences practical instruction in the art of butter making is given, and frequently, as in this case, by that excellent butter maker, W. H. Gilbert of Richland, president of our State Dairymen's Association.

President Gilbert ships his butter nearly 300 miles, to the Hotel Brunswick, New York, and receives a handsome price for it the year round. The same hotel is supplied with cream from President Gilbert's farm. It is shipped in tin cans covered with felt jackets, to preserve an even cool temperature.

At the Cedarsburg dairy conference a churning was made with 200 lbs. of milk from Jersey and Guernsey full bloods and high grades. This milk was produced by 23⅓ cows (so reckoned), or an average of 8.57 lbs. at each milking per cow.

The 200 lbs. of milk produced 191 oz. of butter, or an average, for each cow per milking, of 8.19 oz. Thus it required in round numbers a pound of this milk for an ounce of butter.

At another churning of 200 lbs. of milk from grade Holsteins, produced by eleven cows at one milking each, averaging per cow for milking 18 18 lbs., 101 oz. of butter was made, or an average for each cow per milking of 9.18 oz., requiring nearly 2 lbs. of milk to 1 oz. of butter.

Here we have the actual results of a practical test between full bloods and high grade Jerseys and Guernseys on the one hand and grade Holsteins on the other. In tabulated form the results are as follows:

Breed.	No. of Milkings.	Lbs. of Milk.	Lbs. per Milking.	Oz. of Butter.	Oz. per Cow.
Jerseys, Guernseys and high grades,	21 1-3	200	8.57	191	8.19
Holstein grades, ...	11	200	18.18	101	9.18

The adherents of Jerseys and Guernseys may look at this table, smile complacently, and lecture on the quality of milk of their favorites, dilating on the fact that it required but little over a pound of milk for an ounce of butter, whereas the Holsteins furnished such poor milk that it took nearly 2 lbs. to make 1 oz. of butter.

Why! they say in Massachusetts that Holstein milk does not come up to the standard fixed by law.

The Holstein man who keeps less than half the number of cows (11 to 23⅓) to produce the same amount of milk (200 lbs.), which is more digestible and hence better for man and beast, is not at all troubled, as he is making more money than his friends who are crying skim milk, and at the same time he is furnishing the public with more wholesome milk.

Of course it would be the sheerest folly to attempt to make butter of skim-milk, "milk below the Massachusetts standard," in the opinion of Jersey and Guernsey breeders.

However, the foolish Holstein man fetches his "skim-milk" to the Cedarsburg conference, where it has to compete with that of the special purpose Jersey and Guernsey butter breeds. When lo! and behold! these despised producers of skim-milk, of milk below the Massachusetts standard, in public at this New York State Dairymen's conference at Cedarsburg, make an average of over 10 per cent more butter per cow than the much lauded pet of the fancy farmer, the Jersey and Guernsey.

It is hard to be compelled to bear the taunts of those who are continually throwing the "skim-milk" characteristics of the Holsteins into their owners' faces, but as long as these despised cows produce over 10 per cent more butter and over 100 per cent more milk than the Jerseys or Guernseys, their breeders will probably continue in their foolish ways and stick to the Holstein.

CHAPTER XII.
MICHIGAN AGRICULTURAL COLLEGE.

From a bulletin of the Michigan State College and Experiment Station, we make a liberal extract relating to the three Holstein-Friesian cows, Houwtje D., Belle Sarcastic and Rosa Bonheur. Illustrations of these cows are also given.

Their records of yields of butter fat are, respectively, 600.14 lbs., 632.78 lbs. and 469.31 lbs.

Prof. Clinton D. Smith, under whose continual oversight these animals have been, describes minutely their varying characteristics, food consumed, etc.

For one day, ... 93.0 lbs. milk, 2.96 lbs. fat.
For seven days, ... 628.2 lbs. milk, 18.79 lbs. fat.
For three hundred and sixty-five days, . . 19,025.0 lbs. milk, 660.14 lbs. fat.
Average test for one year, 3.47 per cent fat.

Houwtje D. was calved March 12, 1888, from imported dam and sire, and is described as having in most respects a typical dairy form as to general contour, being distinctly wedge shaped and very deep through the abdomen and udder, and rather too small in girth behind the shoulders. She is another of the famous cows at the Michigan State Agricultural College and Experiment Station which have been tested and considered by Prof. Clinton D. Smith to be one of the three best cows alive. We are enabled, through Prof. Smith's kindness, to here present the pictures of these magnificently handled cows.

Her head is long, inclined to be coarse, and somewhat defective in width at the base of the horns. Her temperament is quiet, almost to the point of stupidity. The neck is thin, long and slightly drooping. The withers are broad rather than sharp, and the crops are full rather than cut out, differing in these two important respects from the ideal form.

The lean, slanting shoulder, uncovered ribs, and serrated, strong, prominent back of the dairy cow are present. The hips are broad and level with the pin-bones unusually high and wide apart. The cow carries a good amount of flesh. The udder, though somewhat uneven, is well developed, slightly meaty in texture and extends well forward.

Her weight varied little from 1,560 lbs. up to the middle of July, when it gradually increased to 1,600 lbs. by the first of January following.

Her last calf was dropped April 25, 1894, at which time she was six years, one month and thirteen days old.

She became with calf on the ninth day of March, 1895.

The records of her yields of milk and butter fat began on the third day of May, 1894, and are given by weeks. As with Rosa Bonheur, the milking was done thrice daily to the third day of March, 1895.

Thereafter she milked twice per day only. Each mess was tested in duplicate by the Babcock test after weighing.

The cow was turned to grass before this record began. The pasture was supplemented by a grain ration of 21 lbs. of the mixture spoken of as being fed to Rosa Bonheur 5th, viz.: 100 lbs. corn meal, 75 lbs. oats and 25 lbs. of bran.

Her yield is given for 455 days, as she failed to get with calf for nearly ten months. During this time she made the following records: For one day, 93 lbs. milk, 2.96 lbs. fat. For seven days, 628.2 lbs. milk, 18.79 lbs. fat. For 365 days, 19,025 lbs. milk, 660.14 lbs. fat. Average test for year, 3.47 per week, 2.47 to 4.71.

From December 19, nearly eight months after freshening, to May 1, a period of 133 days, Houwtje D. consumed the following:

Roots, ... 5,440 lbs. or 41.20 lbs. per day.   Bran, ... 702.25 lbs. or 5.28 lbs. per day
Silage, ... 6,060 "   45.56   "   "   Wheat, . . . 518.02   "   3.89   "   "
Hay, ...   452   "   3.4   "   "   Millet Silage, . 173
Corn, ...   406. 6"   3.05   "   "   Oat and pea hay, 208
Oats, ...   243.68 "   1.83   "   "

This amount of fodder and grain contained 4,490.55 pounds of dry matter, equivalent to 33.8 lbs. dry matter per day. Since the cow weighed on the average during the winter, 1,600 pounds, she had 21.12 lbs. dry matter per day per 1,000 pounds live weight. The German feeding standard for dairy cows in milk requires 24 lbs. of dry matter per day per 1,000 lbs. live weight.

The amount of fat yielded during this period was 189.5 lbs., and its food cost 15.67 cents per pound, or if allowance is made for skim milk, 11.73 cents, equivalent to 10.05 cents for butter.

RECORDS—One day, ... 81.9 lbs. milk,   2.45 lbs. fat.
         Seven days, ... 554.7 lbs. milk, 16.42 lbs. fat.
         One year, ... 21,075.8 lbs. milk, 622.78 lbs. fat.
         Sixteen months, ... 27,626.3 lbs. milk, 887.22 lbs. fat.
PREVIOUS RECORD—1893, eleven months, ... 9,235.5 lbs. milk.

Belle Sarcastic was calved January 18, 1890, and was bred by H. P. Doane, of Duffield, Genesee County, Michigan. She was sired by Sarcastic, 4,720, a bull owned and bred by G. M. Shattuck, Pontiac, Mich., and out of imported pure Dutch-Friesian ancestry.

The dam was Belvisia 2d, 4,553 H. F. H. B., a cow bred by Tousey & Seeley, Pontiac, Mich. She was out of Belvisia, 1,675 D.-F. H. B. The dam of this cow was the famous Pauline 2d, 18 A. R., Vol. 1, and the sire Jelsum, 81 P. R.

The sire of Belvisia 2d was Prince Nicolaas, 361 D.-F. H. B., whose dam, Marie 2d, 232 M. R., was one of the best Holstein cows ever brought into Michigan.

She was selected by Cornelius Baldwin, at that time inspector for the Advanced Register of the Old Dutch-Friesian Herd-Book, and was imported by T. H. McGraw, of Portsmouth, Mich. While not a coarse cow she weighed 1,900 lbs. when fat. She had a wonderful development of the milk veins, and gave over 90 lbs. of milk in a day in the old country.

As a young heifer, Belle was decidedly beefy, broad across the shoulders, and steer-like in general contour. After beginning to give milk, however, the inherited dairy temperament manifested itself until, at the present time, her general form approximates somewhat closely to the ideal dairy type, as is shown by her photograph.

The long head, finely chiseled, broad at the horns, strong and nervous in expression; the thin, shapely neck, but slightly drooping; the sharp withers, the chine straight but open and serrate; the ribs flattened and open, the loin broad and strong, with a high and level rump; the points of the thurl bones far apart and covered with a pad of fat, the thighs incurving, but strong and in good proportion, the udder large, even and with a long connection with the body extending well up behind and well forward and continued in large crooked milk veins ending in large milk wells; the skin, mellow and fine as silk, covered with a coat of soft and glossy hair; these indications point to an ideal dairy cow, capable when carefully managed of producing an extraordinary record.

In disposition she lacks the gentleness and motherly qualities of Rosa Bonheur 5th, and the tendency to stupidity of Houwtje D. She is nervous, quick and highly sensitive, though gentle and perfectly kind to her keeper. Her weight May and June was, on the average, 1,490 lbs., in November it was 1,508 lbs. During the winter it ran up very slowly to 1,600 lbs. by the latter part of April and early May, 1895. The average of her weekly weights in July, 1895, was 1,622 lbs.

Belle's first calf was dropped on the 1st of April, 1893, her second on the 13th of April, 1894. She did not again become pregnant until the 23d day of May, 1895. Her milk and butter record began on the 26th day of April, 1894. As with Rosa Bonheur and Howtje D., she was milked thrice daily, and each mess was separately tested in duplicate by the Babcock test.

The milk record for the year was 21,075.8 lbs., equivalent to an average of 57.74 lbs. per day. In the 490 days she gave 27,626.3 lbs., or an average of 56.38 lbs. per day.

Reducing the butter fat yields to butter, the 632.78 lbs. of fat yielded in the year is equivalent to 738.24 lbs. of butter. This is an average of 14.15 lbs. of butter per week for the year.

The 827.22 lbs. of fat given in the seventy weeks is equivalent to 965.09 lbs. of butter, which is an average of 13.79 lbs. of butter in a week.

At the beginning of this record the cow was but four years and one-quarter old. On account of her square and beefy form she had not been selected as one of the most promising heifers of the herd and given no unusual attention as a calf or heifer. Her previous record of 9,255.5 lbs. of milk was indicative of no unusual powers. She had during the summer of 1894 good pasture and a daily grain ration of 21 lbs. of the mixture of 100 lbs. of corn meal, 75 lbs. of oat meal and 25 lbs. of bran.

Her milk flow was singularly even as to quantity and quality, considering the fact that she was a young cow and somewhat rapidly growing in weight.

Belle had been turned to pasture before this record began. As the pastures dried up they were supplemented by various green fodders, oats and peas, sweet corn and various leguminous crops. During the hottest weather and when the flies were particularly bad, she was confined during the day time in a cool stable and allowed to run in a pasture at night.

On account of her immaturity no attempt was made to crowd the cow, and the ration was kept below the standard.

The American standard ration would require for a cow of her weight, 1,550 lbs., 3.41 lbs. of protein, 20.61 lbs. of carbohydrates and 1.085 lbs. of fat per day.

The cow ate her feed with avidity every day, and was always vigorous, playful and perfectly healthy.

The total dry matter eaten in the twenty-one weeks was 5,276.03 lbs., equal to 35.89 lbs. per day, or 23.18 lbs. per day for 1,000 lbs. live weight, the average weight of the cow for the winter being 1,550 lbs.

The total fat yield for the twenty-one weeks was 230.67 lbs. There was therefore 22.87 lbs. dry matter on the average eaten for each pound of fat yielded.

The cost of the feed for the same period was $40.75. Dividing this sum by 230.67, the number of pounds of fat, we have the feed cost of one pound of fat, viz.: 17.66 cents, if no cognizance is taken of the value of the 6,120 lbs. of skim milk yielded at the same time, which, at 20 cents per hundred, was worth $12.24. Subtracting from the $40.75, total food cost, this value of the skim milk we have the net food cost of the fat $28.51 or 12.35 cents per pound.

After turning to pasture in the early days of May, 1895, the grain feed was continued with some modification. To the 20th of May the daily grain feed consisted of 2 lbs. of oil meal and 18 lbs. of a mixture of 100 lbs. of corn, 60 lbs. of oats, 85 lbs. of bran and 50 lbs. of wheat. After May 20 the wheat was dropped and the cow received 18 lbs. of corn, oats and bran in the proportions just given with 2 lbs. of oil meal. This continued until July 13, after which the daily grain feed was made up of 6 lbs. of a mixture of equal parts of gluten meal and wheat bran, 12 lbs. of the mixture of corn, oats and bran, and 2 lbs. of oil meal.

The drouth was excessive in the early summer, and the pastures were nearly an entire failure after the middle of July. The cow was therefore shut in the stable during the heat of the day and fed on green corn and hay in addition to the grain.

She had been accustomed to receive on the average 35.89 lbs. of dry matter per day while in the yard before turning to pasture. To obtain as much from pasture grass, which contains about 80 per cent water, she would need to consume 179 lbs. daily, the gathering of which alone would be a formidable undertaking, even for as vigorous a cow as this one. To relieve her of the necessity of carying such a mass of succulent material through her stomach and bowels the grain ration was kept up.

The milk flow rose toward the end of May and was fairly constant through June, July and August. The regularity as well as the unusual size of the yield is undoubtedly to be attributed to the grain feed with the pasture.

In the four months of May, June, July and August she consumed $21.77 worth of grain.

The pasture throughout July and August was so poor as to form but an inconspicuous part of the ration. Counting its value with the supplementary green fodder and hay for 123 days as $10.00, the total cost of the feed of the cow for the four months would be $31.77.

The milk yield for the same period was 6,608.5 lbs., containing 195.92 lbs. of fat, equivalent to 228.57 lbs. of estimated butter. Dividing the food cost, $31.77, by this amount, the feed cost of a pound of butter would be 13.89 cents, without reckoning the value of the skim milk, which at 20 cents per hundred would be worth $11.23.

Rosa Bonheur 5th. This most remarkable of Holstein-Friesian cows is another of the Michigan Experiment Station herd which has been so admirably and skillfully handled by Prof. Clinton D. Smith. We make the following extracts from the Station Bulletin:

Rosa Bonheur 5th was calved March 20, 1888. On the 20th of February, 1894, therefore, when this record began, she was 5 years and 11 months old. Her weight at that time and for the months following varied but a few pounds from 1,750, until she became pregnant on the 22d of June, 1894, when it rapidly ran up to 1,850 pounds by the close of the year. She is therefore a very large cow. In general outline she approaches the ideal dairy type, being distinctly wedge shaped, deep through the sacrum and udder, and much less so through the shoulder and brisket, with an immense belly and udder.

The latter measured, a month after calving, five feet and seven inches in circumference, while the girth around the largest part of the belly was eight feet and six inches. The head, in size, is in due proportion to the body, and is long rather than wide. The head back of the horns is broad, giving room for a large brain. The neck is thin, fine, slightly drooping and moderately long. The chine is remarkably open, giving a decided saw-like feeling to the back. The withers are very sharp and thin, while the chest midway between the brisket and the top of the shoulder is broad, giving ample room for the immense lung power required in the digestion of the quantity of food which the cow consumes. There is a decided droop in the back between a point one-third of the distance from the top of the shoulders to the hip bone and the rise of the pelvic arch. The ribs are open, and the distance from the last rib to the point of the hip bone is fourteen inches. The hips and loin are fairly strong and rounded. The height of the cow at the shoulder is four feet and ten inches; at the hips five feet. The udder has a very long connection with the body, extending well up to the vulva behind, and a good distance in from, as is shown by the photograph. There is a strong development of the umbilical region and the milk veins are long and tortuous; ending without extension in large milk wells. The thighs are somewhat thin, but not cathammed. Her skin is mellow and unctuous.

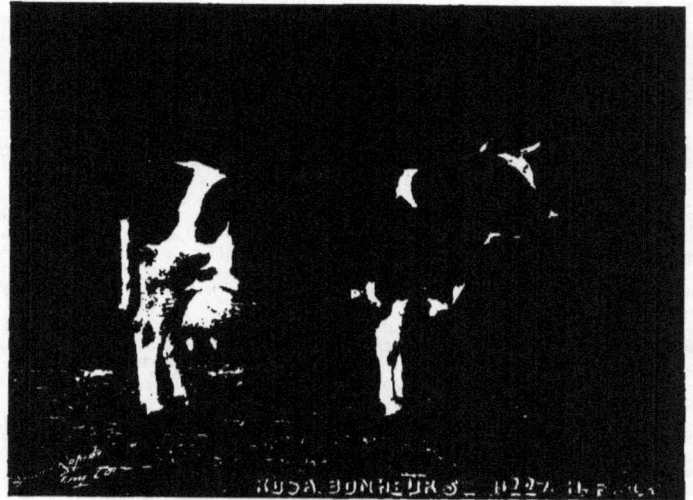

RECORDS—For one day . . . . 106 75 lbs. milk, 3.22 lbs. fat.
For seven days, ... 726.25 lbs. milk, 20.47 lbs. fat.
For thirty days, ... 2,985.50 lbs. milk, 82.16 lbs. fat.
For three hundred and fourteen days, 17,043.45 lbs. milk, 469.31 lbs. fat.
Average per cent of fat for year, 2.75; per week, 2 31 to 3.42.

In disposition she is uniformly quiet, docile and motherly, an enormous eater, never being off her feed, and not dainty in her appetite.

Although the weather was extremely cold during the latter days of February and early March, which immediately succeeded the birth of her calf, she was kept in the box stall shown in the cut without further protection from the extreme cold than was afforded by the battened boards and loose door. Whenever the days were pleasant and sunshiny she was allowed to exercise in the barnyard, and visited the water trough for her water supply. Indeed, the doors of her stall were frequently left open as the cow gave every evidence of enjoyment of the keen and invigorating air.

She was milked thrice daily, at 4.30 a. m., and 12.30, and again at 8.30 p. m., by the same milker.

It is a matter of course that these records were not made without generous feeding. During the winter the cows had silage made from several varieties of dent corn, mixed, fairly glazed when cut and perfectly preserved in the silo; a grain mixture composed of 100 parts corn meal, 75 parts oat meal and 25 parts bran; old process oil meal, mangels and hay. In summer there was pasture, green fodder and grain. For the week ending March 27, Rosa Bonheur 5th ate an average daily ration of 59.22 pounds dry matter, which contained 6.30 pounds digestible protein, 31.34 pounds digestible carbohydrates and 2.34 pounds digestible fat. For the sixty-three days ending April 24, Rosa consumed:

5,181	pounds silage at $2.00 per ton,	. . . .	$5.18
755.5	"	corn meal at $19.00 per ton, ...	7.18
566.63	"	oat meal at $16.00 per ton, ...	4.53
188.87	"	wheat bran at $14.00 per ton, ...	1.32
308	"	oil meal at $22.75 per ton, ...	4.53
1,867	"	mangels at $2.50 per ton, ...	2.33
63	"	hay at $6.00 per ton, ...	19
	Total, ...		$25.26

During this period her milk contained 167.75 pounds of butter fat, thus making its average food cost 15.07 cents per pound, equivalent to 12.92 cents per pound for butter. Prof. Smith gives her credit for 4,497 pounds skim milk (85 per cent of total yield), at 20 cents per hundred pounds and says it was worth more than this to feed to pigs. Deducting the credit for skim milk, the food cost of the butter fat was 9.16 cents per pound, equivalent to 7.85 cents per pound for butter.

When at pasture Rosa had 21 pounds daily of the grain mixture before referred to.

CHAPTER XIII.

IN PUBLIC COMPETITION—BREEDERS' GAZETTE CUP.

Those early victories which called public attention to the wonderful abilities of the Holstein-Friesian cows are very pleasant memories to veteran breeders. The first was the winning of the Breeders' Gazette Challenge Cup by a Holstein-Friesian in 1883. This was the special prize offered by the Breeders' Gazette, for the greatest butter yield for any thirty consecutive days between July 1, 1882, and July 1, 1883. This contest it will be remembered was a close one between the Holstein-Friesian cow Mercedes and the Jersey cow Mary Ann of St. Lamberts, the yield of the former showing 99 lbs. 6 1-2 oz. of unsalted butter for thirty days, and the latter's yield being 97 lbs. 8 1-2 oz. for the same period. The evidence submitted in each case was referred to a committee consisting of Hon. John Landrigan, president; Hon. John P. Reynolds, ex-president, and Hon. D. P. Gilham, also ex-president of the Illinois State Board of Agriculture, all of the above named gentlemen being members of the state board, and men of unquestioned integrity. The substance of the report is as follows: The undersigned, to whom was refered the matter of awarding the silver cup offered by the Breeders' Gazette, "to the owner of the cow that shall produce the largest yield of butter for thirty consecutive days, between the 1st of July, 1882, and the first day of July, 1883," beg leave to report that the following entries have been made for the premium: The Jersey cow Mary Ann of St. Lamberts, 9770, and the Holstein-Friesian cow Mercedes, 723.

The affidavits show the yield of unsalted butter made from the milk of the competing animals during the test of thirty days, to be as follows: Mercedes, 99 lbs. 6 1-2 oz.; Mary Ann of St. Lamberts, 97 lbs. 8 1-2 oz.: in favor of Mercedes, 1 lb. 14 oz. The silver cup is awarded the owner of the Holstein-Friesian cow Mercedes, her record being 1 lb. and 14 oz. better than that of Mary Ann of St. Lamberts.

At the Fat Stock and Dairy Show in 1885, the Minnesota State Fair in 1886, the Iowa State Fair of the same year, the Western Michigan Agricultural and Industrial Society's Fair in 1887, and again at the Chicago Fat Stock and Dairy Show in 1887 were memorable triumphs where Holstein-Friesian butter was awarded first prize in strong competition with Jersey butter.

Especially notable competitions where the Holsteins were awarded first

7

prizes in competition with Jersey cows for making the most butter in a stated time, were at the Chicago Fat Stock Shows of 1885 and 1887, at the Ohio State Fair in 1887, and the Minnesota State Fair of the same year. These tests have been public and open to the world.

The famous Madison Square Garden Show, officially the New York Dairy and Cattle Show of 1887, was a most sweeping Holstein triumph. First, second and third prizes for quality of butter were awarded to this breed. The competitive tests for amount of butter were easily won, though under some disadvantages. It will be remembered that the Holstein-Friesian cows passed almost the entire day in the show ring, yet began a victorious test thirty minutes after returning to their stalls.

The history of the Holstein-Friesian cow when placed in competition with other breeds is most remarkable and satisfactory to her admirers. During the period of years ranging from the time when public tests upon fair grounds were looked upon with so much favor in 1886 and up to 1891, when such contests were openly discouraged by the Association of Exhibitors of Live Stock, the Holstein-Friesian cow was victorious as a butter producer in all sections of the country where exhibited. In 1893 she was not present at the World's Columbian Exposition, from the failure of management of those having her interests in charge.

But her absence at this great contest, regrettable as it was, took nothing from her inherent qualities as a butter cow, and but little from her public esteem. In the system of officially authenticated butter records established in 1894 by the Holstein-Friesian Association of America, a method was found whereby unimpeachable tests could be conducted.

Of the results of these tests which have annually been conducted since, Mr. W. J. Gillett has made a most valuable comparison which we give in full:

Name of Animal.	Age.	Pounds and oz. of milk pr'duced in one week.	Av. per ct. fat.	Total w'k's at, bs.	Am't butter at 80 pr. ct. fat, lbs.	Value of butter at 40c. per lb.	Value of skim milk at 20c. per 100 lbs.	Value of butter and skim milk.	Cost of all food consumd dur'g w'k's test.	Net profit above food cost, butter at 40c. per lb.	Net profit above food cost, butter at 25c. per lb.
Mutual Friend 3d	3	409 3	4.27	17.472	21.840	$ 8.74	$ .654	$ 9.394	$ 2.85	$6.544	$3.264
DeKol 2d	10	536 12	3.96	21,261	26.576	10.63	.858	11.488	2.69	8.800	4.812
Mutual Friend 2d	7	585 2	3.52	20,608	25.700	10.30	.936	11.236	3.92	7.316	3.456
Rosa Bonheur 5th	5	682	2.97	20.270	25.337	10.13	1.091	11.221	2.68	8.541	4.745
Canary's Mercedes	6	409 8	4.92	20.129	25.161	10.06	.654	10.714	2.80	7.914	4.144
Houwtje D	6	625 2	3.00	18.790	23.487	9.39	1.000	10.390	1.46	8.930	5.411
Netherl'd Pietertje Princ's	3	361	4.02	14.496	18.120	7.25	.578	7.828	.99	6.838	4.118
Bell Sarcastic	4	548 8	3.02	16.590	20.737	8.29	.877	9.167	1.46	7.707	4.601
Inka 4th's Pietertje Rose	4	509 6	3.44	17.522	21.902	8.76	.814	9.574	2.24	7.334	4.049
Pietertje Hengerveld	4	492 2	3.55	17.462	21.852	8.74	.787	9.527	2.24	7.287	4.010
Nannette 3d's Pledge	4	361	4.84	17.470	21.837	8.73	.578	9.308	2.24	7.068	3.797
Netherland Hengerveld	6	465	3.48	16.187	20.233	8.09	.744	8.834	2.24	6.594	3.502
Helena Burke	4	412 8	3.41	14.348	17.935	7.17	.659	7.829	.99	6.839	4.152
Jessie Beets	6	412 10	3.74	15.445	19.306	7.72	.659	8.379	.90	7.389	4.495
Weltske's Pappoose	4	353 6	3.53	12.485	15.006	6.24	.564	6.804	2.24	4.564	2.225
Netherland Sada	7	387 2	3.62	14.012	17.515	7.01	.619	7.629	2.24	5.389	2.757
Neth. M. A. Constance	4	439 9	3.15	13.824	17.280	6.91	.702	7.612	1.69	5.922	3.332
Aaggie B	5	412 12	3.32	13.400	16.750	6.70	.659	7.359	.99	6.369	3.856
Aulinda 2d	8	361 4	3.57	13.312	16.640	6.66	.578	7.238	2.84	4.398	1.898
Zur 2d	7	388 14	3.32	12.900	16.250	6.07	.621	7.121	2.24	4.881	2.443
Woodland Queen	7	343 4	3.59	12.320	15.400	6.16	.549	6.709	2.24	4.469	2.150
Bibiana's Pet	7	385 2	3.13	12.137	15.171	6.07	.616	6.686	2.24	4.446	2.163
Johanna 5th	7	592 8	2.98	17.656	22.072	8.83	.947	9.777	1.92	7.857	4.545
Schoone	11	452 11	3.34	15.120	18.900	7.56	.723	8.283	1.24	7.043	4.208
Countess Clothilde	4	316 5	3.84	12.134	15.167	6.07	.506	6.576	1.69	4.886	2.607
Totals		11.242 10			496.834	$198.71	$17.973	$216.683	$51.36	$165.325	$90 814

The Holstein-Friesian Association of America at its annual meeting in March, 1894, for the purpose of stimulating and awakening breeders to a lively interest in the Holstein Cow as a butter producing machine, passed the following resolution:

"Resolved, That the board of officers be authorized to offer not to exceed $1,000 in prizes for authenticated weekly butter records made under the supervision of the superintendent of Advanced Registry, or some inspector designated by him, or made under the direction of the officer of some experiment station or state institution of some state; such tests to be made on the basis of

COPIA, No. 1067 H. H. B. Milk record, 99 1-2 lbs. in one day; 2,747 lbs. 12 oz. in one month.

the rules for admission to the Advanced Registry, and must be entered in that registry. The amount offered to any one cow not to exceed $50; and then the prizes to decrease in amount in ratio to such records. Such prizes to be offered for various ages, as in Advanced Registry rules."

This prize list brought out from the Holstein-Friesian camp thirty-five cows and heifers that were officially tested and entered for prize competition. Of this number ten were two-year-old heifers, ten were three and four years old and the remaining fifteen were from five to eleven years old.

For the purpose of further ascertaining for his own satisfaction as a dairyman and breeder the actual value of a fair type of the Holstein-Friesian cow, the writer has spared no pains to secure an accurate statement of the amount, kind and cost of food consumed by each animal in this test, over the age of three years, incidentally demonstrating to the dairy public that the large black-and-white cow is not only capable of producing a large amount of milk and butter, but that she is capable of doing it profitably and economically, so much so that the following table, showing results of the test, demonstrates conclusively again the oft-repeated statement of those owners of Holstein-Friesian cattle who are business dairymen, that had the Holstein cow been in the Columbian tests she would have been an outstanding winner, when comparing the amount of butter produced, the cost of its production, and the net profit.

In making the calculations of this table, the cost of production was figured on the basis of its actual food cost when purchased, or at its market value if raised upon the farm owned by the competitor. In some cases the cost of the different foods consumed by the Holsteins exceeds that fed at the Chicago test, and vice versa, but as a whole the prices average about the same. My purpose, however, is not to assume the same cost of feed as established by Chief Buchanan for the Chicago test, but I have ascertained from the different breeders having animals in the Advanced Registry test, the actual food cost of producing the results, so that we know exactly what each cow earned for her owner during the week under test.

It is but fair to state that the entire number of animals mentioned in this list represent only six breeding establishments of America, and that there are many other herds from which animals could have been selected that would have been expected to produce records of the same excellent character.

It will be noticed the following list contains but twenty-five animals of the thirty-five tested, the ten two-year-old heifers being omitted so there may be a more direct comparison with the twenty-five fully mature cows (Jerseys) in the dairy test at Chicago. There were sixty-four mature Jersey cows, selected as the best representatives of that breed, sent to the Jersey barn at Chicago, and of this number at least forty-seven calved in their new quarters, which, more than anything else, makes a cow feel at home among new and unusual surroundings. From the above number the final twenty-five cows were selected to enter the ninety days' test, hence it appears that the twenty-five Jerseys reached nearer the very best producers of the breed than do the twenty-five Holstein cows, from the fact that of the twenty-five Holsteins ten were only three and four years old. Many of the leading herds were not represented, and many were tested when it was convenient for the different experiment stations to send a man to supervise the tests. It is, therefore, a question whether there was a Holstein animal tested when actually at her best. On the other hand, the Jerseys were most of them in the fifteen, ninety and thirty days' tests, and we find greater latitude to select from the results of their everyday performance yields of a more extraordinary character. In short, the week each Holstein was tested, she may or may not have been at her best.

At Chicago the butter was credited to the cows at from forty to fifty cents per pound, and, for the purpose of comparison, in this table the butter of the Holsteins is credited at the lowest Chicago test price of forty cents per pound. I desire here to venture an opinion that a test conducted on a basis of fictitious and ridiculously high prices for the product is not a test of greatest value to the average well-to-do dairyman, because not one in 100 can find a market at forty to fifty cents per pound for butter. However, if fair for one breed to assume such a value for its product, it is fair for others, and there can be no comparison otherwise. In this table will also be found a column showing "net profit with butter at twenty-five cents per pound," which will give our readers a practical view of the worth of the Holstein cows when brought down to attainable prices.

The butter of the Holsteins was calculated by the rule established at Chicago of 80 per cent fat. Eighty pounds of skim-milk in the Holstein test are credited to every 100 pounds whole milk, and the skim figured at twenty cents per 100 pounds; and the fact that the tests were personally and directly supervised by representatives of different experiment stations or state institutions of the state from which the cows were entered establishes the absolute accuracy of these tests by the highest authority.

In the Chicago test the cows were credited four and one-half cents per pound for every pound increase in live weight, which factor is not taken into account in the Holstein test; and another point of no little importance is that the Jerseys were, in the language of the chairman of the testing committee, "watched over with the greatest care, and handled with the most wonderful skill," and the Holsteins received their ordinary care by herdsmen, many of them comparatively unskilled.

The total seven days' milk of the twenty-five Holstein cows was 11,242.03 lbs., an average of 64.24 lbs. per day. The average milk per Jersey cow per day for the first week of the ninety days' test at Chicago was 36.6, which is exceeded by the Holsteins by 29.64 lbs. per cow per day.

The total week's butter of the twenty-five Holsteins is 496.83 lbs., an average of 19.87 lbs. per week, or 2.83 lbs. per cow per day. The average amount of butter produced by the Jerseys in the ninety days' test was 170.96 lbs., or 1.89 lbs. per cow per day, which is exceeded by the Holsteins by .93 lbs. per cow per day.

The food cost of one pound of butter for the Holsteins was 10.33 cents and that of the Jerseys 13.75 cents per pound, from which it will be seen that the Holsteins produced a pound of butter by over three cents cheaper per pound than did the Jerseys.

The highest net profit per day of any cow in the ninety days' test was that of Brown Bessie, of eighty-one cents. The average net profit per day of the entire twenty-five Holsteins was ninety-four cents per cow, and coming down to a practical and reasonable basis of twenty-five cents per pound, we find the average net earning of the entire number of Holsteins to be fifty-one cents per day, which is conclusive evidence that the Holstein cow can yield a handsome profit, and is not an expensive cow for the dairyman of this country to keep.

The highest week's yield in butter during the ninety days' test was that of Brown Bessie of 20.163 pounds, which is exceeded by twelve of the twenty-five Holstein cows, and of these one cow was three years old, and four were only four years old.

The best day's production of butter of any cow in the ninety days' test was that of Brown Bessie of 3.48 pounds. The best twenty-four hours' yield of any Holstein was that of De Kol 2d of 4.308 pounds.

During the World's Fair test only eight times was a yield made of upward of three pounds of butter in a day, and in the Holstein tests ten of the twenty-five cows average over three pounds per day for the entire week.

It has often been hurled at us that our breeders dared not enter into the Columbian dairy test to compete with other dairy breeds where cost of production was to be taken into consideration; for my own satisfaction I have made careful analyses of both tests, taking into consideration every point that would give each breed justice and fair play, and have made my calculations from facts.

I think the advantage of the Holsteins being tested at home, though perhaps not entirely, is in a measure offset by some points which favor the Jerseys; viz., scientific feeding, a longer time tested, and a better representation of the highest producing cows of the breed. Anyway, from the conditions under which both breeds were tested, whether on an equal basis or not, I find the Holsteins produced more milk, made more butter per cow and at a less cost than did any of the breeds in the World's Fair test, and this by a very strong lead; so strong that any one examining the above table must concede that the Holsteins produce milk and butter profitably, and the facts here set forth hardly warrant the comments which have been made by thoughtless people and owners of rival breeds for not entering our breed in the World's Fair dairy test.

We also present a copy of the awards made by the Holstein-Friesian Association of America in 1895 and 1896, in tabulated form, a study of which will repay the seeker for truth as to the abilities of the Holstein-Friesian cow as a butter producer.

These scientific tests have awakened great interest not only among breeders but among dairy scientists the world over.*

There seems but one way to present this mass of testimony of Holstein victory, and that is to chronologically arrange and report each test in as full detail as space will permit.

The list of victories begins with the Minnesota State Fair at St. Paul in September, 1886.

Those who were fortunate enough to attend this fair will always recall with pleasure the magnificent appearance of the three hundred dairy cattle upon exhibition. It was a Holstein day, both in the general exhibition and the butter tests. The Holstein herds, in a ring of fourteen dairy herds consisting of five Jersey herds, one Ayrshire, one Swiss, and five Devons, were awarded first and third prizes, while second place was taken by the Jerseys. The awards were made by Hon. W. D. Hoard, editor of Hoard's Dairyman.

The greatest interest centered in the premiums, first, second and third, that were offered for cows from whose milk the most butter is made. Mr. D. W. Curtis was the chairman of the committee conducting the tests. There were eight Jerseys entered and tested, one grade Jersey and seven registered Holsteins.

COLANTHA, No. 6714 H. H. B.
Imported. Milk record at three years old, 12,057 lbs. 8 oz. in ten months. Butter record 31 lbs. 7 oz. in seven days.

The first prize went to the great cow Tritomia upon a yield of 2.393 lbs. of butter; 24.86 lbs. of milk making one pound of butter. Second prize was awarded to Rijaneta and the third to Mink.

This test was the first of the year. A prominent Jersey breeder† had suggested competition of this sort. He hoped that "the Holstein men would not show the white feather this fall, but would enter their cows against the Jerseys in the butter tests to be made at the prominent Western fairs this fall, so that a proper relative comparison could be made between the two." The editor of Hoard's Dairyman said, in accounting for the test, "It should be borne in mind that the Jerseys, owing to their extreme 'nervous character,' were peculiarly affected both in milk-flow and richness by the excitement upon being on exhibition." A slight investigation would have shown that all the Jerseys but

---

*See tables at back of book.   †V. E. Fuller.

one were entered from Minnesota. The longest distance traveled was less than 100 miles. All of the Holsteins entered were from Iowa, and were on board cars not less than twenty-four hours. It will be noted that the eight Jersey cows made a total of 6.15 lbs. of butter from one day's milk, while the seven Holsteins made a total of 10 035 lbs. of butter from one day's milk. Accepting Mr. Hoard's theory, a large allowance would have to be made for the extreme nervous character of the Jersey breed.

At the Iowa State Fair of 1886 occurred another victory for the Holsteins. There were only two entries—a Jersey cow from the herd of Richardson Bros., of Davenport, Ia., and a Holstein cow from the Home Farm Company, of Hampton, Ia. The Holstein cow was loaded at Minneapolis on Saturday afternoon, and was not unloaded until reaching Des Moines on Monday evening. Messrs. Richardson had their cow on the grounds a week previous to the test, which commenced on Tuesday morning. The report of the judge, Mr. C. E. Frink, shows that the Holstein cow made in three days 4.51 lbs. of butter, while the Jersey succeeded in making in the same period 1.13 lbs. of butter, and was then withdrawn, presumably to recuperate from the unusually heavy strain upon her nervous energy.

An interesting dairy test was held at the West Virginia State Fair, also in the fall of 1886. The entries at the start embraced seven aged cows and four two-year-olds from three different breeds. Of the eleven head all but two were Holsteins, the others being Red Polled and Jerseys. The results show that the contest was a close one and that not a cow in the lot failed to do credit to her breed. The testers were directed to make the awards to the cows furnishing the greatest quantity of cream, a fact which prevented the award in all cases accompanying the highest percentage of cream. The management of the test was in the hands of P. L. Kimball of the Vermont Farm and Machine Co., in whose dairy apparatus the milk was set and to Mr. Kimball is due the accuracy with which the many details were kept in hand. The cows and pails were numbered and when the work was finished Mr. Kimball and his assistant had to be furnished a key before they could tell which cows were victorious.

The winner of the first prize, aged class, was Nora of Oatfield, a four-year-old Holstein whose yield of milk was 83.3 pounds showing a percentage of 17.45 cream. The second prize was awarded to the three-year-old cow Princess of Lunenburg upon a yield of 70.10 lbs. of milk showing 17.75 per cent cream. In the class of two-year-olds the first prize was won by Isidore, a Jersey with a yield of 62.10 lbs. of milk showing 17.64 per cent cream. The second prize went to a Holstein, Durkje V of Ohio, upon a yield of 66.9 lbs. of milk containing 15.52 per cent cream.

The year 1887 marks an era in the history of public competitions among dairy cattle breeders. In the middle of February of that year a number of gentlemen interested in dairy cattle met in New York and arranged for a dairy show to be held at the Madison Square Garden, New York City, May 10 to 14. They guaranteed a fund of $20,000 and decided to offer premiums for all dairy breeds and also dairy products. Mr. Edward Burnett was the president, Mr. John I. Holly represented the Jersey cattle, Mr. E. F. Bowditch the Guernseys, Francis H. Appleton represented Ayrshires, and the Hon. Gerrit Smith Miller the Holstein-Friesians. These gentlemen fulfilled the duties of their several offices successfully and called out an exhibition of dairy cattle that had never before been equalled in point of numbers or high quality. With the cattle themselves we have but little to do at this time. Sixteen animals were entered in this test and twelve actually competed, of which five were Jerseys, one Guernsey and six Holstein-Friesians, the prize being a sweepstakes for the best butter cow of any breed, the one producing the largest quantity of butter during twenty-four consecutive hours. The details of the test are indeed meagre, in comparison with the tests of the present day. It will be seen that it was won by a cow from a family which has since become world famous and highly esteemed as a butter producing family.

	AMOUNT OF BUTTER.		FAT.
Clothilde (Holstein),	2 lbs,	7 1-2 oz.	77.55
Clothilde 4th (Holstein),	2 "	1-4 "	81.51
Gold Lace (Jersey),	1 "	14 1-3 "	84.52
Jessie L. Manor (Guernsey),	1 "	14 1-2 "	84.05
Mechtchilde (Holstein),	1 "	14 "	76.75
Lady Fay (Holstein),	1 "	10 1-2 "	81.08
Hilda H. 3d (Jersey),	1 "	9 3-4 "	78.34
I. Chrissie (Jersey),	1 "	8 3-4 "	83.65
Moolke 3d (Holstein),	1 "	2 3-4 "	82.08

When Clothilde astonished the dairy world by this great performance many explanations were attempted by incredulous and envious persons. Public favor, with this victory, largely turned toward the Holstein-Friesians and every argument was resorted to, to show that the Holstein was not valuable nor profitable. We heard of "nervous theories," "musical disturbances," "carelessness on the part of the Jersey people," "unfairness on the part of the Holstein men," to account for the accident. That the full capacity of this great cow, Clothilde, was not shown in the test, is demonstrated by the fact that after being in the show ring, her yield continued increasing until May 31, when she gave in one day, in three milkings, 101 lbs. 2 oz., and made a seven days test of 28 lbs. 2 1-4 oz. of butter; 23.66 lbs. of milk making a pound of butter. She ate about 12 lbs. of grain per day, consisting of two parts corn meal, one part ground oats, two parts wheat bran with a little oil meal. She was on good pasture and had a little green rye when she would eat it.

Holstein-Friesian breeders were not surprised by the victory. They had implicit faith in their cattle and only looked for an opportunity to demonstrate to the world the superiority of their favorite over the Jersey as general dairy cattle. The New York Dairy Show furnished a long looked for opportunity and Holstein breeders made the most of it. One of the pleasant episodes of this show was that an elegant horn cup, handsomely trimmed with silver and engraved with the picture of a Jersey cow, had been donated by a well known Jersey breeder to be awarded to the sweepstakes cow. It was remarked that the engraving upon the cup had been a little premature.

Prizes offered for quality of butter both first, second and third, were also awarded to butter made from Holstein-Friesian milk.

An amusing incident occurred at a lunch in the Garden attended by the expert butter judges from Iowa and the noted Mr. Jackson from Boston. This lunch was being enjoyed after the judges had performed their arduous task of awarding the prizes. Judge Jackson was asked by an innocent if there was any difference in the quality of Jersey and Holstein butter, and in a detailed and elaborate manner kindly answered the inquiry showing conclusively wherein it was impossible for Holstein butter to equal that of his favorites, the Jerseys and Guernseys. Judge Jackson was as ignorant as a babe of the fact that the butter, to which he had just awarded three prizes, designated by numbers only, was made by Mr. F. C. Stevens, of Attica, N. Y., from Holstein milk.

The Ohio Farmer said: "The triumph of the Holstein cow, Clothilde, over the Jerseys, at the recent New York Dairy Show, was a severe blow to the little Jerseys, and a boom for the Holsteins. Seven Jerseys and two Guernseys were pitted against six Holsteins in the sweepstakes for the largest quantity of butter produced during the twenty-four hours competition. The Jerseys were all of famous blood and record and the general expectation was that they would win. The Jersey Bulletin in its last week's issue skirmishes around lively to find out 'who struck Billy Paterson.' It accounts for the failure of the Jerseys on the ground that they are of a higher and more nervous organization. The Holsteins are Dutch cattle, you know, and are therefore of a dull, phlegmatic temperament. A band of music, which played incessantly, was the cause of the whole trouble. Holsteins like music and Jerseys don't. It makes the latter nervous, while the former will close their eyes and chew the cud of sweet contentment as they listen to the familiar strains of 'Yankee Doodle' or 'Peek-a-Boo.' They have probably become accustomed to this in the beer gardens of their native country. Another possible reason for the unexpected result is that the building was too hot and it may be that Jerseys can't stand heat as well as Holsteins. This should be looked after and at the next show let music be banished from the building and the proper temperature maintained."

At the Ohio State Fair in 1887 twelve cows were entered, eight being Holsteins, two Ayrshires and two Jerseys. Three of the Holsteins were drawn on account of injury to udder, and the others because of coming in heat:

The first prize was awarded to Mollie Anderson, whose yield of milk was 142 lbs. 3 oz., containing 29.1 oz. of cream from which was made 4.12 lbs. of butter. The honor of this prize was shared with Nora of Oatfield, whose yield of milk was 137.3 lbs.—containing 34 lbs. 9 oz. of cream, making 4.12 oz. of butter. The next highest cow in this test was an Ayrshire, Lucy Wood, whose milk yield was 134 lbs. 10 oz., containing 21 lbs. 3 oz. of cream, from which was made 4 lbs. 9 oz. of butter. The largest Jersey yield was 2 lbs. 15 oz. of butter, and the next largest 2 lbs. 9 oz. Prize for the best quality of butter in this test was awarded a Holstein cow named Katinka. Amount of the prize was $35.00.

At the Minnesota State Fair in 1888 an official test was made of twenty-four hours for dairy cows, which resulted in giving the first and third premiums to Holstein-Friesian cows and the second prize to a Jersey. The first prize was won by Lena Twisk, whose milk yield was 54 lbs. 12 oz.; butter, 2.16 lbs. The yield of the Jersey cow was 38 lbs. 8 oz. of milk and 1.83 lbs. butter. Third prize to Almee was on a record of 38 lbs. 4½ oz. of milk and a yield of 1.26 lbs. of butter. In this test fourteen head competed, including four Jerseys, one Guernsey and nine Holsteins. Professor Short's oil test was used.

At the Iowa State Fair of 1888 the State Dairy Commissioner, Hon. D. H. Sherman, conducted a comparative test for the best butter cow. The period was a single day, three Jerseys were entered and four Holsteins. First prize was awarded to the Holstein cow Bettina on a yield of 1.90 lbs. of butter. The second to the Holstein cow Rijaneta, who made 1.49 lbs. butter, and the third to a Jersey whose yield was 1.42 lbs. butter. Professor Short's method was used under Mr. Sherman's supervision.

DE KOL 2D, No. 734 H. F. H. B.; 412 ADVANCED REGISTRY.
Butter record, 33 lbs. 6 oz. in seven days; largest one day's record, 6 lbs. 6 1-2 oz. Milk record, 73 lbs. in one day; 1,843 lbs. 4 oz. in thirty days.

At the Bay State Fair held in 1889 sweepstakes prizes were offered for the best milch cow of any age or breed, and the best butter cow. Three entries were finally made in each test, including one Ayrshire, one Jersey and two Holsteins. We extract the following from Mr. James Cheeseman's official report:

The competition for the best milch cow promised to be of more than common interest, but on Saturday evening when the time arrived for stripping the cows preparatory to the two milkings of Sunday, from which the test for milk and butter were to be taken, eleven out of the seventeen entered were withdrawn. The milk from the six cows was sampled morning and evening for analysis, and the whole of the milk of the Jersey cow and the two Holsteins was separated twice to exhaust the butter fat. The morning and evening's cream obtained from each cow's milk were mixed and ripened at 68 degrees until 2 o'clock on Monday. The creams were churned with a weak brine at a temperature of 62 degrees and the following butters were obtained: Queen of the Hill, Holstein, gross, 25 oz., net fat, 17.90 oz.; Della Carr, Jersey, gross, 21.5 oz., net fat, 17.50 oz.; Mink, Holstein, gross, 14.5 oz., net fat, 11.22 oz.

CHEMICAL ANALYSES OF BUTTER.

	1st Holstein.	Jersey.	Holstein.
Water,	26.67	18.63	20.59
Butter fat,	71.60	80.05	77.37
Caseine,	1.30		1.40
Salt,	.43	1.32	.64
	100.00	100.00	100.00

As the quantity of butter churned out was a smaller proportion of the milk than the yield shown by the analysis of the milk, it was thought fairer to base the awards on the chemical results. The awards are based on the following table, which gives each cow's score in the last column, according to the following scale of points: For each pound of milk solids, 8 points; for each pound of butter fat, 30 points; for each twenty days elapsed since calving, 1 point; for each twenty days of gestation, 1 point.

ANALYSES OF TEST COWS' MILK—JUDGE'S AWARD. SWEEPSTAKES FOR THE BEST MILCH COW OF ANY AGE OR BREED.

Breed.	Milk lbs.	Specific gravity.	Solids per cent.	Lbs. of solids.	Fat per cent.	Lbs. of fat.	Days calved.	Days of gestation.	Scores.
Ayrshire,	36	1.033	12.99	4.67	3.35	1.20	35	14	76.04
Holstein,	58	1.0305	11.81	6.85	3.08	1.78	53	—	110.04
Holstein,	46.5	1.0325	11.61	5.14	2.33	1.08	20	—	74.66

SWEEPSTAKES FOR BEST BUTTER COW OF ANY AGE OR BREED.

Breed.	Milk lbs.	Specific gravity.	Solids per cent.	Lbs. of solids.	Fat per cent.	Lbs. of fat.	Days calved.	Days of gestation.	Scores.
Jersey,	30.5	1.032	14.19	3.33	4.26	1.29	51	—	76.07
Holstein,	44.5	1.031	10.62	4.72	1.89	.84	28	—	64.44
Holstein,	53.5	1.0335	12.08	6.46	2.43	1.30	37	—	92.55

The special premiums offered by the Holstein-Friesian Association of America in 1889 were awarded and paid as follows: To the Home Farm Fine Stock Company, of Hampton, Ia., first premium for the best butter cow tested at the Iowa State Fair, $70. To same for third best butter cow at the same fair, $20. To the Friesland Live Stock Company, of Aberdeen, Dak., for best butter cow tested at the Dakota Territorial Fair, $66.66. To I. C. Wade, of Jamestown, Dak., for the second best butter cow, $33.34. To W. M. Chapin, of Sheffield, Mass., for the best butter cow tested at the Bay State Fair, $50. To W. A. Russell, of Lawrence, Mass., for cow producing the largest amount of milk at the Bay State Fair, $50. To B. Waddell, of Marion, O., for duplicate premiums awarded the steer Ohio Champion at American Fat Stock Show, greatest gain per day, $50. Best Holstein-Friesian steer under one year, $30. Sweepstakes, $75. Mr. Waddell also was awarded the first prize for cost of production, which will entitle him to $50 more. To F. C. Stevens, of Attica, N. Y., for duplicates of premiums on butter awarded at the Buffalo International Fair, first on granulated butter, $60. Second on thirty-pound package, $50. Second on package of five to ten pounds, for delivery unbroken to consumer, $30. Second on prints, $30. To N. J. Leavitt, of Waseca, Minn., for duplicate of special butter prize at Minnesota State Fair, $15.24. To Frank A. Leavitt, of Waseca, Minn., for duplicate of special butter prize at Minnesota State Fair, $14.72. To Jere Allis, of Isinours, Minn., for duplicates of the following premiums awarded at the American Fat Stock and Dairy Show at Chicago, Ill.: First on Holstein-Friesian butter, $6. Second on dairy butter made in Minnesota, $5. To Ogden Cole, of Addison, Mich., for duplicates of premiums at same exhibition, first and second on Michigan butter, $15. To the Home Farm Fine Stock Company, of Hampton, Ia., second premium on dairy butter made in Iowa, $5. Second premium on Holstein-Friesian butter, $3.

In the year 1889 only one first prize was won by a Jersey in public dairy tests. Holsteins won all others.

We present a full list of the awards of Special Premiums offered by the Holstein-Friesian Association for 1889 in public competition as below tabulated:

SPECIAL PRIZES OF 1889.

LIST OF COWS WINNING FIRST PREMIUM IN MILK TESTS AT STATE FAIRS AND EXPOSITIONS OF 1889.

Fair.	No. Entries.	Name and No. of Animal.	Lbs. and Oz. of milk.	Owner.
Buffalo,	1	Lutscke, 8356 H. H. B.,	73 12	F. C. Stevens.
New England,	....	Mabel Douglass, 1109 H. H. B.,	66 13	Chas. Robinson & Son.
Nebraska,	8	Rijaneta, 1131 H. H. B.,	66 5	Home Farm Co.
Kansas,	7	Empress Josephine 3d, 1995,	67 15	H. E. Moore.
Detroit,	....	Nicole, 5154 H. H. B.,	65 8	W. C. Munson.
Chicago Fat Stock,	8	May Overton, 2810 H. H. B.,	65 7	F. C. Stevens.
Iowa,	9	Bettina, 2466 H. H. B.,	65	Home Farm Co.
Michigan,	....	Auke, 364 D.-F. H. B.,	64 ½	H. P. Smith.
Minnesota,	14	Pet Texelaar 3d, 7420 H. H. B.,	59 8	N. J. Leavitt.
Detroit,	....	Mechtchilde, 6716 H. H. B.,	58 14	F. C. Stevens.
Georgia,	5	Mooike of Kentucky, 1985 H. H. B.,	49 12	C. A. Bowen.
West Virginia,	....	Nicole, 5154 H. H. B.,	49 4	W. C. Munson.
Ohio,	9	Marjorie Daw, 1830 H. H. B,	45 13	C. W. Horr.
Texas,	....	Neeltje Wit, 2075,	32	J. W. Howard.

The Association National Prize of a gold medal and $100 for the greatest twenty-four-hour milk record at any State Fair or Exposition of 1889, was awarded to F. C. Stevens, of Attica, N. Y., on his cow, Lutscke, 8356 H. H. B., record 73 lbs. 12 oz.

The Premium of $50 for the second best twenty-four-hour milk record made at any State Fair or Exposition of 1889, was awarded to Messrs. Chas. Robinson & Son, Barre Plains, Mass., on their cow, Mabel Douglass, 1109 H. H. B., record 68 lbs. 13 oz.

LIST OF COWS WINNING FIRST PREMIUM IN BUTTER TESTS AT STATE FAIRS AND EXPOSITIONS OF 1889.

Fair.	No. Entries.	Name and No. of Animal.	Lbs. butter.	Owner.
Buffalo,	4	Tirannia, 6716 H. H. B.,	3.12	F. C. Stevens.
Buffalo,	....	Alberta Abbekerk, 9579 H. H. B.,	2.62	F. C. Stevens.
Minnesota,	14	Pet Texelaar 2d, 7420 H. H. B.,	2.37	N. J. Leavitt.
South Dakota,	4	Agie Abbekerk, 9591 H. H. B.,	2.34	I. C. Wade.
Chicago Fat Stock,	8	May Overton, 2810 H. H. B.,	2.26	F. C. Stevens.
Mississippi,	....	Neeltje Wit 2075,	2.25	J. W. Howard.
Nebraska,	8	Rijaneta, 1131 H. H. B.,	2.23	Home Farm Co.
Detroit,	....	Alberta Abbekerk, 9579 H. H. B.,	2.19	F. C. Stevens.
Iowa,	9	Bettina, 2466 H. H. B.,	2.00	Home Farm Co.
Detroit,	....	Parthenia, 1567 H. H. B.,	2.06	F. C. Stevens.
Michigan,	....	Coquette, 900 H. H. B.,	2.	T. D. Seeley & Co.
Kansas,	7	Empress Josephine 3d, 1995,	2.	H. C. Moore.
Georgia,	5	Mooike of Kentucky, 1885 H. H. B.,	1.68	O. A. Bowen.
Ohio,	6	Julia Clifden Mercedes. 2730,	1.54	W. H. S. Foster.

The Association National Prize of a Gold Medal and $100 for the greatest twenty-four-hour butter record made at any State Fair or Exposition of 1889, was awarded to F. C. Stevens, Attica, N. Y., on his cow, Tirannia, 6716 H. H. B., record 3.12 lbs.

The Premium of $50 for the second best twenty-four-hour butter record made at any State Fair or Exposition of 1889, was awarded to F. C. Stevens, Attica, N. Y., on his cow, Alberta Abbekerk, 9579 H. H. B., record 2.62 lbs.

Mr. H. C. Palmer thus comments upon the dairy test of 1889 at Nebraska State Fair: "The Nebraska State Board of Agriculture provided a committee to conduct a public test of dairy breeds at our recent state fair.

"The committee were practical dairymen, fully acquainted with and daily using the methods employed in this test, one being secretary of the Nebraska Dairymen's Association and another operating the largest creamery in the state. The test was carefully conducted and furnishes an array of facts perfectly reliable.

"The committee desired to ascertain:

DE BRAVE HENDRIK, No. 199 N. R. S.; 230 H. F. H. B.

Winner of Committee Prize Alkmaar, 1882; Gouda, 1882; prize bull Alkmaar, 1883; first prize, International Agricultural Exposition, 1884, and prize medal at same exhibition. Selected in Wijde Wormer by the Committee of premiums as first and best bull in the 2d Holland

"1st—The amount of butter each cow would give (as shown by Short's system of computing butter fat).

"2d—The amount of full cream cheese a cow would make (as a total solid in chemical analysis).

"3d—The amount of milk each cow gave by weight.

"4th—The amount of feed consumed to produce the above result.

"Some seven Jerseys and six Holsteins actually commenced in the test, but five Jerseys withdrew on account of the poor showing, and the Holstein heifer Blanch S. was sick from complications following calving and should have been withdrawn in justice to the Holstein men.

"Average live weight, Jerseys 740 lbs., Holsteins 1,190 lbs.

"Average days since calving, Jerseys 65 days, Holsteins 110 days.

"Average daily butter yield, Jerseys .85 lbs. per cow, Holsteins 1.85 lbs. per cow.

"Average daily milk yield, Jerseys 19.75 lbs. per cow, Holsteins 54.50 lbs. per cow.

"Average daily yield of cream cheese, Jerseys 2.57 lbs. per cow, Holsteins 6.52 lbs. per cow.

"Now if we increase the average yield of each Jersey by 60 per cent to correspond with the average difference in live weight between the Jerseys and Holsteins, when we find that pound for pound of live weight a Holstein cow 110 days from calving will produce 40 per cent more butter, 70 per cent more cheese and 75 per cent more milk than a Jersey cow 65 days after calving. That is, a Holstein man owning six cows weighing 7,140 lbs. in all, could sell about 70 per cent more butter, cheese and milk than a Jersey man owning ten cows weighing 7400 lbs. in all.

"As to food consumed the test shows nothing beyond statements of the owners. It was utterly impossible for the committee to stand guard over the various cows for three days to see what they consumed, and one Jersey man making no report a comparison is not possible.

"The vast superiority of the Holsteins in both average yield and yield relative to size will naturally drive the Jersey men to consider the amount of 'food consumed.'

"Now, gentlemen, this is not the question. The true statement is this: Each of the six Holstein cows in the test produced two and one-half times as much total solids as each of the two Jerseys, which may have been due to one of two causes. First, to a more perfect digestion, or: Second, to a larger consumption of food. When we consider that the length of time required to digest the same kind of food is about the same in all cows, it proves that a Holstein could hold more food and thus digest more food than a Jersey. But this would account for a difference of only 60 per cent in yield while we here have a difference of 250 per cent to account for. It must be that the digestive apparatus of the Holstein cow in perfection of work and domestic economy far surpasses that of the Jersey, and that all other differences of size, form and color are not more marked than this greatest of all differences in digestive economy.

"The Dutch are the most thrifty and most economical people on earth. They have bred and culled their black-and-white cattle for over a thousand years, on land worth hundreds of dollars per acre. High priced food, valuable room and urgent demands for beef have been permanent factors continually operating on this breed. No cow's life was safe for a day after she failed to give a good account for her rations. The Dutch ascribe their prosperity to these black-and-white cattle. This test would indicate that an equal prosperity awaits the owners of Holstein cattle in Nebraska." And he might have added, America!

The official report of the test of dairy cows made at the Ohio State Fair of 1889 showed a sweeping victory for Holsteins in various classes, viz., for cow producing the greatest amount of solids, including fat; for the cow producing the greatest amount of milk; and for the cow producing the greatest amount of milk, including fat and solids. There were nine entries in this test—one Red Polled, three Jerseys, five Holstein-Friesians. The test was conducted on the grounds, and a chemical analysis made by H. A. Webber, of the State Board of Agriculture.

The results were calculated from the chemical analysis, and based upon the following rules: One point for each pound of milk, twenty points for each pound of butter fat, four points for every pound of other solids, one point for every ten days since calving after the first twenty days. In the competition for the cow producing the greatest amount of butter fat, there were six entries —three Jerseys, two Holsteins. one Red Polled, with points credited as follows: Julia Clifden Mercedes (Holstein), 92.48; Clissie Coperas (Jersey), 81.27. The milk of Julia Clifden Mercedes analyzed 13.04, total solids showing 8.59 per cent butter fat, and solids not fat, 9.45. Clissie Coperas' milk showed total solids 16.50, fat 5.61, solids not fat 10.89.

In the competition for the greatest amount of solids, including fat, there were three Holsteins and one Jersey. Julia Clifden Mercedes was awarded first premium in this class also, the table showing a production of 92.48 for fat, and solids not fat, 48.69; a total of 140.17.

The Jersey yield was 71.30 fat, and 43.73 solids not fat; total 115.23. The Holstein Margery Daw won second prize, the score being 77.90 fat, and 47.20 solids not fat; total of 125.10. In the competition for the cow producing the greatest amount of milk, the Holstein had no competition, and Margery Daw and Julia Clifden Mercedes took the prizes in the order given.

In the competition for the cow producing the greatest amount of milk, including fat and solids, there were three Holsteins, one Red Polled and one Jersey. In this Julia Clifden Mercedes was again a winner, showing 129 points of milk production, 92.48 on fat, 48.69 for solids not fat, and 4.50 for days since calving; total 274.67. The second prize was awarded to Margery Daw on 128.50 points for milk production, 77.90 for fat, 47.20 for solids not fat, and 16 for days since calving, making a total of 269.60.

These records were followed by the Red Polled, showing total points 239.01, and the Jersey, showing 222.23.

The Nebraska State Fair of 1889 afforded another victory for the breed. This test was for three days. The yields of Holstein cows were as follows: Jewel 2d 5.88 lbs. of butter, Rijaneta 5.56 lbs. of butter, Hortense 5.15 lbs. of butter fat, Empress Josephine 3d 3.8 lbs. of butter fat. The highest Jersey yield was 4.43 lbs. of butter fat.

At the Kansas State Fair in 1889 there were seven entries, six Holsteins and one Jersey. In this test the Holstein cow Jewel made 2.1 oz. butter; Empress Josephine 3d and 4th, 2 lbs. each. Highest Jersey yield was 1.4 oz.

There was a sweeping victory at the Iowa State Fair of 1888. Three Jerseys, one Red Polled and five Holsteins were entered, and the three largest yields were by the Holstein cows. Bettina, Jewel and Rijaneta, whose milk showed butter fat respectively of 2.9, 2.1 and 1.82. The highest Jersey yield was 1.38 and the Red Polled cow showed 1.23 lbs. of butter fat.

In South Dakota in 1889 there was a one day's test by the Lactascope, two Jerseys and two Holsteins were entered. The per cent of butter fat in the milk of the Holsteins—which won—was respectively 2.4 and 1.91. The largest Jersey record was 1.11.

The day's test for dairy cows for butter at the Iowa State Fair of 1889 was a feature of the show. No less than nine cows were entered for competition, three Jerseys, five Holstein-Friesians and one Red Polled. The test was made by C. E. Frink, J. N. Muncey and Prof. G. E. Patrick, the chemist of the Iowa station. The per cent of butter fat was determined by Prof. Patrick's method. There were three premiums offered in this competition and all three were won by Holstein-Friesians from the Home Farm Herd of Hampton, Iowa—Bettina taking first prize with a yield of 2.19 lbs. of butter in twenty-four hours, Jewel second with 2.1 lbs. and Rijaneta third with 1.82 lbs. butter fat. This was the third year in which the Home Farm Herd had supplied the winning cows in this test. The largest Jersey record in this competition was 1.38 lbs. of butter fat.

A test was made at Wheeling, West Virginia, in 1889, which was conducted by A. C. Magruder, of the State Experiment Station. The test was for three days, and the official report shows the following: The first prize for butter was awarded to the Jersey cow, Clissie Coperas, whose yield was 11.5 lbs.; the second prize went to a Holstein cow. Daisy Kroontje, whose yield was 8.7 lbs. She was closely followed by Lady Netherland, whose yield was 8.3 lbs., by Aaggie 4th, whose yield was 7.7 lbs., and by Lotisetta, whose yield was 5.1 lbs. The prize for the largest amount of milk was given to the Holstein cow Nicole, whose yield was 138 lbs. Total yield of milk of the winning Jersey was 71 lbs. 5 oz.

A test of dairy cows at the Detroit Exposition of 1889 was conducted by Mark R. Seeley, of Farmington, Mich. None but Holstein-Friesian cows were entered, and the yields of butter in the twenty-four hours test were as follows: Alberta Abbekerk, 2 lbs. 3¼ oz.; Mechtchilde, 2 lbs. 1 oz.; Parthenea, 2 lbs. 1 oz.; Tirania, 1 lb. 13½ oz.

The result of the butter test at the American Fat Stock and Dairy Show, held in Chicago in 1889, was a substantial victory for the Holstein breed. By the terms of the prize list, the test was open to all recognized recorded breeds of cattle to be judged by the milk product of three successive milkings, the value of the milk to be estimated from the weight and tested butter qualities. Jerseys, Holsteins and Ayrshires were entered in the competition. The Holsteins gained first and second place, the winners being two of the best known cows of the breed with unusual records for show-yard winnings. The first prize went to May Overton, whose yield of milk was 65 lbs. 7 oz., containing 36.12 oz. of butter fat, a percentage of 3.45, and total yield of solids 120.02 oz. The second prize went to Schuiling, whose yield was 57 lbs. 13 oz. of milk, containing 22.66 oz. of butter fat, a percentage of 2.45, and total solids of 91.21 oz. An Ayrshire cow won third prize with a yield of 32 lbs. 9½ oz. of milk, showing 21.54 oz. of butter fat, a percentage of 4.13, and total solids of 64.77 oz. The percentage of fat in the milk of the three Holstein cows averaged 3.17, with a difference of 1.00; of the Ayrshire, 4.04, with a difference of .18; of the Jersey, 5.26, with a difference of 1.75 per cent between the highest and lowest, extreme difference being 3.65 per cent. The milk of the Holstein cow, Schuiling was low in per cent of fat and total solids, although the large yield of milk made the total amount of fat greater than that produced by any other of the lot except one.

At the Minnesota State Fair of 1889 Holstein-Friesian cows won the two highest prizes with the following yields: Pet Texelaar 2d, 66¾ lbs. of milk, of 3.17 per cent butter fat, yielding 2.12 lbs. of butter. Nudine Abbekirk, 58¼ lbs. of milk, 3.65 per cent fat, yielding 1.97 lbs. of butter. The dairy sweepstakes for best herd of dairy cattle in the state was also awarded to a Holstein-Friesian herd, in competition with Brown-Swiss and Jerseys, and the first prize for best cow of dairy breed, as also first prize for best herd of dairy cattle owned by one individual or firm was awarded to the Home Farm Company's animals, a very superior herd of Holsteins.

DE RUITER, No. 80 N. H. B.

At the New England Fair of 1889, held at Worcester, Mass., an interesting single day test was made. The phenomenal yield of milk of the Jersey cow Dandelion, of 55 lbs. 5 oz., carrying 2 lbs. 14¼ oz. of butter, secured the prize. The Holstein yields varying from 1 lb. 10 oz. to 1 lb. 8 oz. were very creditable to the breed.

We make the following excerpt from the official report of the Ohio State test of 1890: "The second public test of dairy cows on the state fair grounds was somewhat of a surprise, not only to visitors but to breeders. This test was open to all breeds without restriction and was broad enough in its scope to give all a fair chance, providing as it did for quantity of milk as well as for quality. Regardless of this fact none but Holstein herds were represented. Can it be possible that the Jersey, the Polled Angus, and other fine stock breeders were afraid to enter representatives of their herds against Holsteins."

The number of entries was five, all Holsteins, entered by three different breeders. The test was conducted upon the grounds and covered a period of three days. The chemical analysis was made by Professor Webber of the State Board of Agriculture, and the results were calculated from the analyses and points scored upon the same rules as in 1889. In the competition for the cow producing the greatest amount of butter fat there were four entries, with results as follows: Lady of Lyons, 4.81 lbs. butter fat, 96.20 points; Nudine 2d, 3.51 lbs. of butter fat. 70.20 points; Shadeland Otley. 3.30 lbs. of butter fat. 66 points; Aurania, 3.16 lbs. of butter fat, 63.20 points. Lady of Lyons was awarded first and Nudine 2d the second premium. For the cow producing the greatest amount of solids including fat there were five entries, with the following results and awards made in the order given: Lady of Lyons—fat produced, 4.81 lbs.; points, 96.20; solids not fat—points, 67.96; total points, 164.16. Nudine 2d—fat, 3.51 lbs.; points, 70.20; solids not fat—points, 51.12; total points, 121.32. Shadeland Otley—fat produced, 3.30 lbs.; solids not fat—points, 43.76; total, 109.76. Aurania—fat, 3,16 lbs.; points, 63.20; solids not fat—points, 32.84. Princess Kroontje—fat, 1.91 lbs.; points, 38.20; solids not fat—points, 35.28; total points, 73.48.

At the Iowa State Fair of 1890 the dairy test was again won by Holstein-Friesian cattle. Eight cows were entered in the competition. Three Shorthorns, two Jerseys and three Holsteins made up the list. The same cows—Bettina, Jewel and Rijaneta—that won in the test last year were again to the front. Bettina's record was 63¼ lbs. of milk containing 2 lbs. of butter fat; Jewel's milk record was 52¼ lbs. of milk, making 1.67 lbs. of fat; Rijaneta's record was 55 lbs. of milk, making 1.66 lbs. of butter. The best Jersey yield was 1.39 lbs. fat, the best Shorthorn 1.05 lbs. of fat. This test was made with the brine bath method, and the committee consisted of State Dairy Commissioner A. C. Tupper, Prof. G. E. Patrick and C. E. Frink.

The usual "breed test" was held at Illinois State Fair in 1890. There were five Holsteins, five Jerseys, seven Ayrshires, and two Shorthorns. Although a noncompetitive test, the Holsteins were the largest producers. The largest Holstein yield, and also the largest of any of the nineteen cows, was made by Bettina, showing 2.51 lbs. of butter fat. The second largest yield was by Jewel, showing 2.18 lbs. of fat. The first prize for three-year-old Holsteins was won by Belle Rijaneta, with a yield of 1.67 lbs. of butter fat. The largest Jersey yield was 1.71 lbs. of fat. The largest Ayrshire yield was 1.19 lbs. of fat, and the largest Shorthorn yield was .95 lbs. of fat.

Two very important sweepstake prizes at the Kansas State Fair of 1890, in the dairy cattle ring, were for any cow of any age or breed, for butter. Seventeen entries were made, including four Jerseys, one Shorthorn and seven Holsteins. The result was determined by chemical analysis made by W. D. Church. The first prize went to the Holstein cow Empress Josephine on a yield of 60 lbs. 12 oz. of milk, containing 1.89 lbs. of fat. The second prize was awarded to the Holstein cow Bessie I 2d of Uplands, whose yield of milk was 49 lbs. 7 oz., containing 1.676 lbs. of butter fat. The third largest yield was made by the Holstein Shadeland Dosky, of 1.348 lbs. of butter fat. The highest Jersey yield was 1.24 lbs. butter fat; the highest Shorthorn giving .893 lbs. of butter fat.

The milk and butter test at the New England Fair at Worcester, Mass., in 1890 presents some interesting points. The test was for 24 hours, among three grades, one Holstein-Friesian and one Swiss cow. The Holstein-Friesian led in requiring less pounds of milk for a pound of butter, while a cross between the pure-bred Holstein-Friesian and pure-bred Jersey led in quantity of milk and butter, and came in second in the amount of milk required for a pound of butter. Her yield was 2 lbs. 9 oz. The Holstein cow showed a pound of butter to 17¼ lbs. of milk, and the grade a pound of butter to 19 lbs. of milk.

At the New York State Fair of 1890, a very interesting competition for a special butter prize of $100 for four cows of any breed, three days' milking, resulted in a victory for the Guernseys, with a yield of 7 lbs. of finished butter. The Holsteins followed with a yield of 6 lbs. 11 oz., and the Jerseys with a yield of 5 lbs. 9 oz. In depth of color of the butter the Guernsey came first, two Holsteins held second and third, and the Jersey fourth place. Finding that the difference in the weight of the butter was very slight, the committee decided to submit four samples to the expert judge, to be uninformed as to the breed of cows that made either lot of butter, and to award the prize to the herd whose butter was pronounced the best in quality. As a result, the judge selected Henry Stevens & Sons' Holstein-Friesian butter, pronouncing it best in quality, grain, flavoring, color, etc. The butter was made by W. H. Gilbert, a Jersey breeder and expert butter maker, and instructor at the New York State Dairy Schools.

DE SCHOTT, No. 5001 H. H. B., AND TWIN CALVES.
Imported. Milk record, 82 lbs. 4 oz. in one day. Butter record, 23 lbs. 8 oz. in one day.

The test for milk cows at the Nebraska State Fair for 1892 was another victory for the Holsteins. There were four Holsteins and one Shorthorn in the test. The official report shows the Holstein-Friesian Empress Josephine 3d to be a winner, on a yield of 3.31 lbs. of butter fat; total value of the product, including the skim-milk, was 98 cents. Second prize was awarded to the Holstein-Friesian Geertje Seffinga, on a yield of 2.67 lbs. of butter fat; total value of the product, 80 cents. The Shorthorn yield was 1.56 lbs. butter; total value, 45 cents. This was a two-days' test.

The Indiana State Fair of 1892 had a competition for the best butter cow, of any age or breed, to be tested by two milkings by the Babcock tester. The first prize went to a Jersey cow showing 1.79 lbs. of butter fat from 37.5 lbs. of milk, and the second prize to cow of the same breed showing 1.84 lbs. butter fat from 28.75 lbs. of milk. The third highest yield was a Holstein showing 1.25 lbs. of butter fat from 43 lbs. of milk. The yield of milk by the Holsteins in this case seems to be a very small one, varying from 29 lbs. to 43 lbs.

Prominent announcement was made in 1892 of the fact that the Ohio State Board of Agriculture would send a competent man to make tests of dairy cows on owners' farms under the most favorable conditions for the best performance of the animals. Entries in this test to be exhibited in the ring at the state fair and there the results announced. Professor Hickman of the State University was the official tester. Five Red Polled cows were tested, and one Holstein, Lady of Lyons 4th, and to the latter was awarded the first premium for the largest amount of butter fat, also first premium for the largest amount of solids not including fat, and the sweepstakes for most milk, most fat and most solids were also awarded this cow. Yields being as follows: Butter fat, 4.74; solids not fat, 9.46; total solids, 14.20. Mr. J. McLain Smith commented as follows: "The new Ohio milk test just closed is a great disappointment in the number of entries, but is very creditable in the record made. The first prize cow, Lady of Lyons 4th, is far and away the best cow ever tested in the state, and the average of all the cows and yields of fat is much above that of any former test in the state, or in the official test reported last year. The most conspicuous feature of the test, however, is the entire lack of the breed that it was intended specially to attract. Jersey breeders have objected to the ordinary fair ground tests, because, as they claim, Jersey cows do not milk so well under the excitement of change of scene and the crowd of people. In this new Ohio test the cows were not subjected to this strain, but the trial was made at her home with the ordinary conditions and with her usual attendants. It was made at any time the owner might select. In addition to this the state board offered the largest money prize ever hung up for a competition in this country, yet not a Jersey cow in the state is found to face the music. There are very many owned in the state that claim in private trials yields of butter far in excess of anything likely to be made. The money prizes were liberal, the honor of success would be great, why did they not appear? There were no Guernseys, Ayrshires or Shorthorns and their absence is much to be regretted, but it does not arouse so much suspicion or so much comment, because they have not claimed so much. There was only one Holstein-Friesian where there should have been ten or twenty, but that one was enough to redeem the breed."

The usual test at the Illinois State Fair of 1892, competitive among animals of the same breed, was held with results which, had there been competition between breeds, would have resulted favorably for the Holsteins. There were three Holsteins over three years old, and three under three years old; ten Jerseys over three years old, and six under three years old; two Ayrshires over three years old, and two under three years old; one Brown Swiss over three years old, and one under. The yields of butter fat of the three Holsteins were: Empress Josephine 3d, 1.696; Gold Leaf 2d, 1.509; Gerben, 1.289. The Holsteins under three years old made 1.267, and .873, and .819 lbs. of butter fat respectively. In comparison with these records, the largest Jersey yield from cow over three years old was 1.585, and the second largest yield, 1.502. The largest Jersey record of cow under three years old was 1.077. The largest Ayrshire yield by cow over three years old was .787, and from cow under three years old, .64. The Brown Swiss made 1.137 and .536 respectively, for the three-year-old and under three years old.

A practical dairy test was given at the Kansas State Fair in 1892. The cows entered consisted of four Jerseys, two Holsteins and three Shorthorns. The grand sweepstakes for dairy purposes was awarded to the Holstein Empress Josephine 3d, on a record of 65 lbs. 1 oz. of milk, showing 2.625 lbs. of butter. The second prize was taken by a Jersey with a record of 1.633 lbs. of butter. The Holstein following third with a record of 1.646. The Shorthorn tests were for two days, in order to compete for the special prizes offered by the Shorthorn Breeders' Association. The winning yield was 2.819, and the next largest, 2.344.

A full official report of a butter test at the Wisconsin State Fair of 1892 developed some very interesting facts. The winner of the sweepstakes for producing the most butter fat during the time allotted was a Holstein cow, Aaggie Beck, whose yield of milk was 44.5 lbs., showing 1.56 lbs. of butter fat. The second prize was won by the Holstein Aaltje Salo, a four-year-old, whose milk record was 38.3 lbs., containing 1.23 lbs. of butter fat.

The Holstein cow Schoone that took sweepstakes at this fair in 1891 had not had a calf since August, 1891, but made a remarkable performance. Her yield of milk was 18.60 lbs., showing .72 lbs. of butter fat. The Brown Swiss cow which competed for this prize had been in milk fourteen months, and on a yield of 19.8 lbs. of milk made .99 lbs. of butter fat.

J. McLain Smith, the Red Poll breeder, commented in the Breeders Gazette as follows upon the tests of 1892: "The important tests for the fall are all now reported, and we are able to make a comparative study of the results attained. In these trials—New York, Ohio, Indiana, Illinois, Wisconsin, Kansas and Nebraska—we have tests of seventy cows and heifers, viz.: twenty-seven Jerseys, twenty Holstein-Friesians, ten Shorthorns, six Ayrshires, five Red Polls and two Brown Swiss. Quite a number of these, however, were heifers milking with first calf, and some were cows very far on in lactation—milking a year or more. Omitting these and confining attention to the cows in full milk, we have the following results by breeds, viz.:

"Sixteen Holstein-Friesians average 45.91 lbs. milk, containing 1.45 lbs. fat.
"Fifteen Jerseys average 25.67 lbs. milk, containing 1.27 lbs. fat.
"Ten Shorthorns average 31.53 lbs. milk, containing 1.07 lbs. fat.
"Five Red Polls average 39.07 lbs. milk, containing 1.57 lbs. fat.
"Four Ayrshires average 29.75 lbs. milk, containing 1.12 lbs. fat.
"One Brown Swiss gave 32.5 lbs. milk, containing 1.23 lbs. fat.

"Comparing individual cows the best by far is a Holstein—Empress Josephine 3d, in the Kansas test—with a yield of 65 lbs. 1 oz. of milk and 2.62 lbs. of fat. And it is not only the best yield reported this fall, but it is the best ever attained in a public test in this country, with the single exception of the Brown Swiss cow Brienz in the Chicago test last fall. The second best cow is also a Holstein-Friesian—Lady of Lyons 4th—in the Ohio test—with a yield of 66 lbs. of milk, containing 2.27 lbs. of fat. But the average made by the breed does not sustain these fine records, though two of the best cows—Empress Josephine 3d and Gold Leaf 2d, belonging to C. F. Stone, Peabody, Kan.—count three times, as they appear in the Kansas, the Nebraska and the Illinois tests, and were the best of the breed in each case. Indeed, judging from the entries in the Western tests and the records made, it looks a little as if there were but one herd of the breed in that section containing any very good milkers. Aside from these two cows, the best record made by a Holstein-Friesian in the West was by Aggie Beck in the Wisconsin test with a yield of 44.5 lbs. of milk, containing 1.56 lbs. of fat.

"Except the two cows referred to—Empress Josephine 3d and Lady of Lyons 4th—there is no yield in any of the tests showing as much as 2 lbs. of fat from twenty-four hours' milk. The best Jersey record was made in the Indiana test by Esther Thorne with a yield of 37.5 lbs. of milk, containing 1.79 lbs. of fat. The best Red Polled cow was Mayflower, with a yield of 44.11 lbs. of milk, containing 1.72 lbs. of fat. The best Shorthorn, Fillpail 7th, in the New York test, gave 42 lbs. 3½ oz. of milk, containing 1.31 lbs. of fat. The best Ayrshire, Cordelia, in the Indiana test, gave 37.5 lbs. of milk, containing 1.12 lbs. of fat. The best Brown Swiss was Mai, in the Illinois test, with a yield of 35.5 lbs. of milk, containing 1.23 lbs. of fat.

"If we consider average yields in the tests of this fall, the Red Polls came to the front with their yield of 1.57 lbs. of fat. They have the advantage in the comparison in that they were tested at home; but the same conditions were offered the Jerseys and the Shorthorns in Ohio, and they failed to respond. How much advantage this is no one knows certainly. Two of these same cows were in the public test on the fair ground last year. One, and the best one, gave almost precisely the same—1.71 lbs. in public, 1.72 at home. The other cow was considerably better in the home test, but the difference is believed to be more in the milker than in the place. In the public test she was milked by a boy not accustomed to her.

"But making reasonable allowance for this, the average of the Red Polls would still be the best, and would show that the breed is entitled to high rank for dairy purposes. This becomes still more manifest if we compare their record with that of the Jerseys at the London Dairy Show. In the tests at this show prior to 1888, 118 Jerseys tested gave an average of 27.87 lbs. of milk, containing 1.27 lbs. of fat. In the years 1888 and 1889, forty-three Jerseys gave an average of 28.41 lbs. of milk a day, containing 1.55 lbs. of fat.

"In this test the prizes are awarded according to the score made, based on the following scale of points, viz.: one point for each pound of milk in twenty-four hours (two milkings), twenty points for each pound of fat in the milk as determined by analysis, four points for each pound of other solids, and one point for each ten days since calving. I have before me the London Live Stock Journal's report for the years of 1887 to 1890, inclusive. No test was held in 1891 and that for this year is not yet received. In these four years 182 cows were tested, chiefly Shorthorns, Jerseys and Guernseys. The best score made by a Shorthorn was 136 points; best Jersey score, 117.2; best Guernsey, 108.1.

"The scores made in the Ohio test, according to the same scale, would be as follows: Lady of Lyons 4th, 142.34; Mayflower, 101.97; Tina, 95.5; Lady of Tillershall, 94.52; Linda, 93.29; Coronet, 86.38. Of these the first is a Holstein-Friesian, the others Red Polls.

"It will be noticed that Lady of Lyons' score exceeds that of any cow of any breed tested at the London Show. Of the sixty odd Jerseys tested in the four years named but one reached a score of 100 points. That was the great Jersey cow, Baron's Progress—the world's champion of the breed for butter. The average of the ten prize Jerseys in these years—the pick of over sixty tested—is 93.33 points; the average of the ten prize Guernseys is 89.99 points; the average of the five Red Polls in the Ohio test is 94.33.

DE VRIES, No. 5433 H. H. B.
Milk record, 95 1-2 lbs. in one day; 2,404 lbs. in thirty days. Butter record, 121 lbs. 12 oz. in thirty days.

"The Red Polls, it will be remembered, are strictly general-purpose cows—milk and beef combined. And yet we are told by our so-called dairy authorities, that in selecting dairy cows we should, of all things, avoid any tendency to beef; and some of our experiment stations are sending out men to preach this doctrine as 'science'! It is pure 'rot,' wholly unsupported by any established *facts*. I begin to think a dairy cow may be of almost any form. Certainly the public records do not sustain the claim that those of a form and capacity to lay on flesh fall behind. And the best dairy cow I ever saw—the best the world has ever seen, according to the public records—the Brown Swiss cow Brienz—is as far removed from the so-called dairy type as it is possible to conceive."

There were but few public tests in 1893. All were saving up their forces for the Columbian Exposition. There was a test at the Kansas City Interstate Fair, and the report shows a Holstein victory. The leading cow was Parana Abbekerk, whose yield was 38 lbs. 12½ oz. of milk, showing 3.45 per cent fat. She was followed by Maryke 3d's Gerben, whose yield of 30 lbs. 10¼ oz. of milk showed 3.875 per cent butter fat. The third cow in the test was a Jersey, with a yield of 24 lbs. 12 oz. of milk, showing 4.135 per cent fat. The fourth cow was also a Jersey, whose 15 lbs. 14 oz. of milk showed 5.145 per cent fat. The Babcock test was also used as a check on one milking, the result being that the chemical test showed a higher per cent fat. It is to be noted that these Holsteins were all three-year-old heifers.

Four Holstein cows were entered in the milk and butter test at the Kansas State Fair at Topeka in 1893. Several Jerseys were entered in this test, but they failed to show up at the milking time, and the prizes were left to the Holsteins, Netherland Curran taking first, with a yield of 39 lbs. of milk, averaging 4.1 per cent butter fat, and showing 2 lbs. of butter; Princess Pel's Mechtchilde second, with a yield of 40 lbs. of milk of the average per cent of 3.19 fat, showing 1 lb. 9¼ oz. of butter. Shadybrook Sylvia, a Holstein heifer twenty-two months old, and in milk since April of that year, showed 1 lb. 2¼ oz. of butter in the test.

The Iowa State Agricultural Society held a dairy cow test at its state fair of 1893. The Jerseys took third place, the Holsteins first and second. The first prize cow was Maryke 3d's Gerben, who, from a milk yield of 51.237 lbs., made 1.628 lbs. of fat, equivalent to 2.034 of 80 per cent butter. She was followed by Empress Josephine 3d's Gerben with a milk yield of 48.563 lbs., showing 1.6 lbs. of fat, equivalent to 2 lbs. of 80 per cent butter. The Jersey yield was .891 lbs. of fat, equivalent to 1.114 lbs. of 80 per cent butter.

In 1893 there was a two days' test of milch cows at the Nebraska State Fair. The Holsteins won all the prizes. The awards were made on the value of the milk for dairy purposes, the fat being counted at 25 cents per pound, and the skim-milk 15 cents per hundred. On this basis, the two days' product of Empress Josephine 3d of 106.11 lbs. and 3.30 butter fat reached 98 cents in value, and she was awarded first premium. The second prize went to Geertje Seffinga, whose yield of milk was 92.28 and 2.67 fat, valued at 80 cents. The Shorthorn cow in this test made a showing of 1.56 fat. A detailed report of this test is found in the proceedings of the Nebraska Dairymen's Association of 1893.

At the test of the California State Fair of 1894 there were eleven entries. The test lasted three days, and the average test made of the butter fat in the three days' milk shows that the highest record was by a Jersey cow, whose milk yield was 116.75 lbs., showing 6.74 per cent fat, with a total of 7.870 lbs. butter fat. The largest Holstein yield was by Rebecca Egmond 3d, whose yield of milk was 127.36 lbs., with an average percentage of 3.2 fat, showing total butter yield of 4.076 lbs. of butter fat. In this test the conditions were hard to contend with. It is always so when a cow giving milk of an average per cent fat of 6.74 is found. Such cows are usually ranked with "hen's teeth," they say in Vermont.

However, some good evidence is found in this test. Butter Witch, a two-year-old Holstein, made 2.13 lbs. of butter, and showed 3.78 per cent average fat. Korvortje 3d, another Holstein, made 3.876 lbs. of fat from milk showing 2.96 per cent. Competition in the California test is classed by ages.

Wisconsin State Fair dairy test of 1894 was made at home, the conditions being that the four winning cows should be exhibited at the fair. Breeders were obliged to make entry by May 20, and had the privilege of selecting the first ten days of June, July, and August or September for the test of their cows. Twenty-one cows were entered by the specified time, and included Red Polled, Shorthorn, Jersey and Holstein-Friesian. In September the test narrowed down to twelve animals, and the first premium of $100 was awarded to the Holstein cow Johanna 5th, on a butter fat record of 5 lbs. in two days. The second premium went to a grade Jersey and Ayrshire, on a record of 4.84 lbs. of fat; and the third premium went to the Holstein Schoone, whose record was 4.17 lbs. of fat. The fourth premium went to a Jersey on a record of 4.03 lbs. of butter fat.

Johanna 5th was fed 22 lbs. of grain daily, consisting of four pounds old process oil meal, and eighteen pounds of a mixture, equal parts by measure, of bran, oats and corn, ground together. The second prize cow was fed one quart of oil meal, barley, oats and pea meal, and two quarts of shorts—six quarts in all, night and morning, and four quarts of oats and bran, equal parts, at noon. Schoone, in addition to green cornstalks and hay, received eight pounds of wheat bran and two pounds of hominy meal each day. The fourth prize Jer-

ETHELKA, No. 1208 H. H. B.

Imported. Milk record, 101 lbs. in one day; 2,682 lbs. 14 oz. in thirty-one days; 18,131 lbs. in one year.

sey is said to have been fed a ration similar to that given the second prize cow.

The usual breed test was held by the Illinois Agricultural State Society on its grounds at Springfield in 1894. The Holsteins made records of 2.94 to 2.52 lbs. of butter fat in the two days as compared with 3.17 lbs. of the Jersey and 3.07 lbs. by the Ayrshire. A Holstein under three years of age made 1.74 lbs. and 1.29 lbs. of butter fat.

A two days' butter test at the Indiana State Fair of 1894 was won by Holstein-Friesian cow, Nahe 2d, with a yield of 3.1061 lbs. of butter fat, which is equivalent to 2.88 lbs. of commercial butter. A Jersey cow was second with a yield of 2.9063 lbs. of butter fat which is equivalent to 3.63 lbs. of commercial butter. Nine animals competed in the test, including three Holstein-Friesians, one Guernsey and four Jerseys. The Guernsey yield was 1.5195, and the Ayrshire 1.5044 lbs. of butter fat.

The Ohio dairy test of 1894 was open to competitors from the middle of January to the 30th of August. The test was made under the abnormal conditions of feeding dry feed and contending with the worst pest of flies that Ohio had experienced for a series of years. Three animals were entered, two Holstein-Friesians and one Jersey. The Holsteins were tested in July, during the very warmest and dryest weather of the season, the Jersey under conditions equally as dry, but with lower temperature exsisting and with less annoyance from flies. The first premium for the largest yield of fat in twenty-four hours was awarded to the Jersey cow upon a yield of 2.00 lbs. of fat; the second to the Holstein-Friesian Peterina 2d, upon a yield of 1.66 lbs. of fat.

The first premium for the largest yield of solids not including fat from twenty-four hours milk was awarded to the Holstein-Friesian Hilton Maid 2d, on a yield of 5.05 lbs. The second premium to Peterina 2d, on a yield of 4.83.

This test, like that of 1892 and 1893, was conducted at the home of the cow, at the season and time most suitable to her owner, and under the same rules as in 1892 and 1893. The representative of the Ohio Experiment Station in each case saw the cow milked out clean, and was present at the morning and evening milkings of the following day to see the animal milked and to weigh and sample the milk, the analysis being made at the Station on the following day.

At the Iowa State Fair of 1894, the prizes offered were $70 to the first, $40 to the second, and $20 to the third, for a three days' test for butter fat, as indicated by testing the samples of the milk of each milking by the Babcock method as the basis of awards. The kinds and quantities of food supplied to the cows was part of the requirements, otherwise the owners had the care and control of their cows. Six cows were entered, and one withdrew after the first milking. There were three Jerseys and two Holsteins.

The first and second prizes were won by Jerseys—Eurodna and Beula Shawhan, with a milk yield of 120.37 lbs. and 120.97 lbs., showing yields of butter fat of 4.84 and 4.77. The margin between these two was so narrow that the committee decided to divide the first and second money equally between them.

The third prize went to the Holstein-Friesian cow Bontje P. 2d's Gerben whose milk record was 133.86 lbs., showing a total of 4.62 lbs. butter fat. The Holstein-Friesian cow Harmetka's Gerben was fourth in the list with a yield of 113.01 lbs. of milk, showing 3.40 lbs. of butter fat.

The remarkable thing about this test is the yield of the milk of the Jersey, which is the largest we have ever seen recorded in a public test. The grain ration fed to the Holstein-Friesian cattle was eight and nine quarts each daily. The winning Jersey consumed nine quarts per day, and the second prize Jersey had a ration varing from eight to nine and three-quarters pounds per day.

Nothing is said about the weight of these cattle but it is true they were very large Jersey cows. The difference between the yield of the winning cow and the Holstein which took third was .15 of a pound.

Prof. H. H. Dean conducted the test at the Provincial Dairy Show, Gananoque, Ontario, in 1894, of sixty hours duration. Nineteen aged cows were entered, and five three-year-olds. Of these four were Jerseys, two Guernseys, five were Ayrshires, one described as a grade, and six were Holstein-Friesians. Of the three-year-olds, two were Holsteins and three were Ayrshires.

The cows were judged according to the product only, as per the following scale: One point for each pound of milk, twenty points for each pound of butter fat, four for each pound of other solids, and one point for each ten days in milk after the first twenty days. Ten points were deducted from the scale for each per cent of fat below three per cent.

The first, second and third prizes were won by Holsteins in the aged class, an Ayrshire took fourth place, while fifth and sixth places were taken by Holstein-Friesians, the grade following seventh. Holstein eighth, Ayrshires filling ninth, tenth and eleventh places, Guernsey twelfth, grade cow thirteenth, Ayrshire fourteenth, Guernsey fifteenth, and the remaining four places by Jerseys.

The winning Holstein cow was Carmen Sylvia, on a record of 261.86 points reckoned from a yield of 138 lbs. of milk, on an average of 2.80 per cent fat, showing 3.827 lbs. of fat and 12.30 lbs. of solids. The cow taking second place was a Holstein-Friesian, Eunice Clay, with a yield of 103 lbs. of milk, showing an average of 3.13 per cent fat, yielding 2.17 lbs. of butter fat and 8.44 lbs. of other solids.

The third place in the test was filled by the Holstein-Friesian cow Aaggie Ida 5th on a yield of 99.50 lbs. of milk showing an average of 3.20 per cent fat, yielding 2.26 lbs. fat and 9.15 lbs. of other solids; the best Guernsey record was 2.25 lbs. of fat and 5.009 lbs. of other solids; the best Jersey record was 2.436 lbs. of fat and 4.597 lbs. of other solids. It will be noted that the difference between the highest Holstein and the highest Ayrshire record in pounds of solids other than fat was 3.781, and between fat yields .535. The difference between the highest Holstein and the highest Guernsey was 6.51 lbs. of solids other than fat, and between fat yields 1.246 lbs. The difference between the highest Holstein and the highest Jersey record in pounds of solids other than fat was 7.343 lbs., and the difference between the fat yield was 1.393 lbs.

In the test for three-year-old heifers, the Holstein-Friesian cow Emery Beauty scored 175.13 lbs. on a yield of 87.75 lbs. of milk with an average of 3.06 per cent fat, showing a yield of 2 666 lbs. of fat and 7.695 lbs. of other solids. She was followed by the Ayrshire, whose yield was 2.247 lbs. of fat and .634 lbs. of other solids.

Mr. C. C. McDonald, the Provincial Dairy Show superintendent, conducted a test at the Winnepeg Industrial Show for 1894. There were six entries in this test, consisting of one Shorthorn, two Ayrshires and three Holstein-Friesians. This was a twenty-four hour test. The first prize was won by the Holstein-Friesian Daisy Teake's Queen, a four-year-old, eighteen days in milk, whose total yield of milk was 72.25 lbs. showing 2.62 lbs. of fat. The second prize went to a Shorthorn five years old and ten days in milk whose milk yield was 56.75 lbs. showing 2.16 lbs. of fat. The third prize went to the Ayrshire with a yield of 1.37 lbs. of fat. Fourth place was taken by a Holstein with 1.35 lbs. of fat, a cow twelve years old that had been in milk thirty-five days.

At the Wisconsin State Butter Test of 1894 the famous Holstein-Friesian cow Johanna 5th was a winner of the first prize over all other breeds. She gave on a forty-eight hours test 169.9 lbs. of milk showing by the Babcock test five pounds of butter.

At the New York State Fair of 1894 a test was conducted by Prof. L. L. Van Slyke, chemist at the Experiment Station. Nine cows were entered, among which were two Jerseys, one Guernsey and six Holstein-Friesians. The first, second and third prizes were awarded to Holstein-Friesians, while the fourth, fifth and sixth places were occupied by the same breed of cattle, the seventh place by the Guernsey, the two Jerseys taking the tail end. The winning cow was Intje Von Holingen, whose milk yield was 234.188 lbs. showing 6.765 lbs. of fat. Clothilde 6th was second with a yield of 184.063 showing 6.683 lbs. of fat. Idene Rooker was third with a yield of 224.125 lbs. of milk showing 6.476 lbs. of fat. Fourth place was taken by Alwina 2d, whose yield was 208.501 lbs. of milk showing 6.419 lbs. of fat. The report of this test in Hoard's Dairyman says: "All the cows in this test were off in butter fat, especially Mr. Wilber's Holsteins, as cows at a fair always are, which accounts for the low per cent of fat recorded. The Jersey and Guernsey milk was rich enough, but the trouble was the cows could not furnish enough of it to get under the wire as winners." The seventh place in the test was taken by the Guernsey with a yield of 4.74 lbs. of butter fat. The eighth and ninth places were held by Jerseys with yields of 4.458 and 4.149 lbs. of butter fat respectively.

At the butter test made in Pennsylvania on the Bethlehem Fair grounds, three cows competed, two Holsteins and one Ayrshire. The test was conducted by Prof. W. H. Hayward of the State Experiment Station and was for one day.

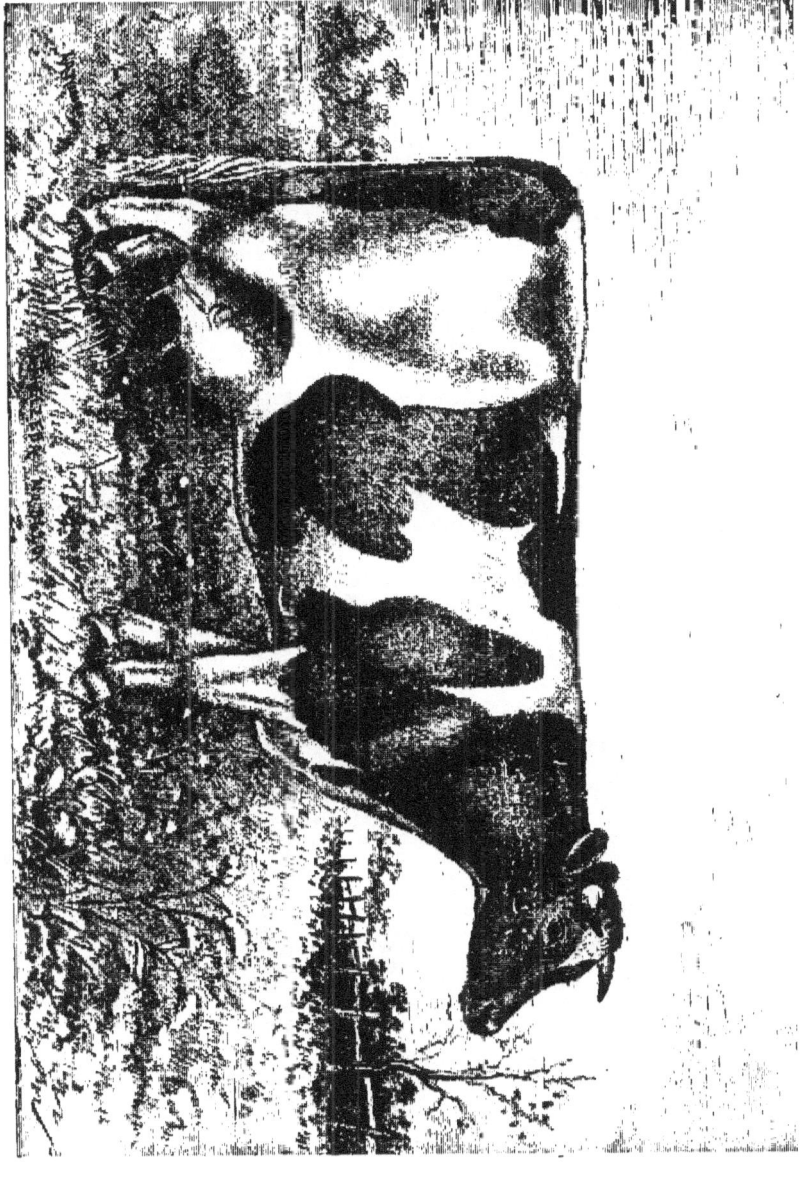

ETHELZEDA, No. 5820 H. H. B.
Imported. Milk record, 69 lbs. in one day without grain, testing 4.3 per cent. fat.

The first prize was taken by the Holstein-Friesian cow Bowen with a yield of 1.404 lbs. of fat. The second place was taken by the Ayrshire with a yield of 1.175. Unfortunately for the Holstein cow Bowen, she was in heat during the last eighteen hours of the test and made a comparatively small record.

At the Fat Stock Show held at Guelph, Ontario, December 12, 1895, the most successful test, under the standard rules of the British Dairy Show, was conducted. Eleven cows competed. Of these, five were Holsteins, three Ayrshires and three grades. The Holstein-Friesian cow Calamity Jane won easily the highest honors with a yield of over 69 lbs. of milk, testing from 3 to 3.6 per cent butter fat, and yielding 2.09 lbs. of butter fat. An Ayrshire cow made the second largest yield of 1.79 lbs. of butter fat, and the grade Shorthorn took third place with a record of 1.79 lbs. of butter fat.

At the Toronto, Ontario, Show a test of forty-eight hours was conducted by Prof. G. E. Day in 1895. There were nine entries, including one Guernsey, two Jerseys, one Ayrshire and four Holstein-Friesians. The Holstein cow Carmen Sylvia took first place with a yield of 122 lbs. 10 oz. of milk showing 14.515 lbs. of solids. An Ayrshire cow followed second with a yield of 111 lbs. 2½ oz. and total solids 12.906. The Holstein-Friesians took third, fourth and fifth places with yields of 12.207, 12.162 and 11.521 lbs. of solids respectively. A Jersey cow took sixth place with a yield of 9.849 lbs. of solids. The difference between this Jersey yield and the winning Holstein yield is 4.666 lbs. of solids.

At the Provincial Dairy Show held at Gananoque, Ontario, in 1895 there were twenty-four cows in competition, among which was the sweepstakes Ayrshire of the Columbian Exposition. She was fresh in milk and had come but a short distance. The winner at Toronto, Carmen Sylvia, was present, having attended four other fairs and travelled about 950 miles. She was then but four years old, and had twice defeated all other breeds in public competition, and held the world's record in the public tests of Canada. She scored 133.36 lbs. more than the best Jersey, and 62.99 lbs. more than the best Ayrshire cow, and 86.73 lbs. more than the best Guernsey.

In this test there were four Jerseys, eight Ayrshires, two Guernseys, two grades and six Holstein-Friesians. Carmen Sylvia's record was 261.86 lbs. upon a yield of 139 lbs. of milk showing 3.827 lbs. of fat and 12.03 lbs. of solids other than fat. The highest Jersey record was 2.436 lbs. of fat, and it was exceeded by the six four-year-old Holsteins in the test, the lowest of which showed 2.606 lbs. of fat.

The highest three-year-old Holstein-Friesian exceeded the Jersey record by 2.30 lbs. of butter fat, and the smallest Holstein record made by one of the three-year-olds equalled the largest Jersey record of the test within .629 lbs. Carmen Sylvia made 12.030 lbs. of solids other than fat, exceeding the highest Jersey yield by .689 lbs.

Interesting records were made at the two-days' test of the Nebraska State Fair of 1895. The winners were both pure-bred Holstein-Friesians, and the famous Geertje Seffinga, a five-year-old, took first place with a product valued at $.90, showing 2 lbs. 13.7 oz. of butter and 119 lbs. 15.3 oz. of skim milk. The second prize was awarded to Lutscke Isabel, a seven-year-old, with a product valued at $.66, containing 2 lbs. 3.1 oz. of butter and 75 lbs. 9 oz. of skim milk.

The California Dairy Test of 1895 was for seven days. The test was competitive between cows of various ages. In the five-year-old class, the Holstein-Friesian cow Sylpha won first prize with a yield of 34.86 lbs. of milk, showing 10.807 lbs. of butter fat, equivalent to 13.509 lbs. of 80 per cent butter.

In the two-year-old class the Holstein cow Windward made 7.215 lbs. of butter fat, equivalent to 9.019 lbs. of 80 per cent butter, and was exceeded by .905 yield by the Durham heifer. There were no entries in the Holstein three-year-old class.

CHAPTER XIV.

TESTS AT EXPERIMENT STATIONS.

Several of our agricultural experiment stations have, within the last few years, undertaken experiments designed to test the relative methods of some of the different breeds of dairy cattle. Of these experiments that of the New York Station at Geneva, which is still in progress, both in the number of cows engaged and in the length of time devoted to it, is by far the most extensive. I have, says Ernest Hitchcock, recently made a somewhat careful examination of the report of this work contained in the Eleventh Annual Report, and the results, owing to defects in the methods employed, seem to be disappointing rather than convincing. While in many respects the work is most valuable, yet so far as the specific aim of the experiments is concerned, namely, "the investigation of the several breeds of dairy cattle with reference to their relative value in the production of milk, butter and cheese," I fear it must be pronounced a failure. While this judgment may appear premature, in view of the fact that the experiment is not yet completed, nevertheless, as there is no indication of a change of methods, I think it is not unfair.

The most serious objections to the character of the work referred to may be summarized as follows:

1st. The character of many of the cows used in the test is not such as to entitle them to be considered fair representatives of their respective breeds.

2d. The use of "periods of lactation" instead of calendar periods renders many of the comparisons grossly unfair, and, further, renders a clear understanding of the merits of the different individuals much more difficult.

EUNICE CLAY, No. 1007 H. F. H. B.

Winner of first prize at Ohio State Fair, 1893, for solids not fat and milk prize, producing in twenty-four hours 84 lbs. 10 oz. of milk, which contained 7.66 lbs. solids not fat. Butter record 23 lbs. 9 oz. in seven days. Winner of butter test at Toronto, 1894, with record of 130 lbs. milk in two days, yielding 3.18 lbs. fat and 14.42 lbs. solids in same period.

3d. The change of the time of calving of many of the cows, during the continuance of the experiment, from spring to fall introduced an element of uncertainty and unfairness entirely destructive of fair competition.

4th. The method of comparing the different individuals and breeds by cost of fat production per pound instead of by net profit for a unit of time, fails to show the most profitable cows and breeds.

5th. The difference in age of the different heifers at the time of commencing their first and subsequent periods of lactation introduced another element of unfairness.

6th. The failure in the tabulation of results to take account of several important items of income and of cost was grossly unfair to certain individuals, and, alone, had the cows been properly selected, might easily have been sufficient to totally change results.

Some of these criticisms, it will be observed, refer to the fundamental methods of conducting the experiment, while others less serious merely refer to the methods of reporting the results. To understand the matter fully, reference should be had to the tables of the report already mentioned.

A few words of further explanation may perhaps be permitted. Where the character of a breed of cows is sought to be tested by the capacity of from one to four individuals of that breed, it is clear that if the test is to be of any value, those individuals must be fair representatives of their respective breeds. The number used is too small for the elimination of individual variations by the process of averaging. The question therefore meets us at the outset—what is "a fair representative" of a breed? Is it one of the best? Is it an average of the entire number of individuals of the breed? Is it one selected by lot? If none of these, what is it? It should be noted that the selection and rearing of heifer calves for the test in no respect meets the difficulty. It merely throws the question of selection back one generation and introduces an additional uncertainty—the question of heredity. Without discussing the matter, I will merely indicate my own impression, that as these tests are conducted for the purpose of assisting practical dairymen in their selection of herds of practical dairy cows, much the same method should be employed in selecting the herd for test as would be employed by an intelligent dairyman in building up his private herd—a somewhat extensive process of selection and weeding. (Compare work of the Cornell Station, Bulletin No. 52.) Were this process applied to the Geneva herd, it is apparent that, notwithstanding Dr. Collier's boast, "one of the finest herds ever brought together" (see page 17 Eleventh An. Rep.), many members of that herd would no longer remain to disgrace the breeds they are supposed to represent. To one who has any knowledge of the Holstein-Friesian cow, the claim that Essel 2d, Tolsma Artis or Beauty Pledge represent that breed is ridiculous. Two of these cows, aged at the date of second calving three years and two months and four years and two months respectively, produced during the first month of their second period of lactation an average of less than 1 lb. of butter fat per day. The weight of the cows was 1,195 and 1,045 lbs. respectively. The average per cent of fat for one during the first three months of lactation was 3.31, of the other 2.36. Beauty Pledge (age not given and record not included in tables for some reason which I have not seen stated) gave in her first seven months, first period, a daily average of 20.8 lbs. of milk testing 3.14. Her best month showed a daily average of nearly 0.71 of a lb. of butter fat. Let us compare the records of these cows with those of others of the same breed at other stations. In 1892 the three mature Holstein cows of the Vermont Station herd gave milk averaging 3.63 per cent fat and 1.11 lb. butter fat per day throughout the entire milking period; the total amounts of butter fat for the three cows for the year being 381, 323 and 364 lbs. respectively, an average butter capacity of over 400 lbs. The Minnesota Station herd, the record of which for 1893, bulletin 35, is before me, contained one Holstein-Friesian and one grade of that breed. The pure-bred cow weighed 1,127 lbs., was milked 331 days, gave 10,087 lbs. of milk and 374 lbs. of butter fat; costing 11.6 cents per lb. The grade gave 408 lbs. butter fat costing 10.4 cents per lb.— the best record of any cow in the herd. As this last cow was only one-half blood Holstein, her dam's breeding being unknown but surmised to be a grade Jersey, her record is perhaps of little pertinence here. The best Jersey cow in the herd gave 354 lbs. of butter fat, costing 10.6 cents per lb. She weighed 877 lbs. and was milked 346 days. No credit was given these cows for skim milk or manure.

The Cornell Station herd for the year 1892 (Bulletin 52) contained nine grade (¼ to ⅞ blood) and two pure-bred Holstein cows. Of these at least two were under specially unfavorable conditions and some were very poor cows. The entire eleven averaged 273 lbs. butter fat. The best six averaged 324 lbs., and the best produced 418 lbs. fat. The seven Jerseys (one pure-bred) averaged 270 lbs. fat, and the best produced 392 lbs. The cost of one pound of fat produced by the Jerseys was fifteen cents, and by the Holsteins seventeen cents, value of manure and of milk solids, not fat, being ignored. It is of some interest that the three pure-bred cows ranked very low.

To hundreds of your readers it is a matter of personal knowledge that the instances I have cited from the Vermont, Minnesota and Cornell Station herds, much as they surpass the animals in the Geneva herd, utterly fail to indicate the butter producing capacity of the best type of the Holstein cow. To such it may seem strange that I have collated none of the well authenticated instances, both public and private, of large records. In reply, I merely say that I hold no brief for the Holstein cow. My purpose is simply to show the unrepresentative character of the Geneva herd. That purpose I believe is best served by comparing it with other station herds. The herds referred to were selected simply because they were the ones, and the only ones, containing cows of the Holstein breed, to the records of which I have access.

Much the same could be said of the selection of Ayrshire cows as of the Holsteins, at Geneva. Suffice it to say, in general, of this matter of the selection of the representative cows for this test, if they are fairly selected it is a waste of time and money to test most of the breeds further. Let the matter as to these breeds be summed up and ended by saying: "No Holstein-Friesian, Shorthorn or American Holderness cow is worth barn-room for dairy purposes. The chance of securing an Ayrshire cow valuable for the dairy is not worth the effort." If these conclusions are unwarranted, most of the inferences sought to be drawn from the results of this test are equally unwarranted.

Of the second and third of the above criticisms, it is hardly necessary to speak. The unfairness of comparing the cost of butter production by a cow that has been continuously milked 761 days with its cost when produced by a cow milked eighty-two days in full flow seems clear. The attempt to change the time of calving of many of the cows from spring to fall, is largely responsible for the difference in the length of the periods of lactation. While perhaps desirable in itself, it was utterly inadvisable during the continuance of a scientific experiment. The use of periods of lactation as the unit of time has produced further confusion in that, even in the same volume, we have different sets of figures given as to the cost of fat production in the first period by the several breeds. If all the cows are to be included, we shall have still another set of figures hereafter for this same period. The figures for the second and subsequent periods will also have to be changed from time to time; so that it is difficult to see when a final result can be reached by this method.

As to the fourth criticism: What a dairyman wants is the cow that will, in a given time, put the most dollars in his pocket. That is not necessarily the cow which produces fat at the lowest cost per pound. For example, in the tables already referred to, the Devon cow, Genevie's Gift, makes a showing much better than the average, producing butter fat during the first period at 19.4 cents per pound and during the second period at 16.5 cents, the average of all the cows being 22.5 and 21.5 for the two periods. Her total production, however, is so small that the net profit would also be comparatively small. No one would for a moment deny that a cow producing 400 pounds of butter at a cost of 15 cents per pound is a better cow than one producing 300 pounds at a cost of 14 cents per pound, butter selling at fair average prices. Yet by the methods of comparison used at the Geneva station, and other stations as well, the reverse would appear to be the case.

On the fifth point comment is needless. As to the sixth, the items omitted are, the manurial value of the excrement, the value of the milk solids not fat, and, I judge, the cost of maintenance of the cows while dry. This last item should certainly be included in the final accounting, but it could not be included in the tables without adding greatly to the unfairness of comparing finished with unfinished periods of lactation. That the manurial value of the excrement is altogether too important an item to be fairly omitted we need not go outside of the present report to learn. We are told "that milch cows gave back in the liquid and solid manure a value in fertilizing constituents, nitrogen, potash and phosphoric acid, equal to 70 per cent of the market value of the feed fed the animals." Of course, even by best methods, there would be some waste of manure. Estimating that waste at the largest reasonable quantity, it still remains true that the total omission of this item is extremely unjust to the heavier feeding animals. On page 40 of the seventh annual report of the Vermont Experiment Station we find an estimate of the combined feeding and fertilizing value of skim-milk of thirty-six cents per 100 pounds. This is approximately four cents per pound for solids not fat, probably a higher valuation than can be realized in ordinary practice. Whatever may be deemed a fair valuation, its inclusion is absolutely necessary in a test of dairy cows. The approximate valuation of skim-milk, of manure and of butter is as easy as that of the foods consumed, and is equally necessary to the conduct of a breed test.

The breed test of the New Jersey Experiment Station was brought to an unhappy end November 1, 1890. Nevertheless, its conductors considered that it afforded ample ground for wide generalizations. "It is assumed," say they, page 32, Bulletin 32, "that the individual animals do represent their respective breeds, and that the average daily results secured from the herds of animals selected as representatives of their breeds are relatively the same as might be expected from a representative animal of each." Unless this assumption is justified, the conclusions are worthless. On this point I mention just two facts. Out of the five breeds represented—Ayrshire, Guernsey, Holstein-Friesian, Jersey and Shorthorn—the smallest quantity of milk was produced by the Jerseys, and next to the smallest (about fifteen per cent less than the next larger) was produced by the Holstein-Friesian. The milk record of one of the Holstein-Friesian cows for the period May 1, 1889, to October 31, 1890, was 3,824 lbs.—an average of about 7 lbs. per day for this "representative" Holstein cow. Upon such a foundation are built the generalizations regarding entire breeds of cows. If the engineers of the coast survey were to guess at the length of their base line, their subsequent work would possess about the same scientific value as that in question.

The only other specific breed test of which I have any report is that of the Maine Station. The number of the animals and breeds is smaller than at either the New York or New Jersey tests. The methods are open to some of the same objections. The premises are altogether too narrow to support the generalizations. For the purpose, however, of illustrating what, in my judgment, a report of such an experiment should show, I append a table giving the results of this station for one year. The table is not copied, but is a compilation from the tables contained in the Maine report for 1890.

Name.	No. of Days in Milk.	Pounds Milk.	Pounds Fat.	Pounds Solids not Fat.	Pounds Butter.	Value Butter.	Value of other Solids.	Value Manure.	Total Income.	Cost of Food.	Profit.
Jansje, H.-F.	365	9991	340	888	397	$99.25	$22.50	$29.28	$150.73	$73.20	$77.53
Nancy Avondale, A.	281	5048	209	542	244	61.00	13.55	23.96	98.51	59.89	38.62
Queen Linda, A.	287	6088	246	648	287	71.25	16.20	25.56	113.51	63.90	49.61
Agnes, J.	340	6873	332	663	411	103.75	16.57	23.86	144.18	59.64	84.54
Ida, J.	322	4107	238	400	277	69.02	10.00	23.18	102.20	57.95	44.25

Note—H.-F., Holstein-Friesian; A., Ayrshire; J., Jersey.

Butter is assumed to be worth twenty-five cents per pound. The quantity is computed by adding one-sixth to the quantity of butter fat. Milk solids not fat are assumed to be worth 2½ cents a pound. It is also assumed that forty per cent of the value of the food consumed is saved in the manure. As to the fairness of this last assumption, see an article by Dr. Collier in the Country Gentleman for December 20 last, page 916, in which he largely quotes Dr. Goessman's bulletins from the Massachusetts Station.

The age, weight and date of calving and average per cent of fat should also be included, but were not given in the 1890 report. Full details as to feeding should also be given. The Maine experiment was continued another year

GERBEN, No. 5562 H. H. B.

with a little Holstein cow included, a much poorer one than Jansje. On the whole, I think the conclusion is fairly warranted that the attempt to settle the relative merits of an entire breed of cows by the test of two or three "representatives" is not a success. I fear further that there is too much haste on the part of some experiment station workers to publish results, and to lay down broad generalizations based on very limited premises. This is the more to be deplored, because very many readers see or hear only the generalizations and never investigate their foundations; in fact, the agricultural press and the experiment station record, from which alone most intelligent readers get their ideas of the work done outside their own state, have no room for more than a mere summary of results.

Since preparing the above, I have seen the Twelfth Annual Report of the New York Station. Tables showing the cost of production of milk and fat for the first, second and third "periods of lactation" are given. I see no reason to modify any of the positions already taken. It is, perhaps, worthy of mention that as a producer of milk (quality ignored), the Holsteins rank, in the second and third periods, fourth, being surpassed by the Ayrshires, American Holderness and Guernseys in the second period, and by the American Holderness, Devon and Ayrshires in the third period.

CHAPTER XV.

HOLSTEIN-FRIESIAN ADVANCED REGISTRY.

This system of registry had its origin in the recognition of a fact largely overlooked by American breeders,—that excellence and public interest in a breed of cattle cannot be maintained permanently without continued selection. The great breeders of England, such as Bakewell, Price and the Collings, recognized this fact more than a century ago. They built and sustained the reputations of the improved breeds they originated by and through constant selection. The same is true of the great breeders on the continent. In Holland the careful selection of bulls for breeding purposes by district authorities has been practiced from time immemorial, and to this is due in large measure the excellence of the Holstein-Friesian breed. More recently in Switzerland this principle has been recognized and brought under the direction of government authority. Thus it will be seen that the idea at the foundation of this system of registry is not original with the founder. It is new only in American breeding.

The formal recognition, however, and embodiment of this principle in a distinct system of registry, is original with the Holstein-Friesian Association of America. At the time of the formation of this association by the union of the Holstein Breeders Association and the Dutch-Friesian Herd Book Association, the need of a greater stimulus to selection than was afforded by the simple system of herd book registry, as practiced both at home and abroad, had become apparent. The great popularity of the breed had stimulated to excessive importation. A class of dealers had already introduced inferior cattle from the Netherlands in the hope simply of immediate profit. These cattle, though not eligible to the herd books of the Netherlands, had from the mere fact of importation and proper coloring been admitted to the herd books here. Moreover, the offspring of these cattle were to be forever eligible to registry. Not only then was there great danger in spite of the herd book registry of the degeneration of the breed, but careful breeders working judiciously with the principle of selection for the improvement of their cattle, were furnished no stimulus and left without protection. It was evident to a close observer, that something further was imperatively demanded in order to advance or even to maintain the standard of excellence of the breed in this country.

A study of the situation by Mr. S. Hoxie, at that time secretary of the Dutch-Friesian Association, convinced him that this object could be attained, and only attained, through a direct recognition of the principle of selection by a further extension of the registry system. Out of this idea has grown the Holstein-Friesian Advanced Registry.

HYKOLINA. 746 H. H. B.
Milk record, 58 lbs. in one day; 11,186 lbs. in one year.

Hitherto in America the only requirements for registry in case of imported cattle, were a standard of color and size and a certification of purity of blood by the European breeder, and in the case of home-bred cattle, descent from stock already registered here. There was no connection with registry in the Netherlands, and no evidence of descent from superior cattle in that country. When importation began there were no herd-books in that country other than those kept by individual breeders. Soon after the Netherlands Herd Book Association was incorporated by the government, followed by the incorporation of the Friesian Association for the province of Friesland. These associations, in addition to blood purity, required excellence of character as tested by standards of structure and appearance indicative of superior milk and flesh producing qualities. Such a test was the first additional requirement that suggested itself as necessary in the construction of an Advanced Registry in America. A brief trial convinced the originator of the idea that such tests were not alone sufficient. From a point of view thus reached, he conceived that a proper stimulus to improvement through selection could only be secured with certainty in a dairy breed by means of tests of actual performance at the pail or churn. This principle of tests by actual performance, embodied in the system, is the distinctive feature of Advanced Registry.

Tentative steps had been taken by the Dutch-Friesian Association as early as 1882, looking toward the requirement of actual tests for registry.* This became one of the distinguishing features of the Dutch-Friesian registry system, and at the meeting of the two associations in 1885, at which time they were merged into the Holstein-Friesian Association of America, the establishment of an advanced registry was made one of the conditions of consolidation. The board of officers of the new association were entrusted with the formulation of its regulations. This board took for the basis of its action a set of rules previously prepared by Mr. Hoxie, and these with slight amendments were adopted. They required in general that all animals received to it should attain a certain standard of structural excellence, and in addition that all cows should reach a certain standard of milk or butter production determined by actual tests. Structural excellence was determined by reference to separate scales of points for cows and bulls. In the case of bulls a score of 80 per cent was the minimum for admission and a weight of at least 1,800 lbs. at full age. Added to these conditions excellence as a stock-getter was required to be shown by examination of at least three of the progeny. Cows were required to score a minimum of 75 per cent of the scale and to weigh at least 1,000 lbs. at full age. A difficulty arose as to the relative milk and butter requirements for cows of different ages. It was manifestly unjust to classify immature cows with mature cows. This difficulty was cleverly solved by Mr. W. G. Powell, who proposed a sliding scale beginning with a minimum requirement of heifers just two years old and increasing the requirement for every day of additional age up to maturity at five years of age. Mr. S. Hoxie was elected superintendent of this registry, and the system was at once put formally into operation.

Though thus formally established, nearly a year elapsed before the first entries were actually made. This was due, in the main, to the fact that the Board of Officers did not complete the Scale of Points till August 12, 1395. Furthermore it was necessary for the new superintendent to formulate a system of measurements and a descriptive nomenclature—a task rendered doubly difficult because with the slight advance in this direction on the part of the

---

* When the Dutch-Friesian Association was organized in 1879, the escutcheon was widely depended upon for the selection of dairy cattle. Investigations by the Government of France and by the Legislature of Pennsylvania had decidedly favored it. This association accepted the conclusions of these investigations and began a system of registry based on the escutcheon. It was called the Main Registry. Its entries contained descriptions of the escutcheon, and in cases where they could be reliably ascertained, measurements, milk records and descriptions of style and build. The requirement of actual tests of milk or butter production was added in 1882. In that year it published the second volume of its Herd-Book in which two forms of registry appeared under the names, Pedigree Registry and Main Registry. The latter required tests of performance of all cows entered. It required animals to be at least two years old at date of entry, bulls to be proved stock-getters and to scale 80 points of the scale of points of the association; and cows to show a high development of udder, mammary veins, escutcheon, and to have records of actual milk production sufficient to satisfy the Official Inspector and Executive Board that they were capable of producing 6,000 lbs. at two years old, 7,000 lbs. at three years old, 8,000 lbs. at four years old, or 10,000 lbs. at five years old or upwards. These requirements were formulated by the Superintendent. He received valuable suggestions from members of the association and from breeders outside. Among those who rendered most assistance were Mr. C. R. Payne, Mr. S. Burchard, Mr. H. Langworthy and Hon. Gerrit S. Miller.

Dutch-Friesian Association and Holland Associations the work was without precedents. Delay also arose out of opposition to the registry on the part of individual breeders growing out of a partisan struggle previously begun entirely foreign to the merits of this system. In this crisis its preservation was due to the combined influence of Mr. T. G. Yeomans and the late W. Brown Smith, leading breeders, who had been active in bringing about the formation of the Holstein-Friesian Association.

The first entries to the Advanced Registry were made in January, 1886. and the first volume was issued a year later. Thirty-one bulls and three hundred and fifty cows were entered in this volume. The result, both in the general make-up of this volume and the number of entries was a surprise even to the friends of the new system. An immediate wave of interest was created, not only in this country, but in Europe. Breeders in England and Scotland wrote for information in regard to it, and discussed the subject before their cattle associations; and in Germany several publications reviewed the system at great length. It was evident that, whatever the fate of this system in America, the fundamental ideas had taken a firm hold on the minds of breeders of improved cattle.

IOLENA FAIRMOUNT, No. 15344 H. F. H. B.
Record: 75 lbs. milk; 2.44 butter fat in twenty-four hours. Winner of first prize for butter, Ohio, 1893.

The permanence of the new registry was not, however, yet assured. It continued to some extent to be an object of disapproval on grounds outside of its purposes or its principles. Gradually it won its way as it was seen that it was a distinct benefit to every breeder, whether he had cattle in it or not, by its service in sustaining and advancing the interests of the breed as a whole. Between 1886 and 1891 three other volumes were published, bringing the total registration to ninety-six bulls and 1,031 cows.

During the next four years occurred the reaction in popular favor that at some time inevitably overtakes every new breed introduced into this country. A typical example of this and perhaps the most pronounced, is that against the Ayrshire breed, commencing about 1880, from which it has not yet recovered. This reaction period against the Holstein-Friesians, from 1891 to 1895, was a critical one for Advanced Registry. But in this crisis of the breed the value of the system was more fully demonstrated. In a measure it saved the breed from the fate of others by furnishing at this trying time, not only indisputable evidence of the great value of the breed, but also held out a continued stimulus to the owners of the best stock to persevere in its improvement. Up to 1895, 921 cows had been registered with records showing a production equivalent to at least 10,700 lbs. of milk for full age animals in the ordinary period of ten months milking, and at the same time 619 cows had been registered that had butter records equivalent to or exceeding 15 lbs. of butter for periods of seven consecutive days. Nearly all of these records, whether of milk or butter, were in fact in excess of these standard requirements. More than ninety different cows and heifers held actual milk records exceeding 14,000 lbs. for periods of ten months or one year, while over 140 held seven-day butter records above 20 lbs. In the presence of such records distrust of the breed could not exist for any extended period and by 1895 it began again to advance in public favor.

Throughout this critical period the experience of breeders had been bringing about an evolution of this Advanced Registry system. Previous to 1893 all cattle registered had been subjected to examination by officials appointed by the Board of Officers of the Association. With the decline of profits to breeders it was found that the expense of such examination prevented the registration of cows fully capable of meeting all the requirements. To clear the way for the entry of such cattle examination by officials was, in that year, made optional with owners. In other words, cows were thereafter admitted to entry simply on sworn records without measurements and descriptions. At the same time provision was made for the acceptance of records of pure butter fat, the ratio of fat to marketable butter being fixed, after correspondence with the officials of leading Agricultural Experiment Stations, at $83\frac{1}{2}$ per cent. A rule was also adopted requiring the superintendent to officially investigate all records of pure butter fat or of marketable butter made in seven consecutive days, exceeding 20 and 25 lbs. respectively, and to publish a summary of such investigation with the entry.

At the meeting of this Association in 1894, to stimulate the making of butter records, a thousand dollars was placed in the hands of the Board of Officers to be offered at their discretion, as prizes, for largest officially authenticated records. At the same time the ratio of butter fat to marketable butter, in determining equivalent production, was reduced to 80 per cent in conformity to the estimates adopted for butter fat tests in the World's Fair competitions. In accordance with such action a contest was inaugurated open to breeders of the Association, with a list of twenty-seven prizes, to be awarded the best seven-day tests conducted under the supervision of the superintendent or some inspector designated by him or by the officer of some Experiment Station or other State institution. The effect of this competition was exceedingly gratifying. The showing of butter production exceeded all unquestioned official records of any breed previously made in America. It reanimated the breeders, stimulated again wide-spread public interest in the breed and went far toward establishing its pre-eminence as butter producers. Apparently all opposition to Advanced Registry ceased with this showing.

The future of Advanced Registry now seems assured. Its value is becoming recognized not only by Holstein-Friesian breeders, but by all breeders of improved cattle. Tentative steps have been taken in other breeders associations and in other breeds for the establishment of similar registries. Vicissitudes no doubt await it. Its requirements will be modified to meet changed conditions; but as the expression of a principle in cattle breeding and registry it will, no doubt, continue as long as the breeding of improved dairy cattle continues.

The following Holstein-Friesian records are taken from the Advanced Register, superintendent, Mr. S. Hoxie, Yorkville, N. Y.:

Milk records—Pietertje 2d. 479 : 1 day, $112\frac{7}{16}$ lbs.: 1 month. $3,289\frac{1}{2}$ lbs.; 10 months, $26,737\frac{7}{16}$ lbs.: 1 year, $30,318\frac{1}{4}$ lbs.; owned by Dallas B. Whipple, Cuba, N. Y. Princess of Wayne 2 : 1 day $113\frac{1}{16}$ lbs.: 1 month, $3,182\frac{1}{4}$ lbs.; 10 months, $25,135\frac{5}{16}$ lbs.; 1 year, $29,008\frac{11}{14}$ lbs.; owned by T. G. Yeomans & Sons, Walworth, N. Y.

Butter records—Pauline Paul : 30 days. $128\frac{11}{14}$ lbs.; 365 days, $1,153\frac{34}{14}$ lbs.; owned by J. B. Dutcher & Son. Pawling, N. Y. Clothilde 2d ; 90 days, $320\frac{7}{16}$ lbs.; owned by Smiths & Powell Co., Syracuse, N. Y. Natsey : 7 days, $34\frac{5}{16}$ lbs.; owned by Ehrich & White, Colorado Springs, Col. Lady Baker : 7 days, $34\frac{1}{16}$

lbs. De Kol 2d : 7 days, 33 7/8 lbs. (age 4 years 9 months 27 days); owned by J. B. Dutcher & Son, Pawling, N. Y.; second owners, Henry Stevens & Sons, Lacona, N. Y.

The great mass of butter records in advanced Registry are for periods of seven consecutive days of twenty-four hours each. As classified March 1, 1897, they are as follows:

Of cows in full-age-form, 290.	Average record, 19 lbs.	11.8 oz.
" " " four-year-form, 98.	" " 18 "	10.2 "
" " " three-year-form, 136.	" " 16 "	6.4 "
" " " two-year-form, 241.	" " 10 "	15.1 "
Heifers under two years, 69.	" " 10 "	10.3 "

Of the total number of records, one hundred and fifty-one are official. These have been under exceedingly strict supervision of disinterested men mainly from our State Experiment Stations. As classified they are as follows:

Of cows in full-age-form, 49.	Average record, 19 lbs.	5.4 oz.
" " " four-year-form, 28.	" " 18 "	5.5 "
" " " three-year-old form, 18.	" " 16 "	3.7 "
" " " two-year-old-form, 40.	" " 12 "	0.7 "
Heifers under two years, 16.	" " 11 "	11.5 "

These figures are worthy of careful study. They reveal the capacity of a large class of our cows. The closeness with which the two divisions of records approach each other is surprising. The difference between the average records of full-age cows in these two divisions is only six and four-tenths ounces; that between cows from four to five years old is four and seven-tenths ounces; while that between heifers from two to three years old is two and seven-tenths ounces. In the other two ages there is a wider difference, by no means excessive. It does not follow that every record from which these averages are calculated is reliable. One of the vital principles of our system of Advanced Registry is that every record rests upon individual separate testimony. While the association inflicts the severest penalties

JAAP 4TH, No. 1337 H. H. B.
Weight at eleven months, 1200 lbs. Gain for thirty consecutive days, 5 1-3 lbs. per day.

on the crime of making fraudulent records, it does not follow that no such records have ever slipped into this registry. But it courts investigation, assured that the closer the records of our breed are examined the more reliable will they appear, and the firmer the ground of this system of registry.

The following instructions for making officially authenticated butter records for Advanced Registry are issued by the superintendent of Advanced Registry of the Holstein-Friesian Association of America, Mr. S. Hoxie, of Yorkville, N. Y.:

1. Such records, to compete for the prizes of the Holstein-Friesian Association of America, may be made by the churn, or by the Babcock test, or by any other method approved by the Association of Official Agricultural Chemists.

2. All such records must be for seven consecutive days, and must be supervised by the officer of some experiment station or state institution, or by the superintendent of Advanced Registry or some inspector designated by him.

3. The person supervising must see the cow milked dry at the beginning of the test and be present at each milking thereafter and weigh the milk, and have such complete control of it in every process of the test as to insure positive accuracy in the results obtained. In his report of the test the supervisor must give full details to the satisfaction of the superintendent of Advanced Registry and make an affidavit to the accuracy and truthfulness of the same.

4. In all cases where possible the supervision should be by an officer or appointee of an experiment station. To obtain such supervision owners of cows contemplating such tests should early begin correspondence with the directors of such stations and also with the superintendent of Advanced Registry. Directors of such stations are always disposed to do such work for their constituency but they sometimes have to employ special assistants for it. In preliminary correspondence with them it is not necessary to give the names of cows or the date of contemplated tests. Its object is simply to induce necessary preparations.

5. It is always wise for owners to know just what their cows are doing. A Babcock testing machine is almost indispensable to this. The method of using it is easily learned. It takes but little time, it takes but little milk, and it is accurate. In addition to the ordinary instructions accompanying the machine the following are suggested. In adding the acid the bottle should be held at an angle so as to cause it to flow slowly down the inside of the wall—the farther the neck of the bottle is from a perpendicular position the better. When about half of the acid is added shake the bottle in the ordinary way until the acid is mixed with the milk, then add the remainder and mix again. After revolving the bottles the usual time fill them with hot water only to the necks, then revolve a minute or more, then complete the filling to raise the fat into the graduated necks and revolve again. Always use hot water and keep the bottles in hot water until the per cent of fat is accurately read. The bottles should be cleansed in hot water after each test.

6. To make an official record eligible to receive a prize it must be entered in Advanced Registry. Application for such entry is made separately from the report of the supervisor. There are no fees for entry.

7. The value of official records can hardly be overestimated. The cost in comparison is trivial. It includes traveling expenses of the supervisor and pay for his time when required. Such charges are moderate.

8. All blank forms are free. There is not a breeder who has made official records but will gladly give information on the subject, and the superintendent of Advanced Registry invites correspondence.

JACOBA HARTOG, No. 2.70. F. H. JB.
Imported. Weight 1,121 lbs (Milk record in sixteen days, 1,185 lbs.

CHAPTER XVI.

SCALE OF POINTS OF THE HOLSTEIN-FRIESIAN ASSOCIATION OF AMERICA, WITH A UNIFORM SYSTEM OF DISCREDITS.

[The items of description following each head of the scale should be passed upon separately, and the amount of discredit marked down on the margin. The uniform discredits to be given are noted under each full description. V. s. means very slight deficiency; s., slight; m., marked; v. m., very marked; e. extreme. The difference between the sum of such discredits and 100 will be the standard of the animal by this scale.]

FOR BULLS.

Discredits. **HEAD.**
Showing full vigor;
Elegant in contour; } 2 points.
Discredit, v. s. 1-8; s. 1-4; m. 1-2; v. m. 3-4; e. 1.

FOREHEAD.
Broad between the eyes;
Dishing. } 2 points.
Discredit, v. s. 1-8; s. 1-4; m. 1-2; v. m. 3-4; e. 1.

FACE.
Of medium length;
Clean and trim especially under eyes;
The bridge of the nose straight;
The muzzle broad; } 2 points.
Discredit, s. 1-8; m. 1-4; e. 1-2.

EARS.
Of medium size;
Of fine texture;
The hair plentiful and soft;
The secretions oily and abundant; } 1 point.
Discredit, m. 1-8; e. 1.4.

EYES.
Large;
Full;
Mild;
Bright; } 2 points.
Discredit, s. 1-8; m. 1-4; e. 1-2.

HORNS.
Short;
Of medium size at base;
Gradually diminishing toward tips;
Oval;
Inclining forward;
Moderately curved inward;
Of fine texture;
In appearance waxy; } 2 points.
Discredit, m. 1-8; e. 1-4.

NECK.
Long;
Finely crested (if animal is mature)
Fine and clean at juncture with the head;
Nearly free from dewlap;
Strongly and smoothly joined to shoulders; } 5 points.
Discredit, v. s. 1-8; s. 1-4; m. 1-2; v. m. 3-4; e. 1.

SHOULDERS.
Of medium height;
Of medium thickness and smoothly rounded at top;
Broad and full at sides;
Smooth over front; } 4 points.
Discredit, v. s. 1-8; s. 1-4; m. 1-2; v. m. 3-4; e. 1.

CHEST.
Deep and low;
Well filled and smooth in the brisket;
Broad between the forearms;
Full in the foreflanks (or through at the heart); } 8 points.
Discredit, v. s. 1-4; s. 1-2; m. 1; v. m. 1 1-2; e. 2.

Discredits. **CROPS.**
Comparatively full;
Nearly level with the shoulders; } 4 points.
Discredit, v. s. 1-4; s. 1-2; m. 1; v. m. 1 1-2; e. 2.

CHINE.
Straight;
Broadly developed;
Open; } 3 points.
Discredit, v. s. 1-8; s. 1-4; m. 1-2; v. m. 3-4; e. 1.

BARREL.
Well rounded;
With large abdomen;
Strongly and trimly held up; } 6 points.
Discredit, v. s. 1-4; s. 1-2; m. 1; v. m. 1 1-2; e. 2.

LOIN AND HIPS.
Broad;
Level or nearly level between hook bones;
Level and strong laterally;
Spreading from the chine broadly and nearly level;
The hook bones fairly prominent; } 5 points.
Discredit, v. s. 1-8; s. 1-4; m. 1-2; v. m. 3-4; e. 1.

RUMP.
Long;
Broad;
High;
Nearly level laterally;
Comparatively full above the thurl; } 5 points.
Discredit, v. s. 1-8; s. 1-4; m. 1-2; v. m. 3-4; e. 1.

THURL.
High;
Broad; } 4 points.
Discredit, v. s. 1-4; s. 1-2; m. 1; v. m. 1 1-2; e. 2.

QUARTERS.
Deep;
Broad;
Straight behind;
Wide and full at sides;
Open and well arched in the twist; } 5 points.
Discredit, v. s. 1-8; s. 1-4; m. 1-2; v. m. 3-4; e. 1.

FLANKS.
Deep;
Full; } 2 points.
Discredit, v. s. 1-8; s. 1-4; m. 1-2; v. m. 3-4; e. 1.

LEGS.
Comparatively short;
Clean and nearly straight;
Wide apart;
Firmly and squarely set under the body;
Arms wide, strong and tapering;
Feet of medium size, round, solid and deep; } 6 points.
Discredit, v. s. 1-8; s. 1-4; m. 1-2; v. m. 3-4; e. 1.

TAIL.
Large at base, the setting well back;
Tapering finely to switch;
The end of the bone reaching to hocks or below;
The switch full; } 2 points.
Discredit, s. 1-8; m. 1-4; e. 1-2.

JAMAICA AND CALF, No. 1236 H. H. B. Imported. Milk record, 112 lbs. 2 oz. in one day; 3039 lbs. 3 oz. in thirty-one days; 19,716 lbs. in one year.

Discredits. **HAIR AND HANDLING.**
Hair healthful in appearance;
Fine, soft and furry;
Skin of medium thickness and loose;
Mellow under the hand;
The secretions oily, abundant, and of a rich brown or yellow color; } 10 points.
Discredit, v. s. 1-4; s. 1-2; m. 1; v. m. 1 1-2; e. 2.

MAMMARY VEINS.
Large;
Full;
Entering large or numerous orifices;
Double extension;
With special developments, such as forks, branches, connections, etc.; } 10 points.
Discredit, v s. 1-4; s. 1-2; m. 1; v. m. 1 1-2; e. 2.

RUDIMENTARY TEATS.
Large;
Well placed; } 2 points.
Discredit, v. s. 1-8; s. 1-4; m. 1-2; v. m. 3-4; e. 1.

ESCUTCHEON.
Largest;
Finest; } 8 points.
Discredit, v. s. 1-2; s. 1; m. 2; v. m. 3; e. 4.

Perfection, 100 points.

GENERAL VIGOR:—For deficiency Inspectors shall discredit from the total received not to exceed eight points.
Discredit, v. s 1; s. 2; m. 3; v. m. 5; e. 8.
GENERAL SYMMETRY AND FINENESS:—For deficiency Inspectors shall discredit from the total received not to exceed eight points.
Discredit, v. s. 1; s. 2; m. 3; v. m. 5; e. 8.
GENERAL STYLE AND BEARING:—For deficiency Inspectors shall discredit from the total received not to exceed eight points.
Discredit, v. s. 1; s. 2; m. 3; v. m. 5; e. 8.
CREDITS FOR OFFSPRING:—A bull shall be credited one point in excess of what he is otherwise entitled to for each and every animal of which he is sire actually entered in the Advanced Register not to exceed ten in number.

In scaling for the Advanced Register, defects caused solely by age, or by accident, or by disease not hereditary, shall not be considered. But in scaling for the show ring, such defects shall be considered and duly discredited.
A bull shall in the judgment of the Examiner will not reach at full age, and in good flesh, 1,800 pounds, live weight, shall be disqualified for entry in the Advanced Register.
No bull shall be received to the Advanced Register that, with all credits due him, will not scale in the judgment of the Examiner at least 80 points.

FOR COWS.

Discredits. **HEAD.**
Decidedly feminine in appearance;
Fine in contour; } 2 points.
Discredit, v. s. 1-8; s. 1-4; m. 1 2; v. m. 3-4; e. 1.

FOREHEAD.
Broad between the eyes;
Dishing; } 2 points.
Discredit, v. s. 1-8; s. 1-4; m. 1-2; v. m. 3-4; e. 1.

FACE.
Of medium length;
Clean and trim, especially under the eyes, showing facial veins;
The bridge of the nose straight;
The muzzle broad; } 2 points.
Discredit, s. 1-8; m. 1-4; e. 1-2.

EARS.
Of medium size;
Of fine texture;
The hair plentiful and soft;
The secretions oily and abundant; } 1 point.
Discredit, m. 1-8; e. 1-4.

EYES.
Large;
Full;
Mild;
Bright; } 2 points.
Discredit, s. 1-8; m. 1-4; e. 1-2.

HORNS.
Small;
Tapering finely toward the tips;
Set moderately narrow at base;
Oval;
Inclining forward;
Well bent inward;
Of fine texture;
In appearance waxy; } 2 points.
Discredit, m. 1-8; e. 1-4.

NECK.
Long;
Fine and clean at juncture with the head;
Free from dewlap;
Evenly and smoothly joined to shoulders; } 4 points.
Discredit, v. s. 1-8; s. 1-4; m. 1-2; v. m. 3-4; e. 1.

Discredits. **SHOULDERS.**
Slightly lower than hips;
Fine and even over tops;
Moderately broad and full at sides; } 3 points.
Discredit, v. s. 1-8; s. 1-4; m. 1-2; v. m. 3-4; e. 1.

CHEST.
Of moderate depth and lowness;
Smooth and moderately full in the brisket;
Full in the foreflanks (or through at the heart); } 6 points.
Discredit, v. s. 1-4; s. 1-2; m. 1; v. m. 1 1-2; e. 2.

CROPS.
Moderately full; 2 points.
Discredit, v. s. 1-4; s. 1 2; m. 3-4; v. m. 1 1-2; e. 2

CHINE.
Straight;
Broadly developed;
Open; } 3 points.
Discredit, v. s. 1-8; s. 1-4; m. 1-2; v. m. 3-4; e. 1.

BARREL.
Of wedge shape;
Well rounded;
With a large abdomen;
Trimly held up (in judging the last item age must be considered); } 4 points.
Discredit, v. s. 1-8; s. 1-4; m. 1-2; v. m. 3-4; e. 1.

LOIN AND HIPS.
Broad;
Level or nearly level between hook-bones;
Level and strong laterally;
Spreading from chine broadly and nearly level;
Hook bones fairly prominent; } 5 points.
Discredit, v. s. 1-8; s. 1-4; m. 1-2; v. m. 3-4; e. 1.

RUMP.
Long;
High;
Broad, with roomy pelvis;
Nearly level laterally;
Comparatively full above the thurl; } 5 points.
Discredit, v. s. 1-8; s. 1-4; m. 1 2; v. m. 3-4; e. 1.

Discredits. **THURL.**
High;
Broad; } 4 points.
Discredit, v. s. 1-4; s. 1-2; m. 1; v. m. 1 1-2; e. 2.

QUARTERS.
Deep;
Straight behind;
Roomy in the twist;
Wide and moderately full at the sides; } 4 points.
Discredit, v. s. 1-8; s. 1-4; m. 1-2; v. m. 3-4; e. 1.

FLANKS.
Deep;
Comparatively full; } 2 points.
Discredit, v. s. 1-8; s. 1-4; m. 1-2; v. m. 3-4; e. 1.

LEGS.
Comparatively short;
Clean and nearly straight;
Wide apart;
Firmly and squarely set under the body;
Feet of medium size, round, solid and deep; } 5 points.
Discredit, v. s. 1-8; s. 1-4; m. 1-2; v. m. 3-4; e. 1.

TAIL.
Large at base, setting well back;
Tapering finely to switch;
The end of the bone reaching to hocks or below;
The switch full; } 2 points.
Discredit, s. 1-8; m. 1-4; e. 1-2.

HAIR AND HANDLING.
Hair healthful in appearance;
Fine, soft and furry;
The skin of medium thickness and loose;
Mellow under the hand;
The secretions oily, abundant, and of a rich brown or yellow color; } 10 points.
Discredit, v. s. 1-4; s. 1-2; m. 1; v. m. 1 1-2; e. 2.

MAMMARY VEINS.
Very large;
Very crooked (age must be taken into consideration in judging of size and crookedness);
Entering very large or numerous orifices;
Double extension;
With special developments, such as branches, connections, etc. } 10 points.
Discredit, v. s. 1-4; s. 1-2; m. 1; v. m. 1 1-2; e. 2.

Discredits. **UDDER AND TEATS.**
Very capacious;
Very flexible;
Quarters even;
Nearly filling the space in the rear below the twist, and extending well forward in front;
Broad and well held up;
Teats well formed, wide apart, plumb, and of convenient size; } 12 points.
Discredit, v. s. 1-4; s. 1-2; m. 1; v. m. 1 1-2; e. 2.

ESCUTCHEON.
Largest;
Finest; } 8 points.
Discredit, v. s. 1-2; s. 1; m. 2; v. m. 3; e. 4.

Perfection, 100 points.

GENERAL VIGOR:—For deficiency Inspectors shall discredit from the total received not to exceed eight points.
Discredit. v. s. 1; s. 2; m. 3; v. m. 5; e. 8.

GENERAL SYMMETRY AND FINENESS:—For deficiency Inspectors shall discredit from the total received not to exceed eight points.
Discredit, v. s. 1; s. 2; m. 3; v. m. 5; e. 8.

GENERAL STYLE AND BEARING:—For deficiency Inspectors shall discredit from the total received not to exceed eight points.
Discredit, v. s. 1; s. 2; m. 3; v. m. 5; e. 8.

CREDITS FOR EXCESS OF REQUIREMENT IN PRODUCTION:—A cow shall be credited one point in excess of what she is otherwise entitled to for each and every eight per cent that her milk or butter record exceeds the minimum requirement.

In scaling for the Advanced Register, defects caused solely by age, or by accident, or by disease not hereditary, shall not be considered. But in scaling for the show ring such defects shall be considered and duly discredited.

A cow that in the judgment of the Examiner will not reach at full age, in milking condition and ordinary flesh, 1000 pounds, live weight, shall be disqualified for entry in the Advanced Register.

No cow shall be received to the Advanced Register that, with all credits due her, will not scale in the judgment of the Examiner at least 75 points.

The Holstein-Friesian Association of America was chartered in New York in 1885. Its records comprise the Holstein Herd Book of nine volumes, the Dutch-Friesian Herd Book of four volumes, the Advanced Registry and the fourteen volumes of the Holstein-Friesian Association of America. The Holstein Breeders Association and the Dutch-Friesian Association united in 1885 under the title of the Holstein-Friesian Association of America, since which time fourteen volumes of its herd book have been printed.

The total registration of the societies up to close of 1896 is as follows: Holstein Herd Book, cows. 10,560; bulls, 4,664; Dutch-Friesian Herd Book, cows, 1,937; bulls, 730; Holstein-Friesian Herd Book to close of Volume 14, cows, 40,516; bulls, 22,586. Thus it appears that there are now upwards of 53,013 cows and 27,980 bulls upon its records.

It is the oldest association in the world founded upon these cattle. Its membership includes 515 breeders and its treasury is in so prosperous condition as to enable it to offer thousands of dollars in special prizes each year. The aggregate sum, so disposed of, is very large indeed and has greatly benefited Holstein-Friesian interests. Nearly $25,000 has been expended in bounties upon bull calves slaughtered or castrated; but this practice is no longer in force. By its enterprise and careful management it has conferred lasting benefit upon breeders and the breed.

It is the only herd book recognized by the United States Government. The fee for life membership is $25. Members' fees for recording cattle are: For males under one year of age $3. Non-members are required to pay for registry

THE HOLSTEIN-FRIESIAN ASSOCIATION.

of males under one year of age $5. The fees for transfers are, to members, 25 cents; non-members, 50 cents.

The attention of applicants for the registry or transfer of animals is called to the following more important By-laws of the Association:

ARTICLE 4. Section 2. The registry shall set forth the number, the name, the date of birth, the name and residence of the breeder and owner, and if imported, the name of the importer, and the names and numbers of both sire and dam.

SEC. 3. In the Herd Book there shall be registered only such animals as are determined under the rules and regulations of this corporation to be pure-bred.

SEC. 4. Pure-bred Holstein-Friesian shall be held to mean and to refer to only those large, improved, black-and-white cattle already registered in the Holstein Herd Book, and such as are descended from them in as to sire and dam, and such imported animals or their ancestry registered in the Netherlands, Friesian or North Holland, and by the affirmation of breeders of the animals satisfactory

Pure-bred animals shall only be registered in the Herd Book made upon forms furnished by the corporation, and the payment of $3 each for males under one year old, and $6 each if over one year to members of the Association; and $5 each if under one year old, and $6 if over one year old, by non-members. The fee for the registry of females under one year old is $1, and if over one year old $2, by members, and $2 each for females under one year old, and if over one year old $4 each for females, must accompany the application. No two animals shall have the same name. Only direct descendants of an animal shall be entitled to the same name with numbers prefixed or added, and after the first generation must be only in combination. Males shall only be entitled to the name in combination in which the family name shall be first. In all cases the names of sire and dam in part or in full may be used as applicants. All titles of distinction, nobility, military or honor, or given names not in use as family names, shall be free for both.

Animals must be transferred to owners before their offspring are registered.

Application for register of animals imported in dam must be made by importer. All animals bred in America shall be registered in the name of owner, in which case a certificate of service is required from the owner of sire, and the signature of the breeder to the application.

In all cases the owner of the dam at time of service.

Blank forms for registry and transfer are furnished from the secretary without charge.

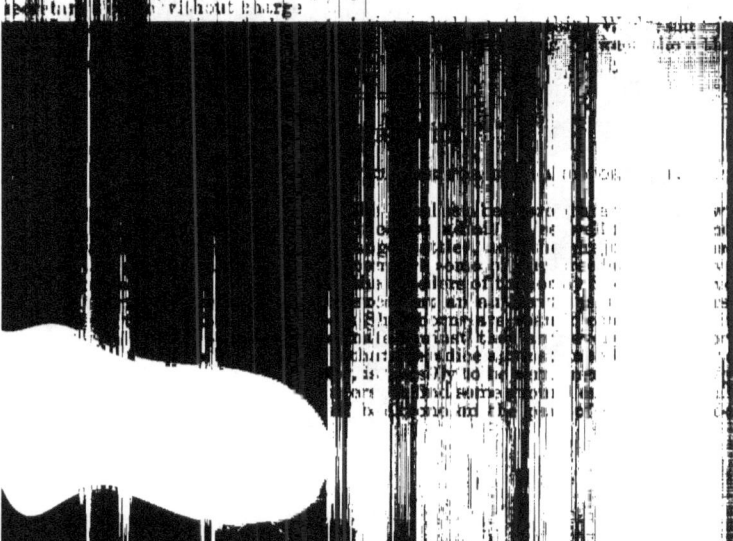

We are aware that the mere presentation of this symposium to our readers will subject us to criticism on the part of so-called "special purpose cow" champions, who believe that it is essential that a good dairy cow should be utterly worthless for beef, and that her calves of either sex should be equally worthless for veal when young, or for beef when older. We confess to a firm belief in the idea of breeding for a special purpose, but we do not intend to allow the belief to close our eyes to facts and to evidence, and that in the Holstein-Friesian cow the very highest dairy quality exists, together with the power to take on flesh readily when dry, and to produce a calf superior to the calves of any other breed, for beef, is a fact fully established by indisputable evidence.

What the farmer wants is the cow that will bring him the most net cash. He cares not whether it is called a special or general purpose cow. To any such farmer seeking light as to the best breed for his purpose, we would ask these questions: Of two cows of different breeds, each netting her owner the same amount from dairy products annually, is it really a disadvantage to one cow that if she loses her udder she will bring for beef $25 more than the other? Of two such cows, is it really a disadvantage to one that she will produce a calf capable of being vealed at a handsome profit? Is it really a disadvantage to a dairy breed that any of its two-year-old heifers proving unsatisfactory in the dairy (and there is no breeder of any breed who does not occasionally draw a blank) can be beefed for a remunerative price? Special purpose champions are too prone to assume that all calves will be heifers, and all heifers profitable cows, and all cows endure the work of the dairy to good old age. They are also fond of assuming that the highest dairy quality is entirely incompatible with any beef producing capacity. To a very important extent the facts are against them.

The late Dudley Miller, the widely known fancier and expert in Holstein-Friesian cattle, writing in February, 1886, says: "No breed of cattle is superior to the Holstein-Friesian for veal; and they and their grades make most excellent beef; juicy, tender and well interlarded with fat.

"The weight of full blood and grade steers at a year and a half or two years old can be put at 1,200 to 1,500 lbs., consequently they can be made to show a handsome profit when bred for beef.

"At birth calves weigh from 80 to 125 lbs. and much heavier are mentioned, but 100 lbs. is not unusual. Cows should weigh 1,200 to 1,400 lbs. and frequently reach 1,600 to 1,800 lbs., and some as high as 2,000 and 2,100 lbs. Bulls and steers

JACOB 2D. FROM A HOLLAND PHOTOGRAPH.
Grandson of Rooker and out of Trintje, No. 35 N. H. B., and the sire of Neptune, De Ruiter, Jacob Wit, Jacob 3d, the great sires of the Aaggie family.

have attained weights of 3,500 lbs. and upwards. The gain in weight by calves of this breed is unprecedented. They frequently gain 100 lbs. per month until about a year old."

At the experiment station of the Michigan Agricultural College, when two each of Galloways, Shorthorns, Holstein-Friesians, Jerseys, and one Hereford and one Devon were selected, and an accurate record kept for seven months of food consumed, daily ration, monthly weight and gains, it was found that the two Holstein-Friesians had the largest gain per day for a given time, and one of the greatest gains per day since birth. It required seven pounds and a fraction of a mixture of food to produce an increase of a pound in weight of Holsteins, and more than ten pounds of the same mixture to produce the same increase in the Shorthorns. The Holstein-Friesians showed themselves the most economical feeders of all that were in the test.

The Fat Stock Show usually held at Chicago has for its object the encouragement of the most economical production of the best quality of meat. The large premiums offered and the emulation among breeders and feeders attract in large numbers each succeeding year to the American Fat Stock Show the choicest specimens of meat producing animals to be found on either continent. The live stock entered for competition at this show most creditably represents the best breeders of England, Scotland and the United States. As the Holstein-Friesian is generally classed and developed as a dairy breed it is not to be expected that entries of them "for competition" with the beef breeds would be numerous.

At the Fat Stock Show in 1886 there were twelve entries in the yearling carcass class. The Holstein steer stood second, weighing 1,250 lbs.; average gain per day since birth, 2.02 lbs.

In rapidity of growth they are seldom equalled, and an example of marvelous growth at the show of 1888 was the calf Ohio Champion, entered for competition by Mr. B. Waddel, of Marion, Ohio. The calf was but nine months old and weighed 1,070 lbs. He attracted marked attention. The feeding possibilities of the breed are thus called to the attention of beef growers. Among the fat cattle butchered at the Chicago Fat Show it was found that Holsteins were the only breed that had the hindquarters heavier than the forequarters. Now it is generally granted that hindquarter beef is the best and most expensive.

At the Fat Stock Show, Chicago, 1890, the heifer Daisy was 285 days old, and weighed 850 lbs., the gain per day was 2.98 lbs.; and the steer Alpine Boy, 197 days old, weighed 495 lbs., or a gain of 2.51 lbs. per day since birth. At this same show, Ben Johnson, 1,298 days old, weighed 1,945 lbs.; Rattler, 1,319 days old, weighed 2,085 lbs.; Madolyn's Leader, 822 days old, weighed 1,470 lbs.; Tom, 789 days old, weighed 1,320 lbs.; Van Asmus, 597 days old, weighed 1,170 lbs.; and Spot, 688 days old, weighed 1,435 lbs. These were all pure-bred Holstein-Friesians, and their weight and gain per day show that they are excellent beef animals.

The claims of the Holstein-Friesian breed as a beef-producer have been presented at this show for a number of years past, but never so strongly as on this occasion (Fat Stock Show, 1890), says the Breeders Gazette. While the numbers of the exhibits were not large it included the best representative of the breed from a beef standpoint yet seen, unless the wonderfully ripe and meaty calf Ohio Champion be excepted. The exhibitors were Mr. B. Waddel, Marion, O., and Mr. M. L. Sweet. Grand Rapids, Mich. A pair of three-year-olds were forward, from which Mr. Imboden selected Mr. Sweet's Ben Johnson as the better. He is a growthy, heavy fellow, large of frame, and carries quite a thick carcass of lean beef. He was better-backed than Mr. Waddel's nicely-finished Rattler, being wider in his spring of rib and better covered on his loin and rib. Positions were reversed in the two-year-olds, as the types of steers shown were also reversed—Mr. Waddel leading with Thomas, a shorter, thicker, wider bullock than Mr. Sweet's level, rather rangy Madolyn's Leader. Thomas has a square, level quarter and is well-meated in his loins Mr. Waddel's spayed yearling heifer Spot was the best of the breed on exhibition by all odds. She is remarkably smooth, neat and deep-fleshed, and should make a very handsome carcass. She was given the blue over Sweet's Van Asmus. Waddel's Daisy, full sister to Ohio Champion, and a calf of much promise, had the ticket in her class over Sweet's Alpine Boy.

JEWEL, No. 668 H. H. B.

Imported. Milk record, ten months, 14,466 lbs. 8 oz.; ten days, 713 lbs. 4 oz.; one day, 85 lbs. 8 oz. Butter record, 20 lbs. 3 oz. in seven days.

Steer or spayed cow three and under four years.					Steer or spayed heifer one and under two years.				
Exhibitor.	Animal.	Age in days, Nov. 13, 1880.	Weight Nov. 13, 1880.	Average gain per day in pounds since birth.	Exhibitor.	Animal.	Age in days, Nov. 13, 1880.	Weight Nov. 13, 1880.	Average gain per day in pounds since birth.
M. L. Sweet,	Ben Johnson,	1293	1945	1.50	M. L. Sweet,	Van Asmus,	597	1170	1.96
B. Waddel,	Rattler,	1319	2085	1.58	B. Waddel,	Spot,	698	1485	2.08
Steer or spayed heifer two and under three years.					Steer or spayed heifer under one year.				
M. L. Sweet,	Madolyn's Leader,	822	1470	1.79	M. L. Sweet,	Alpine Boy,	197	495	2 51
B. Waddel,	Tom,	780	1330	1 68	B. Waddel.	Daisy,	285	850	2.98

The experimental feeding of half-breed yearling steers at the "Record Farm" of William M. Singerly of Philadelphia, Pa., is thus reported January 30, 1886.

We present a statement of the fattening capacity of four half-breed yearling Holstein steers. These cattle were born in May and June, 1884, and will be two years old in May and June, 1886. They demonstrate that the Holsteins will, in the near future be as much sought after for their beef-producing abilities as they are now for their milk-giving capacity. It is believed that these steers can be made to average 1,500 lbs. each by July 1, 1886.

The progress in cattle feeding is as great, if not greater than in the development of trotting horses. For a three-year-old trotter a mile in 2:19, or a two-year-old a mile in 2:28 is so exceptional as to be phenomenal, but in cattle breeding and feeding the advancement is even more notable. A herd can now be made to gain in weight at a rate which would have excited wonder ten years ago. The four-year-old steers that could be made to average 1,400 or 1,500 lbs. were thought to have been successfully fed; today a feeder who cannot successfully turn his steers off with that weight at two-years-old had better get out of the business as being unfitted for it.

The four half-breed steers at the Record Farm were taken from pasture December 4, 1885. The figures in the first column of the table given below show the weight of each steer when put on stall-feed, and the figures in the second column give the weight of each individual on the 22d inst.

```
                 Dec. 4, 1885.      Jan. 22, 1886.
No. 1, . . . .    875 lbs.           1,035 lbs.
No. 2, . . . .    835  "             1,080  "
No. 3, . . . .    880  "             1,045  "
No. 4, . . . .    750  "               885  "
        Total, .  3,340              4,045
```

Gain in 40 days, 705 lbs.; average gain per head, 176 lbs.; average gain per head per day, 3 6 lbs.

"The beef of these Holstein cattle from the Record Farms was slaughtered at the North Philadelphia Stock Yards and placed on sale at John Riley's stalls in the Farmers market, and the splendid meat attracted much admiration. The four steers and the heifer made more pounds of dressed meat for their age than any cattle ever killed in Philadelphia. The live and dead weights, and the number of pounds of dressed to the one hundred pounds of live weight were as follows: Steer No. 1, 1,475 lbs. and 899 and 6; No. 2, 1,450 lbs. 940 and 65; No. 3, 1,550 lbs. 978 and 63; No. 4, 1,350 lbs. 850 and 63; the heifer 1,500 lbs. 996 and 66; the cow 1,725 lbs. 1.104 and 64. The following figures show the weight by quarters, the first two being the hind and the last two the fore quarters: Steer No. 1, 218, 211, 236, 234; No. 2, 213, 210, 256, 261; No. 3, 220, 224, 268, 266; No. 4, 202, 197, 225, 226; the heifer, 224, 233, 270, 269; the cow, 255, 254, 296, 299."

The Smiths & Powell Co. write: In the winter of 1884 and 1885 we caused to be slaughtered the recorded Holstein bull, Syracuse (822), calved April 24,

JEWEL 2D, No. 1119 H. H. B.

1882; the recorded cow, Signet (1817), calved April 6, 1880, and Little Wonder (1788), calved May 14, 1880, with the following result:

Syracuse weighed on day of killing, 2,200 lbs. Dressed beef, 1,430 lbs.; hide, 142 lbs.; rough tallow, 130 lbs. Per cent of dressed beef, 62.44 lbs. Per cent of offal, 26.

Signet weighed alive, 1,470 lbs. Dressed beef, 915 lbs.; hide, 76 lbs.; rough tallow, 126 lbs. Per cent of dressed beef, 62.31. Per cent of offal, 24.

Little Wonder weighed alive, 1,493 lbs. Dressed beef, 791 lbs.; hide, 78 lbs.; rough tallow, 124 lbs. Per cent of dressed beef, 52.93. Per cent of offal, 33.

Syracuse and Little Wonder had not been fattened for beef, and Signet we had fed for some time, but she was not what beef men would regard fat.

Taking everything into consideration we think this shows decidedly to the advantage of Holsteins as beef animals.

The butchers that purchased and cut up the carcasses of Signet and Little Wonder send us the following strong testimonial as to the quality of the beef of these two cows:

SYRACUSE, N. Y., Feb. 11, 1885.

Messrs. Smiths & Powell.

GENTLEMEN: We were much pleased with the two Holstein heifers purchased of you last month. We have been in the meat business for the last twenty-five years and have killed all grades of cattle, the best we could find in this country, but never have we had any that would equal in quality those purchased of you. We had a great many compliments from the leading families of the city in regard to Holstein beef. Respectfully,

W. & J. FAGE,
49 Warren St.

The imported Holstein bull, Ebbo, five years old, was killed at the Remington Farm in Cazenovia:

Weighed, alive, day of killing, 2,260 lbs. Dressed beef, 1,313 lbs.; hide, 156 lbs.; rough tallow, 75 lbs. Per cent of dressed beef, 58¼.

Holstein steers have proved very profitable for feeding. J. S. Lang, writing from North Vassalboro, Me., says: " My experience with half-bloods has been very gratifying; they outstrip all others in growth on the same food, steers averaging in girth at eighteen months six feet, seven inches. My experiments have been conducted with care, and my conviction is, that to institute an impartial test of Holsteins and Shorthorns, it would be found that the Holstein stock would cost the least per pound." As Holsteins have been recently introduced into the West, but little has been done in testing their value strictly for beef, as the best grade bulls have been kept for breeding; but as far as they have been tried, have given good satisfaction.

Half-blood steers in Illinois have attained a weight of over 1,300 lbs. at two years old, and 1,900 lbs. at four years old.

Gray & Van Waters, West Salem, Wis., report as follows: We sold one yoke of half-blood Holsteins, two years and three months old, weighing 2,650 lbs. Andy McEldowny sold thirteen head of half-bloods average two years and three months, average weight 1,345 lbs. The man who bought them said he had bought and shipped cattle for twenty years and they were the best lot he had ever shipped. The oldest of the thirteen was two years and four months old, and weighed 1,600 lbs. They were sold to Daniel Cargle of Sparta, and brought in Milwaukee $5.50 per 100 lbs.

Amos Edmunds, Disco, Ill., writes: I shall give the experience of a few practical feeders as to the fattening qualities of Holstein steers.

I have sold a great many grade steers of this breed to feeders in this vicinity, and all have given satisfaction.

During the winter of 1883–4 L. C. Maynard & Sons of La Harpe, Ill., who are practical men, also perfectly reliable in all respects, fed several grade Holstein steers in the same feed yard with high grade Shorthorns, and they informed the writer that the Holsteins made as large a growth and fatted as readily as the Shorthorns, in fact, they said their best steer, according to their judgment, was a Holstein from my herd. This firm have always bred Shorthorn cattle, but they claim they would just as soon buy a good grade Holstein to feed as a good Shorthorn. I have heard other practical feeders make the same statement.

J. B. Fort of Olena, Ill., raised a carload of grade Holsteins that were sired

by a bull that the writer once owned. They were fed till they were two years old and shipped to Chicago, and brought within ten cents per hundred pounds of the top of the market. Every experienced shipper knows that it takes choice steers to bring them within ten cents of the top of the market, especially after they have been shipped over 200 miles. This entire carload was purchased by an exporter and shipped to England.

William K. Gittings, a neighbor to the writer and a large farmer and stock breeder, says that he never fed a steer of any breed that gave any better satisfaction than a three-fourths Holstein that came from my herd. I could name many other reliable men who have fed Holstein steers with splendid results. The butchers in this vicinity claim that they never slaughtered better beef animals than some grade Holsteins that I sold them.

Now of course some Holsteins are much better formed for beef than others, and some strains of families will fatten better than others.

I have seen some Holstein cows that were as well formed for beef as the best quality of Shorthorns, in fact the writer owns a few such, and my observation and experience is, that they are as deep milkers as those of the so-called milk form.

This assertion may provoke some discussion as the popular opinion is, that a cow of superior beef form cannot be a deep milker.

There are a great many theories and opinions advanced as to deep milkers that are not true, and this is one of them. It is true, however, that a great many deep milkers are of inferior form for beef, but all deep milkers are not of this class. My plan and advice is, to breed for beef as well as milk, and I find that it can be done without injuring in the least the milk and butter producing qualities. My experience and observation is that the shape of a cow has very little to do with her dairy qualities. There are other points that figure more than form, such as good constitution, good appetite, good digestive powers, large paunch, well developed udder and milk veins.

A cow may possess all these points and yet have a splendid form for beef.

In 1880, Judge William Fullerton of New York, writing on the subject of Holsteins for beef, in answer to a Mr. Wright, said:

Those who have seen these splendid cattle, either in this country or in their native polders, would readily conclude upon reading Mr. Wright's article that he had never had the good fortune to see one of them. I have seen tens of thousands of them in Holland, and if they were to be judged by their appearance alone, they would compare favorably with the general average of Shorthorn, either in England or this country. I spent one whole day in examining the cattle at the late Paris Exhibition, and in general appearance the Holstein divided the honors with the best specimens of Shorthorns which England could produce. In size they excelled them; in capacity for taking on flesh they seemed to be quite their equal, and for milking qualities were unapproachable. The owners of the best Shorthorns exhibited were among the principal admirers of these Holsteins. The Hollanders seemed to be quite satisfied with them in every respect, for while London has large daily supplies of beef from Holland, I failed to find a single Shorthorn in the latter country.

For making veal the Holstein stands without a peer. It is very seldom that a calf will consume the milk that a dam gives. The result is that the calves grow rapidly and fatten quickly. If Mr. Wright could stand on the wharf at Flushing in Holland, as I have done, and see a steamboat depart for the London market loaded with veal calves, which for size and condition surpassed anything he ever dreamed of, he would conclude that the English people had a better opinion of the Holsteins than he has. And if he will take the trouble to visit a herd of Holsteins of which I could tell him in this country, numbering now about one hundred head, he would see a number of cows, each of which will turn the scales at 1,600 lbs., and the bull that will do it quickly at 3,000 lbs. He will acknowledge that their hides are no insignificant item in their owners' balance sheet, and he will be forced to conclude from manipulation that there is an ample supply of beef and tallow within them. It is of no use to decry the Holsteins, for they are a very valuable breed of cattle, and will inevitably make their mark in this country. When a cow will give from twenty to forty quarts of milk daily, and when too old for the dairy will yield as much beef and tallow as a Shorthorn, she is not to be despised.

In 1896 the first prize in the beef class at the State Fair of Minnesota was taken by a Holstein. The first prize beef cow weighed 1,965 lbs.

JOHANNA No. 344 H. H. B.

Imported in 1878 as best milch cow recorded in Netherland Herd Book. Milk record, 88 lbs. in one day; 2,407 lbs. 12 oz. in thirty-one days.

H. & W. Bollert, Cassel, Ont., write: We had an opportunity of testing a pure-bred Holstein-Friesian heifer for beef this fall, 1896. She was imported as a calf from North Holland in June, 1883, and was the smallest among the importation. We purchased her in October of the same year, and gave her ordinary good care that winter, and nothing but grass during the summer. Finding then that she had not bred, we kept her thin the next two winters (thinking by this method we could start her to breed). She received no grain whatever during this time. Her feed consisted of straw, chaff and a little corn fodder. Finding now that she would not breed, we concluded to feed her. We stall-fed her just four months and then sold her to Mr. Ben Johnson of Stratford, Ont., for Xmas beef. She was now three years and eight months old and weighed 1,880 lbs. During the last sixty-three days she made a gain of exactly 4 lbs. per day.

She was the best feeder we ever saw of any breed and would easily have carried from 300 to 400 lbs. of beef more if she had been thoroughly fatted. We are thoroughly pleased with the result, and believe that Holsteins can hold their own (even as beefers).

Daniel E. Bandman of Missoula, Mont., writes: For Montana, Shorthorn and Polled Angus are no earthly use; Holsteins are the cattle for us. They milk well and make magnificent beef.

Holstein breeders of the West are well aware of the fact that buyers of feeding cattle discriminate against our breed when selecting their herds for the feed lot. The question has often been asked, why is it? Mr. W. F. Whitney of Mexico, Mo., thus explains: There can be but one answer. When a buyer visits your herd, he does so with the determination to buy for as little money as possible. He knows that at least one-half of the profit in feeding a bunch of cattle is made in the buying, hence it is that he is on the lookout to pick out the flaws in what you offer for sale. He never calls your attention to the best in the lot, and be they ever so even in condition, size and form, if there happens to be a few black-and-white steers, be they Holsteins or of another breed, he is ready to point them out and say something like this: "Well, friend, you have a very nice lot of steers, just such as I am looking for; but I cannot pay your price unless you cut out those black-and-white fellows over there." He knows the objection the farmer has to dividing his cattle, especially when such a division leaves only a few head on his hands. "But," says the farmer, "what's the matter with those steers? Are they not as large and in as good condition and form as the others?" "Well, yes; but they are Holsteins, and when I get to market with them the buyers there will cut the price on them, so if you can not cut them out I can not buy them except you take off $1.00 per head on the bunch." "The cat is out of the bag." The farmer takes off $1.00 per head, cusses the Holsteins up one side and down the other, tells his neighbor if it hadn't been for Holsteins in his lot of cattle, he would have sold for one dollar more on the head. The buyer drives the cattle to his feed lot, very much gratified at the shrewd trick he has played, weighs up the cattle to see what price per cwt. they have cost him, and in so doing, he weighs the black-and-whites separately, puts them all in together and feeds for the market. When he ships out he again weighs up to ascertain what gain in weight his cattle have made. Again he weighs the Holsteins separately and finds that they have gained more pounds per head than any cattle in the lot. Do the market buyers cut the price on his cattle on account of the Holsteins? Well, they may try the same shrewd scheme that he made work so well on the farmer, but the cattle feeder has been to market with cattle before this time and he knows the game too well to let them play him for a "sucker." He knows there is no material difference in the cattle, one is as fat as the other and will dress as much per cwt., live weight, so he declines. The cattle are sold, the hides taken off, and no man on earth can tell which is the Holstein or which is the Shorthorn beef. I have fed cattle for the market and have bought and sold cattle of beef breeds, and am competent to at least judge within a narrow margin of the difference in the value of two beef animals if placed side by side. Some time since I shipped a carload of Holsteins from Kansas into Missouri, and while waiting reshipment in the Kansas City yards, I had the pleasure of meeting a cattle feeder from Eastern Kansas. He was shipping to the Chicago market three cars of four-year-old cattle, every one of which was fully matured and weighed an average of over 1,700 lbs. This gentleman told me that he had bought this lot of cattle when they were two years old, hence he had owned them for two years. They had been pastured and fed together; he had weighed them at intervals during the time he had owned them, commencing at the time of purchase, and in every particular each animal had the same opportunity to grow and fatten. These cattle, strange to say, were made up of Grade Shorthorns, Herefords, Polled Angus and Holsteins, about equally divided as to breeds. In answer to my questions as to the beef and feeding qualities of the Holsteins compared with the beef breeds, he stated that the Holsteins in this lot of cattle had gained in weight from 125 to 375 lbs. more than any of the others. That one Holstein steer had gained 375 lbs. more than any other steer in the lot, and the lightest gain of the Holsteins was 125 lbs. more than the gain of any of the regular beef breeds. I examined these cattle closely and there was no material difference between them as to form; they all showed thick fat and were smooth and straight. I have been told by other feeders that the Holsteins would gain more pounds in a given time than any other breed. Holsteins I admit are not so smooth and symmetrical in form as the purely bred beef breeds, but they compare quite well with the general average of beef cattle that are sent to market. It is all "bosh," this thing of Holstein beef not being as good in quality as the other breeds. I have seen

JOHANNA 5TH, No. 9343 H. F. H. B.
Winner Wisconsin Butter Test of 1894.

them on the block and have it on my own table and can certify as to the good quality of a well fatted Holstein. I want no better. One word to the farmer and I am done. If you have a number of native cows, buy a first-class Holstein bull (dairy form). The progeny of the cross will be a smooth lot of steer calves that will sell to a feeder for as high a price as ordinary steer calves, provided you stand him off when he objects to color, etc. The heifer calves can be bred when 17 or 18 months old and sold to the dairymen when fresh for more money than same age steers of any breed, thereby giving you a market for your heifer increase. The native heifer, a grade of any of the beef breeds, goes begging for a buyer at two years old at $12.50 to $18.00, whereas a grade Holstein of same age will sell to the dairymen at $30 to $50. I have done this very trick and know what I say to be correct.

Mr. W. K. Sexton in an address before the Michigan Holstein Breeders meeting in 1891, said: "The butcher's block is the end of all cattle. While we call the Holstein cattle a dairy breed, we will say they are a large breed, and at the same time are rapid growers of a fine quality of very sweet beef, profitable for the consumer."

HOLSTEIN-FRIESIANS FOR BEEF. 147

J. B. Dutcher & Son, Pawling, N. Y., reported in January, 1891, the slaughter of a Holstein-Friesian cow, Netherland Jewel 3d, that won first prize as best fat cow of any breed at the New York State Fairs of 1889-90, in competition with Herefords, Shorthorns, Aberdeens, Angus, etc. Her live weight was 1,790 lbs., her beef weight, when thoroughly cooled, 1,196 lbs., which was 66.8 per cent of her live weight. The fat weighed 229 lbs.; hide, 90 lbs.; tongue, 11 lbs.; feet, 22 lbs.; and liver 17 lbs. Those to whom the beef was distributed pronounced it of most excellent quality, being juicy, rich and tender. Our experience with Holstein-Friesians not only demonstrates that they are the greatest dairy breed in exsistence, but rate high as beef animals.

Further testimony regarding the quality of Holstein beef comes from no less a judge than William J. Chittenden, of the Russell House, Detroit, writing in 1891 to Mr. Davenport, gave his opinion on the beef from the Michigan college as follows, the test having been independently made by his partner, Mr.

KONINGIN VAN FRIESLAND 5TH, No. 8302 H. H. B.
Milk record, 19,700 lbs. 1-2 oz. in one year as a three-year-old.

McCreary, by his steward and by himself: "We made a thorough test of the qualities of the beef sent to us by Mr. Dixon, with the following result: Devon first, and by all odds the best flavor; Galloway, Holstein, Hereford and Shorthorn in the order I have written. I will add that all were splendid samples of beef. I have never seen better. The poorest would satisfy me for the Russell House. The steaks were all numbered, and we each noted our own opinion, and all agreed."

But California comes with a still brighter bit of evidence in the beef line, and while we are a little bit disposed to chide the late millionaire champion of the black-and-whites on the Pacific coast, one Leland Stanford by name, for not publishing full details regarding so large an experiment as he was carrying on with Holstein steers, we must content ourselves with a Sacramento News item which is, in substance, that C. Swanton, the wholesale butcher, purchased recently (December, 1891) from the Vina ranch, Senator Stanford's Holstein cattle, fattened expressly for the Christmas market. Experts who have viewed the animals declare that no such beef cattle were ever seen in this section. They are as fat as they can roll, and will dress from 1,200 to 1,500 lbs. They have been fed for two years past for the holiday market, and are in the highest state of perfection.

Henry Stevens, of Lacona, N. Y., writes: I had a thoroughbred Holstein-Friesian cow, five years old, that I fattened. She dropped her first calf at twenty-two months old. Owing to her being over-driven, she never has bred since. I milked her until about December 1, 1887. I then fed her until May 7, 1888, when I sold her to Mr. A. R. Cook, a butcher in our village. The morning he took her away she had no grain or water. She was led to the village a distance of three miles and kept without feed or water until about four o'clock in the afternoon, when she was weighed and then butchered, only being off from hay eight hours and grain and water twenty-two hours.

Her live weight was 1,240 lbs. Her dressed weight was as follows: Meat, 690 lbs.; hide, 72 lbs.; tallow, 50 lbs. Total, 812 lbs.; shrinking 428 lbs. or about 33 1-3 per cent. This I consider a good showing when in view of the small amount of tallow she had.

Mr. Cook says he has butchered over fifteen years and never has had a nicer carcass of beef in his market, or beef that gave better satisfaction to his customers. This cow was a granddaughter of Dowager, No. 7 H. H. B., and gave as high as 40 lbs. of milk per day, after being in milk over two years. This is the only thoroughbred I ever fattened. There have been several grades butchered in my neighborhood and all gave good satisfaction. Grade Holstein-Friesian calves have no superior as veal calves.

There are many calves fattened in this section. All buyers say they find nothing equal to them and I think that there is no cow of any breed, when not giving milk, that will take on flesh as fast according to the amount of food consumed as the Holstein-Friesian, and I see no reason why the Holstein-Friesians do not compare favorably for beef with other breeds which are bred especially for that purpose. When we take into account their great milk and butter qualities, they in my opinion far excel any other breed as a general purpose cow.

Gus Head, of Alton Junction, near Alton, Ill., writes: "I sold three two-year-old half-blood Holstein steers last week for Easter beeves, and they made quite a stir in Alton as they passed through the bustling old city. One weighed 1,780, the second 1,640, and third, 1,570 lbs. The leading butchers of Alton, who killed nothing but the very best, say they were as fine beeves as they ever handled. The steers were from common cows, were nearly three years old, had been fed in an open lot, were never in a barn or had any extra care save plenty of feed."

At this rate the Holstein-Friesians or their crosses approach nearer the "all purpose cattle" than any other breed.

Tyson Bros., Berlin, Ont., write: The meat is of uniform color, firm and light in color, the fat white. They are invariably large for their age. We have killed last season calves of 3¼ weeks old which weighed 120 lbs. dressed veal, and 4¼ weeks old which weighed 140 lbs. These were grades. We have also killed quite a number of high-grade and half-bred heifers. They killed well and dressed well, with very little loss in dressing. The meat is fine in the grain, and the fat firm and white. Taking them as a class, they are, in my opinion, far ahead of any of the milking strains, on account of their size and color of beef and veal. The grade calves are very large and fat for their age, and, provided a calf is raised and does not prove a good milker, the animal is large enough to make a good carcass of dressed beef, and bring a good price from the butcher.

William Burton, Brampton, Ont., writes: In reference to the Holstein heifer I got from you last year, I beg to inform you that I was well pleased with it, both as regards weight (862 lbs.) and quality, it being one of the best I have killed since I have been in this country. I have killed a great many of the same breed in England, both as beef and veal, and always found them give good satisfaction. Should you feed any more at any time, kindly give me the offer of them, and I will give you the highest market value for them.

R. Marshall, Edmonton, Ont., writes: A grade Holstein calf raised by me in 1891 weighed 530 lbs. at five months of age. He was a splendid feeder, and took on flesh rapidly, evenly and economically.

William Lang, Sundridge, Ont., writes: I have butchered several of the grade Holsteins, and found them the best of their age I have ever killed. The beef is of the best quality. I killed a calf which I bought from Mr. J. Paget which dressed 350 lbs., it being only seven months old, and was fed only in the common way.

J. A. Awell, Newcastle, Ont., writes: I am pleased to be able to chronicle my testimony in favor of your Holstein breed of calves for vealing purposes, having purchased one from H. A. Adams, Esq. At four weeks old it weighed 145 lbs. dessed, the meat being of good quality and giving entire satisfaction.

James Coulson. Newcastle, Ont., writes: I bought a calf from Mr. H. A. Adams, bred from Hienise's King, which weighed alive at four weeks old 197 lbs., the meat of which gave me entire satisfaction, being a good color, and cut to good advantage, and I might add that I never had as good a calf in every particular of any other breed.

KONINGIN VAN FRIESLAND PIETERTJE.

Mr. George W. Knorr, Clarks Station, Ky., in a prize article which appeared in the Holstein-Friesian Register, March 1, 1802, said: "When Holstein calves are fed with the same care that cows are fed, very satisfactory weights are obtained, equalling or even surpassing those of any beef breed. I do not profess much skill in this line, in fact am just beginning to learn; yet my veals rarely fall below 150 lbs. in weight at six weeks old, and frequently attain 200 lbs. The heaviest veals I have obtained so far were one which weighed 210 lbs. at seven weeks, and another 220 at five weeks. (This last, however, had the phenomenal weight of 124 lbs. at birth to start with.) My skim-milk—separator-skimmed—when fed to calves, returns three and four cents per gallon. Poor produce will fetch poor prices, good produce good prices, and extra good produce extra good prices. This applies to everything sold off of the farm, and to veal as well. Every Holstein calf has the stuff in it to make extra good veal, with proper care, and will realize prices accordingly. My neighbor has to haul to market four 90-lb. calves of indifferent color, for every one which I sell."

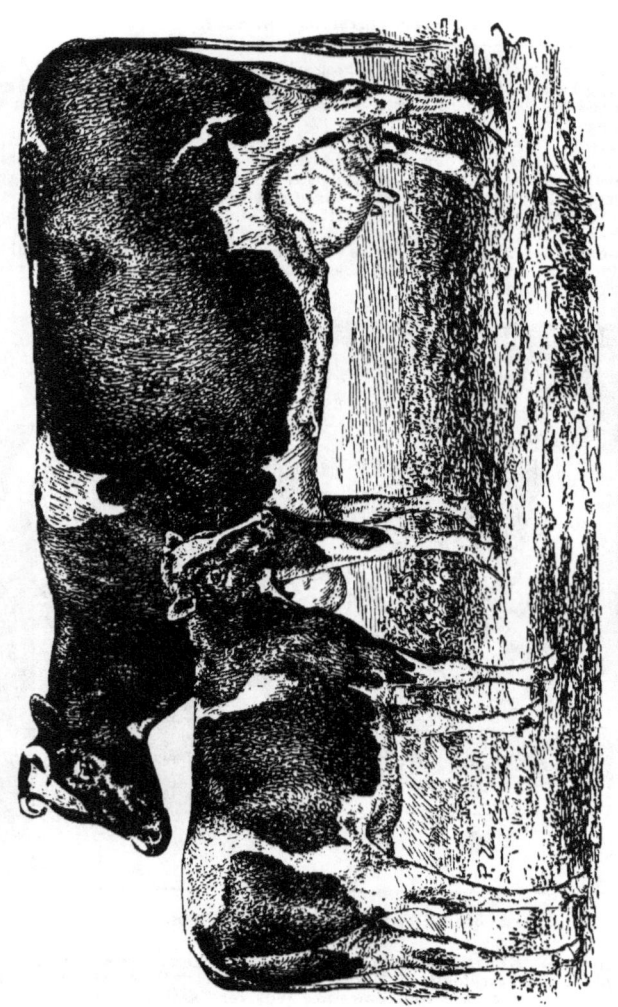

LADY DE VRIES, No. 4056 H. H. B.
Imported. Milk record, 81 lbs. in one day; 18,963 lbs. 4 oz. in one year.

J. V. Cotta & Sons, Nursery, Ill., write (September 15, 1894): "We have had what we believe to be the largest bull-calf on record. He weighed at birth 132 lbs. fair and square. He is another proof of the old saying that 'blood will tell,' his sire being Sir Aaggie Clothilde, 7667, bred by Smiths, Powell & Lamb. Sir Aaggie Clothilde is sired by Clothilde 4th Imperial, that Isaac Damon described as 'colossal in size and a perfect Apollo,' dam of Sir Aaggie Clothilde is Aaggie Lee, a daughter of Napoleon, by Jacob 2d. Aaggie Lee has a butter record of 21 lbs. 5 oz. in 7 days at four years of age. The dam of our great calf is Blanche W., 5228 H. H. B. Her sire, John Clay, 947, a son of Sligo, 621, and Maud Clay, making him a half brother to Lady Baker. Blanche W.'s dam is Memento 2d, 875, a daughter of Pilgrim, 317, consequently a half sister to the great cow Rijaneta. Besides having such great blood back of him, and being colossal in size to start on, this great calf is one of the best individuals we have ever seen."

George M. Westfall of Stockbridge, Mich., reports that his cow Stockbridge Maid, 8826 H. F., on October 23, 1891, dropped a calf weighing 143 lbs. at birth.

H. Fulstone of Carson City, Nevada, writes: I find the Holsteins beat anything for veal I ever raised.

Mr. W. H. Logan, of Seaton, Ill., reports a bull calf from a heifer two years old, which weighed 102 lbs. at birth.

Mr. Jonathan Miller, Nunda, N. Y., reports a bull calf from an imported cow, which at birth weighed 125 lbs. and 194 lbs. when two weeks old.

Mr. B. G. Packard, of Rome, N. Y., reports a male calf which weighed at birth 120 lbs.

Mr. James C. Cobb, of Dodd City, Texas, reports a calf from a two-year-old heifer that weighed 75 lbs. at birth, and at two weeks old weighed 112 lbs., showing a gain of 2¼ lbs. per day.

Cram Bros., Colfax, Wash., write: King Barrington, 2741 H. H. B., weighed at birth 120 lbs., and January 3, 1887, the day on which he was nine months old he turned the scales at 1,014 lbs. This calf had been shipped from New York state to Washington when ten weeks old and confined in transit fourteen days. The gain made was over 3¼ lbs. per day since birth.

Mr. Albert French, president Hamilton County Agricultural Society of Cincinnati, Ohio, in an address before Hamilton County Institute, said: Some of our calves have gained from 90 to 100 lbs. per month, and the males will average an increase of 3 lbs. per day for the first year.

The Holland veal is of great renown, the London market being largely supplied from this source. Calves are shipped in great numbers to Detford on the Thames, at which place they are slaughtered for market.

Newton Bros. of State Center, Iowa, report the weight of bull calf Marquis of Salisbury, 1048 H. F. H. B., as follows: At birth before taking milk, 116 lbs.; at six months, 730 lbs.; on day he was ten months old he weighed 1,012 lbs. 8 oz. This was an average growth of 3¼ lbs. per day.

L. E. Steinmetz, of Carthage, Mo., reports one calf 104 days old that weighed 365 lbs.; another 110 days old weighed 340 lbs.

Mr. E. P. Beauchamp, of Terre Haute, Ind.,writes. All butchers who have had any experience with Holstein bullocks and calves give them a decided preference over all other breeds. The Holstein calves are by far superior to all other breeds both on account of their size and fine fibrous solid flesh. In no case have the calves from my cows weighed less than 80 lbs. at birth and in several cases as high as 115 lbs.

H. C. Jewett & Co., of Buffalo, N. Y., report weight of the calf Ofanto, 1155 H. F. H. B., at six months of age as 702 lbs.

Professor Morrow reports the following comparative experiments with calves in Rural New Yorker, 1886, of different breeds for six months on grass alone, also on a like grain ration. In giving figures we quote the grain fed always first: Ayrshires, 405 and 280; Herefords, 400 and 263; Holsteins, 515 and 530; Shorthorns, 400 and 250. Showing a marked superiority for the Holsteins.

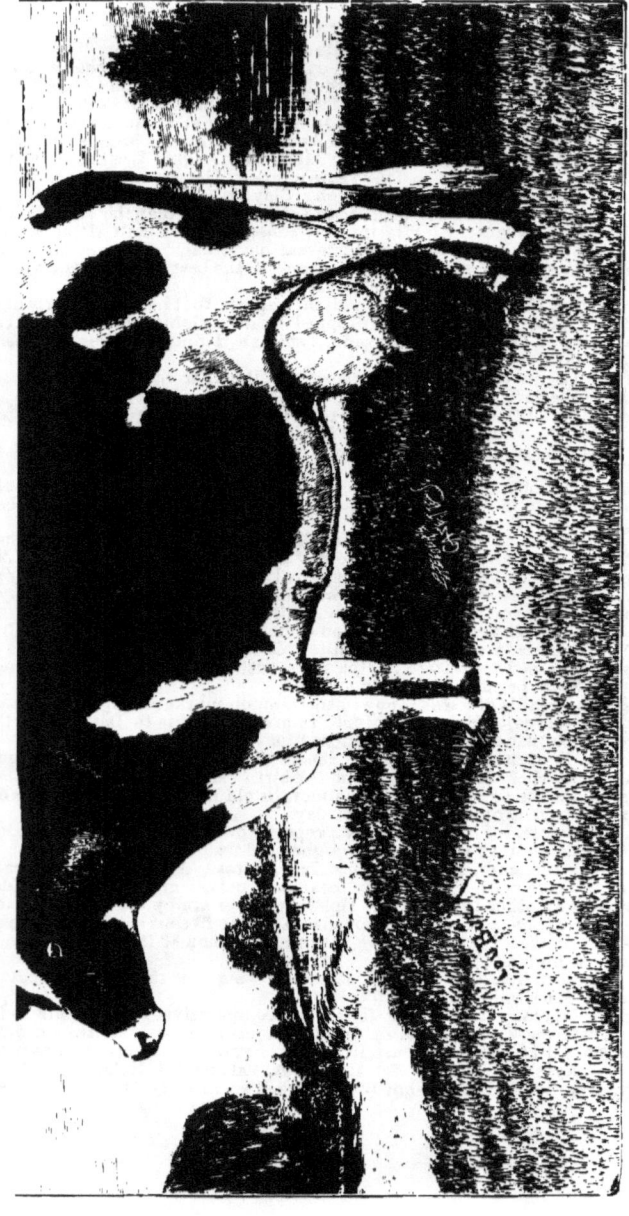

LADY OF BROEK 2D, No.2709 H. H. B.

Milk record, 11,187 lbs. 1 oz. in eight months and six days; 88 lbs. in one day. Butter record, 20 lbs. 3 1-2 oz in seven days.

CHAPTER XVIII.

AS A GENERAL PURPOSE CATTLE.

If the Holstein-Friesian is large and makes a good animal; if she gives immense quantities of rich milk; if her milk makes an abundance of good butter and cheese at a low relative cost for food consumed; if she matures early and breeds freely, then it must be conceded that she is more valuable than the cow that possesses only one or two of these qualities.

There has been much random talk against the general purpose cow. One says it is a dream not to be realized, another that it is a fraud, and that it does not pay to buy a poor milker for your dairy because she will make good beef when you have milked her eight or ten years. And still another says those looking for the general purpose cow do not seem to realize that the highest excellence has been reached only on the line of specialties, and that we cannot combine the milk form and beef producing form in the same animal any more than we can secure in the same horse the best running form and the best draft form. An able writer and editor of one of our best dairy papers says that a cow must be for one thing or the other, for a special purpose or else a failure, and also that nine-tenths of the farmers want a combination of milk, cheese, butter and beef in the same cow, and that is a humbug.

What is a general purpose horse?

Is it the one that is the fleetest runner, the greatest trotter, the strongest draft, the most stylish carriage horse, all combined?

Or is it the horse that excels in none of these specialties, and is more useful than all others, the farm horse, with which to plough, cultivate, harvest and thrash our grain, draw it to the mill, drive twenty or thirty miles a day before buggy or carriage, or saddle and run for the doctor? Will any one say that this horse is a humbug because it is first for no special purpose?

Put your thoroughbred to a plough, your draft horse under the saddle or before a carriage, your Maud S. to draw a load of grain to the mill, and it will readily be seen that the general purpose horse is superior to any of these for all these uses.

What is the general purpose cow that nine-tenths of the farmers want?

Is it one which excels all others in any particular branch, such as producing the greatest quantity or best quality of milk, cheese, butter or beef?

Or is it that cow which is profitable for each of these purposes, without excelling in any one?

Any breed of cows which can be profitably kept for these various uses deserves the name of general purpose cow. Nine-tenths of the farmers are right in wanting a general purpose cow.

When the market is glutted with milk cheese can be made, when cheese is low they can make butter, and if by accident a cow is crippled or is getting on in years, she can be profitably turned to beef, as well as her bull calves.

The wise and prudent farmer, by breeding general purpose cows, runs far less risk than he whose eggs are all in one basket.

The Holstein-Friesian, whose frame is large and well adapted to producing beef, is also superior for the dairy. This breed is nearly, if not quite, as large as those specially bred for beef, and has excelled all others in early maturity, which is of great advantage to the beef producer. No breed of cattle has ever enjoyed the reputation earned by Holstein-Friesians as great milkers nor as cheese producers.

The entire province of North Holland is devoted almost exclusively to cheese making, and in Friesland the principal occupation of the people is butter making.

The Holstein-Friesian also excels as a butter cow. In America many of the largest butter records have been made by them, both individually and also entire herds, when competing with a special purpose cow, and all others, including the famous Jersey.

From the above facts it is evident that the general purpose cow is not only no dream, no humbug, no fraud, but the most useful of all breeds.

The Holstein-Friesian surpasses all others as a general purpose breed, not only because it is profitable for milk, for butter and for beef, but for the reason it has excelled in each and all of these specialties.

Without disparaging other breeds, it must be admitted that the Holstein-Friesian has won its way in this country to popular favor in a remarkably short period of time and to a remarkable degree. It has done this in the face of stronger prejudices and fiercer criticisms than any other breed has ever encountered. It could not have done this without possessing peculiar qualities and adaptations that answered to a wide demand. Foremost among these is its ready adaptation to more than one purpose. Theorists may condemn a "general purpose" cow and by such peculiar logic as "that a draft horse cannot be a race horse or a dump cart a trotting sulky," draw the inference that a superior dairy cow cannot be a good beefing animal, but the fact remains that our dairymen are demanding just such an animal, and that the most popular breeds of the

LAKESIDE CLARISSA, No. 9916 H. H. B.; ADVANCED REGISTRY.
Imported. Milk record, 7,776 lbs. 15 oz. in ten months. Butter record, 12 lbs. 12 oz. in seven days.

world have been characterized by this double adaptation, writes S. Hoxie. Such a breed was the original Shorthorns of England and the early Shorthorns of this country, and such are now the most highly-valued breeds of Belgium, France, Switzerland and Germany. Practical dairymen all over the world have a predilection for such breeds, founded on their necessities and experiences. The Holstein-Friesian is just such a breed. It is a milk and beef breed, the milking qualities leading. In structure the general type is milk and beef form. This involves the lateral wedge shape of the milk form, with the broad, level loins, hips and rump, and rounded body of the beef form. There is nothing in such a body, or in such loins, hips and rump to preclude in the slightest degree the most extraordinary productions of milk or butter.

Its constitutional vigor has also had much to do with its success. Dairymen as a class want vigorous cattle as much as the ranchmen. Especially is this the case with those who handle large herds and who push in every available direction for the largest profits. Vigorous cows can be fattened with comparative ease, should anything occur to stop them from producing milk. If there is a demand for veal, vigorous cows produce large and healthy calves. Vigorous cows need comparatively little care, they make the most of their food and quickly respond to generous feeding. Another characteristic of this breed by which it has won popular favor, is its marked docility. Dairymen do not want nervous cattle, all the fine-spun theories to the contrary. They want cattle that will quietly feed under whatever circumstances they may be placed and then quietly digest their food. Nervous excitability is always a waster of the elements of food that go to make milk, butter and beef. Another of its peculiarities is its ready adaptation to all sorts of climate. It is profitably used in the climate of France and Italy, and at the same time in the climate of Northern Russia, under the Arctic Circle. It readily adapts itself to the conditions of all localities where food is plenty, excepting extremely mountainous districts. Its limbs are too light as compared with its weight of body for such districts.

LUTSCKE, No. 8356 H. H. B.

Imported. Winner of gold medal and $100 from the Holstein-Friesian Association of America in 1889 for best one day milk record at any fair; yield, 73 lbs. 12 oz. First prize two-year-old at World's Exposition, Amsterdam, in 1884.

Nothing need be said here on its capacity to produce either milk or butter. Reports of its records and its triumphs in competitions with other breeds are constantly being published. Within fifteen years it has added more than one-third to the popular idea of the amount of milk that a cow may be made to produce, and the limit is probably not yet reached. In butter production it has taken no secondary place. In veal production it is unequaled. Only in beef production does it take a secondary position, yet by no means an unimportant one. It materially assists in making up a balance on the right side of a dairyman's account. There is another fact in connection with this breed, in this country, that should not be overlooked, which has had and will continue to have much to do with its success. It is largely in the hands of clear-sighted, energetic men. The leading breeders which give character and vitality to the Holstein-Friesian Association of America are progressive and are constantly improving their herds. They are breeding their cattle more and more to symmetrical forms and constantly increasing the richness of the milk. In these respects they have already far surpassed the Holland breeders. The peculiar flexibility of the breed makes it susceptible to such improvements, and the association is stimulating them. There is no indication that this policy will be changed. If it is not, we see no end to the popularity of these cattle.

One of the favorite theories of our times is that the nearer a cow approaches the technical milk form the more profitable she must necessarily be for exclusive dairy purposes. In order to test the truth of this theory let us in imagination place side by side a model of the milk form and a model of the beef form, and construct therefrom the milk and beef form, and see if we have to leave out anything of the former that is really valuable. To begin, we find that both models have fine heads and limbs, indicative of fineness of bones throughout both structures. It follows that this fineness goes into the milk and beef form. We find that in the milk form the chine is high and sharp, and in the beef form broad and flat. The latter goes into the milk and beef form. By it do we lose anything in milking ability or increase the cost of production? We think not, but rather increase the strength and vigor so essential in a profitable dairy cow.

MAID OF VERNON, No. 2372 H. H. B.; 413 ADVANCED REGISTRY.
Milk record, 68 lbs. in one day; 1741 lbs. 3 oz. in thirty days.

We also find that the loin and hips of the milk form are angular and comparatively narrow, while those of the beef form are comparatively broad, smooth and level. The latter style goes into the milk and beef form, and again we ask, by it do we lose anything in milking ability or add anything to the cost of production? Those broad, strong, level hips seem to us just the best possible frame from which a magnificent udder may be suspended. We also find that the rump of the milk form is carried out comparatively narrow and angular, while that of the beef form is broad, smooth and level to the extremity. The latter style goes into the milk and beef form, and once more we ask, by it do we lose anything in milking ability or add anything to the cost of production? Certainly not, for the pelvis is just as roomy or more so than in the milk form, and this is the essential thing at this point in a superior milch cow.

Passing downward we find the twist open and roomy in the milk form, close and full in the beef form. The former goes into the milk and beef form. We also find the lower part of the hams light in the milk form and heavy in the beef form. Again the former goes into the milk and beef form. Passing forward we find the milk form has loose, thin shoulders, a light brisket and a comparatively narrow chest, while the beef form has a broad and deep chest, a heavy brisket and broad, thick, compact shoulders. Neither of these styles go into the milk and beef form, but rather a medium between the two. The shoulders are smoother and more compact than in the milk form, but much lighter in weight than in the beef form, as also is the brisket. The chest is not so deep as in the beef form but the width through at the heart is retained. A degree of strength and vigor is thus obtained that is not found in the milk form. Only one more essential thing remains to be described. In the milk form the abdomen is swung low and its sides are steep and flat, while in the beef form it is no less capacious, though trimly held up and round. The latter style goes to complete the milk and beef form. And as we have repeatedly asked in regard to other parts, by it do we lose anything in milking ability or add anything to the cost of production? The stomach and other internal organs have just as much room and their activity cannot be diminished in the least by this style. And it indicates great constitutional vigor

We venture the assertion that more than half of the superior dairy cows of our country, if classified according to their structures, would be included in this milk and beef form. And in all countries, where dairying is carried on extensively, the same would be true. The dairy Shorthorns of England are of this form, the Brown Schwytzers of Central Europe are of this form, and the great majority of the dairy cattle of Holland, Belgium and Northern France The great cow Clothilde was a perfect milk and beef formed animal. The famous cow Pietertje 2d must be classified in this form. And many of the most famous Ayrshires and Jerseys have closely approached this form. It is the form that practical dairymen, with minds uninfluenced by theories, almost invariably prefer. It would be well if our theorists would rely less upon words, the meanings of which they really know but little, and learn more of the facts about which they presume to express themselves.

The production of fat in an animal is a physiological function, whether the fat is in the tissues or the milk, and must come from the food, and it has been shown beyond a question that the fats of the food are taken into the systems directly, and deposited wherever the idiosyncrasy of the animal favors their disposition, either in the meat or in the milk, writes Henry Stewart.

No doubt cows vary as much in this respect as beeves do in making fat from the food; or any other animals, persons included. There are men like "the lean and hungry Cassius," whom no feeding can make fat, but in general good selected nourishment will have its effect. It is hardly to be supposed that this change can be made in cows in a few days or months. But that it can be made in a few years in almost any cow existing I am fully convinced, while I am quite certain that any good cow can be so fed as to enrich her milk in the short space of a few weeks, so as to affect her yield of butter the same season.

I have a cow which I have had in training now for six years. This cow's history since I bought her when she was three years old for $19, shows that the butter record can be trebled in three years' feeding and her calves can be so improved that the quality will become hereditary. This is a possibility that I think no one can deny in view of all the facts in the long experience of breeders of cattle, both for beef and the dairy, all of which goes to show that it is no longer a question as to the feeding being the foundation of the breeding and this is a most encouraging experience for the owners of the 10,000,000 native cows that are subject to a course of improvement.

CHAPTER XIX.

FEEDING FOR BUTTER FAT—FEEDING FOR MILK

Bulletin No. 14 of the Iowa Agricultural Experiment Station contains an experiment showing the effect of feed on the quantity of milk, indicating that:

1. Quality of milk so far as measured by its percentage of fat was changed by feed to a much greater degree than was quantity. Two-thirds of the increase in average gross yield of butter fat was due to improved quality of the milk and only one-third to increased milk flow.

2. Sugar meal produced .58 of a pound more butter fat per 100 lbs. of milk than did corn and cob-meal; this difference is 17 per cent of the amount of fat in 100 lbs. of milk produced by corn and cob-meal.

3. Sugar-meal produced .73 of a pound more total solids per 100 lbs. of milk than did corn and cob-meal; this difference is 6 per cent of the solids in 100 lbs. of milk produced by corn and cob-meal.

4. As compared with corn and cob-meal, sugar-meal increased the ratio of fat to "solids not fat" in 100 lbs. of milk from 396 per 1,000 of "solids not fat" to 457 per 1,000 of "solids not fat"—an increase of over 15 per cent.

Prof. E. W. Stewart in his very valuable work "Feeding Animals," says: "Since certain very partial experiments were made in Germany * * * dairymen have been told to seek quality of milk in the breed and not in the food. We are always ready to admit and emphasize the value of breed." * * * But "in philosophy and fact the quality and quantity of milk is as perfectly controlled by quality and quantity of food as is the quality and weight of flesh laid upon a stall-fed animal."

Our dairy writers have been very slow to admit the truth of statements of this character. Especially have the advocates of the Jersey breed refused to do so. It is very probable that a majority of them will continue to maintain that quality cannot be fed into milk.

We believe that quality can be fed into milk and that we have in this country the most favorable conditions for so doing. Our climates are dry, our grasses are rich, we have the greatest abundance of rich and cheap grain foods, and our dairymen are among the most skillful feeders in the world. The competition among the dairy breeds, especially between the Holstein-Friesian and Jersey, is stimulating to the highest efforts in this direction.

And furthermore we believe that the work of feeding quality into milk is comparatively rapid.

We wish to add in this connection that we believe the contest between the Holstein-Friesian and Jersey breeds will ultimately depend on their constitutional vigor. The Holstein-Friesian has entered later in the race, but it has immense constitutional vigor. Originally the Jersey is a giver of richer milk but it has less stamina, and produces much less milk. But whatever may be the conclusion of this contest the dairy interests of this country are to be greatly benefited by it. The qualities fed into animals are transmissible, and there is no doubt that certain families in both breeds are being rapidly improved. Ere long our friends embedded in the German experiments will wake up and discover that quality can be fed into the milk of all breeds of dairy cattle.

Bulletin No. 18 of the New York Agricultural Experiment Station contains a report on the "Testing of Dairy Breeds." This report is of more than ordinary interest to breeders of cattle.

In this report there is an introduction, consisting of a description of the breeds represented, the foods used, and a table showing the weights of each animal at the close of each month, which are averaged; then follows a table for each animal tested, showing the total of each variety of food consumed and the daily average of each month and the total of the entire period. These tables also show the increase of live weight and daily gains each month, and the close of the period. Following this are five pages of general averages. In these tables, the summary of the results for each individual are now grouped together according to the breed and averages made. In the Holstein and Ayrshire tables, the average is that of four animals, and for the Guernseys and Holderness two each, while of the Jersey but one is given. There were four Jerseys received at the station according to this report, but no explanation is given for the omission of the data of the other three animals.

In these averages the Jersey test extended during two months, the Guernsey during four months, the Ayrshires during five months, the Holderness during five months and the Holstein during six months. Dr. Collier has calculated the amount of dry matter eaten per 1,000 lbs. of live weight for the same ratio as eaten, that is, the dry matter multiplied by 1,000 and divided by the weight of the animal gives the results. He states that this will be of interest as showing the changes in ratio as the animals come to maturity.

Average per 1000 lbs. live weight,	Holsteins.	Ayrshires.	Am. Holderness	Jerseys.	Guernseys.
Water drunk,	2039.1	2151.0	2247.5	2070.0	2730.0
Water in food,	615.7	779.2	798.4	1161.1	958.18
Dry matter eaten,	510.4	570.4	544.8	588.2	648.1
Ash,	29.48	30.43	34.72	35.10	39.2
Albuminoids,	81.98	93.97	101.71	92.76	106.47
Crude fiber,	115.75	135.40	125.63	138.22	151.82
Nitrogen-free extract,	256.21	280.23	279.42	294.78	321.35
Fat,	21.32	25.19	24.73	27.32	28.76
	3669.94	4065.82	4156.91	4408.48	4984.50
Gain in live weight to Sept. 30,	240 (6 mo.)	178 (5 mo.)	221 (6 mo.)	77 (3 mo.)	104 (5 mo.)
Average monthly gain, lbs.,	48.8	47.0	44.0	38.5	40.5
Dry matter for each lb. increase,	9.6	8.05	7.02	8.7	8.82
Dry matter eaten for 1000 lbs. live wt.,	509.96	570.7	550.1	589.2	660.5
Average age on arrival, days,	305.	317.	231.	300.	273.

In an attempt to present these averages in a way more easy for our readers to comprehend, we have made the above tables, taking the column at the extreme right in the general average tables in the report which is headed "per 1,000 lbs. live weight," which Dr. Collier says "is found by taking the average

MARGARET LINCOLN 2D'S DE KOL, No. 3?006 H. F. H. B.

for the entire period and dividing by the average weight of the animal for the entire period."

The figures are all from the report, excepting the addition of each column which shows the total of the average consumption of the food items enumerated per 1,000 lbs. of live weight.

From the same general average table we have taken the liberty to make still further averages. In these we have made an average of the average of each month and of each breed.

It appears from these figures that the average of consumption of food per 1,000 lbs. live weight was less in the Holstein-Friesian than either the Jersey, Ayrshire, Guernsey or Holderness breed, and that the Holstein-Friesian made a greater gain in weight than either. She consumed 738.54 less than the Jersey per 1,000 lbs. live weight and gained in weight 10.3 more. Of dry matter consumed the figures are 510.4 as to 588.2 for the Jersey, and as to other breeds, very much less. Of albuminoids, crude fiber, nitrogen-free extract and of fat it will be seen the figures all indicate a great economy in the Holstein.

In discussing the importance of the food consumed, as a factor in determining the value of a cow, reference is made to the Ohio test of 1893. Messrs. W. B. Smith & Son, owners of these cows, give the following as the rations actually fed:

In the case of Vasaline, on January 2, 1893, she was put on feed and began milking three times per day, 4 a. m., 12 noon, and 8 p. m. She was started on 3¼ lbs. bran and shorts, equal weights, 1 lb. oil meal, 8 oz. cottonseed meal, 3¼ lbs. chop feed (2 pts. oats, 1 pt. corn) together with two gallons cut mixed hay, and gradually increased in feed until her limit was reached as follows: 4¼ lbs. bran and shorts, 1¼ lbs. oil meal, 12 oz. cottonseed meal, and 4 lbs. chop with cut hay—or 10¼ lbs. of a grain ration, fed three times per day. When she was tested she was getting:

Bran and shorts 13½ lbs. at 14.00,			$.3945
Oil meal 1¾ " " 24.00,			.0468
Cottonseed meal 2¾ " " 28.00,			.1815
Chop feed 7. " " 30.00,			.18
31½			$.3528

This was the amount of grain feed given; she was given all the mixed hay she would eat, which cost $9 per ton; we did not weigh the hay. She produced 2.25 lbs. butter fat, or 2.70 lbs. commercial butter, judging by World's Fair standard. At that time creamery butter was selling in Columbus at 35 cents per pound, or she was making 93¼ cents worth of butter per day; deducting cost of feed (35.28) leaves 59.22 cents profit. This, of course, does not include hay, which would not be more than 20 lbs. nor 9 cents; nor is the by-product taken into consideration. But figuring the hay at 9 cents, cost of producing butter 5 cents, it still leaves 45.22 cents net profit. In justice to this cow, she was fed a larger ration than she could digest two days before the test was made, and shrank some six pounds milk, while her butter fats decreased 1 per cent.

Apropos of the noted Jersey breeder's statement (G. W. Farlee), that a pasture that would keep one Holstein cow would support two Jerseys, it is interesting to note what Jerseys and Holsteins do eat when being tested for butter.

On page one of "Butter Tests of Registered Jersey Cows," is the largest yield in the volume. It is as follows:

"Cromwell Maid, 19024, yield of milk 19¼ qts. per day; yield of butter 29 lbs. 12 oz.; test made from July 21 to 27, 1887; age 5 years and 3 months; estimated weight of cow 900 lbs.; grain fed during test. 6 qts. corn meal, 7 qts. oat meal, 2 qts. pea meal, 1 qt. oil meal and 6 qts. middlings daily."

Twenty-two quarts of grain in one day!

Computing this feed at the standard weights per bushel we find that Cromwell Maid's feed was as follows:

6 qts. corn meal,	10.50 lbs.
7 qts. oat meal,	11.37 lbs.
2 qts. pea meal,	3.75 lbs.
1 qt. oil meal,	1.75 lbs.
6 qts. middlings,	7.50 lbs.
	34.87 lbs.

From this she yielded 19½ qts. of milk per day from which was made 29 lbs. 12 oz. of butter in seven days or 8 3/17 oz. of feed to 1 oz. of butter.

MECHTCHILDE, No. 5718 H. H. B. (AND CALF, SIR MECHTCHILDE, No. 3727 H. F. H. B.)
Milk record, 83 lbs. 4 oz. in one day; 9,033 lbs. in five months. Butter record, 39 lbs. 10 1-2 oz. in seven days.

FEEDING.   163

In the case of Iolena Fairmount, she was started on the 12th, consumed the same amount of feed and gave 2.44 lbs. butter fats, or 2.93 lbs. butter at a value of 1.0255; deducting feed, .4428 cents, cost of making butter 5 cents, leaves .5327 cents net profit. You will also note that feed was counted at top notch prices and could have been procured for less money.

Now for comparison with one of the largest Holstein yields: DeKol 2d, who made 6 lbs. 6¼ oz. in a day and 33 lbs. 6 oz. in seven days She ate 18 lbs. of hominy chop, 7½ lbs. of wheat bran and 3½ lbs. of cotton seed meal, or a total of 29 lbs. Her weight is 1,500 lbs.

She yielded an average of 60 lbs. ½ oz. per day, from which was made 33 lbs. 6 oz. of butter in seven days, or 6$\frac{3}{4}$ oz. of feed to an ounce of butter.

The little 900 lb. Jersey ate 22 qts. of much richer food than did the 1,500 lb. Holstein; the Jersey consumed 34.87 lbs. and the Holstein, weighing 600 lbs. more, consumed 29 lbs. or 5.87 lbs. less and made 4 lbs. 6 oz. more of butter.

DeKol's age is four years and nine months, while Cromwell Maid is five years and three months old.

This shows that the Jersey consumed far more in proportion to her yield than did the Holstein, and we believe she will every day in the week.

CHAPTER XX.

FEEDING.

The profit of the dairy, says Henry Stewart, depends in the greatest measure upon the best use of the materials consumed in the business. A cow is, to a large extent, a machine for the conversion of food into milk. This is her office, for which she has been trained by many years of domestication, feeding, selection and breeding; and it is the business of the dairyman to provide himself with the best cows for the purpose he can get, and until he has the best he must be continually weeding out his herd and replenishing it by breeding or purchase until he is satisfied on this score. This is an easy thing to do; observation and the use of weights or measures only are needed for this. But the feeding depends upon knowledge to be obtained by long continued and exact experiment, and by chemical analyses of the substances used, and this knowledge is beyond the ability of the dairyman to gather for himself. To investigate, experiment and report upon these matters is the work of the chemist, the scientific dairy expert, and those writers who are able to comprehend through scientific knowledge and practical experience, the exact value and the bearings upon the conduct of the dairy, of the knowledge thus gained. In fact "Science with Practice" is the motto of the dairyman and basis on which he must work to reap the full profits of his business

The materials for the use of the dairyman are abundant, but differ not only in specific character but also in quality, depending upon the methods of growing, preparing, storing and using them. There are some food substances that may be cast aside as being so inferior in quality as to be unworthy of consideration along with the large variety which are of the most value, and we propose here to refer only to these latter, which we know from actual use are the most profitable for the production of milk, not for cream or butter, but for milk of good quality for sale, this being the subject at present under consideration.

Milk is now sold under a certain absolute standard of quality, viz., 88 per cent of water and 12 per cent of solid matter, consisting of caseine, sugar, salts and fat, the latter not falling below 3 per cent. Milk of this quality will contain on the average the following proportions, viz.:

	Per Cent.		Per Cent.
Water,	88.00	Salts	75
Caseine,	3 75	Fat	3.00
Sugar,	4.50		
Total,			100.00

Such milk is by no means of the best quality, for the average of well selected dairy cows, fed in the best manner, will give 87 per cent of water and 13 per cent of solids, of which the caseine will amount to 4½ per cent. It is the larger quantity of caseine and sugar upon which the apparent good quality of

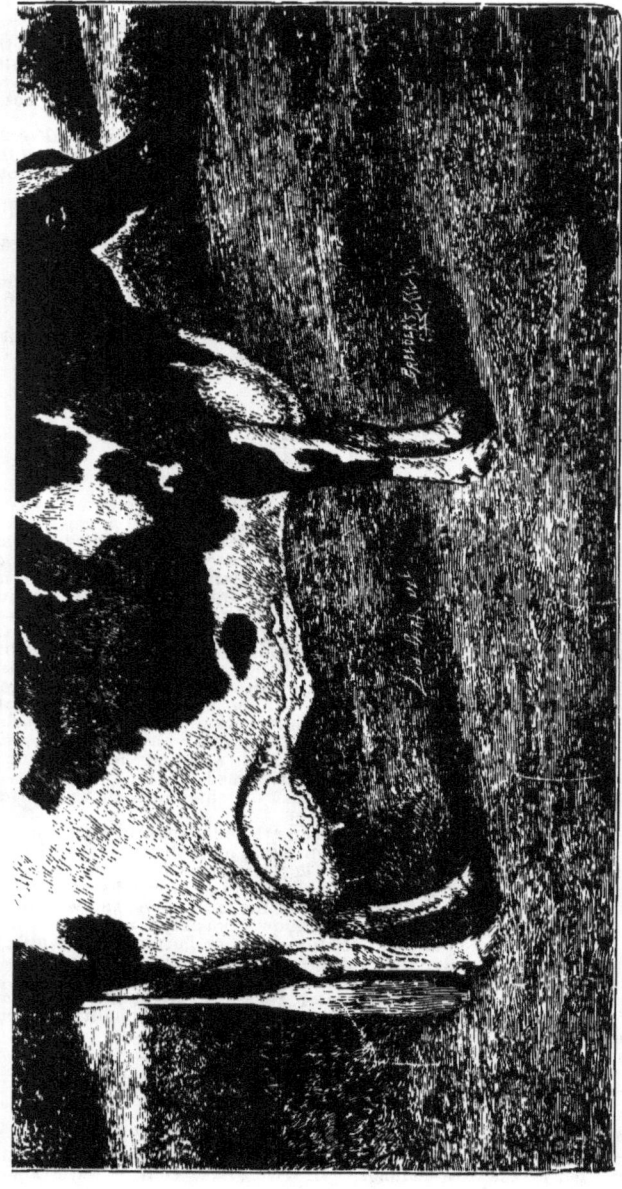

MERCEDES, No. 723 H. H. B.

Imported. Milk record, 88 lbs. in one day; 2,534 lbs. in thirty days. Butter record, unsalted, 3 lbs 10 oz. in one day; 99 lbs 6 1-2 oz. in thirty days, World's record. Winner of Breeders' Gazette Challenge Cup for largest thirty-day record July 1, 1883.

table used milk depends, rather than the amount of fat in it, although the fat is the most important nutritive element in it.

It is a disputed question if the kind of food used has any relative effect upon the quality of the milk. Scientific investigators differ in respect to it, and some very strangely insist upon the negative in regard to it, while their own experiments prove positively the affirmative. This, however, only shows that in some experiments the effort is to sustain previously formed opinions taken up at second hand, rather than to be guided by the results of one's own work. The very careful and accomplished Dr. Vœlcker concluded from his own experiments that "cows should be differently fed according to the purpose for which the milk is used, whether for cheese or butter product," and this being our own belief, formed and strengthened by several years of careful and accurate experimental feeding, we shall be guided by this view in the remarks here made.

Foods, as is well known, are made up of three nutritive elements, viz.: carbo-hydrates, as starch, sugar, gum and digestible cellulose; albuminoids or protein, as albumen, gluten and vegetable fibrine; and fatty matters, which consist of fat, oil and some organic acids, as butyric and others, which are injurious rather than helpful as regards the quality of the milk, giving to it an odor which is not desirable, and for some purposes is wholly destructive to its usefulness, as, for instance, the condensing of the milk. It is known that these foods have certain results in the alimentation of the cow that the carbo-hydrates go to support the vital heat, the albumincids form flesh, and to some extent are convertible into heat and fat, and that the fats are assimilated directly and go to support heat or are deposited in the tissues. When the cow is abundantly supplied with foods rich in these substances the surplus goes to produce milk; the albuminoids furnish material for the caseine and also for fat; the carbo-hydrates furnish the milk, sugar and some of the fat, and the fat goes directly to provide the fat. These products vary in quantity according to the natural ability of the cow to transform them, but in the best cows the product bears some ratio to the materials furnished. Hence it is important to understand the precise nature of the foods available and to make a choice of the best of them. In the following list are mentioned the most common and available food substances for feeding cows, with their constituents and the comparative value both for theoretical feeding and for money:

Kinds of Food.	Digestible.			Value for 100 lbs.
	Albuminoids.	Carbohydrates.	Fats.	
Red clover hay, poor,	5.7	37.9	1.0	$0.50
Red clover, medium,	7.0	38.1	1.2	.70
Red clover, good,	8.5	38.2	1.7	.79
Red clover, extra,	10.7	37.6	2.1	.80
Best pasture grass,	4.5	10.1	1.0	.27
Corn fodder, green,	1.4	8.4	0.5	...
Green leaves of forest trees, young growth,	5.2	15.2	1.5	...
Young clover pasture,	4.6	7.2	0.9	.25
Fodder, rye, green,	3.3	10.4	0.8	.20
Fodder, green peas,	3.2	7.6	0.6	.18
Peas (grain),	0.4	54.5	2.0	.44
Beans (grain),	3.5	50.9	1.6	.51
Cornmeal,	8.4	60.6	4.8	2.11
Cottonseed, whole,	17.1	14.7	27.3	.08
Corn and cob meal,	8.87	49.0	3.5	1.00
Wheat bran,	10.0	48.5	3.1	.01
Wheat middlings,	8.9	54.8	2.6	1.00
Buckwheat bran,	13.5	44.0	3.9	1.15
Hominy waste,	10.13	52.0	7.6	1.40
Gluten meal,	3.2	19.3	1.8	.39
Brewer's grains,	4.8	11.3	1.2	.36
Malt sprouts,	20.8	43.7	0.9	1.33
Palm nut meal,	16.1	55.4	9.5	1.61
Linseed oil meal, new process,	27.8	33.9	2.1	1.61
Cottonseed meal, free from hulls,	33.2	17.6	16.2	2.30

This table should be carefully studied and kept for reference. One should always know his business and have the points of it "at his fingers' ends," so to

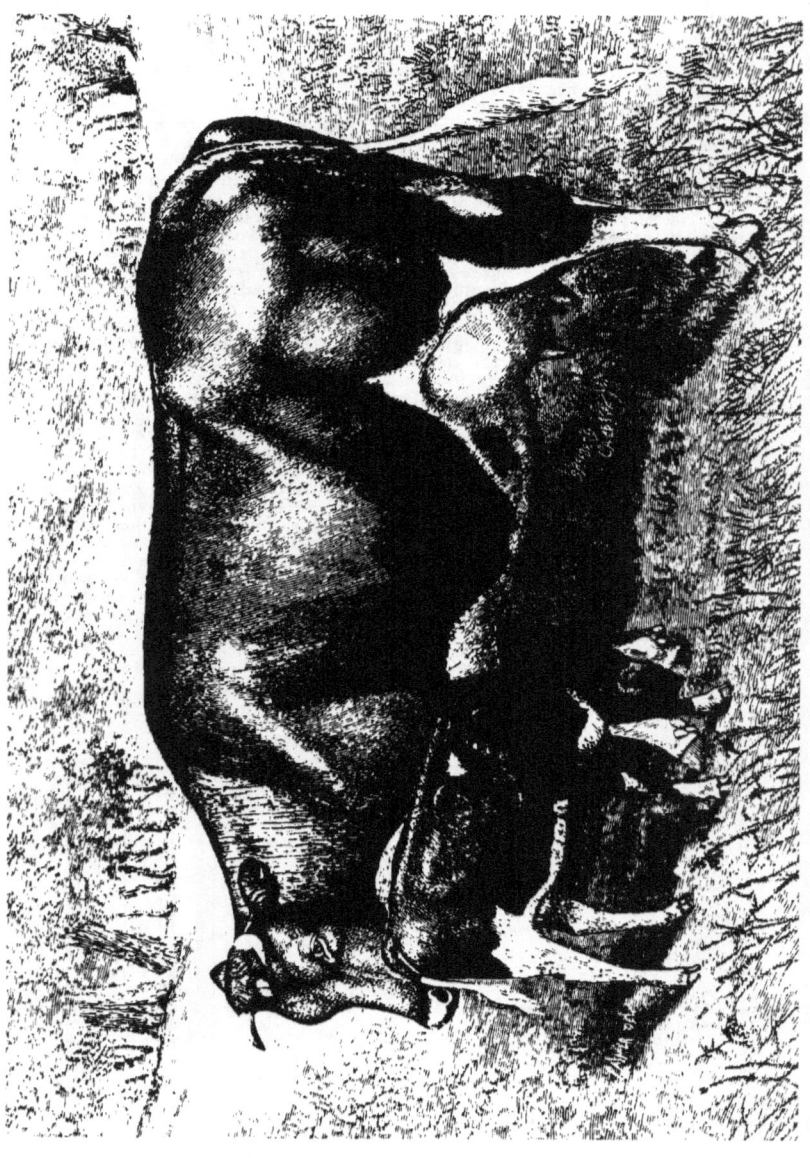

FEEDING.   167

speak, ready for immediate use. And it is the business of the milk dairyman to know what are the best materials for his use, that he may select the most profitable, and when opportunities arise to seize upon them without hesitation. Some years ago the writer was offered a lot of palm nut meal which had been sent here for sale, but no one knowing anything of its value, it was offered at any price that could be procured. Knowing its value for feeding cattle, the writer purchased the lot at once, and it was the cheapest butter-making food he had ever used. In this way a dairyman cannot only choose the cheapest foods, but he may often avoid purchasing other foods at too high prices for profit; so that an accurate knowledge of the characters of the foods in the market should be made a particular study of every dairyman.

Reckoning all nitrogenous matter as albuminoids, the following foods have the nutritive ratio put opposite each :

Clover hay,	1: 5.0	Malt sprouts,	1: 2.2
Meadow hay,	1: 8.	Linseed cake,	1: 2.
Wheat straw,	1:64.4	Linseed cake (new process),	1: 1.2
Oat straw,	1:20.9	Cottonseed cake, decorticated,	1: 1.8
Rye straw,	1:46.0	Rye,	1: 7.
Timothy,	1: 8.1	Barley,	1: 7.9
Hungarian,	1: 7.1	Oats,	1: 6.1
Alsike,	1: 4.2	Buckwheat,	1: 7.4
Orchard grass,	1: 6.5	Parsnips,	1: 7.3
Corn fodder,	1:14.4	Turnips,	1: 5.8
Corn,	1: 0.5	Carrots,	1: 9.3
Wheat middlings,	1: 5.6	Fodder beets,	1: 9.3
Rye bran,	1: 5.3	Wheat bran,	1: 5.6

How to form rations. Suppose we wish to feed meadow hay and rye bran to form a ration having a nutritive ratio of 1:6. We have a problem like this :

$$\begin{array}{cc} 1:8.0 & 1:6.0 \\ 1:6.0 & 1:5.3 \\ \hline 2.0 & .7 \end{array}$$

The meadow hay has an excess of twenty parts of carbohydrates and fats to a lack of seven parts of the same elements in the bran. Hence we will take seven pounds of the hay to twenty pounds of the bran :

$$\begin{array}{l} 1:5.3 \times 20 = 20:106.0 \\ 1:8.0 \times 7 = 7: 56.0 \\ \hline 27:162.0 = 1:6 \end{array}$$

Manifestly we have the proper nutritive ratio, but we must have a greater variety in the food. Suppose we wish to feed orchard grass, wheat bran, rye and turnips in a ration having a nutritive ratio of 1:6. We have this problem:

$$\begin{array}{cccc} 1:6.5 & 1:7.0 & 1:6.0 & 1:6.0 \\ 1:6.0 & 1:6.0 & 1:5.6 & 1:5.8 \\ \hline .5 & 1.9 & .4 & .2 \end{array}$$

In the orchard grass and rye together there is an excess of fifteen parts to a lack of six parts in the wheat bran and turnips. Hence take six parts of grass and six parts of rye to fifteen parts of bran and fifteen parts of turnips :

$$\begin{array}{l} 1:6.5 \times 6 = 6:39.0 \\ 1:7.0 \times 6 = 6:42.0 \\ 1:5.6 \times 15 = 15:84.0 \\ 1:5.8 \times 15 = 15:87.8 \\ \hline 42:252.0 = 1:6 \end{array}$$

But suppose we wish to feed one pound of grass to about one pound of a mixture of the other feeds. In four pounds of hay there would be an excess of twenty parts, and in half a pound of rye an excess of five parts, total twenty-five parts; in a pound of turnips and a pound of wheat bran there would be a total lack of six parts. If we add half a pound of malt sprouts we will have a total lack of twenty-five parts. Hence the ration will have the proper nutritive ratio. To avoid fractions we will double the quantities :

$$\begin{array}{lr} \text{Eight pounds orchard grass,} & 8:52.0 \\ \text{One pound rye,} & : 7.0 \\ \text{Two pounds turnips,} & 2:11.6 \\ \text{Two pounds wheat bran,} & 2:11.2 \\ \text{One pound malt sprouts,} & 1: 2.2 \\ \hline & 14:84.0 = 1:6 \end{array}$$

Here we have eight pounds of grass to six pounds of other feeds. By using more of the grass and of the malt sprouts, or by using part clover, we can get a ration having the proper nutritive ratio, and in which one pound of stover is set against one pound of other feeds. The reader can see that, by using the simple plan I have given, he can form any desired ration.

Now, if linseed cake or cottonseed cake was comparatively cheaper than malt sprouts I would use it. Or, rather than pay high prices for any of them, I would use a ration having a ratio of 1:7 or even 1:8. The point is to keep both ratio and cost in view.

MERCEDES 3D, No. 3769 H. H. B.
Eight months old.

CHAPTER XXI.

BALANCED RATIONS, FOR CALF, FOR MILK AND GROWING WEANLINGS AND YEARLINGS—FOR HEIFERS—FOR COWS DUE IN THE SPRING—FOR MILK, BUTTER AND DEVELOPMENT—FOR LARGE COWS.

The late Prof. E. W. Stewart contributed many valuable suggestions and directions for care and specific feeding of domestic animals to the columns of the Country Gentleman (Albany, N. Y.). He was frequently called upon to suggest rations for Holstein-Friesian cattle. From a large number of these which were reprinted in the Holstein-Friesian Register from time to time, we have made selections and reproduce them here. They are exceedingly valuable and will be found to comprise rations for animals of all ages and conditions.

"I would request instruction as to ration for grade Holstein calf five weeks old. I cannot afford to give her all milk, and am anxious to raise her properly for dairy purposes.

"Does it make any difference with the health of a calf if fed on milk from cow fed with cottonseed meal as a part ration? J. E. W."

1. He may feed his grade Holstein heifer calf by using a small quantity of flaxseed jelly and fine middlings in what milk he can spare. Let him boil flaxseed in eight times its bulk of water for about ten minutes, when it will form a thin jelly. Now let him stir in four times as much fine middlings as he has flaxseed, stirring it all together. Let him put about a gill of this mixture into the milk he can spare for the calf at each feed. As the calf grows older, he can increase the quantity of water and middlings—the quantity of flaxseed jelly remaining the same. Let the calf be fed three times a day, and have a little bright hay to chew at pleasure.

2. It will make no difference with the health of the calf that the cow is fed on cottonseed meal as a part of her ration. But cottonseed meal should never be given to calves; it is too concentrated food for their young stomachs.

"What is best to feed Holstein-Friesian calves besides hay to make them grow—six and seven months old? O. F."

O. P. may compound the following: 5 lbs. cut hay, 2 lbs. wheat bran, 2 lbs. wheat middlings, 1 lb. O. P. linseed meal. The cut hay should be moistened with hot water, then, after mixing the bran, middlings and linseed meal together, mix this with the warm moistened cut hay. It is then ready to feed. This is a combination of food and not a ration per head, although each calf will eat about this amount per day after a few weeks. The calves should be given what they will eat of it twice a day. Wheat bran is perhaps the best single food to grow the bones and frame of calves, but middlings is also a good food for that purpose, as is also linseed meal. These three foods combined with hay in that proportion make a model ration for growing calves of that age. The feeder has much to do with the success of a ration in feeding calves. He should watch carefully the wants of each calf. They will not eat the same every day, and care should be taken not to feed too much. The only improvement that can be made on this combination of food for the most rapid growth of calves would be to use a little cheap molasses in the hot water to moisten the cut hay. This would give them a strong appetite for their food, and would therefore increase their growth. But with careful feeding they will grow fast enough without it. These calves should be fed at the same time each day.

"I have twenty Holstein cows, weighing 1,000 lbs. to 1,100 lbs., on my farm in Orange County, Va., and a number of yearlings and weanlings of last spring. I have abundance of corn ensilage, stover, ground oats and corn and cob meal. Will you oblige me with a proper ration for these several classes of animals out of the material mentioned? J. P. T."

J. P. T. may combine the following foods as a general ration for his Holstein cows: 40 lbs. corn ensilage, 5 lbs. cut corn stover, 5 lbs. ground oats, 4 lbs. cob meal, 3¼ lbs. cottonseed meal. The nutrients of this are shown in the following formula, in pounds:

Imported. Milk record, 532 lbs. 8 oz. in ten days; butter yield from this milk, 23 lbs. 8 oz. MINK, No. 402 H. H. B.; 251 ADVANCED REGISTRY. Best one day's milk yield, 91 lbs; 16,029 lbs. 8 oz. in one year.

BALANCED RATIONS FOR MILK.

	Albuminoids.	Carbohydrates.	Fat.
40 lbs. ensilage,	0.48	4.80	0.20
5 " cut corn stover,	0.12	1.72	0.02
5 " ground oats,	0.45	2.30	0.22
4 " cob meal,	0.27	2.26	0.15
3½ " cottonseed meal,	1.25	0.98	0.87
Total	2.57	12.06	1.46

Nutritive ratio, 1 to 5.4.

This is a fairly-balanced milk ration. The ration could not be properly balanced with any combination of the foods he gives, and we use cottonseed meal because he can easily obtain it at a comparatively low rate, and it is one of the best balancing foods for milk and butter, besides being worth all it costs in that locality as a fertilizer. Nearly all farmers now appreciate the return of fertility to the soil by improved farming. It is nearly always the first beginning of extensive farming. The Cotton States have a great compensating resource in this by-product of the cotton plant.

The 5 lbs. cut corn stover should be well mixed with the ensilage and then the whole slightly further moistened, and the ground oats, cob meal and cottonseed meal being first mixed together dry, should be well mixed with the ensilage and cut stover.

2. The ration for his year-olds may be 30 lbs. ensilage, 5 lbs. ground oats, mixed together and given in three feeds.

3. For the six-months calves he may give 15 lbs. ensilage, 4 lbs. ground oats, mixed together and given in three feeds.

We give these ground oats in the ration for the milch cows and in the ration for the younger animals, because he seems to desire it; yet if the comparative price of oats is as much in that locality as in others, we should think it would be economy to substitute fine bran for the ground oats, the result being practically the same.

"Please compound ration for four Holstein heifers with first calf, two years old, average 980 lbs., with 34 lbs. milk per day. They had no grain, and wintered well on hay and straw, but are falling away considerably in flesh and milk, which you will see by enclosed memorandum:

Weight.	Milk, seven days.							Total.
1,080	32	39	37	38	36	36	35	260
1,040	36	34	36	35	34	34	33	244
950	36	36	33	33	33	33	32	236
850	35	35	33	32	31	30	31	217
3,920								957

(Daily average, 34 lbs.)

"With economy in view, I wish to improve them in flesh and get the greatest flow of milk, from hay, corn, oats, bran and oil meal; have a good hay cutter. Hay is common meadow hay (fine), timothy, clover, red top, and some orchard grass in it. J. V. W."

J. V. W. has, according to his record, four very promising heifers that need only to be properly fed to develop into desirable cows. We should think the following combination would make a very good ration for them. Let him first grind an equal weight of corn and oats together, then make up the following ration for each heifer: 14 lbs. cut mixed hay, 6 lbs. corn and oats ground together, 4 lbs. wheat bran and 2 lbs. oil meal. This ration will have about the following digestible nutrients, in pounds:

	Albuminoids.	Carbohydrates.	Fat.
14 lbs. cut mixed hay,	0.63	6.16	0.15
6 " corn and oats ground,	0.52	3.11	0.28
4 " wheat bran,	0.47	1.84	0.10
2 " oil meal,	0.56	0.56	0.12
Total,	2.18	11.67	0.65

Nutritive ratio, 1 to 6.

This ration is well adapted to quantity and quality of milk, and to put the heifers in good condition and keep up that condition. This ration should be given in three feeds, smallest at noon, and fed at the same times each day. The grain part of the ration is all mixed together dry, and then mixed evenly with the moistened cut hay.

MOOIE, No. 36 D.-F. H. B.

Imported from West Friesland 1878 by Una filla Valley Stock Breeders' Association as best bull that could be procured. Weight, 1,900 lbs. at three years.

If this ration is fed in warm weather, and the ration for the whole day is mixed at once, it should be mixed just before the evening feed, and then it would not ferment to any harm before the next morning feed. We think W. will find this a good ration for stable feeding. But if he turns to good pasture, then to develop his heifers he may feed at evening 3 lbs. cut hay, mixed with 2 lbs. ground corn and oats, 2 lbs. wheat bran and ½ lb. oil meal. This will keep up their improved condition and yield of milk, and assist in establishing a large milking habit.

"Please give ration for Holstein cows weighing 1,000 to 1,200 lbs., coming in in the spring. I want to feed clover ensilage twice a day, and cut corn ensilage once. I have shorts, corn meal, oil meal and cottonseed meal. I am very willing to feed liberally.
I. S. A."

NETHERLAND ALBAN, No. 4584 H. F. H. B.; ADVANCED REGISTRY, 34.

I. S. A., having two kinds of ensilage, and wishing to feed twice of clover and once of corn ensilage, may mix 7 lbs. corn meal with 30 lbs. clover ensilage, and this will form the two feeds, morning and noon, largest half given in the morning. The corn meal should be mixed very evenly with the clover ensilage. Clover is rich in albuminoids, and corn meal in carbohydrates. These will go well together. Now let him mix 4 lbs. of shorts and 1 lb. of cottonseed meal with 20 lbs. corn ensilage, all well mixed together, and let this be the evening feed. This will be safe to feed to the cows coming in in the spring, and it will not be a very large ration for cows of their weight, but as they will become dry the ration should not be larger. The combination with clover ensilage will have the following digestible nutrients in pounds:

	Albuminoids.	Carbohydrates.	Fat.
30 lbs. clover ensilage,	0.69	3.00	0.18
7 " corn meal,	0.59	4.41	0.33
Total,	1.28	7.41	0.51

Ratio 1 to 6.7. The evening feed is as follows:

	Albuminoids.	Carbohydrates.	Fat.
20 lbs. corn ensilage,	0.24	2.40	0.10
4 " shorts,	0.44	1.84	0.11
1 " cottonseed meal,	0.35	0.23	0.06
Total,	1.03	4.47	0.27

Nutritive ratio 1 to 5. When this day's feed is put together we have albuminoids, 2.31; carbohydrates, 11.88; fat .78, and a nutritive ratio of 1 to 6. This should be a successful ration. When the cows go dry feed clover ensilage and 6 to 8 lbs. shorts.

"I want a milk (also a butter) ration made for thoroughbred Holstein-Friesian cattle, and instructions how to change from one to the other. I want it made with reference to good health and development of my herd. My cattle have had good attention, and have been well fed all the time. Foods: Bran, value $19 per ton; clover hay, fine, cured a little too long, $10; ground oats, 35c. per bushel; corn meal, 60c.; corn-heart meal, made in making oil, $20 per ton. My hay is cut, moistened and mixed. I have steam power to cut, grind, etc., and a mill of French buhr stone.

"Please name difference in feed of milch cows and young stock. E. S."

E. S. raises several questions which have been partially discussed in these answers. He seems to take it for granted that a ration may be so constructed as to produce quantity of milk rather than quality, and still be adapted to promote the health of the cow. But this is an error when applied to a permanent ration. For the health of the cow cannot properly be promoted in an extended system, unless it contains a full proportion of all the food elements required in the production of milk. As milk is made from the blood, food best adapted to make healthy blood will best promote the health of the cow. It is true that a ration may be unbalanced by being too nitrogenous, as well as to be too carbonaceous. Some feeders, when they desire to produce the richest milk, give food containing an excess of albuminoids, as was done (as appears by all the published statements) in the tests of the celebrated cows, Princess 2d and Mary Anne of St. Lambert, as well as some others; and it is quite possible, in these tests, that it promoted the temporary increase of butter in the milk. But it is better to have a ration constructed on natural principles, founded on nature's best milk food, good pasture grasses, which have a nutritive ratio of about 1 to 4 or 1 to 4.5.

2. In making a ration with the foods mentioned by S., we are a little doubtful of the precise quality of corn-heart meal, as he says it is "made in making oil," whereas it is usually used in making hominy, and has a large per cent of oil (9.24 per cent). Is this afterwards extracted from the corn-heart? If so, it would change its nutritive ratio—but perhaps make it even better in supplying albuminoids in the milk ration. The analysis of corn-germ feed or corn-heart is as follows: Ash, 2.54; albuminoids, 10.87; carbohydrates, 56.87; fat, 9.24; fibre, 8.30. If the oil is extracted, or a large part of it, it would change its feeding value. And when compared with oats and corn, it is found only the trifle of seven to eight cents per 100 lbs. cheaper, and therefore doubtful economy to use it.

S. uses the only completely reliable mill (French buhr stone), and will be able to do the best grinding, having fine feed and not "chop." Let him grind two bushels of oats with one bushel of corn into a fine meal, or what would be much better, if he had cow peas—grind equal parts by weight of oats, corn and cow peas into a fine meal. This would easily balance his ration for milk. It is not easy to make a proper balance with oats, corn and bran, but the following formula will come very near it:

	Albuminoids.	Carbohydrates.	Fat.
18 lbs. good clover hay,	1.40	7.23	9.25
6 " corn and oats, ground together,	0.53	3.10	0.28
10 " wheat bran,	1.17	4.60	0.25
Total,	3.10	14.93	0.78

This is a nutritive ratio of 1 to 5.4, and may be regarded as a well-balanced milk ration, and it would be sufficient for large cows—would, in fact, be well adapted to the early development of the milk yield in the Holstein-Friesian. But after it had been used for a considerable time, it would be improved by using 8 lbs. of corn and oats ground, or 6 lbs. of wheat bran, with 2 lbs. of cottonseed meal. This would give it a nutritive ratio of 1 to 4.8.

3. In feeding his young stock, it is well to discard corn meal altogether, because it has not the material to grow the bones or frame. The combination would be best as follows: 8 lbs. clover hay, 3 lbs. ground oats, 5 lbs. wheat bran. This combination will develop young heifers without laying on extra fat, and will improve them as breeders. Bran is a peculiarly good food to develop young animals, because of the large per cent it contains of phosphoric acid to grow the bones or expand the frame, and albuminoids to grow the muscles. It is a developing food for the animal. Oats are a good food for the same purpose, and clover hay also assists in the development of the young animal.

NETHERLAND BARONESS, No. 2035 H. F. H. B.; 127 ADVANCED REGISTRY. Imported. Milk record, 72 lbs. 11 oz. in one day; 8,597 lbs. 9 oz. in eight months fifteen days. Butter record, in seven days.

"We have a herd of 100 milch cows, Holstein-Friesians, and are at a loss to know just the cheapest ration to feed this winter for the best results. The fresh ones we milk three times per day for the first four to six months, and we want them to do all they possibly can—1st, for butter ; 2d, milk, quality before quantity. The cows going dry, etc., we are not as particular about. We have 250 tons of excellent corn ensilage, lots of corn, and the finest quality of alfalfa hay; in addition the following feed stuffs: Corn at $20 per ton (we grind it ourselves); wheat bran, $18; cottonseed meal, best quality, $23. Now the question is, Can't we get along with cottonseed meal mostly, as corn and bran are much higher now than a year ago, while the cottonseed remains about the same? We have heard that too much cottonseed is injurious to cows, especially those along in calf four, five or six months. Is it true?

"Would like the best and cheapest grain rations of the three kinds above named, with corn ensilage, and alfalfa hay. The fresh cows we want to feed mostly ensilage, and others not so much ensilage, but more hay. Think the 100 head would be divided half and half.

"As we test all our cows for butter, when first fresh, we want to feed them the best and richest feed possible to get the best results, etc. After they have been tested then all we care for is to have them kept in good shape, and give what milk they can without forcing. C. F. H."

C. F. H. does not properly consider the composition of cottonseed meal when he asks if this cannot be made the principal grain food with ensilage and alfalfa hay in a ration for large milk production. Cottonseed meal is a partial and very much unbalanced food—about as much so as oat straw, the straw having a great excess of carbohydrates and the cottonseed meal a great excess of albuminoids. The two balance each other. To balance corn ensilage alone the largest amount of cottonseed meal might be used. But as H. has both ensilage and the nitrogenous alfalfa hay, which are his cheapest foods, these may be made to very nearly balance each other, and we must add other grain food to make up the ration for large milk yield without much increasing the bulk. Ensilage and alfalfa would have to be eaten in too large quantities to get sufficient nutriment to produce a large yield of rich milk.

The value of cottonseed meal is based upon its excess of albuminoids to balance poor fodders, but in this case we require an additional food rich in carbohydrates, such as corn meal, and next to this is wheat bran. H. is also rightly informed that cottonseed meal in any considerable quantity is dangerous to feed to cows more than four or five months in calf. He may feed to his fresh milkers the largest quantity. If his fodder consisted of corn ensilage and common hay, such as timothy or redtop, he might feed a much larger proportion of cottonseed meal, say four to six pounds per head. But with his excellent alfalfa and corn ensilage he cannot economically feed more than two pounds of cottonseed meal, because when not needed as a balancing food it is not as valuable as corn meal or bran. For his fresh milch cows we should advise the following ration: Fifty pounds corn ensilage, ten pounds alfalfa, four pounds corn meal, five pounds wheat bran and two pounds cottonseed meal. Stated in analytical formula, this shows the following digestible nutrients in pounds :

	Albuminoids.	Carbohydrates.	Fat.
50 lbs. corn ensilage,	0.60	6.00	0.25
10 " alfalfa hay,	0.94	3.00	0.10
4 " corn meal,	0.33	2.52	0.18
5 " wheat bran,	0.58	2.30	0.13
2 " cottonseed meal,	0.71	0.56	0.12
Total,	3.16	14.38	0.78

Nutritive ratio 1 to 5.1. It will be seen that this is a well balanced ration for these large cows, and that it is also the cheapest ration from the foods given. Suppose we were to feed one pound more cottonseed meal in place of two pounds alfalfa, it would not cheapen the ration and would not improve it. This may safely be fed to the cows until four or five months in calf. The only way to improve this ration would be to add one pound more of corn meal. But we think it will be satisfactory. The grain is supposed to be thoroughly mixed with the ensilage and hay.

2. For his cows long in milk, or dry, we would recommend the following ration: Thirty pounds ensilage, fourteen pounds alfalfa hay, two pounds corn meal, four pounds wheat bran. This has the following digestible nutrients in pounds :

	Albuminoids.	Carbohydrates.	Fat.
30 lbs. ensilage,	0.36	3.60	0.15
14 " alfalfa hay,	1.31	4.20	0.14
2 " corn meal,	0.17	1.26	0.09
4 " wheat bran,	0.47	1.84	0.10
Total,	2.31	10.90	0.48

Nutritive ratio 1 to 5.2. This is quite a contrast to the other ration, but the conditions are also very much changed. If they were giving no milk the two pounds corn meal might be left off, but as he feeds his cows in two classes only this ration will be appropriate for the second class.

BALANCED RATIONS FOR MILK AND BUTTER.

"Will you kindly give me the best and most economical milk ration out of the following feeds which I have here, with cost of each as given below: Corn ground with cob and shuck, 50c. per 100 lbs.; wheat bran, 60c. per 100 lbs.; Johnson grass hay, $10 per ton; ensilage from green corn, plenty of which I have put up, at a cost perhaps of $2.50 per ton. I want milk ration for Holstein cows, but do not know how best to mix the above feeds. I can buy cottonseed meal here for $15 to $16 per ton. If it is economy to do so, please include that in the ration. As I have plenty of ensilage you may leave the Johnson grass hay out of the estimate if you think best. I want to feed the corn ground with cob and shuck, as I have just bought the mill for this, and I think it quite a saving. W. E. H."

W. E. H. commands foods at a reasonable price, and can afford to feed a full ration. His cows will do a little better with some hay mixed with ensilage. The following ration in lbs. from his feeds will be successful if properly given:

		Albuminoids.	Carbohydrates.	Fat.
40 lbs.	corn ensilage.	0.40	4.40	0.20
4 "	Johnson grass hay,	0.27	1.64	0.05
6 "	ground corn, cob and shuck.	0.37	3.25	0.21
6 "	wheat bran,	0.70	2.76	0.16
4 "	decorticated cottonseed meal,	1.32	0.88	0.24
	Total,	3.06	12.93	0.86

This has a nutritive ratio of 1 to 4.9, and is a full ration for large cows at the beginning of feeding, but may require a little increase after one month.

Perhaps the amount of corn husk and cob would prove sufficient, with the ensilage as "roughness." He might try it with the Johnson grass left out, and two pounds added to the ground corn, cob, etc., but we think the ration would be more complete with it. This ration should produce a full yield of milk of good quality.

H. will understand that the ground corn, bran and cottonseed meal should be well mixed together, separately, and then mixed with the ensilage and cut hay, if the hay is used.

We think the ration will be very much benefited by the use of cottonseed

NETHERLAND CONSUL AND IDEAL'S LENA.
First prize winners, Toronto, 1896.

meal. But this, being a very concentrated food, it should be thoroughly mixed with the other materials.

As soon as his cows show that they could digest more, he had better give the eight lbs. of corn chop and the four lbs. of cut Johnson's grass hay, for if his cows are of 1,400 lbs. weight they will need it. In profitable milk production the cows should have what food they can digest and assimilate, because the profit all comes from the extra food.

CHAPTER XXII.

FAMILIES OF THE BREED—AAGGIE—NETHERLAND—CLOTHILDE—ARTIS—AEGIS—JOHANNA—WAYNE—MUTUAL FRIEND—PAULINE PAUL.

The experience and observation of the most skillful and observant breeders today, is that the building up of a herd which in the point of production, general excellence, superior quality, uniformity and personal beauty shall fill the ideal, demands that the foundation shall be laid with a well matured and definite plan.

To accomplish this in the most certain manner resort will be had to the selection from the most noted and best established families of the breed.

In the comparatively short period of time covered by Holstein-Friesian cattle in this country a considerable number of prepotent and uniform strains have been developed. We append descriptions of those families which we have been able to obtain and collate. It is needless to say that there are many other nearly or quite as well defined families of which no mention is made herein, but whose characteristics entitle them to recognition. At this time, however, their limited number of members and the absence of detailed information in relation thereto would permit no more than a bare mention of the names by which they are known to breeders.

Those families which are most widely known and stand pre-eminent we present such information about as it has been our fortune to obtain through the assistance of the original founders. In future editions of this work we hope to be able to greatly extend this feature.

NETHERLAND DOWAGER, No. 2032 II. H. B.
Imported. Milk record, 91 lbs. in one day; 17,160 lbs. 11 oz. in one year. Butter record, 16 lbs. 1 2 oz. in seven days.

THE AAGGIE FAMILY.

Those families most widely known to American breeders would probably be included in the following enumeration, which is given without reference to their relative importance: Aaggie, Aegis, Alexander, Artis, Billy Boelyn, Captain, Clothilde, Carlotta, De Kol, Empress, Empress Josephine, Gerben, Jewel, Koningin Van Friesland, Hartog, Johanna, Hengerveld, Pel, Pietertje, Mooie, Keyes, Promoter, Pauline Paul, Queen of the Hill, Mercedes, Opperdoes, Zuider Zee, Wayne, Mutual Friend, Netherland, Texelaar, Tritomia, Twisk, Rijaneta, Florence Herbert, Violet.

One of the earliest families to attract especial attention among breeders was the Aaggie, which was brought before the public by the proprietors of Lakeside.

Aaggie, 901, was imported by them in September, 1879.

The following year, and while carrying twins, she gave 18,004 lbs. 15 oz. of milk in a year—surpassing all records, of all breeds, up to that date.

About the same time, Messrs. Yeomans & Sons imported her daughter, Aaggie 2d, which, as a two-year-old, surpassed all records of her age, by giving 17,746 lbs. 2 oz. of milk in a year. As a cow she gave 20,763 lbs. 3 oz. in a year. She also made 304 lbs. 5½ oz. butter in ninety days—surpassing all records of that time for butter.

NETHERLAND DUCHESS, No. 2498 H. H. B.; ADVANCED REGISTRY 180.

Imported. Milk record, 12,770 lbs. in one year. Butter record, 16 lbs. 15 1-4 oz. in a week; 22.34 lbs. of milk making one pound of butter.

The wonderful showing made by this cow and her daughter induced Messrs. Smiths & Powell Co. to make a special trip to Holland, for the purpose of looking up the family and securing all the choice representatives thereof.

They found that Aaggie was sired by Rooker, a noted prize winner, and that his descendants had proven enormous milkers, the best of which they secured, and imported to this country.

This family is so extensive that it is not practical to go into details regarding the various individuals, but twenty-eight cows, all closely related—either daughters of Rooker, or his son Jacob, or grandson Jacob 2d—have made milk records which average, for the whole number, 16,560 lbs. 13 oz. of milk in a year.

As butter makers they also hold a high position—about twenty of the cows referred to above having made butter records which average 20 lbs. in a week.

BUTTER RECORDS, AAGGIE FAMILY.—ALL MADE AT LAKESIDE.

	Yrs	Lbs.	Oz.		Yrs.	Lbs.	Oz.
Idene Rooker,		25	3 1-2	Sir Henry 2d's Elland,	3	21	10 3-4
Lady Griswold,		24	13	Aaggie Rosa 4th,	4	21	8 1-2
Aaggie Beauty 2d,		23	5 3-4	Aaggie Lee,	4	21	5
Cecelia Rooker,	4	22	13 3-4	Aaggie Beauty,		20	9
Aaggie Rosa,		22	8 1-2	Aaggie Idaline 2d,		20	5

NETHERLAND FAMILY.

	Yrs.	Lbs.	Oz.		Yrs.	Lbs.	Oz.
Aaggie May,	20	2		Aaggie Rosa 2d,	16	2	1-2
Aaggie Constance,	19	14	1-2	Aaggie (two teats),	15	14	1-2
Aaggie Hannah,	19	7	3-4	Aaggie Cora,	15	10	
Aaggie Cornelia 2d,	19	6		Aaggie Idaline 6th,	4	14	14
Aegis 6th,	19	5		Aaggie Cornelia 5th,	4	14	7
Lambertina,	19	4		Topaz 4th,	3	14	8-4
Aaggie Idaline,	19	2	3-4	Ida Rooker	2	13	12 1-2
Aaggie Cornelia,	19	1		Lambertina 2d,	2	13	7
Aaggie Cornelia 4th,	19		1-2	Aaggie Pauline,	4	13	5 3-4
Aaggie Merrell,	18	1	3-4	Margaret Lincoln,	3	12	10
Aaggie Idaline 2d,	17	11	3-4	Jacob Witt's Godiva,	2	12	9 1-2
Aaggie Rachel,	17	0	3-4	Aaggie Rosalia,	2	12	0
Aaggie Cornelia 3d,	17	7		Aaggie Ethel,	2	11	11
Aaagie Sarah 2d,	17	5	3-4	Hannah Rooker,	2	11	9 3-4
Aaggie Eva,	17	3	4	Aaggie May 4th,	2	11	9 1-2
Ambronnetta,	16	15	1-2	Aaggie Bonnie 2d,	3	11	6 1-4
Aaggie Anna,	4	16	3	Phœbe Lincoln,	2	11	2
Aaggie Kate,		16	8 1-2				

These records are all made in our own herd, and from animals imported or bred by us.

MILK RECORDS, AAGGIE FAMILY.—ALL MADE AT LAKESIDE.

	Yrs.	Lbs.	Oz.		Yrs.	Lbs.	Oz.
Aaggie,		18,004	15	Rosalie Somers,	2	12,588	13
Aaggie Rosa,		20,225	3	Aaggie Idaline 6th,	2	12,422	8
Aaggie Cornelia 3d,	4	17,330		Aaggie Bonnie,	4	12,247	10
Aaggie Idaline,		17,129	7	Aegis 6th,		12,196	14
Aaggie Rachel,		7,073	7	De Ruiter's Beatus,	3	12,090	
Lady Griswold,		17,023	7	Aegis 9th,	2	12,088	7
Aaggie Anna,	4	6,993	2	Aaggie Isadora 3d,		12,843	15
Aaggie Sarah,	4	6,933	13	Charity th,	2	12,323	6
Aaggie Rosa 2d,		6,884	13	Netherland Aaggie,	2	11,798	2
Aaggie Cornelia,		6,794	11	Aaggie Pauline,	4	11,599	10
Aaggie Constance,	2	6,761	11	Topaz 4th,	2	11,480	12
Lambertina,		6,744	6	Aaggie Kathleen,		11,390	13
Aaggie Hannah,	4	6,208	6	Aaggie May 2d,	2	11,346	12
Aaggie May,		6,125	10	Kappijne 3d,	2	11,3 4	15
Aaggie Beauty,		5,795		Celeste S.,	2	11,3̄ 4	
Aaggie Idaline 3d,		5,786	1	Aaggie Cornelia 3d's Lass,	2	11,182	6
Idene Rooker,	2	5,157	10	Aaggie's 2d Daughter,	2	11,090	14
Aaggie Beauty 2d,	4	4,058	14	Aaggie Maud 4th,	2	11,025	4
Aaggie Cora,		5,010	1	Margaret Lincoln,	2	10,926	9
Aaggie Cornelia 2d,		4,610	9	Nelly Cooker,	2	10,936	4
Aaggie Idaline 2d,		4,229	1	Aaggie Cornelia 5th,	3	10,879	9
Aaggie Ethel,	2	4,144	1	Miss Lincoln,	2	10,763	8
Aaggie Eva,	3	4,016	9	Hannah Rooker,	2	10,626	1
Aaggie Merrel,	4	3,875	14	Aaggie Bonnie 2d,	2	10,525	4
Aaggie Cornelia 4th,	3	3,818	5	Cecelia Rooker,	2	10,5 4	4
Ambronnetta,	3	3,540	1	Aaggie Camille,	2	10,183	14
Gabrina,	2	3,131	1	Phœbe Lincoln,	2	10,058	10
Aaggie Lee,	3	2,760	9	Princess Aaggie,	2	10,342	15
Aaggie Rosa 4th,	3	2,735	4	Susie Lee 2d,	2	10,1 9	13
Aaggie Sarah 2d,	2	2,682	15	Carrie S.,	2	10,043	
Lady De Ruiter,	3	2,038	12				

The Netherland family was one of the earliest of the breed to make a reputation for the production of butter.

Among the early importations made by Smiths & Powell Co. was the cow Netherland Queen, then rising two years old, and which, commencing at that age, surpassed all former records, by giving 13,574 lbs. 3 oz. of milk in a year. She gave 58 lbs. 12 oz. in a day.

Her trial for butter disclosed the fact that her milk was of very superior quality, and as a four-year-old she made a butter record of 20 lbs. in a week.

These gentlemen then returned to Holland, with a view of making further tests of the quality of the milk of these cows, which proved to be very satisfactory, and they then went to work systematically to secure all the cows of that family to be found in Holland.

Lady Netherland, the dam of Netherland Queen, was bought, and soon gave birth to what was afterwards the famous bull Netherland Prince, 7-6. Netherland Dowager, the grandam of Netherland Prince, was also bought. Several sisters and half sisters to Netherland Queen were then imported, all of which made very large butter records, some of them surpassing anything previously done by the breed.

The daughters of Netherland Prince proved to be remarkably rich milkers. Eight of his daughters, one two-year-old, five three-year-old, one four-year-old, and one five-year-old, made butter records which averaged 20 lbs. 3¼ oz. in a week, averaging 1 lb. of butter from 17.28 lbs. of milk.

NETHERLAND QUEEN, No. 414 H. H. B.; ADVANCED REGISTRY 124.
Imported. Milk record, 70 lbs. 12 oz. in one day; 15,614 lbs. 9 oz. in one year. Butter record, 20 lbs. in seven days.

THE NETHERLAND FAMILY.

Netherland Princess 4th, at 28 months old, made 21 lbs. 10¼ oz. of butter in a week, surpassing all records, of all breeds, for her age, at that time.

Over twenty-five cows of this family have made butter records which average for the whole number over 20 lbs. in a week.

They are also excellent milkers, a large number of them having made large yearly milk records: but their especial value is in the improvement in quality of milk. In this respect probably no other family has done as much for the breed.

The type of the Netherland family is also one which is much desired and sought after by breeders at the present time. They are low, broad, straight, square, blocky, very fine handlers; beautiful show animals; mature at a very early age, and give large yields of milk and butter when young. For the show ring they have very few equals, especially when crossed with the Clothilde family, which cross has become famous for show purposes.

MILK RECORDS, NETHERLAND FAMILY.—ALL MADE AT LAKESIDE.

	Yrs.	Lbs.	Oz.		Yrs.	Lbs.	Oz.
Netherland Belle,	4	19,516	8	Netherland Pet,	4	12,525	3
Netherland Consort		17,873	9	Netherland Grace,	2	12,442	1
Netherland Dowager,		17,160	11	Netherland Waukesha,		12,141	15
Netherland Princess,		16,766	13	Netherland Princess 3d,	2	11,978	3
Netherland Dutchess,		16,520	7	Netherland Aaggie,	2	11,798	2
Clothilde 4th,	3	16,457	9	Kappijne 3d,	2	11,384	15
Netherland Queen,	4	15,614	9	Aaggie Constance Netherland,	2	11,308	13
Netherland Chaperone,		15,414	8	Netherland Monk's Aaggie			
Netherland Peeress,		15,325	13	Constance,	2	11,291	7
Aegis 10th,	3	14,511	13	Netherland Duke's Nierop		11,955	13
Netherland Jewel,	4	14,294	10	Netherland Prince 4th,	2	11,478	2
Netherland Princess 5th,	4	14,153	1	Netherland Countess,		11,472	3
Aaggie Merrel 4th,		14,034	3	Netherland Baroness,		11,240	7
Netherland Baroness 4th,	4	13,922	11	Netherland Baroness 4th,	2	11,201	12
Lady Netherland,		13,875	5	Aaggie's 2d Daughter,	2	11,090	14
Soldene 2d,	4	13,868	11	Executrix 2d,	3	10,898	6
Netherland Dorinda,		13,656	7	Lady Fay's Netherland,	2	10,647	6
Netherland Triumph,	2	13,189	4	Netherland Trifle,	4	10,644	7
Netherland Baroness 2d,		13,047	8	Aaggie Constance Nemo,	2	10,573	15
Netherland Queen 3d,	4	12,770	0	Executrix Netherland,	2	10,290	10
Netherland Queen 2d,		12,022	7	Netherland Baroness 5th,	2	10,202	8
Netherland Pride,	2	12,508	13	Netherland Clara,	2	10,190	14

BUTTER RECORDS OF THE NETHERLAND FAMILY.—ALL MADE AT LAKESIDE.

	Yrs.	Lbs.	Oz.		Yrs.	Lbs.	Oz.
Netherland Peeress,		25	1-4	Netherland Ruth,	2	10	3
Netherland Dorinda,		24	9 1-2	Dream of Holland 3d,		15	3
Netherland Baroness 4th		22	14 1-2	Netherland Duke's Nierop,	3	15	2 1-2
Netherland Princess 5th,	2	21	10 3-4	Aaggie's 2d Daughter,	2	15	1
Lady Netherland,		21	3	Aaggie's 3d Daughter,	4	14	15
Netherland Baroness,		21	3-4	Netherland Gem 2d,	4	14	4
Aegis 10th,	3	21	7	Netherland Chaperon 3d,	4	14	4 2 1-2
Executrix 2d,	3	21	9	Tietsche 2d,	2	14	
Netherland Consort,		20	14 1-2	Netherland Baroness 4th's			
Netherland Queen,		20		Artis,	2	13	14
Netherland Monk's Aaggie				Cecelia Rooker 2d,	3	13	13
Constance,	3	20	1-2	Netherland Aaggie,	3	13	11
Netherland Chaperone,		19	8 1-2	Lady of Vernon,	23 m	13	10 3-4
Netherland Princess 5th,	3	19	6	Netherland Dorinda 2d,	3	13	10 1-2
Princess Idaline,		19	5 1-2	Ruth Artis 2d,	3	13	9 1-2
Netherland Myrrhna,		19	11 1-2	Netherland Grace,	2	13	4 1-2
Netherland Jewel,		18	3-4	Aaggie Constance Nether and,	2	12	5 1-2
Netherland Princess,	4	17	11	Lady Fay's Netherland,	2	12	1 1-2
Daisy Artis 2d,		17	7 1-2	Netherland Statesman's Queen,	2	12	9
Netherland Queen 3d,	4	17	7 1-2	Netherland Grace's Netherland,	2	12	6 1-2
Netherland Countess,		17	4 1-2	Dorinda 3d,	2	11	12
Netherland Triumph,		17	4	Lady Netherland 4th,	2	11	8 1-2
Netherland Baroness 5th,	3	17	1	Carlotta 3d,	2	11	3 1-2
Netherland Pamelia,		17	6	Netherland Dutchess Netherland,	2	11	0
Netherland Duchess,		16	15 1-2	Aegis 2d's Netherland,	2	10	13
Netherland Belle,	3	16	7	Netherland Belle 2d,	2	10	10 1-4
Netherland Dowager,		16	1-2	Netherland Countess 4th,	2	10	4
Executrix Netherland,	2	16	1	Netherland Belva,	2	10	4
Netherland Pride,		16		Netherland Simplicity,	2	10	1 1-2
Kappijne 3d,	4	16	6 1-2	Netherland Countess 3d,	2	10	
Lady Griswold's Netherland,		16	6 1-2	Chloe Artis Netherland,	2	10	12
Aaggie Merrell 4th,	2	16	6 1-2	Netherland Monk's Constance,	2	10	9 1-2
Netherland Queen 2d,		15	7 3-4	Aaggie Constance Nemo,	2	10	10 1-2

*These records were all made by cows bred or imported by us, and all made in our own herd.

NETHERLAND STATESMAN'S CORNELIUS.

THE CLOTHILDE FAMILY.

BUTTER RECORDS OF DAUGHTERS AND GRANDDAUGHTERS OF NETHERLAND PRINCE. BRED AND OWNED AT LAKESIDE.

	Yrs.	Lbs.	Oz.		Yrs.	Lbs.	Oz.
Carlotta 2d,		26		Ruth Artis 2d,	3	13	9 1-2
Clothilde 4th,	3	23	10 1-4	Lambertina 2d,	2	13	7
Netherland Princess 4th,	2	21	10 3-4	Olany,	3	13	1
Clothilde 5th,	3	21	10	Netherland Ruth,	3	12	12 1-2
Executrix 2d,	3	21	9	Aaggie Constance Netherland,	2	12	5 1-2
Aegis 10th,	3	21	7	Clothilde 4th s Netherland,	2	12	11
Netherland Monk's Aaggie Constance,	3	20	1-4	Netherland Grace,	2	12	4 1-2
Netherland Princess 5th,	3	19	6	Lady Fay's Netherland,	2	12	1 1-2
Princess Idaline,		19	5 1-2	Netherland Grace's Netherland,	2	12	6 1-2
Soldene 2d,	3	19	3-4	Clothilde Netherland,	2	11	10 1-2
Clothilde 3d's Countess,	4	19	12 1-4	Netherland Luchess Netherland,	2	11	9
Clothilde 6th,	3	17	10	Duchess of Veragua,	2	11	12
Daisy Artis 2d,	4	17	7 1-2	Netherland Dorinda 3d,	2	11	12 1-2
Aaggie Merrell 4th,	2	16	6 1-2	Princess Netherland Clotilde,	2	11	4 1-2
Executrix Netherland,	2	16	1-2	Netherland Statesman's Clothilde,	2	11	1 1-2
Kappijne 3d,	4	16	6 1-2	Netherland Dowager 2d's Princess,	2	11	1
Lady Griswold's Netherland,	4	16	6 1-2	Carlotta 3d,	2	11	3 1-2
Dream of Holland 3d,	4	15	3	Aegis 2d's Netherland,	2	10	13
Aaggie's 2d Daughter,	2	15	1	Netherland Belle 2d,	2	10	10 1-4
Clothilde 8th,		15	5	Chloe Artis Netherland,	2	10	12
Aaggie's 3d Daughter,	3	14	15	Clothilde 6th's Clothilde,	2	10	2 1-2
Crown Jewel 3d,	3	14	12	Netherland Monk's Constance,	2	10	9 1-2
Aegis 10th's Clothilde,	2	14	7	Aaggie Constance Nemo,	2	10	12 1-2
Tietsche 2d,	2	14		Addie 2d,	2	10	9 1-2
Netherland Chaperon 3d,	2	14	2 1-2	Netherland Simplicity,	2	10	1 1-2
				Netherland Countess 3d,	2	10	

Twenty-nine of the above were daughters of Netherland Prince, and the others are his granddaughters. All were bred and owned at Lakeside.

In 1880 Messrs. Smiths & Powell imported from Holland a yearling heifer of rare beauty of form, finish and promise, selected on account of these qualities, and because her dam possessed all the characteristics of an enormous milker, coupled with the natural beauty and remarkable physical development of the daughter. This heifer was Clothilde, 1308.

She was highly valued by her owners, but they had no conception of the wonderful reputation she was destined to make for herself and family.

As a three-year-old she made herself conspicuous among dairy cows, by producing in a year 15,622¼ lbs. of milk, surpassing all previous records for that age. As a four-year-old she gave 17,970 lbs. 3 oz. in a year, again excelling

NETHERLAND PRINCE No. 716 H. H. B.; ADVANCED REGISTRY, No. 8.

all records for that age. As a six-year-old she gave 26,021¼ lbs. in a year, far surpassing all previous records.

She averaged for five years, commencing before she was two years old, 18,579 lbs. She made 28 lbs. 2¼ oz. of butter in a week.

At the New York Dairy Show at Madison Square Garden in 1887, she was awarded the first prize for butter, over all breeds; her three-year-old daughter, Clothilde 4th, winning second in competition with all ages and all breeds.

Clothilde 2d, as a four-year-old, eclipsed all previous records for that age by giving 23,602½ lbs. of milk in a year.

Commencing with her two-year-old record, she gave in four years 77,212 lbs. 15 oz. of milk, an average of 19,303¼ lbs. per year, surpassing all records for that length of time and age.

She excelled all previous butter records by making 320 lbs. 1¼ oz. in ninety days, while her best week was 30¼ lbs.

Clothilde and four of her daughters (five head) made milk records which averaged 18,156 lbs. 13 oz. per year, one being but three, and two four years old at time of test.

For butter two were tested at three years, and one at four years, and the average record for the five was 24 lbs. 4⅛ oz. per week.

Forty two-year-old heifers of the Clothilde family—all descendants of Clothilde, named above—have been tested at Lakeside for butter, making an average for the whole number of a little over 12 lbs. per week.

Sixteen members of this family have been tested for pure butter fats by the Babcock test, showing an average for the whole number of 4.08 per cent.

The milk records of the Clothilde family are equally as remarkable as its butter production.

MILK RECORDS, CLOTHILDE FAMILY—ALL MADE AT LAKESIDE.

	Yrs.	Lbs.	Oz.		Yrs.	Lbs.	Oz.
Clothilde,		26,021	2	Queen Netherland Clothilde,	2	11,915	10
Clothilde 2d,	4	23,602	10	Clothilde 3d's Beauty,	2	11,839	2
Clothilde 4th,	3	16,457	9	Netherland Clothilde Countess,	2	11,026	2
Netherland Duchess 2d,	3	15,185	1	Clothilde 3d's Clothilde,	2	10,997	12
Clothilde 3d's Countess,		13,189	14	Idene Clothilde,	2	10,942	10
Clothilde 2d's Duchess,	2	13,150	7	Clothilde 6th's Clothilde,	2	10,093	9
Clothilde 6th,		12,612		Clothilde 5th,	3	10,072	14
Clothilde 8th,	4	12,190	13	Duchess of Veragua, in 10 ms.			
Clothilde 4th's Netherland,	2	12,578	12	and 25 days,	2	11,579	
Executrix Clothilde,	2	12,207					

BUTTER RECORDS, CLOTHILDE FAMILY—ALL MADE AT LAKESIDE.

	Yrs.	Lbs.	Oz.		Yrs.	Lbs.	Oz.
Clothilde 2d,		30	8	Intje Von Holingen,	2	13	2 1-2
Clothilde,		28	2 1-4	Clothilde 4th's Netherland,	2	12	11
Clothilde 4th,	3	23	10 1-4	Columbia Clothilde,	2	12	
Clothilde 5th,	3	21	10	Sir Clothilde Carlotta,	2	12	15 1-2
Clothilde 2d's Duchess,		19	15 1-4	Clothilde Netherland,	2	11	10 1-2
Clothilde 3d's Countess,		19	12 1-4	Princess Netherland Clothilde,	2	11	4 1-2
Clothilde 3d's Clothilde,		19	11	Netherland Countess Clothilde,	2	11	8 1-2
Clothilde 6th,		18	11 1-2	Cecelia Clothilde,	2	11	9
Countess Clothilde,	3	18	6 1-2	Clothilde 3d's Beauty,	2	11	3
Netherland Duchess 2d,	3	17	1-2	Duchess of Veragua,	2	11	12
Idene Rooker's Clothilde, under	2	17	2	Aaggie Merrell's Clothilde,		11	13
Clothilde 8th,		15	5	Eva Aaggie Clothilde,	2	11	2 1-2
Clothilde 3d,		15	6	Clothilde 4th's Artis Aaggie Rosa	2	11	11 1-2
Aegis 10th's Clothilde,	2	14	7	Princess Netherland Clothilde,	2	11	4 1-2
Queen Netherland Clothilde,	2	14	12 1-2	Netherland Statesman's Clothilde	2	11	1-2
Idene Rooker's Netherland,	2	14	9 1-2	Clothilde 6th's Netherland,	2	10	13 1-2
Kaan's Marie 2d's Von Holingen,	2	14	3-4	Executrix Clothilde,	2	10	15 1-2
Countess of Clothilde,	2	13	7 1-2	Clothilde 6th's Clothilde,	2	10	2 1-2
Queen of Clothildes,	2	13	9	Clothilde Idaline,	2	10	7

These records were all made at Lakeside, and from cows bred or imported by that establishment.

The Artis family, which has proven very desirable, was brought into prominence at Lakeside.

The founder of this family, Artis, owned by Messrs. Man & Son of Holland, was bred by the government of the Netherlands, his dam and sire both having been kept in the Zoological Gardens at Amsterdam, as choice specimens of the breed.

This bull founded a choice family, a large number of which were brought to America by Smiths & Powell Co.

OAKLAND CHIEF, No. 3259 H. F. H. B.

ONONIS, No. 2366 H. H. B.
Milk record, 68 3-4 lbs. in one day; 1979 lbs. 12 oz. in one month at three years old.

They proved to be animals of fine quality, unusually good handlers, even, desirable milkers, good butter makers, and have added to the quality and finish of nearly every herd into which they have been introduced.

Artis was the most famous bull in Holland. His owner refused $2,000 for him, which was considered an enormous price in that country.

Among the first cows of the black-and-whites to give to the breed a national reputation was Aegis, 69.

She was bred by Hon. G. S. Miller, and sold to Messrs. Smiths & Powell Co., in whose hands she and her nine daughters established the just claim as one of the great families of the breed.

Her sire was Rip Van Winkle, 35, and her dam was Agoo, 1, a daughter of Dowager, 7, the first cow to make a well-authenticated milk record of 12,681¼ lbs. in a year. At six years of age Aegis surpassed all previous records, of all breeds, by giving 16,823 lbs. 10 oz. of milk in a year, and at thirteen years of age she made 2 5lbs. 13¼ oz. of butter in a week, and 100 lbs. 6 oz. in thirty days.

Aegis and four of her daughters, the only ones tested for so long a period, made yearly milk records which averaged for the five 14,714 lbs. 12 oz., and weekly butter records which averaged 20 lbs. 1 oz., although one was but two years, and one but three years at time of test.

Others showed equal promise, on shorter tests, before they were sold. Several granddaughters, at two years, made yearly milk records of 9,000 to 10,000 lbs. in a year, and butter records of from 10 to 14 lbs. in a week.

The Johanna family, which has won its way into distinction as among the best of the breed, has been developed principally by Gillett & Son, whose herd is largely made up of members of this great family of milk and butter producers. Its origin comes from the great Johanna, bought by special order as one of the greatest cows to be found in Holland, for Hon. G. S. Miller, in whose hands she made a milk record of 88 lbs. in one day and 2,407¼ lbs. in one month. It was while under this test she was selected by one of the members of the firm of Gillett & Son at a cost of $537.50, although at the time she was a cow ten years old. She proved herself a valuable acquisition to this great herd and as a breeder of animals of the highest character, certainly one of the best of the breed.

She calved four daughters at Springvale, Johanna 2d, 3d, 4th and 5th; also one son. Johanna 2d and 3d were sent to the block because of being barren, and her son died at one week old. We believe she produced for Mr. Miller two sons and two daughters, viz.: Jonah, formerly at the head of J. W. Stillwell's herd of Ohio; Joe, who was retained for some years at the head of G. S. Miller's herd. Joan of Arc and Joy, who produced in one day 67 lbs. and 76 lbs. of milk respectively, were also kept by the last named gentleman, where they died.

The many Johannas of Springvale herd are direct descendants of Johannas 4th and 5th, whose records follow: Johanna 4th at seven years old made a milk record of 52 lbs. in one day and a butter record of 16 lbs. 10 oz. in one week; at ten years old she reached 76.2 lbs. milk in one day, 2,006.2 lbs. in one month and 20¼ lbs. butter in one week by the Babcock test.

Johanna 5th made as a two-year-old, 42¼ lbs. milk in one day and 14 lbs. 2 oz. butter in one week; at four years old she gave 67 lbs. 10 oz. milk in one day and 16,186 lbs. 5 oz. in one year and made by the Babcock test 23 lbs. 5 oz. butter in one week; at seven years old, after recovering from an attack of parturient paralysis, she was entered in the Wisconsin State Butter Contest and won easily over twenty-one other cows of all breeds. Her record at that time, we believe, has never been surpassed in a similar test by a cow of any breed with one exception. At this age under very adverse circumstances and officially supervised, was 89 lbs. 3 oz. milk in one day, 2,419 lbs. in one month and a butter record of 22 lbs. 1 oz. She will long be remembered as the cow that led us on to victory in the hotly contested butter test in Wisconsin in 1894 in the very hot-bed of Jersey enthusiasm. She not only defeated the Jerseys by a strong lead, but surpassed any work of any cow at the Columbian test for a yield of two consecutive days.

Johanna May, a daughter of Johanna 4th, gave as a six-year-old 74 lbs. 13 oz. of milk in one day, 2,020.1 lbs. in one month, and made 20 lbs. 3 oz. butter in one week.

Johanna Nig, another daughter of Johanna 4th, made as a two-year-old 35 lbs. 7 oz. of milk in one day and 11 lbs. 3 oz. butter in one week. Other daughters of Johanna 4th not yet old enough to milk, are Johanna Aaggie and Johanna Clothilde.

Johanna Rue, the oldest of Johanna 5th's daughters, made as a two-year-old 15 lbs. 7 oz. butter in one week and 44 lbs. 14 oz. milk in one day; as a five-year-old she made 18 lbs. 2 oz. butter in one week and 70 lbs. milk in one day, 14,000 lbs. in one year and 490 lbs. butter fat, equal by rules of Advanced Registry 612¼ lbs. worked butter.

Another daughter is Johanna 5th's Clothilde, who in official tests made the following records: As a two-year-old 45 lbs. 13 oz. milk in one day, 12¼ lbs. butter in one week; as a three-year-old 16 lbs. ¼ oz. butter in one week and 61 lbs. milk in one day.

Johanna Rue 2d, dam Johanna Rue, made as a two-year-old 50 lbs. 10 oz. of milk in one day and 12 lbs. 3 oz. butter in one week; and Johanna 2d's Beauty at three years 52 lbs. milk in one day and 16 lbs. 5 oz. butter in one week.

Weight, 2,500 lbs. Milk record in pedigree: Empress, 109 lbs. in one day; Gude Empress, 114 lbs. in one day. Dam's butter record, 38 lbs. 8 1-2 oz. in seven days.

Young things of the Johanna family now at Springvale are Johannas Aaggie, Clothilde, May 2d, Pauline, De Kol. and Mutual, all of rare individual promise. The esteem that greets the Johanna strain of blood can be best seen from the fact that many of the finest herds in the world are headed by sons and grandsons of Johannas 4th and 5th.

The characteristics of the Johanna tribe are their fine finish, uniformity and individual beauty and style; they are good size, weighing, at maturity, from 1350 lbs. to 1500 lbs., but lack the roughness which one expects to find in cows of this size; on the other hand they are very fine in bone, very broad and smooth, being described from milk to the milk and beef form and are noted prize winners.

Johanna 5th was first prize two-year-old heifer at the Wisconsin Central and Wisconsin State Fairs; as a three-year-old won first at Wisconsin Central and second in aged cow class at Wisconsin State and was in all these shows member of first prize Holstein herd. She was first at La Crosse, second at Minnesota and Wisconsin State Fairs in 1894 and at these was member of sweepstakes Holstein herd. Her daughter, Johanna Rue, was first in two-year-old class at Wisconsin and Inter-State Fairs and member of winning aged and young herds.

Johanna 5th's Clothilde was first in two-year-old class at La Crosse in 1894, second at Minnesota and first at Wisconsin State Fair, being member also of the sweepstakes aged and young herds at La Crosse, all breeds competing; member of produce herd for cow and bull at Minnesota and Wisconsin State Fairs in 1894; and at three years old, in 1895, she was placed third in aged cow class at Wisconsin State.

Johanna Rue 2d, of same age, was second at La Crosse, first at Minnesota and second at Wisconsin State Fairs in 1894, being member of bull and progeny herd that in each case was awarded sweepstakes.

Johanna Aaggie was second prize yearling at Wisconsin State Fair in 1895, member of first prize young herd and first prize aged herd.

Johanna De Kol was first prize calf at Wisconsin and Minnesota State, also Interstate Fair, in 1894, and was member of first prize young herd, sweepstakes and aged herd at last named show; also member first prize aged and young herds at Wisconsin State, the same year; again in 1895 she was member of first prize young herd at Wisconsin State Fair.

Johanna Clothilde and Johanna May 2d were first and third in calf class at Wisconsin State Fair in 1895, the former member first aged herd and both members of the winning young herd.

Cows.	Age at time of record.	Milk in 1 Day.	Milk in 1 Month.	Milk in 1 Year.	Butter in 1 Month.
Johanna,	10	88.	2,407.75	......	14 lbs.
Joan of Arc,	..	76.	......	......	.. ..
Joy,	4	67.	......	......	.. ..
Johanna 4th,	7	52.	......	......	16 " 10 oz.
Johanna 4th,	10	76.2	2,006.2	......	20 " 8 "
Johanna May,	3	50.25	......	......	16 " 6 "
Johanna May,	6	74.13	2,020.1	......	20 " 3 "
Johanna 5th,	2	42.50	......	......	14 " 2 "
Johanna 5th,	4	67.10	2,001.3	16,186.5	23 " 5 "
Johanna 5th,	7	89.3	2,419	......	22 " 1 "
Johanna Nig,	2	35.7	......	......	11 " 3 "
Johanna 2d's Beauty,	3	52.	......	......	16 " 5 "
Johanna 5th's Clothilde,	2	45.13	......	......	12 " 4 "
Johanna 5th's Clothilde,	3	61.	......	......	16 " ½ "
Johanna Rue,	2	44.14	......	......	15 " 7 "
Johanna Rue,	5	70.	1,928.5	14,000	18 " 2 "
Johanna Rue 2d,	2	50.10	......	......	12 " 3 "
Johanna Rue 2d,	3	60.	......	......	14 " 1 "

This list comprises every female of the Johanna family that has ever been tested so far as we know.

WAYNE FAMILY.

This remarkable family of Holstein-Friesians is descended from Queen of Wayne, H. H. B. 955, Advanced Register No. 1, selected personally by Mr. T. G. Yeomans, in Holland in 1879, as the best cow of the breed he was able to find regardless of price. This family is, by many breeders, considered co-equal with the Aaggie. It is not large, sprung as it is from one cow, but what it lacks in numbers it more than makes up in quality. Highest merit has always been the characteristic of the animals with this strain in their veins. We know of no cow which has excelled her in transmitting to her descendants her capacity to give plenty of rich milk. This is a pronounced characteristic of the family, and as inseparable from them as the black and white marks. They are large, vigorous and symmetrical animals.

Queen of Wayne gave 75¼ lbs. of milk in a day, 14,506¼ lbs. in ten months, dropping her next calf within one year. When eleven years old, and after the loss of one-quarter of her udder, she made 17¼ lbs. of thoroughly worked butter in one week, 50 lbs. 2½ oz. in twenty-one days, made by churning the cream by the Cooley process.

Her daughter, Princess of Wayne, H. H. B. 954, Advanced Register No. 2, was the worthy offspring of so remarkable a dam. She gave in her two-year-

old form, 14,008 lbs. 9 oz. of milk in ten months and twenty days, and dropped her next calf within less than one year; she gave in her five-year-old form, 20,469 lbs. 9 oz.; in her eight-year-old form, 20,561 lbs. 8 oz.; in her nine-year-old form, 21,104 lbs. 7 oz.; in her twelve-year-old form, *twenty-nine thousand and eight pounds* and eleven ounces in twelve months, which exceeds any other record ever made by nearly *three thousand pounds*, except one. She gave birth to eleven choice, healthy calves in twelve years and four days, and in twelve years nine and a half months, gave, by actual weighing of each milking, 195,770 lbs. 14 oz. of milk (nearly 200 tons), which is an average of nearly 42 lbs. per day for every day from the date of her first calf including all the time she was dry between calves. Her best day's record is 113 lbs. 1 oz., and 3,182 lbs. 2 oz. in thirty days. She made 24 lbs. 14 oz. of thoroughly worked butter in a week. This record, as a whole, is regarded by many of our best breeders as the most wonderful performance of any cow.

Twenty-seven of this family, including seven two-years, nine three-years, two four-years and only nine mature cows, averaged 16 lbs. 13 oz. of butter in a week, and 58 lbs. 6¼ oz. of milk in a day.

BUTTER RECORDS OF THE WAYNE FAMILY.

	Butter in a Week. Yrs. Lbs. Oz.		Yrs. Lbs. Oz.
Aaggie Cornucopia,	6 21 8	Mutual Friend 2d's Wayne,	6 22 5 3-4
Aaggie Cornucopia 2d,	3 16 12 1-5	Netherland Wayne,	6 16
Aaggie Cornucopia 3d,	2 12 1 4-5	Princess Aaggie, three teats,	6 16 8 1-2
Aaggie Pearl,	2 13 4	Pauline Paul America,	2 13 4 4-5
Aaggie 3d's Wayne,	7 19 10	Princess of Wayne,	10 24 14
America Grant,	3 14 10	Princess of Wayne 3d,	3 18 12
America 2d,	3 13 12	Princess of Wayne 4th,	5 19 8
Brookside Lilith,	2 14 8	Princess of Wayne 5th,	6 21 15
Concordia 2d's America,	2 11 6	Princess of Wayne 5th's Aaggie,	3 14 12
Dorinda Wayne,	3 16 2 7-8	Princess of Wayne 7th,	2 9 6
Dorothy Ondine Wayne,	3 21 5	Queen of Wayne, three teats,	11 17 4
Jetske Wayne,	3 16 7 1-2	Queen of Wayne 2d,	4 16 6 1-2
Lilith Aaggie Wayne,	3 16 1 1-4	Roxie Wayne,	3 21 1 3-5
		Sadie Vale Concordia,	2 18 14 1-3

The entire twenty-seven, comprising seven of two years, nine of three years, two of four years, and nine only of mature cows, averaged 16 lbs. 13 oz. of butter in a week.

MILK RECORDS OF THE WAYNE FAMILY.

	Age.	Milk 1 Day.	One Year.
Aaggie Pearl,	2	55 lbs. 13 oz.	11,305 lbs. 8 oz.
Aaggie 3d's Wayne,	2	48 " 14 "	12,817 " 7 "
Aaggie Wayne,	4	61 " 9 "	12,150 "
America Grant,	2	42 " 14 "	10,241 " 2 "
Concordia 2d's America,	2	47 " 4 "	12,120 " 3 "
Mutual Friend 2d's Wayne,	2	48 "	11,664 " 6 "
Netherland Wayne,	2	55 " 11 "	12,887 " 1 "
Princess Aaggie, three teats,	7	71 " 2 "	12,522 " 2 "
Pauline Paul America,	2	45 " 6 "	9,976 " 1 "
Princess of Wayne,	12	113 " 1 "	29,008 " 11 "
Princess of Wayne 3d,	6	83 " 15 "	19,122 " 8 "
Princess of Wayne 4th,	5	71 " 8 "	14,010 " 11 "
Princess of Wayne 5th,	5	68 "	11,795 " 8 "
Princess of Wayne 5th's Aaggie,	2	51 " 6 "	12,458 "
Princess of Wayne 7th,	3	65 " 1 "	10,998 " 14 "
Queen of Wayne,	8	75 " 8 "	14,506 " 2 "
Queen of Wayne 2d,	4	62 " 9 "	11,567 " 11 "
Sadie Vale Concordia,	2	47 " 2 "	10,258 " 4 "

The nine two-year, two three-year, and one four-year-old averaged 52 lbs. 10 oz. of milk in a day, 11,537¼ lbs. in a year; the six mature cows averaged 80⅞ lbs. in a day, 16,822 lbs. 9⅜ oz. in a year.

The eighteen averaged 61 lbs. 15 oz. in a day, 13,299 lbs. 5¼ oz. in a year.

MUTUAL FRIEND FAMILY.

This is a new family just coming into prominence, noted for the richness, as well as the superior style and finish of its animals.

The cow Mutual Friend, H. H. B. No. 10139, Advanced Registry No. 193, was imported by T. G. Yeomans & Sons of Walworth, N. Y., when a calf in 1884.

In her two-year-old form she gave 56 lbs. 7 oz. of milk in a day; 13,341 lbs. 9 oz. in a year; as a three-year-old, 82 lbs. 5 oz. in a day, 16,281 lbs. 15 oz. in a year, and made 20 lbs. 13 oz. of thoroughly worked butter in a week, by churning the cream by the Cooley process.

Her daughter, Mutual Friend 2d, H. F. H. B. 10513, Advanced Registry 961, has made the following records: At two years, 47 lbs. 15 oz. of milk in a day, 9,892 lbs. 14 oz. in a year, and 13 lbs. 1 oz. of butter in a week; as a four-year-old, 75 lbs. 9 oz. of milk in a day, 12,997 lbs. 3 oz. in a year, and 17 lbs. 3¼ oz. of butter in a week; at six years she tested 23 lbs. 2 oz. by the Babcock test. At seven years she gave 86 lbs. 11 oz. of milk in a day, and made an "officially authenticated" butter record of 25 lbs. 12$\frac{1}{100}$ oz in a week, as tested by the dairy department of Cornell Experiment Station, and was awarded the third butter prize of the Holstein-Friesian Association of $48.00 Her *lowest* amount of butter in one day was 3.583 lbs., which is higher than the *best* day's record of any Jersey cow in the Columbian dairy test. Her average butter fat for the week was 4.4 per cent.

This "official" test fully corroborated all that her owners had ever reported of her as a butter maker.

Another daughter, Mutual Friend 3d, H. F. H. B. 28389, Advanced Registry No. 1119, was "officially" tested when three years old by Prof. H. H. Wing, of

PAUL ALBAN DE KOL, No. 21022 H. F. H. B.

the dairy department of Cornell Experiment Station. Her record was 64 lbs. 2 oz. milk in a day, and 21.84 lbs. of butter in a week. She was awarded the first butter prize of the Holstein-Friesian Association over all the mature cows competing. Under the rules which governed the tests this record of a three-year-old is equivalent to 28 lbs. 8.93 oz. in a week for a mature cow, and nearly 2 lbs. more than any other record of that test. Her average per cent of butter fat for the week was 4.27, and her highest was 4.9 per cent.

Her lowest butter in any day was 3.016 pounds, than which there were only six better records for a day made at Chicago by mature cows. Her record is 1.68 lbs. more than the best week of any mature cow in the Columbian Dairy Test. During that test only eight times was a record made above 3 lbs. of butter in a day, and yet this three-year-old heifer made over 3 lbs. every day during the week of her test.

Mutual Friend 2d's Wayne, H. F. H. B. No. 18456, Advanced Registry No. 1080, a daughter of Mutual Friend 2d, by Aaggie Prince of Wayne, H. F. H. B. 8781, is a very stylish cow, combining the blood of several of the best and most noted families of the breed.

Her record as a two-year-old is 48 lbs. of milk in a day, 11,664 lbs. 6 oz. in a year. At five years she gave 78 lbs. 5 oz. of milk in a day, 2,137 lbs. in thirty days and was "officially" tested for butter by the Dairy Department of Cornell Experiment Station, making a record of 22 lbs. 5.76 oz. of butter in one week.

It must be borne in mind that these "officially authenticated" butter tests are as reliable and accurate as any trotting record made upon a public track, and are made entirely under the personal supervision of a representative of the Cornell University Agricultural Experiment Station, who spends the entire week making the tests at the home of the cows.

These are all of the family which have yet come in milk.

PIETERTJE 2D'S KONINGIN, No. 10625 H. F. H. B.
When nine months old.

PAULINE PAUL FAMILY.

This is a family, few in numbers, which has come into prominence during the past six years through the performance of that grand old cow, Pauline Paul, H. H. B. 2199, Advanced Registy No. 852. She had never been specially tested for milk or butter till she was eight years old, when the Messrs. Dutcher made a test which is the largest butter record ever reported of any cow of any breed for a full year. This record was 31 lbs. 1¼ oz. of butter in a week, 128 lbs. 13¼ oz. in a month, 1,153 lbs. 15¼ oz. in a year, thoroughly worked and salted one ounce to the pound before weighing. It was made by churning the whole milk of each day, and in as public a manner as it is possible to make an unofficial or private record.

An urgent invitation was given to all persons to come and witness the test at any time during the year, and remain as long as they desired. Her milk record during this year was 70 lbs. in a day, 18,699 lbs. 9 oz. in a year, the average for the year being 16¼ lbs. of milk to 1 of butter.

Previous to the making of this record her bull calves had been killed, and she had one heifer calf, Zozo, H. H. B. 10260, Advanced Registry No. 996, of which, in her five-year-old form the Messrs. Dutcher reported a record of 25 lbs. 10¼ oz. of butter in a week, 104¼ lbs. in thirty days, and at eight years of age a milk record of 88¼ lbs. in a day, 7,025⅞ lbs. in three months and fourteen days.

Zozo Princess 2d, H. H. B. 15138, is a granddaughter of Pauline Paul, and has a record, as a two-year-old, of 16¼ lbs. of butter in a week.

Her son, Paul De Kol, H. F. H. B. 14634, Advanced Registry No. 97, was purchased by Messrs. T. G. Yeomans & Sons when a few weeks old, and has been at the head of their herd for the past few years.

The following of his daughters have "officially authenticated" butter records made under the prize offerings of the Holstein-Friesian Association:

De Kol 2d's Pauline, H. F. H. B. 30712, made a record, as a two-year-old, of 12 lbs. 3⅞ oz. of butter in a week, and was awarded the fourteenth prize over eight mature cows competing. Her average per cent of butter fat for the week was 3.92 per cent.

Pauline Paul Georgie, H. F. H. B. 28394, Advanced Registry No. 1120, at three years, 14 lbs. 4¼ oz. in a week.

Pauline Paul Grant, two years, H. F. H. B. 35033, 13 lbs. 1¾ oz. in a week, upon which record she was awarded the eighth butter prize of the Holstein-Friesian Association, in a list of sixty of all ages competing.

Sadie Pauline Paul, H. F. H. B. 35054, two years, 11 lbs. 11¼ oz. in a week, and stood twentieth on the list of sixty competing, of all ages.

Aaggie 3d's Wayne De Kol, H. F. H. B. 37098, two years, 12½ lbs. 12¼ oz in a week, and stood tenth on the list of sixty.

Princess Aaggie's Pauline De Kol, H. F. H. B. 35056, two years, 9 lbs. 13½ oz. in a week.

Prairie Flower's Pauline Paul, H. F. H. B. 32257, Advanced Registry No. 1122, two years, 10¼ lbs. in a week (not official).

Princess of Wayne 7th's Pauline, H. F. H. B. 35055, two years (a granddaughter), 11 lbs. 5⅞ oz. in a week.

The six two-year-olds and one-three-year old, which have made "officially authenticated" records, average 12 lbs. 2.9 oz. of butter in a week.

HARTOG AND TWISK FAMILIES.

Several families originated with the Unadilla Valley breeders in the seventies. The most popular of these are the Hartogs and Twisks. The former sprang from the cow Jacoba Hartog 2 D.-F. H. B. She was a gift to her importer from Burgomaster Jacob Hartog, of Beemster district, North Holland. She was an ideal milch cow in form and appearance. Probably in the history of the breed no more successful prize winner can be found. At two years old she won the sweepstakes prize for the best milch cow of any age, grade or breed, offered by New York State Agricultural Society. The competition was very large, comprising Ayrshires, Jerseys, Devons, Shorthorns and Holsteins. She won the same prize the next year, and the second year following. This career thus remarkably begun continued up to the year of her death. Among her offspring Jacoba Hartog 3d has a record of 42½ lbs. of butter in fourteen days. This was made by the old, wasteful ways of skimming and churning. From this cow the bull Hamilton, for years the pride of the Chenango Valley breeders, was bred. This family is more generally distributed in New York, north of the Mohawk river.

The Twisks originated with Maid of Twisk, 1 D.-F. H. B. She was a prize winner at the International Exhibition held at The Hague, Netherlands, in 1872. Her efficiency in helping to build up the early reputation of the breed in America is universally recognized. At a period when 5,000 lbs. milk in a year was considered a remarkable yield, she produced nearly 16,000. And what is especially remarkable is that this period included the drying up of her milk, and a period of rest and freshening, and the producing of two strong, healthy calves, carried their full time. One of these calves was dropped April 3, 1878, and the other February 23, 1879. There could be no greater evidence of constitutional vigor. Her fine proportions are shown by her measurements, as follows: Height shoulders, 51¼ inches; hips, 54½; width hips, 23¾; length body, 64½; girth, 80. She strongly impressed her descendants. They are found largely as grades in central New York.

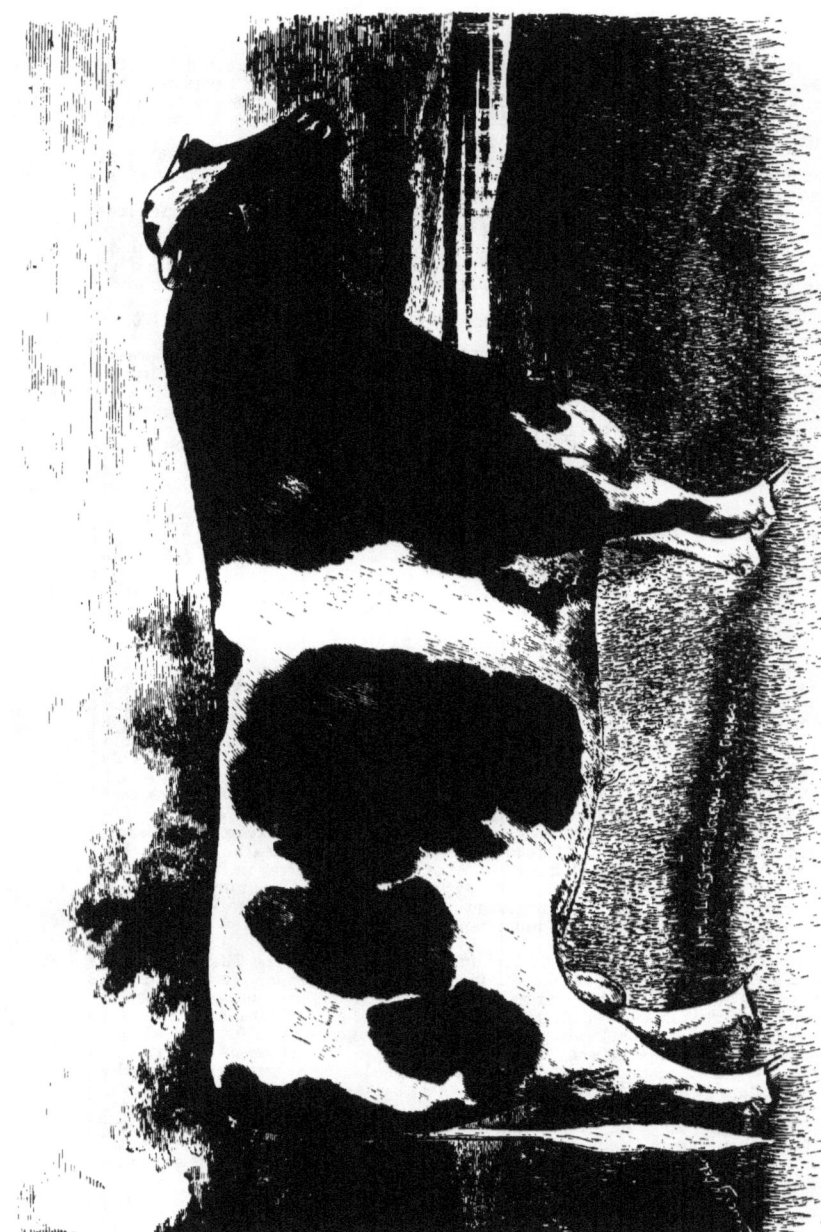

PRINCE OF ALTIDJWERK, No. 61 D.-F. H. B.

Imported. Selected in Friesland by Mr. Cornelius Baldwin as one of the choicest specimens of the breed in 1882.

CHAPTER XXIII.

THE CARE OF THE COW AT CALVING.

No words are needed to emphasize the importance of this subject to the practical breeder and dairyman. A very brief and limited experience is enough to convince any observing man that unless the cow does well at this critical period her usefulness for a long time will be greatly impaired, if her life is not actually lost. Milk fever, caked udder, garget and retention of the placenta are all diseases characteristic of this period, and all much better subjects of prevention than treatment. It is a very unfortunate fact also that as to some of these diseases the best cows are most subject to attack. Even the rugged constitution of our Holsteins does not always exempt them.

Amongst its clientage the Holstein-Friesian Register numbers many of the most skillful and successful breeders of the world. At considerable trouble it has secured from some of these experienced men a statement of their methods of procedure at this decisive time in the cow's life, which we reproduce here.

F. Roe, Sunnybrook Stock Farm, Augusta, N. J.:

"Two months before time to calve, one-half the usual grain ration is taken off, and the cow milked once daily for three days, then she is allowed to go thirty-six hours between milkings, then forty-eight, continuing in this way twelve hours longer each time until she is entirely dry. If she is a very persistent milker, I would take all the grain ration off until dry. Then commence feeding again, lightly at first, but gradually increasing to three-fourths her usual ration. One week before time to calve give one pound Epsom salts at night. If they operate the next morning, all right; if not, give one-half pound more. The evening of same day she is taken from the rest of the dairy, and put in a box stall well bedded with straw, and kept there until calf arrives. If bowels are not right, another pound of salts is given. As soon as the calf will suck, it is moved from one teat to another, so as to draw an equal amount of milk from each quarter. The cow is not milked dry until the end of third day. The feed after calving is bran; drink, water warmed to 100 degrees Fahrenheit, one pailful (four gallons) every hour until she has all she will take. The warm drink is kept up for three days, then gradually cooled until by fifth day she is allowed cold water, and, if all right, is put back with the rest of the dairy. The feed is gradually changed and increased for two weeks, when she will be on full rations again. This winter the ration is five pounds bran, three pounds dried brewers' grains, two pounds Chicago gluten, one pound old process linseed meal, forty pounds corn ensilage well eared, five pounds meadow hay. We do not milk before calf comes, unless the udder is very badly swollen; then she is milked dry every twelve hours until calf comes. We used to lose cows with milk fever, but have not had a single case since we commenced this course. I think the most important point is to leave a part of the milk in udder, and the drink and warm quarters so that the cow never gets chilled, which is very apt to bring on the fever."

Henry Stevens & Sons, Brookside herd, Lacona, N. Y.:

"We prefer to have a cow dry at least four weeks. We think nature demands this. We always avoid feeding any corn meal, or carbonaceous food of any kind, for at least two weeks before a cow is due to calve. We prefer wheat bran, or perhaps wheat bran with one-third ground oats, for a grain ration, and always carefully avoid any kind of food that would be liable to create fever. A week or ten days before a cow is expected to calve we provide her with a roomy, clean and dry pen, well bedded with dry straw and located in the warmest part of the stable.

"If the cow is six years old or over and is in good condition (and we believe it very important she should be) we give her immediately after calf is born one pound of Epsom salts. Always place a warm blanket on the cow, remove all bedding that is damp and replace with dry, then give a pail of bran mash as warm as the cow will eat.

"As soon as the calf has taken a little milk, which we endeavor to assist it

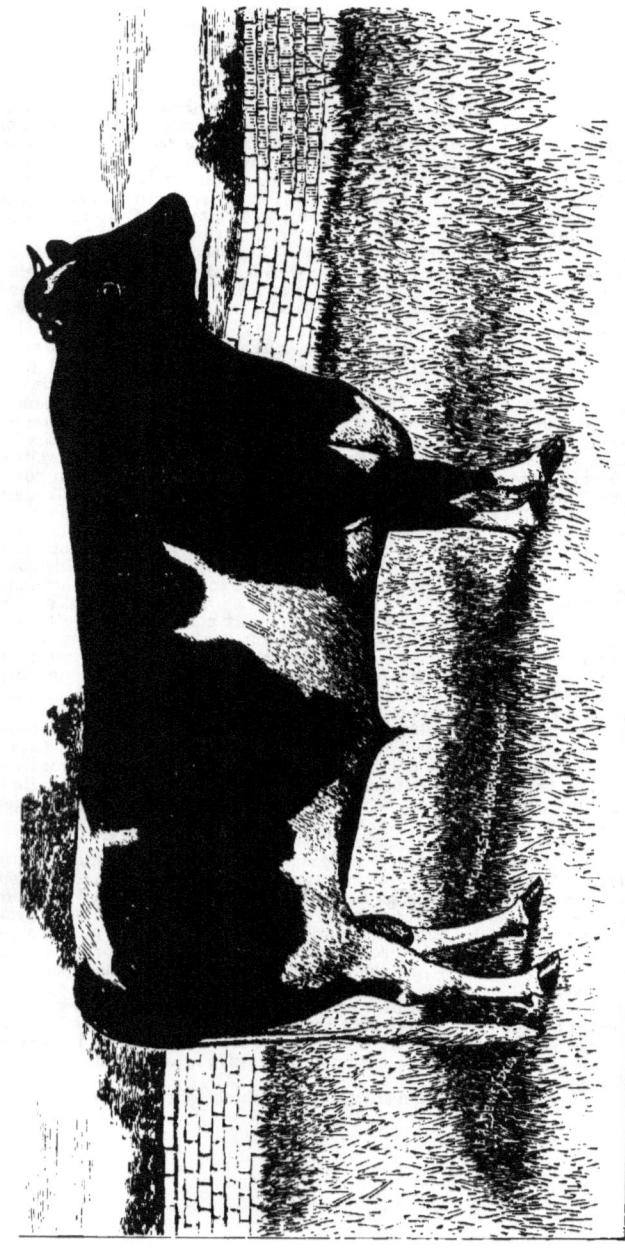

PRINCE OF EDAM, No. 1076 H. H. B.

Imported. First prize at Great Fair, Leyden, open to all the Netherlands. First prize in New York 1882. Weight at four years old 2,410 lbs.

to do as soon as we can conveniently, we milk the dam and feel that we have done everything that can be done for her comfort and safety. If the above precautions are taken, and a cow has proper care, we have but little fear of milk fever. We do not give cow any cold water for several days, and always avoid any cold draft.

"We usually leave the cow blanketed from twenty-four to forty-eight hours. This depends on the temperature of the stable."

William Rankin, Brockton. Mass.:

"First, want my cows to go dry from four to six weeks before the event, and I am very careful during that period to keep them gaining in flesh and other conditions, giving plenty of exercise.

"About four days before calving I put them in a box stall, 10x12, and feed very lightly, no harder grain than coarse shorts. I do this to avoid milk fever. At time of calving I try to be present to give aid if necessary. After the calf is born I sprinkle it over with fine salt. When the calf gets upon its feet I milk about one-half of the milk, and give about four quarts to the cow. I then aid the calf in sucking, let it get what milk it wants, and after about two hours I milk out carefully all the milk left. The calf is left with the cow for about twenty-four hours. The cow is then removed to her stall. About three hours after calving I give the cow two buckets of water, about 80 degrees, and then feed her a warm mash of scalded shorts, and for the first day or two feed lightly on hay, and no hard grain. Afterward I feed all the hay she will eat readily, and about six or eight quarts of shorts and roots per day for a week. I increase gradually on grain till I get to full ration. Warm the water for the first week."

Smiths & Powell Co., Lakeside herd, Syracuse, N. Y.:

"The treatment of cows in the Lakeside herd, preparatory to and during calving time, is as follows: From six to eight weeks prior to date of calving, if grain is being fed to any extent, it is discontinued, and an effort is made to have the cows dry from four to six weeks. Cows usually do better when they have this period of rest. The utmost care should be used in drying cows to avoid injury to the udders. We consider it much better to milk regularly until time of calving, rather than to force the cow dry. Keep the teats and udder flexible and soft.

"Clover hay, with ensilage or roots, we consider a desirable ration at this period. See that the bowels are kept open and regular.

"The cow should be put in a roomy, comfortable box stall a few days before she is due, and kept quiet. About thirty-six to forty-eight hours before the cow is expected to calve, we give one pound of glauber salts. If this dose does not move the bowels freely in twenty four hours, repeat the dose. Repeat the dose as soon as the calf is dropped. This is done to keep the system cool and guard against milk fever.

"The calf is removed from the cow at about three days of age, and taught to drink. The cow should be fed moderately, at first on light food, which can be gradually increased in quantity and richness, as the cow regains her normal condition."

Don J. Wood, West Exeter, N. Y.:

"I prefer that a cow should be thoroughly dry before beginning to spring bag.

"Most of our cows drop calves while on winter feed. They have hay and corn ensilage, as much as they will eat. If cows are not in good condition a light grain ration is given while they are dry, but would not dare to feed cornmeal.

"For a few days before we expect a cow to calve, she is given three or four ears of corn each day, or a few potatoes or other roots.

"Too much should not be given, or any great change in rations be made at this time. The object is to have the cow healthy and thriving, and to avoid a feverish condition.

"When a calf is expected the cow is put in a well-bedded box stall. I always like to be with a cow at time of calving, and help her as much as necessary to avoid too severe labor. She is then given a pail of warm slop, made by scalding four quarts of bran and adding an ounce of saltpetre and water to cool so the cow will drink it.

"If the cow is very feverish, from six to eight drops of extract of aconite is added to the slop, and, after she has cleaned, a pound or more of salts, and

PRINCESS OF WAYNE AND CALF, No. 954 H. H. B.; ADVANCED REGISTRY No. 2.

Milk record, 113 lbs. 1 oz. in one day; 29,008 lbs. 11 oz. in one year, exceeding all other records made by 3,000 lbs., except that of Pietertje 2d. Butter record 24 lbs. 14 oz. in seven days.

three or four heaping tablespoonfuls of ground ginger mixed and dissolved are given. Especial care is taken for a few days not to let the cow get chilled.

"If the udder is badly swollen I continue the aconite night and morning for a few days, and apply hot water slightly salted, and afterwards apply lard and kerosene oil mixed equal parts. If the udder is very painful to the touch, steep hops in water and apply. Warm milk rubbed on the udder after each milking is also good.

"I have usually been very successful with my cows at this period, but occasionally one does not clean. In that case I try to get the cow to eat a good grain ration at once, give her a little Golden Seal in each feed, and an ounce of saltpetre once a day for a few days, and in from seven to nine days she will clean, and usually do well."

S. N. Wright, Elgin, Ill:

"In times past the losing of cows with what is commonly called here milk fever has been a very serious matter with me, as well as with many other dairymen in this great dairy section. I often called on the cow doctor to save my valuable cows, but in almost every case when the cow was down and too late. I came to the conclusion that I had got to do something before the cow came in, and I adopted this simple mode, and have not lost a cow since. I commence about ten days or two weeks before she is due to drop her calf, and give her about four quarts of wheat bran in two feeds—one at night, and one in the morning. To this feed I add at first a large tablespoonful of cream tartar, increasing this to double the amount just before she comes in. About four or five days before she comes in I add to the above feed about two pounds of good linseed meal to each mess and continue this for a week or ten days after she has dropped her calf or until all danger has passed. If in hot weather, I give her to drink cold water, a little at a time and often. Use cow sense, and keep her out of the heat of the sun. If in cool weather, I take the chill off of the water she drinks."

Aug. Knorr: "Whatever the season, I always have the cow calve in the barn, giving her a comfortable, airy box stall, well bedded. I stay by her until her labors are over and calf delivered, leaving nothing to chance. A well-kept Holstein cow is of such rugged health that she will rarely need assistance. When the cow is in good condition previous to calving, nature will do the rest. If on winter rations I withhold constipating food, and give liberally of oil meal, bran, beets, or occasionally a bite of winter pasture. The process of labor loosens the placenta as delivery progresses. Too early or too hasty assistance at this point removes the calf without loosening the afterbirth from its attachments, and the next thing you have on hand is a case of retention of the afterbirth. Occasionally a young cow will have difficulty in calving. The ounce of prevention in this case consists in using only young bulls on the heifers. As soon as the calf is born I give the cow two pailfuls of thin bran and oil meal gruel. Then she is left alone, giving her absolute quiet and rest. During this she will pass the afterbirth, which is promptly removed. Then I look after the udder. When feverish or congested, starvation rations are indicated, a wisp of hay and a couple of beets, if necessary, for days. Put back on regular rations very carefully. After twenty-four hours the calf is taken from the dam."

H. F. W. Breuer, Charleston, S. C.:

"When my cows pass the fourth month of pregnancy I feed them very liberally of concentrated food, ground oats, wheat bran and corn meal. To a cow weighing 1,200 pounds I generally give eight pounds of oats, eight pounds wheat bran, and four pounds of cornmeal daily, divided into two feeds, and what hay or grass they will eat; a smaller cow a little less, a larger one a fraction more.

"Next I dry them off if possible sixty days before calving. About ten days before calving I take them off pasture, and put them in a lot where grass is thin and poor; also, take the corn meal out of their grain ration. Three or four days prior to calving, as near as I am able to judge, if the cow is matured and not over ten years old, I administer two pounds of Epsom salts and one quart of common molasses at one dose; if cow is over ten years old, one pound of salts and a quart of molasses.

"With this treatment, which I have pursued for a number of years, I have had little or no trouble from milk fever or retention of placenta. The advan-

PRINCESS OF WAYNE 3D, No. 1915 H. H. B.; ADVANCED REGISTY No. 6.

Milk record, 83 lbs. 15 oz. in one day; 19,122 lbs. 6 oz. in one year. Butter record, 18 lbs. 12 oz. in seven days; 76 lbs. 12 1-2 oz. in thirty days at three years.

tage in this treatment is in having your cows in the best fix possible for giving largest result at the pail. Should, however, milk fever make its appearance (which is very seldom the case), then I apply the lancet, and take blood away according to age and size—say a cow weighing 1,200 to 1,400 pounds, six years old, not less than from six to seven quarts; and smaller or older cows in proportion. Of course, if above has to be resorted to, she will not do as well in quantity or quality of milk for that season as though depleting had not been necessary."

A. C. Hallman writes as follows: "It is of first importance to have the animal in a strong, healthy condition. When the system is in good tone and health there is very little danger. Nature is so wonderfully perfect that if we only study her conditions there is little fear of trouble. With heavy milkers much stimulating food must be avoided, and laxative food should be provided. The bowels must be kept open. In winter a few roots and corn ensilage are very useful, if given in such quantities as not to cause a rush of milk, only enough to keep up thrift. Precaution must be taken a fortnight before calving and as long after. Before calving the danger is of inflamed udder, after calving garget, milk fever and other troubles of a similar nature. I find a little oil cake meal given daily a month previous is most valuable to throw all impurities out of the blood and remove danger of retention of afterbirth. Prevention is always the best cure. A roomy box stall should always be provided, well littered. The cow should be placed there a week before calving. Tie up before calving to prevent laying against partitions. Assistance can also be rendered more readily when necessary if the cow is tied.

"It is best to remove the calf soon, before the cow and calf get attached. I find it best not to remove the milk all at once. It seems to chill the system, and increases the danger of milk fever. A few pounds of Epsom salts lessens that danger. Light feeding is required for at least a week, and in many cases more. With inflamed udder I have found hot water fomentations very beneficial; afterwards a free application of soap, then rubbed into a thick lather. This has given me very good results. Prevent extreme exposures, either hot or cold. Never allow a draft, nor too close confinement."

Our readers will notice that on most of the points touched upon in the above communications breeders are in close agreement; while details of practice differ, the principles are the same. The salient points may be summed up as follows:

1. Preferably, let the cow go dry from four to eight weeks before calving, but do not force her dry. If she begins to spring before completely dry, continue milking regularly. The best methods of drying off are well stated by Mr. Roe, and there are but few cows that cannot be safely dried in this way.

2. Have the cow in thrifty, vigorous condition, but not fat. Feed no cornmeal, or stimulating, heating grain ration for some weeks prior to calving. Bran is the best grain for this period, with possibly an addition of ground oats or oil meal if the cow is run down.

3. See that bowels are loose. A good many give, in every case, a dose of salts a few days before or just after calving. Some give a dose at both times.

4. Provide a warm, dry, roomy box stall, with plenty of dry bedding, to which the cow should be removed long enough before she calves so that she may become wonted to her new surroundings.

5. Keep from drafts of cold air, and from becoming chilled in any way, especially just at the time of and after calving. One most successful breeder deems this so important that he blankets the cow immediately after calving.

6. Shortly after calving give a bran mash or pail of warm slops. Give no cold water for at least two days, and then only a little at a time at first.

7. Let the cow be kept in the barn, at least nights, whatever the season or the weather, when she is liable to calve. During the day, in the summer season, there is no objection to her running in a pasture where she can be occasionally observed.

QUEEN OF WAYNE AND CALF, No. 955 H. H. B.

CHAPTER XXIV.

THE REARING OF CALVES FOR THE DAIRY.

The general principles applicable to the raising of dairy calves have been well stated by Prof. I. P. Roberts of the Cornell Station as follows:

Having good inherited qualities, the next step is to see to the rearing of the calf. The calf should be well sustained and should make rapid growth, but this should not tend to fat, but the development of those qualities which are to make the value of the cow that is to be.

Warm skim milk in moderate quantities, after the calf is about two weeks old, bright clover hay and unground oats, should form the foundation of the calf's ration. In cold weather some oil meal, old process, or whole corn, or both, should be added, in order to furnish sufficient heat producers.

From the moment the calf is born it should be watched and trained for the dairy as carefully and scientifically as the little foal that is dropped in the trotting stable is trained for the track. It has been discovered that in order to get the best results, trotting colts should be fed and developed towards the uses to which they are to be put when mature. They are not only fed with a view to the track, but they are also exercised with a view to speed. Should the trotting colt be fed like the draught colt, then we might expect marked variation to appear before maturity, and this a marked variation for the worse; and if a trotter were desired, this would be a very foolish and very unscientific method of treating a trotting colt. I use the trotting colt as an illustration, because of its scientific treatment and breeding, which are showing such marked results in colts which have been properly bred, fed, and exercised.

If the dairyman were to use a tithe of the skill in rearing the dairy calf that the horseman does in rearing the trotting colts, we long since would have doubled the average product per cow of our dairies. Taking the dairy calf at birth, we find that it is unable to digest or assimilate coarse or innutritious food. Its delicate digestive apparatus can only take care of those forms of food which are easily broken down and assimilated, such as new milk; but if the calf is fed with new and rich milk, it inclines to put on fat, and this is just what the dairyman does not want. He should teach his animal to put fat in the pail and not on the ribs; and so the utmost care must be taken in balancing the quality and quantity of the food, that it may produce vigorous, healthy growth, and extend to some extent the abdomen, without inducing the animal to store up tallow. Great care should be taken not to have the food so concentrated as to dwarf the viscera and contract the stomach, neither should the food be so innutritious as to distend the stomach to such an extent as to injure the power of digestion and assimilation. We find calves can be reared on whey or watered buttermilk, but the results are not satisfactory, because the calf must take into its stomach so great a bulk that it cannot take care of it, and hence bloating, colic, and indigestion are sure to follow. The dairy calves never should be fed largely on concentrated food, such as corn meal, cotton seed meal, etc. If they lay on some flesh, and even some fat, while on pasture no evil results follow; but flesh and fat laid on by the feeding of concentrated and heat producing foods are sure to affect the usefulness of the future cow.

S. L. Hoxie, Leonardsville, N. Y.:

"No treatment will perfect what is born imperfect. Therefore my calves are raised from the breeds that produce the fewest poor milkers. Milk is the most perfect food. I cannot afford to feed new milk over two weeks. I feed skim milk about two weeks longer. I especially see that my calves are provided with good water from the first. Food should be given with regularity both as to time and quantity. Every individual calf should be watched closely with reference to the condition of its appetite and digestion. I know of no food that is good for dairy cows that is not good for calves, if properly prepared and fed. Calves should never be exposed to cold storms, or left unsheltered during cold nights. I do not favor turning them to pasture, but rather keeping them in clean stables. After they get used to eating wheat shorts they can be

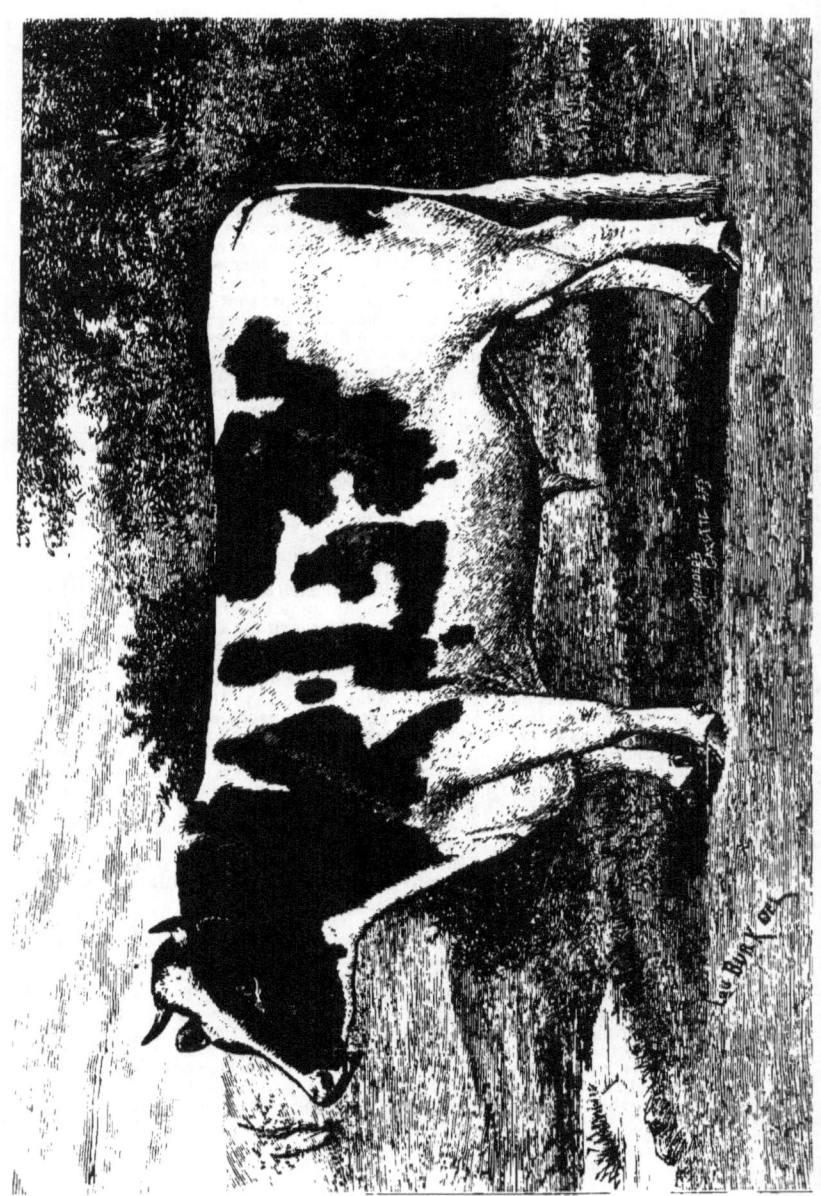

safely given all they will eat. They should always have all the good sweet mixed meadow hay that they relish. They should not be fattened, but kept in a thriving condition. Bulky food should be given that their stomachs may be developed. You cannot get the stomach too large for a dairy cow; providing the animal is kept thrifty. If calves are dropped at other seasons, care should be exercised that growth is not checked during the following winter. I have my heifers take their places in the dairy at about two years of age. After a heifer is bred for her first calf, she should be fed liberally with view of developing her milk glands. I prefer not to have my heifers drop their first calf in winter, they develop their udders more perfectly on grass. Heifers require plenty of succulent food for udder-development. The character of the dairy cow is largely made during the first period of gestation."

Mills Tourtellotte, La Crosse, Wis.:

"We have had good success with our calves for a few years and a compliance with your request on this subject may interest others situated as we were once, in trying to raise a calf as it should be and at the same time preserve the mother's milk for the dairy. If the dairyman could always depend on keeping up his herd to a desired standard of production by purchase, a large expense to him would be saved. But it is pretty generally conceded now that to have a profitable herd of milch cows they must be raised by the owner from calves of his own breeding. No man can buy any considerable number of well bred cows of approved capacity for quantity and quality of milk without paying more than can be invested profitably in the dairy business. This makes the subject of this article important as the foundation of a successful business. It is a very easy matter, if no regard is paid to cost, to rear calves from dairy ancestry so as to produce rapid growth and development; but how to do this cheaply has caused many a man an investment of a good many dollars, and in the last twenty-five years we have had our share of such experience. If what the farmer has to sell is cheap in the market he must produce a good article at a figure that will insure a profit or he must fail in his enterprise.

"Here in Wisconsin for several years it has not been profitable for dairymen to pay much attention to the production of beef. We therefore have not raised any of the male calves, except from the best thoroughbred cows. The female calves that come healthy and strong are matured to take the place of the old cows that must be culled out of every herd to maintain any given standard of production. It will not do to have calves too fat. If the heifer calf is fat she will not make a good dairy cow as a rule. The milk and digestive organs must be cultivated and given every chance to develop. The only safe way to do this is to keep a calf in a good healthy growing condition. Let her hair have a healthy look, skin loose and eyes bright.

"The calf is taken from the cow after the second day and taught to drink; for a week a little whole milk is mixed with skim milk, fresh and warm from the separator, and a very little (about a tablespoonful) of oil meal jelly (boiled oil meal) is stirred in and fed to the calf twice a day. From the start the calf is put in a light, warm, well ventilated and dry pen. Usually two or three calves about the same age and size are put together. We place before them a little bran and whole oats, and some very nice clover or millet hay is always in the rack. The calves will very soon eat freely of this grain and hay. It is always well to keep in a trough some good clean water. They will not drink much at a time but will take a little very often. To calves that are intended for the butcher we give a little more whole milk than is given to the others and continue to give them such until they are about six weeks old when they are ready for market. Always increase the amount of oil meal jelly according to the capacity of the calf, paying attention to the condition of the bowels. If the bowels get too loose stop the oil meal for a few rations, but if care is used the oil meal jelly will not cause any trouble. Always when we used unboiled oil meal our calves had bowel trouble and did not do well. When the calves we intend to keep and mature into dairy cows are about eight weeks old we put them into stanchions and feed them as before, only increasing the amount of grain and hay to what they will eat up clean twice a day.

"Our calves commence coming about the first of September and we find it to be our experience that the late fall and winter calves are reared the easiest and develop the fastest. In the spring they are ready to be turned out to grass and with a little grain they will continue to make rapid growth, and when two years old each one ought to have a calf and commence paying her own way. Those calves that come in the spring and summer we treat in the same way. We do not let them out to grass. The flies and the hot weather are a material damage to them. They are allowed to run each day in an open yard for exercise but go freely to their pens in a basement stable, well lighted and ventilated and dry."

S. A. Langdon, Morrison, Ill.:

"In regard to the matter of rearing calves, I have practiced the following for a number of years with the most satisfactory results in every case: I let the calf draw all the milk it wants from the dam until it is one week old. That gives the calf a good start and I think it is better for the cow. I then feed it the dam's milk until the calf is four weeks old, then gradually get it on to skim milk by mixing it with the new milk. It can be done in three or four days without any bad effect on the calf. I have a calf barn with a row of stalls on each side, and a feed alley through the center. The calves stand head to the alley. The stalls are double, five feet wide for two calves, a hay manger and feed box for each calf. The calves are tied with small chains around the neck. As soon as they will eat I give them hay and a handful of oats and a little oil meal. I like to have them learn to eat before they are put on to skim milk, as the oil meal makes up in part for the fat taken from the milk. I feed one gallon of milk to a feed night and morning. Feed the oats and meal immediately after the milk, as it stops the tendency to suck their stall mates' ears. I never increase the quantity of milk, give more oats and meal as they need it and all the good hay they will eat. I like whole oats better than ground! They eat them slower and are not as apt to clog. I feed the milk as long as I have it, have fed it to calves until twelve months old with the best results. The milk should always be warmed to blood heat. As soon as the calves are old enough to want water they are turned into the yard days where they can get all that

NETHERLAND HENGERVELD, 13106 H. F. H. B.

Was officially tested one week for butter in 1896, and entered in competition for the $1,250 offered in prizes for officially authenticated records by the Holstein-Friesian Association of America, and was awarded second prize upon a record of 21.33 lbs. butter fat, equivalent to 26.66 lbs. commercial butter.

they want. I never allow spring calves to eat any fresh grass until the second season. I am not troubled with calves scouring, and they are always ready for their feed."

Frank Roe, Augusta, N. J.:

"The calves are generally left with their dams until three or four days old, then put in box stalls alone and taught to drink, which they will usually do the second feeding. They are fed morning and evening from three to four quarts of milk from the cow as soon after milking as possible, the quantity depending on size and appetite of the calf, but never give quite all the calf will take as we think it best to keep them a little hungry. After the first week hay and feed are put where the calf may easily reach them.

"The feed is two parts bran or middlings with one part oil meal. It is always fed dry as it is not so liable to scour the calf as when fed in the drink. Will commence with one teaspoonful each feed, increase to one-half pint each feed by the time the calf is four weeks old. If the feed should scour the calf, reduce the quantity. If it does not get better give one-half teaspoonful of tannic acid dissolved with boiling water, with one teaspoonful laudanum twice daily until cure is effected, which will usually be after two doses. This care is continued until about three months old, gradually increasing the feed to one quart daily at this age—when the milk is gradually taken off and water substituted, until about four months old, when it will do very well without the milk ration. At all times the stall is kept dry and with plenty of bedding, for nothing will bring on scours sooner than for a calf to lie down in a filthy stall.

"This is our method, as we sell milk and have no skim milk. If we had the skim milk we would gradually substitute it for the whole milk after the calf was three weeks old, always warming it to about 100 F."

J. R. Beuchler, Leesburg, Va.:

"First, we try to get good healthy calves, then let them to the cow three times a day, for, say, fifteen days. They are then taken off from the cows and given skim milk with a little new milk three times a day for the next fifteen days, and after this skim milk alone with a little oil meal in it, at the same time give what hay and ensilage they will clean up over night. After they are one month old we give in the ensilage or cut feed a little mill feed of any kind we are feeding to the cows. In this way we raise good, healthy, robust calves. Find best results by keeping them in the stable all the first summer.

"For scours in calves a never failing remedy is : 1 oz. of laudanum ; 1 oz. of cannella bark (powdered); 4 oz. of chalk; 4 oz. rain water.

"Shake well and give three or four tablespoonfuls three or four times a day. Attention for one day will generally cure. In very violent cases give 1 to 2 oz. castor oil and one teaspoonful turpentine first. Have used the above over twenty years and never had it fail."

Hoard's Dairyman gives the following instructions for feeding young calves:

"We always prefer the ground flaxseed meal to the oil cake for calf feeding. The object is to replace the lost butter fat with another fat. That in flaxseed seems to be the best substitute.

"We commence with a young calf, say a week old, by feeding not to exceed a tablespoonful a day. This is taken and scalded with boiling water, and when ready divided into the several feeds of the day. As the calf grows, we gradually increase the amount to six or eight tablespoonfuls a day when the calf is four to six months of age. It must be remembered that the calf is a baby bovine. His stomach for the first four weeks will receive solids only in the right form, and then only in a limited quantity. From four to six weeks of age he takes on the ruminating stomach—commences to chew the cud—and when that occurs, it is safer to feed more of the solids. Take special care not to overfeed the first four weeks."

J. L. Stone, Secretary Lackawanna Breeders' Association, Waverly, Pa.:

"I have found it a very simple and easy matter to raise good calves when there was a supply of skim milk available, but thousands of farmers ship their milk to city markets and have no skim milk to feed. Very few of these attempt to raise any calves and consequently can do very little towards improving the character of their dairies. To feed new milk is too expensive and they think they cannot raise calves without milk. I have raised a great many calves with very little milk, and that while they are quite young. I confess it requires a great deal of care and considerable trouble and I have had some failures, but successes enough to warrant the undertaking when one desires to improve the herd.

"I usually allow the calf to nurse the mother a few times, then teach it to drink. For a week or ten days the calf gets nothing but milk, then I very gradually replace the milk with gruel, so that at the end of ten days more very little milk is used. If milk is very expensive it may be dispensed with altogether after a few weeks, but I prefer to use a little for several months.

"To make the gruel referred to I prefer a mixture of equal parts of brown wheat middlings, buckwheat middlings and old process linseed cake meal. Some hours before feeding stir the grain into cold water, stirring thoroughly. At feeding time add warm water to thin, and bring it to the temperature of new milk. I do not give quantities, as they vary so much with the age and condition of the calf. A spoonful of grain to a calf is enough at first, and increase very gradually and watch your animals very closely to see what they will stand. The calves will not look so slick as milk fed calves but they will make just as large two-year-olds and just as good cows. Be particular about the temperature of the gruel and do not overfeed."

RHODA, No. 434 H. H. B.
Milk record, 96 lbs. 12 oz. in one day; 21,309 lbs. in one year. Butter record, 23 lbs. in seven days.

Ernest Hitchcock, Pittsford, Vt.:

"I usually leave the calf with its dam for from thirty-six to forty-eight hours. I then remove it and teach it to drink, allowing it to get hungry before making the first attempt. Feed twice per day, about six pounds per feed, of whole milk warm from the cow. The amount will vary somewhat according to the size and appetite of the calf; better under feed than over feed. Continue this for two weeks. Then feed half skim milk for a week, then all skim milk. Warm the milk for three months, longer in winter. At about ten days old place fine bright hay within easy reach and keep it there. Also teach the calf to eat dry bran, linseed meal, middlings, ground oats or a combination of two or more of these feeds. Perhaps bran and linseed mixed half and half are as good as anything. The calf should eat considerable of this feed by the time it is two or three weeks old. There is little if any danger of its eating too much of this dry feed. The boxes should be kept clean, and don't leave the same feed in them from day to day. After the calf has once learned to eat don't give more than is eaten up clean. I give no gruels of any kind in the milk or out of it and mix no feed of any kind in the milk. Formerly did so, but like my present method much the best. I consider it safer and less trouble. Possibly, if I were trying to force growth for baby beef, might try the other method again. I have tried feeding three times a day but did not see much of any better results than from feeding twice. My chief difficulty comes from not having at all times of the year sweet skim milk, my choice being limited to whole milk or sour milk. At these times I continue the whole milk a week or two longer, according to the vigor of the calf and change at once to sour milk. After the calf has commenced to eat readily of dry bran and hay I consider the critical point has been passed. In case of scouring give an ounce of castor oil, then put on scant rations, feeding perhaps four times a day one or two pounds at a time. A little lime water in water is good. If the case is serious, and the calf valuable, in the absence of a competent veterinary see your family physician and ask what he would do in a similar case amongst human infants. Within the last four months I have seen very successful dairy-

RIJANETA, No. 1431 H. H. B.; 216 ADVANCED REGISTRY.
Butter record, 22 lbs. 1 oz. in one week; 80 lbs. 11 1-4 oz. in thirty days; 26 lbs. 8 1-2 oz. butter in seven days at nine years of age.

men who have adopted the system of dry feeding of grain to young calves instead of making gruel and all are pleased with the change. I have had one experience with calf cholera or white scours. I brought a two-year-old heifer from the pasture one day in September with an apparently healthy calf. The next morning the calf could not stand and by noon it was dead. The stable was thoroughly cleaned and disinfected with a solution of bichloride of mercury. Another cow and calf were placed in it (or if I remember correctly the second calf was dropped in this stable) and the calf went the same road, only he was a little longer in going. From that time on every calf I had for about six months had a more or less severe attack. Those that got a good start of two or three weeks I saved. Those that were attacked at a day or two old died. The disease left as suddenly as it came and I have not had a case for over a year. The leading symptoms as I observed them were extreme and sudden prostration, white watery discharge from the bowels, extremely offensive odor and sinking in of the eyes, the eyes turning dark, and often, if the calf lives long enough, total blindness. In my judgment the best course for a

SCHUILING, No. 3350 H. F. H. B.

Milk record, 88 lbs. one day; 2,500 lbs. 11 1 5 oz. in thirty days; 9,750 lbs. 15 oz. in six months sixteen days.

farmer to pursue, if he has a clear case of this disease, is to bury the calf at once, the sooner the better, at least unless it is an unusually valuable calf. I don't believe a calf a day or two old attacked by the genuine white scour is worth fussing with. I have never seen any explanation of the cause of the disease which seemed to me plausible. To say that it is an outgrowth of simple diarrhœa seems to me much like calling tuberculosis an outgrowth of a common cold. Such calves as my first one have been called living abortions, but I fail to see that that throws any light upon the subject."

Major Henry E. Alvord, of the United States Department of Agriculture:

"Among dairy cattle the best practice is to remove the calf from the cow within twenty-four hours after its birth, and at once teach it to drink. This separation may be delayed until the dam's milk assumes its normal condition, but as a rule the earlier the calf is taken in hand and its feeding regulated, the better for the calf. The younger it is, the easier it learns to drink. It is also better for the dairy cow to be milked by hand regularly than to suckle a calf. The milk of good cows is often too rich for their calves, and the latter are apt to take too much if left to themselves. The calf should have the milk of its dam or some fresh cow, and receive it while warm, and at least three times a day, preferably four, for a week or a month. During this time if the milk is rich it should be diluted with warm water one-fifth to one-third its own bulk according to the richness, or the milk may be kept a few hours, the best of the cream removed, and then warmed and fed. To make a good calf three feedings a day should be kept up for a month or six weeks, and the milk should be fed warm for a longer period, especially if the weather is cold. But after twelve days milk set twelve hours or so, and lightly skimmed, will do, and after ten days more the skimming may gradually be made closer until at the end of a month, or soon after, a skim-milk diet is reached. No rule can be given for quantity in feeding calves, they differ so much in size and food requirements. Judgment must be used and the feeding effects observed, and the calf given enough to thrive and be active, but not too much. More calves suffer from overfeeding than from scant diet. Keep the calf a little hungry and eager for more rather than fill it to dullness. The endeavor should be to prevent the beginning of indigestion which leads to scouring and perhaps to fatal diarrhœa. Nothing causes indigestion sooner than the overfeeding or irregularity in the quantity, time and temperature of the milk, especially while the calf is young, and absolute cleanliness about the feeding vessels is essential, with frequent scalding. If it can with certainty be kept equally clean, some feeding device which compels the calf to suck its milk instead of swallowing it rapidly is preferable to the open pail, but, all considered, the latter is usually the best utensil. If gritting the teeth or other symptoms of indigestion appear, a little limewater in the milk or a little baking soda will usually prove a correction. Keep the calf dry and clean and fairly warm, but in pure air, and allow it to exercise. If its box is small, turn it daily into a covered yard or small paddock. Young calves like company, but if kept together are likely to learn bad sucking habits. Every calf had better have its own box until a month or two old, and then be tied up out of reach of neighbors, but several may exercise together if not turned out until an hour after taking milk. The calf here referred to is not supposed to be for veal, but to be raised for a dairy cow. The foregoing treatment should be accompanied by early lessons inducing it to eat sweet hay and a little grain. The sooner it learns to eat hay, or other rough forage, the better; and the more it eats, the better; but keep up milk feeding as long as possible, if only once a day. Grain should be used sparingly. oats and bran preferred, perhaps a little linseed, and always to judiciously supplement the other food. Do not turn it on to grass too soon. If a spring calf, carry it over to the second summer without pasturage. A fall calf will be in good shape to get its own living from pasture its first summer."

The late Prof. E. W. Stewart (condensed by the editor from "Feeding Animals"):

"Fresh milk is the best food for the young calf, and the natural method is for the calf to draw it from its dam. This method is only practicable among the breeders of pure bred stock grown primarily for beef, and if such breeder is located where milk is valuable, it is unnecessary that he should feed new milk longer than one or two months. After that period the calf may be fed upon the skim-milk and linseed or flaxseed gruel with excellent results. If the

SHADELAND BOON, No. 9887 H. H. B.

Imported. Milk record, 69 lbs. 5 oz. in one day; 1,946 lbs. 6 oz. in thirty days. Butter record at six years old, 81 lbs. 15 1-2 oz. in seven days; 125 lbs. 12 oz. in thirty-one days.

calf is to be taught to drink, it is better to do this when six to ten days old. The calf should have the milk warm from the cow, having the run of a dry yard with a little grass or hay to eat. A small field of grass in summer is still better. When the time comes for feeding skim-milk the ration may be made about as nutritious as new milk by adding to it gruel made by boiling a pint of flaxseed and a pint of oil meal in ten to twelve quarts of water, or flaxseed alone in six times its bulk of water. Mix this one to three parts of skim-milk, and feed warm. Let the calf have its fill twice per day at regular times until six months old. During this time teach it to eat a few oats, and in case of a tendency to scour give for a meal or two, in the milk, a quart of coarse wheat flour, sometimes called by farmers canel. The dairyman may feed whole milk a single week and then substitute skim-milk with a little flaxseed jelly mixed in as above described, or add two tablespoonfuls of oil meal per day dissolved in hot water. This oil meal may be doubled in a week, gradually increasing to one pound per day, but this will be sufficient up to sixty days old, then add a pound of oats, oatmeal or middlings, and continue another sixty days. Twenty pounds of skim-milk per day is sufficient for the first ninety days, but no injury will result from a larger ration as the calf grows older. For the next ninety days, if skim-milk is short, feed only ten pounds per day, and increase the oats or middlings to two pounds per day. Linseed meal, new or old process, is a most excellent feed, but oatmeal or middlings may be used in its place with skim-milk. An excellent calf may be raised on skim-milk alone.

"We have had calves seventy days old fed on one-half pound of flaxseed and one and a half pounds of oatmeal each, with twenty pounds of skim-milk per day, that have gained an average of three and one-fourth pounds per day for ten days. Their average weight at seventy days was 230 pounds. We ordinarily expect thrifty calves to weigh 300 pounds at three months. Flaxseed as a small part of the ration for the calf cannot be too highly recommended. It is a natural antidote to scouring, and a feverish condition of the stomach and intestines. Its large proportion of oil renders it appropriate to mix with other food deficient in the oil."

Prof. James Law—Indigestion, Diarrhea (Simple and Contagious), White Scour (or Calf Cholera):

"Indigestion may occur from many different causes, as costiveness; a too liberal supply of milk; too rich milk; the furnishing of the milk of a cow long after calving to a very young calf; allowing a calf to suck the first milk of a cow that has been hunted, driven by road, shipped by rail, or otherwise violently excited; allowing a calf too long time between meals, so that impelled by hunger it quickly overloads and clogs the stomach; feeding from the pail milk that has been held over in unwashed (unscalded) buckets, so that it is fermented and spoiled; feeding the milk of cows kept on unwholesome food; keeping the calves in cold, damp, dark, filthy or bad smelling pens; feeding the calves on artificial mixtures containing too much starchy matters; or overfeeding the calves on artificial food that may be appropriate enough in smaller amount. The licking of hair from themselves or others, and its formation into balls in the stomach, will cause obstinate indigestion in the calf. The symptoms are dullness, indisposition to move, uneasiness, eructations of gas from the stomach, sour breath, entire loss of appetite, lying down and rising as if in pain, fullness of the abdomen, which gives out a drumlike sound when tapped with the fingers. The costiveness may be marked at first, but soon it gives place to diarrhea, by which the offensive matters may be carried off and health restored. In other cases it becomes aggravated, merges into inflammation of the bowels, fever sets in, and the calf gradually sinks.

"Prevention consists in avoiding the causes above enumerated, or any others that may be detected.

"Treatment consists in first clearing away the irritant present in the bowels. For this purpose one or two ounces of castor oil with twenty drops of laudanum may be given, and if the sour eructations are marked, a tablespoonful of limewater or one-fourth ounce calcined magnesia may be given and repeated two or three times a day. If the disorder continues after the removal of the irritant, a large tablespoonful of rennet, or thirty grains of pepsin, may be given at each meal, along with a teaspoonful of tincture of gentian. Any return of constipation must be treated by injections of warm water and soap, while the persistence of diarrhea must be met as advised below.

SIR JEWEL ECHO MECHTCHILDE, No. 12363 H. F. H. B.

REARING OF CALVES FOR THE DAIRY.

"Scouring is a common result of indigestion, and at first may be nothing more than an attempt of nature to relieve the stomach and bowels of offensive and irritating contents. As the indigestion persists, however, the fermentations going on in the undigested masses become steadily more complex and active, and what was at first the mere result of irritation or suspended digestion comes to be a genuine contagious disease in which the organized ferments (bacteria) propagate the affection from animal to animal, and from herd to herd. In enumerating the other causes of this disease, we may refer to those noted above as inducing indigestion. As a primary consideration any condition which lowers the vitality or vigor of the calf must be accorded a prominent place among the factors which, apart from contagion, contribute to start the disease *de novo*. Other things being equal, the strong, vigorous races are the least predisposed to the malady, and in this respect the compact form, the

DE KOL 2D'S PAULINE, 30112 H. F. H. B.

At four years old awarded first prize by the Holstein-Friesian Association of America for largest officially authenticated yield of butter fat in contests of 1896-7. Record, 19.31 lbs., equivalent to 24.14 lbs. commercial butter.

healthy coat, the clear eye, and the bold, active carriage are desirable. Even the color of the hair is not unimportant, as in the same herd I have found a far greater number of victims among the light colors (light yellow, light brown) than among those of a darker tint. This constitutional predisposition to indigestion and diarrhea is sometimes fostered by too close breeding, without taking due account of the maintenance of a robust constitution, and hence animals that are very much inbred need to be especially observed and cared for unless their inherent vigor has been thoroughly tested. The surroundings of the calf are powerful influences. Calves kept indoors suffer to a greater extent than those running in the open air and having the invigorating influences of sunshine, pure air and exercise. But close, crowded, filthy, bad smelling buildings are especially causative of the complaint. They further weaken the system so that it can no longer resist and overcome the trouble. The condition of the nursing cow and her milk is another potent cause of trouble. The food of the cow is important.

"The symptoms of diarrhea may appear so promptly after birth as to lead to the idea that the cause already existed in the body of the calf, and it usually shows itself before the end of the second week. It may be preceded by constipation, as in retained meconium, or by fetid eructations and colicky pains, as in acute indigestion. The tail is stained by the liquid dejections, which are at first simply soft and mixed with mucus with a sour odor, accompanied by a peculiar and characteristic fetor (suggesting rotten cheese), which continually grows worse. The amount of water and of mucus steadily increases, the normal predominance of fatty matters becoming modified by the presence of a considerable amount of undigested caseine, which is not present in the healthy feces, and in acute cases death may result in one or two days from the combined drain of the system, and the poisoning by the absorbed products of the decomposition in the stomach and bowels. When the case is prolonged the passages, at first five or six per day, increase to fifteen or twenty, and pass with more and more straining, so that they are projected from the animal in a liquid stream. The color of the feces, at first yellow, becomes a lighter grayish yellow, or a dirty white (hence the name white scour), and the fetor becomes intolerable. At first the calf retains its appetite, but as the severity of the disease increases the animal shows less and less disposition to suck and has lost all vivacity, lying dull and listless, and when raised walking weakly and unsteadily. Flesh is lost rapidly, the hair stands erect, the skin gets dry and scurfy, the nose is dry and hot, or this condition alternates with a moist and cool one. By this time the mouth and skin, as well as the breath and dung, exhale the peculiar, penetrating, sour, offensive odor, and the poor calf has become an object of disgust to all that approach it. At first and unless inflammation of the stomach and bowels supervenes (and unless the affection has started an

SIR NETHERLAND CLOTHILDE, No. 8517 H. F. H. B.

Sire, Clothilde 4th's Imperial, Advanced Registry No. 42. Dam, Netherland Princess, Advanced Registry No. 496. His thirteen nearest female ancestors, all there are in this country, have records that average 10,052 lbs. 8 oz. of milk in a year, and 19 lbs. 15 oz. butter in a week, while nine of the nearest ancestors average 21 lbs. 8 oz. butter in a week, two being two years old.

indigestion and colic) the belly is not bloated nor painful on pressure, symptoms of acute colicky pains are absent, and the bowels do not rumble, nor the bubbles of gas mingle with the feces. The irritant products of the intestinal fermentation may, however, irritate and excoriate the skin around the anus which becomes red, raw and broken out in sores for some distance. Similarly the rectum exposed by reason of the relaxed condition of the anus, or temporarily in straining to pass the liquid dejection, is of a more or less deep red, and it may be ulcerated. Fever, with rapid pulse and increased breathing and temperature, usually comes on with the very fetid character of the feces, and is more pronounced as the bowels become inflamed, the abdomen sore to the touch and tucked up, and the feces more watery and even mixed with blood.

"The prevention of these cases is the prevention of constipation and indigestion with all their varied causes as above enumerated, the selection of a strong vigorous stock, and above all the combating of contagion, especially in the separation of the sick from the healthy and in the thorough purification and disinfection of the buildings. The cleansing and sweetening of all drains,

SIR NEWTON OF AAGGIE.

the removal of dung heaps, and the washing and scraping of floors and walls, followed by a liberal application of chloride of lime (bleaching powder) four ounces to the gallon are indicated. Great care must be exercised in the feeding of the cow to have sound and wholesome food and water, so apportioned as to make the milk neither too rich nor too poor, and to her health so that the calf may be saved from the evil consequences of poisonous principles that may be produced in the body of the cow. The calves should be carefully kept apart from all calving cows and their discharges. Similarly each calf must have special attention to see that its nurse gives milk which agrees with it and that this is furnished at suitable times. If allowed to suck, it should either be left with the cow, or it may be fed three times a day. If it comes hungry twice a day it is more likely to overload and derange the stomach, and if left too long hungry it is tempted to take in unsuitable and unwholesome food, for which its stomach is as yet unprepared. So if fed from a pail it is safer to do so three times daily than twice. The utmost cleanliness of feeding dishes should be secured and the feeder must ever be on the alert to prevent the strong and hungry from drinking the milk of the weaker in addition to their own.

SJOERD, No. 71 D.-F. H. B.
Imported. Butter record, 20 lbs. 8 oz. in one week.

REARING OF CALVES FOR THE DAIRY.

In case the cow nurse has been subjected to any great excitement by reason of travel, hunting or carrying, the first milk she yields thereafter should be used for some other purpose, and only the second allowed to the calf. Indeed one and all the conditions above indicated as causes should be judiciously guarded against.

"Treatment will vary according to the nature and stage of the disease. When the disease is not widespread, but isolated cases only occur, it may be assumed to be a simple diarrhea and is easily dealt with. The first object is to remove the irritant matter from the stomach and bowels, and for this one or two ounces of castor oil may be given according to the size of the calf. If the stools smell particularly sour, it may be replaced by one ounce of calcined magnesia, and in any case a tablespoonful or two of limewater may be given with each meal. Great harm is often done by giving opium and astringents at the outset. These merely serve to bind up the bowels and retain the irritant source of the trouble, literally ' to shut up the wolf in the sheepfold.' When the offend-

SOLDENE 2D'S NETHERLAND, No. 819 H. F. H. B.
The great show bull; never beaten in any class.

ing agents have been expelled in this way carminatives and demulcents may be given: One dram anise water, one dram nitrate of bismuth, and one dram gum arabic, three times a day. Under such a course the consistency of the stools should increase until in a day or two they become natural.

"If, however, the outbreak is more general and evidently the result of contagion, the first consideration is to remove all sources of such contamination. Test the milk of the cow with blue litmus paper; if it reddens, reject the milk of that cow until by sound dry feeding with perhaps a course of hyposulphite of soda and gentian root, her milk shall have been made alkaline. The castor oil or magnesia will still be demanded to clear away the (now infecting) irritants, but they should be combined with antiseptics, and, while the limewater and the carminative mixture may still be used, a most valuable mixture will be found in the following: Calomel 10 grains, prepared chalk 1 oz., creosote 1 teaspoonful; mix, divide into ten parts and give one four times a day. Or the following may be given four times a day: 1 dram Dover's powder, 6 grains powdered ipecacuanha; mix, divide into ten equal parts. Injections of solutions

of gum arabic are often useful, and if the anus is red and excoriated, one-half dram coperas may be added to each pint of the gummy solution. All milk given must be boiled, and if that does not agree, eggs made into an emulsion with barley water may be substituted. Small doses (tablespoonful) of port wine are often useful from the first, and as the feces lose their watery character and become more consistent, tincture of gentian in doses of two teaspoonfuls may be given three or four times a day. Counter-irritants, such as mustard, ammonia or oil of turpentine may be rubbed on the abdomen when that becomes tender to the touch."

CHAPTER XXV.

THE SELECTION OF A SIRE.

The amount of experimenting which the average farmer or breeder is able to do in this direction is necessarily limited. In the natural course of events he acquires more experience in calf raising in two or three years than he is able to obtain in the selection of the successive heads of his herd in a lifetime. This fact renders the comparison of ideas and of experiences all the more important in order that we may supplement our own meagre experiences with those of others. The first necessity in the selection of a sire to head a herd is that the breeder shall have in his own mind a clear and distinct idea of what he wants and expects that herd to become. He must have a well defined picture before him of the type of cow which he desires to prevail in his herd. Further than this he must have a decided opinion as to the relative importance of the different elements which go to make up that type of cow. With these ideas firmly fixed, the breeder will then select that animal, from amongst those accessible to him, which he believes will, coupled with the present members of his herd, produce offspring which approach to his ideal as nearly as possible.

Now, what is the ideal which the breeder of Holstein-Friesian cattle should have in mind? First and foremost we believe it should be the economical production of milk solids, and of these solids he should not ignore that fact that at present the fat is by far the more valuable and serves approximately as a measure of the value of the whole. And, under present conditions, we believe the aim of the breeder should be to increase the percentage of solids rather than to increase the total production of milk. In saying this we do not intend to indorse or to countenance those who would condemn all cows that do not come to an abitrary standard in butter fats. The cow giving milk testing three per cent is entitled to be judged simply on the standard of profit or loss, and a cow testing five per cent should be judged in the same way. We have no patience with the sweeping generality of one of our experiment station workers who has undertaken to say that rich milking cows are more profitable than those giving a milk less rich in fat. There is no evidence sufficient to support any such generalizations. But it is true, of course, that of two cows giving the same amount of milk and eating the same food, the one giving the richer milk is the more profitable. All of us are aiming to improve our herds and the breed as a whole, and we believe the possibilities of improvement lie rather in the direction of quality than of quantity. For one thing the amount of milk which a cow can carry in her udder is not unlimited and there are serious doubts whether the practical dairyman will ever care to add to the number of his daily milkings. This does not mean that quantity is to be ignored. No deterioration should be permitted in any direction. We believe our cattle should be bred to the dairy type rather than to the beef type, and here let it be said that there is no connection between dairy type and lack of constitution. The type is too familiar to need description. The scale of points for the Advanced Registry may be referred to. The animal which would score high under that scale must be of the dairy type, though there is room of course for difference of opinion as to some of the individual points, or perhaps better as to their relative importance. There can be but little doubt but that the principal points are udder capacity, digestive capacity and wedge shape. It is one of the valuable characteristics of our breed that in it this type also possesses the capacity to take on flesh economically and rapidly when not milking.

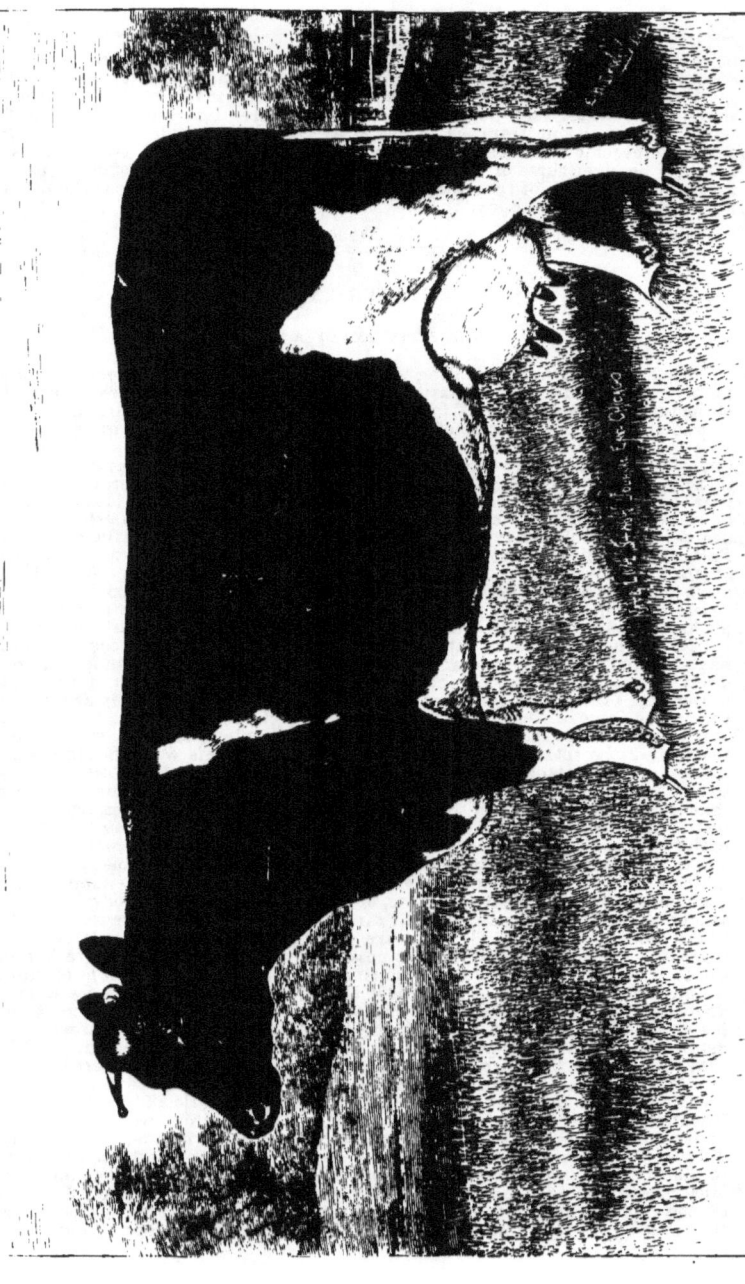

TIETJE 2D, No. 726 H. F. H. B.
Imported. Butter record 20 lbs. in seven days.

The bull of course cannot show the dairy type in the same degree as the cow, nevertheless it is possible that he may have it clearly marked. He may have a decidedly cowy look. He should also have a distinctly vigorous and masculine appearance. The two are not inconsistent. The one is a matter of form chiefly, the other a matter of spirit and bearing.

Every breeder has to do with tendencies. Like tends to beget like. Variations in one generation tend to perpetuate themselves. There is also the tendency, in an artificially created type, like the types of our domestic animals, to revert to the original type. Our large dairy producers have been created by breeders taking advantage of variations in that direction for scores of years. The original type was of course a small producer of dairy products and there is always a possibility of reversion to that type. The farther we get from the original type the smaller the probability or possibility of reversion. Hence the value of the pedigree, hence the prepotency of a well bred animal. A well bred animal is simply one in which the tendency to revert to any other type than the one desired has by a long course of careful selection been thoroughly bred out. We believe also that there can be no question but that a particular type can be more firmly fixed by close inbreeding than by any other method. The difficulty is that undesirable qualities can be firmly fixed in the same way just as easily as the desirable ones.

The fundamental principle, then, is, fix in your own mind the type towards which you wish to breed, then select as your service bull the animal which embodies in himself and through a long line of ancestry the qualities desired in the highest possible degree.

S. Burchard, Hamilton, N. Y.:

"Because we cannot immediately figure out the records that the bull makes (for they must necessarily be second-hand), he is no less the most important animal in the herd. His qualities of excellence or worthlessness are transmitted to every animal that is bred in the herd (unless counteracted by the cow with which he is coupled), and are as fixedly stamped upon his progeny as the eagle is stamped upon the coin at the mint. In my boyhood my father obtained a Shorthorn bull from the Clay stock of Kentucky. He was of the milking strain of Shorthorns, and had the appearance of a very fine and vigorous animal. He was patronized by the farmers for miles around, and was so prepotent that he stamped his qualities of form, style and milk development upon all of his progeny. All of his daughters were superior milkers. About twenty of them were milked in my father's dairy and I have never seen anything that could compare with them, until I came into contact with the black-and-whites. This experience taught in my early life that the bull that is well-bred through a long line of ancestors, possessing a milk development of the highest order, and the power of transmitting his qualities to his descendants, is the only safe bull to be used in a well ordered herd. The bull may be of the finest style and be possessed of the highest order of milk development, yet it will be impossible for him to be a transmitter of his qualities, unless he is endowed with a high order of nervous energy. This force is something that we cannot explain, but still we know that it exists, and we would compare it in the animal kingdom to electricity in the natural world. Like the lightning in the cloud, it is subtly lurking in the system, and when certain conditions occur, it is ready to flash forth and perform its mission. It is this subtle power that enables the horse to trot his mile in 2.30 or better, and it is the same power that enables men to perform business, military and political actions that astonish the world. It always has been and ever will be a potent factor in producing the phenomenal records of horses and cows and men. To be able to detect this power is an important part of the education of the breeder. The most prominent indication of the nervous force element in the bull or the cow is what we call the double chine. In this the points of the vertebræ stand well apart, forming an open space between in which the ends of the fingers may be easily inserted. This indicates a strong spinal cord connecting directly with the brain on one hand, and with every nerve in the system on the other. This, in connection with a prominent, sprightly eye, showing plainly what is called the white of the eye, a mellow, silky skin, and a conformation showing strength and vigor, are the main points to be considered. The law that like begets like has resulted in many failures and much disappointment, but the bull possessing nervous force in a high degree will rarely fail in stamping his qualifications upon his progeny. When such a bull

is once obtained in a herd his days should not be cut short, nor his energies wasted; and he will leave an impress upon the herd that will last for generations."

Edward A. Powell, vice-president Smiths & Powell Co., Lakeside Stock Farm, Syracuse, N. Y.:

"The selection of sires for breeding purposes is the most important matter to be considered in the breeding problem, not only because the sire represents one-half of the herd in breeding, but because uniformity in type, style, etc., is very essential in order to give the herd a nice appearance, and this quality can only be successfully secured through the sire, as the dams are not supposed to be from the same families, or entirely uniform in breeding or quality. If, therefore, the sire be so strongly bred as to impart his characteristics to all his produce, the herd will soon become uniform in appearance. If the sire be just the type desired, fine in form, choice in quality, and of the size preferred, the herd will soon be up to the standard established by the breeder.

"In the dairy production is the first essential, therefore, in selecting the sire the ancestors are first of all to be considered. The dams, for several generations in every line should be large producers of the product desired. If milk be the essential, then they should have large yearly records for milk. Daily records are of little value. If butter alone be essential, then they should have large records for butter. If milk and butter both be desired, we should then select bulls whose female ancestors for many generations have large yearly milk records, and large weekly, monthly or yearly butter records if possible. In connection with this we should also consider the individual excellence of the ancestors, as well as the individual quality of the animal to be chosen.

"Beauty of form, finish and quality, can be secured in connection with the largest production, and hence there is no necessity for breeding from an overgrown, coarse boned, lathy, logy sire, even though his ancestors may have been great producers. We believe the present demand for Holstein-Friesians is for large butter makers, with good milk records, animals of medium size, low, blocky, straight, compact, vigorous, active, with strong constitutions, of superior quality and of high finish. If these be the desiderata, then bulls should be selected which possess in a marked degree all these qualities. Care should also be taken to select animals from families which have been so well established that a reproduction of the characteristics desired may be considered almost a certainty. We should therefore, in selecting a bull, make haste slowly. Study every characteristic of the ancestors, as well as of the individual."

Prof. John A. Craig, of the Wisconsin Experiment Station:

"The most valuable characteristics of the breeding of a dairy bull are the number and merit of the performances that have been made by the cows that enter into his pedigree. The most important feature of this is the degree to which his dam was a good dairy cow, and then in lessening degree the merit of his grandam and great grandam. Next to these facts is the number and performances of the cows that have been gotten by the sires that enter into a pedigree. A bull that has breeding of high order based on performance is as certain as things can be to get good calves, provided as an individual he is satisfactory."

A. P. Foster:

"My earnest advice to dairymen is to use no sire that is unable to claim an unbroken line of dairy ancestors, and, what is better, prove his claim. And right here is found the value of registration. Nothing else can be taken as reliable for any number of consecutive generations. This, too, needs to be supplemented by the best obtainable proof as to the superior individual qualities of his dam and his sire's dam. When our herd books more generally carry along this kind of information, they will become still more valuable."

Editor Hoard's Dairman:

"Considering the importance of the sire in determining the dairy character of his daughters, there is no wonder that thousands of men are asking the question: 'What are the marks of a good bull?' The difficulty is still more enhanced when one tries to make the selection while the animal is a calf. Mr. G. W. Farlee, late president of the Jersey Cattle Club, in answering an inquiry of this sort through the Country Gentleman, confesses that after an experience of twenty-five years in breeding, he is unable to name the external points of excellence in a bull save that of constitution, a deep barrel and an open twist. His greatest reliance, however, is in pedigree. If the bull

TEXELAAR, No. 51 H. H. B.

Imported in 1861 by W. W. Chenery, Belmont, Mass. Milk record, 76 lbs. 5 oz. in one day; 744 lbs. 12 oz. in ten days. Butter record, 17 lbs. 14 oz. in seven days. Milk showing by analyses 22 72-100 cream.

has a long line of ancestors on both sides, of decided dairy performance he very sensibly, we think, counts that worth more than anything else. We would suggest, however, that the development of the navel is a more unerring indication of constitution or natural vitality than the deep barrel. In men and animals both we often find specimens of wonderful vigor and endurance who are not marked by large development of the barrel. But we never saw such an instance where the construction of the navel and surrounding walls of the abdomen were weak. Every physician has noticed that where the umbilical cord at birth was small and weak the child is correspondingly low in vitality, and usually it is hard to raise such a child. This shows that the mother failed to endow the foetus with sufficient vitality because the channel through which that vitality is conveyed was weak and imperfect. A strong umbilical development is, in our judgement, the surest indication of vital force and endurance, or, as it is generally called, constitution."

V. E. Fuller:

"If breeders and dairymen would only realize the truth of the adage that 'the bull is half the herd,' and how thoroughly in the course of years the blood and characteristics of the bull impregnate and dominate any herd where he is used, there would be more care in the selection of a breeding bull for use in our herds.

"Let me make a suggestion, first of all, to those who are not raising thoroughbred herds, but are rather in the dairying business for the profit of the cows either at the pail or the churn. Use none but a thoroughbred bull. Remember that the bull should impress upon his get either 'his own likeness or the likeness of an ancestor,' but unless a bull be extraordinarily prepotent, he more often impresses upon his offspring a likeness of a remote ancestor rather than give any fixed characteristics from himself.

"Therefore, in using any bull it does not follow that his daughters will have the characteristics of his dam—the chances are that his get will partake more closely in resemblance and characteristics to a more remote ancestor than the dam of the bull. It therefore follows if there be any impure blood in the sire used, there is a chance that his get may partake of the 'impure' characteristics and that he will not impress upon his get the sought for qualities to the same extent as if he were pure. If you seek to produce milk and milk only, without regard to what is contained in it, use a bull of a breed whose characteristic is to give a large flow of milk, but let it be one of the milking breeds. If you are seeking to produce animals for the butcher's block, breed from a pure bull of one of the beef breeds.

"To those who are seeking to breed cows for the dairy, whether they be thoroughbred or whether they be grades, I would say, remember the adage that 'like produces like, or the likeness of an ancestor.' See that the dam of your bull that you propose to use has the characteristics, in either milk giving or butter making, and in form and size of udder, that you desire to see perpetuated in your herd; that his grandams are possessed of like characteristics and so back by at least four generations. If the female ancestors be possessed of those characteristics you seek to have perpetuated in your herd, then you may be reasonably assured that the bull will, when coupled properly with desirable dams, produce you satisfactory offspring.

"To those using what is known as an 'inbred sire,' namely, one inbred to a common ancestor on the part of both sire and dam, bear in mind that while the bull so inbred will probably have the ability to fix the characteristics of the common ancestor to whom he is inbred, he will as surely fix and exaggerate the undesirable features of the ancestor as he will desirable ones. Therefore it is especially necessary to see that the ancestor to whom he is inbred, or his descendants through whom your bull traces to him, be not possessed of characteristics that you do not desire to perpetuate in your cows."

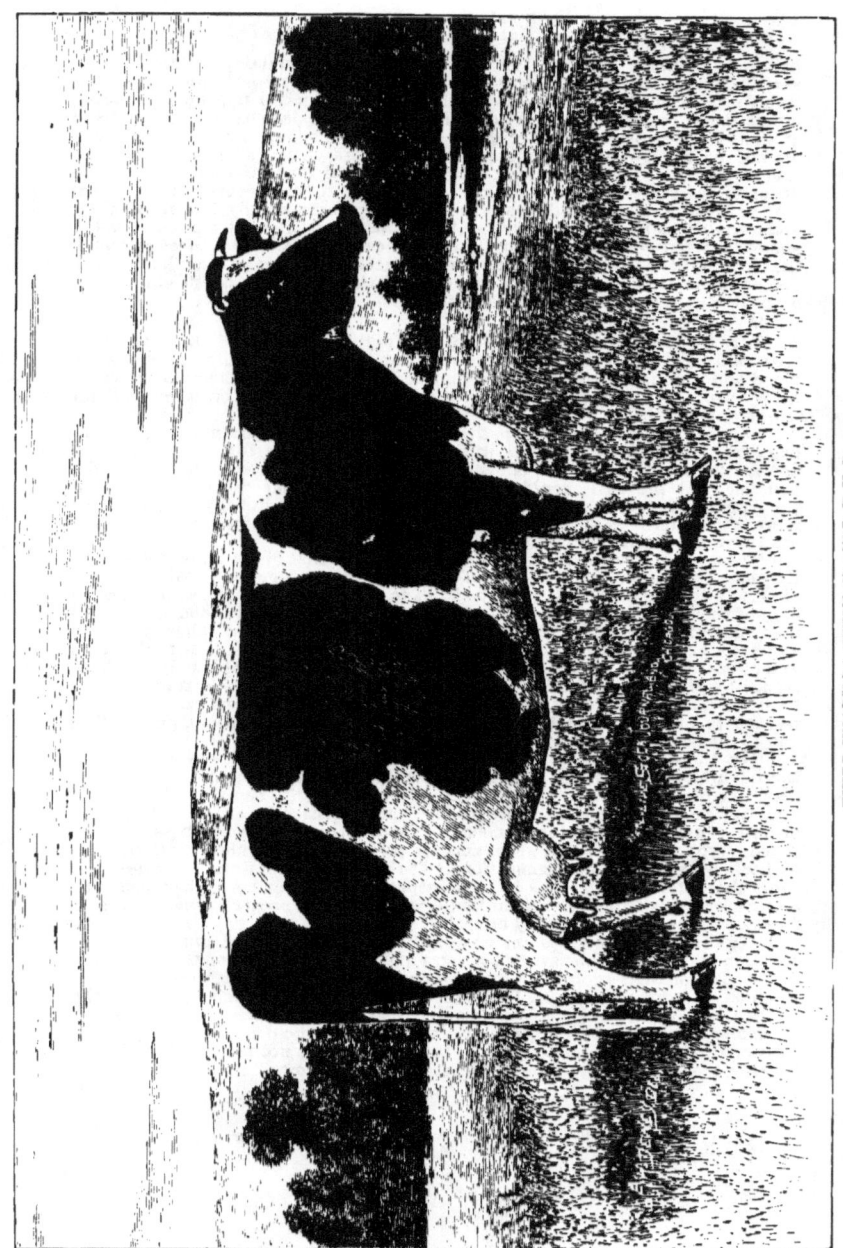

THIRD UNADILLA TWISK, No. 230 D.-F. H. B.

CHAPTER XXVI.

PREPARING FOR THE SHOW RING.

"The condition of stock shown at fairs always has a marked influence on judges and no exhibitor can afford to neglect showing his stock in the most favorable light," says the Agricultural Gazette.

"Grooming is as necessary with show cattle as with horses; that is, if the cattle are to be shown in perfection. In the case of cattle, grooming need not be commenced until within three months of the date of the show. The cattle, it is presumed, have for some time previous been well fed and kept in clean lairs. In this condition to begin with, three months' grooming should put them in form.

"Cattle, it is true, come into the show yard with all kinds of coats, some with long hair, others short, and, worse than all, some with the hair partly off. But half the game in showing cattle is in having them good in their coats, and stock owners who fail to handle their animals so as to make them look their very best, need not expect to win against those who do. When the show happens to be about mid-summer, the spring shedding of the coat will save the trouble of having to take it off by other means, but when the exhibitions take place late or early in the year, then we adopt measures to cause the hair to shed and the new hair to be again well up, and shining like the new spring coat, even in mid-winter.

"Provide a good warm rug, the same as are used for horse clothing, and about three months previous to the show put one on each of the animals to be prepared. The rugs do not require to be on all the time, but as much as possible, and may be taken off during the night, or when the cattle go to pasture, or are turned out into the yards for exercise, when they are apt to get torn. If the blankets are kept on about twelve or fourteen hours daily they will soon do their work in taking the old hair off. A good washing with carbolic soap and tepid water should be given at the commencement of the sheeting. This will help to lessen the dandruff in the hide. Once a month will be often enough to wash if the bedding be well looked after. There is a great difference in the skins of cattle for being easily cleaned. Some are rough and so full of dandruff that it needs special means to get them into good condition. An extra washing, however, and a heavier blanket will help to smooth them down, and with a little oil rubbed in will soon raise all the scurf clean off the skin. Until the scurf be thoroughly got rid of, the coat will never shine. It takes rubbing and brushing, brushing and rubbing, day after day, and a great amount of elbow grease to put on the shine. Cattle have far finer coats and take a 'brighter polish than horses; yet we generally see horses brighter-coated than cattle. The reason is, the cattle do not get the same amount of rubbing.

"A dandy brush, a soft brush and a chamois skin are the tools required for putting on the polish. The skin becomes soft under this treatment, and a curry comb should never be used but for the purpose of combing down the hips when necessary, as the comb, unless very lightly applied, is certain to scratch and irritate the skin. In rubbing down with the cloth, it must be done quickly. The friction raises a certain amount of heat on the surface of the thing polished, and this heat is the main agent in putting on the shine. It takes an enormous amount of rubbing to make the skin of cattle shine, but nothing else will do it.

"For putting on the final touch, no brush or cloth can equal the bare hand. The heat of the hand is more effective than that produced by friction with a brush or cloth, and as a man can rub considerably quicker without either of these appliances, the bare palms make the best polishing paste that can be used. Hand rubbing will also take off the old hair quicker than either comb or brush. It is not easy to say when grooming is perfect, but when the skin will no longer soil a white kid glove with either dust or hair there is not much to complain of. This condition is not, however, reached without many days of careful sheeting and rubbing. Some fancy they can, with one washing and a few times groomed, do all that can be done; but it is a mistake. There is the greatest difference imaginable between the one that has been prepared by months of labor and the other hastily got up. The one article is genuine, and will last; the other will fade between the stall and the ring."

A. C. Hallman:

"In order to be a successful exhibitor a man must have the proper qualifications. He should be a good judge of cattle, be punctual in all his doings, pay strict attention to the little details, have a proper method of doing things, and a love for what he is undertaking.

"It is generally supposed that a successful exhibitor has some secret method of doing things; such is not the case; it's the right man at the right place, with the proper conditions. He should have a thorough knowledge of what he is undertaking. The selection of proper animals for their different classes is very important. It is a waste of time and feed to fit an animal not suited for its class.

"Blood will tell. See that your cattle have a good lineage. Select them from a line of ancestors that have been successful prize winners, heavy performers and rich milkers. It is the 'breedy' looking animal with careful fitting that wins. Have some fixed standard, then model after it. The females should be a very select lot of the true type at which you are aiming, with rich breeding; but the male is the most important factor: he must have rich blood coursing through his veins, he should be very symmetrical and have a vigorous constitution, with strong conformation, and be of the type you are aiming to breed; if he has the correct breeding and is of the right stamp individually, he is almost sure to strongly impress his mark on his offspring. Remember, he is the fountain head of your show animals. One mistake in the selection of a sire will cripple a herd for years. Get the best, it is always the cheapest.

"We now begin with the calf, for in it lies the future prize winner. We suppose the breeding is correct. We have no different method for show animals except for the last two months. If cattle are kept as they ought to be that length of time is quite sufficient for fitting dairy cattle. I might also add that I never turn show calves out to pasture. Our calves are weaned from

TRITOMIA, No. 4004 H. H. B.; 252 Advanced Registry.

Imported. Milk record, 74 lbs. 8 oz. in one day; 2,062 lbs. 8 oz. in thirty-one days. Butter record, 25 lbs. 8 4-5 oz. in seven days. First prize as best butter cow at Minnesota, 1886. Later private butter test, 3 lbs. 12 oz. in one day; 36 lbs. 11 oz. in seven days.

their dams at from one to three days old; fed on their mothers' milk three times a day for one week, twice a day after that. We continue to feed new milk for three weeks, then make a gradual change to sweet skim; as we start to change we add a little oil meal, scalded, with enough water added to heat the milk to blood temperature; as the new milk is withdrawn the oil meal is increased in such proportions as to make a good substitute for the cream. Sweet hay is placed before them and often changed. Bran is put in a box when they can eat, but this also must be often changed. As soon as they learn to eat nicely only so much is given as will be eaten up clean. A little meal is added at three weeks old. One part peas, one part oats, and one part barley, the other part bran, forms a very good mixture for calves, given three times a day in such quantities as will be eaten up clean before the next meal. Never allow food in a manger over one meal, give less. Pulped roots should also be given, or ensilage, enough to keep the bowels nice and open. Feed enough milk and oil cake, scalded, twice a day so that they need no other drink except for the noon meal; give water as the calf grows older and the weather warm. At six months old all our calves are weaned except our show calves. They are now carefully looked over and the ones coming nearest to our ideal are fitted for the show; in this we use no forcing system. Our calves now eat well; the milk is continued till after the exhibitions. The meal ration is a little changed, a little more concentrated food added, but always feed half bran. They can eat as much as they like and it will never hurt them. Our object is not to get them fat, but in good condition, to keep them vigorous and growing, form lots of bone and muscle, and have a nice loose, mellow skin with soft hair. The age I consider most suitable for showing calves is from seven to nine months old.

"Yearling heifers if raised in the manner described, and kept well through the winter, require nothing but good pasture and plenty of water until the first of July or later if in good condition. We have repeatedly taken heifers out of pasture, with little or no fitting, and won honor prizes. When pasture is scant, four quarts meal, two parts peas, two parts oats, one part bran, and one part oil cake will soon put them in good shape, with fodder corn added (we also like fodder corn for the calves as soon as in season). The best age to show a yearling is about twenty months old, bred to be starting to spring at show time. Two year-olds need careful attention; they should be in good condition before calving, which should be in the end of June; this will give them a grand

chance to build up on the succulent pasture, and sufficient time after to get in nice shape for exhibition. When in milk they should be fed twice a day in sufficient quantities as to keep up the flow of milk and the system. In older animals the object should be almost the same as with young animals—to keep them in good, healthy condition, and if pasture becomes scarce, add other foods to keep up the condition and the flow of milk. We don't want dairy animals (females) to enter the ring fat (it tells against them), but in nice condition, and in the pink of health; they must look thrifty. To strike a medium is about right. I have seen dairy cattle too thin for exhibition. Such animals should never be brought out; they are a disgrace to the breed and breeder. While we allow cows heavy in milk to be rather thin, it will not do with young stock. The public will judge the breed, not the conditions.

"Males should be in good condition always; however, not too beefy. Feed to keep a good coat and rich, mellow skin. Give exercise, but not to excess; keep the feet in proper trim. Bulls will not thrive when their feet are sore, and they soon will become sore if care is not taken. They should be laid down, and trimmed from the bottom. Wash cattle with soap and water thoroughly, rinse well, and blanket, a day before going to exhibition. We never use a blanket before. If an animal's coat won't get in proper shape for the ring after

TIRANNIA.

a few days' blanketing there is something wrong and it should be left at home. However, grooming will always help to make them comfortable and improve their coats, and cattle that are stabled should be groomed regularly.

"In conclusion, would say, make the right selection; show your cattle in a good, healthy condition; aim not to have them too fat; while we allow it with males, it is never admissible with females. If a dairy animal has the proper treatment from calfhood, and the correct breeding, there is no reason why any animal intended for breeding purposes should be ruined by being fitted for exhibition. The aim and object should always be to secure early development, but not to impair their future usefulness.

"Much as I admire the care and attention of the skillful breeder and feeder whose sole object is to promote growth and pile on flesh, and much as I admire the results of such labor, I question very much if it pays even with the beef breeds, while it surely will injure their future usefulness as breeders. The best breed and most valuable animal is often ruined as a breeder, while the milking qualities are surely injured and often destroyed. Dairy cattle must be judged on points. Any man that does not judge in that way has no business in the ring; he must have a thorough knowledge of what he is undertaking, and do it skillfully."

W. M. Benninger:

"In order to prepare a herd for the show ring you must first have the animals to prepare, and this is the keynote to the whole business. One must be an expert judge of cattle, or employ an expert to select the animals. The selection must not be made to suit a particular person's fancy, but must be all 'round first-class individuals that will score as near as possible 100 on the scale of points adopted by the association of the breed you wish to show. Be sure to have a bull to show in the aged class. If you win first in this class, you have won half the battle.

"The preparing should be done continually, commence immediately after you come in from the last fair or show in fall to get ready for the next season.

"The main feature is plenty of good food, comfortable quarters, good clean water, and extra care and attention. A show herd should be thoroughly cleaned every day, plenty of arm muscle work with the brush should be used, and the stables kept perfectly clean. The herd should be kept in a cool barn

UNCLE TOM, No. 168 H. H. B.

Weight, 2200 lbs. First prize at New York State Fair and Onondaga County Fair for four successive years.

during the hot hours of the day, with thin blankets on them during the fly season, and should go to pasture and exercise at night. Plenty of good, fresh grain is the best feed that can be fed.

"In the young class select animals as old as you can get them; that is, in the class for calves select one as near a year old as possible, and so on till you get to the aged class; then a bull from three to six years generally in his prime, a cow may be shown that is older, say from six to twelve years.

"Let me here emphasize, be sure to have the herd in good condition, the animals of strong constitutions and large frames. By saying in good condition, I do not mean fat like the beef breeds, or so fat that you would injure the dairy points, but in fair, good flesh. I even saw Mr. T. W. Cooper select, or prefer, at the New York State Fair at Syracuse, Jerseys in extra good condition with strong constitution in preference to the finer, slick, so-called dairy type.

"I am pleased to note that some of the most intelligent breeders of all the dairy breeds are now trying for Holstein frames and constitutions, even if some editors of leading dairy journals criticise expert judges for favoring dairy cattle in good condition.

"In conclusion, let me say when you appear in the ring be sure that you are in good shape, horns polished, hoofs trimmed, your animals perfectly clean and well broken, and show them in a natural position, standing a little high in front. Answer all questions asked by the judge correctly and honestly, and never kick if you don't win; if you do, you generally kick yourself the most. Cows in milk should always be shown with a well-filled, square udder, which greatly adds to the general appearance."

O. P. Thompson, manager Home Farm herd:

"While our experience in showing has not been so extensive as that of some others, it has been exceedingly varied, as we have exhibited at state fairs when we were awarded practically no premiums, as well as when we secured nearly every prize for which we had an entry. The first year we made a showing at the Iowa State Fair, in 1884, I think. We selected as cows only those that were rolling fat at the time, and necessarily such cows were dry and had been for some time previous, or were always very poor milkers. That they were pretty, fat, sleek, and world beaters in the eyes of a novice, none

VASELINE, No. 15,923 H. F. H. B.
Winner first prize as butter cow, Michigan State Fair, 1895, 4.50 lbs. butter; also second prize, Ohio, 1893, 2.70 lbs. butter in one day.

could gainsay, but that year these state fairs had as judges experts who were worthy of the name, than whom there are none better—S. N. Wright, at Iowa, and W. D. Hoard, of Minnesota. As at both these fairs we had in competition with us Holsteins of the strict dairy type that were shown in moderate flesh, thus not having the dairy points covered up with fat, and the cows in full flow of milk, we got practically nothing in the way of premiums and scarcely enough to pay our freight. After the premiums were awarded at Minnesota the writer hereof requested Mr. Hoard (he had not at that time been Governor of Wisconsin), if he would have the kindness to tell us why he awarded us so few prizes. He answered by saying that we were exhibiting in the wrong ring; that if we should go over among the beef breeds we would stand a much better chance of winning. This was the last time we showed cattle in high flesh. I was much surprised lately in reading a communication from a leading breeder of Holstein-Friesian cattle to note that he recommended for exhibition cattle in high flesh. This may be all right if you are to exhibit at county fairs or even at state fairs when they have picked up judges, usually

VIOLET, No. 743 H. H. B.

Imported. Milk record, 86 lbs. 12 oz. one day; 18,677 lbs. 4 oz. in one year. Butter record, 19 lbs. 9 oz. in seven days.

three of them, and when the crowd practically decides the honors; but I want to say that when you face such judges as those named above you want to have dairy cattle in dairy condition.

"Before again starting out with a show herd we secured the cows Jewel, Jewel 2d, and Colantha, when in their prime, and filled out our show herd with selections of cattle of their type. In those days the big money was hung for herd to consist of one male and four females over three years of age.

"These three cows, together with Rijaneta and Bettina, made us almost impregnable on cows, and they were always able to carry our bull with them. We were a little weak on bull until a son of Jewel 2d arrived at an age when he could be shown with the herd. At this time every animal in our show herd was of the strictly dairy type.

"It would take up too much of your valuable space to enumerate all the premiums won by Home Farm during the seasons of 1889 and 1890. Suffice it to say we came home at the end of the season of 1889 with $1,300 and in 1890 with $1,800 above all expenses.

"Those were the years when public butter tests were so popular at the leading Western state fairs and we also made entries therein. In thirteen such tests we won first prize twelve times.

"We aim to have our cattle perfectly broken to halter and trained to stand squarely on their feet with heads erect and to stand quiet. Those to be shown as a herd are frequently led into line at home and made to stand just as they are expected to when the trying time comes, in order.

"With such a judge as Mr. Wright no cow with a defective udder or teats stands any chance of winning no matter how superior she may be in other points. We are also much in favor of his way of selecting the best cows. After standing them all in line he selects perhaps one-half of them and advances them to another line just in front, and those in the back row might just as well go to their stalls. This front row is again selected from and advanced as before and so on until the best three or four cows stand in the front row, and to them are awarded the premiums. In this way the public can learn something of the comparative value of the cows.

"The main point in making an exhibit is to advertise your herd and hence you should at all times have some one in attendance whose business it is to answer questions and who is well informed as to the entire herd, both those on exhibition and at home. Be on the lookout for possible customers. Talk up your own cattle, but do not try to build up merit for them by depreciating the good points of other breeds. In fact if an exhibitor has had no experience sufficient to justify him in expressing an opinion, he had best refer all inquiries as to them to their respective breeders."

H. B. Daggett:

"In entering cows for public tests, breeders should give the cows a chance to win, and not put them out of the race before it begins—by this I mean the bad management after reaching the grounds. Nearly any of the breeders will start from home with their cows in good fix; if they will then cut down the feed while on board the cars they will do a wise act, as the jar and confinement will tend to produce scours. But it is after reaching the fair grounds that the trouble usually occurs; when they look over the opposition their hearts fail them and in goes the feed, here is where you make a mistake. Don't crowd your cows; let the other fellow do that, and he generally does it too. I am sure more premiums have been lost by over than under feeding. As to a ration, will say that only the intelligent feeder can tell the amount to be given to each animal; it may consist of equal parts by measure of bran and ground corn and oats with good clover hay and ensilage of green corn, if it can be had."

AUGUSTINE R. AYERS.

SOME AMERICAN BREEDERS.

AUGUSTINE R. AYERS, North Boscawen, N. H. The dairy interest in New Hampshire has grown in importance to a wonderful extent in the past few years, in both the milk and butter-producing lines, so that the attention of the progressive farmers of the state has been called to the matter of improved stock, and the Holsteins have come in for a generous share of consideration and approval.

Among dairymen adopting this breed is Augustine R. Ayers, of North Boscawen, N. H., an enthusiastic milk producer, who is now wholesaling his product to dealers in Concord in preference to selling at the cars for the Boston market, as a majority of the producers in that section of the state are doing.

Mr. Ayers is a native of Gilmanton, N. H., born December 28, 1839, but he spent his childhood and youth on a farm in the town of Canterbury, manifesting in this early period of his career a strong love for domestic animals and adapting himself with special readiness to the training of colts and steers, milking the cows and caring for lambs and poultry. Before attaining manhood, however, he was impelled by various considerations to devote himself to mercantile life in the city of Concord, which he followed in different lines— with the exception of a term of service in the Union army in the late war as a member of the Fifteenth Regiment, New Hampshire Volunteers—from the age of eighteen until 1890. Feeling the need of a change for the benefit of his health, and inspired by his early love for farm life, he determined to engage in agriculture. His love for good horses had been indulged to considerable extent while in business in Concord, and upon commencing farm operations upon the old Jacob Gerrish place at North Boscawen, which came into his possession practically as an abandoned farm, he first turned his attention to the breeding of trotting horses, which he pursued with a fair measure of success for two or three years; but with the decline in horses he determined to change to the dairy.

His attention being directed favorably to the Holstein-Friesian cattle, through ex-Governor Goodell and others, and being favorably impressed with their beautiful form and size, great dairy capacity, uniform health and strong constitution, he procured a few good registered animals of this breed from the Russell importation and has steadily increased and improved his herd. He has now about thirty-five head altogether, including some very fine specimens of the Netherland, Pauline Paul and Pietertje families. His bull, Jean Paul, two years of age, is a splendid animal, a great-grandson of Pauline Paul, and won a premium at the New Hampshire Grange State Fair at Tilton, last fall.

Mr. Ayers milks about eighteen cows, giving them ordinary care and no fancy feeding, making no effort for extra records. Yet some of his cows have averaged 600 cans of milk each per annum, and one has given 81 lbs. in twenty-four hours.

The farm, which embraces 275 acres altogether, is finely located on the line of the Boston & Maine Railroad, Concord Division, just above the Merrimack County Farm at North Boscawen, bordering on the west bank of the Merrimack river, and extending back upon the hill a mile and a half, with seventy-five acres of easily-tilled river land, and the balance pasture and woodland. When Mr. Ayers took possession it was in a neglected and run-down condition, but by care and labor he has greatly improved it, and already has forty acres in superior condition. He has eleven acres in corn this year, and several acres in oats and potatoes, having raised from 300 to 1,200 bushels of the latter each year since he has been on the farm.

He has built a new 100-foot barn with cellar under the whole, and a large

poultry house and carthouse, and has put in a silo of seventy-five tons capacity. He puts his corn into the silo after breaking off the best ears. In feeding he gives one ration of hay and one of ensilage each day, and a supplementary feed of gluten, linseed, bran, and corn and cobmeal combined.

Mr. Ayers is an earnest worker, pushing whatever he undertakes with vigor. He keeps eight horses, and they are generally busily employed, with two or three men, besides his son and himself, at work on the place. He is an enthusiastic member of the order Patrons of Husbandry, having joined Capital Grange, at Concord, ten years ago, and transferred his membership to Ezekiel Webster Grange, of Boscawen, after his removal. He is at present overseer of the latter grange, while his wife is secretary, and his eldest son, John F., is assistant steward. Mr. Ayers is also a member of the Holstein-Friesian Association of America.

Mr. E. T. BEDELL of Springville, Ia., was born in the state of New York in 1852. He came to the then pioneer state of Iowa as a two-year-old and has lived in Linn county, Iowa, ever since, or over forty-two years. When the Bedell family settled here, there was not a railroad west of the Mississippi river; now the Belmont Stock Farm lies almost in sight of two of the greatest roads in America, viz.: The Chicago & Northwestern R. R. and the Chicago, Milwaukee & St. Paul R. R.

Mr. Bedell was the youngest of a family of seven children, and, his parents being in limited circumstances, he was early taught the necessity of perseverance and self-reliance and to make the best of the hardships and privations incidental to any one starting in a new country; and having a fair share of Western pluck and "get there" in his make-up, he was capable, at his father's death—which occurred when Mr. Bedell was in his seventeenth year—to take the management of his father's farm and run it successfully. This he did for about ten years.

In 1880 he bought the farm he now occupies, comprising nearly a quarter section, which has since taken on the name of "Belmont Stock Farm." A firm believer in tile draining and good cultivating, he at once began to improve this farm by building good fences and draining all the wet land and also building a large and commodious barn and other out-buildings, and today the farm is one of the best improved and most valuable in the country.

Mr. Bedell was always a lover of fine stock. In 1888 he started out to acquire a herd of Holsteins. Steadily the herd increased in number and value, and now it is considered one of the best in the state. It is at the present time headed by one of the grandest bred Holstein bulls in the world, whose dam has a record of 33¼ lbs. of butter in one week. Six cows in the herd have an average record of over 90 lbs. of milk in one day, and an average yield of over 20 lbs. of butter in one week.

The foundation stock of this herd was purchased at a great price, but it has been a profitable investment to the owner. There has been shipped from this herd, cows, bulls and heifers to many states of the Union. There is evidently no place in the Union better adapted to the growing of fine cattle than the state of Iowa.

Mr. W. M. BENNINGER of Walnutport, Pa., was born at Lehigh Gap, Lehigh county, Pa., in 1854. In the same year his parents moved across the Lehigh river to Lehigh Township, Northampton county, Pa., where he has since remained, and where his noted stock farm, nursery and creameries are located. In addition to a common-school education he attended one term of the Keystone State Normal School.

He was raised and worked on his father's farm up to 1873, when he started on the road as a nursery agent, selling trees. In 1874 he started in the nursery business as a dealer, employing quite a number of agents, and met with great success, making increased sales over the same territory every year; continuing in this till 1885, when he partly abandoned the retail department of the business, having then become widely recognized in furnishing the Grange and Alliance in Pennsylvania and a number of other states with nursery stock. In the same year he made his first investment in Holstein-Friesian cattle, making his first purchase from James Black and Mr. Cole of New York state. He afterwards purchased some of the finest specimens from different breeders, and in

W. M. BENNINGER.

1898 bought two carloads—a first selection—from the noted Maplewood herd at Attica, N. Y., amongst them the noted bulls Parthenea's Sir Henry and Sir Jewel Echo Mechtchilde; also, the famous cows Paladin, Cynthiana, Aaggie Hopeful, Alexina, Carl Henry's Beatitude, and others.

Mr. Benninger has made special personal efforts in fitting up a show herd with remarkable success, winning over three-fourths of the premiums competed for, and exhibiting at such fairs as Trenton, N. J.; Waverly, N. J.; Hagerstown, Md.; Raleigh, N. C.; Syracuse, N. Y.; Bethlehem, Pa.; Atlanta Exposition and other fairs.

Mr. Benninger has also had unusual success in selling bulls to beginners, and finds it a great success to grade up other herds with Holstein bulls. He had sold hundreds of bulls for that purpose without having a single complaint, his customers being well satisfied with the cross.

Mr. Benninger is also well known as a lecturer, being on the staff of the Pennsylvania State Grange, and also lecturing at farmers' institutes, etc., and is a member of the Holstein-Friesian Association of America. He also contributes articles on dairying, stock breeding, etc., to a number of the leading agricultural and stock-breeding journals, and lately assumed editorial management of the Breeders' Magazine, Dairyman and Horticulturist, published at High Point, N. C.

MR. H. F. W. BREUER of Charleston, South Carolina, was born on the 13th of January, 1841, at Bederkesa, Hanover, Germany, and came to America with his parents while quite young; located at Charleston, S. C., where he has resided ever since, and engaged in mercantile business at an early age. Having a natural fondness for cattle, as early as 1860 he established a dairy, which he managed in conjunction with other business. For foundation stock, Mr. Breuer first used Shorthorns of the Princess and Rose of Sharon families, which proved good milkers, but with every new bull introduced it was found that the beef characteristics would more and more predominate and the Shorthorns were replaced with Ayrshires, which gave good results.

After visiting the land of his nativity on many occasions and observed and admired the ideal Netherland or Friesian cow grazing on those enormously rich pastures of the Netherlands, Mr. Breuer decided that this was the true dairy cow and the cow of the future for our country. In 1877 he purchased his first Holsteins from George E. Brown, and later on bought more foundation stock from Messrs. Smiths & Powell, Edgar Huidekoper. S. L. Hoxie, T. B. Wales, Hon. Gerrit S. Miller and others. In 1884 he purchased a tract of land containg 2000 acres in close proximity to the city of Charleston, S. C., where was then established the Sea Side Herd of Holstein-Friesians and through the use of the best bulls only that money could buy to head the herd, results were obtained that far exceeded all expectations; many a cow in the Sea Side Herd has given forty quarts of milk daily, of a quality that would compare favorably with any breed, and the average of the herd is about ten quarts of milk to one pound of butter.

S. BURCHARD of Hamilton, N. Y. Sylvester Burchard was born September 17, 1834, at Remsen, Oneida county, New York. He came of sturdy New England stock. His father, Sylvester Burchard, Sr., moved from Granby, Mass., with his parents when sixteen years of age. Jabes Burchard, the grandfather, settled upon the old Baron Stuben farm in the town of Stuben.

Sylvester Burchard, Sr., was the village blacksmith of Remsen until the year 1840; he then moved with his wfe, Anna Platt Burchard and his family on the farm in the town of Eaton, Madison county, which he owned and occupied until his death in 1853.

Sylvester Burchard, Sr., established the first large dairy in Madison county. His pride was the old red Durham stock, and his cows were bred from a sire brought from Kentucky. He was an expert judge of dairy cows, and his dairy was the pride of the county.

Sylvester Burchard, the subject of this sketch, was proud of his father's stock, and his first work on the farm consisted of driving the cows to and from the pasture, and in assisting his father in those numberless litt e things which distinguish the successful dairyman.

Upon the death of the father, the son, then eighteen years of age, under-

H. F. W. BREUER.

took the care and management of a large and fertile farm and a choice dairy of cows.

The laws of heredity and environment have their influence upon the man, and Sylvester Burchard has been a successful dairyman for over forty years.

He commenced breeding Holsteins in 1879, and in 1882 he was sent as an expert judge of cattle to Holland, to purchase stock for parties in the United States. He selected 217 head and brought them to this country. The high character of stock purchased by him is sufficient evidence of ability to select the best. He has probably adjudged Holstein stock at more fairs than any other man in this country.

Sylvester Burchard has been a member of the Holstein-Friesian Association since its organization, and has attended all its meetings and has been deeply interested in its work.

The high standing and popularity of Mr. Burchard among Holstein breeders was never better attested than by his nomination for the presidency of the Holstein-Friesian Association at its annual meeting in March, 1894, when he received a unanimous vote for that position. In his annual address as president, delivered at the meeting of the association in March, 1895, in speaking of the great work carried on by the Holstein-Friesian Association, Mr. Burchard said:

"We have a powerful incentive to stimulate us in this great work, inasmuch as the cow we represent laid the foundation of all dairy industries, and taught the generations that it was her mission to nourish and bless the world. We may well boast of her ancient lineage and the blue blood that courses through her veins, and also feel proud of the purity of her pedigree and the great antiquity of her origin, for long before the stately Shorthorn chewed her cud on the banks of the Tees, or the beautiful Ayrshire cropped the grasses on the bleak hillsides of Scotland, or the golden Jersey became queen of the islands of the Channel, the black-and-white cow was feeding in the green pastures and lying down beside the still waters of Holland.

"In the land of her adoption she has helped to make picturesque the landscape, and added to the contentment and happiness of the home, has helped to keep the boys on the farm, and has opened up to our people such possibilities as had never been dreamed of. She has added much to the welfare of our country, and her unprecedented performances at the churn and pail have stimulated many a poor dairyman to a triumphant success. Her gentle disposition and kindly nature have taught us many a lesson in patience and forbearance, and if there is a place for the cow among the immortals, we shall find the Holstein-Friesian happily feeding in the green fields of Paradise."

He has been inspector of imported cattle, and also an inspector for Advanced Registry since the association was formed, and is now a director and member of the executive committee.

Sylvester Burchard is a man of perfect integrity of character; he has large ability, quick perception, good judgment, and his past experience has fully ripened his powers.

FRANK H. BURKE, San Francisco, Cal. Possibly no one on the Pacific coast has had more experience with Holsteins than Mr. Frank H. Burke, of La Siesta ranch, Menlo Park, Cal.

Prior to investing in Holsteins he had practical experience in butter dairying on the largest scale in the world, at the Shafter ranch, in Marin county, Cal., where 4,000 cows are milked daily during the season. Before establishing a herd himself he examined the best herds in the United States, no matter what the breed, and though from past experience he leaned toward the Jersey and Shorthorn cattle, this careful inspection demonstrated to him, as a practical man, that the black-and-whites would be the money-makers.

Nine years ago he purchased largely of these in the East, and the following year so greatly was he pleased with the pecuniary returns that he sent orders for seven carloads, and from time to time has given other orders for "the best."

His herd, notwithstanding numerous sales all over the Pacific coast, from British Columbia to Chili, consists of over sixty head of pure-breds, mostly Clothilde 5th's Clothilde heifers, out of King Aaggie Clothilde cows, with foundation crosses of Aaggie, Netherland, Artis Twisk and Mercedes blood.

Mr. Burke's success in the show ring in the past seven years has been phenomenal, over 700 prizes, including every sweepstakes in the past three years,

S. BURCHARD.

and numerous gold medals in competition with all-milk breeds, have been awarded to him.

At the last state fair (Sacramento), 1895, he won first with a Holstein in the ten-days' butter test, competing with the pick of the coast Jerseys, Ayrshires and Durhams, which victory is the more creditable as millionaire Henry Pierce, whose herd of Jerseys was also in the test, has spared neither money or pains to secure the best by repeated drafts from the Island of Jersey and the East.

While on this side of the Rockies Mr. Burke is only known through the fast race horses bred by him, on the Pacific side he is given credit for using the same skill in mating and handling his herd of Holstein-Friesians that has brought his horses so often first to the wire. His ranch adjoining that of Hon. Leland Stanford, at Palo Alto, is one of the show places of California, and is inspected by many visiting horsemen.

Mr. Burke is not only one of the most popular horsemen in the state of California, but he is also one of San Francisco's most successful business men. Mr. Burke was born in Milwaukee, Wis., but went to this state with his parents while a babe, and is a thorough Californian. For years Mr. Burke was one of the best-known road drivers in San Francisco, and naturally drifted into breeding trotters, at which he had eminent success. He was fortunate enough to secure Eros, 2:20¼, by Electioneer, dam Sontag Mohawk, and, placing this stallion at the head of the La Siesta Stock Farm, at Menlo Park, bred a number of fast ones whose names are known all over the country.

Mr. Burke was one of the organizers of the Pacific Coast Trotting Horse Breeders' Association, and is at the present time one of its directors and chairman of the executive committee. As a member of the well-known real estate firm of Madison & Burke, 626 Market street, he gives his personal attention to the management of one of the longest-established and best-known business houses in the city. As a business man Frank Burke is thorough and straightforward, and none stand higher in the community than he. As a lover of "man's best friend," he is known from one end of California to the other, and has done much to advance the breeding as well as the racing interests toward that high standard which all true sportsmen hope to see them attain in California.

MR. WINTHROP W. CHENERY, first president of the association of the breeders of thoroughbred Holstein cattle, was born in 1819, in Watertown, Mass. He was descended from Lambert Chenery, who came from England with Sir Richard Saltonstall, and settled in Watertown in 1630. At an early age he sought occupation in mercantile life. He became clerk and bookkeeper, and afterwards partner of Abel Phelps, importer and commission merchant, on Long Wharf, Boston. At the death of Mr. Phelps he succeeded to the business, and carried it on for more than twenty-five years.

Early in life he purchased a small farm in his native town, where he delighted in gratifying his taste for fine horses and stock of all kinds. In 1856 he established the Highland Stock Farm at Belmont, Mass., which soon became famous for the display of horses, imported cattle, sheep, swine and other choice stock.

Reasoning from the similarity of the climate of Holland and New England, he conceived the idea that the cattle of that country, so famed for its dairy products, would be a valuable acquisition here in the United States. His first importation of cattle from Holland was made in 1852—a single cow, whose good qualities encouraged him to make other importations in 1857, 1859 and 1861. The cattle of these early importations were kept by the side of Jerseys, Ayrshires, Devons and Guernseys, and the comparison thus made soon convinced him of their superiority as a dairy breed to any of these. The performances of some of this stock are matters of record, and although not remarkable in comparison with some of the records of late years, were far in advance of anything known at that time, and did much to first call attention to the merits of the breed.

Mr. Chenery possessed unbounded enthusiasm, energy and perseverance in the prosecution of any enterprise which he undertook. Like the pioneers in every good cause, he met with many discouragements, but his faith in the Holsteins as the coming stock was never shaken. In 1860, when he had just

17

FRANK H. BURKE.

fairly started in breeding the stock, occurred the pleuro-pneumonia panic in Massachusetts. The State Cattle Commissioners, claiming that some of Mr. Chenery's stock had been exposed to the contagion, ordered the entire herd to be slaughtered. On the same day when this order was executed, Mr. Chenery sent to Holland for another lot of cattle.

One of the early criticisms on the breed was that quantity of milk was produced at the expense of quality. Mr. Chenery took some pains to refute this charge, claiming that they excelled not only in milk but in butter and cheese production. Probably the first butter test of a Holstein cow ever made was his test of the cow Texelaar, in which she produced 17 lbs. 14 oz. of butter in six days.

Mr. Chenery was a frequent contributor to the agricultural press on matters connected with live stock, and his pen was always ready to promote the interests of the Holsteins, or defend them from any aspersions. An article on Holstein cattle which he contributed in 1864 to the Report of the United States Department of Agriculture probably did more than anything ever published to disseminate a knowledge of the race in all parts of the country.

He early recognized the importance of keeping a record of the pure-bred stock in this country, and kept such a record of his own stock from the beginning. Upon the formation of the association of breeders of thoroughbred Holstein cattle, he was authorized to prepare the herd-book of the society. The first volume was published in 1872 (the small beginning of the present bulky volumes)—a book of sixty-seven pages, of which forty-two pages were devoted to a sketch of the Holstein race of cattle prepared by Mr. Chenery. In 1875 he published the second volume, and was engaged in the preparation of the third volume at the time of his death in July, 1876.

Mr. Chenery was a man of commanding presence, standing over six feet four inches, and weighing upwards of 300 pounds. His qualities of mind and heart corresponded to his physical proportions—liberal in his views, generous in disposition, upright in life, having the respect of all, and most highly esteemed by those who knew him best. He was possessed of an excellent memory and keen powers of observation. He not only brought to his work great zeal and enthusiasm, but, like his friend, Prof. Agassiz, had the rare gift of imparting this enthusiasm to others. In fine, he seemed to be peculiarly fitted for the task which he undertook—the introduction of a new breed of cattle, in the face of opposition arising as well from ignorance and apathy as from prejudice in favor of other and well-known breeds of stock. The Holsteins were fortunate in having just such a man to present their claims.

Mr. J. W. Coley of New Woodstock, N. Y., a member of the Holstein-Friesian Association of America, was born May 17, 1836, upon the farm where he now resides in the town of Cazenovia, Madison county, New York. The farm, consisting of 200 acres of fine farming land, is devoted to the raising of wheat, corn and clover, and carries about fifty head of cattle, forty of which are pure-bred Holstein-Friesians.

Mr. Coley has been a dairyman for forty years. During part of that period he has been a breeder and admirer of Shorthorns, among which he found some fine milkers, but too many of them were failures for the dairy and he found their strong tendency to take or flesh a disadvantage. Mr. Coley also had a limited experience with Jerseys, but concluded that the breed lacked constitution.

Passing through these experiences, he decided to buy some Holsteins, which he finds to be very hardy and yield a large quantity of milk and of good quality, and are presistent milkers.

Mr. Coley's herd of registered cattle now numbers upwards of forty head and are of the great butter families of the breed. Prominent in the blood lines are to be noted the Pauline Paul, Mechtchilde, Colantha, Parthenia and Pietertje strains. The herd is at present headed by Sir Ononis Netherland, a son of Soldene 2d's Netherland out of the famous Ononis. This bull has strong resemblance to his famous prize-winning sire and is a half-brother to Sir Henry of Maplewood, and unquestionably of high breeding.

WINTHROP W. CHENERY.

THOMAS H. DODGE. Among those who have taken a deep and active interest in breeding Holstein-Friesian stock of the best and highest type, Thomas H. Dodge, a member of the Holstein-Friesian Association of America, ranks and stands among the first, since he has spared no expense in securing the very best foundation stock from which to raise the choicest representatives of this famous breed of cattle, and has thereby added greatly to its standing and credit in the public estimation, as compared with other favorite breeds.

As proprietor of the New England Stock Farm in Worcester, Mass., he secured at a great cost, New England Queen, Oriana 2d, Marie Wortel 3d, and Planetta, the three latter imported, and they all proved to be great milkers. New England Queen's milk record for thirty days being 2,152¼ lbs., an average of 71¼ lbs. per day; the largest day's record being 79¼ lbs. of milk.

Oriana 2d's milk record for thirty days being 2,064⅛ lbs., an average of 68.8 lbs. per day; the largest day's record being 78 lbs. of milk.

Marie Wortel 3d's milk record for thirty days being 2,004¾ lbs., an average of 66.82 lbs. per day; largest day's record being 78¼ lbs. of milk.

Planetta's milk record for thirty days being 1,999¼ lbs., an average of 66.65 lbs. per day; largest day's record being 75 lbs. of milk.

These cows and their female descendants being bred to such noted stock bulls as Netherland Prince, Iroquois, Uncle Pete, Netherland Emperor and Elijah S., have produced some of the finest and most valuable stock in New England, and among which may be mentioned the bulls, Netherland Emperor 2d, Netherland Crown Prince, Netherland the Great, Netherland Renowned, Netherland Prince's Grandson, Netherland Emperor 3d, Netherland Preferred, Netherland Planetta and Quinsigamond Chief, and the cows, Marie Netherland, with a milk record of 51 lbs. per day as a two-year-old, she being a daughter of Netherland Prince; Princess of Worcester, daughter of Iroquois; Eastern Queen, Netherland Milk Queen, Holstein-Friesian Queen, Netherland Crown Princess, Netherland Crown Princess 2d, and Queen of Bedford, the latter a daughter of Princess of Worcester, making the largest and best milk record as a two-year-old ever made in New England. Although this noted herd has been dispersed in consequence of the growth of the city of Worcester, a broad avenue of eighty feet in width having been laid out through Mr. Dodge's farm, he nevertheless retains an indirect interest in many of the finest animals, and will therefore still keep up his old-time efforts in behalf of Holstein-Friesian stock.

Mr. Dodge was born in the town of Eden, Vermont, in 1823. He is a lawyer by profession. His early training among manufacturers of textile fabrics pre-eminently fitted him for that branch of his profession in which he attained so great a success, that of a patent lawyer.

As an inventor but few men have contributed more in the improvement of labor-saving machinery than he; an adequate notice of his efforts in this direction would completely fill a book.

As a philanthropist Worcester is indeed fortunate in having him as a citizen. He has become widely known as a public benefactor by his handsome gifts to the Natural History Society, and by his contribution to the living as well as to the generations to come in the donation of a tract of thirteen acres of land in the northerly part of the city of Worcester to be used as a public park, and for his generous gift to the Odd Fellows of a very valuable tract of land of eleven acres in the same city as a site for the Massachusetts Odd Fellows' Home, the corner stone of which was laid in October, 1890.

By these and countless minor acts, Mr. Dodge has demonstrated his interest in public charities and his great love for the welfare of mankind. He has always been a generous contributer to public enterprises, and in Worcester has greatly aided in the building of Trinity Methodist Church.

The National Cyclopedia of American Biography closes its sketch of Mr. Dodge with the statement that "to young men, however limited their means, his success and useful life is a most encouraging example of the possibilities of energy and well-directed effort, both in the accumulation and distribution of wealth."

MR. L. A. DOWNER of Cave City, Ky., a member of the Holstein-Friesian Association of America, and stanch admirer of the breed, was born in Hopkinsville, Christian county, Ky., on March 22, 1834. In early childhood his parents located in Todd county, Ky., near Fairview.

His father, J. S. Downer, established the Forest nursery at that place, and

his son grew up in that business, working in all the details till January, 1864. At that time Mr. L. A. Downer purchased the place known as Prewett's Knob, and commenced the cultivation of fruit, which proved fairly remunerative. Having from boyhood a fondness for cattle, on changing from the nursery to the orchard business he commenced devoting a portion of his time to the improvement of the cattle found among the people. His first effort in this direction was the purchase of the best Durham bull that could be found, and commenced grading up.

It was not satisfactory however, and a pair of pure Devons was obtained, which proved far from being what was desired. The next effort was a trial of the Jersey breed—pure-breds and grades—with no better results. Mr. Downer now began to doubt his ability to make any success with cattle, but disliked to surrender. He had read much about the new breeds, and his attention was especially attracted to the Holstein-Friesians by their size, quick growth and wonderful performances at the pail and churn. In May, 1894, a purchase was made of four calves—three females and a bull—which were watched with great solicitude.

One heifer died after a few weeks, and another after a few years; but the heifer that survived, named Duchess of Beemster, when she came in milk Mr. Downer found that he had not expected too much. When she reached five years Mr. Downer had never seen anything to compare with her, her yield being as high as 100 lbs. of milk in a day in midwinter.

This heifer's milk was tested by three impartial men, with the result that it made 24 lbs. 15½ oz. of merchantable butter in seven days. The first heifer calf from Duchess of Beemster was Lady Ollie Artis, sired by Artis Jr.

When fresh for the fourth time Lady Ollie Artis gave in eight and one-half months 14,842¼ lbs. of milk, and made 29 lbs. ¼ oz. of merchantable butter in seven days, to the great surprise of her breeder, and proved an education to the neighbors, many of whom came to see her. While this yield is surpassed by many others in other sections, it demonstrates what this breed will do under the care of an ordinary handler unversed in the ways of feeding and caring for a dairy cow. Mr. Downer states that this breed has given him entire satisfaction for beef, and he easily makes a good calf weigh 1,000 pounds as a yearling. The grades also have given satisfaction as milkers and feeders in this section.

Mr. Solomon Du Bois of New Paltz, N. Y., was born in New Paltz in 1839, and is a descendant of Louis Du Bois, a French Huguenot who was driven from his own country by bitter persecution and fled to America in 1660 and settled in Kingston, N. Y. In 1677, he, with eleven others of his countrymen obtained a grant of a tract of 36,000 acres of land on the west side of the Hudson, comprising the present town of Loyd, a great part of Esopus, New Paltz, Rosendale and Gardiner in Ulster county, N. Y.

Solomon Du Bois is the sixth in descent from Louis. His ancestors since the first settlement at New Paltz have all been farmers, and his place, known as "Fruit and Dairyland Farm," has been in the Du Bois family over two hundred years. About thirty years ago Mr. Du Bois embarked quite extensively in fruit growing, then in its infancy in Ulster county. This business he conducted and has continued to the present time with success.

In 1883 he commenced the breeding of Holstein-Friesian cattle, and later became a member of the Holstein-Friesian Association of America. Making his selections with greatest care from the very best strains, by skilful breeding and weeding, his herd at present ranks among the first in the state. At the head of the herd is Sir Keyes Mechthilde, bred by Henry Stevens & Sons, and in the herd are many fine representatives and descendants of the Aaggie, Netherland, Echo and Pietertje families. The milk produced is sold to the Borden Condensed Milk Company at Wallkill, which is evidence of its fine quality.

The farm is located two and one-half miles from New Paltz, on Wallkill Valley railroad. It lies on the east side of the Wallkill river, and from the lowland there is a gentle rise to the east. This western slope is occupied by vineyards and orchards and from the tableland above, on which is the residence, magnificient views are obtained of the surrounding valley, and the Catskill and Shawangunk Mountains, Lake Mohonk and Minnewaska, the famous summer resorts, being about four miles distant.

THOMAS H. DODGE.

MR. MALCOLM H. GARDNER was born in the town of Sharon, Walworth county, Wis., in 1853. When five years of age his father left the farm, and his childhood was passed in the village of Delavan, Wis. Nine years after his father returned to the farm, and it again became his home, when not away at school, or teaching. Mr. Gardner gained his education at the Delavan high school and Beloit college, where he was a member of the class of '78. His health breaking near the close of his course, he gave up the law as a profession, and returned to the farm, completing his college course at his leisure.

In 1879 he formed a partnership with his brother, W. A. Gardner, and the business is still carried on under the firm name of Gardner Brothers. Seeing that the dairy industry, with hogs as accessory, was especially adapted to southern Wisconsin, the firm turned its attention in that direction, and was among the pioneers in improved dairying in the West. Their first Holstein-Friesian bull was purchased of ex-Secretary T. B. Wales, in January, 1883, and cows, of the same party, in the spring of '85. Other fine animals have been obtained from other sources, and the net profits from the herd have always been highly satisfactory. After losing two of their most promising cows by milk fever, Gardner Brothers gave up all forcing for records, and depend on plain, everyday yields for their showing, believing that this plan gives better satisfaction to customers in the long run.

Mr. Gardner has long been an earnest supporter of the Holstein-Friesian breed, and has written much, mostly for Hoard's Dairyman and the Breeders' Gazette. He is at present secretary and financial manager of the Darien Creamery Company, Darien, Wis., and is a director in the Western Holstein-Friesian Association.

MR. WILLIS JUDD GILLETT of Rosendale, Wis., was born of Eastern parents, July 26, 1864, and up to the age of twenty-one spent the greater part of his time in school. He entered Wayland University, from which he graduated with honor in the class of 1886, and in June the same year he delivered the honorary oration of this his final school year.

After taking his college course Mr. Gillett returned to his father's stock farm at Rosendale, Wis., and took an active interest in the black-and-whites, of which there were then in the stables of Springvale about fifty head of superior animals. He has long been a great admirer of our favorite Hollander, and in the line of working for the interests of the breed and breeder we find his "footprints in the sands of time." Though that time has been short, they are not easily blotted out.

His fine herd has already attained a position second to none in the Northwest as one of great uniformity and beauty, performance and rich breeding. Among the members of his herd may be seen:

Colantha, butter record, 31 lbs. 7 oz. in seven days; milk record, 89 lbs. 5 oz. in one day; 2,375 lbs. 5 oz. in one month, and well known in both East and West as among the greatest.

Johanna 5th, another beauty, has four-year-old records as follows: Butter, 23 lbs. 5 oz. in seven days; milk records, 67 lbs. 10 oz. in one day; 2,001 lbs. 5 oz. in one month; and over 14,500 lbs. in nine months.

Rijaneta, the veteran beauty beast of the leading Western shows, is also there. Her butter record is 26 lbs. 8¼ oz. in seven days; milk record, 83 lbs 12 oz. in one day; 2,013 lbs. 6 oz. in one month.

Nor would it be well to pass without a mention of Johanna Rue, with two-year-old butter record of 15 lbs. 7 oz. in seven days; Elgin Bell 2d, Colantha 3d, Rijaneta's Jewel, Johanna 5th's Clothilde, and many others of rare individuality and remarkable pedigree.

Mr. Gillett will be remembered as a young man of energy, honorable and upright in his dealings, and, if we are to take warnings from the past and adopt them as indications for the future, we can but predict, as his movements in the line of breeding prompt us, the building up in the future of one of the choicest herds to be found in America.

To Mr. Gillett Wisconsin in no small degree owes her State Holstein-Friesian Association, of which he is secretary.

Mr. Gillett has, for some years, been a member of the Holstein-Friesian Association of America, and his success and high standing as a breeder has been recognized by that association in his election as a director, and his elec-

L. A. DOWNER.

tion in 1896 as vice-president. His interest in matters pertaining to the breed has always been very great, and his work in the interests of the breed has been invaluable both in a practical way, and with his pen.

Holstein breeders will long remember his famous contribution to the literature of the breed, which was published in nearly every agricultural paper in the United States, and known as "Gillett's Comparison." In this article he demonstrated by the records of twenty-five leading cows in the Columbian Test compared with twenty-five largest records made under the Holstein-Friesian system of Advanced Registry, and officially authenticated by the officers of institutions and state experiment stations, the superior qualifications of the Holstein-Friesian breed as butter cows.

MR. A. C. HALLMAN of New Dundee, Ont., was born October 25, in the year 1858, in Waterloo county on the old homestead near the village of New Dundee, Ontario, and is of Canadian birth and German parentage.

His father, J. S. Hallman, was also born in the same county of Waterloo, and his grandfather, Rev. Jacob Hallman, was born in Montgomery county, Pennsylvania, being one of the pioneer settlers there, and went to the province early in the "twenties," and cleared up the old homestead. He had nothing to start with but lots of ambition, but amassed a nice fortune. In his day he had walked the distance between the two countries. On the mother's side was Mary Clemons, who was born in Waterloo county, a daughter of A. D. Clemons, also of Pennsylvania origin.

The subject of this sketch was raised on the old homestead and received a common school education. His intentions were to obtain a thorough education and become a professional man, but his help was needed on the farm and his pleadings were unheeded; his training from youth up was on a large well-regulated farm, operated as a grain and stock farm. High-grade and full-blood Shorthorns constituted the live stock until the last four years of his stay under the parental roof, when pure-bred Holstein-Friesians were adopted. Mr. Hallman's love was for domesticated animals of all kinds, and increased as he grew older and served to retain him contentedly on the farm.

The foundation of the celebrated herd known as the Spring Brook Herd of Holstein-Friesians was laid in the spring of 1883. Mr. Hallman's father, with two other gentlemen, became dissatisfied with the milking qualities of the Shorthorns, and, going West, selected three imported heifers and two imported bulls from the herd of George E. Brown, then of Aurora, Ill. These cattle were imported not with the intention of starting a breeding concern, but merely for their own private farm use. His delight in fine cattle was greatly increased when these noble black-and-white beauties graced the farm of which he then had charge, and he decided to establish a herd for breeding purposes. In the year 1884 Mr. Hallman started farming a few miles away from the old homestead, on a farm nicely situated on the public highway between St. Petersburg and New Dundee, and now known as the Spring Brook Stock Farm. A partnership was formed with H. Hilgartner as silent member and the firm established, known for years as A. C. Hallman & Co.

Another importation, or rather a selection from an importation, was made in Toronto from a large consignment of about 100 head then passing through Canada, also owned by Mr. Brown. Out of this lot were selected seven head, six females and one male. Another importation was made in 1886, selected from the famous Lakeside herd at Syracuse, N. Y., and that of T. G. Yeomans & Sons of Walworth, N. Y., and still another in 1888 from the Lakeside herd and that of G. S. Miller of Peterboro, N. Y. The herd numbered for years about sixty head. A dispersion sale was held in 1895, when the partnership was dissolved by mutual consent, and the herd reduced to about thirty head, which in connection with about 100 head of the celebrated bacon hog, the "Red Tamworth," now constitutes the breeding stock.

The object in the selection of foundation stock was always to obtain the best representatives of the most popular families and richest breeding, backed with high records. Mr. Hallman has exhibited stock since 1885, and claims that there is no other herd in Canada that can make such 'showing of successful winnings as the Spring Brook herd, which he thinks has carried away more honor, first silver medals and prizes on bull and progeny, and single prizes, than any other herd.

SOLOMON DU BOIS.

Many of the warmest competitors in the show ring today are animals bred from or descendants of this herd. Other large herds have sprung up and flourished for a season, but Spring Brook is still in it and at the top, as was proven in the show rings of 1895.

Mr. Hallman's connection with the Canadian Holstein-Friesian Association has been prominent from its organization in 1892, and it was largely due to his efforts that this independent record was established. He is at present one of its vice-presidents and prominently identified with the Holstein-Friesian interests of the Dominion.

MR. JOHN M. HAM of Washington Hollow, N. Y., was born at Washington Hollow, Dutchess county, N. Y., upon the farm where he now resides—Lynfeld—which has been the homestead of the family since about 1745, when it was settled upon by the great-grandfather of the present owner, and has been occupied by the Ham family in direct line since that date.

He received his early education at home in the common schools, and at the Poughkeepsie Military Institute, and later pursued a special course in engineering at Lafayette College.

In politics he is a Democrat, and has for several years represented the town of Washington in the Board of Supervisors, which, as the town is largely Republican, speaks highly of the consideration in which he is held by those who know him best.

As a breeder and handler of live stock, his experience has been, it might be said, lifelong. When eighteen years old he was interested with the selection and purchase of stock cattle and sheep, the business at that time being the feeding of cattle and sheep for the New York markets, which in later years was succeeded by the dairy business. The first pure-bred Holstein-Friesian cattle for Lynfeld were purchased by Mr. Ham after his attention had been drawn to the breed through the successful handling of the grades as dairy animals. The business was increased by breeding and the purchase of choice animals until the entire herd were pure-breds. It has been his aim to conduct his herd on a paying basis from a dairy standpoint, and in the selling of breeding stock he has paid particular attention to supplying the local demand of dairymen and farmers for animals to improve their herds.

As a breeder of horses Mr. Ham brought the first pure-bred Percheron stallion to stand for public service into Dutchess county, and later successfully established the first breeding stud of pure-bred horses of that breed in this part of the state. He has a wide reputation as a breeder of Berkshire swine, this branch of his pure-bred live stock antedating that of any other. He was one of the early breeders in America of Dorset Horn sheep, and one of the organizers of the registry association of that breed, and at present is one of the executive committee. In addition to the local business in pure-bred stock, shipments have been made from Lynfeld in the past year into every Eastern and Middle state, Canada, South America and the West Indies.

MR. JOHN D. HARP of Benevola, Md., was born at Benevola, Washington county, Md., in 1853, and became a member of the Holstein-Friesian Association of America in 1895.

The farm upon which he resides is a fertile tract of land, well watered by fine springs and a small stream called Beaver Creek running through it. Mr. Harp is the elder of two sons of Rev. Joshua Harp. From early youth he was given the care of his father's sheep and swine, and in riper years the horses and cattle were added to his charge. As a young man he took little interest in cattle, but was greatly devoted to horses. In 1879 his father retired from business, and sold his entire live stock to the subject of our sketch.

The horses were of a good class, and the cattle were grade Durhams. Mr. Harp, still pursuing his love for horses, was a pioneer in the introduction of the Clydesdale in Washington county. His early experience in the horse business was very discouraging from the loss of a number, but perseverance and great courage overcame these difficulties, and he now raises some very superior horses.

Mr. Harp's experience with Holstein-Friesian cattle began in 1887, when he purchased his first bull of Roberts, Durnall & Hicks, and several cows from the Lackawanna Breeders' Association in Pennsylvania. Proceeding carefully

MALCOLM H. GARDNER.

with these, and carefully selecting and retaining the choicest females from the increase, in 1892 he disposed of his remaining grade cattle at public sale, and now maintains a select herd of recorded cattle only.

While Mr. Harp feels that his herd is not fully up to the high standard which he desires to attain, he is eminently well satisfied with the practical results, and is an enthusiastic admirer of the breed. The herd is now headed by Cynthiana's Echo Colanthus, 20469, a superior sire, whose breeding assures fine progeny, and which fact is now being demonstrated by the young stock now at the farm.

Among the fine animals of this flourishing herd is Maud, 46 D.-F. H B., now giving 84 lbs. in one day of rich milk, and yielding 21 lbs. of butter in one week. Regola, 4501, is another superior cow who made a fair-ground record of 64 lbs. of milk in one day, from which was made more than 3 lbs. of choice butter. Regola has already won three first prizes in the show ring.

Mr. Harp is a believer in officially authenticated records, and is arranging to so test the entire herd.

MR. FRED E. HARRIMAN of Appleton, Wis., was born in that town October 12, 1862, and is the second son of the late Judge J. E. Harriman and Celia Pratt Harriman. Besides Fred, there are three children now living, Frank W. Harriman, attorney at law, who has held many places of trust and honor, including judge of probate and postmaster of Appleton under President Harrison's administration; Florian J. Harriman, the third son, who is now county surveyor of Outagamie county, Wis., and Flora L. Harriman, now wife of B. W. Jones of Appleton.

Fred E. Harriman is a cousin of Judge Thomas M. Cooley of Michigan, and is by profession an attorney at law. In 1884 Mr. Harriman engaged quite extensively in the real estate business.

Mr. Harriman seemed to be endowed with a love for pure-bred live stock from a child up, always having pure-breds of the highest type of whatever breed they belonged. But it was not perhaps till 1889 that Mr. Harriman became extensively interested with live stock, and on March 4, 1890, together with others, he organized and incorporated the Wisconsin Live Stock Association of Appleton, Wis., whose dealings have been almost exclusively in the Holstein-Friesian cattle. This company purchased for foundation stock the very best specimens of the breed to be found. Mr. Harriman has been the general manager of the association since its origin, and the extensive trade which the association enjoys is almost wholly due to Mr. Harriman's energy and skill.

The first importation of this breed of cattle ever received at Jamaica, West Indies, was selected by Hon. C. S. T. Fursdon in person from this herd. Their sales have included almost every state in the Union, many foreign countries and islands of the seas. This herd, often numbering 150 head, is unable to supply the demand, so great has it been.

In February, 1892, Mr. Harriman with others incorporated the Holstein-Friesian Breeders' Association of Wisconsin, which is today the largest and most powerful state association in the Union. Its object is to promote the welfare of the breed and its members, and it is largely through the push of Mr. Harriman, who has been its secretary for several years, ably assisted by its president. J. Rust of North Greenfield, Wis., that this success has been attained. "Fred," as he is usually called, is an extensive reader of dairy and agricultural papers; receiving weekly about twenty leading journals, and is willing to admit the good and bad qualities of all breeds, but is a staunch and fearless advocate of the Holstein-Friesian cow, a pure-bred and none other.

For several years past, a portion of the stock under Mr. Harriman's care, numbering from forty to sixty head, has been kept in the city for inspection and sale. The stable is modern in construction, light and warm, the cattle brushed daily, water within their reach at all times, and the stables cleared whenever droppings begin to accumulate therein. The milk from each cow is weighed at each milking and the amount recorded. It is then aerated, chilled, bottled and delivered to customers in the city, which trade is rapidly growing and giving the best of satisfaction. It is now Mr. Harriman's desire to furnish such a quality of milk from the Holstein cow that it will find a market for 2,000 bottles daily.

W. J. GILLETT.

On November 3, 1886, Mr. Harriman was united in matrimony to Ida E. Robinson of Neenah, Wis., a remarkable woman of business activity and social qualities. To them was born on July 28, 1888, Fred E. Harriman, Jr., and on July 18, 1890, Ray Marshall Harriman, both of whom still bless the household.

Mr. Harriman keeps well posted with the pedigrees of the several breeds of dairy cattle as well as the different families of the various breeds, and is pleased to have all who are interested in the live stock industry visit him.

Mr. JOSEPH HAVILAND of Glens Falls, N. Y., was born in the town of Queensburg, Warren county, N. Y., in the year 1826, where he now resides (post office Glens Falls). His father, Joseph Haviland, was a successful farmer on what is known as Sanford's Ridge, and an admirer of fine stock.

Mr. Haviland's experience in handling and caring for stock has been that of a life-time.

In March, 1880, he purchased a Holstein bull and heifer of, and imported by, the Unadilla Valley Stock Breeders' Association, and later the bull Jacob Hartog, each of which proved to be of such superior quality that he was induced in 1883 to buy more cattle of Smiths & Powell.

Among this last lot was Carrie Dean, an imported heifer bred to Netherland Marquis. Carrie Dean's sire, Willem, was a noted bull in Holland. This animal has been one of the foundation animals of the herd; the other foundation animals were obtained from H. Stevens of Lacona and F. C. Stevens of Attica, N. Y.

The herd is now headed by America 2d's Wayne Paul De Kol, from T. G. Yeomans & Sons' herd.

With all the former experience of Mr. Haviland, he has found the Holsteins excel for butter as well as milk producing, and that feeding for either will produce the desired object, and also that they will readily take on flesh when not in milk, thus making the most profitable cow for the owner.

Mr. Haviland in visiting Holland in the year 1887, where the black-and-whites stand higher than all other breeds, was struck with admiration to find them so little pampered, and the almost only source of profit to the farmer.

Butter and cheese were there sold the highest in Amsterdam for the London market, and proved to him that the Hollanders were reaping the reward of their ancestors' skill, and are going on improving their most desirable breed of cattle, and it is their never-tiring effort to excel all others in the future as well as in the past.

Mr. H. N. HOLDEMAN of Carthage, Mo., was born in Wooster, O., December 27, 1854; was raised on a farm where his father early taught him to be accurate in the feeding and handling of his live stock, though he only kept good high-grade stock.

In 1878 Mr. Holdeman moved on to a farm of his own near Congress, O., on which he farmed and raised stock, dealing principally in sheep and horses. In 1885 he sold the farm and bought and shipped calves to Carthage, Mo., and sold them at a good profit. Being well pleased with the country, and not liking the long, cold winters of northern Ohio, he concluded to move with his family to Missouri. Finding here much inquiry for grade Holstein calves, he returned to Ohio, and bought 110 head of grade Holstein calves and yearlings, and shipped them to Carthage, Mo.

In 1885 he bought a farm of 140 acres near Carthage, and sold all his Holsteins but about thirty head. Mr. Holdeman now realized that in buying the cattle in Lorain and Medina counties, Ohio, he had hitherto been breeding the wrong breed of cattle, namely, Shorthorn. This was also proved to him on looking at the mature Holstein cows owned by such men as Mr. C. W. Harr, Mr. Phelon, and others, and he was easily converted to the fact that the Holsteins were the true dairy cows, and were also hard to beat for beef. With this in mind, in the spring of 1886 he went to Kansas City and purchased two registered yearling Holsteins—a heifer and a bull. They were from the herd of Mr. Buckingham, of Cleveland, O.

He took these home, and bred the grade heifers to the bull, and in the fall of the same year made a sale and disposed of the heifers, except three or four of the choicest ones. In 1887 Mr. Holdeman went to Aurora, Ill., and from the herd of George E. Brown selected a cow and a two-year-old heifer. The bull,

A. C. HALLMAN.

weighing over 1,300 pounds at the age of eighteen months, proved a magnificent breeder. The cow Kero gave 14,000 lbs. of milk in one year on common feed, testing 4.4 lbs. butter fat.

The heifer Nettie Langspeen has never been defeated in the show ring since owned by him, and she is now giving 25 lbs. of milk daily, and has been milking eight months.

In the same year, 1887, the neighboring farmers concluded that they wanted a creamery built at Carthage, and erected one at the cost of $8,000, of which Mr. Holdeman took two shares, and was selected to act as secretary and manager. After starting, some of the patrons, especially the Jersey men, said they could not afford to sell their rich milk for the same price Mr. Holdeman was getting for his "blue Holstein" milk.

Mr. Holdeman had in the meantime traded for another herd of registered cows, and was sending a big lot of the "blue milk" to the creamery. The creamery patrons then purchased a Babcock test, and the butter maker was instructed to test the "blue Holstein milk," but, to their great surprise, they found the "blue milk" was second to none, testing as high as 5 per cent fat.

In 1892 Mr. Holdeman made a sale on his farm, disposing of forty head of registered and grade cows and heifers. The registered cattle averaged $83. His present herd is not a large one, but of excellent quality, consisting of such strains as Mechthilde, Kere, Parthenea and Mahomet. The milk is at present sold on the retail market in Carthage for ten cents per gallon at the door.

Mr. Holdeman finds the Holsteins very gentle and docile cattle, giving plenty of good milk, and he does not have to feed them twelve months to get milk six months of the time. The calves are large and strong, easily trained to drink out of a bucket, and grow faster and larger than those of other breeds. They give more milk, which makes more butter and cheese, than any other breed which he has milked, including Shorthorns and Jerseys, of which latter he thinks that, if he had them to keep, he would have to do so at a loss, and thus concludes that the breed of cattle that an enterprising farmer should keep is one that excels in the product of milk, butter, cheese and beef, and which he states is most certainly the large black-and-white sort, called Holstein-Friesian.

Mr. Charles Houghton of Boston, Mass., the first secretary of The Association of Breeders of Pure-bred Holstein Cattle and of the Holstein Breeders' Association, died on May 18, 1891, at his residence in Brookline, Mass., at the age of 70 years. He was born and reared upon a farm at Putney, Windham county, Vermont, and was a thorough farmer and was known as the most expert handler of live stock of all sorts in that section when a young man.

He was a graduate of the famous old academy at Chester, Vt., and afterwards studied law with Hon. E. W. Stoughton. He was admitted to the Suffolk bar in Boston in 1856, and immediately entered into active practice, which he continued up to the time of his sudden demise.

After several years in Boston he turned his attention more especially to patent law, and was widely known from his connection with inventions relating to the manufacture of boots and shoes, particularly the famous McKay sewing machine. Many other inventions of a highly important character were by him brought out and placed before the public. He achieved great success in his profession, and was highly esteemed in legal circles and socially.

Having always retained the old homestead in Putney, he set about its improvement and fitted it up in a practical manner and improved it in every way, until it became known as one of the finest and model farms of New England.

He was intimately acquainted with the late W. W. Chenery of Belmont, Mass., the pioneer importer and breeder of the Holstein-Friesian cattle, and early recognizing their great value, made his first purchase and founded the Houghton Farm herd in 1866. He was the first customer that Mr. Chenery had, and therefore the second man in America to establish a herd of the famous Dutch cattle, as they were then called.

In 1871, in connection with Mr. Chenery, Mr. Thomas B. Wales, Mr. C. C. Walworth and Mr. William A. Russell, he organized the Association of Breeders of Thoroughbred Holstein Cattle, and became its secretary and treasurer, thus starting the first record of purity of blood of this breed that the world

J. M. HAM.

had known. Upon the death of Mr. Chenery, who had prepared and published a volume of the Herd-Book at his own risk financially, but "by authority" of the association, Mr. Houghton began to keep the records and prepare the herdbooks from time to time as secretary. He thus, in his early days, largely conceived and carried out the plans which have resulted in placing the present association before the world, the most successful organization of its kind.

He drew the charter and by-laws for the Holstein Breeders' Association, which was the successor of the original association, and was, during his long connection with the breed, a most careful conservator of what he believed to be its true interest, and was active and vigilant in everything which had any bearing upon the subject and would advance the breed.

MR. SOLOMON HOXIE of Yorkville, N. Y., was born at Brookside, N. Y., in 1829, and in 1833 his parents moved to Edmeston, N. Y., which town was at the time largely owned by the heirs of Col. Robert Edmeston, who had received it by grant from the King of England. Owing to circumstances connected with foreign ownership, this tract of country was only partly settled, and the privations and experiences of the settlers were somewhat similar to those of earlier pioneer life.

Mr. Hoxie in 1874 united with others in forming the Unadilla Valley Stock Breeders' Association, which for many years was one of the largest and most progressive societies of its kind in the country. It was located in the northern part of the Unadilla Valley, in the counties of Otsego, Chenango and Madison, and for convenience of access to the public a fine farm was purchased in 1876 at Whitestown, in Oneida county. Here a part of their herd was kept for exhibition and sale, under the care of Mr. Hoxie, who was one of the executive committee of the association. The remainder of the herd was kept in various parts of the Unadilla Valley, in charge of another member of the committee. The history of this association would form a long and interesting story, for its part in the introduction of the Holstein-Friesian breed was a series of skillful, aggressive moves which placed their cattle in the front ranks as prize-winners and producers.

In 1876 Mr. Hoxie moved to Whitestown, to better look after the association's interests, and still resides there, though through the establishment of a new post-office his address was changed to Yorkville.

In 1879 he went to Europe as the agent of the Unadilla Valley Stock Breeders' Association, for the purpose of purchasing and importing cattle; and again in 1880, accompanied by Mr. Irwin Langworthy, he visited Holland and selected the noted bull Mooie, 26 D.-F. H. B. In 1882 he made another trip, this time in company with Mr. S. Burchard, of Hamilton, N. Y., who is one of the inspectors of the Holstein-Friesian Association; Mr. Cornelius Baldwin, of Nelson, O., the famous expert on dairy cattle; and Mr. L. C. Payne, of Garrettsville, O., who has long been prominent as a breeder. This visit was the longest which Mr. Hoxie had yet made, and he remained in Europe for six months, studying not only the characteristics of Holstein-Friesian cattle, but also those of the Islands of Jersey and Guernsey, and other places.

In 1879 Mr. Hoxie was made the secretary of the Dutch-Friesian Herd Book Association, and filled the position with rare ability and good judgment until the formation of the Holstein-Friesian Association in 1885. He was also during these years the editor of the herd book, and prepared and published volumes containing a large amount of interesting and valuable information. In 1885 he was elected an honorary life member of the Friesian Herd Book Association of Europe, an honor we believe possessed by no other American breeder.

Mr. Hoxie has written much on the subject of Holstein-Friesian cattle, and portions of his work have been translated into Hollandish, and published in Europe. He is a most interesting writer. One of his best efforts, perhaps, was an article which was published by Harper's Monthly, in August, 1888, though many articles of equal value have been prepared for, and published in, the Register, which have called out much praise from its readers and have been widely quoted by the agricultural press.

But Mr. Hoxie's life work, and that which must survive to distinguish him in the history of the improvement of live stock, is the Advanced Registry, several volumes of which he has most carefully edited and prepared for the Holstein-Friesian Association, which has adopted the system. We regret we are

JOHN D. HARP.

unable in this short sketch to do justice to his work in this direction, but it is sufficient, perhaps, for our purposes to say that the idea (which, by the way, Mr. Hoxie modestly declines to claim as of his origin) is regarded in all countries by the associations whose object is the improvement of live stock as the most valuable and progressive step taken since the registration of pure breeding began. Upon this point Mr. Hoxie says:

"I think I have no claim to the origin of the idea of advanced registry. It seems to have existed in many minds in a nebulous form; in fact, it was hinted at in some of our leading agricultural journals. If I can claim any credit, it is only that of having given distinct form to it. And in this I must say that I think Gerrit S. Miller, Cornelius Baldwin, W. G. Powell, E. A Powell, and perhaps others, are deserving of quite as much credit as myself. After it was thus given form it would have failed, for a time, had it not received the support of such men as T. G. Yeomans and W. Brown Smith. My confidence in advanced registry has always been unlimited, and now I look forward to a necessary adoption of its fundamental principles by breeders of all kinds of thoroughbred stock. It must be so, and in the near future, for this simple reason: As such stock multiplies, two opposite movements are constantly going on—one of improvement, the other of degeneration: the former in the hands of skillful breeders, the latter in the hands of unskillful breeders; the difference between the extremes constantly widening, until, on the one hand, it is no better than scrub stock, while on the other it is royal in character. As time goes on a separation in registry as well as in character is inevitable, and the easiest and most natural way by which it can take place is through a system of advanced registry."

Mr. EDGAR HUIDEKOPER of Meadville, Pa., was born in Meadville March 10, 1845, attended the Phillips Exeter Academy, 1862-1864, graduated at Harvard, 1868, and took a degree of A. M., 1871. He has been secretary and treasurer of The Meadville Agricultural Works; assistant treasurer of the Meadville Theological School, 1869, and treasurer since October 4, 1879; secretary of the Meadville Water Company since 1886 and treasurer since January 2, 1894; president of Spencer Hospital, Meadville since 1888; president Holstein-Friesian Association of America, 1889-1890; president Meadville, Conneaut Lake & Linesville railroad, 1891; treasurer Meadville Conservatory of Music since 1890.

Mr. Huidekoper has been one of the most extensive importers of Holstein-Friesian cattle, going to Holland for this purpose no less than eight times, and bringing over 312 very choice animals.

On March 31, 1878, Mr. Huidekoper imported two bulls, Akkerman, 461, and Anton, 462, and ten heifers, among them the well known Violet, 743, and Hykolina, 746, Wilhelmina, 737, Cecilia, 748, and Saapke, 736, all having made large records. On December 5, 1878, he imported four bulls and four heifers, including Wouter, 460. On November 10, 1881, he imported two bulls and twenty-one cows and heifers, including the beautiful show cow Klara, 3020. On September 18, 1882, he imported two bulls and thirty-two heifers, including Peterina, 2960, a successful prize winner. On December 8, 1883, he imported nine cows and ninety-two heifers, among which was Cybele, 5291, now having a record of 100¼ lbs. of milk in a day. On February 27, 1884, he imported 100 cows and heifers, including the grand cows, Jenny Wren, 10377 (Isabella, 885 N. R. S.), and her dam, Isabella, 884 N. R. S. On September 29, 1884, he imported thirty-four cows and heifers. On May 7, 1385, he imported the celebrated prize bull of Holland, De Brave Hendrik.

In 1880 when on a visit to Gerrit S. Miller, of Peterboro, N. Y., Mr. Huidekoper saw Billy Boelyn, 189, and quietly determined to own him when possible. After waiting two years he found Mr. Miller ready to name a price on the bull, and Mr. Huidekoper immediately bought Billy Boelyn, which he showed with such wonderful success through the seasons of 1882-83. Upon this remarkable trip the following list of prizes was won with this bull, viz.: Billy Boelyn, with his herd, winner of the gold medal prize for the best herd at New York State Fair, 1880; first prize, Ohio State Fair, 1882; first prize, Pennsylvania State Fair, 1882; first prize, best bull any age, Pennsylvania State Fair, 1882; first prize, sweepstakes herd (one bull and four cows), Pennsylvania State Fair, 1882; first prize, Mahoning and Chenango Valley Fair, 1882; first prize, sweepstakes best herd, Mahoning and Chenango Valley Fair, 1882; first prize sweep-

FRED E. HARRIMAN.

stakes herd (one bull and four cows), Ohio State Fair, 1883; first prize, best bull three years old and over, Tri-State Fair, 1883; first prize, best herd (one bull and four cows), sweepstakes, Tri-State Fair, 1883; first prize, best herd, sweepstakes, Mahoning and Chenango Valley Fair, 1883.

The Bulletin of the Ohio State Board of Agriculture for 1882 reports: "Before entering upon the examination of this breed the awarding committee agreed upon the following rules, by which their decision would be guided:

"1st. Considered in their relation to the dairy.

"2d. Considered in their relation to the shambles. Any animal, in their judgment, combining the greatest amount of excellence, viewed from this standpoint, would be entitled to the first premium, etc.

"The practical application of this rule tied the red ribbon on Billy Boelyn's horn, the finest bull of the breed I ever saw. Short legged, broad, level back, straight on rump, ribs well sprung, and covered with a mellow hide, resting on wonderfully soft tissues. He is modelled more after the Shorthorn than Friesian type. The second premium went to Mooie, a large animal of the true Holstein type, one that has been a successful campaigner. Taken as a whole, this was a fine show of Holstein bulls."

Mr. Huidekoper states that Billy Boelyn has won more prizes and sired more prize bulls and bulls which stand at the head of leading herds than any bull living or dead. His weight in prime condition is 2,080 lbs. Ten of Billy Boelyn's descendants won prizes at the New York Dairy Show in May, 1887, including Sir Henry of Maplewood, who with his get won the most coveted prize offered, for best bull and progeny. He imparts his good qualities to his offspring. His daughters are, as a rule, better milkers than their dams. Billy Boelyn is the sire of Copia, 97 lbs. one day, and 2,747¼ lbs. in thirty-one days, and sire of Pledge, 92¼ lbs. in one day, 2,577¼ lbs. in thirty-one days. No other bull has the honor of two daughters which give 90 lbs. of milk in a day.

Mr. Huidekoper was awarded during the years 1879 to 1883 at the only State fairs where his herd was exhibited, thirty first prizes in all classes, many of them sweepstakes. In addition to these were 130 other prizes at county fairs, and Mr. Huidekoper for twelve years had in his herd the great prize bull of Holland, De Brave Hendrik, No. 199 N. R. S., 230 H. F. H. B., who won the following prizes there: Committee prize, Alkmaar. March, 1882; committee prize, Holland Agricultural Society, Gouda, September, 1882; prize bull, Alkmaar, August, 1883; first prize, International Agricultural Exhibition, Amsterdam, August, 1884; prize medal, International Agricultural Exhibition, Amsterdam, August, 1884.

In March, 1883, the Committee of Agriculture selected fifty bulls in Holland, and from those fifty selected and designated De Brave Hendrik as the first and best bull to stand in North Holland. De Brave Hendrik comes from a great milking family. He indicates the great milking tendency in his breeding, and imparts to his heifers perfect model udders. His sons have teats like heifers' teats. Mr. Huidekoper confidently believes that De Brave Hendrik was the most magnificent Holstein bull in the world.

Mr. Huidekoper is a breeder who always fully appreciated the saying that "a bull is one-half of the herd," and, when Billy Boelyn increased in age, he imported De Brave Hendrik, 230, the grandest bull that Holland could produce. Billy Boelyn remained in the herd until fifteen years of age, and De Brave Hendrik until twelve years old. Later bulls in the herd have been: Pietertje Netherland, 12804, a descendant of Lady Netherland and Pietertje 2d; Violet Prince, 4209, and Violet King, 4210, sons of the dairy queen, Violet; Peterina's Billy Boelyn, 3156, a son of Billy Boelyn and Peterina, a cow who never met defeat in the show ring.

At the present time the bulls at the head of the herd are: Lady Fay's Monk, 17253, a son of Netherland Monk and Lady Fay; together with Brandi, 20770 a double grandson of Billy Boelyn, and grandson of De Brave Hendrik.

Mr. Huidekoper whose wide experience amply qualifies him to speak, says: Holland, or Holstein cattle, combine more desirable qualities than any other breed of cattle. Their color is black and white, in picturesque and distinct marks, variegated or mottled. They possess wonderfully strong and vigorous constitutions. They are extremely hardy and of healthy digestive organization. Both bulls and cows are docile and quiet in disposition. They mature early, both as milkers and as beef cattle. They readily adapt themselves to change of soil and climate. They are unrivalled as milk producers, and as

JOSEPH HAVILAND.

butter makers surpass any other breed. As beef cattle they will compare favorably with any of the noted beef breeds. Holsteins combine milk, cheese, butter and beef far more successfully than any other breed, and therefore are the most desirable for general purposes.

Heifers two years old give from 30 to 50 lbs., 60 lbs., and even 80 lbs. and over of milk per day; yielding 6,000 to 10,000 lbs. during the first year. Older cows give 50 to 80 lbs., with many records of 90 lbs., and as high as 112 lbs per day, and yield usually 10,000 to 15,000 lbs per year; while some yield 16,000 to 30,000 lbs. per year. They hold out nearly the whole year. Large milkers are the rule, not the exception. My cows have never been forced with feed nor they ever been fed any milk.

It is only recently that special attention has been paid to the butter qualities of Holstein cows, and the results prove that they far surpass all other breeds as butter makers, in quality of butter as well as quantity. Young cows two years old have made from 8 to 21 lbs of butter in one week, and mature cows make from 12 to 30 lbs. per week. At the New York Cattle and Dairy Show, May, 1887, unquestionably the largest and best exhibition of the kind ever held in this country, between 400 and 500 choice representatives of the various breeds being represented, sweepstakes for best milch cow of any breed was won by a Holstein. Sweepstakes for best butter cow of any breed, the one producing the largest quantity of butter during twenty-four consecutive hours of the exhibition, was won by a Holstein, in competition with Jerseys and a Guernsey. She made 2 lbs. 7½ oz. butter in twenty-four hours from 63 lbs. 1½ oz. milk. Holstein butter won first prize on 5 lbs. package, thirty-eight entries representing the various dairy breeds in competition. Holstein butter won second and third prizes on 30 lbs. package, eighteen entries in competition. Holsteins now wear the laurels for butter.

The readiness with which Holstein cows take on flesh when dry is not surpassed by that of any other breed, and the quality of the beef is of the finest, the fat being well distributed among the lean. Calves frequently weigh from 90 to 120 lbs. They gain rapidly in growth, making from 2½ to 5 lbs. per day. Matured bulls usually weigh 2,000 to 2,500 lbs. One-year-old heifers frequently weigh 800 lbs.; cows two years old and older weigh from 1,000 to 1,800 lbs.

Holstein grades and crosses are a great success; the heifers make great milkers and the steers attain a rapid growth and large size at early age.

MR. LE ROY F. JUDD of Lancaster, Wisconsin, of whom the engraving is a fair likeness at the age of twenty-one, is a descendant of the old Judd family so well and popularly known in agricultural circles in southern New York, the region around Elmira and Attica.

Le Roy is the son of Henry C. Judd with whom he is associated in the stock business. Henry C. was born in Genesee county, one of New York's richest counties.

The old Judd estate lies in the rich valley of the Genesee river, about sixteen miles out from Attica. This valley is among the most productive in the great banner state of the Union. It is equal in fertility to the richest of the Mohawk valley. Here is where he has spent his boyhood days in agricultural pursuits and the rearing and handling of fine stock.

Henry C. Judd early in life acquired a love for the rich prairies of our Western country. He visited the then pioneer counties of western Wisconsin and took a great delight in the valley lands of the great Mississippi. After some time spent in careful observation as to the best point in which to settle, he pitched his tent in Grant county, Wisconsin, twenty miles from the bank of the Mississippi. For nearly thirty years he has been prominent among the citizens of western Wisconsin.

No one farmer has probably done more to advance the agricultural interests in this part of the great state of Wisconsin than Henry C. Judd. He was married in Grant county to Ella Paterson, a member of the Paterson family so favorably known in this part of the state among the leaders in agricultural pursuits. Mr. H. C. Judd and his son Le Roy F. made a strong team of workers in the building up of one of the finest farm homes in western Wisconsin.

Although coming from a dairy state, Mr. Judd has been engaged in the rearing of Shorthorns from pure-bred stock. But for a number of years past he has been in the dairy business, during which time he has tested a number of

H. N. HOLDEMAN.

different breeds for the dairy business, and settled on the Holstein as the profitable breed to handle.

Henry C. is now advanced in years, but his eldest son, Le Roy F., is the active manager of the stock farm. He is handling one of the fine herds of purebreds in Wisconsin. He was reared in this rich valley where crops never fail and rains come about to suit the convenience; and has been a handler of fine stock all his life. "Turn the cows in at the gate" is the family joke upon him, which simply means to the reader that Le Roy F. is a great lover of fine cows. He was graduated from the agricultural department of the State University, and is consequently up with the theory as well as the practice of handling fine stock. He states: "We are Holstein men from the ground up. We know what we are doing because we have tried all of the best breeds, and find the Holstein a long way in the lead. We have in our herd a member of the distinguished Parthenea family as a herd bull; Mercedes, Aaggie, Netherland, Astrea, Echo and Scholton families are also represented here. Our Nettie Scholton is hardly equalled by any other cow in the state. Her record of 93 lbs. of milk in one day and 30 lbs. 14 oz. of butter in one week stands among the lead of great cows. We are here to stay in the Holstein business."

MR. C. H. KRUEGER of Lisbon, Ia., proprietor of the Lisbon Valley Stock Farm, was born in Germany. He came to this country in 1872, and has handled fine cattle all his life. He moved to Iowa in 1879, and settled in Lisbon.

Mr. Krueger was married in 1888, as he states, to "the best woman in Iowa." She was a farmer's daughter, and took great delight in fine cows; and together they embarked in the business of handling Holsteins a little less than ten years ago. They had tried common cows for dairying, but soon learned that the Holsteins were far more profitable, and began to keep them exclusively. They now have one of the best-bred herds, and some of the best individual cows, in Iowa. A large number of their cows are in Advanced Registry.

An agricultural college man who examined this herd not long ago said it was the finest herd of cows he had ever seen. Three cows in this herd this season (1896) took premiums in the competitive test for officially-authenticated records made by the Holstein-Friesian Association. The Kruegers have sold during the past few years a large number of bulls, and heifers, and cows, and their customers are always highly pleased with the stock. A member of their herd, Bryonia Albia, won second prize in the great test, in which there were nearly a hundred cows in competition, and about twenty winners. Mechthilde's Sir Henry of Maplewood is one of the sires of this herd, and by them is considered the greatest of sires.

MR. SAMUEL A. LANGDON, now of Morrison, Ill., was born on June 17, 1833, in Berkshire county, Massachusetts. His father, Amos Langdon, was an extensive farmer and stock breeder and was a member of the Massachusetts Legislature in 1840 and in 1852. Young Langdon remained on the farm with his father during his minority, and received his education in the common schools and a business course at Bacon's Commercial College at Cincinnati, O.

At the age of twenty-two years he went to Ross county, Ohio, and was for several years station agent at the town of Lyndon on what is now the Baltimore & Ohio Southwestern railroad. He was also engaged in the grain trade and merchandise up to 1865, when he was elected treasurer of Ross county and re-elected in 1867 and removed to Chillicothe, the county seat, and served four years in that capacity.

His health being somewhat impaired by the close application to business, and his family also being in poor health and thinking a change of climate would be beneficial, he removed in 1871 to Whiteside county, Illinois, and purchased a farm near the city of Morrison. His first intention was to engage in the breeding of Shorthorn cattle, but this breed not proving satisfactory, in 1881 he purchased his first Holstein cattle, five cows and a bull. In this lot was the celebrated cow Minnie Winkle, No. 405 H. H. B.; a cut of this cow will be found in Vol. 3, H. F. H. B. She was a noted show animal at that time and one of the best of the breed.

The starting of this herd was the first herd of pure bred Holsteins in Whiteside county. They were a great curiosity as many had never seen anything of the kind.

CHARLES HOUGHTON.

From this herd has been produced many splendid animals; but as Mr. Langdon has not kept his stock for the purpose of making large records, his animals do not appear in the advanced records. The object has been to produce animals that with the ordinary keeping given by dairy farmers will produce the best results.

One animal now in the herd produced in seven days 21 lbs. 11 oz. of butter; this on pasture feed only, having no grain feed for four weeks previous to the test, and making 1 lb. of butter to 20 lbs. of milk. This, Mr. Langdon thinks, is the true test of the value of a cow without any forcing.

He has always had at the head of the herd the best sires, such as the descendants of Mink, Mercedes and Pietertje 2d.

Mr. Langdon removed from the farm to Morrison in February, 1894, his health being such that he was not able to give his stock his personal attention; but the farm is still stocked with Holstein-Friesian cattle.

Mr. Langdon's family consists of a wife and five children; the oldest, a daughter, Elsie L., and a son, Porter B., are married, and are residents of Sterling, Ill. Buel A. is one of the proprietors of the Morrison Record, a paper published at Morrison, Ill. The two younger sons, Ross S. and Clark E., are at home and are members of the Morrison High School. Not a member of the family either drinks whiskey or uses tobacco in any form.

Mr. J. W. LA GRANGE of Franklin, Ind., was born November 1, 1865, on the farm where he resides. He moved to Franklin with his parents when nine years old, and was educated in the public schools there, and finished his studies at Hanover College, where he was graduated in 1886. He then took charge of the old homestead.

That fall the editor of one of the local papers had a Holstein heifer, which he bought for a milch cow, but concluded he did not have time to care for her, and she was purchased by the firm of W. H. La Grange & Son. She was a good one, and since then has made a record of 84 lbs. of milk in one day, and 23 lbs. and 4 oz. of butter in seven days. Thus encouraged the firm bought a bull and subsequently picked up many other Holsteins, until, with the natural increase, they now have about seventy head of pure-bred cattle. Messrs. La Grange state that they are in the business to stay, and are making money in the dairy with their cows, and have a good trade, both for young cattle and their dairy products, selling cream in Indianapolis.

In the show yards the Wellswood Place herd has a most creditable record, and in eight years' showing has never lost the herd prize, but on two occasions to a Jersey herd when coming into competition with them.

Mr. La Grange is a member of the Indiana State Board of Agriculture from the Fourth District, having been elected in 1894, and re-elected in 1896.

Mr. M. E. MOORE of Cameron, Mo., is a native of Parkman, Geauga county, Ohio, and was born January 6, 1847. He was reared at his birthplace, spending his boyhood days on a dairy farm where were made some of what is known as the "Western Reserve Cheese." He received his early education at the common schools of that vicinity; then attended Western Reserve Seminary and College at Hiram, Ohio, and finished with a commercial course at Poughkeepsie, N. Y.

At the age of twenty-one he "emigrated" to Missouri and engaged in the mercantile business at Cameron, Mo., when, after two years of successful trade, his love for the dairy returned, and he started the first successful cheese factory in the state, and continued increasing it in this direction until he had in successful operation four factories in as many different counties.

It was at this time that he saw the great need of improvement in the dairy cows of the state, and after a thorough investigation and study of the breeds in 1881 decided that the Dutch-Friesian (Holstein) cow was to be his choice. He purchased one cow at Gilman, Ill. It was the first registered cow of the breed in the state of Missouri, and Mr. Moore was so well pleased that he purchased four heifers from the Unadilla Valley Stock Breeders' Association of West Edmeston, N. Y., which were just imported and had been bred to the famous bull Mooie; and in 1884 he purchased a carload from the same asssociation, all of which were imported.

At this time Mr. Moore saw the great necessity of a breeder being thoroughly

SOLOMON HOXIE.

conversant with all the points that combine to make a typical dairy cow, and determined to visit his old neighbor and noted cattle expert, Cornelius Baldwin of Nelson, Ohio. From him Mr. Moore received instruction on the points and anatomy of a dairy cow. With his own experience and the aid of Mr. Baldwin, he has been able to secure, breed and develop some of the greatest performers in public and private tests of Holstein-Friesian history.

A few of these will be mentioned in detail; first is the Empress Josephine family, the foundation of which is Empress Josephine, 429 D.-F. H. B., which was selected in Holland by Cornelius Baldwin of Nelson, Ohio, and bred by R. Witema Tjummazurn, Friesland. She is a very large and typical dairy cow, a great producer, making 353 lbs. 8 oz. of milk in seven days, from which was churned 25 lbs. 14 oz. of butter. Prof. W. A. Henry of the Agricultural Experiment Station at Madison, Wis., sent Prof. Short to the farm at Cameron, Mo., taking three samples of her milk, which tested by Prof. F. W. A. Woll 3.01, 3.67 and 4 per cent fat. She has made 88 lbs. 14 oz. milk in one day, 10,119¾ lbs. in 139 days, and has won many prizes in public tests for butter and milk. She transmits her remarkable qualities of production to her offspring.

Empress Josephine 3d, 642 Advanced Registry, was calved February 22, 1885, was exhibited at St. Joe Exhibition as a two-year-old and won first prize for quality of milk in competition with Jerseys. She has been shown at state fairs for ten years, and it is safe to say that no other cow of Holstein-Friesian fame has won as many prizes in public tests, competing with Holsteins and other breeds. Her record for seven days is 603 lbs. 12 oz. of milk, yielding 31 lbs. 2 oz. butter. Analysis of her milk by Prof F. W. A. Woll showed 3.74 butter fat.

Empress Josephine 4th, now at the Kansas Agricultural College farm, when she was three years old, at the Kansas State Fair, made in public test 50 lbs. milk in a single day, from which was churned 2 lbs. of butter, winning first prize.

Perhaps one of the greatest cows of the breed is Gerben 4th, 643 Advanced Registry, selected in Holland by Cornelius Baldwin, who said to Mr. K. N. Kuperus at the time that she showed better points for quality than any heifer he had ever seen, and her subsequent development and production of 32 lbs. butter in seven days, being at that time (1889) the largest of any cow of the breed, proved that his judgment was correct.

Prof. W. A. Henry of the Wisconsin Agricultural Experiment Station, and whose authority no one questions, sent Prof. Short to the farm at Cameron himself, taking three samples of her milk, which analyzed by Prof. F. W. A. Woll 4.91, 3.85, 3.53 per cent butter fat. She is now about fourteen years old and in good health and captured first prize at Iowa State Fair last fall (1895). Although a regular breeder she has never produced but one female, Gerben 2d, 18677 H. F. H. B. The latter is a great prize winner : one of the many silver cups won by this herd is placed to her credit. She made 39 lbs. milk in a single day at 22 months old ; analysis of her milk showing 4 and 4.2 per cent butter fat.

Not only there have been bred and developed in this herd some of the greatest butter producers and prize winners, but they have been added to the herd by purchase also at long prices. Among those whose blood now permeates this herd may be mentioned Parthenea, 9597 H. H. B., imported, whose butter record for seven days is 38 lbs. 8½ oz. She was acquired at a cost of $1000. Another is Parana Abbekerk, 9594 H. H. B., imported, whose butter record for seven days is 30 lbs. 8 oz.; and Carlotta 2d, 3555 H. H. B., whose butter record for seven days is 31 lbs. 12 oz., at a cost of $1098. Others might be mentioned did space permit.

MR. B. NAUMAN of Frankfort, Kansas, was born in the Duchy of Saxe-Altenburg, Prussia, on July 9, 1840.

Early in the spring of 1849 his parents started with him and seven other children for Marion, Linn county, Iowa. While passing through Illinois the father and two eldest children died of cholera. The mother, worn with grief and the care of so large a family lived to reach their destination, but in a few days thereafter she, too, was taken away.

He was, with the other children under sixteen years of age, bound out until sixteen years of age, among the farmers of the surrounding country. When he arrived at the age of sixteen, with the consent of his guardian (who

EDGAR HUIDEKOPER.

was pleased to escape further responsibility), he took charge of his own affairs, and a year or two later apprenticed himself to learn the cabinet trade, attending the high school during the winter, working his board by doing chores.

In the spring of 1860, times being dull, and not finding profitable employment, he concluded to try his fortune in California. As it happened that no one from that locality crossed the plains that year, he set out on foot and alone, with $13 in his pocket to reach the golden shore. Of course he did not expect to complete the journey in this fashion, but he rightly judged that at some one of the "outfitting points" on the frontier he would not fail of getting the opportunity of procuring a passage in some manner. He trudged nearly the entire width of Iowa on foot, and at Council Bluffs found the opportunity he sought for arranging for a passage. He had to pay $90, after earning it, on getting through.

He spent the first winter west of Santa Rosa, near the Pocket Redwoods, employed in teaming, farming, and chopping.

The next summer he went to Nevada Territory, and spent five years there, farming, chopping, mining, teaching, carpentering, and all manner of other ways to make a living and accumulate a little wealth. Of course, he had to have his little experience with dabbling in mining stock, and spent a good share of his hard-earned dollars on wild-cat claims. A spell of hard times coming on in the spring of 1866, and employment being scarce, he struck out after a mining rush to Colombia, South America. The mines were about a town called Barbucous, in the southern extremity of Colombia, and almost under the equator. Some very lucky finds were made in these mines, but he was not of the fortunate ones, and, his money being gone, and health giving way in October, 1868, he turned again toward California, being obliged to beg his way back.

He arrived in San Francisco in November, in time to take in the great earthquake. Through the aid of a friend he reached San Jose and, after recuperating a short time, got employment at carpenter work. In July, 1869, he returned to Nevada, and struck carpenter work at Reno.

The next year he taught school at Glendale, four miles below Reno, and in the winter returned to Iowa. In May, 1871, he came to Marshall county, Kansas, and located on a 100-acre lot of land which he had acquired while on the Pacific coast. He built a little 12x14 shanty, and went to work making a farm, teaching the district school during the winter. Early in 1874 he married, having during this time "bached it." He applied himself so closely to his work that for fifteen years he was not outside the limits of his county. The farm was added to as opportunity favored, until now it embraces 560 acres. The quality of the land and the value of the improvements are not surpassed by any in the county.

Having noted the changes demanded in the different farming processes by the changes occurring in the environment, he became satisfied that there was no profit in raising scrub stock and after carefully studying the situation, he concluded that the black-and-white breed of cattle was the one best adapted to his circumstances. He decided to begin in a small way by grading up common stock, and, if that proved satisfactory, to venture more and start a herd of registered cattle. In 1885 he purchased a bull of H. Langworthy, out of a herd the latter was showing at Western fairs; and being pleased with the result of the trial, he bought two cows and a male calf at T. B. Wales' dispersion sale in Kansas City, September, 1887.

In October, 1892, he bought most of the good things at Kirkpatrick & Sons' dispersion sale at Connors, Kansas, and he now has a herd of about thirty-five head. As he is still building up his herd, he has made no effort to attract public attention; but in good time he expects to give a creditable account of it, and in the meantime he remains a stanch supporter of the breed.

MR. EDWARD ALEXANDER POWELL, the subject of this sketch, has been prominently identified with the growth and development of the Holstein-Friesian breed of cattle in America for many years, commencing when this breed was comparatively little known in this country.

He was born in Crawford county, Pennsylvania, January 27, 1838, on the farm, now widely known as "Shadeland," which is noted for its fine stock. His father, Hon. Howell Powell, was one of the first breeders of pure Devon cattle in the state and his earliest memory recalls a large herd of these beautiful red cattle, the descendants of which are still on the farm.

LEROY F. JUDD.

Before reaching his majority a large herd of Herefords was added to the stock of the place, but being inferior for dairy purposes, and their value for beef not being then appreciated in this country, the breeding of these cattle did not prove a success and the herd was sold for beef. Fine horses were also extensively bred on the place. As a member of the firm of Powell Bros., he commenced business at a very early age. The brothers all having a natural fondness and cultivated taste for fine animals, it was only natural that the firm should become interested therein, and breeding of blooded horses and cattle soon became an important department of their business. Thus was laid the foundation of one of the most noted fine stock establishments in this country.

In 1868 Mr. Powell was united in marriage to the only daughter of W. Brown Smith of Syracuse, N. Y., and disposing of his interest in Pennsylvania to his brothers, he became a partner in the Syracuse Nurseries and a resident of that city. The live-stock department was then added to the nursery business. Jerseys and Shorthorns were both bred, but neither proved satisfactory. About 1872 the attention of the firm—Smith & Powell—was called to the Dutch breed of cattle by Hon. C. B. Sedgwick, upon his return from Europe.

Some time was spent in investigating the merits of this breed, and in 1875 was established the herd now owned by Smiths & Powell Co., which is known to all our readers.

On the organization of the Holstein Breeders' Association of America, under the charter of the State of New York in 1880, Mr. Powell was elected its first president, to which office he was re-elected for four successive years. He has continually taken a deep and active interest in the affairs of the association. He has ever been progressive and liberal in his ideas regarding the development of the breed, and enthusiastic regarding its future possibilities.

In connection with Smiths & Powell Co., of which firm he is a member, he has done much for the development of the breed in the production of both milk and butter, and also in bringing these cattle prominently and favorably before the public. He early advocated a system of breeding for a specific purpose, as the quickest, surest and most progressive means of developing desired qualities and characteristics. Believing that "like would produce like," that if large yields of butter and milk were to be an established fact in the offspring, these qualities must be developed in a long, unbroken line of ancestors, running far back through every channel, by putting these principles into practice at an early date, by breeding only from dams with large records, and using only sires of such breeding. Lakeside Herd now possesses many young animals whose fifteen or twenty nearest female ancestors have butter records which average from 19 to 20 lbs. of butter in a week, and milk records of from 15,000 to 17,000 lbs. in a year. These facts are mentioned to show what could be accomplished by the persistent, intelligent application of a fundamental principle of breeding.

Mr. Powell was one of the earliest advocates of the possibilities of the breed as butter producers. The system of careful weekly butter tests, which has been the means of bringing the breed up to its present standard, was first begun on a liberal scale, in Lakeside herd, in 1879, when Netherland Queen, Maid of Purmer, Holland Beauty, Neilson, Aegis, Juniata, etc., were carefully tested. Prior to this or ly occasionally single cows of the breed had been tested.

It was during this year that, by careful tests, by ascertaining the amount of milk required to make a pound of butter, when fresh, and near the close of the season, and the amount of milk given during the year, it was shown by a careful estimate that Maid of Purmer could have made 400 lbs., and Netherland Queen 388 lbs., of butter during the year, both being two years old. Commercing in 1879 a large number of cows have each year been tested at Lakeside, and the result is generally known to all breeders.

Mr. Powell was, as far as records in our possession indicate, the first to publicly announce his belief that this breed could be made to equal any other breed for the production of butter.

In his annual address to the Holstein Breeders' Association in March, 1883, he said: "From all the information and data at command I am confident that the general average of Holsteins for butter will fully equal that of any other breed. With proper encouragement from this association, and continued efforts on the part of all its members, records comparing favorably with the highest made by any other breed will, in my judgment, soon be attained." He probably had no idea that this prediction would soon be fully verified.

C. H. KRUEGER.

Mr. Powell has led a very busy life, confining himself closely to business, but he has found time to give much personal attention to the breeding and development of live stock. Few breeders have made it so much of a study, and probably no one has had a larger experience in breeding and developing Holstein-Friesian cattle.

The firm has imported and bred over 3,000 head of cattle of this breed. The herd at Lakeside has frequently exceeded 600 head at one time, and yet nearly all the cows in milk have been tested for both milk and butter. Some idea of the amount of time and labor expended in this direction can be conceived when it is known that over 100 cows of this herd have made weekly butter records which average over 19¼ lbs., and about fifty cows have made yearly milk records which average over 17,000 lbs.

All who have made tests can appreciate what an amount of careful intelligent work must have been done to have attained such wonderful results. We know of no other herd, of any breed, that can show such results from an equal number of cows. The benefits of this work have not been confined to this herd, or to this firm, but they have been shared by every breeder of Holstein-Friesian cattle in the land.

Mr. FRANK ROE was born on the farm now owned by him, on March 12, 1854, near Augusta, Sussex county, New Jersey; was married in 1875 to Maggie C. Dalrymple, a neighbor's daughter and a schoolmate, who has always taken as great an interest in the development of their new dairy of Holsteins as her husband and children—one boy and one girl, who are both interested in the business at this time. The farm was bought by Mr. Roe's grandfather, from William Roe, of Orange county, N. Y., in the year 1799. From this date the farm has been owned by the Roe family, and always used as a dairy farm. The father of the present owner, William H. Roe, was a fancier of fine cows, and kept a high-grade dairy of Shorthorns.

The Shorthorn in those days was strictly a dairy breed, as much so as the Ayrshire and Holstein are at the present time. This dairy produced more than 300 lbs. of butter a year, and always brought the top price in market. When Mr. Roe bought the farm in 1878 eighteen cows and four heifers came into his possession. In this lot there were a number that would give 60 lbs. of milk daily with ordinary feed and care. The following year, 1879, thirteen of the lot aborted, and the following year four more. As they were nearly all old cows, they were used as long as they gave milk, then turned into beef, and their places filled with the best native cows that could be bought in the neighborhood, and a pure-bred Ayrshire bull was obtained for use on this dairy. This course was continued until the whole dairy was turned into grade Ayrshires, by raising their heifer calves from the best milking cows. This dairy gave good satisfaction as milk producers of a fair quality, the only trouble being their tendency to turn too much of their feed into beef. In fact, they were always fat, but gave a good-paying mess of milk, and were always ready for the butcher as soon as dry.

The next step was to buy a pure-bred Holstein-Friesian bull to breed on these grade Ayrshire cows. From this cross was obtained a very fine animal, larger than the Ayrshire, a trifle coarser, and a cow that turned feed into milk and not into beef. They gave as much as 25 per cent more milk than their dams. But it had fallen off very much in quality, and soon complaints were received from the milkman about it. The milk was finally stopped, and the accusation made that it had been watered. Another milkman was obtained, but in a short time the same trouble followed, and the milk was stopped the second time. Then the milk was sold for a number of years to a near-by creamery. While selling to the creamery there were so many complaints about the quality that it was about decided to give up the Holsteins, and try the little Jersey or Guernsey. About this time C. H. Vandevort, of Amity, N. Y., a breeder of pure-bred Holstein-Friesians, was about to sell his whole dairy at public auction. While on an advertising trip to this county he stayed one night with Mr. Roe. Of course, he was informed of the trouble with the grade Holsteins, and was asked if he was not selling his pure ones for the same reason. This he denied, and insisted on Mr. Roe's going to his sale, and trying to buy some cows from his dairy. This Mr. Roe consented to do, with the understanding that he could test the whole dairy for cream before the sale, so that he would be able to buy intelligently on the day of the sale.

S. A. LANGDON.

One week before the date of sale the visit was made, and Mr. Roe saw each cow milked both night and morning, and the milk placed in graduated cream gauges. Seventeen in all were tested, the milk showing from 9 per cent to 22 per cent of cream. From these seventeen cows tested he selected four of the best cream producers, and bought them on the day of the sale, paying a good round sum for them. These four, with four heifers bought of Gerrit S. Miller and one from N. F. Sholes the same year, constituted the foundation of the present herd of pure-breds. As fast as they were raised the pure-bred calves took the places of the grades which were sold mostly for beef.

Mr. Roe has at this time fifty-seven head of pure-breds nearly all raised from the nine foundation cows. He had received a bitter lesson with the grades and resolved to buy one of the best butter-bred bulls that could be found to use on these nine foundation cows. After considerable time had been spent in looking at different herds, he finally selected the bull, Aaggie Prince of Wayne, No. 8781 H. F. H. B., and bought him of T. G. Yeomans & Sons. This bull's dam is Princess of Wayne, No. 954 H. H. B., Advanced Registry No. 2 ; milk record, 29,008 lbs. 11 oz. in one year ; butter record, 24 lbs. 14 oz. in seven days. His sire is Royal Aaggie, No. 3463 H. H. B., a son of De Schot ; milk record, 82½ lbs. in one day ; butter record, 23 lbs. 8 oz. in seven days. From this bull's calves was anticipated great results, for both the Wayne and Aaggie families are great milk and butter producers. Mr. Roe was not disappointed, and he has the calves now, five, four, three and two years old, in milk from this sire.

They are great producers of rich milk, very few of them falling below four per cent butter fat, and many of them have tested as high as five per cent butter fat. The trouble in selling milk is a thing of the past, as the milk from the dairy has gone to the same dealer for the past five years in glass jars and gives entire satisfaction and is frequently complimented for its fine quality.

Mr. Roe feels very thankful to Mr. Vandevort for insisting so hard upon his giving the Holstein another trial and for the privilege given to test the dairy and prove that all Holstein-Friesians did not give poor milk. Those Mr. Roe has now are proving their value as dairy cows exclusively, for they are paying well for the money invested in the first foundation cows in the sale of milk alone, and Mr. Roe insists that the pure-bred Holstein-Friesian cow at present prices will pay the dairyman better than any other breed, grade or scrub cow for the production of milk and butter. If the average dairyman can not or will not use the pure-bred as dairy cows, he can at least afford to put a pure-bred bull at the head of his dairy, but should be careful in the selection of this bull and get one from a butter-producing family. Then if the heifer calves from the best cows are raised, in a few years he can nearly double the quantity of milk without its falling off in quality. The breeding of pure-breds with Mr. Roe is merely a side issue. The money from the sale of their milk is the main business ; only the increase that is not needed to keep up the dairy is offered for sale.

In the spring of 1894 an eight-bottle Babcock test was procured and every cow in milk at that time was tested at once. From these tests it was concluded that very few if any of the dairy would fall below the requirements to admit them to Advanced Registry. Mr. Roe resolved that he would give every cow that came fresh, at least a seven-day test for butter. The first cow to calve was Zanca, No. 10703 H. F. H. B., in the last part of July, 1894. Although this was a very unfavorable time to test on account of flies (buffalo horn fly) and very hot weather, and with her worrying for the rest of the dairy. She could not be separated from them in the pasture to milk her at noon and so was put in stable with a run in barnyard for exercise and water.

The test commenced on August 7, ended on August 13, the result being 18 lbs. 15$\frac{18}{100}$ oz. butter. Mr. Roe was very much pleased to have her do so well under such unfavorable conditions, and was quite sure that all the rest would get there if they were in proper condition after calving. In this he was not mistaken, as a reference to the records made by the dairy will show. The whole lot were entered on their butter records after being examined by Mr. S. Hoxie and pronounced all right. In fact Mr. Hoxie said at the time of examination that in his opinion they were capable of making much larger records than were made from them, which proved true even with the same handling, for several were officially tested by Mr. Voorhees of the New Jersey Experiment Station after their next calving time, and all made much larger records than they had under the testing of the year before.

J. W. LA GRANGE.

Mr. Roe's aim has been to breed for a large flow of rich milk, the standard being an average of four per cent butter fat from the mixed milk from the entire dairy, a mark that has been very nearly reached with the heifers from the bull Aaggie Prince of Wayne.

To avoid inbreeding this bull was sold for beef in the summer of 1894, and another one bought to breed on the heifers. This time Mr. Roe had a long hunt to find the right kind of a bull; one that would improve the offspring of these Aaggie-Wayne heifers in the production of butter. It was a long hunt and a very long price was obliged to be paid for such a bull, but he was secured in De Kol 2d's Paul De Kol, No. 20735 H. F. H. B., Advanced Registry No. 107. His dam is the great cow De Kol 2d, who holds the world's four-year-old butter record of 33 lbs. 6 oz. in seven days, and also the largest official butter record of 26 lbs. 9$\frac{81}{100}$ oz. De Kol 2d's daughter, De Kol 2d's Queen, has the largest three-year-old butter record, 28 lbs. 7 oz. in seven days. Another daughter has the largest thirty-day butter record of 82 lbs. 7$\frac{3}{4}$ oz. at two years of age. His sire is the great butter-bred bull, Paul De Kol, now at the head of the herd of T. G. Yeomans & Sons. His dam, Pauline Paul, is the world's largest butter producer of any breed, having the world famous record for one year of 1,153 lbs. and 15$\frac{1}{4}$ oz. His sire is De Kol 2d's Prince, a son of De Kol 2d. This bull contains 62$\frac{1}{4}$ per cent of the blood of De Kol 2d, 25 per cent of Pauline Paul, 12$\frac{1}{4}$ per cent of Neptune, Jr., an Aaggie bull. Is it possible to get better butter breeding in any Holstein-Friesian bull? As an individual he is all that any one can expect. He has a long body, very fine head and neck, large full eye, very yellow skin, a wonderful milk vein development, large escutcheon of fine quality. With this bull on the daughters of Aaggie Prince of Wayne, it is expected to obtain heifers that will fully come up to the standard of four per cent fat with a large flow of milk. A number of his calves are already on the farm. They are very fine individuals with soft silky hair, straight backs, very yellow skins and with indications of making animals of the highest quality.

Mr. Eldon F. Smith of Columbus, Ohio, one of the proprietors of Ohio's famous herd of Holstein-Friesians, was born in the county of Athens, November 23, 1861, the son of a farmer. He attended the district school until thirteen years of age, when an academy opened, which offered special advantages that he availed himself of for two years, and when sixteen years old entered the Ohio University at Athens. Four years were occupied at this institution and six months were passed in a law office.

Mr. Smith had then about reached his majority. New fields of enterprise were now opened to his father, W. B. Smith, who secured the contract for furnishing milk to the Columbus Hospital for the Insane. This institution is the largest of its kind. Young Mr. Smith, desiring to assist his father, dropped his legal studies for a time and joined in establishing a dairy suited to the needs of this institution, and again resumed his studies for two years with a leading law firm in Columbus. Failing health, however, compelled him to abandon all thoughts of practicing law, and he again turned his attention to out-door life and his father's dairy.

Mr. Smith soon became proficient in the details of this work and began a systematic study of the comparative merits of the various breeds of cattle. It was apparent that the results produced with grade Shorthorns in quantity and quality of milk were unprofitable. The methods of care and feeding must be improved with corresponding increase in results or a larger yielding breed of cattle found that would respond profitably to present conditions of reasonable care and feeding. It was found that some improvement in handling could be made, and improved methods were adopted, yet it still appeared that the cattle were the great source of loss.

Mr. Smith then determined that among the special purpose dairy breeds would be found the profitable milk and butter producer, and the questions that confronted him were, which is the breed, what breed has the requisite qualifications of size and constitution and capacity. A careful study determined the choice of the Holstein as more nearly filling the requirements.

Ten years use of the Holstein breed warrants the statement made by Mr. Smith that by their use he is enabled to obtain almost double the yield of milk and butter over that yielded by other stock.

M. E. MOORE.

MR. HENRY STEVENS of Lacona, N. Y., the subject of this sketch, was born in 1840, on the place where he now resides. His life has been so checkered, adversity and prosperity having followed each other in quick succession, that the story of his career is a most interesting one.

He started when a young man with 126 acres of land, on which the buildings were very poor, and he owed all it was worth. He was climbing slowly but surely along the road of prosperity as a farmer, when the dishonesty of a partner in the cattle trade (whose debts he was obliged to pay) so embarrassed him that he had to commence again at the foot of the ladder. Perseverance and energy had once again begun to pay their reward of success when he suddenly became blind, in November, 1886. With the bright and beautiful world shut out from view, and the most important of all his business senses paralyzed, he was well-nigh discouraged; but his natural energy, his untiring perseverance, and his indomitable pluck did not allow him to remain long in a condition of inactivity.

Although deprived of sight, his ever active mind was still at work. Its thinking could not be suppressed. The result has been that although he is blind he has not been groping in the dark, for his mental vision has discerned the road to success.

Today he owns a farm of 400 acres, on which he has erected a large and handsome house and a barn built according to the most modern improvements, containing every convenience for the breeding and rearing of stock. During these dark days his beautiful herd of Holstein-Friesian cattle has been his consolation and his hope. He is proud of their attainments and success, and their increasing development and improvement is a joyous light that illumines his life.

Mr. Stevens has bought the best cattle obtainable. His first purchase was made in the spring of 1876, of C. R. Payne, of Hamilton. In the spring of 1877 he made another purchase of Gerrit S. Miller. From that time on he has made choice selections from the best herds in the country. The wisdom of his selections is proved by the admiration that his herd receives, by his many sales to the most fastidious breeders, and by the fabulous prices that he has obtained. He sold one cow for $2,500, and received the enormous sum of $2,800 for one bull eleven months old, being the largest price, we think, ever paid for any animal of the breed. Many other animals of this herd have brought large prices for the reason that, in the first place, they were well selected, and have since been well bred and intelligently developed.

In 1892 Mr. Stevens took his two sons into partnership. This firm was the first to make official butter records under the rules of the Holstein-Friesian Association, and they now have about forty cows which have been tested out of their herd of 100 head.

Henry Stevens was elected a member of the Board of Directors of the Holstein-Friesian Association in 1895. His sound judgment and good common sense make him a valuable member.

The elevation and strength of his character are derived from nature, while its direction and control are the result of reflection and discipline. In his home, surrounded by his devoted family who are ever ready to minister to his wants, he is far from being a discontented or unhappy man.

J. L. STONE of Waverly, Pa., secretary of the Lackawanna Breeders' Association, Waverly, Pa., was born on the farm now occupied by him, on July 6, 1852. His grandfather came to this vicinity from Rhode Island in 1807, and the family have occupied this territory since. All have been frugal, industrious, and prosperous farmers and public-minded citizens.

Mr. J. L. Stone was educated in the village academy at Waverly, Pa., and at Cornell University, Ithaca, N. Y., graduating in the course of agriculture with the class of 1874.

A few months were passed clerking in Scranton, Pa. This with the four years spent at Cornell mark the extent of his separation from the paternal acres.

Mr. Stone bought his first Holstein—a bull calf, a son of old Burgomaster of Beemster—of Mr. S. Hoxie, in 1879. So well was he pleased with his growth and appearance that in the fall of 1881 he bought of another member of the Unadilla Valley Stock Breeders' Association, Mr. H. Langworthy, two three-

B. NAUMAN.

year-old heifers—Boukje, 116 D.-F. H. B., and Winkje, 136 D.-F. H. B. The former developed into the heaviest milker he has ever owned, her record being 26,679 lbs. 10 oz. in one year. Her largest day's yield was 85 lbs. 10 oz., and when she closed the year, being three months in calf, she was producing over 60 lbs. of milk per day. At that time (1885) this was by far the best record that had been made in Pennsylvania, and took fourth or fifth position in the United States. Boukje dropped but one heifer, however, but through her sons her blood was quite generally diffused through the herd.

In 1882 the Lackawanna Breeders' Association was organized, including L. W. Stone, father of J. L. Stone; J. W. Miller, E. G. and G. M. Carpenter. The combined area of their farms aggregated about 700 acres.

In this year combined importation of the Dutch-Friesian Association was participated in, the Lackawanna Association securing seven females and one male direct from Holland.

In 1884 Mr. Stone visited Holland, and selected thirty head to add to the herd. En route he stopped in England, and selected twenty-one head of Shropshire sheep from some of the best flocks there, to add to a small flock already started.

Through natural increase and an occasional purchase the herd soon reached about 120 head, at which point it has been quite steadily maintained for the past eight or ten years. There are also a few head of pure-bred Jerseys.

Among the bulls that have been purchased outside of this herd are: Mooie Sjoerd, 235 D.-F. H. B., whose dam Sjoerd was the first Holstein cow to be tested for butter, and produced 20 lbs. per week under very unfavorable conditions in a test made by S. Hoxie; Aaggie Rachel's Imperial, 8694; Amleto 2d's Sir Mechthilde, 14835; Count Clothilde Beauty, 19706; and Paul De Kol America, 21718. The last two named are now doing duty in the herd.

Count Clothilde Beauty's dam produced 26 lbs. butter in seven days, his four nearest female ancestors produced an average of over 24 lbs. butter in seven days, and his seven nearest female ancestors produced over 20 lbs. butter in seven days.

Paul De Kol America carries in his veins 31¼ per cent of the blood of Princess of Wayne, 25 per cent of that of Pauline Paul, 12¼ per cent of De Kol 2d, and 12½ per cent of America.

The milk from these herds goes to the Scranton Dairy Company, which has a large trade in Scranton, Pa., and whose manager is Mr. G. M. Carpenter, of the Lackawanna Association.

Mr. J. L. Stone has always been actively identified with the religious, educational, and reform movements of the locality, and has twice been a candidate for the Legislature as a representative of a righteous but unpopular cause, but luckily escaped serving a term at Harrisburg. Mr. Stone is secretary of the Lackawanna County School Directors' Association, president of the Lackawanna County Agricultural Society, and member of the Pennsylvania State Board of Agriculture from Lackawanna county, also secretary of the Abington Mutual Fire Insurance Company. He has visited a large number of the counties of the state in farmers' institute work.

MR. EDWIN W. TREXLER of Allentown, Pa., the subject of this sketch, was born in October, 1826, on the farm still owned by him in Upper Milford township, Lehigh county, Pa. The family to which he belongs is one of the oldest in eastern Pennsylvania, the original settlers having immigrated prior to 1720. Mr. Trexler worked on the farm until he was fourteen years of age, when he left home and became a clerk in a general store at Emaus, Lehigh county, from which place he removed to Easton, where he for a number of years engaged in the store business, but was compelled to abandon it owing to failing health due to the confinement incident to the business. He then removed to Allentown, Pa., where he has been in the lumber business since 1856.

Mr. Trexler has always taken a great interest in farming and has owned a farm since 1847, he first became a breeder of Holsteins in 1885; he began in a small way, rather by way of experiment than with any idea of discarding other breeds, but the superiority of the breed over others became so apparent that he now has no other kind. He joined the Holstein-Friesian Association of America in 1894.

He has been largely instrumental in introducing the Holsteins into general

E. A. POWELL.

use in the section of the country where he resides, and many of the finest herds are the progeny of stock purchased from him.

He has been an exhibitor at the local agricultural fairs and his cattle have uniformly drawn a large number of prizes.

Mr. Trexler married in 1852 and has three sons, who are Col. H. C. Trexler, a member of the E. W. Trexler Lumber Co. of Allentown and of the Trexler & Turrell Lumber Co. of Ricketts, Pa.; E. G. Trexler, also in the lumber business at Ricketts, and Frank M. Trexler, an attorney at law, now and for many years city solicitor for the city of Allentown, Pa.

MR. DON J. WOOD of West Exeter, N. Y., was born in 1860 in the town of Plainfield, Otsego county, N. Y., on the farm which has ever since been his home.

After a course of study in the West Winfield Academy he taught school during the winter of 1878-9, and the next winter attended Eastman's National Business College at Poughkeepsie, N. Y., from which he was graduated in March, 1881.

Mr. Wood's first acquaintance with the Holstein-Friesian cattle was in the fall of 1874, when his father and uncle bought an imported cow and bull calf. He helped to raise and develop the grade Holsteins which gradually replaced the old dairy of mixed blood, and then in turn to replace these with registered Holstein-Friesians.

In the spring of 1883 Mr. Wood in connection with his brother, A. C. Wood, commenced to conduct the home farm.

In 1884 he became a member of the Holstein Breeders' Association, and in 1886 he purchased his brother's interest in the herd, which at that time contained a number of pure-bred Holstein-Friesians descended from his father's original purchase and from subsequent additions to the herd.

He early commenced to make systematic tests of his cows and has been an enthusiastic supporter of the system of Advanced Registry since its adoption by the Holstein-Friesian Association in 1885.

He has also taken advantage of the opportunities offered by the association for making officially authenticated butter records and has had several members of his herd officially tested for butter fat with excellent results.

As a result of careful testing and selection, aided by judicious purchases, Mr. Wood now has a herd of nearly fifty registered Holstein-Friesians of high average production and containing descendants of many of the most noted animals of the breed.

MR. J. F. WOODYARD, Parkersburg, W. Va., was born April 28, 1850, in Wood county. He was reared on the farm and acquired a good common school education. When seventeen years of age he took charge of a flour and grist mill and successfully ran it for several years. At the age of twenty he returned to the farm and at twenty-one was married.

He then purchased a tract of land in the woods near Parkersburg, for which he paid $35 per acre and went in debt for the larger portion of the purchase money. In a short time he cleared this land and seeded it down to blue grass, and was occupied in the buying and shipping of stock to the Baltimore and Philadelphia markets from 1876 to 1885.

In 1886 he engaged in the dairy business, and purchased his first pure-bred Holstein cattle in 1887. This foundation consisted of a bull and two cows, which Mr. Woodyard, relying upon his own experience and ability, selected himself. Mr. Woodyard believes that a successful judge of dairy stock must have actual experience in the milking, testing and handling of dairy cows, and that the selection of animals by persons not having this experience is apt to result disastrously.

Mr. Woodyard long since discarded the idea of a combination beef and dairy cow, and believes them to be unprofitable cattle. He is of the opinion that a medium sized animal is the better dairy cow, though he is inclined to cite a few exceptions, such as Pietertje 2d, a large cow and one which made the world's record of 30,318 lbs. of milk in one year; but he accounts for this enormous yield in conjunction with the size by stating that she was not a large boned beefy animal in appearance, but was possessed more nearly of a pure milch type.

Among the foundation animals which he purchased was the bull Shadeland

19

FRANK ROE.

Hyles. This animal was a grandson of Netherland Prince and his dam was a true type of a dairy cow. His progeny proved to be superior dairy animals. In his study of dairying and dairy cattle, Mr. Woodyard availed himself largely of the journals devoted to those subjects, and also travelled extensively in the dairy states. At the end of the year he felt that he had learned many things. He then purchased a fine lot of Holstein-Friesian cattle on very advantageous terms in Ohio, which proved to be the best lot of dairy cattle which he ever owned.

Two years later he purchased of J. B. Dutcher & Son four fine two-year-olds for $1,000. In this lot were Lady De Kol, Kitty Artis and De Freule 2d's Queen, all of which developed into very fine cows, Lady De Kol leading the lot. A misfortune overtook Mr. Woodyard at this time and his entire herd including these animals and thirty-one others were destroyed by fire, leaving him but eight head of Holsteins and three Jerseys.

He proceeded at once to construct a model dairy farm containing every improvement suggested by the best methods of the day. In acquiring a new stock of Holsteins, he attended the dispersion sale of the Belle Mead herd, owned by Senator J. B. McPherson of New Jersey, and acquired several head. In York, Mich., he procured eighteen head more. He also purchased from the famous Jersey herd of L. T. Bailey twelve of his finest animals. With this collection he was enabled to make a new start, and a fine opportunity was offered to contrast the merits of each breed, and to determine which was the more profitable.

His dairy business at this time was the sale of milk and cream. Systematic methods were adopted, and the scales and the Babcock tester and a record book were kept in constant use. The amount of the yield from each animal was separately kept, as was also the amount of feed consumed. Lack of space prevents our giving a summary of this very interesting comparison in this book.

From this experience he determined that the Holsteins consumed more food than the Jerseys, but proportionately to their size and yield. As milk producers the Holsteins showed thirty per cent more profit than the Jerseys. It was found that those customers who desired a high colored milk were better satisfied with the mixed milk from each breed, using one-third from the Jerseys.

Considering all factors Mr. Woodyard determined that the Holsteins were largely the most profitable animals. For more than five years his yearly average per cow varied from $110 to $125. The milk was sold at prices varying from eighteen cents wholesale to twenty-eight cents retail per gallon, and seventy cents per gallon for cream, 4½ gallons of milk making one of cream; and the number of Holstein animals in milk varied from forty to fifty head.

The products of these cattle were handled and sold by Mr. Woodyard's two sons, who were ten and twelve years of age when they began the business. His oldest son, Frank, ran the milk wagon for three consecutive years and had no advantages other than what schooling he obtained at home and upon the wagon. He was then sent to the high school at Parkersburg, and shortly obtained the appointment of a cadet at the West Point Military Academy, where he now is. Mr. Woodyard's younger son then succeeded to the duties of his brother upon the milk wagon.

Misfortune again overtook Mr. Woodyard at this period and his buildings, horses, machinery and nearly everything excepting his herd of cattle were destroyed by fire, compelling him for the time to sell his herd and abandon the dairy business. Mr. Woodyard is a firm believer in dairying as a money making operation with Holstein cattle. He is strongly in favor of the silo and after eight years experience, during which time he has been burned out twice, he has now built his third silo and believes ensilage to be a most valuable adjunct in farming.

MR. SAMUEL NEWITT WRIGHT of Elgin, Ill., was born at De Ruyter, Madison county, N. Y., March 6, 1824. From his eighth year until he was seventeen years old, Mr. Wright worked for an uncle, who owned a farm on Quaker Hill, De Ruyter. He then went to Ithaca and worked a short time for Ezra Cornell. On returning home and finding some relatives had moved to New Jersey, he followed, and worked for an uncle near Camden, still sticking to farming, which he always liked, especially the live-stock part.

The Virginia fever breaking out, he went with an uncle to that State and

E. F. SMITH.

engaged in farming on his own account, meeting with indifferent success. In the year 1857 he engaged as manager on the farm of A. S. Abel near Balt more, Md., and while here he saw the first black and white cattle, consisting of three head, which had been sent over from Holland to a Mr. Barnum. He liked them from the first and made up his mind if he ever was able, he would have some. After three years work there, he picked up his possessions, consisting of a wife, three children and a few hundred dollars in money, and went to Elgin, Ill.

For three years he worked the land of B. W. Raymond, within the city limits, and then bought his present home, struggling along under difficulties until 1874, when, in partnership with Messrs. Tefft and Hoag, he bought the first Holstein bull owned in Kane county. Since then he has worked for the advancement of the Holstein cattle to the best of his ability with hands, tongue and pen.

Those who have been so fortunate as to examine Mr. Wright's herds have discovered a master's skill in selection and breeding these famous cattle. Mr. Wright is an old and highly esteemed member of the Holstein-Friesian Association of America.

Evidence of his skill in selection and his intimate knowledge of a milch cow may be observed in various sections of the West, where there are many large herds whose foundation animals Mr. Wright has been called upon as an expert to select.

MR. J. H. D. WHITCOMB of Beaver Brook Stock Farm, Littleton, Mass., was born June 15, 1861, upon the farm which he now occupies. This farm has been in the Whitcomb family for no less than eight generations and the various members of the family have been prominently identified with agricultural matters.

In the fall of 1879 Mr. Whitcomb completed the course of study at the Bryant and Stratton Commercial School at Boston, acted as his father's foreman until 1893. He then purchased the herd of Ayrshire cows owned by his father and began business.

In January, 1984, he visited the Lakeside Stock Farm, the great Holstein-Friesian breeding establishment of Smiths & Powell Co., at Syracuse, N Y., and selected two very choice animals, a bull and a heifer. These animals were fine representatives of the breed and from the Aaggie and Alexander families, the bull being Sir Rupert of Aaggie, and the heifer, Amy A.exander. These constituted the foundation of the now widely known Beaver Brook Herd of Holstein-Friesians, which has been gradually increased until at present it numbers about fifty pure-bred recorded cattle.

Mr. Whitcomb found in his early experience with the breed that it was considered too large for New England pastures, but with trial and investigation this unfounded prejudice disappeared, and he now finds it difficult to supply the demand. As milk and butter producers Mr. Whitcomb considers the breed has no equal and probably no family in New England has had longer or greater experience in milk producing than the Whitcombs.

For the past few years Mr. Whitcomb has been a large and successful exhibitor at the Bay State and New England Fairs. The high quality of his herd has here been demonstrated to the public by the many prizes awarded to its members by expert judges of the breed.

The blood lines followed in the breeding of Beaver Brook herd are those whose performances have been the means of their popularity as great producers. Most prominent are the Aaggie, Netherland, Queen of the Hill and Clothilde families. The leading sire of the herd, Sir Netherland Soldene Clothilde, is also of these lines and has the additional qualifications of much beauty and symmetry of form. In the public competitions at the various fairs, this grand bull has never failed to bring the highest award to Beaver Brook.

Mr. THERON G. YEOMANS was born in Cairo, Greene county, N. Y., January 31, 1815. He removed to Walworth, Wayne county, N. Y. in 1830, where he has since resided. Until sixteen years of age his home was on a farm, and for the next fifteen years he was engaged in mercantile business. In 1840, in connection with his other interests, he engaged in the nursery business, which for more than forty years has been known as the Walworth Nurseries, in connection with which he planted extensive orchards embracing about 150 acres,

HENRY STEVENS.

which have for many years borne abundance of fruit; a part of his orchards consisted of about 3,000 dwarf pear trees which he imported from France in 1851, which have been in good bearing condition more than thirty years.

In 1879 he went to Holland where he selected for their firm (T. G. Yeomans & Sons) the foundation herd of Holstein-Friesian cattle, which has become noted for its uniform and superior excellence.

Mr. Yeomans was the first president of the Holstein-Friesian Association of America, and gave active and efficient influence in accomplishing the union of the Holstein and Dutch-Fresian Associations, both of which were propagating the same breed of cattle.

He also earnestly co-operated in establishing the system of Advanced Registry of the Association, and the firm of T. G. Yeomans & Sons caused of their herd the entry of the first forty animals in this register, and every one upon both their milk and butter records. They were the pioneers also in testing their herd for butter, which has led to such wonderful development of the butter qualities of this breed of cattle. They have not aimed to have a very large herd, but have persistently and very successfully sought to have one of the greatest uniform excellence.

Mr. Yeomans has resided in Walworth for sixty years and for fifty years in the house in which he now lives. He is a widely known and highly esteemed citizen. His sterling integrity and true manly qualities have made him recognized and honored in many high positions of trust and responsibilty in local affairs. In 1851 and 1852 he was a member of the New York State Legislature. In the Holstein-Friesian Association his wise, conservative counsels have been highly valued and he has served almost continuously as a member of its board of officers.

MILK AND BUTTER RECORDS
OF
RECORDED HOLSTEIN-FRIESIAN COWS.

A LIST OF ALL PUBLISHED BUTTER AND MILK RECORDS OF HOLSTEIN-FRIESIAN COWS, SHOWING ALSO THE SIRE AND
DAM OF EACH COW.

NOTE.—The name of the animal is followed by its Herd-Book number, its sire and dam and then a statement of its record. The letters A. R. after any record indicate that it is an Advanced Registry test. P. indicates a private test. A. R. A. indicates an Officially Authenticated Advanced Registry test. H. indicates registry in the Holstein Herd-Book. H. F. the Helstein-Friesian Herd-Book. C. the Canadian Herd-Book. W. the Western Holstein-Friesian Herd-Book. D.-F. the Dutch-Friesian Herd-Book. N. H. B. the American Branch of the North Holland Herd-Book.

Persons noting errors or omissions in this list will confer a favor by promptly informing the editor and giving a correct statement of the record, which will be published in the revised edition of this work.

AAFJE 3D, 1522 H. Imp. Milk 71 lbs. 1 day, 2356 lbs. 1 oz. 31 days, A.R.
AAGGIE, 901 H. Imp. Milk 84 lbs. 12 oz. 1 day , 18,004 lbs. 5 oz. 1 year, A.R. Butter 17 lbs. 12 oz. 7 days.
AAGGIE 2D, 1360 H. Jacob 2d, 56 Neth. Aaggie, 901 H. Milk 85 lbs. 1 day, 20,763 lbs. 3 oz. 1 year, A.R. Butter 26 lbs. 7 oz. 7 days. 105 21-32 lbs. 30 days, 304 11-32 lbs. 1 year, A.R.
AAGGIE 3D, 1676 H. Sentinel, 512 H.; Aaggie 2d, 1360 H. Milk 68 lbs. 1 day, 13,810 lbs. 2 oz. 1 year, A.R. Butter 19 lbs. 1 oz., A.R.
AAGGIE 3D's WAYNE, 10516 H. F. Prince Aaggie Wayne, 1027 H. F.; Aaggie 3d, 1676 H. Milk 48 lbs. 14 oz. 1 day, 12,817 lbs. 7 oz. 1 year, A.R. Butter 19 lbs. 10 oz., P.
AAGGIE 3D's WAYNE DE KOL, 27098 H. F. Paul De Kol, 14634 H. F.; Aaggie 3d's Wayne, 10516 H. F. Butter 12 lbs. 12 1-6 oz.
AAGGIE 4TH, 3018 H. Burly, 304 H.; Aaggie 2d, 1360 H. Milk 72 lbs. 11 oz. 1 day, P.; 8155 lbs. 3 oz. 1 year, A.R. Butter 12 lbs. 11 oz. 7 days, A. R.
AAGGIE 4TH's PRINCESS, 18454 H. F. Royal Aaggie, 3463 H.; Aaggie 4th, 3018 H. Milk 43 lbs. 7 oz. 1 day, P.; 11,290 lbs. 2 oz. 1 year, A.R. Butter 9 lbs. 7 days, A.R.
AAGGIE 5TH, 4759 H. Burly, 304 H.; Aaggie 2d, 1360 H. Milk 59 lbs. 2 oz. 1 day, 9698 lbs. 10 oz. 1 year, P. Butter 12 lbs. 15 oz., A.R.
AAGGIE 6TH, 4760 H. Foil. 1237 H.; Aaggie 3d, 1676 H. Milk 45 lbs. 13 oz., P.; 10,430 lbs. 3 oz., P. Butter 19 lbs. 1 oz., P.
AAGGIE ADA, 4320 H. Imp. Milk 42 lbs. 15 oz. 1 day, P.; 1182 lbs 30 days, P.
AAGGIE ALBA, 4335 H. Sir Henry of Aaggie. Milk 81 lbs.
AAGGIE ALLIS, 4330 H.; Willem, 84 Neth.; Aaggie Isadora, 4403 H. Milk 40 lbs. 1 day, P.; 8315 lbs. 4 oz, 8 months 3 days.
AAGGIE ALLIS ARTIS, 15050 H. F. Sir Palox, 4113 H. F.; Sarah Artis, 4856 H. F. Milk 10,000 lbs. 1 year. Butter 10 lbs. 9 1-2 oz. 7 days.
AAGGIE AHNA, 26994 H. F. Shadeland Tara 2d's Albion, 12210 H. F.; Molette 2d's Beauty, 13737 H. F. Milk 38 lbs. 4 oz. 1 day, 1110 lbs. 10 oz. 1 month 3 1-2 oz. 7 days, A.R
AAGGIE ANNA, 2602 H. Imp. Milk 69 lbs. 1 day. P.; 16,993 lbs. 2 oz. 1 year. Butter 16 lbs. 13 oz. 7 days.
AAGGIE AURELIA, 2630 H. Imp. Milk 2203 lbs 4 oz. 3 months 16 days, P.
AAGGIE B., 13607 H. F. Aaggie Grace's Lad, 896 H. F.; Aaggie Grace 2d, 8494 H. F. Milk 412 lbs. 12 oz. 7 days, A.R. Butter 16 lbs. 12 oz. 7 days, A.R.
AAGGIE BEATRICE, 4336 H. Imp. Milk 4320 lbs. 10 oz. 6 months 25 days, P.
AAGGIE BEATRICE 2D, 5243 H. Tromp, 188 Neth. Imp. Milk 9612 lbs. 14 oz. 8 months 23 days, A.R.
AAGGIE BEAUTY, 2907 H. Imp. Milk 51 lbs. 6 oz. 1 day, P.; 13,573 lbs. 15 oz. 1 year, P. Butter 20 lbs. 9 oz. 7 days, 85 lbs. 7 3-4 oz. 30 days.
AAGGIE BEAUTY 2D, 2631 H. Jacob 2d, 56 Neth. Imp. Milk 49 lbs. 4 oz. 1 day. P.; 14,958 lbs. 14 oz. 1 year. Butter 23 lbs. 5 3-4 oz. 7 days. 94 lbs. 15 3-4 oz. 30 days, A.R.
AAGGIE BEAUTY 5TH, 3870 H. F. Ryse Dike, 3073 H.; Aaggie Beauty, 2907 H. Milk 529 lbs. 14 oz. 10 days, A.R.
AAGGIE BELLE, 2607 H. Jacob 2d, 56 Neth.; Trijntje, 35 Neth. Milk 9673 lbs. 14 oz. 11 months, P.
AAGGIE BERTHA, 2020 H. Imp. Milk 45 lbs. 1 day.
AAGGIE BONNIE, 2608 H. Imp. Milk 66 lbs. 1 day, 12,267 lbs. 12 oz. 10 months 16 days, P.
AAGGIE BONNIE 2D, 6053 H. Sir Henry 2d of Aaggie, 1451 H.; Aaggie Bonnie, 2608 H. Milk 14,525 lbs. oz 1 year. Butter 11 lbs. 6 1-2 oz. 7 days.
AAGGIE BOONSTRA, 10603 H. F. De Kol 2d's Prince, 2767 H. F.; Boonstra 5th, 2419 H. F. Butter 15 lbs. 13 oz. 7 days.

MILK AND BUTTER RECORDS. 307

AAGGIE CAMILLE, 4349 H. Sir Henry of Aaggie, 1450 H.; De Schot, 573 Neth. Milk 11,103 lbs. 14 oz. 1 year, P.
AAGGIE CATHARINE, 4573 H. Lincoln, 120 Neth. Imp. Milk 58 lbs. 1 day, 2922 lbs. 8 oz. 30 days, A.R. Butter 21 lbs. 8 oz. 10 days, A.R.
AAGGIE CLARA, 2626 H. Imp. Milk 64 lbs. 4 oz. 1 day, P.; 4085 lbs. 60 days. Butter 2 lbs. 8 oz. 1 day.
AAGGIE CLEORA, 4567 H. Imp. Milk 4501 lbs. 12 oz. 6 months 12 days, P.
AAGGIE CONSTANCE, 2629 H. De Ruiter, 89 Neth. Imp. Milk 76 lbs. 6 oz. 1 day, P.; 16,761 lbs. 11 oz, 1 year, A.R. Butter 19 lbs. 14 1-2 oz. 7 days.
AAGGIE CONSTANCE's NETHERLAND, 10582 H. F. Netherland Prince, 716 H.; Aaggie Constance, 2629 H. Butter 12 lbs. 5 oz.
AAGGIE CORA, 2609 H. Jacob 2d, 56 Neth. Imp. Milk 65 lbs. 8 oz. 1 day, 13,996 lbs. 1 year, P. Butter 15 lbs. 10 oz. 7 days, P.
AAGGIE CORNELIA, 4410 H. Imp. Milk 78 lbs. 3 oz. 1 day, 16,754 lbs. 11 oz. 1 year, P. Butter 19 lbs. 1 oz. 7 days, P.
AAGGIE CORNELIA 2D, 4341 H. Alexander, 83 Neth.; Aaggie Cornelia, 4410 H. Milk 63 1-6 lbs. 1 day, 14,610 lbs. 9 oz. 1 year, P. Butter 19 lbs. 6 oz. 7 days, P.
AAGGIE CORNELIA 2D's GRACE, 9816 H. Netherland Prince, 713 H.; Aaggie Cornelia 2d, 4341 H. Milk 37 lbs. 8 oz. 1 day, 4134 lbs. 12 oz. 5 months 20 days, P. Butter 18 lbs. 14 oz. 7 days, P.
AAGGIE CORNELIA 3D, 4342 H. Alexander, 83 Neth.; Aaggie Cornelia, 4410 H. Milk 78 lbs. 2 oz. 1 day, P.; 17,350 lbs. 1 year, A.R. Butter 17 lbs. 7 oz. 7 days, P.
AAGGIE CORNELIA 3D's LASS, 6735 H. Tromp, 188 Neth.; Aaggie Cornelia 3d, 4342 H. Milk 41 lbs. 9 oz. 1 day, 11,152 lbs. 6 oz. 1 year, P. Butter 9 lbs. 1 oz. 7 days, P.
AAGGIE CORNELIA 4TH, 4343 H. Alexander, 83 Neth.; Aaggie Cornelia, 4410 H. Milk 60 lbs. 1 oz. 1 day, P.; 13,818 lbs. 5 oz. 1 year A.R. Butter 19 lbs. 8 oz. 7 days, A.R.
AAGGIE CORNELIA 5TH, 6733 H. Tromp, 188 Neth.; Aaggie Cornelia, 4410 H. Milk 10,870 lbs. 9 oz. 1 year, P. Butter 14 lbs. 7 oz., P.
AAGGIE CORNELIA 6TH'S PRINCESS, 1566 H. F. Netherland Prince, 716 H. Aaggie Cornelia 5th, 6733 H. Milk 10,578 lbs. 6 oz. 1 year, A.R. Butter 18 lbs. 14 1-2 oz. 7 days, A.R.
AAGGIE DIAMOND, 4975 H. F. Royal Aaggie, 3405 H.; Aaggie 6th, 4760 H. Milk 58 lbs. 6 oz. 1 day, P.; 8919 lbs. 2 oz, 12 days, A.R. Butter 24 lbs. 7 days, A.R.; 10 lbs. 8 oz. 3 days, P.
AAGGIE DOROTHY, 4352 H. Imp. Milk 63 lbs. 1 day, P.
AAGGIE DOUGLAS, 10009 H. F. Princess Aaggie's Royal, 4492 H.; Ada Douglass, 4202 H. Butter 20 lbs. 4 oz. 7 days, 78 lbs. 11 oz 30 days, P.
AAGGIE ELLA, 6382 H. F. Careno Prince, 2353 H.; Aaggie Alba, 4335 H. Milk 78 lbs. 2 oz. 1 day, P.
AAGGIE ETHEL, 4353 H. Sir Henry of Aaggie, 1450 H. Imp. Milk 58 lbs. 5 oz. 1 day, 14,144 lbs. oz. 1 year, P. Butter 11 lbs. 11 oz. 7 days, P.
AAGGIE ETTA, 4555 H. Lincoln, 120 Neth.; Matilda, 444 Neth. Milk 38 lbs. 12 oz. 1 day, P.
AAGGIE EVA, 4354 H. De Ruiter, 89 Neth. Imp. Milk 36 lbs. 1 oz. 1 day, 14,016 lbs. 9 oz. 1 year, P. Butter 17 lbs. 12 oz. 7 days, P.
AAGGIE FANNIE, 4358 H. Jacob 4th, 2 0 Neth. Imp. Milk 37 lbs. 1 day, P.
AAGGIE FIDELIA, 4357 H. Jacob 4th, 2 0 Neth. Imp. Milk 50 lbs. 6 oz. 1 day, 11,412 lbs. 12 oz. 1 year, P.
AAGGIE FLORA, 2600 H. Jacob 2d, 56 Neth.; De Schot, 573 Neth. Milk 82 lbs. 8 oz. 1 day, 3329 lbs. 2 months 18 days, P. Butter 11 lbs. 13 oz. 7 days, P.
AAGGIE GERALDINE, 4360 H. Imp. Milk 43 lbs. 1 day, P.
AAGGIE GERTRUDE, 4350 H. Sir Henry of Aaggie, 1450 H.; Lijsje, 700 Neth. Milk 32 lbs. 1 day, P.
AAGGIE GRACE, 2618 H. Imp. Milk 63 lbs. 2 oz, 8 months 15 days, A.R.
AAGGIE GRACE 2D, 8404 H. Prince Imperial, 1164 H.; Aaggie Grace, 2618 H. Milk 397 lbs. 10 oz. 10 days, A.R.
AAGGIE GRACE'S BOY'S QUEEN, 22041 H. F. Aaggie Grace's Boy, 7008 H. F.; Queen of the Valley 4th, 1294 H. F. Milk 10,869 lbs. 4 oz. 10 months, A.R.
AAGGIE GRACE'S BOY'S TOPSY, 22046 H. F. Aaggie Grace's Boy, 7008 H. F.; Judith W. 2d, 1287 H. F. Milk 360 lbs. 4 oz. 10 days, A.R.
AAGGIE GRANT, 86 H. F. Royal Aaggie, 3463 H.; Nellie Grant, 943 H. Milk 53 lbs. 1 day, P.
AAGGIE HANNAH, 4361 H. Jacob 2d, 56 Neth. Imp. Milk 71 lbs. 15 oz. 1 day, P.; 16,268 lbs. 6 oz. 1 year, A.R. Butter 19 lbs. 7 3-4 oz. 7 days, A.R.
AAGGIE HANNAH 2D, 1587 H. F. Prince Imperial, 1164 H.; Aaggie Hannah, 4361 H. Milk 5232 lbs. 15 oz. 8 months 12 days, P.
AAGGIE HARTOG, 3 D. F. Imp. Milk 54 lbs. 1 day, 13,498 lbs. 1 year, P.
AAGGIE HARTOG, 2D. 48 D. F. Ellswout 2d, 2 A.; Aaggie Hartog, 3 D. F. Milk 30 lbs. 1 day, P.
AAGGIE HARTOG 3D, 48 D. F. Paul Potter, 2 D. F.; Aaggie Hartog, 3 D. F. Milk 50 lbs. 1 day, P.
AAGGIE HENRIETTA, 0026 H. F. Sir Henry Lambert, 1203 H. F.; Aaggie Cornelia 3d's Lass. 6735 H. Milk 13,491 lbs. 4 oz. 1 year, A. R. Butter 21 lbs. 11 oz. 7 days, A.R.
AAGGIE HOPEFUL, 6003 H. F. Aaggie Rosa's Prince, 8132 H.; Myth, 8006 H. Milk 48 lbs. 18 oz. 1 day, P.
AAGGIE IDA, 2000 H. Imp. Milk 47 lbs 1 day, 1294 lbs. 30 days, P.
AAGGIE IDALINE, 4362 H. Jacob, 20 Neth. Imp. Milk 60 lbs. 1 day, 17,129 lbs. 7 oz. 1 year, P. Butter 19 lbs. 2 3-4 oz. 7 days, P.
AAGGIE IDALINE 2D, 4363 H. Jacob 2d, 56 Neth. Imp. Milk 66 lbs. 1 oz. 1 day, 14,229 lbs. 1 oz. 1 year, P. Butter 20 lbs. 5 oz. 7 days, P.
AAGGIE IDALINE 3D, 4364 H. Jacob 2d, 35 Neth. Imp. Milk 69 lbs. 10 oz 1 day, 15,785 lbs. 1 oz. 1 year, P. Butter 17 lbs. 11 3-4 oz. 7 days, A.R.
AAGGIE IDALINE 4TH, 4365 H. Imp. Milk 3642 lbs. 8 oz. 7 months 6 days, P.
AAGGIE IDALINE 6TH, 4366 H. Willem, 84 Neth.; Aaggie Idaline, 4362 H. Milk 46 lbs. 4 oz. 1 day, 12,402 lbs. 8 oz. 1 year, P. Butter 14 lbs. 14 oz. 7 days, P.
AAGGIE IDALINE 7TH, 8470 H. F. Netherland Monk, 4124 H.; Aaggie Idaline, 4362 H. Milk 50 lbs. 10 oz. 1 day, P.; 8564 lbs. 4 oz. 10 months, A.R. Butter 20 lbs. 3 oz. 7 days, A.R.
AAGGIE IRENE, 4509 H. Jacob 2d, 56 Neth. Imp. Milk 60 lbs. 8 oz. 1 day, P.
AAGGIE ISADORA, 4493 H. Jacob 2d, 56 Neth. Imp. Milk 54 lbs. 4 oz. 1 day, 11,968 lbs. 3 oz. 1 year, P.
AAGGIE JENNIE, 2625 H. De Ruiter, 85 Neth. Imp. Milk 50 lbs. 15 oz. 1 day, 5104 lbs. 6 oz. 4 months 13 days, P.
AAGGIE JOSEPHINE, 4476 H. Imp. Milk 11,526 lbs. 8 oz. 10 months. A.R.
AAGGIE JOSEPHINE 2D, 1635 H. F. Uncle Tom 2d, 1163 H.; Aaggie Josephine, 4476 H. Milk 44 lbs. 3 oz. 1 day, 8757 lbs. 3 oz. 10 months, A.R.

DON J. WOOD.

MILK AND BUTTER RECORDS. 309

AAGGIE JOSEPHINE 3D, 4002 H. F. Billy Bawn, 3087 H.; Aaggie Josephine, 4476 H. Milk 43 lbs. 15 oz. 1 day, 8500 lbs. 10 months, P.
AAGGIE JOSIE, 4367 H. Lincoln, 120 Neth. Imp. Milk 46 lbs. 6 oz. 1 day, 4605 lbs. 8 oz. 4 months 12 days, P.
AAGGIE JULIET, 4474 H. Sir Henry of Aaggie, 1450 H.; Blokker, 390 Neth. Milk 75 lbs. 1 day, 12,170 lbs. 10 months 20 days, P. Butter 15 lbs. 10½ oz. 7 days, P.
AAGGIE JULIET 2D, 2180 H. F. Netherland Prince, 716 H.; Aaggie Juliet, 4474 H. Milk 48 lbs. 1 day, P.
AAGGIE KATE, 4516 H. Imp. Milk 54 lbs. 13 5-7 oz. 1 day, P. Butter 16 lbs. 8 1-2 oz. 7 days, P.
AAGGIE KATHLEEN, 4492 H. Jacob, 20 Neth. Imp. Milk 56 lbs. 8 oz. 1 day, 11,390 lbs. 13 oz. 9 months 6 days, P.
AAGGIE LAMBERT, 8556 H. F. Sir Henry Lambert, 1263 H. F.; Aaggie Hannah 2d, 1587 H. F. Milk 10,000 lbs. 1 year, P.
AAGGIE LAURA, 2616 H. Napoleon, 129 Neth. Milk 54 lbs. 1 day, P. Butter 17 lbs. 7 days, P.
AAGGIE LAURA, 2D, 250 H. F. Sir Henry of Aaggie, 1450 H.; Aaggie Laura, 2616 H. Milk 42 lbs. 11 oz. 1 day, P.; 9054 lbs. 11 1-2 oz. 1 year, A.R. Butter 15 lbs. 6 1-2 oz., P.
AAGGIE LEE, 2613 H. Napoleon, 129 Neth.; Marie, 373 Neth. Milk 12,760 lbs. 9 oz. 11 months 9 days, P. Butter 21 lbs. 5 oz. 7 days, P.
AAGGIE LEILA, 2603 H. Imp. Milk 52 lbs. 1 day, P.; 1612 lbs. 31 days, A.R. Butter 17 lbs. 4 oz. 7 days, A.R.
AAGGIE LEILA 2D, 6007 H. Sir William of Aaggie, 1455 H. F.; Aaggie Leila, 2603 H. F. Milk 73 lbs. 1 day, P.
AAGGIE LEILA'S INKA, 5481 H. F. Inka's Duke, 1161 H.; Aaggie Leila, 2603 H. F. Milk 62 lbs. 3 oz. 1 day, P. Butter 20 lbs. 8 oz. 7 days, P.
AAGGIE LILY, 4393 H. Lincoln, 120 Neth. Imp. Milk 41 lbs. 1 oz. 1 day, 1104 lbs. 1 year, P.
AAGGIE LILY 3D, 1128 H. F. Lad of Prescott, 2389 H.; Aaggie Lily, 4393 H. Milk 367 lbs. 6 oz. 10 days, A.R. Butter 9 lbs. 14 oz. 7 days, A.R.
AAGGIE LILY 5TH, 8638 H. F. Otsego Chief, 893 H. F.; Aaggie Lily, 4393 H. Milk 370 lbs. 10 oz. 10 days, A.R.
AAGGIE LOTTA, 4405 H. Tromp, 188 Neth. Imp. Milk 10,562 lbs. 15 oz. 9 months, P. Butter 19 lbs. 5 oz. 7 days, P.
AAGGIE LOTTA 3D, 11796 H. F. Netherland Carl, 3279 H.; Aaggie Lotta, 4405 H. Butter 16 lbs. 12 oz. 7 days, P.
AAGGIE LOUISE, 2022 H. Jacob 2d, 56 Neth.; Fispal. Milk 12,229 lbs. 4 oz. 1 year, P.
AAGGIE LULA, 2621 H. Imp. Milk 60 lbs. 8 oz. 1 day, P.
AAGGIE MARIA, 2004 H. Imp. Milk 48 lbs. 1 day, P.
AAGGIE MARY, 3648 H. F. Sir Henry 2d of Aaggie, 1451 H.; Jacob Wit's Berylla, 7792 H. Milk 38 lbs. 14 oz. 1 day, P. Butter 17 lbs. 4 oz. 7 days, P.
AAGGIE MAUD, 2615 H. Imp. Milk 40 lbs. 8 oz. 1 day, 2550 lbs. 72 days, P.
AAGGIE MAXIMA, 6001 H. F. Aaggie Rosa Prince, 3132 H.; Magna Charta, 8102 H. Milk 64 lbs. 1 day, P.
AAGGIE MAY, 2601 H. Imp. Milk 57 lbs. 12 oz. 1 day, 16,125 lbs. 10 oz. 1 year, P. Butter 20 lbs. 2 oz. A.R.
AAGGIE MAY 2D, 3501 H. Sir Henry of Aaggie, 1450 H.; Aaggie May, 2601 H. Milk 43 lbs. 8 oz 1 day, 11,346 lbs. 12 oz. 1 year, P. Butter 4 lbs. 6 1-2 oz. 7 days, P.
AAGGIE MAY 4TH, 8478 H. F. Clothilde 4th's Imperial, 1281 H. F.; Aaggie May 2601 H. Butter 11 lbs. 9 1-2 oz. 7 days, P.
AAGGIE MERREL, 2024 H. De Ruiter, 89 Neth. Imp. Milk 46 lbs. 4 oz. 1 day, 13,818 lbs. 5 oz. 1 year P. Butter 18 lbs. 1 3-4 oz. 7 days, P.
AAGGIE MERREL 2D, 1577 H. F. Netherland King, 1924 H.; Aaggie Merrel, 2628 H. Milk 10,173 lbs. 15 oz. 1 year, P. Butter 17 lbs. 6 oz. 7 days, P.
AAGGIE MERREL 4TH, 8330 H. F. Netherland Statesman, 3280 H.; Aaggie Merrel, 2028 H. Milk 11,035 lbs. 4 oz. 1 year, P. Butter 6 lbs. 6 1-2 oz. A.R.
AAGGIE OF ASHLEY, 3883 H. Neptune, 71 H.; Arminda, 2658 H. Milk 38 lbs. 2 oz. 1 day, P.
AAGGIE OF HOORN, 4481 H. Imp. Milk 51 lbs. 1 day, P.
AAGGIE OF HOORN'S NETHERLAND, 10655 H. F. Netherland Marquis, 2484 H.; Aaggie of Hoorn, 4481 H. Milk 50 lbs. 8 oz. 1 day, 20 10 months, P. Butter 14 lbs. 7 days, A.R.
AAGGIE OF MIDWOUD, 4482 H. Imp. Milk 53 lbs. 1 day, P.
AAGGIE OPTIMA, 6002 H. F. Aaggie Rosa Prince, 3132 H.; Magna Charta, 8102 H. Milk 29 lbs. 8 oz. 1 day, P.
AAGGIE PANSY, 4434 H. Napoleon, 129 Neth. Imp. Milk 1794 lbs. 30 days, A.R. Butter 15 lbs. 12 oz. 7 days, A.R.
AAGGIE PANSY 2D, 6072 H. F. Netherland Convoy, 2034 H.; Aaggie Pansy, 4434 H. Milk 51 lbs. 8 oz. 1 day, P.; 1249 lbs. 8 oz. 31 days, A.R.
AAGGIE PANSY 3D, 14128 H. F. Netherland Convoy, 2034 H.; Aaggie Pansy, 4434 H. Milk 31 lbs. 4 oz. 1 day, P. Butter 15 lbs. 12 oz. 7 days, P.
AAGGIE PAULINE, 2623 H. De Ruiter, 89 Neth. Imp. Milk 11,599 lbs. 11 oz. 10 months, P. Butter 18 lbs. 8 oz. 7 days, P.
AAGGIE PEARL, 9783 H. Prince of Wayne 5th, 1910 H.; Aaggie 4th, 3618 H. Milk 55 lbs. 13 oz. 1 day, P.; 11,305 lbs. 8 oz. 1 year, A.R. Butter 18 lbs. 4 oz. 7 days, A.R.
AAGGIE RACHEL, 4473 H. Sir Henry of Aaggie, 1450 H. Imp. Milk 14,959 lbs. 13 oz. 1 year, A.R. Butter 17 lbs. 9 3-4 oz. 7 days, P.
AAGGIE ROSA, 2605 H. Jacob 1st, 20 Neth.; Jansje, 88 Neth. Milk 91 lbs. 1 day, P.; 20,225 lbs. 3 oz. 1 year, A.R. Butter 22 lbs. 8 1-2 oz. 7 days, 87 lbs. 30 days, P.
AAGGIE ROSA 2D, 2610 H. Jacob 2d, 56 Neth.; Wemeltein, 323 Neth. Milk 65 lbs. 4 oz. 1 day, 16,834 lbs. 13 oz. 1 year, P. Butter 16 lbs. 2 1-2 oz. 7 days, P.
AAGGIE ROSA 2D'S NETHERLAND, 7006 H. F. Netherland Statesman, 3280 H.; Aaggie Rosa 2d, 2610 H. Milk 7372 lbs. 10 oz. 7 months 10 days, P.
AAGGIE ROSA 3D, 2611 H. De Ruiter, 89 Neth.; Aaggie Rosa 2d, 2610 H. Milk 8175 lbs. 10 months, A.R.
AAGGIE ROSA 4TH, 3485 H. Sir Henry of Aaggie, 1450 H.; Aaggie Rosa, 2605 H. Milk 12,735 lbs. 4 oz. P. Butter 21 lbs. 8 1-2 oz. 7 days, 88 lbs. 11 oz. 30 days, P.
AAGGIE ROSALIND, 4404 H. Imp. Milk 89 lbs. 2 oz. 1 day, 10,800 lbs. 6 months, P. Butter 19 lbs. 12 oz. 7 days, P.
AAGGIE ROSA PRINCESS, 9036 H. F. Aaggie Rosa's Prince, 3132 H; Saboa, 7959 H. Milk 46 lbs. 8 oz. 1 day, 1129 lbs. 27 days, P.

MILK AND BUTTER RECORDS. 311

AAGGIE ROZALIA, 4939 H. F. Sir Henry 2d of Aaggie, 1451 H.; Aaggie Rosa 3d's Diora, 8465 H. Butter 12 lbs. 9 oz. 7 days, P.
AAGGIE SADIE, 4472 H. De Ruiter, 89 Neth. Imp. Milk 64 lbs. 7 oz. 1 day, 11,809 lbs. 2 oz. 1 year, P.
AAGGIE SADIE VALE, 4979 H. F. Royal Aaggie, 3463 H.; Sadie Vale, 958 H. Milk 36 lbs. 8 oz. 1 day, P.; 8620 lbs. 23 days, A.R. Butter 22 lbs. 6 oz. 7 days, A.R.
AAGGIE SAPHIRA, 4568 H. Imp. Milk 35 lbs. 4 oz. 1 day, 1006 lbs. 1 oz. 30 days, P.
AAGGIE SAPHIRA 2D, 4568 H. Imp. M lk 8579 lbs. 8 oz. 10 months, A.R.
AAGGIE SAPHIRA 3D, 1289 H. F. Lad of Prescott, 2389 H.; Aaggie Saphira, 4568 H. Milk 7703 lbs. 12 oz. 8 months 10 days, A.R.
AAGGIE SAPHIRA MAY, 7329 H. F. Lad of Prescott 2d, 968 H. F.; Aaggie Saphira 3d, 1289 H. F. Milk 371 lbs. 10 days, A.R.
AAGGIE SAPHIRA W., 2530 H. F. Lad of Prescott 2389 H.; Aaggie Saphira 2d, 8483 H. Milk 5331 lbs. 6 months 26 days, P.
AAGGIE SARAH, 4412 H. Jacob 2d, 56 Neth. Imp. Milk 80 lbs. 8 oz. 1 day, 16,993 lbs. 18 oz. 1 year, P.
AAGGIE SARAH 2D, 7142 H. Imp. Milk 12,682 lbs. 15 oz. 1 year, P.; 10,926 lbs. 12 oz. 10 months, A.R. Butter 17 lbs. 5 3-4 oz. 7 days, P.
AAGGIE SOPHIA, 4394 H. Sir Henry of Aaggie, 1450 H. Imp. Milk 54 lbs. 7 oz. 1 day, 7528 lbs. 14 oz. 6 months, P.
AAGGIE'S SECOND DAUGHTER, 8700 H. Netherland Prince, 716 H.; Aaggie, 901 H. Milk 40 lbs. 2 oz. 1 day, P.; 11,090 lbs. 14 oz. 1 year A.R. Butter 15 lbs. 1 oz. 7 days, A.R.
AAGGIE STELLA, 4477 H. Imp. Milk 44 lbs. 14 oz. 1 day, 1365 lbs. 12 oz. 30 days, P.
AAGGIE STELLA 2D, 574 H. F. Captain Daw, 2088 H.; Aaggie Stella, 4477 H. Milk 47 lbs. 8 oz. 1 day, P.; 7717 lbs. 8 oz. 8 months 14 days, A.R.
AAGGIE STELLA 3D, 4000 H. F. Captain Daw, 2088 H. Aaggie Stella, 4477 H. Milk 7343 lbs. 11 oz. 10 months, A.R.
AAGGIE'S THIRD DAUGHTER, 1597 H. F. Netherland Prince, 716 H.; Aaggie, 901 H. Milk 7710 lbs. 3 oz. 10 months, A.R. Butter 14 lbs. 15 oz. 7 days, 51 lbs. 4 1-4 oz. 30 days, P.
AAGGIE TEHEE, 8226 H. F. Aaggie Grace's Lad, 895 H. F.; Tehee, 8484 H. Milk 452 lbs. 15 oz. 10 days, A.R.
AAGGIE WAYNE, 9780 H. Prince of Wayne 5th, 1910 H.; Aaggie 2d, 1360 H. Milk 61 lbs. 9 oz. 1 day, 12,156 lbs. 1 year, P. Butter 9 lbs. 14 1-2 oz. 7 days, P.
AAGGIE WAYNE 3D, 13747 H. F. Koningin Van Friesland 5th's Netherland, 3515 H. F.; Aaggie Wayne, 9780 H. Milk 41 lbs. 4 oz. 1 day, 9247 lbs. 5 oz. 10 months, A.R.
AAGGIE WAYNE 4TH, 28386 H. F. Duke Netherland, 1271 H. F.; Aaggie Wayne, 9780 H. Milk 7977 lbs. 1 oz. 10 months, A.R.
AAGGIE WIT, 9391 H. Jacob, 20 Neth. Imp. Milk 68 lbs. 9 oz. 1 day, P.
AAGJI 2D, 981 H. Imp. Milk 1293 lbs. 9 oz. 30 days, P
AALTJE, 711 Neth. Imp. Milk 85 lbs. 13 oz. 1 day, P.
AALTJE 2D, 982 H. Imp. Milk 44 lbs. 12 oz. 1 day, 6255 lbs. 4 oz. 6 months 10 days, P.
AALTJE LEE 2D, 3237 H. Imp Milk 55 lbs. 1 day, P.
AALTJE TOLSMA 2D, 221 D. F. Mooie, 25 M. R.; Aaltje Toisma, 69 M. R. Milk 80 lbs. 1 day, P.
AALTJE TOLSMA 3D, 1110 D. F. Prince Kuperus, 121 P. R.; Aaltje Tolsma, 69 M. R. Milk 69 lbs. 12 oz. 1 day, P.; 14,316 lbs. 2 oz. 7 months 25 days, A.R. Butter 19 lbs. 4 oz. 7 days, A.R.
AALTJE TWISK, 9682 H. F. Twisk's Price, 1208 H.; Aaltje Wessels 2d, 8339 H. Milk 8121 lbs. 4 oz. 10 months, A.R.
AALTJE WESSELS, 5710 H. Imp. Milk 84 lbs. 8 oz. 1 day, P.
AALTJE WESSELS 2D, 8339 H. Imp. Milk 47 lbs. 8 oz. 1 day, P.; 12,912 lbs. 1 year. A.R. Butter 15 lbs. 11 oz. 7 days, A.R.
AALTJE HENGERVELD, 11 D. F. Imp. Milk 11,856 lbs. 292 days, P.
AALTJE HENGERVELD 3D, 18 D. F. Paul Potter, 2 D. F.; Aaltje Hengerveld, 11 D.F. Milk 65 lbs. 1 day, 10,006 lbs. 12 oz. 1 year, P. Butter 2 lbs. 1 day, P.
AALQUI, 1691 D. F. Dirk; Aaltje. Milk 55 lbs. 1 day, 31 lbs. 4 oz. 7 days, P.
AARDZAK, 2021 H. F. De Prins, 310 Neth..; Anna, 1024 Neth. Milk 13,859 lbs. 1 year, P.
ABANAKA, 7152 H. Imp. Milk 7333 lbs. 1 year, P.
ABDA, 872 H. Imp. Milk 72 lbs. 1 day, P. Butter 18 lbs. 14 oz. 7 days, P.
ABBA 2D, 3864 H. Banjo, 564 H.; Abba 372 H. Milk 63 lbs. 1 day, P.
ABBEKERK PRINCESS, 3829 H. F. Abbekerk, 206 Neth.; Trijntje, 735 H. F. Milk 53 lbs. 1 day, P. Butter 11 lbs. 2 oz. 7 days, P.
ABBY, 586 H. Imp. Milk 55 lbs. 1 day, P.
ABDALETTA, 6847 H. Imp. Milk 987 lbs. 30 days, P.
ABINADE BOER, 377 F. H. Imp. Milk 55 lbs. 1 day, P.
ABRA, 9312 H. F. Sancho, 3902 H.; Pavia, 7162 H. Milk 9322 lbs. 1 year, P.
ACHSAH, 5002 H. Imp. Milk 40 lbs. 8 oz. 1 day, 10,550 lbs. 8 oz. 1 year, P.
ACME, 547 H. Imp. Milk 62 lbs. 8 oz. 1 day, P. Butter 20 lbs. 1 1-2 oz. 4 days, P.
ACRA, 7150 H. Imp. Milk 11,202 lbs. 4 oz. 1 year, P.
ADA, 1872 H. Imp. Milk 76 lbs. 8 oz. 1 day, P.
ADA ALEXANDER, 4563 H. Imp. Milk 42 lbs. 1 day, P.
ADA ARTIS, 4839 H. F. Imp. Milk 7387 lbs. 2 oz. 5 months 12 days, P.
ADA DOUGLAS, 4202 H. Lord Russell 2d, 622 H. Belle Douglas, 1108 H. Milk 55 lbs. 1 day, P. Butter 18 lbs. 7 days, P.
ADDIE, 873 H. Imp. Milk 51 lbs. 2 oz. 1 day, 17,164 lbs. 15 oz. 1 year, P. Butter 21 lbs. 14 oz. 7 days, P.
ADDIE 2D, 8467 H. Netherland Prince, 736 H.; Addie, 873 H. Milk 8752 lbs. 10 oz. 11 months, P. Butter 10 lbs. 19 1-2 oz., P.
ADDIE 2D'S AAGGIE, 6931 H. F. Sir Henry 2d of Aaggie, 1451 H.; Addie 2d, 8467 H. Milk 49 lbs. 8 oz. 1 day, 1212 lbs. 8 oz. 30 days, P
ADELIA ARTIS 4840 H. Artis, 127 Neth.; Pastelijntje, 2580 Neth. Milk 11,467 lbs. 14 oz. 10 months, A.R. Butter 81 lbs. 3 3-4 oz. 30 days, P.
ADELIA ARTIS 2D, 7003 H. F. Artis America, 3938 H.; Adelia Artis. 4840 H. Milk 6216 lbs. 5 oz. 7 months 10 days, P. Butter 19 lbs. 9 oz. 7 days, 81 lbs. 3 3-4 oz. 30 days, A.F.
ADELIZA, 7431 H. Lord Bantam, 1011 H.; Marie Wortel 2d, 1838 H. Milk 8009 lbs. 3 oz. 0 months, P.
ADMIRALDA, 7838 H. Imp. Milk 36 lbs. 1 day, P.
ADMIRATION, 6235 H. Consolation, 2661 H.; Gwendolen, 2329 H. Butter 12 lbs. 3 oz. 7 days, P.
ADRIAANTJE, 9461 H. Imp. Milk 55 lbs. 3 oz. 1 day.
ADRIANE 2D, 7146 H. Imp. Milk 10.840 lbs. 9 months 17 days, A.R.

MILK AND BUTTER RECORDS. 313

ADRIEMA 1681 D.-F. Halbe, 280 F. H.; Jonge Stienser, 2350 H. F. Butter 9 lbs. 6 oz. 7 days, A.R.
ADRIENNE, 2196 H. Banjo, 564 H.; Abba, 672 H. Butter 16 lbs. 10 oz. 7 days, P.
ANURINE, 3884 H. Jaques, 765 H.; Mebuta, 1135 H. Butter 13 lbs. 9 oz. 7 days, P.
ADVENTURESS 3D, 6452 H. F. De Brave Hendrik, 230 H. F.; Adventuress 6152 H. Milk 53 lbs. 8 oz. 1 day, 7240 lbs. 8 oz. 1 year, P. Butter 15 lbs. 5 oz. 7 days, P.
AEGIS, 1587 D.-F. Rip Van Winkle, 523 P. R.; Agoo, 1585 P. R. Milk 82 lbs. 11 oz. 1 day, 16,323 lbs. 10 oz. 1 year, A.R. Butter 25 lbs. 13 1-4 oz. 7 days, 100 lbs. 6 oz. 30 days, A.R.
AEGIS 2D, 235 H. Uncle Tom, 163 H.; Aegis 69 H. Milk 79 lbs. 1 day, 17,807 lbs. 9 oz. 1 year, P. Butter 23 lbs. 7 1-2 oz. 7 days, 93 lbs. 5 1 4 oz. A.R.
AEGIS 2D'S NETHERLAND, 3726 H. F. Netherland Prince, 716 H.; Aegis 2d, 235 H. Milk 5014 lbs. 10 oz. 6 months 27 days, P. Butter 10 lbs. 13 oz., A.R.
AEGIS 3D, 563 H. Uncle Tom, 163 H.; Juniata, 154 H. Milk 35 lbs. 6 oz, 1 day, P.
AEGIS 4TH, 1276 H. Beaconsfield, 401 H.; Aegis 2d, 235 H. Milk 10,318 lbs. 1 year, A.R.
AEGIS 6TH, 2088 H. Neptune, 711 H.; Aegis 2d, 235 H. Milk 44 lbs. 9 oz. 1 day, 10,556 lbs. 1 oz. 1 year, P. Butter 19 lbs. 5 oz. 7 days, P.
AEGIS 9TH, 3014 H. Neptune, 711 H.; Aegis, 69 H. Milk 44 lbs. 1 oz. 1 day, 12,098 lbs. 7 oz. 1 year, P. Butter 10 lbs. 5 oz. 7 days, A.R.
AEGIS 10TH, 4041 H. F. Netherland Prince, 716 H.; Aegis, 69 H. Milk 10,216 lbs. 11 oz. 10 months, A.R. Butter 21 lbs. 7 days, A.R.
AELODIA, 4016 H. Imp. Milk 60 lbs. 1 day, P.
AELODIA 2D, 235 H. F. Duke of Niagara, 2030 H.; Aelodia, 4016 H Milk 51 lbs. 8 oz. 1 day, P.
AFKA DE VRIES, 5558 H. Imp. Milk 75 lbs. 1 day, 12,837 lbs. 13 oz. 1 year, P.
AFKE, 156 D.-F. Imp. Milk 40 lbs. 1 day, P.
AFKE LEE, 5714 H. Imp. Butter 16 lbs. 14 1-2 oz. 7 days, A.R.
AFRA, 2854 Neth. Imp. Milk 91 lbs. 1 day, P.
AFRA BRANTJES, 6012 H. Bouwke, 100 Neth.; Cato, 475 Neth. Milk 50 lbs. 1 day, P.
AFRICAN MAID, 6000 H. Imp. Milk 12,155 lbs. 15 oz. 1 year, P.
AFTON, 13516 H. F. Nannette's Ondit, 839 H. F.; Wavelet, 3369 H. Milk 966 lbs. 5 oz. 30 days, P.
AGATHA, 2025 H. Imp. Milk 84 lbs. 1 day, P. Butter 18 lbs. 12 oz. 7 days, P.
AGATE, 236 H. Imp. Milk 12,528 lbs. 0 oz. 10 months, A.R.
AGATHA, 1612 D.-F. Rembrandt, 172 F. H.; Jetske, 2035 F. H. Milk 90 lbs. 8 oz. 1 day, P. Butter 18 lbs. 12 oz. 7 days, P.
AGAWAN, 1491 D.-F.; De Nette, 280 F. H.; Jantje 1455 F. H. Butter 10 lbs. 2 oz. 7 days, A.R.
AGIE ABBEKERK, 9591 H. Abbekerk, 296 Neth. Imp. Milk 72 lbs. 1 day, P.; 730 lbs. 10 days A.R.
AGILITY, 1856 H. Imp. Milk 5618 lbs. 3 oz. 8 months 20 days, P.
AGILITY 2D, 2664 H. Imp Milk 48 lbs. 1 day, 1468 lbs. 15 oz. 30 days, P.
AGNES DE KOL, 20200 H. F. De Kol 2d's Prince, 2767 H. F.; Boonstra 5th, 2419 H. F. Butter 29 lbs. 5 oz. 7 days, 133 lbs. 4 oz. 60 days, A.R.
AGNES DE KOL'S ELLEN, 30228 H. F. Petertje 2d's Koningen, 10625 H. F.; Agnes De Kol, 2020 H. F. Milk 312 lbs. 7 days, A.R. Butter 13 lbs. .075 oz. 7 days, A. R.
AGNETA, 1117 H. F. Cossack, 2008 H. Amulet, 3421 H. Milk 9113 lbs. 9 oz. 1 year A.R.
AGNITA, 990 H. F. Prius, 124 Neth.; Haartje, 3269 Neth. Milk 71 lbs. 1 day, P. Butter 14 lbs. 7 days, P.
AGOSTINA, 501 H. Imp. Milk 58 lbs. 1 day, 11,387 lbs. 1 year. P.
AGRIPPINA, 7301 H. Imp. 9370 lbs. 7 oz. 1 year, P.
AGKJE 2D, 2540 H. Imp. Milk 75 lbs. 1 day, 1472 lbs. 15 oz. 30 days, P. Butter 14 lbs. 7 oz. 7 days, P.
ALAMEDA, 8717 H. Friesland Prince, 1397 H.; Clara Vaughn, 2686 H. Milk 48 lbs. 1 day. P.
ALBANI, 592 D.-F. Friesian Bull, Van Scheltinga 2d, 370 P. R. Milk 56 lbs. 1 day, 7720 lbs. 4 oz. 328 days, P.
ALBARDA, 1175 H. Imp. Milk 48 lbs. 8 oz. 1 day, 1217 lbs. 8 oz. 30 days, P.
ALBERT, 74 H. Imp. Milk 45 lbs. 1 day, P.
ALBERTA ABBEKERK, 9579 H. Abbekerk, 296 Neth. Imp. Milk 88 lbs. 4 oz. 1 day, 2304 lbs. 5 oz. 1 month, P. Butter 3 lbs. 3 oz. 1 day, 24 lbs. 7 days, P.
ALBERTA ABBEKERK 2D, 12702 H. F. Sir Mechthilde, 2224 H. F.; Alberta Abbekerk, 9579 H. Milk 64 lbs. 12 oz. 1 day, 1822 lbs. 8 oz. 30 days, P. Butter 21 lbs. 7 days, P.
ALBERTA ABBEKERK 3D, 16405 H. F. Orlantha's Sir Henry, 3733 H. F.; Alberta Abbekerk, 9579 H. Butter 18 lbs. 6 oz. 7 days, P.
ALBERTI NIKO, 9612 H. Nico, 207 Neth. Imp. Milk 61 lbs. 4 oz. 1 day, 7154 lbs. 8 oz. 10 months, P.
ALBERTJE, 2923 H. Imp. Milk 86 lbs. 1 day, P. Butter 19 lbs. 12 oz. 7 days, P.
ALBINO, 2654 H. Imp. Milk 71 lbs. 5 oz. 1 day, P.; 13,701 lbs. 4 oz. 1 year, A.R. Butter 17 lbs. 13 oz. 7 days, A.R.
ALBINO 2D, 3500 H. Imp. Milk 65 lbs. 2 oz. 1 day, P.; 18,484 lbs. 13 oz. 1 year, A.R. Butter 25 lbs. 14 1-4 oz. 7 days, 106 lbs. 14 oz. 30 days, A.R.
ALDA, 5305 H. Imp. Milk 71 lbs. 1 day, P.
ALDINE, 2643 H. Peter, 103 Neth. Imp. Milk 14,683 lbs. 6 oz. 1 year, P.; 12,950 lbs. 10 oz. 10 months, A.R.
ALENA, 2644 H. De Valk, 160 Neth.; De Goede, 600 Neth. Milk 9173 lbs. 1 year, P.
ALENA 2D, 3808 H. F. Viking, 2002 H.; Alena, 2644 H. Milk 52 lbs. 8 oz. 1 day, P.
ALEPH, 8724 H. Netherland Prince, 716 H.; Hermstine, 1871 H. Milk 50 lbs. 1 day, P.
ALETJE, 17209 H. F. Imp. Milk 50 lbs. 1 day, P.
ALEXANDER'S QUEEN, 6998 H. Alexander, 83 Neth. Imp. Milk 52 lbs. 3 oz. 1 day, 11,295 lbs. 1 year, P. Butter 15 lbs. 4 oz.
ALEXANDER'S QUEEN 2D, 1582 H. F. Sir Henry 2d of Aaggie, 1451 H.; Alexander's Queen, 6998 H. Milk 8782 lbs. 10 oz. 10 months, A R. Butter 20 lbs. 7 days, A.R.
ALEXANDRA, 9270 H. Imp. Milk 70 lbs. 1 day, P.
ALEXANDRINA, 9284 H. Imp. Milk 87 lbs. 1 day, P. Butter 79 lbs. 6 oz. 28 days, P.
ALEXINA, 9577 H. Imp. Milk 60 lbs. 1 day. 10,032 lbs. 8 oz. 10 months, P.
ALGINA BELLE, 8604 H. F. Prins Midlu m, 2430 H.; Lina Alberdina, 4106 H. Milk 50 lbs. 1 day. 101 lbs. 7 days, P.
ALICA D, 721 H. F. Imp. Milk 48 lbs. 1 day, P.
ALICE D 2D, 5745 H. F. Parole, 391 H. F.; Alice D, 731 H. F. Milk 66 lbs. 1 day, P.; 400 lbs. 6 oz. 7 days, A. R. Butter 19 lbs. 7 days, A.R.
ALICE D 3D, 14004 H. F. Duke of Fair Haven, 4650 H. F.; Alice D. 731 H. F. Butter 12 lbs. 4 oz. 7 days, P.
ALICE OF PACIFIC, 621 H. F. Imp. Milk 11,461 lbs. 3 oz. 237 days, A.R.
ALIDA, 238 H. Imp. Milk 83 lbs. 4 oz.

J. H. D. WHITCOMB.

MILK AND BUTTER RECORDS. 315

ALIDA JONGENS, 6443 H. Imp. Milk 43 lbs. 8 oz. 1 day, 1200 lbs. 30 days, P.
ALISON, 5086 H. Imp. Milk 78 lbs. 1 day, P.
ALISON 2D, 17000 H. F. Mahomet, 289 H.; Alison, 5086 H. Milk 46 lbs. 1 day, P.
ALEO HAMMING, 2028 H. Imp. Milk 65 lbs. 1 day, P.
ALLETA TWINK, 742 H. Imp. Milk 80 lbs. 1 day, P.
ALLIE, 5963 H. Baron, 2133 H.; Dora Bleeker 2d, 5601 H. Milk 60 lbs. 1 day, P.
ALLIKY, 2357 H. Stentor, 346 H.; Valeria, 896 H. Milk 40 lbs. 1 day, P.
ALLIQUIPPA, 8506 H. Uranus of Shade and, 2575 H.; Shadeland Alma, 4911 H Milk 63 lbs. 8 oz. 1 day, 8445 lbs. 14 oz. 8 months, P.
ALMA, 1418 D.-F. De Watergus, 293 R. R.; Lady Potsma, 631 P. R. Milk 9506 lbs. 283 days, P.
ALMA DAWN, 5339 H. F. Netherlaud Convoy, 2084 H.; Cassendena, 7260 H. Milk 60 lbs. 10 oz. 1 day, 1600 lbs. 2 oz. 30 days, A.R. Butter 18 lbs. 2 oz. 7 days, 51 lbs. 4 oz. 31 days, A.R.
ALMEE, 9605 H. Imp. Milk 85 lbs. 1 day, P.; 760 lbs. 10 days, A.R. Butter 810 lbs. 10 days, P.
ALMET OF LYNWOOD, 6778 H. Imp. Milk 41 lbs. 9 oz. 1 day, P.
ALMINA, 699 H. Hector, 107 H.; Alma, 76 H. Milk 75 lbs. 1 day, P.
ALPHEA 3D, 2707 H. F. Consolation, 2431 H.; Alphea, 1158 H. Milk 45 lbs. 1 day, P.
ALPHEOLIA, 4014 H. De Valk, 160 Neth. Imp. Milk 2101 lbs. 31 days, A.R. Butter 19 lbs. 8 oz. 7 days, 36 lbs. 2 oz. 14 days, P.
ALSIE, 1631 H. Imp. Butter 15 lbs. 7 days, P.
ALTONA, 2 H. Imp. Butter 17 lbs. 14 oz. 7 days, 35 lbs. 3 oz. 14 days, P.
ALTONE, 6599 H. Imp. Milk 8245 lbs. 6 oz. 10 months 20 days, P. Butter 12 lbs. 6 oz. 7 days, P.
ALTHEA PROMOTER, 1738 H. F. Promoter, 1518 H.; Arrumer, 5768 H. Milk 1620 lbs. 7 oz. 30 days, P.
ALWINA, 6508 H. F. First Duke of Oneida, 189 D.-F. Maid of Osterend, 625 L.-F. Milk 38 lbs. 1 day, P.
ALYDA NEKO, 8074 H. Imp. Butter 16 lbs. 2 1-2 oz. 7 days, A.R.
AMAGANSETT, 8254 H. F. David, 402 F. H ; Bouthles, 1655 Neth. Milk 43 lbs. 1 day, P.
AMANDA GROYNEDD, 1009 H. Aagoo, 2*8 H.; Talma, 528 H. Milk 54 lbs. 1 day, 1516 lbs. 30 days, P.
AMARANTH, 4332 H. Imp. Milk 43 lbs. 1 day, P.
AMARILLA, 9180 H. Imp. Milk 92 lbs. 5 oz. 1 day, P.; 10,053 lbs. 12 oz. 7 months 6 days, A.R.
AMARILLA'S KONINGEN, 11948 H. F. Furness, 4270 H.; Amarilla, 9180 H. Milk 22 lbs. 1 day, P.
AMARYLLIS, 5316 H. Imp. Milk 62 lbs. 4 oz. 1 day, 10,444 lbs. 4 oz. , P. Butter 74 lbs. 5 oz. 7 days, P.
AMARYLLIS 2D, 6435 H. F. De Brave Hendrik, 230 H. F.; Amaryllis, 5316 H. Milk 46 lbs. 4 oz. 1 day, P.
AMAZON, 1833 H. Imp. Butter 9 lbs. 5 1-2 oz. 7 days, P.
AMBRA, 487 H. Imp. Milk 86 lbs. 1 day, 5279 lbs. 12 oz. 212 days, P.
AMBRONETTA, 6851 H Napoleon, 129 Neth. Imp. Milk 13,540 lbs. 1 oz. 1 year. P. Butter 16 lbs. 15 1-2 oz. 7 days, A.R.
AMEINON, 1611 D.-F. Otto Von Bismarck, 227 F.; Jannigje. Milk 68 lbs. 1 day, P. Butter 11 lbs. 7 oz. 7 days, P.
AMELANDER, 6523 H. Imp. Milk 60 lbs. 1 day, P. Butter 18 lbs. 14 oz. 7 days, A.R.
AMELANDER'S MERCEDES, 640 H. F. Mercedes Prince, 2150 H.; amelander, 6523 H. Milk 30 lbs. 8 oz. 1 day, P.; 377 lbs. 7 oz. 10 days, A.R. Butter 17 lbs. 7 days, A.R.
AMELIA, 1076 H. Aurora, 180 H.; Antjeal, 517 H. Milk 11,947 lbs. 1 year, P.
AMERICA, 8683 H. Imp. Milk 97 lbs. 1 oz. 1 day, 17,085 lbs. 11 oz. 1 year, A.R. Butter 21 lbs. 10 oz. 7 days, A.R.
AMERICA 2D, 10500 H. F. Prince of Wayne 5th, 19 Lo H.; America, 8683 H. Milk 54 lbs. 2 oz. 1 day, 8501 lbs. 8 oz. 8 months 15 days, P. Butter 13 lbs. 12 oz. 7 days, A.R.
AMERICA GRANT, 13740 H. F. America's Champion, 4056 H. F.; Nellie Grant 4th, 6024 H. Milk 42 lbs. 14 oz. 1 day, 10,241 lbs. 2 oz. 1 year, P. Butter 14 lbs. 10 oz. 7 days, P.
AMERICANA B, 16358 H. F. Promoter, 1518 H.; Americana, 8448 H. Milk 58 lbs 1 day, 1349 lbs. 4 oz. 30 days, P.
AMERICAN GIRL, 962 H. Imp. Milk 36 lbs. 1 oz. 1 day, 15,001 lbs. 1 year, P.
AMERIQUITA, 5532 H. Kurt, 120 IL ; Camilla, 102 H. Milk 956 lbs. 1 month, P.
AMETHYST, 1802 H. Imp. Milk 54 lbs. 1 day, 12,000 lbs. 1 year, P.
AMI, 7762 H. Willem, 82 Neth.; Aaltje. 711 Neth. Milk 40 lbs. 1 day, P.
AMIE, 1075 H. Keike, 266 H.; Agostina, 501 H. Milk 91 lbs. 9 oz. 1 day, P.
AMINIA, 9274 H. Imp. Milk 40 lbs. 8 oz. 1 day, P.
AMLETO, 8351 H. Imp. Milk 70 lbs. 4 oz. 1 day, 1955 lbs. 30 days, P.
AMOUR, 2046 H. De Valk, 160 H.; Hiltje 610 Neth. Milk 70 lbs. 1 day, P. Butter 1072 lbs. 30 days, P.
AMRI, 8597 H. Imp. Milk 54 lbs. 12 oz. 1 day, 9785 lbs. 8 oz. 10 months, P.
AMSTERDAM DOETJE, 10550 H. De Jouster Stier, 102 F.; Doetje, 800 F. Milk 62 lbs. 7 oz. 1 day, P.; 623 lbs. 5 oz. 10 days, A.R. Butter 23 lbs. 5 oz. 7 days, A.R.
AMY ROBSART, 1293 H. Imp. Milk 35 lbs. 1 day, 8340 lbs. 8 oz. 10 months 28 days, P.
ANAH, 9275 H. Imp. Milk 51 lbs. 8 oz. 1 day, 547 lbs. 4 oz. 10 days, P.
ANGIE, 1568 H. Jagoo, 270 H.; Tinaj, 522 H. Milk 48 lbs. 1 day, P.
ANCY, 9134, H. Imp. Milk 40 lbs. 8 oz. 1 day, 11,924 lbs. 8 oz. 1 year, P. Butter 17 lbs. 8 1-2 oz. 7 days, A.R.
ANGELINA, 1858 H. Dirk Hatterick, 219 H.; Agate, 236 H. Milk 9002 lbs. 2 oz. 10 months, A.R.
ANNA, 81 H. Imp. Milk 77 lbs. 1 day, 13 481 lbs, 11 months, P.
ANNA 2D, 473 D.-F. Nijdam, 70 F.; Anna, 535 F. Butter 14 lbs. 12 oz. 7 days, A.R.
ANNA A, 5723 H. Imp. Milk 125 lbs. 14 oz. 10 days, 1181 lbs. 1 oz. 30 days, A.R.
ANNA B 2D, 12058 H. F. Bob. Belcher, 83 H. F.; Anna B. 3943 H. Butter 7915 lbs. 6 months, P.
ANNA BATTELS, 2471 H. Sligo, 621 H.; Lady Battels, 1064 H. Milk 91 lbs. 1 day, 891 lbs. 10 days, P. Butter 26 lbs. 4 oz. 7 days, A.R.
ANNA BATTEL'S AAGGIE, 7735 H. F. Sir Newton of Aaggie, 1858 H ; Anna Battels, 2471 H. Milk 60 lbs. 1 day, P.; 679 lbs. 10 days, A.R Butter 21 lbs. 13 oz. 7 days, A.R.
ANNA BEETS, 2640 H. F. Midnight, 125 D.-F.; Dora Beets 2d, 205 D.-F. Milk 681 bs. 8 oz. 1 day, P.; 459 lbs. 7 days, A.R. Butter 21 lbs. A. oz. 7 days, A.R.
ANNA BOELYN OF SEASIDE, 3534 H. F. Halda's Empire, 3149 H.; Arminda, 2658 H. Milk 43 lbs. 1 day, P.
ANNA DEWDROP, 5407 H. Imp. Milk 720 lbs. 8 months 2 days, P.
ANNA EDMOND, 6454 H. Imp. Milk 66 lbs. 2 oz. 1 day, 2709 lbs. 4 1-2 oz. 49 days, P.
ANNA HILL, 1188 H. Imp. Milk 66 lbs. 1 day, P.
ANNA PRESTO, 3920 H. F. Presto, 390 Neth ; Anna, 5123 Neth. Milk 48 lbs. 1 day, P.
ANNA SCHOUTEN 3D, 4235 H. Imp. Milk 36 lbs. 4 oz. 1 day.

T. G. YEOMANS.

MILK AND BUTTER RECORDS. 317

ANNE, 1644 Neth. Imp. Milk 80 lbs. 3 oz. 1 day, P.
ANNEKE 4TH, 551 D.-F. Imp. Milk 62 lbs. 12 oz. 1 day
ANNELE, 53304 H. Arnold, 274 Neth. Imp. Milk 522 lbs. 2 oz. 10 days, 13,642 lbs. 2 oz. 1 year A.R. Butter 19 lbs. 6 oz. 7 days, P.
ANNELE'S MERCEDES, 10157 H. Mercedes Prince, 2150 H.; Annele, 5336 H. Milk 312 lbs. 8 oz. 10 days, A.R. Butter 12 lbs. 3 1-2 oz. 7 days, A.R.
ANNELIDA, 1678 D. F. De Nette, 324 F.; Bruinsma, 1007 F. Milk 7533 lbs. 12 oz. 8 months 1 day, A.R. Butter 9 lbs. 3 oz. 7 days, A.R.
ANNESS, 2237 H. F. Prince Opperdoes 4th. 847 H.; Alice C, 3066 H. Milk 36 lbs. 1 day, P.
ANNETTE, 957 H. Imp. Milk 40 lbs. 2 oz. 1 day, 7170 lbs. 10 months 5 days. P.
ANNIE, 242 H. Holland Prince, 113 H.; Jufron, 153 H. Milk 9018 lbs. 4 oz. 1 year, P.
ANNIE DARLING, 243 H. Holland Prince, 113 H.; Jufron, 153 H. Milk 10,510 lbs. 9 months 17 days, P.
ANNIE ELSWOUT, 78 H. Elswout Prince 95 H.; Gentle Annie, 135 H. Milk 9021 lbs. 5 oz. 1 year, P.
ANNIE LOURIE, 2752 H. Imp. Milk 1827 lbs. 7 oz. 61 days, P.
ANNIE VAN KAMPEN, 740 H. F. Hoogsearpel 1, 362 Neth.; Maartje, 4150 Neth. Milk 52 lbs. 5 oz. P. Butter 16 lbs. 10 1-4 oz. 7 days. P.
ANNIE WOOD, 244 H. Imp. Milk 53 lbs. 1 day, P.
ANTHEM, 2653 H. Imp. Milk 9146 lbs. 12 oz. 11 1-2 months, P.
ANTIGUA, 8425 H. F. Imp. Milk 82 lbs. 1 day, 703 lbs. 10 days, P. Butter 18 lbs. 7 oz. 7 days, P.
ANTIQUE, 2648 H. Imp. Milk 42 lbs. 1 day, 1976 lbs. 5 oz. 2 months, P.
ANTJE, 233 H. F. Slot, Pluisker. Milk 83 lbs. 1 day, P. Butter 19 lbs. 12 oz. 7 days, P.
ANTJE 2D, 3460 F. H. Imp. Milk 72 lbs. 8 oz. 1 day, P.
ANTJE A, 5719 H. Ruurd, 241 F. Imp. Milk 70 lbs. 1 day, P.; 19,487 lbs. 12 oz. 1 year, A. R. Butter 16 lbs. 7 oz. 7 days, A.R.
ANTJEAL, 517 H. Imp. Milk 11,387 lbs. 9 months 27 days, A.R.
ANTJE ALMA, 5857 H. Imp. Milk 86 lbs. 1 day, P.
ANTJE VRIEND, 3990 H. Imp. Milk 88 lbs. 1 day, P. Butter 28 lbs. 8 oz. 7 day, P.
ANTONION BEETS, 6420 H. Imp. Milk 65 lbs. 4 oz. 1 day, P.
ANTOINETTE, 0276 H. Imp. Milk 62 lbs. 9 oz. 1 day, 1608 lbs. 30 days, P.
ANTONE, 2512 H. Imp. Milk 42 lbs. 1 day, P. Butter 1 lb. 9 oz. 1 day, P.
ANT POEL, 6039 H. Imp. Milk 72 lbs. 1 oz. 1 day, 13,317 lbs. 10 oz. 10 months 18 days, A.R. Butter 14 oz. 7 days, A.R.
ANTRIM 2D, 246 H. Fifth Prince of Orange, 243 H.; Lady Antrim. 352 H. Milk 53 lbs. 8 oz. 1 day, 7593 lbs. 12 oz. 325 days, P.
ANVILINA, 5190 H. F. Empyrean, 1006 H.; Amulet, 3421 H. Milk 60 lbs. 1 day. P.
ANZE, 6186 H. F. Bonny Burly, 4252 H.; Orpha, 9004 H. Milk 7593 lbs. 8 months 17 days, A.R.
APHRODITE 2D, 2662 H. Imp. Milk 30 lbs. 1 day.
APPY, 1761 Neth. Imp. 82 lbs. 1 day, P.
AQUILA, 6937 H. Eilern 3d, 190 Neth. Imp. Milk 3343 lbs. 9 oz. 4 months 25 days, P.
ARAMINTA, 4831 H. Imp. Milk 43 lbs. 8 oz. 1 day, 1221 lbs. 30 days, P.
ARANZA, 6274 H. Imp. Milk 42 lbs. 1 day, P.
ARATONIE, 6412 H. F. No No, 4076 H.; Amazura, 4887 H. Milk 36 lbs. 4 oz. 1 day, P.
ARBUTUS, 2397 H. General Arthur, 720 H.; Netherland Beauty, 968 H. Milk 12,000 lbs. 1 year, P.
ARDELIA, 13519 H. F. Nannette's Ondie, 839 H. F.; Namur, 7173 H. Milk 944 lbs. 7 oz. 30 days, P.
ARDELLE, 5988 H. Imp. Milk 40 lbs. 1 day, 8061 lbs. 2 oz. 8 months 7 days, P.
ARGYREA 3D, 6696 H. F. Herder, 2331 H.; Argyrea, 9277 H. Milk 3774 lbs. 7 oz. 4 months 9 days, P. Butter 15 lbs. 5 1-4 oz. 7 days, A.R.
ARISTA, 1614 D.-F. Imp. Milk 438 lbs. 6 oz. 10 days, A.R.
ARMEDA, 8162 H. Imp. Milk 8915 lbs. 4 oz. 10 months, A.R.
ARMIDA, 1230 H. Imp. Butter 10 lbs. 8 oz. 7 days, P.
ARMINDA, 2658 H. Imp. Milk 69 lbs. 8 oz. 1 day, P.
ARNY, 1480 D.-F. Jonker, 210 F.; Afke, 2519 F. Butter 10 lbs. 8 oz. 7 days, A.R.
ARNY JACOBA HARTOG, 2800 H. F. Mooie U. Twisk, 251 D.-F.; Jacoba Hartog 5th, 219 D.-F. Milk 53 lbs. 8 oz. 1 day, 237 lbs. 8 oz. 7 days, P. Butter 13 lbs. 7 days, P.
AROOSTOOK, 7814 H. Imp. Milk 1500 lbs. 30 day, P.
ARRUMER, 5768 H. Imp. Milk 91 lbs. 1 day, P. Butter 4 lbs. 1 day, P.
ARSENIA, 7445 H. Imp. Milk 67 lbs. 6 oz. 1 day, P.
ARSENIA 2D, 2831 H. F. Sir Henry of Maplewood, 2933 H.; Atsenia, 7445 H. Milk 58 lbs. 3 oz. 1 day. Butter 21 lbs. 7 days, P.
ARTEMIA, 2657 H. Imp. Milk 8045 lbs. 10 oz. 10 months, A.R.
ARTESIA 2D, 2965 H. Imp. Milk 15,320 lbs. 10 oz. 1 year, P. Butter 13 lbs. 3 oz. 7 days, P.
ARTIS' ADIANTUM, 6012 H. Artis, 127 Neth. Imp. Milk 48 lbs. 1 day, P.; 12,622 lbs. 8 oz. 1 year, A.R. Butter 14 lbs. 4 3-4 oz. 7 days, P.
ARTIS' CARISA, 7798 H. Imp. Milk 21,934 lbs. 8 oz. 1 year, A.R.
ARTIS' EDMONIA, 7805 H. Imp. Milk 47 lbs. 8 oz. 1 day, 11,552 lbs. 1 oz. 1 year, P. Butter 15 lbs. 7 days, P.
ARTIS' EDMONIA 2D, 2903 H. F. Neptune, 711 H.; Artis' Edmonia, 7805 H. Milk 5965 lbs. 6 oz. 8 months 4 days, P. Butter 10 lbs. 6 1-2 oz. 7 days, A.R.
ARTIS' EVA, 9892 H. Artis, 127 Neth. Milk 53 lbs. 15 oz. 1 day, 7879 lbs. 9 oz. 6 months 27 days, P. Butter 16 lbs. 15 oz. 7 days, P.
ARTIS EVA'S NETHERLAND, 7005 H. F. Netherland Statesman, 3280 H.; Artis Eva, 9892 H. Milk 64 lbs. 8 oz. 1 day, 10,178 lbs. 10 months, P. Butter 2 lbs. 8 oz. 1 day, P.; 18 lbs. 10 oz. 7 days, A.R.
ARTIS' HELEN, 9906 H. Artis, 127 Neth. Milk 52 lbs. 14 oz. 1 day, P.; 16,105 lbs. 10 oz. 1 year, P. Butter 17 23-32 lbs. 7 days, A.R.
ARTIS HENGEVELD, 6079 H. Artis, 127 H.; Klasina Hengeveld 2d, 4908 H. Milk 67 lbs. 1 day, 1608 lbs. 30 days, P. Butter 23 lbs. 7 days, P.
ARTIS' JACQUETTA, 7003 H. Artis, 127 Neth. Imp. Milk 40 lbs. 14 oz. 1 day, P.; 12,041 lbs. 15 1-2 oz. 1 year, A.R. Butter 31 lbs. 12 oz. 7 days, P.
ARTIS' KASSIE, 9921 H. Artis, 127 Neth. Milk 49 lbs. 2 oz. 1 day, P.
ARTIS' KATY, 9934 H. Artis, 127 Neth.; Kaatje, 1139 Neth. Milk 42 lbs. 11 oz. 1 day, 12,423 lbs. 1 year, P. Butter 16 lbs. 8 1-2 oz. 7 days, P.
ARTIS MARTHA, 9001 H. Artis, 127 Neth.; Marijtje, 570 Neth. Butter 18 lbs. 4 oz. 7 days, P.
ARTIS' ROLLORA, 7000 H. Artis, 127 Neth. Imp. Milk 62 lbs. 2 oz. 1 day, 11,907 lbs. 3 oz. 10 months, P. Butter 22 lbs. 10 oz., P.

VIOLET FAMILY.

ARTIS ROSA, 4684 H. F. Prince of Artis, 2479 H.; Aaggie Rosa 4th, 3485 H. Milk 6829 lbs. : oz. 9 months, 16 days, P.
ARTIS' SURPRISE, 9035 H. Artis, 127 Neth. Imp. Milk 48 lbs. 2 oz. 1 day, P., 10,260 lbs. 13 oz. 10 months, P.
ARTIS VAN DER MEER, 3400 H. F. Artis, 127 Neth.; Van Der Meer, 2496 Neth. Milk 60 lbs. 1 day, P.; butter 15 lbs. 4 1-2 oz. 7 days, P.
ARUNA HARTOG, 6694 H. Mooie Hartog 4th, 418 D.-F.; Amarilla, 9189 H. Milk 65 lbs. 4 oz. 1 day, P.; 12,510 lbs. 10 oz. 9 months, A.R.
ARVINE, 2507 H. Imp. Milk 26 lbs. 1 day, P. Butter 1 lb. 9 oz. 1 day, P.
ASPASIA, 6452 H. De Graaf, 166 Neth.: Trijntje, 1080 Neth. Milk 14,745 lbs. 1 year, P.
ASTELLA, 6087 H. Imp. Milk 51 lbs. 1 day, 0372 lbs. 9 months 10 days. P.
ASTERIA, 5334 H. Arnold, 274 Neth. Imp. Milk 80 lbs. 1 day, P.
ASTORA, 2655 H. Imp. Milk 11,850 lbs. 9 months 4 days, A.R. Butter 16 lbs. 10 oz. 7 days, P.
ASTORA 2D, 2603 H. Imp. Milk 43 lbs. 1 day, P.
ASTRID, 3032 H. F. American Prince, 1430 H.; Primrose, 2205 H. Butter 20 lbs. 4 1-2 oz. 7 days, P.
ASTRID 2D, 11772 H. F. Disco, 4008 H ; Astrid, 3032 H. F. Butter 12 lbs. 10 1 2 oz. 7 days, A.R.
ATALA, 9313 H. F. Nannette's Ondit, 639 H. F.; Sumach, 453 H. Milk 7334 lbs. 7 oz. 1 year, P.
ATOSSA, 2204 H. Prince of Twisk, 1022 H.; Aafje 3d, 1522 H. Milk 57 lbs. 10 oz. 1 day, P.
ATOSSA 2D, 4569 H. F. Duplicate, 2325 H.; Atossa, 2204 H. Milk 518 lbs. 9 oz. 10 days, A.R.
ATTECA, 3817 H. F. Willem 2d, 183 Neth.; Aaltje 879 Neth. Milk 45 lbs. 1 day, 286 lbs. 8 oz. 7 days, P. Butter 16 lbs. 3 oz. 7 days, P.
AU BON MARCHE, 6378 H. Imp. Milk 54 lbs. 3 oz. 1 day, P. Butter 1 lb. 10 oz. 1 day, P.
AUBURN DAISY, 1795 D.-F. Major Pell, 53 M. R.; Dutch Girl, 427 P. R. Milk 48 lbs. 1 day, P.
AUGUSTA OF TIMBER POINT, 10280 H. Imp. Milk 63 lbs. 12 oz. 1 day, P.
AUGUSTA, 616 H. Highland Chief, 18 H.; Betti, 98 H. Milk 80 lbs. 4 oz 1 day, P.
AUKE, 364 D.-F. Imp. Milk 78 lbs. 10 oz. 1 day; 12,680 lbs. 1 oz. 9 months, P.
AULINDA 3D, 5083 H. F. Brambo, 3257 H.; Aulinda, 2362 H. Milk 316 lbs. 4 oz 7 days, A.R. Butter 16 lbs. .64 oz. 7 days, A.R.
AUNT POLLY 2D, 3556 H. F. Willem 2d 183 Neth.; Aunt Polly, 541 H. Milk 43 lbs. 3 oz. 1 day, P. Butter 10 lbs. 7 oz. 7 days, P.
AURANIA, 3337 H. F. Willem II, 190 Neth.; Trijntje, 272 Neth. Milk 65 lbs. 1 day, P.
AURELIA, 1814 D.-F. Ykema, 322 P. R.; De Gravere's Wopkje, 904 R. R. Milk 55 lbs. 1 day, P
AURORA FLOYD, 344 H. F. Imp. Milk 8 lbs. 4 oz. 1 day, P.
AURUNA HARTOG, 6694 H. F. Mooie Hartog 4th, 418 D.-F.; Amarilla, 9180 H. Milk 65 lbs. 4 oz. 1 day, 12,510 lbs. 10 oz. 9 months, P.
AUTENA, 2008 H. F. Willem 3d, 375 Neth.; Antje, 3346 H. Milk 3744 lbs. 1 year, P.
AUTOM MAID, 8712 H. F. William of Oakwood, 2005 H.; Octie, 9457 H. Milk 43 lbs. 8 oz. 1 day, P.
AUWENA, 2024 H. F. Stumpius, 312 Neth.; Annie, 2694 Neth. Milk 48 lbs. 9124 lbs. 1 year, P.
AVENA, 5902 H. Empyrean, 1006 H.; Angelina, 1808 H. Milk 10,796 lbs. 5 oz. 1 year, P.
AVENHILL, 2923 H. F. De Prins, 310 Neth.; Adeline, 1027 Neth. Milk 10,817 lbs. 11 months, P.
AVERLO, 2026 H. F. De Valk, 160 Neth ; Antje, 2009 Neth. Milk 11,006 lbs. 11 months 24 days, P.
AVOND, 2010 H. F. Adam, 270 Neth.; Aaltje, 3707 Neth. Milk 11,575 lbs. 1 year, P.
AYDELOTT, 9534 H. Imp. Milk 1875 lbs. 9 months, P.
AYESHA PEL, 10964 H. F. Commodore Pel, 349 D.-F.; Gwendoline Pel, 1072 D.-F. Milk 50 lbs. 1 day, P.
AZALEA, 7453 H. Imp. Milk 8323 lbs. 1) months, P.
AZALIA 3D, 3364 H. Billy Boelyn, 189 Neth.; Azalia, 1559 H. Butter 8 lbs. 1 day, P.
AZELDA, 1482 D.-F. Bismarck, 183 F.; Amelia, 793 F. Milk 7244 lbs. 13 oz. 8 months, 1 day, A.R. Butter 9 lbs. 3 oz. 7 days, A.R.
AZELIE, 9278 H. Imp. Milk 32 lbs. 8 oz. 1 day, P.
AZELLA, 8157 H. Imp. Milk 41 lbs. 2 oz. 1 day, P.
AZELO, 2018 H. F. Imp. Milk 48 lbs. 1 day, P.
AZUCEAH, 6881 H. Imp. Milk 12,025 lbs. 5 oz. 1 year, P.
BABY BELLE, 4053 H. Imp. Milk 50 lbs. 4 oz. 1 day. 2788 lbs. 15 oz. 62 days, P.
BAILLIE, 9753 H. Venture, 1315. H.; Negress, 5550 H. Milk 7163 lbs. 2 oz. 8 months 1 day, P.
BAISE, 9752 H. Venture, 1315 H.; Caprice, 2679 H. Butter 21 lbs. 3 1-2 oz. 7 days, P.
BAKKER, 47 D.-F. Imp. Milk 40 lbs. 1 day, P.
BAKKER 2D, 215 D.-F. Aac, 17 M. R.; Dekker, 47 D.-F. Milk 79 lbs. 1 day, P.
BAKKERDJE 2D, 5004 H. Imp. Milk 45 lbs. 8 oz. 1 day, 10,354 lbs. 2 oz. 9 months 21 days, P. Butter 17 lbs. 2 oz. 7 days, A.R
BAKKER'S BEST, 1831 D.-F. Mooie Twisk, 85 D.-F.; Bakker 2d, 215 D. F. Milk 44 lbs. 1 day, P.
BALTINA, 7217 H. Imp. Milk 9685 lbs. 9 months 25 days, P.
BANCO, 7587 H. Imp. Butter 20 lbs. 7 3 4 oz. 7 days, A.R.
BANKJE, 983 H. Imp. Milk 30 lbs. 12 oz. 1 day, 5025 lbs. 8 oz. 6 months 9 days, P.
BARBARA, 1107 H. Tegus, 373 H.; Cora, 271 H. Milk 73 lbs. 3 oz. 1 day, P.
BARBARA OF TIMBER POINT, 1360 H. F.; De Brave Hendrik, 230 H. F. Imp. Milk 52 lbs. 1 day, P.
BARNA, 12030 H. F. Jan, 686 H. Van der Lei, 4496 F. Milk 52 lbs. 1 day, P.; 503 lbs. 10 days, A.R.
BARONESS S, 5008 H. Milk 79 lbs. 1 day, 565 lbs. 10 days, P.
BASHFUL, 10154 H. Imp. Milk 40 lbs. 9 oz. 1 day, 9092 lbs. 2 oz. 1 year, P. Butter 8 lbs. 2 oz. 7 days, P.
BATJE, 2030 H. Wartena, 16 Neth.; Boukje, 94 Neth. Milk 81 lbs. 1 day, P. Butter 18 lbs. 3 oz. 7 days, P.
BAUKJE, 2670 F. H. Imp. Milk 50 lbs. 1 day, P.
BEATITUDE, 7972 H. Prince Imperial, 1164 H.; Bridesmaid, 2676 H. Milk 60 lbs. 1 day, 2120 lbs 14 oz. 2 months, P.
BEATRICE, 247 H. Von Bismarck, 169 H.; Princess Alexandra, 204 H. Milk 60 lbs. 1 day, P.
BEATRICE OF SHADELAND, 2418 H. Imp. Milk 10,063 lbs. 4 oz. 9 months, A.R.
BEAUTY, 91 H. Imp. Milk 54 lbs. 1 day, 11.313 lbs. 8 oz. 1 year, P.
BEAUTY BLOSSOM, 16141 H. F. Wacabuc. 3163 H. F.; Bertie's Beauty, 11942 H. F. Milk 7404 lbs. 1 year, P.
BEAUTY NETHERLAND, 1755 H. F. Netherland Duke, 1571 H.; Autje Loan, 4237 H. Milk 2176 lbs. 30 days, A.R.
BEAUTY OF HAMILTON 2D, 5212 H. F. Hamilton, 686 D.-F.; Beauty of Hamilton, 1908 D.-F. Milk 7546 lbs. 11 oz. 9 months 10 days, A.R.
BEAUTY OF NINON, 4541 H. Imp. Milk 28 lbs. 15 oz. 1 day, 5360 lbs. 4 oz. 7 months 13 days, P.
BEAUTY OF PINE GROVE, 4032 H. F. Netherland Monarch 2d, 1120 H. F.; Senorita, 2103 H. Milk 36 lbs. 1 day, P.

VREDA, No. 2239 H. H. R.

Imported. Milk Record, 67 lbs. one day; 1878 lbs. in thirty-one days.

MILK AND BUTTER RECORDS. 321

BEETGUMER 2D, 565 H. F. Delaware Moole, 233 D.-F.; Beetgumer, 608 D.-F. Milk 1150 lbs. 30 days, A. R.
BEETS, 1588 Neth. Imp. Milk 84 lbs. 1 day, P.
BEETJE, 8103 H. Imp. Milk 70 lbs. 8 oz. 1 day, P.
BEL, 0272 H. F. First Duke of Oneida, 180 D.-F.; Sijbrandij, 650 D.-F. Milk 55 lbs. 1 day, 1501 lbs. 30 days, P.
BELANGIA, 6650 H. F. Aaggie Idaline 4th's Roland, 4365 H.; Jacob Wit's Bernie, 7790 H. Milk 3642 lbs. 8 oz. 7 months 6 days, P.
BELASCA, 9573 H. Imp. Milk 65 lbs. 1 day, P.
BELLE, 95 H. Imp. Milk 9931 lbs. 12 oz. 323 days, P.
BELLE ALEXANDER, 4408 H. Imp. Milk 46 lbs. 11 oz. 1 day, P.; 11,318 lbs. 3 oz. 1 year, A.R. Butter 16 lbs. 9 1-2 oz. 7 days, P.
BELLE ARTIS, 4520 H. Artis, 127 Neth.; Doortje, 598 Neth. Milk 43 lbs. 13 oz. 1 day, 7850 lbs. 15 oz. 8 months, 5 days, P.
BELLE BARNUM, 2422 H. F. Forster, 2771 H.; Lady Barnum, 6281 H. Milk 46 lbs. 1 day, P. Butter 17 lbs. 15 3-4 oz. A.R.
BELLE BOYD, 4565 H. Imp. Milk 73 lbs. 1 oz. 1 day, 10,143 lbs. 7 oz., P.
BELLE CLAY, 1052 H. First Consul, 100 H.; Maud Clay, 300 H. Milk 48 lbs. 1 day, P.
BELLE DOUGLAS, 1108 H. Lord Clifden, 572 H.; Lady Douglas, 1648 H. Milk 74 lbs. 1 day, 15,506 lbs. 1 year, P.
BELLE HERBERT, 9630 H. F. Don Quixote, 1324 H.; Maquoketa Belle, 1164 H. Butter 11 lbs. 14 oz. 7 days, P.
BELLE MARGO 2D, 4846 H. Tenth Lord of Texelaar, 160 H.; Belle Margo, 1196 H. Milk 60 lbs. 1 day, P.
BELLE OF ASHLEY, 2373 H. Wouter, 450 H.; Hendrina 2d, 1558 H. Milk 47 lbs. 1 day, P.
BELLE OF LAKEVIEW, 252 H. Dictator, 82 H.; Lady Andover, 16 H. Milk 73 lbs. 1 day, 12,444 lbs. 7 months 16 days, P.
BELLE OF LAKEVIEW 3D, 1161 H. Fifth Prince of Orange, 243 H.; Belle of Lakeview, 252 H. Milk 68 lbs. 1 day, P.
BELLE OF OPPERDOES, 1232 H. Imp. Milk 54 lbs. 1 day, 8616 lbs. 1 year, P.
BELLE OF OPPERDOES 3D, 2438 H. F. Clarion, 870 H.; Belle of Opperdoes, 1232 H. Milk 7280 lbs. 10 months, P.
BELLE OF OPPERDOES 3D A, 9128 H. F. Mooike 2d's Clarion, 1995 H. F.; Belle of Opperdoes 3d, 2438 H. F. Milk 6784 lbs. 15 months, P.
BELLE OF OPPERDOES 4TH, 5273 H. F. Robert S, 3210 H.; Belle of Opperdoes, 1232 H. Milk 59 lbs. 1 day, 9433 lbs. 1 year, P.
BELLE OF OPPERDOES 5TH, 9125 H. F. Hilda's Empire, 3562 H.; Helle of Opperdoes, 1232 H. Milk 51 lbs. 1 day, 7238 lbs. 11 months, P.
BELLE OF OPPERDOES 6TH, 14245 H. F. Copia's Empire, 3559 H.; Belle of Opperdoes, 1232 H. Milk 36 lbs 1 day, P.
BELLE OF ORCHARDSIDE, 235 D.-F. Mooie, 26 M. R.; Siepkje, 120 M. R. Milk 1037 lbs. 4 oz. 1 month, P.
BELLE OF ORCHARDSIDE 2D, 6256 H. F. Rothmore, 326 D.-F.; Belle of Orchardside, 235 D.-F. Milk 54 lbs. 8 oz. 1 day, 8303 lbs. 8 oz. 230 days, P.
BELLE OF OXFORD, 461 H. F. Sterling, 215 D.-F.; Jassma Goudgeld, 42 D.-F. Milk 10,001 lbs. 10 months, A.R.
BELLE OF PACIFIC, 627 H. F. Imp. Milk 9876 lbs. 10 days, A.R.
BELLE OF RIVERVIEW, 6197 H. F. Commodore Preble, 3191 H.; Slyra of Shadeland, 9100 H. Milk 33 lbs. 12 oz. 1 day, 805 lbs. 30 days, P.
BELLE OF THE VALE, 9662 H. Alexander 2d, 171 Neth.; Trijntje, 577 Neth. Milk 8075 lbs. 1 oz. 1 year, A.R. Butter 19 lbs. 6 oz. 7 days, A.R.
BELLE OF VERONA, 8216 H. F. Neptune Fairview, 3886 H.; Mantel 2d, 2146 H. Milk 41 lbs. 1 day, P.
BELLE OF WOODSIDE, 1676 D. F. Ykema, 322 P. R.; Tiet Kaastra, 082 P. R. Milk 106 lbs. 12 oz. 1 day, P. Butter 4 lbs. 1 day, P.
BELLE PALSIFER, 166 H. F. Harold of Shadeland, 1499 H.; Kulffer 2d, 2486 H. Butter 10 lbs. 7 days, P.
BELLE RIJANETA HERBERT, 13030 H. F. Rijaneta's Don, 3507 H.; Maquoketa Girl, 1164 H. Butter 17 lbs. 8 oz. 7 days, P.
BELLE SARCASTIC, 23030 H. F. Sarcastic, 4720 H. F.; Belvisia 2d, 4353 H. F. Milk 780 lbs. .99 oz. 10 days, 18,142 lbs. .4 oz. 10 months, A.R. Butter 20 lbs. .73 oz. 7 days, 679 lbs. .88 oz. 10 months, A.R.
BELLE SETSKE, 185 H. F. Cesar, 3189 H; Setske W, 6578 H. Milk 110 lbs. 1 day, P. Butter 38 lbs. 7 oz. 7 days, P.
BELLE TOLSMA, 584 H. F. Netherland Knight, 1852 H.; Aaltje Tolsma 5th, 4689 H. Milk 30 lbs. 1 day, P.
BELLE VIKING, 2429 H. F. Viking, 2062 H.; Fanchon, 1879 H. Milk 8773 lbs. 12 oz. 8 months. A.R.
BELLE WINKLE, 1150 D. F. Wouter, 30 Neth.; Cato, 236 Neth. Milk 65 lbs. 12 oz. 1 day, 10,000 lbs. 200 days, P.
BELLE WITTOP, 1277 H. F. Don Quixote, 1324 H.; Maquoketa Belle, 1164 H. Milk 37 lbs. 12 oz. 1 day, 252 lbs. 7 days, P. Butter 13 lbs. 1 oz. 7 days, A.R.
BELLE PENTAUR, 20361 H. F. Pentaur, 3849 H ; Bell W., 6676 H. F. Milk 8212 lbs 8 months 3 days, P.
BELL WINKLE, 919 H. Imp. Milk 69 lbs. 12 oz. 1 day, P.
BELL WINKLE 4TH, 2066 H. Piet Heim. 886 H.; Bell Winkle, 919 H. Milk 34 lbs. 1 day, P.
BELL WINKLE 5TH, 3929 H. Prince of Fairview, 1138 H.; Bell Winkle 3d, 2065 H. Milk 61 lbs. 9 oz. 1 day, P.
BELSUMER, 2915 F. H. Imp. Milk 59 lbs. 1 day, P.
BENNETT, 0015 F. H. Billy Draper, 479 D. F.; Pierkje 4th, 1915 D. F. Butter 17 lbs. 7 days, P.
BENOLA FLETCHER, 6801 H. Alexander 2., 1552 H.; Bakker, 1266 Neth. Milk 13 150 lbs. 4 oz. 1 year, A. R. Butter 22 lbs. 4½ oz. 7 days P.
BENOLA FLETCHER 2D, 9817 H. Prince Imperial, 1164 H.; Benola Fletcher, 6801 H. Milk 7667 lbs. 10 months, A.R. Butter 11 lbs. 9 oz. 7 days, A.R.
BEPPO, 8418 H. Eckke, 681 H.; Maquoketa Belle, 1164 H. Milk 46 lbs. 1 day, 317 lbs. 11 oz. 7 days, P. Butter 14 lbs. 7 oz. 7 days, A.R.
BERBER, 111 D. F. Imp. Milk 40 lbs. 1 day. P.
BERGMITA, 2494 H. F. Duke of Vernon, 2399 H.; Kate 2d. 3543 H. Butter 11 lbs. 17 oz. 7 days, P.
BERKHOUT 3D, 2433 H. F. Clarion, 870 H.; Berkhout, 665 H. Milk 38 lbs. 1 day, 7397 lbs. 10 months, P.

21

YUINNE, No. 8353 H.H.B.; No. 1535 N. H. B.
Imported. Milk record, 91 lbs. in one day.

ZOZO, No. 10,260 H. H. B.; 906 ADVANCED REGISTRY.
Butter record, 25 lbs. 10 1-4 oz. in seven days; 104 lbs. 12 oz. in thirty days. Milk record, 83 lbs. 2 oz. in one day; 7025 lbs. 14 oz. in three months and fourteen days.

MILK AND BUTTER RECORDS. 323

BERKSHIRE BELLE, 530 H. Berkshire Boy, 184 H.; Gretel, 321 H. Milk 85 lbs. 1 day, P. Butter 18 lbs. 7 days, P.
BERLIKUMER, 1978 F. H. Imp. Milk 58 lbs. 8 oz. 1 day, P.
BERNADINE, 2020 H. Imp. Milk 48 lbs. 1 day, P.
BERNARDIENTJE, 6364 H. Imp. Milk 53 lbs. 1 day, P. Butter 15 lbs. 5 oz. 7 days, P.
BERNICO, 8266 H. F. Gerrit, 345 F. H.; De Zwarte, 946 F. H. Milk 58 lbs. 1 day, 571 lbs. 10 days, P.
BEROE, 5340 H. Imp. Milk 76 lbs. 1 day, P.
BERTHA ARTIS, 4526 H. Artis, 127 Neth.; Pietertje, 521 Neth. Milk 8318 lbs. 2 oz. 1 year, P.
BERTHALDA, 6860 H. Imp Milk 918 lbs. 30 days, P.
BERTHA OF SHADELAND 4TH, 16709 H. F. Netherland Monarch, 2570 H.; Bertha of Shadeland, 2406 H. Milk 6794 lbs. 12 oz. 8 months, P.
BERTHA S, 3970 H. Imp. Milk 42 lbs. 1 day, P.
BERTHINE, 2358 H. F. Pactol, 3497 H. Tinateen, 4724 H. Milk 36 lbs. 8 oz. 1 day, P.
BERTIE BRANCH, 2486 H. F. Wacabuc, 3163 H. F.; Bertie, 1084 H. Milk 7877 lbs. 1 year, P.
BERTIE's BUD, 16140 H. F. Wacabuc, 3163 H. F.; Bertie, 1084 H. Milk 8102 lbs. 1 year, P.
BERTINA, 4402 H. Imp. Milk 37 lbs. 8 oz. 1 day, 1039 lbs. 30 days, P.
BERTJE, 1729 H. Imp. Milk 48 lbs. 1 day, 10,950 lbs. 1 year, P.
BERYL, 1069 H. Billy Boelyn, 189 H.; Queen Bess, 429 H. Milk 38 lbs. 1 day, P.
BESERTA P. 5000 H. Imp. Milk 61 lbs. 1 day, P.
BESIKA, 2669 H. Imp. Milk 44 lbs. 1 day, P.
BESSIBEL, 5387 H. Imp. Milk 54 lbs. 3 oz. 1 day, 11,194 lbs. 2 oz. 9 months 3 days, P.
BESSIE ALEXANDER, 4413 H. Alexander, 83 Neth. Milk 45 lbs. 8 oz. 1 day, 9250 lbs. 1 year, P.
BESSIE ARTIS, 4522 H. Imp. Milk 48 lbs. 14 oz. 1 day, P.; 10,632 lbs. 7 oz. 1 year, A.R. Butter 13 lbs. 1 oz. 7 days, A.R.
BESSIE ARTIS 3D. 7427 H. F. Neptune, 711 H.; Bessie Artis, 4522 H. Milk 66 lbs. 15 oz. 1 day, 1942 lbs. 5 oz. 30 days, A.R. Butter 1½ lbs. 13 oz. 7 days, A.R.
BESSIE B, 1195 H. Imp. Valeria, 896 H. Milk 59 lbs. 12 oz. 1 day, 9243 lbs. 8 oz. 10 months 12 days, P.
BESSIE BELLE, 4084 H. F. Netherland Monarch 2d, 1128 H. F.; Marion 3d, 6092 H. Milk 54 lbs. 13 oz. 1 day, 11,194 lbs. 2 oz. 9 months 3 days, P.
BESSIE BLACK, 7109 H. F. Nimbus 2d. 2381 H.; De Boerin, 5311 H. Butter 15 lbs. 0 oz. 7 days, A.R.
BESSIE BLEEKER, 602 D. F. Theo, 70 H. R.; Cjietje Bleeker 4th, 167 M. R. Milk 44 lbs. 1 day, P.
BESSIE HARTOG, 10361 H. F. Moole Hartog 4th, 418 D. F.; Inara, 9428 H. Milk 63 lbs. 8 oz. 1 day, P. Butter 19 lbs. 3 oz. 7 days, P.
BESSIE I, 1686 H. Stentor, 346 H.; Rosebel, 803 H. Milk 59 lbs. 12 oz. 1 day, 650 lbs. 6 oz. 6 months, P.
BESSIE L 2D OF UPLANDS, 9804 H. Lord Bantam, 1011 H.; Bessie I, 1686 H. M lk 50 lbs. 1 day, P.
BESSIE KIZERIN, 8096 H. F. Van Kon Friesland, 1940 H. F.; Kizerin 2d, 9488 H. Butter 15 lbs. 2½ oz. 7 days, A.R.
BESSIE LOEMAN, 11717 H. F. Oakland Chief, 8250 H.; Bientje 3d. 1654 H. Milk 34 lbs. 15 oz. 1 day, 493 lbs. 13 oz. 15 days, P. Butter 11 lbs. 3 oz. 7 days, P.
BESSIE LYLE, 4538 H. Imp. Milk 60 lbs. 4 oz. 1 day, 1753 lbs. 4 oz. 30 days, P.
BESSIE PH, 5754 H. Imp. Milk 61 lbs. 1 day, P.
BETH CORNWALL, 1005 H. F. Lord of Cornwall, 3429 H.; Steady Dame, 7235 H Milk 66 lbs. 1 day P.
BETH R, 4473 H. F. Graaf Adolf, 203 Neth.; Susanna, 6123 Neth. Milk 66 lbs. 1 day, P.
BETJE, 730 H. Imp. Milk 61 lbs. 10 oz. 1 day, P.
BETSEY PRIG. 964 H. Opperdoes 4th, 2 H.; Electra, 286 H. Milk 70 lbs. 1 day, 14,000 lbs. 1 year, P.
BETSEY J, 3344 H. Imp. Milk 45 lbs. 1 day, P.
BETSY PERK, 975 H. F. Bouwke 2d, 262 Neth.; Friesin 2d, 2927 Neth. Milk 49 lbs. 1 day, P. Butter 9 lbs. 5 oz. 7 days, P.
BETSY TROTWOOD, 4418 H. Imp. Milk 4151 lbs. 10 oz. 6 months 11 days, P.
BETSY VON HOLINGEN, 17217 H. F. Lolawijk, 557 Neth. Imp. Milk 50 lbs. 1 day, P.
BETTINA, 2466 H. Midox, 986 H.; Rijaneta, 1131 H. Milk 71 lbs. 4 oz. 1 day, 409 lbs. 15 oz. 7 days, P. Butter 32 lbs. 1½ oz. 7 days, A.R.
BETTINA'S RIJANETA, 6206 H. F. Don Quixote, 1324 H.; Bettina, 2466 H. Milk 35 lbs. 8 oz. 1 day, 243 lbs. 12 oz. 7 days, P. Butter 13 lbs. 14 oz. 7 days, P.
BETTY ALEXANDER, 4403 H. Alexander, 83 Neth.; Lamberta, 576 Neth. Milk 43 lbs. 1 day, P.
BETTY MINK, 10404 H. Imp. Milk 414 lbs. 7 days, P. Butter 19 lbs. 4 oz. 7 days, P.
BEWUNDE, 1670 H. Dirk Schilp, 220; Lady Kurt, 358 H. Milk 80 lbs. 1 day, P.
BEWUNDE'S AAGGIE, 5242 H. F. Sir Newton of Aaggie, 1858 H.; Bewunde, 1670 H. Milk 89 lbs. 1 day, 869 lbs. 10 days, P. Butter 29 lbs. 3 oz. 7 days, A.R.
BIANCA, 859 H. Imp. Milk 42 lbs. 8 oz. 1 day, P.
BIBIANA'S PET, 6778 H. F. Armory, 33 H.; Bibiana, 7045 H. M lk 74 lbs. 1 day, 1610 lbs. 4 oz. 30 days, P. Butter 21 lbs. 4 oz., P.
BIENTJE 3D, 1654 H. Lord Le Baron, 538 H.; Bientje 2d, 901 H. Milk 50 lbs. 1 day, P. Butter 17 lbs. 8 oz. 7 days, P.
BILDA, 4504 H. Imp. Milk 36 lbs. 1 day, P.
BIRDIE, 897 H. Imp. Milk 44 lbs. 6 oz. 1 day, 1227 lbs. 4 oz. 30 days, P.
BIXX FUNNY 2D, 17147 H. F. Norm Ells, 4663 H. F.; Bixx Funny, 9808 H. F. Milk 5584 lbs. 180 days, P.
BLACK DELL, 4829 H. Geneva Duke, 234 H.; Almina, 609 H. Milk 54 lbs. 1 day, P.
BLACK VENUS, 1863 H. Imp. Milk 43 lbs. 1 day, P.
BLADE OF GRASS, 1421 D. F. De Watergens, 29 P. R.; Janke, 026 P. R. Milk 61 lbs. 1 day, P.
BLAINTJE 3D, 8204 H. Imp. Milk 60 lbs. 1 day, P.
BLANKSMA. 524 D. F. Imp. Milk 430 lbs. 8 oz. 10 days, P.
BLANKSMA ZWARTE 3D, 620 D. F. Leuwa der, 71 F.; Engelum. Butter 12 lbs. ⊢ oz. 7 days, A.R.
BLESKE, 2267 H. Imp. Milk 42 lbs. 1 day, P. Butter 14 lbs. 2 oz. 7 days, P.
BLISSFUL, 10155 H. Imp. Milk 48 lbs. 6 oz. 1 day, P.; 7808 lbs, 8 oz 7 months 14 days, A.R. Butter 10 lbs. 5 1-2 oz. 7 days, A.R.
BLOKJEY, 3823 H. F. Columbus, 460 Neth.; Blokje. 4515 Neth. Milk 84 lbs. 1 day, P.
BLOKKER, 390 Neth. Imp. Milk 82 lbs. 5 oz. 1 day, P.
BLOKKER 2D, 391 Neth. Imp. Milk 89 lbs. 2 oz. 1 day, P.
BLONDINE, 8397 H. Imp. Milk 61 lbs. 1 day, 10,000 lbs. 1 year, P.
BLOSSOM, 256 H. Imp. Milk 84 lbs. 1 day, P.
BLOXONI, 4423 H. F. Dirk, 33 F. H.; Sigrandi, 186 F. H. Milk 36 lbs. 1 day, P.
BLUE BERRY, 2671 H. Imp. Milk 75 lbs. 1 day, 5120 lbs. 10 oz. 4 months, P. Butter 2 lbs. 1 day, P.
BLUETTE, 1778 D. F. Cæsar, 810 F.; Koolstra, 1438 F. Milk 43 lbs. 8 oz. 1 day, P.
BODEREA LINCOLN, 9610 H. Imp. Milk 65 lbs. 12 oz. 1 day, P. Butter 8 lbs 6 oz. 1 day, P.
BOELYN ARTIS, 8021 H. F. Johnnie Boe rn, 2494 H. F.; Artis Martha, 9901 H. F. Milk 41 lbs. 1 day, P.

BACKELTJE, 1106 Neth. Imp. Milk 86 lbs. 1 day, P.
BOFIE, 3554 H. F. Nicolaas, 322 Neth.; Grietje, 1211 Neth. Milk 6120 lbs. 4 months, P. Butter 12 lbs. 4 oz. 7 days, P.
BOLSWARD, 8924 H. F. Imp. Milk 7321 lbs. 10 oz. 10 months 4 days, P.
BOMAZ 2D, 20460 H. F. Uncle Dan, 2011 H. F.; Bomaz, 20458 H. F. Milk 66 lbs. 8 oz. 1 day, 15,733 lbs. 1 year, P.
BONA, 7774 H. Walter Scott 4th, 1398 H.; Rowena B, 2592 H. Milk 80 lbs. 1 day, P. Butter 19 lbs. 7 days, P.
BONANZA MAID, 4544 H. Imp. Milk 62 lbs. 2 oz. 1 day, 14,065 lbs. 10 oz., P. Butter 25 lbs. 3½ oz. 7 days, 91 lbs. 12 oz. 30 days, P.
BONNIE ETHEL, 9510 H. Imp. Milk 62 lbs. 11 oz. 1 day P.; 606 lbs. 14 oz. 10 days, A.R. Butter 15 lbs. 11 oz. 7 days, A.R.
BONNIE JEAN, 783 H. Imp. Milk 12,152 lbs. 11 oz. 10 months 28 days, P. Butter 20 lbs. 2 oz. 7 days, P.
BONNIE NETHERLAND, 11792 H. F. Netherland Carl, 3279 H.; Bonnie Jean, 783 H. Butter 18 lbs. 11½ oz. 7 days, P.
BONNIE QUEEN, 10278 H. Imp. Milk 10,000 lbs. 6 months, P.
BONNIE SADIE, 9751 H. Venture, 1315 H.; Geddes Girl, 2735 H. Milk 40 lbs. 1 day, P.
BONNY LASS, 950 H. Imp. Milk 40 lbs. 8 oz. 1 day, 9107 lbs. 14 oz. 1 year, P. Butter 14 lbs. 7 days, P.
BONTBLES, 1665 Neth. Imp. Milk 64 lbs. 1 day, P.
BONTE TWEELING, 4332 F. H. Imp. Milk 68 lbs. 1 day, P.
BONTJE 2D, 3234 F. H. Imp. Milk 70 lbs. 1 day, P.
BONTJE P 2D, 8455 H. Major Pel, 2763 H.; Bontje P, 6216 H. Milk 69 lbs. 1 day, 645 lbs. 8 oz. 10 days, P. Butter 19 lbs. 13 oz. 7 days, P.
BONTJE P 2D's GERBEN, 23958 H. F. Consul Gerben, 4304 H. F.; Bontje P 2d, 8455 H. F. Milk 55 lbs. 12 oz. 1 day, P.
BONTJIE, 9279 H. Imp. Milk 82 lbs. 1 day, P.
BONTSCHONK, 1518 D F. David, 222 F. H.; Mooye, 202 F. H. Butter 8 lbs. 11 oz. 7 days, P.
BONTSCHONK 2D, 4717 H. F. Moole Hartog 2d, 407 D. F.; Bontschonk, 1518 D. F. Milk 58 lbs. 1 day, P.; 11,633 lbs. 12 oz. 10 months, A.R. Butter 15 lbs. 9 oz. 7 days, A.R.
BONZILLA, 6926 H. Imp. Milk 85 lbs. 8 oz. 1 day, P.; 8000 lbs. 8 oz. 90 days, A.R. Butter 22 lbs. 7 oz. 7 days, A.R.
BOONSTRA 2D, 732 H. Imp. Milk 84 lbs. 8 oz. 1 day, 2160 lbs. 30 days, P. Butter 20 lbs. 6½ oz. 7 days, A.R.
BOONSTRA 4TH, 7409 H. Endymion, 817 H.; Boonstra 2d, 732 H. Milk 48 lbs. 1 day, P.
BOONSTRA 4TH's PRINCESS, 3380 H. F. Forster, 2771 H.; Boonstra 4th, 7409 H. Milk 46 lbs. 14 oz. 1 day, P.; 10,264 lbs. 1 oz. 10 months, A.R.
BOONSTRA'S LIEUWKJE 2D, 1401 D. F. Jan; Lieuwkje. Milk 89 lbs. 8 oz. 1 day, P.
BOQUETTE, 6089 H. Imp. Milk 52 lbs. 1 day, P.
BORNIA, 2016 H. F. Veldbeer, 349 Neth.; Bontje, 1911 Neth. Milk 11,234 lbs. 11 months 10 days, P.
BOSMA, 770 F. H. Imp. Milk 75 lbs. 1 day, P.
BOSTON QUEEN 2D, 15422 H. F. Bartholdi, 4393 H.; Boston Queen, 6948 H. Milk 60 lbs. 1 day, P.
BOTJE, 5314 H. Imp. Milk 81 lbs. 1 day, P. Butter 18 lbs. 3 oz. 7 days, P.
BOUKJE, 116 D. F. Imp. Milk 21,679 lbs. 8 oz. 1 year, A.R.
BOUNTIFUL MAID, 4411 H. Imp. Milk 40 lbs. 1 day, P.
BOUNTY, 133 Neth. Imp. Milk 78 lbs. 1 day, P.
BOUTBEE's, 1655 Neth. Imp. Milk 64 lbs. 1 day, P.
BOWEN, 19041 H. F. Pel Posma, 673 F. H.; Tietje, 1084 F. H. Milk 69 lbs. 1 day, 1982 lbs. 30 days, P.
BOUWMAN, 372 Neth. Imp. Milk 76 lbs. 1 day, P.
BRACELET, 1567 D. F. Willem II, 183 Neth.; Doortje, 1812 Neth. Milk 84 lbs. 4 oz. 1 day, 12,815 lbs. 8 months, P.
BRAKENHOF, 6449 H. Imp. Milk 11,937 lbs. 11 oz. 8 months 10 days, A.R.
BRAZITJE, 8280 H. F. Imp. Milk 81 lbs. 1 day, 1975 lbs. 30 days, P. Butter 21 lbs. 3 oz. 7 days, P.
BREDA, 257 H. Imp. Milk 64 lbs. 8 oz. 1 day, 11,165 lbs. 7 months 10 days, P.
BREGJE SWART 3D, 29208 H. F. Krootje's Champion, 10179 H. F.; Bregje Swart, 2045 H. F. Milk 40 lbs. 6 oz. 1 day, 381 lbs. 10 days, P.
BREMA, 6300 H. Imp. Milk 12,837 lbs. 416 days. P.
BRENDA, 258 H. Imp. Milk 11,582 lbs. 1 year, P.
BRENTA, 2368 H. F. Dennis, 1344 H.; Meyd 3d, 2246 H. Milk 36 lbs. 12 oz. 1 day, P.
BRIDE, 653 H. Fifth Prince of Orange, 243 H.; Belle of Lakeview, 252 H. Milk 6923 lbs. 1 year, P.
BRIDE GWYNEDD, 1666 H. Iagoo, 270 H.; Evangeline, 293 H. Milk 12,331 lbs. 1 year, P.; 10,721 lbs. 9 months, 24 days, A.R.
BRIGHT PROMISE, 5799 H. Imp. Milk 100 lbs. 1 day, P.; 13,085 lbs. 11 oz. 10 months, A.R.
BRILLIANTE, 101 H. Kaiser, 22 H.; Texelaar 8th, 55 H. Milk 80 lbs. 1 day, P.
BRIMFUL, 165 Neth. Imp. Milk 92 lbs. 1 day, P.
BRIMFUL 2D, 35713 H. F. Nutford 2d, 18006 H. F.; Brimful, 8926 H. F. Milk 53 lbs 1 day, P.
BRIMSMA, 4088 H. Imp. Milk 441 lbs. 8 oz. 10 days, 7920 lbs. 1 oz. 9 months 21 days, A.R.
BRINDISI, 8434 H. F. Kalma, 86 F. H.; Ulbe, 92 F. H. Milk 404 lbs. 10 days, A.R
BRINKA, 5186 H. Imp. Milk 72 lbs. 1 day, 10,146 lbs. 8 oz. 6 months 21 days, P.
BROUKJE, 94 Neth. Imp. Milk 8 lbs. 1 day, P.
BRUGMAN, 6760 H. Imp. Milk 33 lbs. 8 oz. 1 day, P.
BRUIDJE, 1410 H. Imp. Milk 81 lbs. 8 oz. 1 day, P. Butter 19 lbs. 11 oz., P.
BRIMSMA RIKA, 5769 H. Imp. Milk 66 lbs. 8 oz. 1 day, P.
BRUNETTE, 1251 H. Imp. Milk 30 lbs. 1 day, P.
BRUNHILD, 3002 H. Napoleon, 706 H.; Christabel, 1247 H. Milk 60 lbs. 10 oz. 1 day, P.
BUCKEYE, 155 Neth. Imp. Milk 69 lbs. 1 day, P.
BUCKEYE BELLE, 1198 H. Anton, 462 H.; Saapke, 736 H. Milk 50 lbs. 1 day, 10,000 lbs. 10 months, P.
BUENIE, 4886 H. Promoter, 1518 H.; Charetta, 533 H. Milk 10,061 lbs. 4 oz. 10 months, A.R.
BUITH, 178 D. F. Imp. Milk 40 lbs. 1 day, P.
BUMBLE BEE, 8853 H. Imp. Milk 55 lbs. 8 oz. 1 day, 8002 lbs. 4 oz. 9 months, P.
BURDETTA, 8434 H. Imp. Milk 54 lbs. 1 day, P.
BURDETTA's DUCHESS, 12538 H. F. Reserve Prince, 1915 H. F.; Burdetta, 8434 H. Milk 32 lbs. 1 day, P.
BURGER, 2028 H. F. Nicholaas, 348 Neth.; Betji, 2802 Neth. Milk 49 lbs. 1 day, 1200 lbs. 30 days, P.
BURLY's WONDER, 8706 H. Burly, 394 H.; Wonder, 952 H. Butter 12 lbs. 5 oz. 7 days, A It.
BUTTER BELLE, 10143 H. Lincoln, 120 Neth. Imp. Milk 59 lbs. 4 oz. 1 day, P.; 8661 lbs. 12 oz. 6 months 14 days. A.R. Butter 10 lbs. 7 days, A.R.
BUTTERCUP, 593 H. Imp. Butter 11 lbs. 7 oz. 7 days, A.R.

MILK AND BUTTER RECORDS. 325

BUTTERFLY, 906 H Imp. Milk 88 lbs. 1 day, 9967 lbs. 1 year, F. Butter 24 lbs. 15 oz. 7 days, P.
BYRONETTE, 4506 H. F. Byron, 1101 H.; Lady Winthrop, 10130 H. Milk 41 lbs. 1 day, 1178 lbs. 8 oz. 30 days, P.

CALISTRA, 6870 H. Imp. Milk 50 lbs. 10 oz. 1 day, P.; 10,348 lbs. 1 oz. 10 months, A.R. Butter 11 lbs. 15 1-2 oz. 7 days, P.
CALPHURNIA, 5030 H. Imp. Milk 77 lbs. 1 day, 2025 lbs. 30 days, P. Butter 10 lbs. 7 oz. 7 days, P.
CAMBODIA, 8432 H. F. Jelle, 202 F.; Berlikumer, 1978 F. Milk 51 lbs. 1 day, 1386 lbs. 30 days, P.
CAMBY, 8265 H. F. Philip, 645 F. H.; Gerbug, 3941 F. H. Milk 41 lbs. 1 day, 1163 lbs. 30 days, P.
CAMEO, 1267 H. Imp. Milk 64 lbs. 7 oz. 1 day, 11,475 lbs, 1 year, P. Butter 11 lbs. 8 oz. 7 days, P.
CAMEO 2D, 3554 H. Neptune, 711 H.; Cameo, 1267 H. Milk 71 lbs. 8 oz. 1 day, P.; 5400 lbs. 4 oz. 3 months, A.R. Butter 24 lbs. 2 oz. 7 days, P.
CAMILLA, 102 H. Fourth Duke of Belmont, 12 H.; Belle of Essex, 3 H. Milk 73 lbs. 1 day, P.
CAMILLE S, 3060 H. Uncle Tom, 163 H.; Porceleintje, 508 H. Milk 9504 lbs. 11 months 3 days, P.
CAMOMILE, 8850 H. Imp. Milk 67 lbs. 8 oz. 1 day, 11,046 lbs. 4 oz. 1 year, P. Butter 15 lbs. 6 oz. 7 days, P.
CANARY, 4284 H. Imp. Milk 76 lbs. 1 day, P.
CANARY'S MERCEDES, 12596 H. F. Antje Vriend's Mercedes Prince, 2865 H. F.; Canary, 4284 H. Milk 409 lbs. 8 oz. 7 days, A.R. Butter 25 lbs. .16 oz. 7 days, A.R.
CANBY, 8265 H. F. Philips, 645 F.; Gerbug, 3941 F. Milk 59 lbs. 1 day, P.; 574 lbs. 10 days, P. Butter 19 lbs. 7 oz. 7 days, P.
CAREME, 7469 H. Imp. Milk 100 lbs. 12 oz. 1 day, 2591 lbs. 30 days, P. Butter 35 lbs. 9 oz. 7 days, 134 lbs. 10 oz. 30 days, 259 lbs. 8 oz. 60 days, P.
CAREME 3D, 12696 H. F. Sir Henry of Maplewood, 2033 H.; Careme, 7469 H. Butter 26 lbs. 7½ oz. 7 days, P.
CAREME 4TH, 15861 H. F. Colantha's Sir Henry, 3733 H. F.; Careme, 7469 H. Milk 48 lbs. 1 day, P. Butter 28 lbs. 1 day, P.
CAREME 5TH, 23135 H. F. Colantha's Sir Henry, 3733 H. F.; Careme, 7469 H. Milk 44 lbs. 1 day, P. Butter 2 lbs. 6 oz. 1 day, P.
CARENO, 1859 H. Imp. Milk 14,706 lbs. 11 oz. 10 months, 17,108 lbs. 15 oz. 1 year, A.R. Butter 20 lbs. 3 oz. 7 days, A.R.
CARENO 2D, 2102 H. Imp. Milk 40 lbs. 1 day, P.
CARL HENRY'S BEATITUDE, 21350 H. F. Carl Henry, 5654 H. F.; Beatitude, 7972 H. Milk 58 lbs. 1 day, P. Butter 17 lbs. 3½ oz. 1 day, P.
CARLOKA, 5337 H. Imp. Milk 74 lbs. 8 oz. 1 day, P.
CARLOTTA, 1266 H. Imp. Milk 71 lbs. 11 oz. 1 day, P.; 12,603 lbs. 4 oz. 1 year, A.R. Butter 22 lbs. 4 oz. 7 days, 91 lbs. 2½ oz. 30 days, P.
CARLOTTA 2D, 3555 H. Netherland Prince, 716 H.; Carlotta, 1266 H. Milk 76 lbs. 8 oz. 1 day, 8394 lbs. 2 oz. 8 months 11 days, P. Butter 31 lbs. 12 oz. 7 days, 119 lbs. 12 oz. 30 days, 230 lbs. 8 oz. 60 days, P.
CARLOTTA 3D, 5073 H. F. Netherland, 716 H.; Carlotta, 1266 H. Milk 7611 lbs. 13 oz. 10 months, A.R. Butter 11 lbs. 3½ oz. 7 days, A.R.
CARMELINE 2D, 10243 H. Primate, 880 H.; Carmeline, 1570 H. Milk 52 lbs. 1 day, P.
CARNATION, 571 H. Imp. Milk 68 lbs. 1 day, P.
CAROL, 1422 H. F. Cossack, 2008 H.; Agrippina, 7201 H. Milk 9-77 lbs. 8 oz. 1 year, 10,433 lbs. 10 oz. 14 months, A.R.
CAROLYN, 7704 H. F. Prins Midlum, 2139 H.; Anna Jelsum, 4135 H. Milk 3425 lbs. 2 oz. 5 months, P.
CARREN WASE, 3249 H. Klaas, 2201 H.; Sjnt, 6586 H. Milk 91 lbs. 8 oz. 1 day, P. Butter 36 lbs. 13 oz. 7 days, P.
CARRICK'S CLIFDEN, 6345 H. F. Lord Clifden 2d, 616 H. F.; Carrick, 7282 H. Butter 13 lbs. 12 oz. 7 days, A.R.
CARRIE, 589 H. Imp. Milk 61 lbs. 1 day, P.
CARRIE ASTREA, 520 H. F. Black Boy, 2176 H.; Astrea 3d, 1907 H. Milk 99 lbs. 1 day. Butter 32 lbs. 3 oz. 7 days, P.
CARRIE FAIR, 4415 H. Imp. Milk 36 lbs. 10 oz. 1 day, P.
CARRIE FAIR 2D, 1574 H. F. Neptune, 711 H.; Carrie Fair, 4415 H. Milk 940 lbs. 30 days, P.
CARRIE S, 3056 H. Neptune, 711 H.; Valley Queen, 851 H. Milk 50 lbs. 1 day, 1601 lbs. 30 days, P.
CARRIE SLADE, 8856 H. F. Turk, 3244 H.; Snapke 2d, 6180 H. Milk 7933 lbs. 9 oz. 10 months, A.R.
CASSENDENA, 7269 H. Imp. Milk 92 lbs. 8 oz. 1 day, P.; 4739 lbs. 60 days, A.R. Butter 23 lbs. 10 oz. 7 days, A.R.
CASSIE HECKENDOWN, 3315 H. Sir William, 155 H.; Vesta of Potsdam, 470 H. Milk 76 lbs. 1 day, P. Butter 71 lbs. 10 oz. 30 days, P.
CASSIE HECKENDOWN 2D, 8357 H. Mr. Chuffy, 556 H.; Cassie Heckendown, 3315 H. Milk 62 lbs. 1 day, P.
CASSIE HECKENDOWN 3D, 8358 H. Prince of Twisk, 1055 H.; Cassie Heckendown, 3315 H. Butter 71 lbs. 10 oz. 30 days, P.
CASTINE, 3796 H. Imp. Milk 98 lbs. 10 oz. 1 day, 1898 lbs. 30 days, P. Butter 21 lbs. 7 days, 98 lbs. 10 oz. 30 days, P.
CASTOR'S ISABELLE, 4803 H. F. Imp. Milk 52 lbs. 1 day, P.
CATALPA 2D, 2099 H. Imp. Butter 8 lbs. 14½ oz. 7 days, P.
CATHARINA, 105 H. Imp. Milk 70 lbs. 1 day, P.
CATO 2D, 1224 H. Imp. Milk 41 lbs. 8 oz. 1 day, P.
CATO BRANTJES, 6015 H. Bouke, 100 Neth.; Princes, 407 Neth. Milk 69 lbs. 1 day, P.
CATRINA, 100 H. Imp. Milk 70 lbs. 1 day, P.
CAVI, 7837 H. Imp. Milk 42 lbs. 1 day, P.
CECILIA ROOKER, 9056 H. Jacob Wit, 34 Neth. Imp. Milk 44 lbs. 13 oz. 1 day, P.; 10,514 lbs. 4 oz. 1 year, A.R. Butter 22 lbs. 13½ oz. 7 days, 93 lbs. 14½ oz. 30 days, P.
CECILIA ROOKER 2D, 3179 H. F. Prince Imperial, 1164 H.; Cecilia Rooker, 9056 H. Butter 13 lbs. 13 oz. 7 days, P.
CELANDINE 3D, 6438 H. F. De Brave Hendrik, 230 H. F.; Celandine, 8850 H. Milk 50 lbs. 8 oz. 1 day, 7637 lbs. 12 oz. 9 months, P. Butter 8 lbs. 8 oz. 7 days, P.
CELESTE, 1836 H. Imp. Milk 50 lbs. 1 day, P.
CELESTE 2D, 3900 H. Iriquols, 1074 H.; Celeste, 1836 H. Milk 65 lbs. 1 day, 1880 lbs. 30 days, P.
CELESTE 3D, 2866 H. F. Viking, 2002 H. Celeste, 1836 H. Milk 107 lbs. 8 oz. 1 day, P.; 10,071 lbs. 12 oz. 6 months, A.R.
CELESTE 4TH, 5927 H. F. Viking, 2002 H.; Celeste, 1836 H. Milk 14,102 lbs. 11 months 12 days, P.

CELESTE S, 3052 H. Neptune, 711 H.; Isis 2d, 337 H. Milk 40 lbs. 1 day, P.; 12,524 lbs. 9 months 26 days, A.R.
CELIA S, 3760 H. Bounce Gwynne, 1005 H.; Ancle, 1568 H. Milk 8052 lbs. 1 year, P.
CELINE, 1828 H. Imp. Milk 10,903 lbs. 9 oz. 1 year, P.
CESNA, 8332 H. Imp. Milk 47 lbs. 8 oz. 1 day, P.
CHARITY, 1804 H. Imp. Milk 35 lbs. 6 oz. 1 day, 11,575 lbs. 4 oz. 1 year, P.
CHARITY 6TH, 1677 H. F. Viking, 2026 H.; Charity, 1804 H. Milk 56 lbs. 1 day, 8183 lbs. 4 oz. 7 months A.R.
CHARITY 7TH, 5098 H. F. Viking, 2026 H.; Charity, 1804 H. Butter 10 lbs. 12½ oz. 7 days, A.R.
CHARLINE, 6845 H. Imp. Milk 45 lbs. 1 day, 1327 lbs. 30 days, P.
CHATERDAAM, 8260 H. F. Oneides, 817 F.; Walma, 1504 F. Milk 60 lbs. 1 day, P.
CHAUTAUGUA GIRL, 1177 H. Imp. Milk 85 lbs. 1 day, 2400 lbs. 30 days, P.
CHERI, 321 Neth. Imp. Milk 39 lbs. 1 day, P.
CHERRY CREEK GIRL, 4196 H. Imp. Milk 6½ lbs. 1 day, 325 lbs. 7 days, P. Butter 16 lbs. 4 oz. 7 days, P.
CHERRY CREEK QUEEN, 2582 H. Imp. Milk 51 lbs. 1 day, P. Butter 2 lbs 4 oz. 1 day, P.
CHESTER MAID, 12239 H. F. Robet, 4610 H.; Kiola, 402 H. F. Milk 50 lbs. 1 day, P.
CHICOPA, 984 H. Imp. Milk 40 lbs. 1 day, P.
CHLOE, 670 H. Imp. Milk 75 lbs. 1 day, P.; 9,771 lbs. 6 oz. 11 months 26 days, A.R. Butter 16 lbs. 14 oz. 7 days, A.R.
CHLOE ARTIS, 4848 H. F. Artis, 127 Neth.; Princesje, 520 Neth. Milk 39 lbs. 3 oz. 1 day, 5297 lbs. 6 months 2 days, P. Butter 15 lbs. 1 oz. 7 days, P.
CHLOE VON HARLINGEN, 12378 H. F. Archibald, 383 D. F.; Chloe H, 16 D. F. Milk 6516 lbs. 14 oz. 7 months, P.
CHRISTABEL, 1247 H. Imp. Milk 70 lbs. 1 day, P. Butter 27 lbs. 6 oz. 7 days, P.
CHRISTABEL 2D, 8080 H. Nicolaas 2d, 451 H.; Christabel, 1247 H. Milk 60 lbs. 1 day, P.
CHRISTATA, 7855 H. Imp. Milk 52 lbs. 5 oz. 1 day, 4104 lbs. 5 oz. 3 months, P.
CHRISTINA, 719 H. Imp. Milk 80 lbs. 4 oz. 1 day, 13,099 lbs. 10 months, P.
CICILY, 9282 H. Imp. Milk 39 lbs. 1 day, P.
CJRIETJI BLEEKER, 5 D. F. Imp. Milk 14,220 lbs. 1 year, P.
CLACK, 9310 H. Imp. Milk 38 lbs. 1 day, P.
CLARA, 2852 Neth. Imp. Milk 90 lbs. 1 day, P.
CLARA ARTIS, 4524 H. Artis, 127 Neth.; Princesje 520 Neth. Milk 7408 lbs. 12 oz. 290 days, P.
CLARA PEL, 17638 H. F. Prince Serraris, 1726 H. F.; Pel 4th. Milk 44 lbs. 1 day, P.
CLARA S, 3058 H. Iagoo, 270 H.; Antjeal, 517 H. Milk 9808 lbs. 9 months 20 days, P.
CLARA VAUGHN, 2086 H. Imp. Milk 63 lbs. 1 day, P.
CLARDIE, 8539 H. Imp. Milk 45 lbs. 1 day, P.
CLARICE S, 3761 H. Bounce Gwynne, 1005 H.; Amanda Gwynedd, 1609 H. Milk 9407 lbs. 10 months 4 days, P.
CLARINDA, 1042 H. Tenth Lord of Texelaar, 160 H.; Zuider Zee 17th, 485 H. Butter 10 lbs. 12 oz. 7 days, A.R.
CLARIONET, 8922 H. Imp. Milk 38 lbs. 1 day, 8058 lbs. 12 oz. 11 months 2 days, P.
CLARISSA, 2288 H. Imp. Milk 51 lbs. 1 day, 1431 lbs. 1 month, P.
CLASINA, 1212 Neth. Imp. Milk 87 lbs. 1 day, P.
CLASINA OF TIMBER POINT, 1358 H. F. Imp. Milk 44 lbs. 1 day, P.
CLAUDE, 6144 H. Imp. Milk 10,156 lbs. 1 year, P.
CLEARY, 8277 H. F. Rintje, 427 F. Baukje, 2610 F. Milk 53 lbs. 1 day, P.; 466 lbs. 10 days, A.R. Butter 19 lbs. 13 oz. 7 days, P.
CLEMENTINE, 1789 H. Imp. Milk 62 lbs. 7 oz. 1 day, 11,721 lbs. 1 year, P.
CLINTONIA 3D, 10830 H. F. Barrington, 2103 H.; Clintonia, 6294 H. Milk 56 lbs. 1 day, 1600 lbs. 30 days, P.
CLOTHILDE, 1308 H. Imp. Milk 101 lbs. 2 oz. 1 day, P.; 26,021 lbs. 2 oz. 1 year, A.R. Butter 28 lbs. 2¼ oz. 7 days, 95 lbs. 2¼ oz. 30 days, A.R.
CLOTHILDE 2D, 1541 H. Imp. Milk 97 lbs. 14 oz. 1 day, P.; 23,602 lbs. 10 oz. 1 year, A.R. Butter 30 lbs. 8 oz. 7 days, A.R.; 119 lbs. 14¾ oz. 30 days, P.; 320 lbs. 1¾ oz. 90 days, A.R.
CLOTHILDE 2D's DUCHESS, 6401 H. Duke of Manheim, 2118 H.; Clothilde 2d, 1451 H. Milk 11,524 lbs. 15 oz. 10 months, A.R. Butter 19 lbs 15¼ oz. 7 days, P.
CLOTHILDE 3D, 2091 H. Uncle Tom, 103 H.; Clothilde, 1308 H. Milk 10,718 lbs. 1 year, P. Butter 15 lbs. 6 oz. 7 days, A.R.
CLOTHILDE 3D's COUNTESS, 2902 H. F. Prince Imperial, 1164 H.; Clothilde 3d, 2091 H. Milk 9300 lbs. 8 oz. 1 year. Butter 13 lbs. 14¼ oz. 7 days, A.R.
CLOTHILDE 4TH, 3480 H. Netherland Prince 716 H.; Clothilde, 1308 H. Milk 68 lbs. 14 oz. 1 day, 26,021 lbs. 8 oz. 1 year, P. Butter 23 lbs. 10¼ oz. 7 days, A.R.; 93 lbs. 1½ oz. 30 days, P.
CLOTHILDE 5TH, 8460 H. Netherland Prince, 716 H.; Clothilde, 1308 H. Milk 10,072 lbs. 14 oz. 1 year, P. Butter 21 lbs. 10 oz. 7 days, A.R.
CLOTHILDE 6TH, 1561 H. F. Netherland Prince, 716 H.; Clothilde, 1308 H. Milk 9519 lbs. 8 oz. 10 months 8 days, P. Butter 18 lbs. 11½ oz. 7 days, A.R.
CLOTHILDE 8TH, 11094 H. F. Netherland Prince, 716 H.; Clothilde, 1308 H. Butter 14 lbs. 5 oz. 7 days, P.
CLOTHILDE NETHERLAND, 17957 H. F. Netherland Prince, 716 H.; Clothilde 2d, 1451 H. Butter 11 lbs. 10 oz. 7 days, P.
CLOVERDALE QUEEN, 11734 H. F. Shadeland Mars, 2384 H F.; Ramonia W, 9325 H. F. Milk 50 lbs. 1 day, P.; 300 lbs. 10 days, A.R.
CLOVER LEAF 2D, 2684 H. Imp. Milk 57 lbs. 1 day, P.
CLOVER TOP, 1082 H. Saladin, 336 H.; Milk Maid, 194 H. Milk 46 lbs. 1 day, P.
CLYTE, 549 H. Imp. Milk 63 lbs. 8 oz. 1 day, 1768 lbs. 8 oz. 31 days. Butter 9 lbs. 12 oz. 7 days, A.R.
CLYTE B, 4509 H. F. Mooie, 26 D. F.; Clyte, 549 H. Milk 85 lbs. 8 oz. 1 day, 6501 lbs. 8 oz. 10 months, P.
CLYTE VAN TIEL JANET, 11929 H. F. Sir Van Tiel, 3681 H. F.; Clyte B, 4509 H. F. Milk 438 lbs. 10 oz. 7 days, P. Butter 21 lbs. 2½ oz. 7 days, A.R.
CNOSSEN, 780 F. II. Imp. Milk 78 lbs. 1 day, P.
COBA 2D, 1358 D F. Justus, Coba. Milk 70 lbs. 1 day, P.; 14,127 lbs. 6 oz. 10 months 18 days, A.R.
COBWEB, 10156 H. Imp. Milk 45 lbs. 12 oz. 1 day, 8286 lbs. 14 oz. 1 year, P. Butter 8 lbs. 9 oz. 7 days, P.
COIRA, 3142 H. Imp. Milk 67 lbs. 1 day, P.
COLANTHA, 6714 H. Imp. Milk 70 lbs. 1 day, 12,057 lbs. 8 oz. 10 months, P. Butter 31 lbs. 7 oz. 7 days, P.

COLANTHA 2D, 21933 H. F. Sir Henry of Maplewood, 2933 H.; Colantha, 6714 H. Butter 20 lbs. 13 oz. 7 days, P.
COLANTHA 3D, 30837 H. F. Aaggie Cornelia 5th's Clothilde Imperial, 11822 H. F.; Colantha, 6714 H. Milk 287 lbs. 5 oz. 7 days, A.R. Butter 12 lbs. 8 oz. 7 days, A.R.
COLANTHA ECHO, 7601 H. F. Echo's Prince of Wayne, 31 H. F.; Colantha, 6714 H. Milk 47 lbs. 5 oz. 1 day, P. Butter 5 lbs. 2 oz. 2 days, P.
COLO, 5298 H. Imp. Milk 72 lbs. 8 oz. 1 day, P.
COLOMBA, 3144 H. Imp. Milk 56 lbs. 1 lay, P.
COLUMBIA CLOTHILDE, 33365 H. F. Sir Netherland Clothilde, 8517 H. F.; Clothilde 2d's Duchess, 6401 H. Milk 278 lbs. 3 oz. 7 days, A.R. Butter 9 lbs. .77 oz. 7 days, A.R.
COMEDIA, 6097 H. Imp. Milk 51 lbs. 6 oz. 1 day, 13,501 lbs. 1 oz. 1 year, P. Butter 17 lbs. 8½ oz. 7 days, P.
COMLY KOOPMAN, 8398 H. Imp. Milk 64 lbs. 1 day, 1730 lbs. 30 days, P. Butter 2 lbs. 9 oz. 1 day, P.
COMO, 8083 H. Imp. Milk 74 lbs. 1 day, 1975 lbs. 8 oz. 30 days, P.
CONCORDIA, 10148 H. Roel, 184 F.; Groete Bles, 203 F. Milk 86 lbs. 5 oz. 1 day, P.; 17,146 lbs. 6 oz. 1 year, A.R. Butter 25 lbs. 8½ oz. 7 days, P.; 94 lbs. 8½ oz. 30 days, A.R.
CONCORDIA 2D, 10511 H. F. Royal Aaggæ, 3463 H.; Concordia, 10148 H. Milk 58 lbs. 11 oz. 1 day, 14,433 lbs. 13 oz. 1 year, P. Butter 18 lbs. 15 4-5 oz. 7 days, P.
CONCORDIA 2D'S AMERICA, 22979 H. F. America's Champion, 4056 H. F.; Concordia 2d, 10511 H. F. Milk 47 lbs. 4 oz. 1 day, P.; 12,120 lbs. 3 oz. 1 year, A.R. Butter 11 lbs. 4 oz. 7 days, A.R.
CONSTANCE, 111 H. Imp. Milk 8634 lbs. 8 oz. 1 year, P. Butter 9 lbs. 3 oz. 7 days, A.R.; 353 lbs. 1 year, P.
CONSTANCE S, 3057 H. Crown Prince 3d, 625 H.; Kathrin, 510 H. Milk 83 lbs. 1 day, 2287 lbs. 30 days, P.
COPIA, 1067 H. Billy Boelyn, 189 H.; Coronet, 544 H. Milk 90 lbs. 8 oz. 1 day, 2747 lbs. 12 oz. 31 days, P.
COPIA 2D, 1045 H. F. Empire, 588 H.; Copia, 1067 H. Milk 40 lbs. 1 day, P.
COQUETTE, 909 H. Imp. Milk 60 lbs. 1 day, P.
CORA ARTIS, 4321 H. Imp. Milk 51 lbs. 15 oz. 1 day, 10,566 lbs. 6 oz. 1 year, P. Butter 18 lbs. 13½ oz. 7 days, P.
CORA BELLE SPAANZ, 2077 H. Brithart, 633 H.; Mina Spaanz, 1104 H. Milk 63 lbs. 8 oz. 1 day, A.R.; 14,453 lbs. 12 oz. 1 year, P.
CORA GUTHRIE, 4147 H. Benson, 1506 H.; Carnation, 571 H. Milk 42 lbs. 1 day, P.
CORAI, 907 H. Imp. Milk 12,141 lbs. 12 oz. 8 months 13 days, A.R.
CORA S, 3759 H. Crown Prince 3d, 625 H.; Katinka 2d, 491 H. Milk 48 lbs. 1 day, 9626 lbs. 10 months 13 days, P.
CORDELIA, 922 H. Imp. Milk 91 lbs. 1 day, 8725 lbs. 12 oz. 6 months, P.
CORELIA YKEMA, 4527 H. F. Ykema, 322 D. F.; Antje Santema, 945 D. F. Milk 62 lbs. 8 oz. 1 day, 10,000 lbs. 240 days, P.
CORIANDER, 3568 H. Imp. Milk 400 lbs. 7 days, P.
CORIANDER 2D, 3568 H. Imp. Milk 464 lbs. 7 oz. 10 days, 8768 lbs. 12 oz. 7 months 20 days, A.R.
CORINGA, 3134 H. Imp. Milk 51 lbs. 1 day, P.
CORINNE OF OAKHURST, 2773 H. F. Clovis, 3303 H.; Loulie, 6052 H. Milk 1975 lbs. 8 oz. 1 month, P.
CORMOREND, 6458 H. Imp. Milk 10,671 lbs. 9 months 27 days, A.R.
CORNELIA, 570 H. Imp. Milk 87 lbs. 1 day, P.
CORNELIA 2D, 563 D. F. Douwe Cornelia. Milk 68 lbs. 6 oz. 1 day, P.
CORNELIA BRANTJES, 6017 H. Bouwke, 180 Neth.; Elizabeth, 724 Neth. Milk 60 lbs. 1 day, P.
CORNELIA COOK, 4529 H. Imp. Milk 70 lbs. 8 oz. 1 day, P.
CORNELIA DEKKER, 6447 H. Imp. Milk 50 lbs. 1 day, P.
CORNELIA KOL, 5703 H. Imp. Milk 46 lbs. 1 day, P.
CORNELIA KOL 2D, 1656 H. F. Imp Cornelia Kol, 5703 H. Milk 38 lbs. 1 day, P.
CORNELIA L, 3049 H. Imp. Milk 68 lbs. 1 day, P.
CORNELIA TENSEN, 1817 H. F. Clymax, 70 Neth.; Cornelia, 750 Neth. Milk 81 lbs. 1 day, 10,000 lbs. 10 months, P. Butter 3 lbs. 4 oz. 1 day, 19 lbs. 7 days, P.
CORNELIA V, 4243 H. Imp. Milk 58 lbs. 1 day, P.
CORNELISJE, 1672 Neth. Imp. Milk 70 lbs. 1 day, P. Butter 10 lbs. 2 oz. 7 days, P.
CORNELISJE, 971 H. F. Imp. Milk 48 lbs. 1 day, P. Butter 10 lbs. 2 oz. 7 days, P.
CORNUCOPIA, 8087 H. Imp. Milk 35 lbs. 14 oz. 1 day, P.; 7969 lbs. 13 oz. 10 months, A.R. Butter 12 lbs. 11½ oz. 7 days, A.R.
CORONET, 544 H. Imp. Milk 66 lbs. 1 day, P. Butter 10 lbs. 1 day, P.
CORRENNA, 5994 H. F. Billnoble, 3729 H. Bedott, 4828 H. Milk 2648 lbs. 3 oz. 3 months 12 days. Butter 10 lbs. 2½ oz. 7 days, A.R.
CORINNE, 1396 H. Imp. Milk 50 lbs. 10 oz. 1 day, 1304 lbs. 30 days, P.
CORINNE OF OAKHURST, 2773 H. F. Clovis, 3303 H.; Loolie, 6052 H. Milk 2515 lbs. 10 oz. 2 months 18 days, P. Butter 13 lbs. 13 oz. 7 days, P.
CORTICELLI, 5386 H. Imp. Milk 18,776 lbs. 12 oz. 10 months, A.R.
COSMELLA, 7828 H. Imp. Milk 40 lbs. 1 day, P.
COUNTESS, 843 H. Imp. Milk 50 lbs. 1 day, P.
COUNTESS CLOTHILDE, 21580 H. F. Count Clothilde, 9915 H. F.; Clothilde 6th's Netherland, 8329 H. F. Milk 316 lbs. 5 oz. 7 days, A.R. Butter 15 lbs. 2 oz. 7 days, A.R.
COUNTESS OF CLOTHILDE, 33364 H. F. Sir Netherland Clothilde, 8517 H. F.; Clothilde 3d's Countess 2802 H. F. Milk 305 lbs. 9 oz. 7 days, A.R. Butter 10 lbs. 4 oz. 7 days, A.R.
COUNTESS OF FLANDERS, 112 H. Imp. Milk 67 lbs. 1 day, P.
COUNTESS OF FLANDERS 3D, 273 H. Bleecker, 3 H.; Countess of Flanders, 112 H. Milk 72 lbs. 1 day, P.; 11,411 lbs. 8 oz. 9 months 18 days, A.R. Butter 18 lbs. 1 oz. 7 days, 25 lbs. 9 oz. 10 days, A.R.
COUNTESS OF FLANDERS 4TH, 1240 H. Beaconsfield, 401 H.; Countess of Flanders, 112 H. Milk 1835 lbs. 30 days, P. Butter 14 lbs. 10 oz. 7 days, P.
COUNTESS OF FLANDERS 8TH, 3430 H. Van Strader, 1043 H.; Countess of Flanders 6th, 1511 H. Butter 25 lbs. 9 oz. 7 days, P.
COUNTRY GIRL, 1882 H. Imp. Milk 54 lbs. 3 oz. 1 day, 7421 lbs. 8 oz. 7 months, P.
COUSIN PENSIE, 9914 H. F. Prins Maurits, 4633 H.; Madam Monica, 2102 H. Milk 50 lbs. 4 oz. 1 day, 12,061 lbs. 8 oz. 1 year, A.R. Butter 31 lbs. 6½ oz. 7 days, A.R.
COVEY, 8272 H. F. Hobbema 2d, 682 D. F.; Terpstra 2d, 4765 F. Milk 63 lbs. 1 day. 613 lbs. 10 days, P.
COWSLIP, 274 H. Imp. Milk 690 lbs. 10 days, P.
CRARY HENGERVELD, 807 H. F. Prince Kaperus, 121 D. F.; Aaltje Hengerveld 2d, 13 D. F. Butter 16 lbs. 6 oz. 7 days, A.R.

CREAMER, 9401 H. Imp. Milk 41 lbs. 1 day, 10,022 lbs. 2 oz. 1 year, P. Butter 13 lbs. 3 oz. 7 days, A.R.
CRESCENT, 276 H. Rip Van Winkle, 35 H.; Fraulein, 9 H. Milk 37 lbs. 1 day, P.
CRISTATA, 7835 H. Imp. Milk 52 lbs. 5 oz. 1 day, P.
CROCALE, 5360 H. Imp. Milk 71 lbs. 1 day, P.
CROWN JEWEL, 2000 H. Imp. Milk 81 lbs. 13 oz. 1 day, P.; 14,724 lbs. 1 oz. 1 year, A.R. Butter 19 lbs. 9 oz. 7 days, A.R.
CROWN JEWEL 2D, 2607 H. Imp. Milk 53 lbs. 8 oz. 1 day, 9742 lbs. 5 oz. 1 year, P.
CROWN JEWEL 3D, 317 H. F. Netherland Prince, 716 H.; Crown Jewel, 2000 H. Milk 8153 lbs. 0½ oz. 10 months, A.R. Butter 14 lbs. 12 oz. 7 days, P.
CROWN PRINCESS, 6 H. Imp. Milk 74 lbs. 8 oz. 1 day, 14,027 lbs. 1 year, P.
CRYSTAL, 048 H. Imp. Milk 59 lbs. 10 oz. 1 day, P.; 13,143 lbs. 5 oz. 10 months, A.R. Butter 16 lbs. 7 days, A.R.
CUSHA 2D, 9747 H. Jacob Wit, 2662 H.; Cusha, 5026 H. Milk 41 lbs. 1 day, P.
CYBELE, 5291 H. Imp Milk 100 lbs. 8 oz 1 day, 13.031 lbs. 8 oz. 1 year, P. Butter 15 lbs. 8 oz. 7 days, P.
CYNTHIA, 8100 H. Imp. Milk 84 lbs. 1 day, 11,333 lbs. 8 months, P.
CZARINA, 1837 H. Imp. Milk 53 lbs. 1 day, 4726 lbs. 122 days, P. Butter 8 lbs. 7 days, P.

DAFFODIL, 1318 H. Imp. Milk 9488 lbs. 5 oz. 1 year. Butter 18 lbs. 3½ oz. 7 days, P.
DAINTY DOT, 1805 H. Imp. Milk 65 lbs. 1 day, 12,790 lbs. 1 year, P.
DAINTY NICO, 4053 H. Imp. Milk 58 lbs. 4 oz. 1 day, P.; 13,305 lbs. 8 oz. 10 months, A.R. Butter 25 lbs. 7 days, P.
DAINTY NICO 2D, 15109 H. F. Jacob Clifden, 2318 H.; Dainty Nico, 4653 H. Butter 10 lbs. 5⅜ oz. 7 days, A R.
DAINTY RUTH, 9515 H. F. Furst Heksl, 3809 H.; Rustle, 7818 H. Milk 8887 lbs. 1 oz. 10 months, A.R.
DAINTY S, 3787 H. Crown Prince 3d, 625 H.; Dairy Maid, 610 H. Milk 11,586 lbs. 1 year, P.
DAIRY MAID, 610 H. Imp. Milk 11,019 lbs. 9 months 24 days, A.R.
DAISY, 113 H. Hamilcar, 17 H.; Hebe, 12 H. Milk 36 lbs. 1 day, P.
DAISY A, 3450 H. Promoter, 1518 H.; Aafje 3d, 1522 H. Milk 42 lbs. 1 day, P.
DAISY ALEXANDER, 4400 H. Imp. Milk 7749 lbs. 1 year, P.
DAISY ARTIS, 4523 H. Imp. Milk 9000 lbs. 1 year, P. Butter 13 lbs. 11 oz. 7 days, P.
DAISY ARTIS 2D, 8005 H. Netherland Prince, 716 H.; Daisy Artis, 4523 H. Milk 9394 lbs. 2 oz. 1 year, P. Butter 17 lbs. 7 oz. 7 days, 72 lbs. 12½ oz. 30 days, P.
DAISY BURKE, 22014 H. F. Lord Burke, 11731 H. F; Daisy H 3d, 13021 H. F. Milk 35 lbs. 8 oz. 1 day, P.
DAISY COOK 3D, 2555 H. F. Remington, 1716 H.; Daisy Cook, 1681 H. Milk 47 lbs. 1 day, P.; 9640 lbs. 8 oz. 1 year, A.R. Butter 15 lbs. 7 oz. 7 days, A.R.
DAISY DALE, 2604 H. Imp. Milk 38 lbs. 1 day, 1085 lbs. 2 oz. 30 days, P. Butter 9 lbs, 8 oz. 7 days, P.
DAISY DE KOL, 20201 H. F. De Kol 2d's Prince, 2767 H. F.; Bella Barnum, 2422 H. F. Butter 17 lbs. 8½ oz. 7 days, A.R.
DAISY H 3D, 13621 H. F. Burr, 1460 H.; Daisy H., 732 H. Milk 45 lbs. 1 day, P. Butter 14 lbs. 7 days, P.
DAISY SINDT, 24141 H. F. Beppo's Rijaneta Herbert, 11241 H. F.; Nora Sindt, 9251 H. F. Butter 21 lbs. 7 oz. 7 days, P.
DAKOLAR NICO, 0632 H. Imp. Milk 59 lbs. 7 oz. 1 day, 6600 lbs. 10 months, P. Butter 2 lbs. 12 oz. 1 day, P.
DAKOTA PLUM, 7803 H. F. Jewel's Prince of Wayne, 32 H. F.; Erna Abbekerk, 9006 H. Milk 52 lbs. 1 day, P.
DAKOTA QUEEN, 7898 H. F. Jewel's Prince of Wayne, 32 H.; Arline, 5027 H. Milk 42 lbs. 1 day, P., 560 lbs. 10 da· s, A.R.
DAME DURDEN, 6867 H. Imp. Milk 53 lbs. 12 oz. 1 day. P.; 10,724 lbs. 14 oz. 10 months, A.R.
DAMSEL, 1808 H. Imp. Milk 6242 lbs. 3 oz. 11 months 15 days, P.
DANDELION, 2692 H. Imp. Milk 65 lbs. 1 day, P.
DANGLE S, 3786 H. Crown Prince 3d, 625 H.; Gretje 2d, 516 H. Milk 53 lbs. 1 day, P.; 12,227 lbs. 11 months 14 days, P.
DAPHNE, 596 H. Imp. Milk 44 lbs. 1 day, 9475 lbs. 12 oz. 1 year, P.
DAPHNE 2D, 1312 H. Uncle Tom, 163 H.; Daphne, 596 H. Milk 37 lbs. 1 day, P.
DAPHNE 3D, 596 H. Keys, 53 Neth. Imp. Milk 6049 lbs. 11 oz. 10 months, A.R.
DAWN 277 H. Billy Boelyn, 180 H.; Modjeska, 407 H. Milk 13,586 lbs. 12 oz., P.
DAY, 4649 H. F. J. Corwin, 3623 H.; Damie, 8423 H. Butter 18 lbs 5 oz. 7 days, P.
DAZIEL, 6920 H. Imp. Milk 70 lbs. 1 day, P.; 6014 lbs. 4 oz. 3 months 18 days, A.R. Butter 21 lbs. 7 oz. 7 days. A.R.
DAZIE MC, 10546 H. F. Netherland Convoy 2934 H.; Taffy, 6035 H. Milk 44 lbs. 1 day, P.; 419 lbs. 8 oz. 10 days, A.R. Butter 9 lbs. 15 oz. 7 days, A.R.
DE BLES, 806 D. F. Imp. Milk 81 lbs. 1 day, 16,148 lbs. 11 months 28 days, P. Butter 21 lbs. 12 oz. 7 days, A.R.
DE BLESS 2D, 2588 H. Promoter, 1518 H.; Cordelia, 922 H. Milk 63 lbs. 4 oz. 1 day, P.; 15,042 lbs. 1 year, A.R.
DE DIKKE, 7145 H. Imp. Milk 10,103 lbs. 5 oz. 10 months, A.R.
DE DIKKERT, 1158 D. F. Zan Dikkert. Milk 71 lbs. 1 day, P.
DE FLORA, 10851 H. F. Fell, 128 D. F.; Eradne, 8446 H. Milk 10,097 lbs. 15 oz. 10 months, P.
DE FREULE, 4249 Neth. Imp. Milk 80 lbs. 1 day, 5759 lbs. 11 oz. 6 months, P.
DE FREULE, 742 H. Bismark, 224 Neth.; De Freule, 4249 Neth. Milk 80 lbs. 8 oz. 1 day, P.; 10,683 lbs. 9 oz. 10 months, A.R.
DE FREULE 2D, 3381 H. F. Neptune, Jr., 1916 H. F.; DeFrenle, 742 H. F. Milk 9846 lbs. 6 oz. 10 months. A.R.
DE FREULE 3d, 7031 H. F. Forster, 2771 H.; De Freule, 742 H. F. Butter 20 lbs. 12 oz. 7 days, A.R.
DE GOEDE, 5568 H. Imp. Milk 91 lbs. 8 oz. 1 day, 12,460 lbs. 6 oz. 1 year, P. Butter 14 lbs. 2 oz. 7 days, A.R.
DE GOEDE 2D, 357 D. F. Imp. Milk 618 lbs. 12 oz. 10 days, 11,078 lbs 8 oz. 266 days, A.R.
DE GOEDE GEEFSTER, 4078 H. Imp. Milk 84 lbs. 1 day, P.
DE GROOT'S GRIETJE 3D, 853 D. F. Prins; Grietje. Milk 10,056 lbs. 4 oz., P. Butter 17 lbs. 8 oz 7 days, A.R.
DEKKERTJE 3D, 4303 H. F. Burghorn, 4075 H.; Dekkertje, 8069 H. Butter 14 lbs. 5 oz. 7 days, A.R.
DE KOL, 6245 H. Imp. Milk 80 lbs. 1 day, 886 lbs. 10 days, P.
DE KOL 2D, 784 H. F. Willem III, 190 Neth.; De Kol, 6245 H. Milk 73 lbs. 1 day, P.; 11,953 lbs. 9 oz. 7 months 22 days, A.R. Butter 6 lbs. 6½ oz. 1 day, 33 lbs. 6 oz. 7 days, P.

DE KOL 2D'S PAULINE, 30712 H. F.   Paul De Kol, 14643 H. F.; De Kol 2d, 734 H F.   Milk 249 lbs. 6 oz 7 days, A.R.   Butter 12 lbs. 2 oz. 7 days, A.R.
DE KOL 2D'S QUEEN, 6324 H. F.   Forster, 2771 H. F.; De Kol 2d, 734 H. F.   Milk 71 lbs. 4 oz. 1 day, 9750 lbs. 3 oz. 10 months, A.R.   Butter 28 lbs. 7 oz. 7 days, A.R.
DELIGHT, 1774 H.   Dirk Hatterick, 219 H.; Dawn, 277 H.   Milk 12,421 lbs. 15 oz. 1 year, A.R.
DELIGHTFUL, 1536 D. F.   Willem, 20 F.; Sophia, 865 F.   Butter 10 lbs. 7 days, A.R.
DELLAH, 2600 H.   Imp   Milk 8000 lbs. 1 year. P.
DELORES, 8440 H.   Imp.   Milk 70 lbs. 1 day, P.
DE MOOIE, 1654 F. H.   Imp.   Milk 70 lbs. 1 day, P.
DE ONDE VROW, 480 Neth   Imp.   Milk 84 lbs. 8 oz. 1 day, P.
DE RUITER'S BEATUS, 6888 H.   Imp.   Milk 48 lbs. 14 oz. 1 day; 12,099 lbs. 1 year, P.
DE SCHOT, 5001 H.   Imp.   Milk 82 lbs. 4 oz. 1 day. P.   Butter 23 lbs. 8 oz. 7 days, P.
DESDEMONA, 1237 H.   Trump, 354 H.; Clematis, 270 H.   Milk 51 lbs. 1 day, P.
DESDEMONA 3D, 10779 H. F.   Jonge Carre, 2305 H.; Desdemona, 1237 H.   Butter 24 lbs. 15 oz. 7 days, P.
DETT BEAUTY, 20457 H. F.   Mazda, 2072 H.; Beauty Zwaan, 242 H,   Milk 64 lbs. 12 oz. 1 day, 1844 lbs. 8 oz, 30 days, P.
DE VRIES 5433 H.   Imp.   Milk 95 lbs. 8 oz. 1 day; 2404 lbs. 30 days, P.   Butter 30 lbs. 7 days, 122 lbs. 12 oz. 30 days, P.
DE VRIEN CASSIE, 7318 H. F.   De Vries' Jacob, 883 H. F.; Cassie Heckendown 2d, 8357 H.   Milk 36 lbs. 8 oz. 1 day P.; 7872 lbs. 12 oz. 9 months 18 days, A.R.   Butter 22 lbs. 12 oz. 7 days, 28 lbs. 4 oz. 14 days, A.R.
DEWDROP, 960 H.   Imp.   Milk 68 lbs. 3 oz. 1 day, 9408 lbs. 2 oz. 1 year, P.   Butter 18 lbs. 6½ oz. 7 days, A.R.
DEW DROP OF SEA SIDE, 8560 H. F.   Leander, 520 H.; Aaggie of Ashley, 3883 H.   Milk 44 lbs. 10 oz. 1 day, P.
DE WIT, 1758 Neth.   Imp.   Milk 77 lbs. 12 oz. 1 day, P.
DE WIT'S JANSJE 2D, 1653 H. F.   Lincoln, 120 H.; De Wit's Jansje, 5699 H.   Milk 50 lbs. 1 day, P.
DE ZWARTE, 946 H.   Imp.   Milk 61 lbs. 1 day, P.
DE ZWARTKOP, 1049 Neth.   Imp.   Milk 61 lbs. 12 oz. 1 day, P.
DIAMEDE, 7006 H, Porcelein, 142 Neth.   Hollander, 843 Neth.   Milk 50 lbs. 12 oz. 1 day, 7856 lbs. 14 oz. 8 months 15 days. P.
DIAMOND S, 3975 H.   Imp.   Milk 510 lbs. 10 days, P.
DIANA, 115 H.   Imp.   Milk 88 lbs. 1 day, P.   Butter 9 lbs. 14 oz. 7 days, A.R.
DIANA S, 3766 H.   Crown Prince 3d, 625 H.; Carrie, 583 H.   Milk 48 lbs. 1 day, 1320 lbs. 30 days, P.
DICENTRA, 7934 H.   Imp.   Milk 61 lbs. 1 day, P.   Butter 12 lbs. 1 oz. 7 days, P.
DIENTJE, 2571 H.   Imp.   Milk 51 lbs. 1 day, P.
DIEUWERA, 9320 H.   Imp.   Milk 52 lbs. 1 day, 1451 lbs. 30 days, P.
DIEWERTJE, 2020 H. F.   De Prins, 310 Neth.; Dieuwertje, 1025 Neth.   Milk 88 lbs. 1 day, 15,225 lbs. 1 year, P.
DIEUWERTJE ROGGEVEEN, 3831 H. F.   Roggeveen, 420 Neth.; Dieuwertje, 1973 Neth.   Milk 6840 lbs. 6 months.   Butter 9 lbs. 8 oz. 7 days, P.
DIEWKJE, 145 D. F.   Imp.   Milk 40 lbs. 1 day, P.
DIJKSTRA 2D, 358 D. F.   Imp.   Milk 76 lbs. 5 oz. 10 days, 10,024 lbs. 3 oz. 8 months 12 days, A.R.
DIKKE KOE, 4247 H.   Imp.   Butter 16 lbs. 8 oz. 7 days, P.
DIKKERT 2D, 4741 H.   Johannis 428 H.   Dikkert 664 H.   Milk 6398 lbs. 9 months, P.
DINA, 715 Neth.   Imp.   Milk 84 lbs. 1 day, P.   Butter 17 lbs. 8 oz. 7 days, P.
DINAH, 1892 H.   Imp.   Milk 30 lbs. 6 oz. 1 day, 6486 lbs. 1 oz. 7 months 18 days, P.   Butter 7 lbs. 3 oz. 7 days, P.
DINA OF THE PINES, 3509 H. F.   Neptune, Jr., 1916 H.; Dina T, 1815 H.   Milk 48 lbs. 8 oz. 1 day, 318 lbs. 8 oz. 7 days, P.
DINGLE DELL 2701 H.   Imp.   Milk 73 lbs. 8 oz. 1 day, 10,680 lbs. 7 oz. 228 days, A.R.
DINGLE DELL 2D, 5576 H.   Sir Henry of Aaggie, 1459 H.; Dingle Dell, 2701 H.   Milk 9050 lbs. 3 oz. 8 months 26 days, P.
DINNIE, 1415 H. F.   Constantyn, 2040 H.; Tessa Abbekerk, 6722 H.   Butter 18 lbs. 15 oz. 7 days, P.
DINOLA, 1529 D. F.   David, 222 D. F.; Jonge Jeltje, F. H. B.   Butter, 9 lbs. 6 oz. 7 days, A.R.
DINORA, 5355 H.   Imp.   Milk 66 lbs. 1 day, P.
DIRKJE VON HOLINGEN, 17221 H. F.   Imp.   Milk 60 lbs. 1 day, P.
DISSE, 92 D. F.   Imp.   Milk 56 lbs. 1 day, P.
DIVINIA, 6006 H.   Imp.   Milk 40 lbs. 12 oz. 1 day, P.; 10,451 lbs. 9 oz. 1 year, P.
DOCIA, 3429 H. F.   Billy Bawn, 3087 H.; Rustic Lass 2d, H.   Milk 35 lbs. 10 oz. 1 day, 6739 lbs. 3 oz. 9 months 6 days, A.R.
DOCKUMER 2D, 556 D. F.   Imp.   Milk 60 lbs. 12 oz. 1 day, P.
DOCKUMER 6TH, 13496 H. F.   Dockumer 3d's Mooie, 4260 H. F.; Dockumer 2d, 556 D. F.   Milk 40 lbs. 1 day, P.
DOEDE BINNEMA, 6215 H.   Imp.   Milk 75 lbs. 1 day, P.
DOEDE BINNEMA 4TH, 5048 H. F.   Major Pel, 53 M. F.; Doede Binnema, 6215 H.   Milk 69 lbs. 12 oz. 1 day, 9250 lbs. 1 year, P.
DOEDTJE, 7616 H. F.   Imp.   Milk 59 lbs. 1 day, 904 lbs. 8 oz. 20 days, P.
DOEKES 2D, 4708 H.   Imp.   Milk 64 lbs. 1 day, 15,000 lbs. 1 year, P.
DOEKES SCOTT, 1478 H. F.   Walter Scott, 606 H.; Doekes 2d, 4708 H.   Milk 81 lbs. 1 day, P.
DOETJE KONING, 56 D. F.   Imp.   Milk 11,700 lbs. 8 oz. 9 months 17 days, P.
DOETJE WELLING, 3241 H. F.   Imp.   Milk 67 lbs. 8 oz. 1 day, 10,740 lbs. 7 months 4 days, A.R.
DOLLY VARDEN, 972 H.   Jacob 2d, 56 Neth.; Aaggie, 501 H.   Milk 50 lbs. 1 day, P.
DOMINGO S' MABEL, 13671 H. F.   Domingo S, 3411 H.; Mabel of Pacific, 625 H. F.   Milk 10,308 lbs. 1 year, A.R.
DOMINU, 8261 H. F.   Jan, 376 F. H. B.; Janneke, 798 F. H. B.   Milk 71 lbs. 1 day, 691 lbs. 10 days, P.
DONIA KONING, 37 D. F.   Imp.   Milk 62 lbs. 1 day, P.
DOUNA S, 6204 H. F.   Prince of Twisk, 1055 H.; Wegdal Ray, 7685 H.   Butter 14 lbs. 7 days, A.R.
DORA BARNUM, 6322 H. F.   Forster, 2771 H.; Jessie Barnum, 10262 H.   Milk 6748 lbs. 1 oz. 9 months, A.R.   Butter 20 lbs. 4 oz. 7 days, P.
DORA BEETS 2D, 265 D. F.   Burg Hartog, 3 M. R.; Marianna Beets, 7 M. R.   Milk 75 lbs. 1 day, P.
DORA BEETS 3D, 269 D. F.   Burg Hartog, 3 M. R.; Marianna Beets. 7 M. R.   Milk 78 lbs. 3 oz. 1 day, 18,510 lbs. 3 oz. 1 year, P.   Butter 17 lbs. 14 oz. 7 days, A.R.
DORA BEETS 4TH, 889 D. F.   Prince Kuperus, 121 P. R.; Marianna Beets, 7 M. R.   Milk 65 lbs. 1 day, P.

22

HOLSTEIN-FRIESIAN CATTLE.

DORA BLEEKER 2D, 19 D. F. Paul Potter, 2 D. F.; Dora Bleeker 6 D. F. Milk 12,000 lbs. 9 months 24 days, P.
DORA DEAN, 2925 H. Imp. Milk 51 lbs. 1 day, P.
DORA DUMPLING, 14160 H. F. Tell, 128 D. F.; Vellinga, 302 D. F. Milk 8940 lbs. 2 oz. 1 year, P.
DORA MERRILES, 5181 H. Artemus Ward, 1428 H.; Meg Merriles 2d, 1485 H. Milk 41 lbs. 7 oz. 1 day, 6831 lbs. 9 months 6 days, P.
DORA S, 1418 H. Imp. Milk 40 lbs. 1 day, P.
DORINDA, 7962 H. Imp. Milk 58 lbs. 1 day, P.
DORINDA S, 3763 H. Crown Prince 3d, 625 H.; Vineta 473 H. Milk 50 lbs. 1 day, 8731 lbs. 9 months 3 days, P.
DORIS, 885 H. Imp. Milk 40 lbs. 8 oz. 1 day, 1160 lbs. 8 oz. 30 days, P.
DOTINGA, 1538 D. F. De Nette 281 F. H. B.; Foekje 2050 F. H. B, Milk 91 lbs. 11 oz. 1 day, A. R.; 2427 lbs. 10 oz. 30 days, P. Butter 20 lbs. 9 oz. 7 days, A. R.
DOTINGA 3D, 6919 H. F. Prince Kerbel 1727 H. F.; Dotinga 1538 D. F. Milk 60 lbs 1 day, P.
DOWAGER, 7 H. Imp. Milk 62 lbs. 8 oz. 1 day, 12,681 lbs. 8 oz. 1 year, P. Butter 19 lbs. 12 oz. 7 days, P.
DOWAGER MAY, 1438 H. F. Midnight, 128 D. F.; May 2d, 401 D. F. Milk 71 lbs. 1 day, P.; 15,237 lbs. 10 months 29 days, A.R. Butter 19 lbs. 12 oz. 7 days, A. R.
DRAMANTJE, 3466 Neth. Imp. Milk 87 lbs. 1 day, P.
DREAM OF HOLLAND, 2703 H. Imp. Milk 77 lbs. 1 day, 11,860 lbs. 5 oz. 11 months, P. Butter 5 lbs. 5 oz. 3 days, P.
DREAM OF HOLLAND 3D, 8469 H. Netherland Prince 716 H.; Dream of Holland, 2703 H. Milk 11,860 lbs. 5 oz. 1 year, P. Butter 15 lbs. 3 oz. 7 days, P.
DREAMY EYES, 10451 H. Imp. Milk 60 lbs. 6 oz. 1 day, P. Butter 13 lbs. 12 oz. 7 days, P.
DREDA, 8354 H. Imp. Milk 62 lbs. 1 day, 6797 lbs. 4 oz. 4 months, P.
DRUSILLA S, 8764 H. Bristol, 927 H.; Rebecca 2d, 400 H. Milk 10,215 lbs. 1 year, P.
DRUYF 2D, 917 H. Imp. Milk 82 lbs. 1 day, P.
DRUYF 3D, 921 H. Imp. Milk 60 lbs. 1 day, P.
DUANNA, 1780 D. F. Prins, 153 F. H. B.; De Bakker, 944 F. H. B. Butter 9 lbs. 5 oz. 7 days, A.R.
DUCHESS, 2705 H. Imp. Milk 13,673 lbs. 8 oz. 9 months 17 days, P.
DUCHESS OF BEEMSTER, 4621 H. Imp. Milk 92 lbs. 12 oz. 1 day, 576 lbs. 7 days, P. Butter 18 lbs. 2 oz. 7 days, P.
DUCHESS OF FRIESLAND, 382 H. Wartena 16 Neth.; Oliver, 91 Neth. Milk 52 lbs. 3 oz. 1 day, 13,454 lbs. 12 oz. 1 year, P.
DUCHESS OF PAWLING, 6318 H. F. Forster, 2771 H.; Maid of Pawling, 7408 H. Milk 51 lbs. 1 day, P.
DUCHESS OF SPRINGVALE, 845 H. Imp. Milk 42 lbs. 8 oz 1 day, 9873 lbs. 1 year, P.
DUCHESS OF YORK, 120 H. Imp. Milk 87 lbs. 8 oz. 1 day, 841 lbs. 10 days, P.
DUDGEMONA, 1522 H. F. Leonatus, 2139 H.; Clara Vaughn. 2686 H. Milk 38 lbs. 1 day, P.
DUKE OF OBISPO'S MABEL OF PACIFIC, 16891 H. F. Duke of Obispo, 6810 H. F. Mabel of Pacific, 625 H. F. Milk 9711 lbs. 1 year, A.R.
DULCINA, 5358 H. Imp. Milk 82 lbs. 1 day, 2212 lbs. 30 days, P.
DULCINA 2D, 6487 H. F. De Brave Hendrik, 230 H. F.; Dulcina 5358 H. Milk 42 lbs. 4 oz. 1 day, 7105 lbs. 4 oz. 8 months, P. Butter 12 lbs. 7 days, P.
DUMFRIES, 12029 H. F. August, 717 F. H. B.; Jorritsma, 522 Aux, F. Milk 67 lbs. 1 day, 1215 lbs. 30 days, P. Butter 19 lbs. 6 oz. 7 days, P.
DURKJE, 1641 H. Imp. Milk 13,000 lbs. 10 months, P.
DURKJE BAKER, 569 D. F. Imp. Milk 80 lbs. 1 day, 4773 lbs. 150 days, P.
DURKJE VEEMAN, 478 D. F. Imp. Milk 84 lbs. 1 day, 748 lbs. 10 days, P.
DURKJE VEEMAN 2D, 479 D. F. Imp. Milk 55 lbs. 1 day, 550 lbs. 10 days, P.
DURKJE VEEMAN 8TH, 2687 H. F. Mooie Hartog, 418 D. F.; Durkje Veeman, 478 D. F. Milk 8490 lbs. 12 oz. 10 months, A.R.
DUSTY, 6536 H. Imp. Milk 54 lbs. 14 oz. 1 day, 1158 lbs. 1 month, P.
DUTCH GIRL, 427 D. F. Imp. Milk 48 lbs. 1 day, P.
DUTY, 8606 H. Imp. Milk 36 lbs. 5 oz. 1 day, 7792 lbs. 11 oz. 1 year, P.
DUYNTJE KOOPMAN, 8229 H. Imp. Milk 40 lbs. 4 oz. 1 day, 432 lbs. 10 days, P.

EADBURGH S, 8573 H. Crown Prince 3d, 625 H.; American Girl, 902 H. Milk 8158 lbs. 1 year, P.
EALINE, 2057 H. Imp. Milk 76 lbs. 1 day, P.
EARLY DAWN, 3547 H. F. Pell 2d, 327 D. F.; Pauline 3d, 425 D. F. Milk 9903 lbs. 10 oz. 1 year, P.
EARLY SUNRISE, 14164 H. F. Duke of Woodrid, 2461 H. F.; Early Dawn, 5347 H. F. Milk 7755 lbs. 1 year, P.
EASTER MAID, 4511 H. Imp. Milk 12,539 lbs. 9 months 28 days, P.
EBBA, 13518 H. F. Nannette's Ondit, 839 H. F.; Heliotrope, 352 H. Milk 625 lbs. 10 oz. 19 days, P.
EBOLI, 8078 H. Imp. Butter 25 lbs. 9 oz. 7 days, P.
ECHO, 121 H. Rip Van Winkle, 35 H.; Crown Princess, 6 H. Milk 82 lbs. 1 day, 23,775 lbs. 8 oz. 1 year, P. Butter 17 lbs. 3 oz. 7 days, P.
ECHO 2D, 1355 H. Mahomet, 289 H.; Echo, 121 H. Milk 67 lbs. 3 oz. 1 day, 9230 lbs. 8 oz. 10 months, P. Butter 18 lbs. 2 oz. 7 days, P.
ECHO 3D, 2189 H. Mahomet, 289 H.; Echo, 121 H. Milk 73 lbs. 1 day, 2116 lbs. 4 oz. 1 month, P.
ECHO 4TH, 3599 H. Prince of Wayne 2d, 736 H.; Echo, 121 H. Milk 9608 lbs. 8 oz. 10 months, P.
EDGING S, 8577 H. Bristol, 927 H.; Molly S, 3055 H. Milk 9288 lbs. 9 months 27 days, A.R.
EDINA, 3798 H. Imp. Milk 11,991 lbs. 4 oz. 9 months 19 days, A.R.
EDINA 2D, 10,315 H. F. Haywood 738 H. F.; Edina 3798 H. Milk 10,120 lbs. 1 year, A.R. Butter 12 lbs. 13 oz. 7 days, A.R.
EDITH, 721 H. Imp. Milk 60 lbs. 1 day, P.
EDITH GRAY, 4587 H. Imp. Milk 43 lbs. 1 day, P.
EDITH PRESCOTT, 2708 H. Imp. Milk 9730 lbs. 10 months, A.R.
EDITH PRESCOTT 2D, 1127 H. F. Admiral, 1648 H.; Edith Prescott, 2708 H. Milk 384 lbs. 12 oz. 10 days, A.R. Butter 10 lbs. 6 oz. 7 days, P.
EDMA, 8432 H. Imp. Milk 45 lbs. 1 day, P.
EDNA, 1490 D. F. Fritz, 293 F. H. B.; Frouwkje, 1282 F H. B. Milk 67 lbs. 14 oz. 1 day, P.; 17,855 lbs. 10 months, A. R.
EDNAH, 6104 H. F. Promoter, 1518 H.; Metamora, 8433 H. Milk 10,575 lbs. 6 oz. 1 year, P.
EDWEWA 8921 H. Imp. Milk 38 lbs. 1 day, 6733 lbs. 6 oz. 11 months 9 days, P.
EDWINA 2D'S ROSE, 10673 H. F. Prince of Rose, 1429 H. F.; Edwina 2d, 1766 H. F. Milk 62 lbs. 4 oz. 1 day, 5012 lbs. 3 months, A.R. Butter 17 lbs. 11 oz. 7 days, A.R.

MILK AND BUTTER RECORDS. 331

EDWINNA, 6983 H. Imp. Milk 55 lbs. 1 day, P. Butter 12 lbs. 7 days, P.
EEFJE, 5085 Neth. Imp. Milk 84 lbs. 1 day, P.
EKE 2D, 1737 D. F. Imp. Milk 534 lbs. 2 oz. 10 days, A.R.
EFFIE DEANS, 1284 H. Imp. Milk 47 lbs. 1 day, 11,085 lbs. 1 year, P.
EOBERTA, 6897 H. Imp. Milk 6837 lbs. 12 oz. 8 months 13 days, P.
EGILONA S, 8578 H. Bobbie, 928 H.; Abby, 586 H. Milk 50 lbs. 1 day, 8010 lbs. 10 months, P.
EIGHTH MAID OF TWISK, 324 D. F. 2d Maid of Twisk, 20 M. R.; Dick Swivler, 35 M. R. Milk 30 lbs. 1 day, P.
EILIE, 7700 H. F. Jonge Carre, 23CF H.; Zwart Bonte Truitje, 4133 H. Milk 1615 lbs. 16 oz. 2 months 12 days, P.
EKE, 2865 F. H. B. Imp. Milk 59 lbs. 1 day, P.
EKSTER, 661 H. Imp. Milk 11,227 lbs. 8 oz. 10 months, A.R.
EKSTER 2D, 1543 H. Johannis, 428 H.; Ekster, 661 H. Milk 72 lbs. 1 day, P.
EKSTER 2D A, 2437 H. F. Clarion, 870 H.; Ekster 2d, 1543 H. Milk 72 lbs. 1 day, P.
EKSTER 3D B, 9121 H. F. Clarion, 870 H.; Ekster 2d, 1543 H. Milk 43 lbs. 1 day, 7874 lbs. 11 months 6 days, P.
EKSTER 3D A, 9123 H. F. Hilda's Empire, 3562 H.; Ekster, 3d, 8480 H. Milk 35 lbs. 1 day, 8,501 lbs. 3 months, P.
EKSTER 3D B, 14249 H. F. Copia's Empire, 3539 H.; Ekster 3d, 8480 H. Milk 4684 lbs. 11 months, P.
EKSTER 4TH, 8481 H. Johannis 428 H.; Ekster, 661 H. Milk 7070 lbs. 11 months 4 days, P.
EKSTER 4TH A, 14250 H. F. Clarion 870 H.; Ekster 4th, 8481 H. Milk 4056 lbs. 10 months 11 days, P.
ELEANOR, 2710 H. Imp. Milk 7008 lbs. 8 oz. 10 months 28 days, P.
ELEANOR R, 5340 H. F. Netherland Convoy, 2934 H.; Bonzilla, 6936 H. Milk 76 lbs. 1 day, 1871 lbs. 30 days, P. Butter 19 lbs. 4 oz. 7 days, A.R.
ELGEE, 8186 H. Neptune, 711 H.; Satinette, 2885 H. Milk 54 lbs. 2 oz. 1 day, 8916 lbs. 7 months 20 days, P. Butter 14 lbs. 11 oz. 7 days, A.R.
ELGERSMA, 1934 D. F. Simon; Dieuwke. Milk 63 lbs. 1 day, 14,616 lbs. 1 year, P.
ELGIN BELLE, 4640 H. Imp. Milk 74 lbs. 1 day, 20,109 lbs. 4 oz. 1 year, A.R. Butter 31 lbs. 5 oz. 7 days, 100 lbs. 6 oz 30 days, A.R.
ELGIN BELLE 2D, 8292 H. Imp. Butter 18 lbs. 1 oz. 7 days, P.
ELGIN GIRL 3D, 1787 H. F. Jan Wit, 2524 H.; Elgin Girl, 4675 H. Milk 42 lbs. 3 oz. 1 day, P.
ELITE, 20843 H. F. Seer, 5027 H. F.; Latina, 8161 H. Milk 5441 lbs. 8 oz. 10 months, P.
ELIZA, 6102 H. Imp. Milk 32 lbs. 1 day, P.
ELIZABETH, 724 Neth. Imp. Milk 69 lbs. 1 day, P.
ELLA, 122 H. Imp. Milk 10,850 lbs. 1 year, P.
ELLA ALEXANDER, 1181 H. Imp. Milk 74 lbs. 1 day, P.
ELLA ARTIS, 4848 H. F. Artis, 127 Neth.; Theodora, 3760 Neth. Milk 6630 lbs. 4 oz. 6 months 27 days, P. Butter 13 lbs. 3 oz. 7 days, A.R.
ELLA MCKINNEY, 5403 H. Imp. Milk 67 lbs. 8 oz. 1 day, P. Butter 17 lbs. 12 oz. 7 days, P.
ELLEN, 9296 H. Imp. Milk 66 lbs. 1 day, P.
ELLERBROCK 2D, 3652 H. F. Millerndecerde, 3643 H.; Ellerbrock 8104 H. Milk 58 lbs. 1 day, 23,616 lbs. 1 year, P.
ELLIDA, 3133 H. Imp. Milk 55 lbs. 1 day, P.
ELLIE, 4023 H Imp. Milk 2946 lbs. 10 oz. 2 months, P.
ELOISE OF ISLIP, 10296 H. F. Milk 30 qts. 1 day, P.
ELSE, 1848 D. F. Tell, 128 P. R.; Vellinga, 302 P. R. Milk 9245 lbs. 8 oz. 1 year, P.
ELSIE ARTIS, 4518 H. Imp. Milk 43 lbs. 10 oz. 1 day, P.; 12,407 lbs. 9 oz. 1 year, A.R. Butter 40 lbs. 11 oz. 7 days, A.R.
ELSIE CHESTER, 4370 H. Imp. Milk 64 lbs. 1 day, P.; 1667 lbs. 8 oz. 30 days, A.R.
ELSIE S, 3054 H. Jubilee, 276 H.; Carrie, 583 H. Milk 65 lbs. 1 day, 1923 lbs. 11 months 25 days, P.
ELSPIE, 817 H. Fourth Prince of Orange, 246 H.; Leah 3d, 815 H. Milk 84 lbs. 1 day, P.
ELTJE, 2805 F. H. B. Imp. Milk 66 lbs. 1 day, P.
ELTONA, 2881 H. Imp. Milk 68 lbs. 12 oz. 1 day, 11,906 lbs. 12 oz. 1 year, P. Butter 2 lbs. 10 oz. 1 day, 35 lbs. 3 oz. 14 days, P.
ELVINA, 7826 H. Imp. Milk 30 lbs. 1 day, P.
ELVIRA, 3179 H. Imp. Milk 70 lbs. 1 day, P.
ELKJE 2D, 3527 H. F. Hague, 104 D. F.; Elkje, 172 D. F. Milk 74 lbs. 11 oz. 1 day, P.
EMA ABBEKERK, 9606 H. Imp. Milk 80 lbs. 1 day, 755 lbs. 10 days, P.
EMBLEM 2D, 2625 H. F. Bounce, 873 H.; Emblem, 1858 H. Milk 58 lbs. 1 day, 1588 lbs. 5 oz. 1 month, P.
EMERALD, 559 H. Uncle Tom, 163 H.; Lady Fisher, 355 H. Milk 31 lbs. 1 day. P.
EMMA, 327 D. F. Imp. Milk 83 lbs. 1 day, 400 lbs. 10 days, P.
EMMA 2D, 1143 H. Schuyler, 338 H.; Emma, 289 H. Milk 86 lbs. 1 day, P.
EMMA DE KOL, 20203 H. F. De Kol 2d's Prince, 2707 H. F.; Maartje van Kampen, 739 H. F. Milk 14 lbs. 2 oz. 7 days, P.; 55 lbs. 11 oz. 30 days, A.R.
EMMA J, 10050 H. Barrington, 2103 H.; Jessie B. 5173 H. Milk 48 lbs. 1 day, 1.
EMMA J NEPTUNE, 9417 H. F. Neptune Jr., 1916 H.; Emma J, 10,350 H. Milk 48 lbs. 1 day, P.
EMMA OF SHADELAND, 2413 H. Imp. Milk 69 lbs. 2276 lbs. 8 oz. 31 days, P.
EMMA OF SHADELAND 3D, 10783 H. F. Netherland Conqueror, 2476 H.; Emma of Shadeland, 2-13 H. Milk 8230 lbs. 2 oz. 8 months, A.R.
EMMA POSCH, 741 H. F. Bismarck, 224 Neth; Emma 2d, 4251 Neth. Milk 46 lbs. 12 oz. 1 day, P.
EMMA POSCH 2D, 4610 H. F. Emma Posch, 741 H. Butter 18 lbs. 1 oz. 7 days, P.
EMOGENE TWISK, 8636 H. F. Moode Twisk, 85 D. F.; Hiltje Kuperus, 34 M. R. Milk 45 lbs. 1 day, P.
EMPORIA, 4165 H. Joe, 1002 H.; Empress, 549 H. Milk 43 lbs. 1 day, P.
EMPRESS, 196 Neth. Imp. Milk 49 lbs. 1 day, 19,714 lbs. 4 oz. 1 year, P.
EMPRESS, 539 Neth. Imp. Milk 108 lbs. 1 day, 2276 lbs. 8 oz. 31 days, P.
EMPRESS JOSEPHINE, 429 D. F. Imp. Milk 88 lbs. 14 oz. 1 day, P.; 10,119 lbs. 12 oz. 4 months 19 days, A.R. Butter 23 lbs. 14 oz. 7 days A.R.
EMPRESS JOSEPHINE 2D, 1783 D. F. Reeloff, 179 D. F.; Empress Josephine, 429 D. F. Milk 40 lbs. 1 day, 504 lbs. 10 oz. 10 days, P.
EMPRESS JOSEPHINE 3D, 1995 H. F. Major Pel, 2763 H.; Empress Josephine, 429 D F. Milk 40 lbs. 5 oz. 1 day, 862 lbs. 12 oz. 10 days, A.R. Butter 31 lbs. 2 oz. 7 days, A.R.
EMPRESS JOSEPHINE 3D'S GERBEN, 22739 H. F. Consul Gerben, 6304 H. F.; Empress Josephine 3d, 1995 H. F. Milk 48 lbs. 12 oz. 1 day, P.
EMPRESS JOSEPHINE 4th, 4405 H. F. Major Pel, 2763 H.; Empress Josephine, 429 D. F. Milk 57 lbs. 10 oz. 1 day, 601 lbs. 2 oz. 10 days, P. Butter 2 lbs. 12 oz. 1 day, P.
EMPRESS OF ONDINE, 1041 H. F. Empire, 588 H.; Onyx, 1066 H. Milk 43 lbs. 1 day, P.

332   HOLSTEIN-FRIESIAN CATTLE.

ENCHANTRESS, 884 H. Imp. Milk 50 lbs. 3 oz. 1 day, 1505 lbs. 30 days, P.
ENCHANTRESS 2D, 3499 H. Ebbo, 236 H.; Enchantress, 884 H. Milk 95 lbs. 1 day, 1026 lbs. 30 days, P.
ENGLEWOOD S, 8531 H. Prince Neptune, 2093 H.; Dorinda S, 9763 H. Milk 53 lbs. 1 day, P.; 7864 lbs. 9 months 26 days, A.R.
ENSENORE, 4512 H. Porcelain, 142 Neth.; Powele, 564 Neth. Milk 816 lbs 12 oz. 10 days, 17,864 lbs. 14 oz. 1 year, A.R.
EOLA, 9140 H. Imp. Milk 82 lbs. 1 day, P. Butter 17 lbs. 7 days, P.
ERADNE, 8446 H. Imp. Milk 12,347 lbs. 1 year, P.
ERIE BELLE 2D, 18812 H. F. Tecumseh Witzyde, 5967 H. F.; Erie Belle, 1008 D. F. Milk 59 lbs. 1 day, 8933 lbs. 237 days, P.
ERINA, 1848 H. Imp. Milk 11,065 lbs. 1 year, P.
ERIX 2D, 6711 H. F. Alveri, 3158 H.; Erix, 6786 H. Butter 11 lbs. 10 oz. 7 days, A.R.
ERMINA, 2278 H. Imp. Milk 78 lbs. 1 day, P.
ERMINE OF SEA SIDE, 3910 H. F. Second Duke of Ashley, 1426 H.; Lady Berkley, 6139 H. Milk 18 qts. 1 day, P.
ERNESTA, 3700 H. Imp. Milk 58 lbs. 1 day, 1650 lbs. 30 days, P. Butter 11 lbs. 7 days, P.
ESCHJE, 1708 Neth. Imp. Milk 83 lbs., P.
ESCONE, 7292 H. F. Tobin, 2268 H.; Tzerelfa, 5503 H. Butter 15 lbs. 7 oz. 7 days, A.R.
ESEL, 2505 H. Imp. Milk 81 lbs. 1 day, P.
ESSENCE, 7137 H. Gortus, 649 H.; Iris 2d, 660 H. Milk 47 lbs. 12 oz. 1 day, P.
ESSENCE 2D, 9678 H. F. Flora Clifden's Mercedes Prince, 3545 H.; Essence, 7137 H. Milk 3684 lbs. 4 oz. 3 months, A.R. Butter 12 lbs. 10 oz. 7 days, A.R.
ESTHER, 1026 H. Egmont, 89 H.; Duchess of Holstein, 8 H. Milk 70 lbs. 1 day, P.
ESTHER ABBEKERK, 4483 H. F. Abbekerk, 206 Neth.; Christine, 1512 Neth. Milk 40 lbs. 1 day.
ESTHER ALEXANDER, 4406 H. Imp. Milk 66 lbs. 10 oz. 1 day, 1867 lbs. 1 year, P.
ETELKA, 1431 H. Banjo, 564 H.; Abba, 872 H. Milk 50 lbs. 1 day, P. Butter 9 lbs. 8 oz. 7 days, P.
ETHEL, 905 H. Imp. Milk 45 lbs. 1 day, 10,262 lbs. 8 oz. 1 year, P.
ETHELKA, 1208 H. Imp. Milk 101 lbs. 1 day, 18,137 lbs. 7 oz. 1 year, P.
ETHELKA PRINCESS, 3897 H. F. Sir Henry Artis, 4418 H.; Ethelka 3d, 4817 H. Milk 46 lbs. 8 oz. 1 day, 900 lbs. 11 months 15 days, P.
ETHLENE, 5118 H. Imp. Milk 83 lbs. 1 day, P.
ETIENETTE, 5117 H. Imp. Milk 61 lbs. 1 day, P.
ETONA, 1006 D. F. Imp. Milk 62 lbs. 1 day, P.
ETTA, 876 H. Imp. Milk 42 lbs. 8 oz. 1 day, P.
EULA LEE, 1846 H. Imp. Milk 45 lbs. 1 day, 867 lbs. 1 oz. 8 months 25 days, P.
EUNICE, 291 H. Kossuth, 119 H.; Grand Duchess, 10 H. Milk 69 lbs. 1 day, P.
EUNICE CLAY, 1007 H. F. Lord of Cornwall, 3429 H.; Emma Clay, 1588 H. Milk 60 lbs. 1 day, P. Butter 23 lbs. 9 oz. 7 days, P.
EUNICE MIDWOULD, 1486 H. F. Walter Scott, 606 H.; Eunice, 291 H. Milk 46 lbs. 8 oz. 1 day, P.
EUSEBIA, 9289 H. Imp. Milk 45 lbs. 1 day, P. Butter 20 lbs. 15 oz. 7 days, P.
EUSEBIS 2D, 9487 H. Imp. Butter 20 lbs. 15 oz. 7 days, A.R.
EUTOPIA, 8933 H. Imp Milk 68 lbs. 4 oz. 1 day, P.
EVADNE, 5005 H. Imp. Milk 9376 lbs. 5 oz. 10 months 15 days, A R. Butter 24 lbs. 9 oz, 7 days, A.R.
EVALENA OF SHADELAND 2D, 8601 H. Shadeland Duke, 1093 H.; Evalena of Shadeland, 2411 H. Milk 373 lbs. 8 oz. 10 days, P.
EVALENA OF SHADELAND 3D, 6043 H. F. Shadeland Monarch, 2570 H.; Evalena of Shadeland, 2411 H. Milk 373 lbs. 8 oz. 10 days, A.R.
EVALENA OF SHADELAND 4TH, 10764 H. F. Shadeland Monarch, 2570 H.; Evalena of Shadeland, 2411 H. Milk 7063 lbs. 8 oz. 9 months, A.R.
EVAS ILIAS, 17075 H. F. Mazda, 2672 H.; Ilias Bonne, 5369 H. Butter 18 lbs. 9 oz. 7 days, A.R.
EVELYN S, 3977 H. Imp. Milk 63 lbs. 1 day, P. Butter 11 lbs. 1 oz. 7 days, P.
EVENTJE 2D, 3300 H. Imp. Milk 25 qts. 1 day, 422 lbs. 6 oz. 10 days, P.
EVERTJE, 1498 D. F. Heeg, 141 F. H. B.; Akke, 849 F. H. B. Milk 67 lbs. 1 day, P.
EXCELLENTJE 2D, 1365 H. F. Jacob Wit, 2662 Neth.; Excellentje, 9182 H. Milk 21 qts. 1 day, P.
EXCELSIOR'S BARONESS, 9944 H. Excelsior, 266 Neth.; Ham, 1090 Neth. Milk 60 lbs. 9 oz. 1 day, 13,831 lbs. 13 oz. 1 year, A.R. Butter 15 lbs. 8 oz. 7 days, A.R.
EXCELSIOR'S DUCHESS, 9038 H. Imp. Milk 8392 lbs. 11 months, P.
EXCELSIOR'S LADY, 9940 H. Imp. Milk 9783 lbs. 1 oz. 10 months 11 days, P.
EXCELSIOR'S MARQUISE, 9939 H. Imp. Milk 11,842 lbs. 10 oz. 1 year, P.
EXCELSIOR'S PRINCESS, 9941 H. Imp. Milk 11,301 lbs. 14 oz. 1 year, P. Butter 13 lbs. 5 oz. 7 days, P.
EXCELSIOR'S PRINCESS 2D, 3180 H. F. Prince Imperial, 1164 H.; Excelsior's Princess, 9041 H. Butter 10 lbs. 8 oz. 7 days, A.R.
EXECUTRIX, 4410 H. Imp. Milk 16,587 lbs. 14 oz. 1 year, P. Butter 21 lbs. 12 oz. 7 days, 86 lbs. 13 oz. 30 days, A.R.
EXECUTRIX 2D, 1591 H. F. Prince Imperial, 1164 H.; Executrix, 4401 H. Milk 9009 lbs. 13 oz. 11 months, P. Butter 21 lbs. 9 oz. 7 days, A.R.
EXECUTRIX NETHERLAND, 4942 H. Netherland Prince, 716 H.; Executrix, 4401 H. Milk 10,299 lbs. 10 oz. 1 year, A.R. Butter 16 lbs. 8 oz. 7 days, A.R.
EXQUISITE 2D, 1811 H. Imp. Milk 48 lbs. 12 oz. 1 day, 7800 lbs. 14 oz. 6 months 13 days, P.

FABIOLA, 2717 H. Imp. Milk 67 lbs. 1 day, 6239 lbs. 8 oz. 6 months 14 days, P.
FADETTA, 2718 H. Imp. Milk 41 lbs. 1 day, 1143 lbs. 30 days, P.
FADHA S, 2559 H. F. Bobbie, 928 H.; Dairy Maid, 610 H. Milk 9632 lbs. 10 months 21 days, P.
FADLADINIDA S, 2097 H. F. Bobbie, 928 H.; Amanda Gwynedd, 1669 H. Milk 8899 lbs. 11 months 11 days, P.
FAIRALL A, 511 H. Imp. Milk 71 lbs. 1 day, P. Butter 2 lbs. 11 oz. 1 day, 17 lbs. 7 days, P.
FAIR BLOSSOM, 4431 H. Imp. Milk 40 lbs. 1 day, P.
FAIRMONT PRIDE, 3157 H. F. Jacob, 608 H.; Orphia, 2851 H. Milk 48 lbs. 1 day, P.
FAIR PENITENT S, 2144 H. F. Violet King, 4210 H.; Thistledown, 7890 H. Milk 8572 lbs. 11 months 13 days, P.
FAIRSTAR S, 209 H. F. Joe S, 1592 H.; Constance S, 3057 H. Milk 54 lbs. 1 day, 10,428 lbs. 11 months 8 days, P.
FAIR VIEW, 2719 H. Imp. Milk 49 lbs. 8 oz. 1 day, 6025 lbs. 1 year, P.
FAIRY, 295 H. Imp. Milk 46 lbs. 1 day, 9957 lbs. 8 oz. 335 days, P.
FAIRY BELLE, 1849 H. Imp. Milk 46 lbs. 11 oz. 1 day, 9754 lbs. 10 oz. 11 months, P.
FAIRY S, 2139 H. F. Violet Prince, 4209 H.; Cinora, 6744 H. Milk 8784 lbs. 10 months, P.

MILK AND BUTTER RECORDS. 333

FAIRY VENUS, 5099 H. F. Sir Henry Artis, 4418 H.; Venus 4th, 3755 H. Butter 14 lbs. 3 oz. 7 days, P.
FANCHETTE, 5380 H. Pel, 122 F. H. B.; Eirdaarder, 755 F. H. B. Milk 33 lbs. 7 oz. 1 day, P.
FANCMONETTE LINCOLN, 10032 H. Imp. Milk 8019 lbs. 1 oz. 8 months 15 days, P.
FANCIFUL, 10146 H. David, 222 F. H. B.; Mooj¼, 202 F. H. B. Milk 37 lbs. 12 oz. 1 day, 8844 lbs. 4 oz. 1 year, P. Butter 10 lbs. 6 oz. 7 days. A.R.
FANNELL, 684 H. Imp. Milk 70 lbs. 1 day, P. Butter 2 lbs. 6 oz. 1 day, P.
FANNIEDELL, 52 H. F. Jacob, 215 Neth.; Sara, 2031 Neth. Milk 60 lbs. 1 day, P.
FANNIE CLARK, 8394 H. F. Prins Midlun , 2439 H.; Betje Havinga, 4070 H. Milk 1377 lbs. 12 oz. 1 month 4 days.
FANNIE DAW, 3430 H. F. Billy Bawn, 3087 H.; Marjorie Daw 3d, 5577 H. Milk 43 lbs. 6 oz. 1 day, 11,132 lbs. 8 oz. 1 year, P.
FANNY, 760 H. Bishop, 190 H.; Alma 2d. 240 H. Butter 12 lbs. 13 oz. 7 days, P.
FANNY ARTIS, 4850 H. F. Artis. 127 Neth.; Ariaantje, 1326 Neth. Milk 42 lbs. 1 oz. 1 day, 10,040 lbs. 14 oz. 1 year, P. Butter 12 lbs. 13 oz. 7 days, P.
FANNY FERN, 1289 H. Imp. Milk 68 lbs. 1 day, P.
FANNY FERN 2D, 1481 H. Imp. Milk 6445 lbs. 7 months 11 days, P.
FANNY OGDEN, 4430 H. Imp. Milk 57 lbs. 1 day, P. Butter 12 lbs. 2 oz. 7 days.
FANSJE, 6032 H. Imp. Milk 11,656 lbs. 6 oz. 10 months, A.R.
FANSJE 2D, 9052 H. F. Patrol, 864 H.; Fansje, 6032 H. Milk 61 lbs. 5 oz. 1 day, 13,923 lbs. 14 oz. 1 year, P.
FANTIBEL SCHAGEN, 7253 H. Imp. Milk 60 lbs. 1 day, P.
FARMINGTON BELLE, 294 D. F. Roscoe, 134 H.; Antje, 233 H. Milk 56 lbs. 1 day, P.
FASHION, 946 H. Imp. Milk 37 lbs. 3 oz. 1 day. 9427 lbs. 13 oz. 1 year, P.
FATINA, 5535 H. Snow Boy, 2046 H.; Maid of Mayfield, 5531 H. Milk 1220 lbs. 1 month, P.
FATINITZA, 2723 H. Imp. Milk 61 lbs. 3 oz. 1 day, 14,368 lbs. 1 year, P. Butter 16 lbs. 4 oz. 7 days, P.
FATINITZA 2D, 2724 H. Imp. Milk 11,798 lbs. 13 oz. 10 months, A.R. Butter 9 lbs. 10 oz. 7 days, A.R.
FATINITZA 4TH, 1703 H. F. Compeer, 200 H.; Fatinitza, 2723 H. Milk 8055 lbs. 6 oz. 9 months, P. Butter 10 lbs. 12 oz. 7 days, P.
FAW S, 2099 H. F. Joe S, 1592 H.; Elsie S, 3054 H. Milk 47 lbs. 1 day, 10,205 lbs. 11 months 23 days, P.
FEA S, 2146 H. F. Prince David, 2076 H ; Annie Wood, 244 H. Milk 51 lbs. 1 day, P.
FEDELLA, 1410 H. F. Cossack, 2008 H.; Harriet, 2456 H. Milk 10,105 lbs. 3 oz. 1 year, P.
FEDORA, 5893 H. Imp. Milk 90 lbs. 1 day, P.
FEDORA BELLE, 6514 H. Kurl, 1243 H.; Frankie Belle. 2482 H. Milk 655 lbs. 10 days, A.R.
FEKSTRA 2D, 4341 F. H. B. Imp. Milk 42 lbs. 1 day, P.
FELICITY, 878 H. Imp. Milk 40 lbs. 1 day, P.
FENELLA S, 2102 H. F. Bobbie, 923 H.; Kathrin, 510 H. Milk 10,261 lbs. 10 months. P.
FERN, 883 H. Imp. Milk 64 lbs. 1 day. 1980 lbs. 30 days, P. Butter 17 lbs. 7 days, 64 lbs. 30 days, P.
FERN SIDE, 2060 H. F. Norfolk, 1701 H. Schuurman's Port, 5851 H. Milk 49 lbs. 1 day, 2526 lbs. 60 days, P.
FERONIA, 7175 H. Imp. Milk 12,345 lbs. 8 oz. 1 year, A.R.
FETJE, 3702 H. Imp. Milk 72 lbs. 1 day.
FETJE HEIDERBROESEM, 4082 H. Imp. Milk 52 lbs. 1 day, P.
FETNAR S, 2103 H. Bobbie, 928 H.; Bessie Gwynedd, 1608 H. Milk 9608 lbs. 1 year, P.
FEZON S, 2106 H. F. Bobbie, 928 H.; Zepha, 1176 H. Milk 41 lbs. 1 day, 8942 lbs. 11 months 22 days, P.
FIAMETTA S, 2410 H. F. Hindoo, 2649 H.; Lurancy. 6137 H. Milk 49 lbs. 1 day, 1334 lbs. 30 days, P.
FIB S, 2141 H. F. Hindoo, 2649 H.; Gudmare, 6119 H. Milk 40 lbs. 1 day, 1181 lbs. 30 days, P.
FIDELIA OF SHADELAND, 2408 H. Imp. Milk 3235 lbs. 4 oz. 2 months, P.
FIDELIA ROI,, 5708 H. Imp. Milk 400 lbs. 10 days. P.
FIDES, 120 H. Imp. Milk 86 lbs. 1 day, P.
FIDES S, 2105 H. F. Prince Neptune, 2193 H.; Drusilla S, 3764 H. Milk 8610 lbs. 1 year, P.
FIDESSA S, 2143 H. F. Bonny, 3070 H.; Cormorend, 6358 H. Milk 11,228 lbs. 1 year, P.
FIELD SIGHT 2D, 3297 H. Imp. Milk 74 lbs. 1 day, P.
FIELD SIGHT 3D, 3298 H. Imp. Milk 50 lbs. 1 day, P.
FIDGETY, 5204 H. F. Neptune Jr., 1916 H.; Geertrui, 3332 H. Milk 72 lbs. 1 day, 1900 lbs. 30 days, P.
FIDGETY 2D. 14994 H. F. Zymel's Barrington, 1841 H F.; Fidgety, 5204 H. F. Milk 45 lbs. 1 day, P.
FILIA S, 2145 H. F. Clovis, 3303 H.; Charline, 6845 H. Milk 44 lbs. 1 day, P.; 7204 lbs. 9 months 26 days, A.R.
FINESSE, 298 H. Imp. Milk 87 lbs. 1 day, 17,337 lbs. 8 oz. 1 year, P.
FINESSE 2D., 561 H. Uncle Tom, 163 H.; Finesse, 298 H. Milk 12,983 lbs. 8 oz. 10 months, P.
FINETTA S, 2107 H. F. Oswald, 3331 H ; Gomora, 7236 H. Milk 7738 lbs. 1 year, P.
FLATTERY, 14158 H. F. Tell, 128 D. F ; Jallia, 3794 H. Milk 0700 lbs. 10 oz. 1 year, P.
FLAVONA, 7766 H. Imp. Milk 55 lbs. 12 oz. 1 day, 2722 lbs. 2 months, P.
FLIPPANTA S, 2148 H. F. Violet Prince, 4209 H.; Vitesse, 6137 H. Milk 36 lbs. 1 day, P.
FLOCKHEART S. 2111 H. F. Bristol, 297 H.; Modjeska, 407 H. Milk 11,821 lbs. 1 year, P.
FLORA 2D, 120 H Imp. Milk 9176 lbs. 296 days, P.
FLORABEL, 1702 H. Imp. Milk 62 lbs. 2 oz. 1 day, P.; 15,597 lbs. 10 oz. A.R. Butter 17 lbs. 1 oz. 7 days, A.R.
FLORA CLIFDEN'S MERCEDES, 1001 H. F. Mercedes Prince, 2150 H.; Flora Cliiden, 2408 H. Milk 35 lbs. 4 oz. 1 day, P.; 325 lbs. 13 oz. 10 days, A.R. Butter 12 lbs. 4 oz. 7 days, A.R.
FLORA FAIRFAX, 4733 H. F. Khan, 1144 H ; Belle Fairfax, 1117 H. Milk 62 lbs. 1 day, P.
FLORA KONING, 18 D. F. Imp. Milk 40 lbs. 1 day, P.
FLORAL, 1854 H. Imp. Milk 800*** lbs. 5 oz. 1 year, P.
FLORANTHA S, 2110 H F. Netherland Courtier, 2474 H.; Baltina, 7217 H. Milk 46 lbs. 1 day, P.
FLORDELICE S, 2112 H. F. Joe S, 1592 H.; Fondling, 7880 H. Milk 36 lbs. 1 day, 8749 lbs. 1 year, P.
FLORENCE HERBERT, 3093 H. Hugo 261 H.; Wittof, 675 H. Milk 62 lbs. 1 day, 18,163 lbs. 1 year, P. Butter 27 lbs. 13 oz. 7 days, A.R.; 101 lbs. 7 oz. 1 year, P.
FLORENCE REED, 2009 H. F. Lord's Jambo, 1588 H.; Jenny Reed, 712 H. Milk 65 lbs. 1 day, P.
FLORENTENA, 3357 H. Lord LeBaron, 248 H.; Index, 987 H. Milk 481 lbs. 4 oz. 7 days, P. Butter 23 lbs. 7 oz. 7 days, A.R.
FLORETTA, 915 H. Imp. Milk 40 lbs. 1 day, P.
FLORIDA, 5121 H. Imp. Milk 61 lbs. 1 day.
FLOSSY DILL, 11070 H. F. Pierre 1348 H.; Tygerin Pyzn 5693 H. Milk 50 lbs. 1 day, P.
FLY AWAY, 2792 H. F. 1st Duke of Oreida, 189 D. F.; Zuidma, 180 D. F. Milk 46 lbs. 2 oz. 1 day, P.
FONDLING, 7880 H. Imp. Milk 10,000 lbs. 1 year, P.
FOREST MAID, 4421 H. Imp. Milk 64 lbs. 6 oz. 1 day, 2130 lbs. 30 days, P.
FOUNTAIN, 953 H. Imp. Milk 8227 lbs. 4 oz. 1 year, P.
FOXIE, 2732 H. Imp. Milk 34 lbs. 9 oz. 1 day; 6200 lbs. 15 oz. 9 months 21 days, P.

FOZINA, 3195 H. Imp. Milk 595 lbs. 10 days, 11,908 lbs. 8 oz. 10 months 19 days, A.R.
FRAGRANT, 10152 H. Imp. Milk 47 lbs. 8 oz. 1 day, 12,618 lbs. 10 oz. 1 year, P. Butter 9 lbs. 13 oz. 7 days
FRANC, 886 H. Imp. Milk 32 lbs. 1 day, 10,000 lbs. 10 months P.
FRANCES, 1887 H. Imp. Milk 70 lbs. 7 oz. 1 day, P.
FRANCESCA, 5354 H. Imp. Milk 54 lbs. 1 day, 10,096 lbs. 1 year, P.
FRANCISCA, 578 H. Imp. Milk 40 lbs. 1 day, P.
FRANKIE BELLE, 2482 H. Tom Karl, 1009 H.; Geske, 317 H. Milk 608 lbs. 12 oz. 10 days, P.
FRANEJE, 88 D. F. Imp. Milk 63 lbs. 8 oz. 1 day, P.
FRANSEJE, 7094 H. Imp. Milk 46 lbs. 1 day, P.
FRAU, 131 H. Imp. Milk 1021 lbs. 1 month, P.
FRAU 2D, 303 H. Prince of Orange, 138 H.; Frau, 131 H. Milk 7916 lbs. 1 year, P.
FRAU 5th, 1436 H. Crown Prince, 80 H.; Frau 2d, 303 H. Milk 1779 lbs. 4 oz. 30 days, P. Butter 17 lbs 9 oz. 7 days, P.
FRAULEIN, 9 H. Imp. Milk 70 lbs. 1 day, 8588 lbs. 1 year, P.
FREDERIKA 2D, 5443 H. Saul 1435 H.; Frederika, 2255 H. Milk 6485 lbs. 10 months 15 days, P.
FRENESTA, 3530 H. F. International Prince, 4600 H.; Maas Nymph, 10401 H. F. Milk 40 lbs. 4 oz. 1 day, P., 8590 lbs. 6 oz. 10 months, P.
FRESCOE, 761 H. Imp. Milk 68 lbs. 1 day, P.
FRET, 6476 H. Imp. Milk 58 lbs. 1 day, P.
FRIEDA, 306 H. Imp. Milk 16.076 lbs. 1 year, P. Butter 6 lbs. 8 oz. 1 day, P.
FRIESIN 2D, 2997 Neth. Imp. Milk 73 lbs. 1 day, P.
FRIESLAND MAID, 1624 H. Imp. Milk 71 lbs. 8 oz. 1 day, 2153 lbs. 31 days, P.
FRIESLAND QUEEN, 3274 H. Imp. Milk 34 lbs. 1 day, P.
FROLIC, 2342 H. Burly, 394 H.; Dewdrop, 960 H. Milk 52 lbs. 12 oz. 1 day, P.; 8160 lbs. 3 oz. 1 year, A.R. Butter 10 lbs. 3 oz. 7 days, A.R.
FROLICSOME, 879 H. Imp. Milk 79 lbs. 12 oz. 1 day, 8404 lbs. 10 oz. 1 year. Butter 13 lbs. 7 days, P.
FRONAH, 10174 H. Imp. Milk 50 lbs. 1 day, P.
FROUKJE, 5494 H. Imp. Milk 57 lbs. 8 oz. 1 day, P.
FYRA BEAUTY, 1525 H. F. Mazda, 2672 H.; Beauty Zwaan, 240 H. Milk 72 lbs. 12 oz. 1 day, 19,027 lbs. 1 year, P.

GAASTRA, 637 D. F. Imp. Milk 529 lbs. 10 days, A.R.
GAASTRA 2D, 9608 H. F. Hamilton, 686 D. F.; Gaastra, 637 D. F. Milk 7631 lbs. 8 oz. 10 months.
GAASTRA 3D, 19813 H. F. Hamilton, 686 D. F.; Gaastra, 637 D. F. Milk 7750 lbs. 8 months 10 days, A.R.
GABRETTA S, 5278 H. F. Netherland Courtier, 2474 H.; Valley Queen, 851 H. Milk 9518 lbs. 1 year, P.
GABRIELLE, 792 H. Imp. Milk 45 lbs. 1 day, P.
GABRIELLE 2D, 4849 H. F. Joe Jefferson, 273 H.; Gabrielle, 792 H. Milk 40 lbs. 1 day, P.
GABRIELLE S, 5277 H. F. Cornelis, 563 Neth.; Diewertje, 2020 Neth. Milk 9274 lbs. 1 year, P.
GABRINA, 6890 H. F. Imp. Milk 13,131 lbs. 1 oz. 1 year, A.R. Butter 13 lbs. 9 oz. 7 days, P.
GABRINA 2D, 1590 H. F. Sir Henry 2d of Aaggie, 1451 H.; Gabrina, 6890 H. Butter 10 lbs. 7 days, P.
GALATEA, 308 H. Imp. Milk 57 lbs. 4 oz. 1 day, 8247 lbs. 8 oz. 10 months, P.
GALATIA 2D, 4588 H. F. King Estmere, 4255 H.; Galatia, 9565 H. Milk 39 lbs. 8 oz. 1 day, P.
GALERANA S, 5281 H. F. Cornelis, 563 Neth.; Langedyk, 2030 H. F. Milk 7245 lbs. 9 months 25 days, A.R.
GALIANA S, 5282 H. F. Rembrandt 2d, 620 Neth.; Maartje, 2037 H. F. Milk 9094 lbs. 1 year.
GALLIA, 5794 H. Imp. Milk 75 lbs. 14 oz. 1 day, 14,222 lbs. 12 oz. 1 year, P.
GALLICUA S, 5284 H. F. Prince David, 2076 H.; Vineta, 473 H. Milk 43 lbs. 1 day, 1148 lbs. 30 days, P.
GAMBIA, 7202 H. Imp. Milk 10,379 lbs. 13 oz. 1 year, P.
GANDIOSA S, 5289 H. F. Prince Neptune, 2098 H.; Jenury Jones, 6112 H. Milk 45 lbs. 1 day, 1211 lbs. 30 days, P.
GARGANELLA, 5287 H. F. Netherland Courtier, 2474 H.; Joel 6128 H. Milk 39 lbs. 1 day, 108 lbs. 30 days, P.
GARRETTY 3D, 13455 H. F. Washington Mahomet, 3857 H. F.; Garretty, 9035 H. Butter 10 lbs. 11 oz. 7 days, A.R.
GAWREY S, 5290 H. F. Prince Neptune, 2098 H.; Orbona, 7203 H. Milk 33 lbs 1 day; 990 lbs. 30 days. P.
GAYNESHA, 1928 D. F. Johan; Klaske. Milk 58 lbs. 1 day, 13,423 lbs. 1 year, P.
GAYETY, 8098 H. Imp. Milk 57 lbs. 1 day, P.
GAZELLE. 312 H. Imp. Milk 40 lbs. 8 oz. 1 day; 6188 lbs. 260 days. P. Butter 16 lbs. 4 oz. 7 days, P.
GAZELLITA, 7532 H. F. No-No, 4076 H.; Gaznel, 8940 H. Milk 46 lbs. 3 oz. 1 day, P.
GEBKE (OTIS), 2185 H. Imp. Milk 12,000 lbs. 1 year. Butter 16 lbs. 9 oz. 7 days, P.
GEDDES GIRL, 2735 H. Imp. Milk 65 lbs. 1 day, P.
GEELE, 1506 D. F. Carre, 255 F. H. B.; Trijntje, 448 F. H. B. Milk 51 lbs. on grass, P.
GEERTJE, 313 H. Imp. Milk 88 lbs. 6 oz. 1 day, P.
GEERTRUDE NICO, 6720 H. Imp. Butter 19 lbs. 7 days A.R.
GEERTRUI, 3332 H. F. Pieter, 209 Neth.; Geertrui, 3934 Neth. Milk 71 lbs. 4 oz. 1 day, 1996 lbs. 8 oz. 7 days, P.
GEERTRUIDA NIENHUIS, 4091 H. Imp. Milk 48 lbs 1 day, P.
GEERT VAN DIEPEN, 6018 H. Imp. Milk 79 lbs. 12 oz. 1 day, P.; 12,188 lbs. 11 oz. 9 months 27 days, A.R.
GEESJE, 5916 Neth. Imp. Milk 73 lbs. 8 oz. 1 day, P.
GELDERTJE, 11612 H. F. Imp. Milk 84 lbs. 1 day, 20,138 lbs. 8 oz. 10 months, P. Butter 21 lbs. 7 days, P.
GELSCHE, 173 D. F. Imp. Milk 100 lbs. 1 day, 22,863 lbs. 1 year, A.R.
GELSKE, 715 H. Imp. Milk 80 lbs. 1 day, P. Butter 15 lbs. 15 oz. 7 days, P.
GELUK, 3226 H. Imp. Milk 33 lbs. 1 day, P.
GENESTA, 9566 H. Artis, 127 Neth.; De Goede, 606 Neth. Milk 8076 lbs. 4 oz. 10 months. Butter 24 lbs. 9 oz. 7 days.
GENESTA 2D, 4592 H. F. Sir Henry of Maplewood, 2633 H.; Genesta, 9566 H. Milk 78 lbs. 10 oz. 1 day. Butter 51 lbs. 7 oz. 1 day, 23 lbs. 5 oz. 7 days, P.
GENESTA ECHO, 7600 H. F. Echo's Prince of Wayne, 31 H. F.; Genesta, 9566 H. Milk 53 lbs. 10 oz. 1 day, 5138 lbs. 1 oz. 6 months, P.
GENOVEFA S, 5292 H. F. Netherland Courtier, 2474 H.; Antjeal, 517 H. Milk 39 lbs. 1 day, 7811 lbs. 10 months, P.

GENTLE ANNIE, 135 H. Elswout, 94 H.; Jufrou, 153 H. Milk 9572 lbs. 4 oz. 1 year. Butter 375 lbs. 1 year, P.
GENTLE MAID, 672 H. Imp. Milk 65 lbs. 1 day, 12,903 lbs. 8 oz. 1 year, P.
GENTLE MAID 2D, 1160 H. Ebbo, 236 H.; Gentle Maid, 672 H. Milk 8884 lbs. 11 oz. 8 months 26 days. P. Butter 16 lbs. 12 oz. 7 days, A.R.
GEORGIA OF LYNWOOD, 6787 H. Imp. Milk 56 lbs. 12 oz. 1 day, 5923 lbs. 13 oz. 4 months, P.
GEORGIE, 944 H. Imp. Milk 76 lbs. 5 oz. 1 day, 13,209 lbs. 9 oz. 343 days, P. Butter 21 lbs. 15 oz. 7 days, 63 lbs. 4 oz. 21 days, A.R.
GEORGIE 2D, 3549 H. Burly, 394 H.; Georgie, 944 H. Milk 54 lbs. 8 oz. 1 day, 9680 lbs. 14 oz. 1 year, P. Butter 13 lbs. 11 oz. 7 days, A.R.
GEORGIE 2D'S AAGGIE, 5385 H. F. Royal Aaggie, 3463 H.; Georgie 2d, 3549 H. Butter 17 lbs. 9 oz. 7 days, A.R.
GEORGIE 3D, 6623 H. Burly, 394 H.; Georgie, 944 H. Milk 77 lbs. 1 day, 15,370 lbs. 13 oz. 1 year, A.R. Butter 19 lbs. 3 oz. 7 days, A.R.
GEORGIE CLAY, 1350 H. F. Lord of Cornwall, 3429 H.; Belle Clay, 1052 H.
GERBEN 2D, 18677 H. F. Chief of Maple Hill, 1674 H. F.; Gerben, 5562 H. Milk 39 lbs. 1 day. Butter 32 lbs. 7 days, P.
GERBEN 4th, 1080 D. F. Gerben, 7 F. H. B.; Gerben 3d. 250 F. H. B. Milk 77 lbs. 14 oz. 1 day, 13,570 lbs. 4 oz. 8 months, P. Butter 32 lbs. 7 days, A.R.
GERBIG, 3941 F. H. B. Imp. Milk 60 lbs. 1 day, P.
GERDA, 5309 H. Imp. Milk 66 lbs. 6 oz. 1 day, 11,000 lbs. 10 months, P.
GERDA BAWN, 3996 H. F. Billy Bawn, 3087 H.; Gerda, 5309 H. Milk 6777 lbs. 4 oz. 9 months 16 days, A.R.
GERRITJE, 4252 H. Imp. Milk 76 lbs. 1 day, P.
GERSTER, 1917 H. Imp. Milk 48 lbs. 8 oz. 1 day, 1228 lbs. 30 days, P.
GERTJE, 8250 H. Imp. Milk 79 lbs. 8 oz. 1 day, P.
GERTIE ROOKER, 9879 H. Imp. Milk 7337 lbs. 9 oz. 10 months, P.
GERT MET 2D. Imp. Milk 71 lbs. 8 oz. 1 day, P.
GERTRUDE, 690 D. F. Caesar, 77 P. R.; Gretje, 221 M. R. Milk 70 lbs. 1 day; 3440 lbs. 90 days. Butter 76 lbs. 30 days, 203 lbs. 90 days, P.
GETA, 5288 H. Imp. Milk 70 lbs. 1 day.
GETA 2D. Griff, 1719 H.; Geta, 5288 H. Milk 40 lbs. 1 day, P.
GEUKER 2D, 1776 D. F. Hobbema, 319 F. H. B.; Geuker, 2320 F. H. B. Milk 4648 lbs. 8 oz. 8 months 1 day, A.R. Butter 11 lbs. 13 oz. 7 days, A.R.
GIANETTA, 3704 H. Imp. Milk 48 lbs. 1 day, P.
GIFT, 2344 H. Burly, 394 H.; Oatka, 945 H. Milk 44 lbs. 9 oz. 1 day, P.; 10,145 lbs. 14 oz. 1 year, A.R. Butter 10 lbs. 10 oz. 7 days, A.R.
GIFT'S AAGGIE, 4984 H. F. Royal Aaggie, 3463 H.; Gift, 2344 H. Milk 8638 lbs. 9 months, P. Butter 19 lbs. 13 oz. 7 days, A.R.
GILDIPPE S, 5299 H. F. Imp. Milk 37 lbs. 1 day, P.; 7632 lbs. 10 months 3 days, A.R.
GILLIAN S, 5300 H. F. No Shirk, 3561 H.; Nierda, 2007 H. F. Milk 38 lbs. 1 day, P.; 9619 lbs. 1 year, A.R.
GILT EDGE, 2736 H. Imp. Milk 57 lbs. 14 oz. 1 day, 11,585 lbs. 14 oz. 9 months 6 days, P.
GILT EDGE 2D, 495 H. F. Captain Daw, 2088 H.; Gilt Edge, 2736 H. Milk 39 lbs. 9 oz. 1 day, P.; 7931 lbs. 6 oz. 10 months, A.R.
GIPSEY QUEEN, 1209 H. Imp. Milk 8577 lbs. 14 oz. 10 months 27 days, P.
GITANA, 3166 H. Imp. Milk 72 lbs. 8 oz. 1 day, 12,156 lbs. 1 year, P.
GLADIOLA, 1865 H. Imp. Milk 46 lbs. 4 oz. 1 day, 3307 lbs. 12 oz. 3 months, P.
GLADIS, 7957 H. Imp. Milk 50 lbs. 8 oz. 1 day, P.
GLAD TIDINGS, 6869 H. Imp. Milk 12,325 lbs. 1 year, A.R. Butter 11 lbs. 3 oz. 7 days, A.R.
GLANCE S, 5303 H. F. No Shirk, 3561 H.; Meddo, 2113 H. Milk 40 lbs. 1 day; 9893 lbs. 1 year, P.
GLENARA, 1413 H. F. Cossack, 2008 H.; Grisette, 2479 H. Milk 5839 lbs. 8 oz. 10 months.
GLENBURINE, 8788 H. Imp. Milk 20, 38 lbs. 8 oz. 1 year, P.
GLENDORA, 2737 H. Imp. Milk 57 lbs. 12 oz. 1 day, P.
GLENEIDA 4TH, 5929 H. F. Viking, 2062 H.; Gleneida, 1397 H. Milk 372 lbs. 4 oz. 10 days, A.R.
GLORIA, 3811 H. Imp. Milk 60 lbs. 1 day, P.
GODVIVA S, 5304 H. F. No Shirk, 3561 H.; Burger, 2028 H. F. Milk 37 lbs. 1 day, 8520 lbs. 9 months 24 days, P.
GOLD FRINGE, 6673 H. F. Sir Edwin of Aaggie, 1861 H.; Almet of Lynwood, 6778 H. Milk 41 lbs. 14 oz. 1 day, P.
GOLDIE KONING, 241 D. F. Paul Hartog, 6 M. R.; Katje Koning, 40 M. R. Milk 64 lbs. 8 oz. 1 day, P.; 1868 lbs. 8 oz. 30 days, A.R Butter 20 lbs. 1 oz. 7 days, P.; 26 lbs. 4 oz. 10 days, A.R.
GOLD LEAF, 6547 H. Milk 64 lbs. 1 day, P.; 519 lbs. 11 oz. 10 days, A.R. Butter 20 lbs. 3 oz. 7 days, A.R.
GOMORA, 7236 H. Imp. Milk 52 lbs. 1 day, 13,071 lbs. 1 year, P.
GONERIL S, 5305 H. F. Joe S, 1592 H.; Remmetji, 2012 H. F. Milk, 4957 lbs 4 months, P.
GOOD CHEER, 4423 H. Imp. Milk 40 lbs. 1 day, P.
GORI PEL, 2246 H. F. Prince of Altijzverk, 178 D. F.; Pel 4th, 525 D. F. Milk 60 lbs. 1 day.
GORTER, 662 H. Imp. Milk 84 lbs. 1 day, P.; 11,511 lbs. 10 months, A.R.
GORTER 2D, 663 H. Imp. Milk 10,236 lbs. 10 months.
GORTER 2D A, 1545 H. Johannis, 428 H.; Gorter 2d, 663 H. Milk 7846 lbs. 10 months, P.
GOULDINA, 8701 H. Imp. Milk 10,264 lbs. 6 oz. 11 months, P.
GOVERNESS, 4371 H. Imp. Milk 40 lbs. 1 day.
GOVERS, 1809 Neth. Imp. Milk 57 lbs. 8 oz. 1 day, P.
GRACE, 503 H. Imp. Milk 60 lbs. 1 day, P.
GRACE ANDOVER, 1046 H. Dictator 82 H.; Lady Andover, 16 H. Milk 85 lbs. 1 day, P.
GRACE LINCOLN, 10004 H. Lincoln, 120 Neth.; Trijntje, 35 Neth. Milk 55 lbs. 11 oz. 1 day, P.; 11,823 lbs. 1 oz. 10 months, A.R. Butter 15 lbs. 12 oz. 7 days, A.R.
GRACIENNE, 9297 H. Imp. Milk 60 lbs. 1 day.
GRACIENNE 2D, 4058 H. F. Netherland Knight, 1852 H.; Gracienne, 9297 H. Butter 14 lbs. 14 oz. 7 days. A.R.
GRACIOSA S, 5307 H. F. Netherland Courtier, 2474 H.; Gomora, 7236 H. Milk 39 lbs. 1 day, 1,095 lbs. 30 days, P.
GRASSY S, 5293 H. F. Joe, 1592 H.; Neefjes, 9473 H. Milk 37 lbs. 1 day, P.
GREAT RIVER GLORIE, 1304 H. F. Imp. Milk 25 qts. 1 day, P.
GREENWOOD GIRL, 4428 H. Imp. Milk 50 lbs. 4 oz. 1 day, 604 lbs. 10 oz. 10 days, P. Butter 14 lbs. 1 oz., A.R.

HOLSTEIN-FRIESIAN CATTLE.

GRENDA DORREBOOM, 8409 H. Imp. Milk 43 lbs. 4 oz. 1 day, P.
GRETCHEN 3D, 819 H. William, 56 H.; Gretchen, 11 H. Milk 72 lbs. 1 day, P.
GRETCHEN 5TH, 1556 H. Karl, 278 H.; Gretchen 3d, 319 H. Milk 60 lbs. 1 day, P.
GRETJE, 875 Neth. Imp. Milk 60 lbs. 1 day, P.
GRETJE 2D, 1528 H. Imp. Milk 65 lbs. 1 day, P.
GRETTA THORNE, 10951 H. F. Pierre, 1848 H.; Duyn's Koopman, 8231 H. Milk 54 lbs. 1 day, P.
GRETT HARTOG, 13101 H. F. Mooie Hartog, 418 D. F.; Gretje, 221 D. F. Milk 60 lbs. 8 oz. 1 day, 6053 lbs. 5 oz. 1 year, P. Butter 20 lbs. 3 oz. 7 days, P.
GRIEJKE BEAUTY 2D, 1712 H. F. Jacob Clifden, 2318 H.; Griejke Beauty, 4658 H. Milk 29 lbs. 4 oz. 1 day, P.
GRIETJE, 250 D. F. Jacob; Pietje. Milk 73 lbs. 1 day. P.
GRIETJE BOOTS, 6429 H. Imp. Milk 53 lbs. 8 oz 1 day. 5432 lbs. 10 oz. 4 months 28 days, P.
GRIETJE COLUMBUS, 3822 H. F. Columbus, 400 Neth.; Grietje, 5415 Neth. Milk 52 lbs. 1 day, P.
GRIETJE EGMOND, 6456 H. Imp. Milk 23 lbs. 8 oz. 1 day, P.
GRIETJE KEYES, 8357 H. F. Druyfs Keyes, 2371 H. F.; Grietje W, 5718 H. Milk 55 lbs. 1 day.
GRIETJE L, 3040 H. Imp. Milk 80 lbs. 8 oz. 1 day. Butter 9 lbs. 4 oz. 7 days, P.
GRIETJE P. Imp. Milk 11,230 lbs. 1 year, P.
GRIETJE RAUWERD, 5728 H. Imp. Milk 15 qts. 1 day, P.
GRIETJE V, 2339 H. Imp. Milk 51 lbs. 4 oz. 1 day, P.
GRIETJE VESTER 2D, 2289 H. F. Saul, 1435 H.; Grietje Vester, 5701 H. Milk 4979 lbs. 7 months, P.
GRIETJE W, 5718 H. Imp. Milk 55 lbs. 1 day, P.
GRIFFITH S, 5291 H. F. Joe S, 1592 H.; Katrina, 510 H. Milk 39 lbs. 1 day, P.
GRILLA, 4865 H. Duke of Anjon, 1250 H.; Minnie Scholton, 1906 H. Milk 71 lbs. 1 day, P.
GRISKINISSA S, 5309 H. F. Joe S, 1592 H.; Bornia, 2016 H. Milk 9423 lbs. 1 year, P.
GRIZZIE S, 5310 H. F. Prince David, 2076 H.; Adria, 7190 H. Milk 53 lbs 1 day, 1534 lbs. 30 days, P.
GROH, 8276 H. F. De Hoop, 311 F. H. B.; Weijer, 2311 F. H. B. Milk 48 lbs. 1 day, 1240 lbs. 30 days, P.
GRONINGEN MAID, 1179 H. Imp. Milk 70 lbs. 1 day. Butter 21 lbs. 13 oz. 7 days, P.
GROOTANNA, 7742 H. Imp. Milk 84 lbs. 1 day, P.
GROTON PET 2D, 2524 H. Duke of Groton, 1710 H.; Groton Pet, 6821 H. Milk 21 qts. 1 day, P.
GUDULA, 6122 H. Imp. Milk 56 lbs 1 day, 11,652 lbs. 8 oz. 1 year, P. Butter 16 lbs. 7 oz. 7 days, P.
GUESSNOT, 9361 H. F. Archibald, 383 D. F.; Chloe, 816 D. F. Milk 7427 lbs. 10 oz. 8 months 5 days, P.
GUILELESS S, 5296 H. F. No Shirk, 3561 H.; Fonsel, 2001 H. F. Milk 7332 lbs. 10 months 7 days, P.
GUNSTIG, 3448 H. Dick Schlip, 220 H.; Lady Kurt, 358 H. Milk 52 lbs. 1 day, P.
GURGLE, 8099 H. Imp. Milk 67 lbs. 1 day, P.
GUSKE, 1727 F. H. B. Imp. Milk 80 lbs. 1 day, P.
GUSKER, 2320 F. H. B. Imp. Milk 59 lbs. 1 day, P.
GUSTINA, 806 H. Imp. Milk 60 lbs. 1 day. Butter 16 lbs. 8 oz. 7 days, P.
GUSTY, 6536 H. Imp. Milk 54 lbs. 14 oz. 1 day, 1158 lbs. 30 days, P.
GUTHRIEBELLE, 7744 H. Klaas, 216 Neth.; Jacoba, 1352 Neth. Milk 44 lbs. 1 day, P.
GUURTJE, 5116 Neth. Imp. Milk 77 lbs. 1 day, 15,152 lbs. 1 year, P.
GUURTJE ROGGEVEEN, 3821 H. F. Roggeveen, 420 Neth; Guurtje, 5116 Neth. Milk 5443 lbs, 7 months. Butter 10 lbs. 3½ oz. 7 days, P.
GWENDOLINE, 9299 H. Imp. Milk 52 lbs. 1 day, 10,308 lbs. 9 months 14 days, P.
GWENDOLINE PEL, 1072 D. F. Witema, 125 F. H. B.; Pel 4th, 194 M. R. Milk 65 lbs. 1 day. Butter 32 lbs. 7 days P.

HAARSMA, 5080 H. Imp. Milk 40 lbs. 1 day, P.
HAGA DORREBOOM, 8406 H. Imp. Milk 66 lbs. 8 oz. 1 day. Butter 14 lbs. 7 days, P.
HAGAR 2D, 6555 H. Gortus, 642 H.; Hagar, 1006 H. Milk 46 lbs. 8 oz. 1 day, P.
HAIZUM, 4702 H. Imp. Milk 20 qts. 1 day, P.
HALBE 5721 H. Imp. Milk 62 lbs. 1 day, P.
HALEYZAAM, 8262 H. F. Frisco 2d, 676 F. H. B.; Jantje, 1444 F. H. B. Milk 48 lbs 1 day, P.
HALITJE, 8263 H. F. David 2d, 492 F. H. B.; Sophia, 1657 F. H. B. Milk 61 lbs. 1 day, 1261 lbs. 30 days, P.
HALKINA, 5186 H. F. Empyrean, 1006 H.; Harriet 2456 H. Milk 6439 lbs. 3 oz. 1 year, P.
HALMIDE, 3007 H. F. Imp. Milk 9680 lbs. 5 oz. 10 months, A.R.
HALQUI, 8627 H. Imp. Milk 65 lbs. 1 day, 1,611 lbs. 8 oz 30 days, P.
HALQUI 2D, 4124 H. F. Lubbert, 3384 H.; Halqui, 8627 H. Milk 395 lbs. 10 days, A.R.
HAMER SCHOTSMAN, 8390 H. Imp. Milk 49 lbs. 8 oz. 1 day, 400 lbs 10 days, P.
HAMMING, 3851 H. Imp. Milk 99 lbs. 1 day, P.
HAMMOLEKETH S, 9472 H. F. No Shirk, 3561 H.; Pastelein, 2011 H. F. Milk 8023 lbs. 7 months 24 days, P.
HANDSOME, 8695 H. Imp. Butter 11 lbs. 14 oz. 7 days, P.
HANNAH, 323 H. Imp. Milk 7891 lbs. 1 year, P.
HANNAH ROOKER, 9007 H. Imp. Milk 46 lbs. 5 oz. 1 day, 10,026 lbs. 1 oz. 1 year, P. Butter 11 lbs. 9 oz. 7 days, P.
HANS 2D, 3276 H. Imp. Milk 48 lbs. 1 day, P. Butter 14 lbs. 7 days, P.
HARLOWE S, 9455 H. F. Prince David, 2076 H.; Faw S, 2099 H. F. Milk 45 lbs. 1 day, 1323 lbs. 30 days, P.
HARMENKE, 6219 H. Imp. Milk 72 lbs. 1 day, P.
HARMONIA, 3094 H. Imp. Milk 54 lbs. 4 oz. 1 day, P.; 50½ lbs. 2 oz. 10 days, A.R. Butter 16 lbs. 11¾ oz. 7 days, A.R.
HAROLDINE, 2742 H. Imp. Milk 47 lbs. 15 oz. 1 day, 1,822 lbs. 7 oz. 45 days, P. Butter 15 lbs. 11 oz. 7 days, 30 lbs. 5 oz. 15 days, P.
HARREL S, 9450 H. F. Netherland Courtier, 2474 H.; Dainty S, 3787 H. Milk 411 lbs. 10 days, A.R.
HARRIET, 2456 H. Dirk Hatterick, 219 H.; Hetty, 327 H. Milk 6583 lbs. 8 months 3 days, P.
HARRIET ANN, 696 H. York, 171 H.; Betsey Prig, 694 H. Milk 12,840 lbs. 11 months, P.
HARRIETTA, 856 H. F. Ulitje, 267 F. H. B.; Pietje, 1911 F. H. B. Milk 30 lbs. 1 day, P.
HASKELL S, 9463 H. F. Netherland Courtier, 2474 H.; Evangeline, 203 H. Milk 37 lbs. 1 day, P.
HASSAN VEER, 8404 H. Imp. Milk 48 lbs. 8 oz. 1 day, P.
HATIE S, 9469 H. F. Prince David, 2076 H.; Fairy S, 2139 H. F. Milk 370 lbs. 10 days, A.R.
HATTIE, 3042 H. Silas, 592 H.; Linka, 1132 H. Milk 72 lbs. 1 day, P.
HATTIE FAIR, 4441 H. Imp. Milk 45 lbs. 1 day, P.
HAVILAH S, 9444 H. F. Netherland Courtier, 2474 H.; Avenhil, 2023 H. F. Milk 36 lbs. 1 day, 1048 lbs. 30 days, P.
HAWKEYE, 5270 H. Imp. Milk 50 lbs. 1 day, P.; 15,533 lbs. 8 oz. 10 months 25 days, A.R.

MILK AND BUTTER RECORDS. 337

HAZEL, 3390 H. Imp. Milk 42 lbs. 8 oz. 1 day, P.
HE, 7792 H. F. Neptune, 711 H.; Rustic Lass, 1821 H. Milk 25 qts. 1 day, P.
HEABELTJE, 11826 H. F. Uiltje, 411 F. H. B.; Abina de Boer, 377 Aux F. H. B. Milk 54 lbs. 1 day,
1508 lbs. 30 days, P.
HEABELTJE 2D, 11895 H. F. Cleveland, 1091 F. H. B.; Heabeltje, 11826 H. F. Milk 72 lbs. 1 day, 771
lbs. 10 days. Butter 18 lbs. 7 oz. 7 days, P.
HEBE LINCOLN. 10019 H. Imp. Milk 46 lbs. 13 oz. 1 day, P.
HECATE 3D, 17934 H. F. Violet Prince, 42000 H. F.; Hecate, 6117 H. Milk 74 lbs. 4 oz. 1 day, 18,821
lbs. 10 months 9 days, P.
HEDDA 2D, 6808 H. F. Dime, 3161 H. F.; Hedda, 3399 H. Milk 1307 lbs. 30 days, 8430 lbs. 238 days, P.
Butter 41 lbs. 9 oz. 30 days, P.
HEEG'S REINKJE 4TH, 1359 D. F. Johan; Reinkje. Milk 10,952 lbs. 12 oz. 12 months 27 days, F.
HEILTJE, 1006 Neth. Imp. Milk 68 lbs. 1 day, P.
HEINSE, 999 D. F. Imp. Milk 72 lbs. 5 oz. 1 day, P.
HELA S, 9443 H. F. Netherland Courtier, 2474 H.; Merlo, 2014 H F. Milk 29 lbs. 1 day, 1107 lbs. 30
days, P.
HELDER, 324 H. Imp. Milk 60 lbs. 1 day, P.
HELENA 2D, 17988 H. F. Duplicate, 2225 H.; Helena, 1625 D. F. Butter 13 lbs. 2 oz. A.R.
HELENA BURKE, 22916 H. F. Lord Burke, 11731 H. F.; Sicha, 733 H. F. M lk 51 lbs. 8 oz. 1 day,
1404 lbs. 31 days, P. Butter 17.03 lbs. 7 days. A.R.
HELENA S, 9445 H. F. Netherland Courtier, 2474 H.; Astella, 6087 H. Milk 389 lbs. 8 oz. 10 days, A.R.
HELENE'S VIOLET 2D, 7914 H. F. Remington, 1716 H. F.; Helene's Violet, 792 H. F. Milk 40 lbs. 1
day, 10,956 lbs. 12 oz. 1 year, A.R. Butter 10 lbs. 3 oz. 7 days, A.R.
HELEN S, 1415 H. Imp. Milk 53 lbs. 1 day, P.
HELIOTROPE, 325 H. Imp. Milk 12,614 lbs. 10 months, A.R.
HENDRIKA, 140 H. Imp. Milk 75 lbs. 8 oz. 1 day, P.
HENNA, 9677 H. Imp. Milk 50 lbs. 1 day, 1300 lbs. 30 days, P.
HERE S, 9475 H. F. No Shirk, 3561 H.; Englewood S, 8531 H. Milk 5400 lbs. 5 months 20 days. P.
HERINGA, 10848 H. F. Tell, 128 D. F.; Norrissa, 1842 D. F. Milk 42 lbs. 1 oz. _ day, 10,856 lbs. 12 oz.
1 year, P.
HERMANA, 9318 H. F. Sultan, 3496 H. F.; Agneta, 1417 H. F. Milk 30 lbs. 1 dry, P.
HERMESIND S, 9451 H. F. Prince David, 2076 H.; Clara S, 3058 H. Milk 382 lbs. 10 days, A.R.
HERMION S, 9453 H. F. Prince David, 2076 H.; Diewertje, 2020 H. F. Milk 635 lbs. 10 months 15
days, P.
HERNSTINE, 1871 H. Imp. Milk 70 lbs 1 day, 5921 lbs. 15 oz. 6 months 13 days, P. Butter 8 bs. 12
oz. 7 days, P.
HERODIAS S, 9474 H. F. Prince David 2076 H.; Orbona, 7203 H. Milk 6894 lbs. 10 months, P.
HERTIE, 3340 H. Imp. Milk, 43 lbs. 1 day, P.
HETTY 327 H. Imp. Milk 12,613 lbs. 3 oz. 10 months, A.R.
HETTY W, 3064 H. Sir William 2d, 342 H.; Queen of the Valley, 4301/2 H. Milk 12.223 lbs. 4 oz., A.R.
HETTY W 2D, 1288 H F. Lad of Present, 2389 H.; Hetty W, 3074 H. Milk 560 lbs. 4 oz. 10 days,
8141 lbs. 12 oz. 8 months 15 days, A.R.
HETTY W's ARTIS CLOTHILDE, 31543 H. F. Artis Adiantum's Clothilde, 15202 H. F.; Hetty W,
3064 H. Milk 380 lbs. 12 oz. 10 days, 7776 lbs 8 oz. 10 months, A.R.
HIATOGA, 3308 H. Dirk Hatterick, 219 H.; Heliotrope, 325 H. M lk 5834 lbs. 4 oz. 1 year, P.
HIAWATHA MAID, 3448 H. Compeer, 209 H.; Bonnie Jean, 783 H Milk 1012 bs. 5 oz. 30 days, 5755
lbs. 1 oz. 5 months 3 days, P.
HIEKE, 2810 F. H. B. Imp. Milk 66 lbs. 1 day, P.
HIEMKE, 6267 H. Imp. Milk 65 lbs. 1 day, P.
HIEMSTRA'S FAVORITE, 6377 H. Imp. Milk 10,555 lbs. 1 year, P.
HIGHLAND MARY, 6158 H. Imp. Milk 68 lbs. 1 day, P. Butter 15 lbs. 2 oz. 1 day, P.
HIGHT ULAR, 11479 H. F. Juror, 2295 H.; Ulah, 7184 H. Milk 59 lbs. 1 day, P.
HIJKE 2D, 1012 D. F. Imp. Milk 6764 lbs. 5 months. Butter 18 ls. 7 days, P.
HILDA, 556 H. Imp. Milk 64 lbs. 1 day, P.
HILDA ALBAN, 8631 H. F. Netherland Alban, 4584 H.; Topaz 3d's Henrietta, 1580 H. F. Butter 14
lbs. 10 oz. 30 days, A.R.
HILDA OF PACIFIC. 619 H. F. Milk 56 lbs. 1 day, P.
HILDA SPAANZ, 2535 H. F. Senboer, 3227 H.; Pride O'Dec. 4903 H. Milk 63 lbs. 1 day, 14,591 lbs. 1
year, A. R. Butter 20 lbs. 7 oz. 7 days, A.R.
HILLEGONDA KA, 5681 H. Imp. Milk 6 lbs. 1 day, 9,164 lbs. 8 oz. 5 months, P.
HILLEGONDA KA'S BOELYN, 14418 H. F. Johnnie Boelyn, 2494 H. F.; Hillegonda Ka, 5681 H. Milk
7,759 lbs. 4 oz 9 months, P.
HILLETJE, 2008 H. Lincoln, 120 Neth. Hillegonda, 4332 Neth. Milk 10,384 lbs 1 year, A.R.
HILLSBOROUGH MAID, 1099 H. F. Promoter, 1518 H ; Gentle Maid 2d. Milk 3889 lbs. 7 oz. 5 months
14 days, P.
HILTJE KUPER'S, 34 D. F. Jacob, 58 Neth.; Letske. Milk 70 lbs. 1 day, P.
HILTON MAID, 1993 H. Imp. Milk 80 lbs. 1 day, P.
HILTON MAID 2D, 4936 H. Gortus, 642 H.; Hilton Maid, 1993 H. Milk 68 lbs. 4 oz. 1 day, 638 lbs. 10
days, P.
HINKE, 216 D. F. Mooie, 26 M. R.; Winkje, 136 M. R. Butter 17 lbs. 1 oz. 7 days, A.R.
HINKE 3D, 27169 H. F. Hamilton 2d. 5608 H. F.; Hinke, 216 D. F. Milk 50 lbs. 12 oz. 1 day, P.
HIPPOLITA, 6115 H. Imp. Milk 7738 lbs. 13 oz. 10 months, A.R.
HIPPOLYTA S. 9457 H. F. Joe S, 1592 H.; Zwartkof, 2025 H. F. Milk 7254 lbs. 11 months, P.
HISKE, 80 D. F. Imp. Milk 50 lbs. 1 day, P. Butter 15 lbs. 7 days, A.R.
HOBIA, 8712 H. Paragon, 1175 H.; Hokwerda 3d, 3268 H. Milk 50 lbs. 1 day, 1206 lbs. 3 oz. 1 month.
Butter 2 lbs. 6 oz. 1 day, P.
HOBNELIA S, 9458 H. F. Joe S, 1592 H.; Celeste S, 3052 H. Milk 57 lbs. 1 day, P.
HOKEMA 2D, 3249 H. Imp. Milk 54 lbs. 1 day, P.
HOKWERDA 3D, 3208 H. Imp. Butter 18 lbs. 14 oz. 7 days, A.R.
HOLLAND BEAUTY, 330 H. Imp. Milk 600 lbs. 1 year, P.
HOLLANDER, 3706 H. Imp. Milk 75 lbs. 6 oz. 1 day, 14,053 lbs, 12 oz. 10 months. P.
HOLLANDER 2D, 5782 H. Constantyn, 2040 H.; Hollander, 3706 H. Milk 75 lbs. 8 oz. 1 day, 9817 lbs.
12 oz. 10 months. Butter 13 lbs. 2 oz. 7 days, P.
HOLLAND JEWEL, 960 H. Imp. Milk 62 lbs. 4 oz. 1 day, P.; 10,360 lbs. 15 oz. 1 year, A.R. Butter 15
lbs. 8 oz. 7 days, A.R.
HOLLAND PRIDE, 2745 H. Imp. Milk 54 lbs. 8 oz. 1 day, 5720 lbs. 10 oz. 4 months, P.

23

HOLSTEIN-FRIESIAN CATTLE.

HOLLAND PRINCESS, 143 H. Holland Prince, 113 H.; Holland Queen, 144 H. Milk 7401 lbs. 11 oz. 1 year, P.
HOME COUNTESS, 4094 H. Eckke, 681 H.; Wittof, 675 H. Milk 1511 lbs. 8 oz. 30 days, P. Butter 14 lbs. 1 oz. 7 days, P.
HOMESPUN, 5184 H. F. Empyrena, 1006 H.; Hippolita, 6115 H. Milk 5234 lbs. 10 oz. 6 months 7 days, P.
HONORIA, 1230 H. Imp. Milk 530 lbs. 10 days, P.
HOPSIE, 9169 H. Imp. Milk 65 lbs. 1 day. Butter 16 lbs. 8 oz. 7 days, P.
HORTENSE, 1500 H. Milk 68 lbs. 1 day. Butter 18 lbs. 4 oz. 7 days, P.
HORTENSE, 1527 D. F. Penninga. 164 F. H. B ; Auke Ankes, 961 F. H. B. Milk 74 lbs. 8 oz. 1 day, 1924 lbs. 1 month. Butter 3 lbs. 2 oz 1 day, 15 lbs. 11¼ oz. 7 days, P.
HORTENSIA, 4019 H. Imp. Milk 57 lbs. 4 oz. 1 day, 393 lbs. 12 oz. 7 days. Butter 19 lbs. 3 1-2 oz. 7 days, P.
HORTENSIA'S BLACK MERCEDES, 2731 H. F. Mercedes Prince, 2150 H.; Hortensia, 4019 H. Butter 16 lbs. 13 oz. 7 days, P.
HORTENSIA'S MERCEDES, 9492 H. Mercedes Prince, 2150 H.; Hortensia, 4019 H. Milk 45 lbs. 15 oz. 1 day, P.; 449 lbs. 6 oz. 10 days, A.R. Butter 17 lbs. 8¼ oz. 7 days, A.R.
HORTENSIA'S SECOND MERCEDES, 11240 H. F. Mercedes Prince, 2150 H.; Hortensia, 4019 H. Milk 7000 lbs. 1 year, P.
HOTSKE 2D, 1777 D. F. Adam, 298 F. H. B.; Hotske, 1294 F. H. B. Butter 10 lbs. 12 oz. 7 days, A.R.
HOUWTJE D, 12005 H. F. Jumbo Boy, 1993 H.; Houwtje, 2041 H. Milk 92 lbs. 1 day, 17475 lbs. 10 months, A.R. Butter 23.48 lbs. 7 days, P.; 727.42 lbs. 10 months, A.R.
HOYDEN S, 9464 H. F. No Shirk, 3561 H.; Fea S, 2146 H. F. Milk 396 lbs. 10 days, A.R.
HUBBARD, 8245 H. Imp. Butter 14 lbs. 6 oz. 7 days, P.
HUBERTA, 6820 H. Imp. Milk 84 lbs., P.
HULDA, 550 H. Imp. Milk 69 lbs. 1 day, P.
HUNETJE. 8256 H. F. Groote Jan, 534 F. H. B.; Hieke, 647 F. H. B. Milk 47 lbs. 1 day, 1360 lbs. 30 days, P.
HUNNIWELL, 8436 H. Albert, 342 F. H. B.; Pietje, 2482 F. H. B. Milk, 59 lbs. 1 day, 1454 lbs. 30 days, P.
HUZZY, 1190 H. Billy Boelyn, 189 H.; Hulda, 550 H. Milk 35 lbs. 1 day, P.
HYACINTH S, 9465 H. D. Prince David, 2076 H.; Fair Penitent S, 2144 H. F. Milk 438 lbs. 10 days, A.R.
HYKE 2D, 4311 H. F. Brick, 3222 H. F.; Hyke, 6532 H. Milk 64 lbs. 8 oz. 1 day, P.
HYKOLINA, 746 H. Imp. Milk 58 lbs. 1 day, 11,183 lbs. 1 year, P.
HYKOLINA 2D, 754 H. F. Billy Boelyn, 189 H.; Hykolina, 746 H. Milk 10,952 lbs. 1 year, P.
HYLA, 5290 H. Imp. Milk 7495 lbs. 4 oz. 7 months 24 days, P.
HYLKU, 741 H. Imp. Milk 83½ qts. 1 day, P.
HYPSA, 20840 H. F. Seer, 5027 H. F.; Justina, 1845 D. F. Milk 5.407 lbs. 6 oz. 10 months, P.

IBIS, 293 Neth. Imp. Milk 36 lbs. 1 day, P.
IDAARD 2D, 5704 H. F. Gilroy 3079 H.; Idaard, 4983 H. Milk 57 lbs. 8 oz. 1 day, 11,423 lbs. 8 oz. 11 months 15 days, A.R.
IDALAH S, 14745 H. F. Netherland Courtier, 2474 H.; Aardzak, 2021 H. F. Milk 40 lbs. 1 day, P.
IDA MAY, 947 H. Imp. Milk 52 lbs. 10 oz. 1 day, 10,958 lbs. 2 oz. 1 year, P.
IDA ROOKER, 4859 H. F. Ruiter 4th; Trijntje, 4224 Neth. Butter 13 lbs. 12½ oz. 7 days, A.R.
IDEAL, 8691 H. Imp. Milk 38 lbs. 8 oz. 1 day, 9,167 lbs 1 oz. 1 year, P. Butter 14 lbs. 1½ oz. 7 days, A.R.
IDENE ROOKER. 9995 H. Imp. Milk 15,157 lbs. 10 oz. 1 year, A.R. Butter 25 lbs. 3½ oz. 7 days, A.R.; 98 lbs. 5½ oz. 30 days, P.
IDENE ROOKER 2D, 3167 H. F. Sir Henry 2d of Aaggie, 1451 H.; Idene Rooker, 9995 H. Milk 1,004 lbs. 5 oz. 1 month, 6,143 lbs. 1 oz. 8 months 3 days, P. Butter 10 lbs. 2 oz. 7 days, A.R.
IDRIA, 7190 H. Imp. Milk 61 lbs. 1 day, P.
IFKJE, 799 F. H. B. Imp. Milk 61 lbs. 1 day, P.
IJNTENA 2D, 4139 H. F. Mooie, 26 D. F.; Ijntena, 1506 D. F. Milk 36 lbs. 8 oz. 1 day, 1038 lbs. 8 oz. 30 days, P.
IJSBRANDIA 3D, 3912 H. F. De Brave Hendrik, 230 H. F.; Ijsbrandia, 5300 H. Milk 36 lbs. 8 oz. 1 day, 5726 lbs. 8 months, P.
ILIONE S, 14753 H. F. Prince David, 2076 H. F.; Lurancy, 6137 H. Milk 45 lbs. 1 day, 1191 lbs. 30 days, P.
IMAGENA S, 14734 H. F. Prince David, 2076 H.; Thistledown, 7899 H. Milk 6351 lbs. 8 months, P.
IMKJE'S MERCEDES, 9490 H. Mercedes Prince, 2150 H.; Imkje, 5310 H. Milk 47 lbs. 13 oz. 1 day, P.; 312 lbs. 6 oz. 7 days, A.R. Butter 25 lbs. 15¼ oz. 7 days, P.
IMOGENIA, 500 H. Stentor, 346 H.; Isis, 148 H. Milk 47 lbs. 1 day, 10,925 lbs. 9 oz. 1 year, P.
IMOGENIA 2D, 3923 H. St. Elmo, 714 H.; Imogenia. 500 H. Butter 16 lbs. 6 oz. 7 days, P.
IMPERIAL ROSA, 1583 H. F. Prince Imperial, 1164 H.; Aaggie Rosa 2d, 2010 H. Milk 9408 lbs. 6 oz. 10 months, P.
INARA, 9428 H. Imp. Milk 70 lbs. 1 day, P.; 9787 lbs. 3 oz. 7 months, A.R. Butter 18 lbs. 14 oz. 7 days, A.R.
INA S, 14758 H. F. No Shirk, 3561 H.; Galiana S, 5282 H. Milk 5024 lbs. 6 months 25 days, P.
INDEX, 987 H. Imp. Milk 3270 lbs. 60 days, P.
INDI, 2508 H. Imp. Milk 66 lbs. 1 day, P.
INDI 2D, 3650 H. Promoter, 1518 H.; Indi, 2508 H. Milk 63 lbs. 8 oz. 1 day, P.; 7781 lbs. 15 oz. 9 months 22 days, A.R.
INDI MINNIE, 6277 H F. Lad of Prescott, 2389 H.; Indi 2d, 3650 H. Milk 426 lbs. 4 oz. 7 days, A.R.
INDRANI S, 14736 H. F. Netherland Courtier, 2474 H.; Lilio, 2019 H. F. Milk 35 lbs. 1 day, P.
INGA NEKO. 8557 H. Imp. Milk 37 lbs. 1 day, 964 lbs. 12 oz. 30 days, P.
INKA, 334 H. Imp. Milk 14,046 lbs. 7 months, A.R. Butter 20 lbs. 2 oz. 7 days, A.R.
INKA 2D, 1013 H. Baron Steuben, 66 H.; Inka, 334 H. Milk 82 lbs. 1 day, 17,345 lbs. 1 oz. 1 year, P. Butter 18 lbs. 2 oz. 7 days, A.R.
INKA 4TH, 1093 D. F. Victor Bruinsma, 88 F. R.; Inka, 222 M. R. Milk 85 lbs. 1 day, 20,640 lbs. 12 oz. 1 year, P. Butter 19 lbs. 2 oz. 7 days, A.R.
INKA 4TH'S PIETERTJE ROSE, 23481 H F. Milla's Pietertje Netherland, 7825 H. F.; Inka 4th, 1093 D. F. Milk 54 lbs. 1 day, 1535 lbs. 5 oz. 1 month, P. Butter 21.9 lbs. 7 days, A.R.
INKA 5TH, 4288 H. F. Prince of Monroe, 1630 H.; Inka, 480 D. F. Milk 68 lbs. 1 day, P.; 8529 lbs. 12 oz. 8 months 10 days, A.R. Butter 11 lbs. 6 oz. 7 days, A.R.

MILK AND BUTTER RECORDS. 339

INKA 6TH, 7968 H. F. Mooie Hartog 4th, 418 D. F.; Ilka, 486 D. F. Milk 72 lbs. 1 day, 13,977 lbs. 3 oz. 1 year, P. Butter 20 lbs. 5 oz. 7 days.
INKA 6TH'S QUEEN PIETERTJE, 17791 H. F. Milla's Pietertje Netherland, 7825 H. F.; Inka 6th, 7968 H. F. Milk 54 lbs. 1 day, 1537 lbs 30 days, P. Butter 16 lbs. 7 days, P.
INKA 7TH, 13102 H. F. Mooie Hartog 4th, 418 D. F.; Inka, 486 D. F. Milk 5126 lbs. 2 oz. 2 months. Butter 20 lbs. 7 days, P.
INKA 7TH'S PIETERTJE, 24136 H. F. Milla's Pietertje Netherland, 7825 H. F.; Inka 7th, 13102 H. F. Milk 52 lbs. 8 oz. 1 day, 1531 lbs. 14 oz. 30 days. Butter 15 lbs. 7 days, P.
INKA BELLE, 1447 D. F. Midnight, 125 P. R.; Inka 2d, 488 P. R. Milk 65 lbs. 1 day, P.
INKA DARKNESS, 273 D. F. Unadilla, 71 P. R.; Inka 2d, 488 P. R. Milk 84 lbs. 1 day, P.; 1901½ lbs. 4 oz. 1 year, A. R. Butter 19 lbs. 8 oz. 7 days, A. R.
INKA DARKNESS 2D, 1335 H. F. Mooie Kleiterp, 319 D. F.; Inka Darkness, 273 D. F. Milk 68 lbs. 8 oz. 1 day, 1728 lbs. 12 oz. 30 days, P.
INKA DARKNESS 2D'S NETHERLAND, 13915 H. F. Aaggie Leila's Prince, 4419 H.; Inka Darkness 2d, 1335 H. F. Milk 63 lbs. 4 oz. 1 day, P.
INKA HARTOG, 7909 H. F. Mooie Hartog 4th, 418 D. F.; Inka 4th, 1093 D. F. Milk 77 lbs. 5 oz. 1 day, P.; 10,460 lbs. 12 oz. 8 months, A.R. Butter 23 lbs. 14 oz. 7 days, P.
INKA PIETERTJE MECHTHILDE, 30608 H. F. Tirania's Sir Meehthilde, 16409 H. F.; Inka 4th's Pietertje Rose, 23481 H. F. Milk 309 lbs. 4 oz. 7 days, A. R. Butter 12.92 lbs. 7 days, A. R.
INKA PRINCESS, 7970 H. F. Aaggie Leila's Prince, 4419 H.; Inka Darkness, 273 D. F. Milk 68 lbs. 14 oz. 1 day, 16,132 lbs. 4 oz. 1 year, P. Butter 15 lbs. 10 oz. 7 days, A. R.
INTJE 2D, 5002 H. Imp. Milk 48 lbs. 1 day, 20,011 lbs. 14 oz. 11 months 16 days, A.R. Butter 19 lbs. 9 oz. 7 days, P.
IONA, 335 H. Imp. Milk 12,033 lbs. 8 oz. 346 days, P.
IONTHA, 8240 H. Imp. Milk 54 lbs. 1 day, 16,060 lbs. 1 year, P.
IOLA, 809 H. Imp. Milk 43 lbs. 14 oz. 1 day, 10,294 lbs. 13 oz. 1 year, P.
IOLENA FAIRMONT, 15544 H. F. Fairmont Tom, 2448 H. F.; Orphia, 2851 H. Milk 53 lbs. 1 day, 503 lbs. 10 days.
IONA, 335 H. Imp. Milk 12,033 lbs. 8 oz. 346 days, P.
IONE, 844 H. Imp. Milk 35 lbs. 1 day, P.
IONIA, 3964 H. Imp. Milk 1,054 lbs. 5 oz. 30 days, P.
IONIA 2D, 4294 H. F. Robertus, 3300 H.; Ionia, 3964 H. Milk 4,106 lbs. 5 months 28 days, P.
IPHIS H, 14748 H. F. No Shirk, 3051 H.; Finetta S, 2107 H., Milk 37 lbs. 1 day, P.
IRENA, 2494 H. Apollot, 402 H.; Sylvia, 573 H. Milk 52 lbs. 1 day, P.
IRENE, 1260 H. Imp. Milk 20 quarts 1 day, P.
IRENE ARTIS, 4844 H. F. Artis, 127 Neth.; Haarlemmermeer, 1020 Neth. Milk 43 lbs. 10 oz. 1 day, 5675 lbs. 11 oz. 5 months 29 days, P. Butter 15 lbs. 10 oz. 7 days, P.
IRIS 3D, 1542 H. Johannis, 428 H.; Iris, 147 H. Milk 68 lbs. 1 day, P.
IRIS 3D A's 1st, 18043 H. F. Copia's Empire, 3559 H.; Iris 3d A, 4747 H. Milk 28 lbs. 1 day, P.
IRIS 3D C, 10336 H. F. Copia's Empire, 3559 H.; Iris 3d, 1542 H. Milk 5,546 lbs. 10 months 20 days, P.
IRIS 4TH, 4748 H. Johannis, 428 H.; Iris, 147 H. Milk 40 lbs. 1 day, P.
IRMENA, 201 F. H. B. Tulener, 1448 F. H. B. Butter 9 lbs. 14 oz. 7 days, A. R.
ISABEL, 1050 Neth. Imp. Milk 54 lbs. 1 day, P.
ISACA S, 14746 H. F. Prince David, 2076 H.; Edging, 8577 H. F. Milk 31 lbs. 1 day, P.
ISADORA, 1800 H. Imp. Milk 69 lbs. 8 oz. 1 day, 9386 lbs. 5 oz. 1 year, P. Butter 10 lbs. 13½ oz. 7 days, P.
ISANTHE, 9300 H. Imp. Milk 32 lbs. 3 oz. 1 day, P.
ISIS, 148 H. Imp. Milk 4140 lbs. 14 oz. 4 months, P.
ISIS 2D, 337 H. Uncle Tom, 163 H.; Isis, 148 H. Milk 34 lbs. 7 oz. 1 day, 9114 bs. 12 oz. 1 year, P.
ISLIP MAID, 10290 H. Imp. Milk 20 qts. 1 day, P.
ISSAQUENNA, 6767 H. Imp. Milk 60 lbs. 1 day, P.
ISMA, 5529 H. Blythe, 2208 H.; Camilla, 102 H. Milk 1067 lbs. 30 days, P.
ITA, 8917 H. Imp. Milk 45 lbs. 1 day, 8482 lbs. 10 oz. 10 months 13 days, P. Butter 17 lbs. 7⅝ oz. 7 days, P.
IVA, 4831 H. Silas. 522 H.; Rialvia, 1130 H. Milk 9662 lbs. 10 months, P.
IVA S, 1474 H. F. Prince David, 2076 H.; Langedijk, 2030 H. F. Milk 31 lbs. 1 day.
IVAS PRIDE, 13005 H. F. Tjkma. 436 H. F.; Rienstra's Jaantje, 960 D. F. Butter 42 lbs. 6 oz. 30 days, P.
IVAS PRIDE 2D, 21568 H. F. D. W. D., 9999 H. F.; Ivas Pride, 13005 H. F. Milk 4464 lbs. 110 days, P.
IVY, 5678H. F. Farmington Pel, 329 L. F.; Rienstra's Jaantje, 960 D. F. Milk 11,580 lbs. 13 oz. 1 year, P.

JAARSMA, 5976 H. Imp. Milk 40 lbs. 1 day.
JACOB, 950 F. H. B. Imp. Milk 58 lbs. 1 day, P.
JACOBA, 1347 H. Imp. Milk 79 lbs. P.
JACOBA BRANTJES, 6023 H. Imp. Milk 61 lbs. 1 day. Butter 12 lbs. 2 oz. 7 days, P.
JACOBA HARTOG, 2 D. F. Imp. Milk 87 lbs. 8 oz. 1 day, 10,430 lbs. 1 year, P.
JACOBA HARTOG 2D, 24 D. F. Burgomaster of Beemster, 1 D. F.; Jacoba Hartog, 2 D. F. Milk 87 lbs. 8 oz. 1 day, 10,230 lbs. 1 year, P.
JACOBA HARTOG 3D, 166 D. F. Burgomaster of Beemster, 1 D. F.; Jacoba Hartog, 2 D. F. Milk 98 lbs. 10 oz. 1 day, A.R. Butter 22 lbs. 14 oz. 7 days, 42 lbs. 8 oz. 14 days, A.R.
JACOBA HARTOG 4TH, 169 D. F. Burgomaster of Beemster, 1 D. F.; Jacoba Hartog, 2 D. F. Butter 18 lbs. 7 days, A.R.
JACOBA HARTOG 5TH, 219 D. F. Mooie, 26 M. R.; Jacoba Hartog 2d, 24 M. R. Butter 15 lbs. 8 oz. 7 days, A.R.
JACOBA HARTOG 6TH, 220 D. F. Mooie, 26 M. R.; Jacoba Hartog 3d, 166 M. R. Butter 17 lbs. 7 days, A.R.
JACOBA HARTOG 7TH, 309 D. F. Mooie, 26 M. R.; Jacoba Hartog 2d, 24 M. R. Butter 14 lbs. 12 oz. 7 days, A.R.
JACOBA HARTOG 8TH, 699 D. F. Mooie Twisk, 85 P. R.; Jacoba Hartog 5th. Milk 365 lbs. 10 days, A. R.
JACOBA HARTOG 9TH, 583 D. F. Mooie, 26 M. R.; Jacoba Hartog 3d, 166 M. R. Butter 12 lbs. 4 oz. A.R.
JACOBA HARTOG T, 5319 H. F. Mooie Twisk 4th, 706 D. F.; Jacoba Hartog 2d, 24 D. F. Milk 307 lbs. 14 oz. 7 days, P. Butter, 14 lbs. 5 oz. 7 days, A.R.

JACOBA LEEGHWATER, 976 H. F. Leeghwater, 279 Neth.; Jacoba, 4515 Neth. Milk 52 lbs. 1 day. Butter 9 lbs. 10 oz. 7 days, P.
JACOB'S BLANCHE, 1957 H. F. Jacob, 608 H.; Zig Mayo, 7533 H. Milk 49 lbs. 4 oz. 1 day, P.
JACOB'S LIZZIE, 9679 H. F. Jacob, 608 H.; Lizzie C, 5399 H. Milk 3723 lbs. 12 oz. 3 months, A.R. Butter 11 lbs. 7½ oz. 7 days, A.R.
JACOB WIT'S BELVA, 7791 H. Jacob Wit, 2662 H.; Breggar, 1738 Neth. Milk 45 lbs. 1 oz. 1 day, 9516 lbs. 1 oz. 1 year, P.
JACOB WIT'S BERYLLA, 7792 H. Jacob Wit, 2662 H.; Alkmaria, 1525 Neth. Milk 66 lbs. 7 oz. 1 day, P.
JACOB WIT'S DE SCHOT, 3802 H. F. Jacob Wit, 2662 H.; De Schot, 5001 H. Milk 5235 lbs. 7 oz. 10 months 1 day, P.
JACOB WIT'S GODIVA, 6919 H. Imp. Milk 51 lbs. 12 oz. 1 day, 7023 lbs. 3 oz. 6 months 15 days, P. Butter 12 lbs. 9¼ oz. 7 days, P.
JACOB WIT'S MINELLA, 7785 H. Imp. Milk 964 lbs. 30 days, P.
JACOB WIT'S MURILLO, 2472 H. F. Jacob Wit, 2662 H.; Murillo, 5053 H. Milk 61 lbs. 1 day, 691 lbs. 30 days, P.
JACQUELINE BELLE, 13972 H. F. Carrick's Porcelain, 4705 H. F.; Jacqueline's Pet, 4730 H. F. Milk 43 lbs. 1 day, 1244 lbs. 30 days. Butter 13 lbs. 8½ oz., P.
JAMAICA, 1336 H. Imp. Milk 112 lbs. 2 oz. 1 day, 19,546 lbs. 15 oz. 1 year, P.
JAMAICA 2D, 4818 H. Iroquois, 1074 H.; Jamaica, 1336 H. Milk 7402 lbs. 4 oz. 319 days, P.
JAMESANNA, 2911 H. Imp. Milk 82 lbs. 8 oz. 1 day, P.
JAMESTOWN BELLE, 7897 H. F. Jewel's Prince of Wayne, 32 H. F.; Meala, 9578 H. Milk 42 lbs. 8 oz. 1 day, P.
JAN 3D, 3225 H. Imp. Milk 76 lbs. 6 oz. 1 day, 312 lbs. 7 oz. 10 days, P.
JANE ARTIS, 4842 H. F. Artis, 127 Neth.; Saartje, 597 Neth. Milk 11,561 lbs. 14 oz. 10 months, A.R. Butter 21 lbs. 11 oz. 7 days, A.R.
JANE EYRE, 1281 H. Imp. Milk 10,117 lbs. 11 oz. 9 months 25 days, P.
JANEKA, 149 H. Imp. Milk 54 lbs. 1 day, 10,448 lbs. 1 oz. 1 year, P. Butter 409 lbs. 1 year, P.
JANET GRAY, 2752 H. Imp. Milk 5436 lbs. 11 months, P.
JANINA, 7172 H. Imp. Milk 647 lbs. 6 oz. 10 days, A.R.; 14,181 lbs. 5 oz. 1 year, P.
JANKE 5TH, 3713 H. Imp. Milk 63 lbs. 4 oz. 1 day, 601 lbs. 14 oz. 10 days, P. Butter 2 lbs. 12 oz. 1 day, P.
JANKE HIBMA, 626 D. F. Imp. Milk 61 lbs. 1 day, P.
JANNA, 1632 H. Imp. Milk 60 lbs. 1 day. Butter 3 lbs. 8 oz. 1 day, 24 lbs. 7 oz. 7 days, P.
JANNEK, 871 H. Imp. Milk 71 lbs. 12 oz. 1 day, 13,015 lbs. 15 oz. 1 year. Butter 19 lbs. 15 oz. 7 days, P.
JANNEK 3D, 1458 H. Uncle Tom, 163 H.; Jannek, 871 H. Milk 53 lbs. 6 oz. 1 day, P.
JANNEK BEAUTY, 1283 H. Lad of Prescott, 2389 H.; Jannek 5th, 4858 H. Milk 505 lbs. 4 oz. 10 days, A.R.
JANNEK BELLE 2D, 28660 H. F. Aaggie Grace's Boy, 7068 H. F.; Jannek Belle, 6280 H. F. Milk 357 lbs. 4 oz. 10 days, A.R.
JANNEK BRIGHT, 1285 H. F. Lad of Prescott, 2389 H.; Jannek 4th. Milk 383 lbs 4 oz. 10 days, A.R.
JANNEK BRIGHT 2D, 22943 H. F. Aaggie Grace's Boy, 7068 H. F.; Jannek Bright, 1285 H. F. Milk 392 lbs. 12 oz. 10 days, 7015 lbs. 8 oz. 10 months, A.R.
JANNEKER, 798 F. H. B. Imp. Milk 61 lbs. 1 day, P.
JANNEK LASS, 10021 H. F. Lad of Prescott 2d, 968 H. F.; Jannek 5th, 4858 H. Milk 406 lbs. 4 oz. 10 days, 8352 lbs. 8 oz. 10 months, A.R.
JANNEK WORTEL, 2659 H. Imp. Milk 15,542 lbs. 14 oz. 1 year. Butter 18 lbs. 8 oz. 7 days, 35 lbs. 11 oz. 14 days, A.R.
JANNETJE, 3027 H. Imp. Milk 84 lbs. 1 day, P.
JANNETJE K. Imp. Milk 601 lbs. 12 oz. 7 days, 14,436 lbs. 8 oz. 7 months. Butter 20 lbs. 7 days, A.R.
JANNETJE K 3D, 6805 H. F. Mazda, 2072 H.; Jannetje K, 5074 H. Milk 64 los. 1 day, 10,270 lbs, 9 months 4 days, P.
JANSJE, 596 Neth. Imp. Milk 80 lbs. 2 oz. 1 day. Butter 3 lbs. 2 oz. 1 day, P.
JANSMA, 5313 H. Imp. Milk 74 lbs. 1 day, P.
JANTINA, 2914 H. Imp. Milk 65 lbs. 1 day, P.
JANTJE, 2221 H. Imp. Milk 90 lbs. 8 oz. 1 day, 2623 lbs. 8 oz. 31 days. P.
JANTJE 2D, 497 D. F. Imp. Milk 12,623 lbs. 8 oz. 1 year, P.
JANTJE 2D, 8017 H. Imp. Milk 64 lbs. 1 day, P.; 522 lbs. 10 days, A.R. Butter 16 lbs. 7 days, A.R.
JANTJE DE VRIES, 432 D. F. Imp. Milk 74 lbs. 1 day, P.
JAPONICA, 3714 H. Imp. Milk 82 lbs. 8 oz. 1 day, 5345 lbs. 3 oz. 6 months 19 days, P.
JAPONICA'S NETHERLAND, 9839 H. F. Netherland Duke, 1571 H.; Japonica, 3714 H. Milk 41 lbs. 1 day, P.
JASAMINE, 1782 D. F. Excelsior, 206 Neth.; Elizabeth, 1092 Neth. Butter 10 lbs. 6 oz. 7 days, A.R.
JAUKE, 2879 F. H. B. Imp. Milk 70 lbs. 1 day, P.
JEANETTE OF SHADELAND, 2419 H. Imp. Milk 60 lbs. 2 oz. 1 day, 9704 lbs. 4 oz. 10 months, A.R.
JEAN INGELOW, 1305 H. Imp. Milk 64 lbs. 1 day, 10,757 lbs. 9 months. Butter 18 lbs. 8 oz. 7 days, P.
JELEJE B, 6541 H. Imp. Milk 40 lbs. 1 day, P.
JELLE TRINTJE, 5727 H. Imp. Milk 76 lbs. 12 oz. 1 day, 11,732 lbs. 12 oz. 10 months, A.R. Butter 21 lbs. 11½ oz. 7 days, A.R.
JELLUM, 5500 H. Imp. Milk 9661 lbs. 10 oz. 26 days, A.R.
JELLUM 2D, 7591 H. F. Isaiah, 2539 H.; Jellum, 5500 H. Butter 22 lbs. 7 days, P.
JELTJE, 1629 H. Imp. Milk 61 lbs. 1 day, P.
JELTJE 2D, 3779 H. Jaap, 452 H.; Jeltje, 1209 H. Milk 64 lbs. 5 oz. 1 day, 422 lbs. 9 oz. 7 days, P. Butter 16 lbs. 7½ oz. 7 days, A.R.
JELTJE S, 5760 H. Imp. Milk 76 lbs. 1 day, P.; 2201 lbs. 30 days, A.R.
JELTJE S NETHERLAND, 9335 H. F. Netherland Duke, 1571 H.; Jeltje S. Milk 37 lbs. 8 oz. 1 day, P.
JENNE B 2D, 2910 H. Imp. Milk 86 lbs. 8 oz. 1 day, 2387 lbs. 8 oz. 1 month, P. Butter 18 lbs. 8 oz. 7 days, P.
JENNE B 3D, 5132 H. Imp. Milk 82 lbs. 8 oz. 1 day, P.
JENNE B 5TH, 5134 H. Imp. Milk 46 lbs. 1 day, P.
JENNIE, 4633 H. F. Ulrich, 567 H.; Schenk, 1045 H. Milk 66 lbs. 1 day, P.
JENNIE A, 4270 H. Imp. Milk 40 lbs. 8 oz. 1 day, P.
JENNIE DEANS, 1905 H. Duke of Washington, 575 H.; Nauchy, 698 H. Milk 60 lbs. 1 day, P.
JENNIE G, 339 H. Ajax, 63 H.; Anna, 81 H. Milk 83 lbs. 3 oz. 1 day, 2218 lbs. 8 oz. 30 days, P.
JENNIE RICHARDSON, 6073 H. F. Netherland Convoy, 2934 H.; Elsie Chester, 4370 H. Milk 47 lbs. 8 oz. 1 day, A.R.; 3351 lbs. 12 oz. 90 days, P.

MILK AND BUTTER RECORDS. 341

JENNY CLIFDEN, 151 H. Imp. Butter 18 lbs. 6 oz. 7 days, P.
JENNY CLIFDEN 2D, 2184 H. Sligo, 621 H.; Jenny Clifden, 151 H. Milk 49 lbs. 14 oz. 1 day. Butter 18 lbs. 6 oz. 7 days, P.
JENNY JONES, 6112 H. Imp. Milk 57 lbs. 1 day, 12,019 lbs. 11 months 3 days, P.
JENNY LIND, 966 H. Imp. Milk 77 lbs. 1 day, 8318 lbs. 4 oz. 1 year, P. Butter 22 lbs. 7 days, A.R.
JENNY WREN, 10377 H. Imp. Milk 63 lbs. 1 day, 11.823 lbs. 1 year, P. Butter 18 lbs. 8 oz. 8 days, P.
JENNY WREN 2D, 12172 H. F. Violet V Boelyn, 768 H. F.; Jenny Wren. Milk 50 lbs. 1 day, P.
JENNY WREN 3D, 16993 H. F. De Brave Hendrik, 230 H. F.; Jenny Wren, 10377 H. Milk 40 lbs. 1 day, P.
JENTJE, 732 F. H. B. Imp. Milk 68 lbs. 1 day, P.
JEPMA 2D, 733 H. Milk 53 lbs. 1 day, P.
JESSE, 490 D. F. Unadilla, 71 P. R.; Juno, 484 P. R. Milk 75 lbs. 1 day, P.
JESSE 2D'S AAGGIE, 15933 H. F. Aaggie Leila's Netherland, 2527 H. F.; Jesse 2d, 1445 H. F. Milk 65 lbs. 1 day, P.; 429 lbs. 7 days, A.R. Butter 17 lbs. 8 oz. 7 days, A.R.
JESSIE, 342 H. Imp. Butter 10 lbs. 15 oz. 7 days, A.R.
JESSIE 2D, 4403 H. F. De Jongh, 3465 H.; Jessie, 342 H. Milk 70 lbs. 1 day, P.
JESSIE ARTIS, 4857 H. F. Artis, 127 Neth.; Anna, 3363 Neth. Milk 11,540 lbs. 3 oz. 1 year, P. Butter 15 lbs. 4 oz. 7 days, P.
JESSIE BARNUM, 10362 H. Picador, 304 H.; Lady Barnum, 6281 H. Milk 45 lbs. 1 day, 9449 lbs. 4 oz. 9 months, P. Butter 15 lbs. 2½ oz. 7 days, A.R.
JESSIE BEETS, 8123 H. F. Mooie Hartje 4th, 418 D. F.; Dora Beets 3d, 268 D. F. Milk 64 lbs. 8 oz. 1 day, 8081 lbs. 8 oz. 6 months, P. Butter 19 lbs. 8 oz. 7 days, A.R.
JETTA, 5025 H. Imp. Milk 64 lbs. 1 day, P.
JETTA 2D, 0230 H. Royal Aaggie, 3458 H.; Jetta, 5025 H. Milk 41 lbs. 8 oz. 1 day, P.; 12,458 lbs. 1 year, P.
JETT TOPSY, 20450 H. F. Mazda, 2672 H.; Topsy Beauty, 1710 H. Milk 71 lbs. 1 day, P.
JEWEL, 668 H. Imp. Milk 100 lbs. 1 day, 9439 lbs. 271 days, P. Butter 5 lbs. 3 oz. 1 day, P.; 31 lbs. 3½ oz. 7 days, A.R.
JEWEL 2D, 119 H. Ebbo, 236 H.; Jewel, 608 H. Milk 70 lbs. 12 oz. 1 day, 10,227 lbs. 10 months, P. Butter 27 lbs. 13 oz. 7 days, A.R.
JEWEL 3D, 2188 H. Mahomet, 289 H.; Jewel, 608 H. Milk 69 lbs. 1 day, 2,376 lbs. 3 oz. 31 days, P.
JEWEL ECHO, 7744 H. F. Echo's Prince of Wayne, 31 H. F.; Jewel 2d, 1119 H. Milk 56 lbs. 6 oz. 1 day. Butter 17 lbs. 6 oz. 7 days, P.
JIKKE HERBERT, 9641 H. F. Florence Herbert's Kazoo, 4053 H.; Jikke, 6548 H. Butter 14 lbs. 8 oz. 7 days, A.R.
JOAN, 846 H. Imp. Milk 63 lbs. 1 day P.
JODIN, 10403 H. Imp. Milk 70 lbs. 3 oz. 1 day, Butter 18 lbs. 7 oz. 7 days, P.
JOEL, 6128 H. Imp. Milk 56 lbs. 1 day, 9990 lbs. 1 year, P.
JOHANNA, 1421 Neth. Imp. Milk 77 lbs. 1 day, P.
JOHANNA, 344 H. Imp. Milk 88 lbs. 1 day, 12,364 lbs. 1 year, P.
JOHANNA 2D'S BEAUTY, 5415 H. F. Oakland Chief, 3259 H.; Johanna 2d, 3088 H. Milk 44 lbs. 8 oz. 1 day, 301 lbs. 8 oz. 7 days, P. Butter 16 lbs. 5 oz. 7 days, P.
JOHANNA 5TH, 9343 H. F. Oakland Chief, 3259 H.; Johanna, 344 H. Milk 84 lbs. 1 day, 402 lbs. 7 oz. 10 days. Butter 23 lbs. 5 oz. 7 days, P.
JOHANNA 5TH'S CLOTHILDE, 30836 H. F. Aaggie Cornelia 5th's Clothilde Imperial, 11822 H. F.; Johanna 5th. Milk 287 lbs. 6 oz. 7 days, A. R. Butter 12.56 lbs. 7 days A.R.
JOHANNA LEE 2D, 3278 H. Imp. Milk 72 lbs. 1 day, P.
JOHANNA NIG, 17664 H. F. Ben Loeman, 1607 H. F.; Johanna 4th, 2129 H. F. Milk 35 lbs. 7 oz. 1 day, 238 lbs. 2 oz. 7 days. Butter 11 lbs. 3 oz. 7 days, P.
JOHANNA RUE 2D, 33788 H. F. Aaggie Cornelia 5th's Clothilde Imperial, 11822 H. F.; Johanna Rue, 21223 H. F. Milk 324 lbs. 6 oz. 7 days, A.R. Butter 12 21 lbs. 7 days, A.R.
JONELLA 2D, 8060 H. F. Bugle, 3033 H.; Jonella, 6249 H. Milk 305 lbs. 4 oz. 10 days, A.R.
JONGE LUITZEN, 8217 H. Imp. Milk 67 lbs. 8 oz. 1 day, 455 lbs. 13 oz. 7 days, P. Butter 22 lbs. 12 oz. 7 days, A.R.
JONGSTE AAGGIE, 398 D. F. Gerben Antje. Milk 74 lbs. 8 oz. 1 day, 1,074 lbs. 8 oz. 30 days, P.
JONKER, 3245 F. H. B. Imp. Milk 68 lbs. 1 day, P.
JOSEPHINA, 661 H. F. Angus, 907 H ; Tedora, 1206 H. Milk 85 lbs. 1 day, P.
JOSIE LYLE, 4450 H. Imp. Milk 99½ lbs. 30 days, P.
JOY, 1189 H. Conqueror, 388 H.; JeLanna, 344 H. Milk 76 lbs. 1 day, P.
JOZEFIA, 959 H. F. Bouwke 2d, 262 Neth.; Jozefia, 1048 Neth. Milk 46 lbs. 1 day. Butter 9 lbs. 3 oz. 1 day, P.
JUANITA, 5025 H. Imp. Milk 71 lbs 1 day, 2086 lbs. 30 days. P.
JUDITH, 152 H. Imp. Milk 60 lbs. 1 day, P.
JUDITH W 2D, 1287 H. F. Lad of Prescott, 2389 H.; Judith W, 3065 H. Milk 7936 lbs. 4 oz. 10 months, A.R.
JUFROU, 153 H. Imp. Milk 12,011 lbs. 1 year, P. Butter 471 lbs. 1 year, P.
JULIA 2D, 25171 H. F. Milk Prince, 2805 H.; Julia, 5073 H. Milk 2136 lbs. 30 days, P.
JULIETTA OF SHADELAND, 2404 H. F. Imp. Milk 51 lbs. 1 day, P.
JUNA LUSKA, 7049 H. Imp. Milk 40 lbs. 1 day, P.
JUNIATA, 154 H. Rip Van Winkle, 8 H.; Juno, 15 H. Milk 13,880 lbs. 1 oz. 1 year, P.
JUNIATA 2D, 562 H. Uncle Tom, 163 H.; Juniata, 154 H. Milk 34 lbs. 1 d·y, P.
JUNIE AARDE, 10339 H. Imp. Milk 72 lbs. 1 day, 11,014 lbs. 8 oz. 1 year, P.
JUNO, 155 H. Imp. Milk 74 lbs. 1 day, P.
JURRE, 648 D. F. Imp. Milk 88 lbs 1 day, P.
JUSTINA, 1646 H. Imp. Milk 50 lbs. 1 day, P.
KAAN'S MARIE, 810 D. F. Graaf Adolph, 98 Neth.; Johanna, 422 Neth. Milk 13,997 lbs. 14 oz. 1 year, A.R. Butter 17 lbs. 12 oz. 7 days, A.R.
KAASJE, 846 F. H. B. Imp. Milk 70 lbs. 1 day, P.
KAATJE, 1189 Neth. Imp. Milk 51 lbs. 1 day, P.
KAATJE BONNY, 8395 H. F. Bonny, 3070 H.; Kaatje Oley, 5095 H. Milk 48 lbs. 8 oz. 1 day, P. Butter 1 lb. 12 oz. 1 day, P.
KABAGE, 11043 H. F. Wacabuc, 8165 H. F.; Katydid, 2053 H. Milk 9508 lbs. 1 year. Butter 378 lbs. 1 year, P.
KALMA 2D. 3299 H. Imp. Milk 56 lbs. 1 day, 704 lbs. 14 oz. 7 days, P.
KANSAS, 9236 H. Netherland Baron, 1573 H.; Kitty Fisher, 5827 H. Milk 57 lbs. 1 day, P.

KAPPIJNE, 9998 H. Imp. Milk 15,227 lbs. 7 oz. 1 year. Butter 19 lbs. 12¼ oz, 7 days, P.
KAPPIJNE 2D, 10039 H. Jacob de Hollander, 357 N.; Kappijne, 9998 H. Butter 11 lbs. 1 oz. 7 days, P.
KAPPIJNE 3D, 9364 H. F. Netherland Monk, 4424 H.; Kappijne, 9998 H. Milk 11,344 lbs. 11 oz. 1 year, A.R. Butter 9 lbs. 12 oz. 7 days, A.R.
KASHMANN, 9059 H. Imp. Butter 19 lbs. 9 oz. 7 days, P.
KASSIE, 2802 H. F. Mooie, 26 D. F.; Kastaleintje 2d, 1483 D. F. Milk 64 lbs. 1 day, P.; 8,753 lbs. 8 oz. 10 months, A.R. Butter 28 lbs. 12 oz. 7 days, A.R.
KATE 2D, 3543 H. Prince of the Meadows, 359 H ; Kate, 156 H. Milk 52 lbs. 1 day, P. Butter 2 lbs. 9 oz. 1 day, 17 lbs. 7 oz. 7 days, P.
KATE EDGE, 5401 H. Imp. Milk 64 lbs. 1 day, P. Butter 17 lbs. 7 days, P.
KATHLEEN SPOFFORD, 10734 H. F. Mooie Hartog 4th, 418 D. F.; Nannie Spofford, 1785 H. Milk 38 lbs. 1 day, 868 lbs. 30 days, P.
KATHRIN, 510 H. Imp. Milk 12,810 lbs. 1 year, P.
KATIE D, 14430 H. F. Ironville, 7556 H. F.; Rotha, 6506 H. Butter 14 lbs. 7 days, P.
KATIE NETHERLAND, 7873 H. Netherland Duke, 1571 H.; Blueberry, 2671 H. Milk 80 lbs. 1 day, P.
KATINKA, 350 H. Imp. Milk 12,116 lbs. 8 months 3 days, P.
KATINKA 2D, 491 H. Motley, 126 H.; Katinka, 350 H. Milk 12,548 lbs. 1 year, P.
KATISHA, 2852 H. F. Imp. Milk 36 qts. 1 day, P.
KATRINA, 1071 H. Second Consul, 339 H.; Clasina, 269 H. Milk 68 lbs. 1 day, P.
KATYDID 2053 H. Imp. Milk 60 lbs. 1 day, 8,600 lbs. 8 months. Butter 15 lbs. 7 days, P.
KATY HIJLAARD, 5404 H. F. Mooie Hartog, 418 D. F.; Vrouwkje of Hijlaard 2d. Butter 20 lbs. 6 oz. 7 days, A.R.
KATY K, 5466 H. Imp. Milk 74 lbs. 8 oz. 1 day. Butter 19 lbs. 8 oz. 7 days, P.
KATY SPOFFORD, 5074 H. F. Glendale, 3417 H.; Nannie Spofford, 1785 H. Milk 66 lbs. 1 day, 416 lbs. 8 oz. 7 days, P. Butter 11 lbs. 8 oz. 7 days, P.
KEAY, 360 Neth. Imp. Milk 43 lbs. 8 oz. 1 day, P.
KEETJE VON HOLINGEN, 17215 H. F. Lodewijk, 557 Neth.; Keetje, 5027 Neth. Milk 50 lbs. 1 day, P.
KEKA OF WOODSIDE, 928 D. F. Rauward, 25 M. R.; Guschen 2d, 909 D. F. Milk 10,89d lbs. 15 oz. 1 year, P.
KEKKE 3D, 887 D. F. Burg Hartog, 3 M. R.; Kekke, 74 M. R. Milk 72 lbs. 1 day, 3709 lbs. 4 oz. 73 days, A.R. Butter 17 lbs. 7 days, A.R.
KENTUCKY BELLE, 861 H. Imp. Milk 80 lbs. 1 day, P.
KETELAAR, 3231 F. H. B. Imp. Milk 73 lbs. 1 day, P.
KETURAH, 1182 H. Imp. Milk 72 lbs. 1 day. Butter 16 lbs. 8 oz. 7 days, P.
KETURAH 2D, 1567 H. Imp. Milk 61 lbs. 1 day, P.
KEWAUNEE, 8911 H. Friesland Prince, 1597 H.; Venus 3d, 2398 H. Milk 50 lbs. 1 day, P.
KHRONE, 8279 H. F. Jelle, 202 F. H. B.; Dina, 832 F. H. B. Milk 58 lbs. 1 day, 1,342 lbs. 30 days, P.
KINNIE, 15775 H. F. Duke of St. Anna, 614 D. F.; Lady Gretchen, 428 D. F. Milk 53 lbs. 1 day. 551 lbs. 8 oz. 11 days, P.
KIOLA, 402 H. F. Imp. Milk 59 lbs. 1 day, P.
KIRSTINA, 3131 H. Imp. Milk 65 lbs. 1 day, P. Butter 18 lbs. 7 days, P.
KISMET, 1784 H. Imp. Milk 64 lbs. 1 day. Butter 11 lbs. 2 oz. 7 days, P.
KITTIE EDLER, 4048 H. F. Sterling, 315 D. F.; Jassma Goudgeld, 42 D. F. Milk 7,626 lbs. 12 oz. 10 months, A.R.
KITTY C. ARTIS, 17893 H. F. Artis Peer, 9048 H. F.; Kitty Chatham 2d, 7234 H. F. Milk 56 lbs. 1 day, P. Butter 16 lbs. 1 oz. 7 days, P.
KITTY CHATHAM, 248 H. F. Sir Henry of Aaggie, 1450 H.; Carlotta 2d, 3555 H. Milk 43 lbs. 2 oz. 1 day, 8016 lbs. 8 months 11 days, P. Butter 22 lbs. 4¼ oz. 7 days, P.
KITTY CLOVER, 1537 D. F. Willem, 204 F. H. B.; Trintje, 1213 F. H. B. Butter 10 lbs. 4 oz. 7 days, A.R.
KITTY CLOVER 3D, 15323 H. F. Mooie Twisk 4th, 703 D. F.; Kitty Clover, 1537 D. F. Butter 18 lbs. 12½ oz. 7 days, P.
KITTY FISHER, 5627 H. Imp. Milk 69 lbs. 1 day, 1999 lbs. 30 days, P.
KITTY K 2D, 4707 H. Imp. Milk 61 lbs. 1 day, P.
KITTY POSCH, 13630 H. F. Uncle Dan Barnum, 5070 H. F.; Emma Posch 2d, 4610 H. F. Butter 13 lbs. 15½ oz. 7 days, A.R.
KIZERIN, 9285 H. Imp. Milk 60 lbs. 1 day, P.
KIZERIN 2D, 9488 H. Don Karlos, 50 Neth.; Kizerin, 9285 H. Milk 50 lbs. 1 day. Butter 13 lbs. 12½ oz. 7 days, P.
KLAASJE, 2565 H. Imp. Milk 70 lbs. 1 day, P.; 11,109 lbs. 3 oz. 260 days, A.R.
KLAASJE VEEMAN 2D, 1432 D. F. De Watergeus, 229 P. R.; Klaasje Veeman, 659 P. R. Milk 8605 lbs. 12 oz. 10 months, A.R.
KLAATJE, 10409 H. Pel, 122 F. H. B.; Klaasje, 846 F. H. B. Milk 82 lbs. 1 day, P. Butter 14 lbs. 10 oz. 7 days, P.
KLARA, 3020 H. Imp. Milk 87 lbs. 8 oz. 1 day, 14,506 lbs. 1 year, P.
KLASKE L, 5860 H. Imp. Milk 81 lbs. 6 oz. 1 day, P.; 11,978 lbs. 3 oz. 8 months 10 days, A.R.
KLASINA HENGEVELD, 656 Neth. Milk 102 lbs. 1 day, 956 lbs. 8 oz. 10 days. Butter 26 lbs. 5½ oz. 7 days, 97 lbs. 5 oz. 30 days, P.
KLASINA HENGEVELD 2D, 4998 H. Imp. Milk 91 lbs. 6 oz. 1 day, 2465 lbs. 30 days, P. Butter 21 lbs. 13 oz. 7 days, P.
KLASINA HENGEVELD 3D, 9387 H. Imp. Milk 59 lbs. 8 oz. 1 day, P.
KLASINA PAYNE, 5896 H. Imp. Milk 102 lbs. 1 day, P.; 905 lbs. 8 oz. 10 days, P. Butter 26 lbs. 7 days, 97 lbs. 5 oz. 30 days, P.
KLASKE, 1639 H. Imp. Milk 85 lbs. 1 day, 2374 lbs. 30 days, P.
KLAY, 5000 H. Imp. Milk 91 lbs. 9 oz. 1 day, P.
KLAY 3D, 304 H. F. Jacob Wit, 2662 H.; Klay, 5000 H. Milk 48 lbs. 2 oz. 1 day, 10,820 lbs. 4 oz 10 months, P. Butter 13 lbs. 7 days, A.R.
KLAY 7TH 1169 D. F. Teunis, 85 Neth.; Klay, 360 Neth. Milk 39 lbs. 1 day, P.
KLAYTONIA, 4999 H. Imp. Milk 82 lbs. 5½ oz. 1 day, P. Butter 26 lbs. 2 oz. 7 days, P.
KLAY WINKEE, 4085 H. F. Keyes 6th, 1692 H.; Klay 7th. 3249 H. Milk 3771 lbs. 10 oz, 4 months 27 days, P. Butter 11 lbs. 7½ oz. 7 days, A.R.
KLAZIENTJE, 10396 H. Imp. Milk 88 lbs. 1 day. Butter 19 lbs. 12 oz. 7 days, P.
KLAZIENTJE 3D, 3529 H. F. International Prince, 4600 H.; Klazientje, 10396 H. Milk 6802 lbs. 7 oz. 9 months, A.R.
KLAZINA 2D, 7395 H. Billy Boelyn, 189 H.; Klazina, 2989 H. Milk 46 lbs. 1 day, 10,006 lbs. 1 year, P. Butter 15 lbs. 3 oz. 7 days, P.

KLEINE 2D, 4721 H. Imp. Milk 25½ qts. 1 day, P.
KLEITERP 4TH, 228 D. F. Kleiterp, 70 M. R.; Mooie, 26 M. R. Milk 1,000 lbs. 20 days, P.
KLEITERP 5TH, 311 D. F. Mooie, 26 M. R.; Kleiterp 3d, 162 M. R. Butter 14 lbs. 4 oz. 7 days A.R.
KLIMENIA, 4149 H, F. Mooie, 26 M. R.; Klimenia, 1772 D. F. Milk 50 lbs. 1 day, 8,371 lbs. 9 months, A.R.
KNUTELTJE, 5422 H. Imp. Milk 1763 lbs. 8 oz. 30 days. Butter 62 lbs. 12 oz. 30 days, P.
KOL, 1036 F. II. B. Imp. Milk 68 lbs. 1 day, P.
KOLLIE LINCOLN. 5666 H. Imp. Milk 90 lbs. 1 day, P.
KOLTJE 2D, 4626 H. F. Harrold, 381 D. F.; Koltje, 634 D. F. Milk 7000 lbs. 4 oz. 10 months, A.R.
KONENGEN, 9283 H. Imp. Milk 80 lbs. 1 day, P.
KONINGEN 2D, 6504 H. Billy Boelvn, 80 H.; Koningen, 3002 H. Milk 52 lbs. 1 day, 8,227 lbs. 1 year, P. Butter 14 lbs. 1 oz. 7 days, P.
KONINGIN VAN FRIESLAND 3D, 3266 H. Imp. Milk 89 lbs. 11 oz. 1 day, 23,616 lbs. 14 oz. 1 year. P.
KONINGIN VAN FRIESLAND 4TH. Imp. Milk 90 lbs. 1 day, P.
KONINGIN VAN FRIESLAND 5TH, 3302 H. Imp. Milk 62 lbs. 8 oz. 1 day, 19,700 lbs. 2 oz. 1 year, P.
KOOS, 6822 H. Imp. Milk 65 lbs. 1 day, 7067 lbs 1 year, P.
KOOY, 8118 H. Imp. Butter 18 lbs. 5 oz. 7 days, P.
KORNELISKA, 7811 H. F. Imp. Milk 85 lbs. 1 day, P.
KORNELISKA 2D, 23710 H. F. Netherland Lincoln, 2554 H. F.; Korneliska, 781. H. F. Milk 61 lbs. 1 day, 1503 lbs. 30 days, P.
KOSTER 3D, 3260 H. Imp. Milk 99 lbs. 12 oz. 1 day, 2483 lbs. 31 days, P.
KROMHOORN. 5775 H. Imp. Milk 73 lbs. 1 day, P.
KROONTJE, 5584 H. Gerben, 7 F. H. B ; Kroontje, 248 F. H. B. Butter 3 lbs. 8 oz. 1 day, P.
KROONTJE 2D, 25725 H. F. Klasina Payne's Gold Dust, 12746 H. F.; Kroontje 5584 H. Butter 3 lbs. 1 day, 25 lbs. 7 oz. 7 days, P.
KRYERS, 8537 H. Imp. Milk 41 lbs. 8 oz. 1 day, P.
KTRINA, 987 Neth. Imp. Milk 77 lbs 8 oz 1 day. P.
KULA, 7843 H. Pierre, 1348 H.; Meyd, 941 H. Milk 43 lbs. 1 day P.
KYKNIT, 2026 H. Imp. Milk 70 lbs. 1 day, P.

LAAN, 3207 H. Imp. Milk 84 lbs. 8 oz 1 day, P.
LAANTJE, 321 Neth. Imp. Milk 82 lbs. 1 day, P. Butter 16 lbs. 5½ oz. 7 days, A.R.
LA BELLE FARMINGTON, 5949 H. Meadow Prince, 1154 H.; Mabe. Livingston. Milk 62 lbs. 1 day, P.
LADY AKERSLOOT, 6678 H. Imp. Milk 45 lbs. 1 day, P.
LADY AKKRUM, 8153 H. Duke of Heilron, 1607 H.; Lodema Akkrum, 1908 H. Milk 69 lbs 1 day. Butter 21 lbs. 8 oz. 7 days, P.
LADY AKKRUM 2D, 9302 H. F. Lad Deane, 579 H. F.; Lady Akkrum, 8153 H. Milk 67 lbs. 8 oz. 1 day. Butter 24 lbs. 7 days, P.
LADY ALLIS, 7141 H. Copal, 1142 H.; Siebereu 3d, 2302 H. Milk 59 lbs. 8 oz. 1 day. Butter 15 lbs. 7 days, P.
LADY ALMA BREEZE, 26053 H. F. Shadeland Consul, 8761 H. F.; Shadeland Breeze 2d, 2955 H. F. Milk 36 lbs. 4 oz. 1 day, 1,036 lbs. 30 days, A.R. Butter 9 lbs. 5 oz. 7 days, A.R.
LADY ALTJE, 730 H. F. Imp. Milk 47 lbs. 1 day, P.
LADY ANDOVER, 16 H. Zuider Zee 2d. 57 H.; Midwould 4th, 26 N. Milk 68 lbs. 1 day, P.
LADY ANNA'S AAGGIE 1115 H. F. Sir Newton of Aaggie, 1851 H.; Lady Anna, 3314 H. Butter 30 lbs. 14½ oz. 7 days, P.
LADY ANNIE, 1083 H. Saladin, 336 H.; Milk Maid, 194 H. Milk 50 lbs. 8 oz. 1 day, P.
LADY ANTRIM, 352 H. Dictator, 82 H.. Anja, 80 H. Milk 72 lbs. 4 oz. 1 day, 11,820 lbs. 7 months 14 days, P.
LADY ARIAN, 5890 H. F. Arian, 3256 H.; Hettie Rose. 10511 H. Milk 48 lbs. 4 oz. 1 day, P.; 4,888 lbs. 4 months. A. R. Butter 11 lbs. 15 oz. 7 days, A.R.
LADY ARTIS, 4525 H. Artis, 127 Neth.; Jansje, 596 Neth. Milk 57 lbs. 1 day, 11,677 lbs. 10 oz. 1 year, P. Butter 17 lbs. 9 oz. 7 days, P.
LADY ASHLEY, 4374 H. Imp. Milk 65 lbs. 1 day, P.
LADY ASTREA, 4863 H. Duke of Anjou, 1250 H.; Astrea, 88 H. Milk 733 lbs. 10 days, A.R. Butter 22 lbs. 5 oz. 7 days, A.R.
LADY BAKER, 1112 H. Sligo, 621 H.; Ariel, 85 H. Milk 77 lbs, 8 oz. 1 day, P. Butter 5 lbs. 11½ oz. 1 day, P.; 34 lbs. 6 oz. 7 days, A R.
LADY BAKER 2D, 2473 H. Dalrymple, 618 H.; Lady Baker, 1112 H. Milk 67 lbs. 1 day, 1,83- lbs. 12 oz. 30 days, A.R. Butter 18 lbs 6¼ oz. 7 days, A.R.
LADY BANTA, 11340 H. Imp. Milk 65 lbs. 1 day, P.
LADY BARNUM, 6281 H. Imp Milk 50 lbs. 1 day, P. Butter 20 lbs. 6¾ oz. 7 days, A R.
LADY BATTELS 2D, 8497 H. Sligo, 621 H.; Lady Burk, 353 H. Milk 75 lbs. 1 day, P.
LADY BELLE, 216 H. Imp. Milk 9,708 lbs. 3 oz. 1 year, P.
LADY BIRD, 6125 H. Imp. Milk 57 lbs. 8 oz 1 day, P.
LADY BOERSMA, 7514 H. Imp. Milk 78 lbs, 1 day, 11,449 lbs. 4 oz. 7 months 27 days, P. Butter 17 lbs. 8 oz. 7 days, A.R.
LADY BONAPARTE, 5038 H. F. Duon, 012 D. F.; Lady of St. Anna. Milk 70 bs., P.
LADY BOONSTRA, 6926 H. F. Forster, 2771 H.; Boonstra 4th, 7408 H. Butter 16 lbs. 7 days, P.
LADY BYRON, 4378 H. Imp. Milk 71 lbs. 1 day, P.
LADY CLARINA, 7249 H. Imp. Milk 43 lbs. 1 day, P.
LADY CLAY, 15 H. Imp. Milk 80 lbs. 1 day, P.
LADY CLIFDEN, 159 H. Imp. Milk 7" lbs. 8 oz. 1 day, P.; 17,746 lbs. 2 oz. 1 year, P.
LADY COLLINS, 2949 H. Joe Jefferson, 273 H.; Hepsey, 1674 H. Milk 50 lbs 1 day, P.
LADY DE HAAN, 615 D. H. Imp. Milk 72 lbs, 1 day, P.; 2018 lbs. 14 oz. 30 days, P. Butter 20 lbs. 7 days, P.
LADY DE HAAN 2D, 1761 D. F. De Watergeus, 229 P. R.; Lady De Haan, 615 P. R. Butter 20 lbs. 7 days, A.R.
LADY DELIGHT, 782 H. Imp. Milk 10,890 lbs. 347 days. Butter 2 lbs. 12 oz. 1 day, 18 lbs. 12 oz. 7 days, P.
LADY DE RUTTER, 6942 H. Imp. Milk 12,638 lbs. 12 oz. 1 year, P.
LADY DE VRIES, 4056 H. Imp. Milk 91 lbs. 12 oz. 1 day, 18,848 lbs. 4 oz. 1 year, P.
LADY DE VRIES KLASINA, 25726 H. F. Klasina Payne's Gold Dust, 12746 H. F.; Payne's Lady De Vries 2d, 903 H. Milk 72 lbs. 1 day, P.
LADY DUCHESS, 6363 H. F. My Favorite's Lad, 4314 H.; Duchess, 2705 H. Milk 6630 lbs. 1 oz. 10 months, A.R. Butter 19 lbs. 4 oz. 7 days, P.

HOLSTEIN-FRIESIAN CATTLE.

LADY ECHO 2D, 16410 H. F. Sir Henry of Maplewood, 6296 H. F.; Lady Echo, 5783 H. Milk 50 lbs. 1 day. Butter 14 lbs. 12 oz. 7 days, P.
LADY ELGIN 2D, 1793 H. F. Jan Wit, 2594 H.; Lady Elgin, 2183 H. Milk 35 lbs. 1 day, P.
LADY ETHELIND, 1871 H. Pride of Lakeside 2d, 322 H.; Lady Eva, 161 H. Milk 40 lbs. 15 oz. 1 day, 7676 lbs. 8 oz. 6 months 28 days, P.
LADY ETHELIND 2D, 6398 H. Syracuse, 822 H.; Lady Ethelind, 1371 H. Milk 49 lbs. 11 oz. 1 day, 1383 lbs. 14 oz. 1 month, P.
LADY EVA, 161 H. Imp. Milk 106 lbs. 1 day. 7205 lbs. 115 days, P.
LADY FAY, 4470 H. Imp. Milk 97 lbs. 5 oz. 1 day, P.; 20,412 lbs. 1 year, A.R. Butter 22 lbs. 3½ oz. 7 days, A.R.
LADY FISHER, 355 H. Imp. Milk 62 lbs. 1 day, P.
LADY FLORA, 2168 H. Crown Prince. 80 H.; Opperdoes 17th, 198 H. Milk 93 lbs. 12 oz. 1 day, 2654 lbs. 4 oz. 30 days, P. Butter 22 lbs. 8 oz. 7 days, P.
LADY FLORA 3D, 3634 H. F. Jaques, 765 H.; Lady Fisher, 2168 H. Milk 60 lbs. 8 oz. 1 day, P.; 5087 lbs. 3 months 18 days, A.R. Butter 17 lbs. 5 oz. 7 days, A.R.
LADY FLOYD, 9764 H. Roman Chief, 1151 H.; Niobe, 816 H. Milk 70 lbs. 1 day, P.
LADY GARSON 2D, 2726 H. F. No-No, 4076 H.; Lady Garson, 10423 H. Milk 36 lbs. 1 day, P.
LADY GERDA, 806 H. F. Mercedes Prince, 2150 H ; Gerda, 5309 H. Milk 6877 lbs. 4 oz. 10 months, P.
LADY GERDA 2D, 8768 H. F. Billy Bawn, 3087 H.; Lady Gerda, 806 H. F. Milk 7600 lbs. 1 oz. 10 months, A.R.
LADY GRETCHEN. Imp. Milk 800 lbs. 10 days, P.
LADY GRISWOLD, 6878 H. Imp. Milk 77 lbs. 1 day, 17,023 lbs. 7 oz. 1 year, A.R. Butter 24 lbs. 13 oz. 7 days, 101 lbs. 10 oz. 30 days, P.
LADY GRISWOLD'S NETHERLAND, 11102 H. F. Netherland Prince, 716 H.; Lady Griswold, 6878 H. Milk 8420 lbs. 7 oz. 11 months 12 days, A.R. Butter 16 lbs. 7 days. A.R.
LADY HARRISON, 12849 H. F. Sir Archie, 2298 H. F.; Jelkje, 6541 H. Milk 48 lbs. 1 day, P.
LADY HELEN, 1849 H. Imp. Milk 39 lbs. 1 day, P.
LADY HENDRICK, 10376 H. F. Imp. Milk 74 lbs. 1 day. P.
LADY HENDRICK 3D, 28715 H. F. Murillo's Mercedes Prince, 12363 H. F. Milk 80 lbs 1 day, 871 lbs. 10 days, P. Butter 2 lbs. 8 oz. 1 day, P.
LADY H'SKE. Imp. Milk 488 lbs. 8 oz. 10 days, A.R.
LADY HORN, 2873 H. F. Birghorn, 4075 H.; Aafge, 8973 H. Milk 40 lbs. 8 oz. 1 day, 8849 lbs. 1 year, P. Butter 20 lbs. 6½ oz. 7 days, A.R.
LADY HORNELL 786 H. F. Jacob Wit, 2662 H.; Little Muffits, 5016 H. Milk 62 lbs. 1 day, 606 lbs. 10 days, P.
LADY JANS, 4883 H. Imp. Milk 70 lbs. 12 oz. 1 day, A.R.; 15,706 lbs. 1 year, A.R. Butter 18 lbs. 5 oz. 7 days, A.R.
LADY KIRBY OF MAPLEWOOD, 5969 H. F. Osman Digma, 3007 H.; Sallie Kirby, 2879 H. Milk 549 lbs. 10 days, A.R.; 5680 lbs. 4 months, A.R. Butter 15 lbs. 2 oz. 7 days, A.R.
LADY K OF RIVERVIEW, 6731 H. F. Commodore Preble, 3191 H.; Evalena of Shadeland, 8601 H. Milk 41 lbs. 8 oz. 1 day, 1095 lbs. 30 days, P.
LADY KOSTER, 1404 H. Imp. Milk 69 lbs. 1 day P.; 3442 lbs. 60 days, P.
LADY KURT, 358 H. Kurt, 120 H.; Lea. 169 H. Butter 13 lbs. 7 days, P.
LADY LINCOLN, 5694 H. Imp. Milk 62 lbs. 12 oz. 1 day, P.
LADY LOCKSPUR, 8220 H. F. Neptune Fairview, 3886 H.; Lockspur 2d, 2906 H. Milk 36 lbs. 1 day, 6519 lbs. 10 months, 20 days, P.
LADY LORAINE, 1091 H. F. Bonny, 3070 H.; Lady Lauree, 6366 H. Butter 12 lbs. 5 oz. 7 days, P.
LADY MABEL, 371 H. Imp. Butter 17 lbs. 5 oz. 7 days, A.R.
LADY MAC, 1366 H. Col. Fox, 206 H.; Jennie G, 339 H. Milk 72 lbs. 1 day, 2022 lbs. 7 oz. 1 month, P.
LADY MAC 2D, 3617 H. F. Turk. 3244 H.; Lady Mac, 1366 H. Milk 8572 lbs. 2/₇ oz. 9 months, A.R.
LADY MARION, 1825 H. Imp. Butter 15 lbs. 2 oz. 7 days, A.R.
LADY MARRINGA 2D, 16255 H. F. Staveren, 3639 H.; Lady Marringa, 7978 H. Milk 71 lbs. 1 day, P. Butter 21 lbs. 10 oz. 7 days, P.
LADY MARY, 3452 H. Trump, 354 H.; Blossom. 256 H. Milk 68 lbs. 1 day, 641 lbs. 10 days, P.
LADY MEB, 6649 H. Prince Alexander; Meb, 1417 Neth. Milk 8117 lbs. 280 days, P.
LADY MEINSMA 4TH, 5052 H. F. Major Pel, 2763 H.; Lady Meinsma, 8563 H. Milk 56 lbs. 1 day, 501 lbs. 10 days, P.
LADY MIDWOULD, 17 H. Imp. Milk 62 lbs. 1 day, P.
LADY MIGNONETTE, 3591 H. Bounce, 873 H.; Dahlia, 1835 H. Milk 39 lbs. 1 day, P.
LADY MOTLEY, 2763 H. Imp. Milk 64 lbs. 5 oz. 1 day, 10,500 lbs. 9 months, P.
LADY NEKO, 19675 H. F. (Governor 11th, 7748 H. F.; Antonia Neko, 8553 H. Milk 61 lbs. 1 day. P.
LADY NETHERLAND, 1263 H. Imp. Milk 73 lbs. 11 oz. 1 day, 13,875 lbs. 5 oz. 1 year, P. Butter 21 lbs. 3 oz. 7 days, A. R.; 88 lbs. 6 oz. 30 days, P.
LADY NETHERLAND OF BROOKSIDE, 23478 H. F. Aaggie Leila's Prince, 4419 H.; Madame Hengerveld, 1333 H. Butter 15 lbs. 7 days, P.
LADY NUDINE, 3432 H. F. Billy Bawn, 3087 H.; Nudine 2d, 9413 H. Milk 54 lbs. 8 oz. 1 day, 11,000 lbs. 10 months, P.
LADY OF BROEK 2D, 2799 H. Imp. Milk 88 lbs. 1 day, P.; 11,187 lbs. 1 oz. 8 months, 6 days, A.R. Butter 20 lbs. 3½ oz. 7 days, P.
LADY OF LYONS, 2767 H. Imp. Milk 72 lbs. 14 oz. 1 day, P.; 8761 lbs. 5 oz. 10 months, A.R.
LADY OF LYONS 2D, 6399 H. Neptune, 711 H.; Lady of Lyons, 2767 H. Milk 63 lbs. 6 oz. 1 day, P.; 8008 lbs. 5 oz. 7 months, 30 days, A.R.
LADY OF LYONS 3D, 572 H. F. Uncle Tom 2d, 1163 H.; Lady of Lyons, 2767 H. Milk 8123 lbs. 6 oz. 10 months, A.R.
LADY OF LYONS 4TH, 4001 H. F. Billy Bawn, 3087 H.; Lady of Lyons, 2767 H. Milk 58 lbs. 4 oz. 1 day, 12,000 lbs. 10 months, P.
LADY OF ST. ANNA, 413 D. F. Wassenaar; Groote. Milk 68 lbs. 8 oz. 1 day, P.; 612 lbs. 12 oz. 10 days, A.R. Butter 28 lbs. 7 days, 7 lbs. 7 oz. 2 days, P.
LADY OF THE LAKE, 574 H. Imp. Milk 45 lbs. 13 oz. 1 day, 12,201 lbs. 4 oz. 1 year, P.
LADY OF VERONA, 4750 H. F. Neptune Fairview, 3886 H.; Lockspur 2d's Netherland, 8750 H. Milk 9135 lbs. 10 months 11 days, P. Butter 15 lbs. 10 oz. 7 days, A.R.
LADY OLLIE ARTIS, 2300 H. F. Artis Jr., 2723 H.; Duchess of Beemster, 4621 H. Milk 65 lbs. 1 day, 360 lbs. 6 days, P. Butter 5 lbs. 10 oz. 1 day, 26 lbs. 6¼ oz. 6 days, P.
LADY OOSTERBAAN, 526 D. F. Imp. Milk 55 lbs. 1 day, P.
LADY PANSY, 5572 H. David Copperfield, 404 H.; Janna, 1632 H. Milk 40 lbs. 1 day, 14,600 lbs. 1 year, P. Butter 14 lbs. 8 oz. 7 days, P.

MILK AND BUTTER RECORDS.   345

LADY PARAGON, 2005 H. F.   Paragon, 2275 H.; Queen of the Hill 4th, 3793 H.   Butter 16 lbs. 4 oz. 7 days, A.R.
LADY PERCY, 4375 H.   Imp.   Milk 42 lbs. 1 day, P.
LADY PHILPAIL, 10394 H.   Imp.   Milk 35 lbs. 12 oz. 1 day, 11,040 lbs. 5 months, P.   Butter 25 lbs. 3 oz. 7 days, P.
LADY PHILPAIL 2D, 937 H. F.   Nicholas, 567 Neth.; Lady Philpail 10394, H.   Milk 80 lbs. 1 day, P.
LADY PHILPAIL 3D, 4208 H. F.   International Prince; Lady Philpail, 10394 H.   Milk 49 lbs. 6 oz. 1 day, P.   Butter, 12 lbs. 14 oz. 7 days, P.
LADY PHILPAIL 4TH, 12551 H. F.   Matehet; Lady Philpail, 10394 H.   Milk 48 lbs. 8 oz. 1 day, P.
LADY PLAS, 4628 H.   Imp.   Milk 85 lbs. 8 oz. 1 day, 2323 lbs. 12 oz. 30 days, A.R.   Butter 15 lbs. 10¼ oz. 7 days, A.R.
LADY PLUISTER, 6712 H.   Imp.   Butter 18 lbs. 4 oz. 7 days, P.
LADY PORTAGE, 434 H. F.   Major Pel, 2763 H.; Kroontje, 5584 H.   Milk 65 lbs. 1 day, P.
LADY PYM, 8236 H.   Jonge Prins, 197 Neth.; Antje, 146 Neth.   Milk 75 lbs. 12 oz. 1 day, P.   Butter 22 lbs. 12 oz. 7 days, P.
LADY QUEEN, 1003 H.   Heike, 256 H.; Aileen, 237 H.   Milk 47 lbs. 1 day, P.
LADY REX, 4376 H.   Imp.   Milk 44 lbs. 1 day, P.
LADY SALATINE, 10285 H.   Imp.   Milk 9048 lbs, 10 months, P.
LADY SAPPHO, 10550 H. F.   Netherland Convoy, 2934 H.; Aaggie Sappho, 4574 H.   Milk 40 lbs. 8 oz. 1 day, 1103 lbs. 8 oz. 30 days, P.   Butter 9 lbs. 13 oz. 7 days, A.R.; 26 lbs. 9 oz. 3 weeks, P.
LADY SCHOLTON, 1054 H.   Imp.   Milk 38 lbs. 1 day, P.
LADY SCHOLTON 3D, 1056 H.   Stadtholder, 157 H.; Lady Scholton 2d, 1055 H.   Milk 50 lbs. 1 day, P.   Butter 21 lbs. 5 oz. 1 day, 20 lbs. 8 oz. 7 days, P.
LADY SCHOORL, 6764 H.   Imp.   Milk 37 lbs. 9 oz. 1 day, P.
LADY SIFFINGA 2D, 554 D. F.   Imp.   Milk 59 lbs. 4 oz. 1 day, P.
LADY SMYTHE, 9063 H.   Imp.   Milk 9700 lbs. 1 year, P.
LADY SOCIAL, 9062 H.   Imp.   Butter, 17 lbs. 10 oz. 7 days, P.
LADY SPARKLE, 5259 H. F.   Promoter, 518 H.; Sophie Sparkle, 5385 H.   Milk 35 lbs. 1 day, P.
LADY SPOFFORD, 9642 H. F.   Imp.   Milk 43 lbs. 1 day, P.
LADY STANLEY, 4377 H.   Imp.   Milk 78 lbs. 8 oz. 1 day, P.; 1682 lbs. 8 oz. 30 days, A.R.   Butter 17 lbs. 11 oz. 7 days A.R.
LADY STOUT, 1891 H.   Imp.   Milk 484 lbs. 7 days, P.
LADY SUTTON, 10330 H.   Imp.   Milk 59 lbs. 1 day, P.
LADY TEXAL 4TH, 10 D. F.   Imp.   Milk 81 lbs. 1 day, P.   Butter 4 lbs. 1 day, P.
LADY THURSTON, 6818 H.   Imp.   Milk 65 lbs. 1 day, P.   Butter 24 lbs. 6 oz. 7 days, P.
LADY THURSTON 2D, 3141 H. F.   Tamerlund, 4568 H.; Lady Thurston, 6818 H.   Milk 60 lbs. 1 day, P.
LADY TIMBER POINT, 10291 H. F.   Bouwke, 100 Neth.; Antje, 624 Neth.   Milk 40 lbs. 1 day, P.
LADY TRONI, 4659 H.   Imp.   Milk 70 lbs. 4 oz. 1 day, 1946 lbs. 30 days, A.R.   Butter 18 lbs 12 oz. 7 days, A.R.
LADY TWISK OF MEADOWVALE, 4173 H.   Baron, 2133 H.; 6th Maid of Twisk, 3891 H.   Milk 8048 lbs. 10 months, A.R.
LADY VALENCIA, 6382 H,   Prince Oppendoes, 387 H.; Detmara, 3147 H.   Milk 68 lbs. 1 day, P.   Butter 23 lbs. 15 oz. 7 days, P.
LADY VAN, 929 D. F.   Wijndert, 102 P R.; Tjerk, 234 P. R.   Milk 9514 lbs. 9 oz. 9 months, A.R.
LADY VAN 4TH, 27166 H. F.   Hamilton 2d, 5608 H. F.; Lady Van, 929 D. F.   Milk 54 lbs. 7 oz. 1 day, P.
LADY VAN BEERS, 6651 H.   Imp.   Milk 65 lbs. 1 day, 9242 lbs. 230 days, P.   Butter 19 lbs. 12 oz. 7 days, P.
LADY VET, 2518 H.   Kees.   Imp.   Milk 55 lbs. 1 day, P.
LADY WAIBOER, 6772 H.   Imp.   Milk 50 lbs. 1 day, P.
LADY WALWORTH, 956 H.   Imp.   Milk 81 lbs. 4 oz. 1 day, P.; 14,287 lbs. 5 oz. 10 months, A.R.   Butter 19 lbs. 7 days, 37 lbs. 6 oz. 14 days, A.R.
LADY WESTWOUD, 11611 H. F.   Peter, 113 Neth.; Glenburine, 8788 H.   Milk 80 lbs. 8 oz. 1 day, P.
LADY WINKEL, 4656 H.   Imp.   Milk 80 lbs. 1 day, P.
LA FAVORITA, 6715 H.   Imp.   Milk 47 lbs. 8 oz. 1 day, 760 lbs. 10 days, P.
LA FAVORITE, 1255 H.   Imp.   Milk 60 lbs. 1 day, P.
LAHASKA, 7040 H.   Imp.   Milk 70 lbs. 4 oz. 1 day, P.
LAKESIDE ADELA, 9047 H.   Imp.   Milk 11,939 lbs. 1 oz. 1 year, A.R.   Butter 13 lbs. 10½ oz. 7 days, P.
LAKESIDE BERTA, 10012 H.   Imp.   Butter 11 lbs. 12¾ oz. 7 days, P.
LAKESIDE CLARISSA, 9915 H.   Imp.   Milk 7776 lbs. 15 oz. 10 months, A.R.   Butter 12 lbs. 12 oz. 7 days, A.R.
LAKESIDE DAISY, 9899 H.   Imp.   Milk 10,249 lbs. 13 oz. 1 year, P.
LAKESIDE HESTER, 9981 H.   Imp.   Milk 11,063 lbs. 7 oz. 1 year, P.   Butter 16 lbs. 6¼ oz. 7 days, P.
LAKESIDE PRIZE, 9973 H.   Imp.   Milk 60 lbs. 2 oz. 1 day, P.; 15,052 lbs. 8 oz. 1 year, A.R.   Butter 10 lbs. 6½ oz. 7 days, P.
LAKESIDE RUTH, 9975 H.   Imp.   Milk 44 lbs. 13 oz. 1 day, 10,518 lbs. 6 oz. 1 year, P.   Butter 9 lbs. 8 oz. 7 days, P.
LAKESIDE THEO, 9890 H.   Imp.   Milk 71 lbs. 4 oz. 1 day, P.; 11,513 lbs. 9 oz. 1 year, A.R.   Butter 14 lbs. 6½ oz. 7 days, A.R.
LAKESIDE THEO 3D, 8325 H. F.   Sir Henry Lambert, 1263 H. F.; Lakeside Theo, 9890 H.   Milk 64 lbs. 8 oz. 1 day, P.   Butter 6 lbs. 8 oz. 3 days, P.
LAKESIDE VIOLA, 9919 H.   Imp.   Milk 34 lbs. 7 oz. 1 day, P.
LAKESIDE WINONA, 10029 H.   Imp.   Milk 61 lbs. 1 day, P.
LAMBERTINA, 6889 H.   Imp.   Milk 66 lbs. 2 oz. 1 day, 10,744 lbs. 6 oz. 1 year, P.   Butter 19 lbs. 4 oz. 7 days, 101 lbs, 10 oz. 30 days, P.
LAMBERTINA 2D, 9365 H. F.   Netherland Prince, 716 H.; Lambertina, 6889 H   Butter 17 lbs. 9 oz. 7 days, A.R.
LAMPASAS, 7008 H.   Imp.   Milk 79 lbs. 8 oz. 1 day, P.; 640 lbs. 8 oz. 10 days, A.R.   Butter 3 lbs. 12 oz. 1 day, 26 lbs. 4 oz. 7 days, P.
LANDRUS 3D, 8164 H. F.   Duchess of York's Barent, 88 H. F.; Landrus, 7275 H.   Milk 60 lbs. 1 day, P.
LANGEDIJK, 2030 H. F.   De Prins, 310 Neth.; Langedijk, 600 Neth.   Milk 45 lbs. 1 day; 1307 lbs. 30 days, P.
LANGMEER LASS, 10412 H.   Imp.   Milk 300 lbs. 8 oz. 7 days, P.   Butter 12 lbs. 12 oz. 7 days, P.
LANGTRY, 2447 H.   Burley, 394 H.; Silver Bell, 971 H.   Milk 56 lbs. 8 oz. 1 day, 1568 lbs. 30 days, P.
LA REINA, 2164 H.   Imp.   Milk 60 lbs 8 oz. 1 day; 1910 lbs. 30 days, P.
LARONTA, 7471 H.   Imp.   Milk 67 lbs. 1 day, P.   Butter 18 lbs. 7 days, P.

24

LASSIE JEAN, 19630 H. F. Meadowbrook Chief, 1069 H. F.; Annie Laura, 9354 H. F. Milk 1525 lbs. 30 days, 9386 lbs. 8 oz. 8 months, P.
LAUNA, 11953 H. F. Davalos, 1964 H. F.; Pride of Elgin, 11061 H. F. Milk 8089 lbs. 8 oz. 10 months, A.R.
LAURA, 205 D. F. Paul Hartog; Laurel. Milk 70 lbs. 1 day, 9467 lbs. 13 oz. 1 year, P.
LAURA OF SHADELAND, 2426 H. Imp. Milk 67 lbs. 11 oz. 1 day, 6487 lbs. 7 oz. 4 months, P. Butter 15 lbs. 8¼ oz. 7 days, P.
LAURA ROOKER, 9906 H. Royal Aaggie, 3463 H. Imp. Milk 42 lbs. 3 oz. 1 day, 11,079 lbs. 1 year, P.
LAURENTINE, 6079 H. Imp. Milk 52 lbs. 1 day, 1500 lbs. 30 days, P.
LAURIE, 6685 H. Imp. Milk 41 lbs. 8 oz. 1 day, P.; 9154 lbs. 7 oz. 10 months, A.R. Butter 13 lbs. 7 oz. 7 days, A.R.
LAURINA, 1363 H. F. Imp. Milk 46 lbs. 1 day, P.
LAURINDA, 9303 H. Imp. Milk 37 lbs. 8 oz. 1 day, P.
LAVINIA, 168 H. Imp. Milk 50 lbs. 1 day, P.
LAWRENCE BEAUTY, 15359 H. F. Judge Mulkey, 985 H. F.; Spierdyk 2d, 4302 H. F. Butter 10 lbs. 14 oz. 7 days, A.R.
LAZINEA OF MAPLEWOOD, 6532 H. F. Tennessee Prince, 3130 H.; Cameo 2d, 3554 H. Milk 53 lbs. 14 oz. 1 day, 1474 lbs. 30 days, P. Butter 16 lbs. 13 oz. 7 days, P.
LEA 2D, 170 H. Imp. Milk 13768 lbs. 1 year, P.
LEAH VEEMAN, 5526 H. F. Hamilton, 686 D. F.; Sixth Durkje Veeman, 1904 D. F. Milk 8100 lbs. 10 months, A.R.
LEDA, 1269 D. F. Johannes; De Jong's Sjut. Milk 67 lbs. 1 day, P.
LEDA, 1677 D. F. De Nette, 324 F.; Pieter, 1006 F. Milk 58 lbs. 1 day, 1611 lbs. 4 oz. 30 days, P. Butter 18 lbs. 8 oz. 7 days, P.
LEENTJE, 2972 H. Imp. Milk 76 lbs. 12 oz. 1 day, P.
LEENTJE 2D, 2587 H. Imp. Milk 56 lbs. 3 oz. 1 day, P. Butter 17 lbs. 8¼ oz. 7 days, P.
LEENTJE MAID, 4652 H. Imp. Milk 13,328 lbs. 8 oz. 10 months, P.
LEILA, 5143 H. Imp. Milk 48 lbs. 8 oz. 1 day, P.
LEILA PROMOTER, 1744 H. F. Promoter, 1518 H.; Cordelia, 922 H. Milk 51 lbs. 1 day, P.
LEMABEL, 6987 H. Imp. Milk 48 lbs. 14 oz. 1 day, 10,314 lbs. 15 oz. 1 year, P.
LENA, 7019 Neth. Imp. Milk 78 lbs. 1 day, P.
LENAWEE, 1682 D. F. Jonge Carr, 231 F.; Koltje, 1808 F. Butter 9 lbs. 11 oz. 7 days, A.R.
LENAWEE 2D, 2806 H. F. Mooie, 26 D. F.; Lenawee, 1082 D. F. Milk 32 lbs. 1 day, P.
LENTJE GLENDIVE, 14357 H. F. Glendive, 315 H. F.; Lentje 2d, 2587 H. Milk 538 lbs. 10 days, P.
LEONIA TWEEDE, 1521 D. F. Groote Pier, 194 F.; Siebrigje, 2660 F. Butter 9 lbs. 6 oz. 7 days, A.R.
LESBIA, 6159 H. Imp. Milk 10,089 lbs. 9 months 27 days, A.R.
LETHEA, 2082 H. F. Imp. Milk 38 lbs. 1 day, P.
LEUWKJE, 90 D. F. Imp. Milk 50 lbs. 1 day, P.
LIBBIE C, 1178 H. Imp. Milk 77 lbs. 12 oz. 1 day, 2263 lbs. 6 oz. 30 days, P. Butter 19 lbs. 11 oz. 7 days, P.
LIDA, 2778 H. Imp. Milk 53 lbs. 12 oz. 1 day, 8536 lbs. 12 oz. 7 months 6 days, P. Butter 11 lbs. 13½ oz. 7 days, P.
LIEVIA, 5717 H. Imp. Milk 75 lbs. 1 day, P.
LIGHTNING'S BUTTERFLY, 11874 H. F. Lightning, 4117 H.; Butterfly, 906 H. Milk 56 lbs. 1 day, 548 lbs. 10 days, P. Butter 15 lbs. 10 oz. 7 days, P.
LIGHTSOME, 2784 H. Imp. Milk 16,793 lbs. 13 oz. 1 year, P. Butter 18 lbs. 8 oz. 7 days, P.
LIGHTSOME'S NETHERLAND, 6980 H. F. Aegis Netherland Prince, 4585 H.; Lightsome, 2784 H. Butter 16 lbs. 1 oz. 1 day, A.R.
LIJE (OTIS), 1744 H. Imp. Milk 63 lbs. 1 day, 12,000 lbs. 1 year, P.
LIJSBERT, 12821 H. F. Karel, 254 F. H. Imp. Milk 68 lbs. 1 day, P.
LILIO, 2019 H. F. Imp. Milk 45 lbs. 1 day, 1280 lbs. 30 days, P.
LILITH, 5138 H. Imp. Milk 82 lbs. 1 day, 562 lbs. 4 oz. 7 days, P. Butter 18 lbs. 4 oz. 7 days, P.
LILLA, 2783 H. Imp. Milk 45 lbs. 7 oz. 1 day, 5674 lbs. 13 oz. 5 months, 17 days, P.
LILLIAN OLCOTT, 2063 H. Imp. Milk 61 lbs. 13 oz. 1 day, P.
LILY, 964 H. Imp. Milk 66 lbs. 8 oz. 1 day, P.; 17,302 lbs. 7 oz. 1 year, A.R. Butter 21 lbs. 4½ oz. 7 days, 83 lbs. 11½ oz. 30 days, A.R.
LILY DALE, 4301 H. Milk 70 lbs. 1 day, P.
LINA 2D, 1413 H. Imp. Milk 42 lbs. 1 day, P. Butter 15 lbs. 6 oz. 7 days, P.
LINARIA, 5144 H. Imp. Milk 94 lbs. 1 day, P.
LINDA, 645 H. Nestor, 127 H; Frieda, 306 H. Milk 34 lbs. 1 day, 6117 lbs. 1 year, P.
LINDA LEE, 4387 H. Imp. Milk 51 lbs. 1 day, 620 lbs. 10 days, P.
LINESKA, 1136 H. Colonel Fox, 206 H.; Lina, 172 H. Butter 2 lbs. 12 oz. 1 day, 18 lbs. 11 oz. 7 days, P.
LIPKJE, 112 D. F. Imp. Milk 13,021 lbs. 1 year, P.
LIPKJE 3D, 6459 H. F. Wolters, 146 D. F.; Lipkje, 112 D. F. Milk 9000 lbs. 10 months, P.
LIPKJE 4TH, 6460 H. F. Fritts, 4735 H.; Lipkje, 112 D. F. Milk 41 lbs. 8 oz. 1 day, 1126 lbs. 12 oz. 30 days, P. Butter 13 lbs. 14 oz. 7 days, P.
LITTLE GIFT, 11018 H. F. Jan Wit 13th, 633 H. F.; Mina Spaanz, 1104 H. Milk 7315 lbs. 9 months, 7 days, A.R.
LITTLE KATE, 5035 H. Imp. Milk 45 lbs. 1 day, P.
LITTLE WONDER, 1788 H. Imp. Milk 6262 lbs. 8 oz. 11 months, 20 days, P.
LIZABEL, 6103 H. Imp. Butter 16 lbs. 7 days, P.
LIZE, 6292 H. Imp. Milk 61 lbs. 12 oz. 1 day, P.
LIZZIE C, 5399 H. Imp. Milk 60 lbs. 1 day, P.
LIZZIE D, 3313 H. Sir William, 155 H. Paula, 200 H. Milk 54 lbs. 1 day, P.
LIZZIE G, 5396 H. Imp. Milk 8595 lbs. 9 months 15 days, P.
LIZZIE H. BATTELS, 5909 H. F. Sir Foreest, 4000 H.; Lady Battels 2d, 8479 H. Milk 40 lbs. 1 day, P.
LIZZIE J, 7903 H. F. Prince Rival, 33 H. F.; Vinnie 3d, 200 H. F. Milk 11,000 lbs. 1 year, P.
LIZZIE J's JEWEL, 28643 H. F. Aimee's Jewel, 10089 H. F.; Lizzie J, 7903 H. F. Milk 7000 lbs. 1 year, P.
LIZZIE NICHOLS, 5520 H. F. Honest Abe, 749 H.; Lizzie D, 3313 H. Milk 42 lbs. 1 day, P.
LIZZIE OF ALLENTOWN, 20992 H. F. Prince Philpail, 2853 H. F.; Maaz, 10070 H. Milk 60 lbs. 1 day, P.
LOBELIA, 9436 H. Imp. Milk 75 lbs. 6 oz. 1 day, 14,797 lbs. 12 oz. 1 year, P. Butter 14 lbs. 7 days, P.
LOCKSPUR 2D, 2906 H. Imp. Milk 55 lbs. 1 day, 8010 lbs. 7 year, P.
LODEWIKA, 11821 H. F. Johan, 456 F.; Pesch, 2011 F. Milk 54 lbs. 1 day, 1532 lbs. 30 days, P.
LOHRVILLE, 7534 H. Imp. Milk 62 lbs. 8 oz. 1 day, P.

MILK AND BUTTER RECORDS. 347

LOKING, 12036 H. F. Terpstra, 37 F. H.; Van der Goot, 4456 F. H. Milk 44 lbs. 1 day, P.; 414 lbs. 10 days, A.R.
LOLA, 2789 H. Imp. Milk 40 lbs. 6 oz. 1 day, 996 lbs. 9 oz. 30 days, P.
LONEMMA, 3341 H. F. Willem LLL, 130 Neth.; Emma, 95 Neth. Milk 54 lbs. 1 day, P.
LONE STAR, 1430 D. F. De Watergens 229 P. R.; Lily, 646 P. R. Milk 427 lbs. 8 oz. 10 days, A.R.
LORA SADIE VALE, 11967 H. F. Koningen Van Friesland 5th's Netherland, 2515 H.; Aaggie Sadie Vale, 4979 H. F. Milk 5474 lbs. 14 oz. 10 months, P.
LOREA NIKO, 9618 H. Imp. Milk 79 lbs. 1 oz. 1 day, P. Butter 28 lbs. 6 oz. 7 days, P.
LOREA NIKO 2D, 4597 H. F. Sir Henry of Maplewood, 2933 H.; Lorea Niko, 9618 H. Milk 48 lbs. 1 day, P.
LOREA NIKO 3D, 7597 H. F. Sir Henry of Maplewood, 2933 H.; Lorea Niko, 9618 H. Milk 4" lbs. 6 oz. 1 day, P. Butter 2 lbs. 6 oz. 1 day, P.
LOREA NIKO 3D's ONONIS, 16404 H. F. Ononis Echo's Prince of Wayne, 6293 H. F.; Lorea Niko 3d, 9618 H. Milk 56 lbs. 1 day, P.
LORELEIL, 3336 H. F. Imp. Milk 84 lbs. 8 oz. 1 day, P.
LORINDA, 7840 H. Imp. Milk 40 lbs. 1 day, P.
LOTJE, 7276 H. Imp. Milk 79 lbs. 1 day, P.
LOTTA, 595 H. F. Imp. Milk 40 lbs. 1 day, P.
LOUIE S, 3684 H. Imp. Milk 5598 lbs. 7 months, P.
LOUISA, 2928 Neth. Imp. Milk 84 lbs. 4 oz. 1 day, P.
LOUISE, 1429 Neth. Imp. Milk 88 lbs. 1 day, P.
LOUISE S, 4039 H. Imp. Milk 68 lbs. 12 oz. 1 day, P.
LOUIZA, 445 Neth. Imp. Milk 80 lbs. 3 oz. 1 day, P.
LOU MINK, 10298 H. F. Mink Prince, 5865 H.; Sooez, 2916 H. F. Butter 13 lbs. 7 oz., P.
LOURINDA P, 1564 H. Imp. Milk 45 lbs. 1 day, P.
LOUVERSE, 675 H. Imp. Milk 406 lbs. 4 oz. 7 days, P. Butter 12 lbs. 4 oz. 7 days, P.
LOVLIE, 6952 H. Imp. Milk 65 lbs. 6 oz. 1 day, 1798 lbs. 8 oz. 30 days, P.
LOWLAND LASSIE, 2704 H. Imp. Milk 16,745 lbs. 4 oz. 1 year, P. Butter 22 lbs. 3½ oz. 7 days, P.
LUCENA, 3903 H. Napoleon, 706 H.; Jean Ingelow, 1305 H. Milk 43 lbs. 9 oz. 1 day, P.
LUCENA 3D, 9203 H. F. Mercedes' Mahomet, 2943 H.; Lucena, 3903 H. Milk 1240 lbs. 59 days. P.
LUCIA ARTIS, 4851 H. Artis, 127 Neth.; Marie, 3363 Neth. Milk 9500 lbs. 1 oz. 9 months 14 days, A.R. Butter 22 lbs. 5½ oz. 7 days, P.
LUCIANA, 377 H. F. Jan Wit, 2524 H. Imp. Milk 7820 lbs. 259 days, P.
LUCILE, 1358 H. Col. Fox, 206 H.; Duchess of Erie, 119 H. Milk 30 lbs. 1 day, P.
LUCK, 2061 H. Smike, 660 H.; Ulrica, 1192 H. Milk 8215 lbs. 4 oz. 9 months 21 days, A.R.
LUCKY DEAL, 5279 H. Figurehead, 336 H.; Bellwort, 253 H. Milk 620 lbs. 10 days, P.
LUCRETIA, 3009 H. Ben Butler, 533 H.; Myra, 409 H. Milk 65 lbs. 8 oz. 1 day, P.
LUCRETIA L, 2038 H. Imp. Milk 78 lbs. 8 oz. 1 day, P. Butter 18 lbs. 4 oz. 7 days, P.
LUCRETIA MOTT, 1262 H. Imp. Milk 11,101 lbs. 10 months, P.
LUCY, 176 H. Imp. Milk 40 lbs. 15 oz. 1 day, 6650 lbs. 6 oz. 7 months 21 days, P.
LUCY OF PACIFIC, 623 H. F. Imp. Milk 507 lbs. 8 oz. 10 days, 12,160 lbs. 10 months, A.R.
LUCYQUIN, 1600 D. F. Jamie, 207 P. R.; Van Scheltinga 2d, 370 P. R. Milk 45 lbs. 1 day, P.
LUCY ROOKER, 9905 H. Royal Aaggie, 3463 H.; Porcelein, 147 Neth. Milk 40 lbs. 15 oz. 1 day, 7280 lbs. 8 oz. 9 months, P. Butter 11 lbs. 4 oz 7 days, P.
LUCY VAN BEERS, 8392 H. F. Duke of Portland, 1721 H. F.; Dinah Van Beers, 1218 H. F. Milk 36 lbs. 1 day, P. Butter 13 lbs. 8 oz. 7 days, P.
LUELLA, 1577 H. Gen. Grant, 497 H.; Lady Black, 809 H. Milk 43 lbs. 8 oz. 1 day, P.
LUITJE JONGENS, 6442 H. Imp. Milk 43 lbs. 8 oz. 1 day, P.
LUITZEN'S MERCEDES, 6912 H. F. Mercedes Prince, 2150 H.; Jonge Luitzen, 8217 H. Milk 52 lbs. 1 day, 500 lbs. 10 days, P. Butter 15 lbs. 7 oz. 7 days, P.
LUNDE, 1513 D. F. Phillipus, 156 F. H.; Bos, 2346 F. H. Milk 360 lbs. 4 oz. 10 days, A.R.
LURANCY, 6137 H. Imp. Milk 66 lbs. 1 day, 12,908 lbs. 10 months 13 days, P.
LURLINE, 2797 H. Imp. Milk 10,213 lbs. 4 oz. 8 months 15 days, A.R. Butter 20 lbs. 8 oz. 7 days, P.
LUSTRE 2D. 3664 H. Imp. Milk 406 lbs. 4 oz. 7 days, P. Butter 20 lbs. 4 oz. 7 days, A.R.
LUTSCKE, 8356 H. Imp. Milk 84 lbs. 13 oz. 1 day, P. Butter 28 lbs. 5 oz. 7 days, P.
LYCAGHT, 8275 H. F. Dirk, 439 F.; Grietje, 4370 F. Milk 60 lbs. 1 day, 1666 lbs. 30 days, P. Butter 18 lbs. 4 oz. 7 days, P.
LYNDORA, 6796 H. Sir Edwin of Aaggie, 1861 H.; Trintjean, 6775 H. Milk 54 lbs. 2 oz. 1 day P.
LYNTJE, 738 H. F. Hoogearspel I, 562 Neth.; Lyntje, 4151 Neth. Milk 84 lbs. 1 day, P. Butter 24 lbs. 2 oz. 7 days, P.
LYNTJE 2D, 6022 H. F. Forster, 2771 H.; Lyntje, 738 H. Butter 20 lbs. 4 oz. " days.
LYRA, 2801 H. Imp. Milk 10,242 lbs. 9 oz. 1 year, P. Butter 9 lbs. 3 oz. 7 days, P.
LYSKJE, 2822 F. H. Imp. Milk 57 lbs. 1 day, P.
LYTAE, 5304 H. Imp. Milk 71 lbs. 1 day, P.

MAAIKE 2D, 3267 H. Freerk, 14 F. H. Imp. Milk 45 lbs. 1 day P.
MAART, 6047 H. Imp. Milk 52 lbs. 1 day, P.
MAART D, 0021 H. Imp. Milk 52 lbs. 1 day, P.
MAARTJE, 584 H. Imp. Milk 89 lbs. 1 day, P.; 10,072 lbs. 9 months, 37 days, A.R.
MAARTJE 2D, 6410 Neth. Imp. Milk 42 lbs. 1 day, P.
MAARTJE ROGGEVEEN, 3830 H. F. Roggeveen, 420 Neth.; Maartje, 1974 Neth. Milk 6710 lbs. 6 months, P. Butter 10 lbs. 7 days, P.
MAARTJE SYMMES, 950 H. F. Imp. Milk 86 lbs. 1 day, 1920 lbs. 30 days, P.
MAARTJE SYMMES 2D, 988 H. F. Imp. Milk 80 lbs. 4 oz. 1 day, P. Butter 20 lbs. 4 oz. 7 days, P.
MAARTJE SYMMES 3D, 989 H. F. Maartje Symmes, 950 H. F. Milk 72 lbs. 1 day, P. Butter 14 lbs. 3 oz. 7 days, P.
MAARTJE VAN KAMPEN, 730 H. F. Hoogearspel I, 802 Neth.; Maartje, 4150 Neth. Milk 55 lbs. 5 oz. 1 day, P.; 564 lbs. 10 days, A.R
MAAZ, 10070 H. Imp. Milk 50 lbs. 1 day, P.
MABEL, 571 H. Imp. Butter 20 lbs. 9 oz. 7 days, P.
MABEL ARTIS, 4853 H. F. Artis, 127 Neth.; Trijntje, 4238 Neth. Milk 42 lbs. 14 oz. 1 day, 4923 lbs. 6 oz. 4 months 26 days, P. Butter 10 lbs. 11¼ oz. 7 days, P.
MABEL DOUGLAS, 1109 H. Lord Clifden, 572 H.; Alcmaria, 75 H. Milk 70 lbs. 8 oz. 1 day, 9000 lbs. 1 year, P.
MABEL LIVINGSTON, 2812 H. Imp. Milk 78 lbs. 1 day, 2010 lbs. 30 days, P.

MABEL OF PACIFIC, 625 H. F. Nicolaas, 348 Neth.; Aaltje, 1718 Neth. Milk 550 lbs. 10 days, 7949 lbs. 8 oz. 10 months, A.R.
MABEL S, 1414 H. Imp. Milk 61 lbs. 1 day, P. Butter 9 lbs. 5 oz. 7 days, P.
MABEL SPAANZ, 3353 H. Panic, 871 H.; Mina Spaanz, 1104 H. Milk 64 lbs. 8 oz. 1 day, 11,828 lbs. 10 months, A.R.
MABEL ZEEMAN, 9965 H. Imp. Milk 40 lbs. 11 oz. 1 day, P.; 8604 lbs. 15 oz. 10 months, A.R. Butter 9 lbs. 14 oz. 7 days, A.R.
MABELLE SPAANZ, 3353 H. Panic, 871 H.; Mina Spaanz, 1104 H. Milk 64 lbs. 8 oz. 1 day, 1809 lbs. 30 days, P. Butter 18 lbs. 5¼ oz. 7 days, A.R.
MACAO, 7176 H. Imp. Milk 10,008 lbs. 3 oz. 10 months, A.R.
MADAM AUGUSTA, 2806 H. Imp. Milk 88 lbs. 1 day, 8024 lbs. 8 oz. 7 months 7 days, P.
MADAME HENGERVELD, 1333 H. F. Mooie Kleiterp, 319 D. F.; Aaltje Hengerveld 3d, 18 D. F. Milk 60 lbs. 8 oz. 1 day, 3170 lbs. 2 months, P. Butter 18 lbs. 4 oz. 7 days, A.R.
MADAM HENDRIK, 4470 H. F. Hendrik, 300 Neth.; Aafje, 4088 Neth. Milk 55 lbs. 1 day, P.
MADAM STAPEL, 7799 H. Willem 3d, 190 Neth.; Antje, 107 Neth. Milk 60 lbs. 1 day, 1390 lbs. 1 month, P.
MAID OF CEDERSIDE, 2207 H. Cyclone, 392 H.; Galaxy 3d, 311 H. Milk 95 lbs. 1 day, 2000 lbs. 30 days, P.
MAID OF CLIFDEN, 9681 H. F. Flora Clifden's Mercedes Prince, 3545 H.; Maid of Eddyes, 7708 H. Milk 7885 lbs. 10 months A.R.
MAID OF CLINTON, 8979 H. F. Rothmere, 326 D. F.; Kleiterp 4th, 228 D. F. Milk 1573 lbs. 8 oz. 30 days, P.
MAID OF CLOVERDALE, 1305 H. Alkmaar, 459 H.; Saapke, 736 H. Milk 67 lbs. 12 oz. 1 day, P.; 10,887 lbs. 10 months, A.R.
MAID OF COLUMBUS, 1457 H. Mark Tapley, 558 H.; Vesta 3d, 469 H. Milk 40 lbs. 1 day, P.
MAID OF EDDYES, 7708 H. Imp. Milk 65 lbs. 8 oz. 1 day, P.; 10,821 lbs. 21 oz. 10 months, A.R. Butter 12 lbs. 7¾ oz. 7 days, P.
MAID OF ERIN, 3615 H. F. Turk, 3244 H.; Ola, 3375 H. Milk 5299 lbs. 15 oz. 9 months 16 days, P.
MAID OF GOSHEN, 182 H. Imp. Milk 1178 lbs. 30 days, P.
MAID OF LYONS, 8431 H. F. Billy Bawn, 3087 H.; Lady of Lyons 2d, 6399 H. Milk 40 lbs. 1 oz. 1 day, 7810 lbs. 4 oz. 10 months, A.R.
MAID OF MAPLECROFT, 7499 H. Japoon, 1287 H.; Maid of Vernon, 2372 H. Milk 10285 lbs. 6 oz. 10 months, A.R. Butter 16 lbs. 5¼ oz. 7 days, A R.
MAID OF MARION, 38057 H. F. Sir Jewel Echo Jeuzen Mechtbilde, 17562 H. F.; Susie Wicks, 13402 H. F. Milk 11,112 lbs. 1 year, P.
MAID OF MENALDUM, 7021 H. Imp. Milk 49 lbs. 1 day, P.; 476 lbs. 2 oz. 10 days, A.R. Butter 13 lbs. 7 days, A.R.
MAID OF ORLEANS, 2201 H. Climax, 204 H.; Katrina, 1071 H. Milk 55 lbs. 1 day, 11,880 lbs. 11 oz. 8 months, P.
MAID OF PAWLING, 7408 H. Japoon, 1287 H.; Maid of Orleans, 2201 H. Milk 50 lbs. 1 day, P.
MADGE, 374 H. Monitor, 299 H.; Mekia, 395 H. Milk 55 lbs. 1 day, P. Butter 16 lbs. 3 oz. 7 days, P.
MADONNA, 1885 H. Imp. Milk 58 lbs. 1 day, 1575 lbs. 30 days, P.
MAGDALENE, 1873 H. Imp. Milk 48 lbs. 3 oz. 1 day, 8844 lbs. 10 months, P.
MAGENICA, 9832 H. Imp. Milk 40 lbs. 1 day, P.
MAGGIE, 375 H. William, 56 H.; Midwould 6th, 29 H. Milk 78 lbs. 1 day, P.
MAGGIE ARTIS, 4852 H. F. Artis, 127 Neth.; Bathje, 3465 Neth. Milk 55 lbs. 12 oz. 1 day, 5052 lbs. 4 oz. 8 months 5 days, P. Butter 21 lbs. 4 oz. 7 days, P.
MAGGIE CLIFDEN, 5265 H. Imp. Milk 782 lbs. 10 days, 16,720 lbs. 7 oz. 10 months, A.R. Butter 19 lbs. 9 oz. 7 days, A.R.
MAGGIE KEYES, 1743 H. F. Keyes 6th, 1692 H.; Koningin Van Friesland 5th, 3302 H. Milk 82 lbs. 8 oz. 1 day, 19,434 lbs 4 oz. 1 year, P. Butter 26 lbs. 10 oz. 7 days, P.
MAGGIE MIDWOULD, 1485 H. F. Walter Scott, 606 H.; Maggie, 375 H. Milk 70 lbs. 1 day, P.
MAGGIE MIDWORLD OF MARLBORO, 4332 H. F. Yohd Gimel, 3736 H.; Maggie, 375 H. Milk 78 lbs. 8 oz. 1 day, P.
MAGNA CHARTA, 8102 H. Imp. Milk 82 lbs. 12 oz. 1 day, 13,000 lbs. 1 year, P.
MAID MARION, 181 H. Imp. Milk 11,112 lbs. 1 year, P.
MAID OF AMSTERDAM, 1250 H. Imp. Milk 51 lbs. 1 day, P.
MAID OF AUBURN, 5794 H. F. Major Pel, 53 M. F.; Dutch Girl, 427 D. F. Milk 40 lbs. 1 day, P.
MAID OF BEACHWOOD, 2251 H. Halifax, 385 H.; Lily of the Valley, 1007 H. Milk 41 lbs. 8 oz. 1 day, P. Butter 117 lbs. 8 oz. 65 days, P.
MAID OF PURMER, 382 H. Imp. Milk 11,473 lbs. 1 year, P.
MAID OF THE OAKS, 2127 H. F. Second Duke of Springvale, 1785 H.; Nonpareil, 2056 H. Milk 37 lbs. 8 oz. 1 day, P. Butter 9 lbs. 7 days, P.
MAID OF THE VALLEY, 4579 H. Imp. Milk 81 lbs. 4 oz. 1 day, 501 lbs. 8 oz. 7 days, P. Butter 16 lbs. 1 oz. 7 days, P.
MAID OF TWISK, 1 D. F. Imp. Milk 88 lbs. 1 day, P.; 15,960 lbs. 10 oz. 1 year, P. Butter 18 lbs. 8 oz., P.
MAID OF VERNON, 2372 H. Cresco, 730 H.; Camella, 752 H. Milk 68 lbs 1 day, P.; 11,880 lbs. 11 oz. 8 months, A.R. Butter 22 lbs. 2½ oz. 7 days, A.R.
MALLENA, 7765 H. Imp. Milk 36 lbs. 1 day, P.
MAMIE S, 4041 H. Imp. Milk 49 lbs. 5½ oz. 1 day, P. Butter 1 lb. 15½ oz, 1 day, 6 lbs. 7½ oz. 4 days, P.
MA'MZELLE, 9827 H. Gilderoy, 2025 H.; Lady of Broek 2d, 2799 H. Milk 2424 lbs. 11 oz. 2 months 16 days, P.
MANANA, 9699 H. Imp. Milk 70 lbs. 1 day, P.
MANAQUA, 12037 H. F. Siebe, 600 F.; Lipkje, 2822 F. Milk 63 lbs. 1 day, 615 lbs. 10 days, P. Butter 18 lbs. 7 oz. 7 days, P.
MANDE, 1512 D. F. Philippus, 156 F. H.; Frouwkje, 1480 F. H. Milk 10,211 lbs. 10 months 24 days, A R.
MANTEL, 1009 H. Imp. Milk 83 lbs. 1 day, 9374 lbs. 8 oz. 11½ months, P.
MANTEL 2D, 2146 H. Piet Hein, 316 H.; Mantel, 1009 H. Milk 57 lbs. 1 day, 1550 lbs. 9 months, P.
MANTEL 3D, 2148 H. Ranger, 635 H.; Mantel, 1009 H. Milk 68 lbs. 1 day, 10,907 lbs. 9 months, P.
MANTEL 5TH, 8141 H. Paragon, 1175 H.; Mantel, 1009 H. Milk 48 lbs. 1 day, 10,087 lbs. 1 year, P.
MANTEL 6TH, 8225 H. F. Neptune Fairview, 3886 H.; Mantel, 1009 H. Milk 6072 lbs. 11 months, P.
MANTISSA, 6031 H. Imp. Milk 47 lbs. 10 oz. 1 day, 10,610 lbs. 3 oz. 1 year, P.
MANTISSA ARTIS, 6688 H. F. Prince of Artis, 2479 H.; Mantissa, 6931 H. Milk 41 lbs. 1 day, P.

MILK AND BUTTER RECORDS.   349

MAPLE LEAF'S MERCEDES, 6295 H. F.   Mercedes Prince, 2150 H.; Maple Leaf, 6543 H.   Butter 16 lbs. 9 oz. 7 days, A.R.
MARCELLA LINCOLN, 9928 H.   Imp.   Milk 42 lbs. 7 oz. 1 day, 8949 lbs. 11 oz. 10 months 11 days, P.
MARCELLE, 15774 H. F.   Duke of St. Anna, 614 D. F.; Lady Gretzhen, 428 D. F.   Milk 50 lbs. 4 oz. 1 day, 551 lbs. 10 days, P.
MARCELLUS QUEEN, 5953 H.   Promoter, 1518 H.; Kalma 2d, 3299 H.   Milk 49 lbs. 1 day, 1333 lbs. 30 days, P.
MARCIA, 847 H.   Imp.   Milk 60 lbs. 1 day, P.
MARFA, 1248 H.   Imp.   Milk 10,600 lbs. 11 months, P.
MARGARET, 386 H.   Zaandam, 369 H.; Dora, 117 H.   Milk 10,986 lbs. 9 oz. 11 months 23 days, P.
MARGARET 4TH, 18813 H. F.   Tecumseh Witzyde, 5067 H. F.; Margaret, 1015 D. F.   Milk 62 lbs. 1 day, 10,000 lbs. 1 year, P.   Butter 21 lbs. 7½ oz. 7 days, P.
MARGARETHA, 1585 Neth.   Imp.   Milk 68 lbs. 1 day, P.   Butter 19 lbs. 8 oz. 7 days, A.R.
MARGARET LINCOLN, 9927 H.   Imp.   Milk 50 lbs. 11 oz. 1 day, 10.986 lbs. 9 oz. 11 months 23 days, P.   Butter 12 lbs. 10 oz. 7 days, A.E.
MARGARY, 1502 D F.   Bismarck, 300 F.; Swarte, 1339 F.   Milk 72 lbs. 14 oz. 1 day, P.; 1994 lbs. 9 oz. 30 days, A.R.
MARGE, 2047 H.   Beaconsfield, 401 H ; Genevieve, 314 H.   Milk 68 lbs. 1 day, 1062 lbs. 8 oz. 30 days.   Butter 16 lbs. 8 oz. 7 days, P.
MARGERY, 6000 H.   Jaap, 211 Neth ; Mina, 1351 Neth.   Milk 48 lbs. 1 day, 7286 lbs. 1 year, P.
MARGOT, 8806 H.   Imp.   Milk 84 lbs. 8 oz. 1 day, 13,734 lbs. 12 oz. 1 year, P.   Butter 15 lbs. 6 oz. 7 days, P.
MARGOT 3D, 778 H. F.   Imp.   Milk 66 lbs. 1 day, 10,437 lbs. 1 year, P.   Butter 5 lbs. 12 oz. 2 days, P.
MARIA, 1260 Neth.   Imp.   Milk 94 lbs. 1 day, P.
MARIAN, 1812 D. F.   Nicolaas 2d, 29 M. R.; Yep Yma, 401 P. R.   Milk 88 lbs. 1 day, 20 lbs. 4 oz. 7 days, P.
MARIANNA BEETS, 7 D. F.   Imp.   Milk 13,895 lbs. 1 year, P.
MARIANNA BEETS 3D, 22 D. F.   Burgemaster of Beemster, 1 D. F.; Marianna Beets, 7 D. F.   Milk 57 lbs. 8 oz. 1 day, 3191 lbs. 68 days, P.
MARIANNE, 101 D. F.   Radbout, 25 Neth.; Marianne, 25 Neth.   Milk 67 lbs. 12 oz. 1 day, 14,712 lbs. 12 oz. 1 year, P.
MARIANNE PHELPS, 4010 H. F.   Fyn, 29 D. F.; Marianne, 101 D. F.   Milk 50 lbs. 8 oz. 1 day, 1424 lbs. 30 days, P.   Butter 15 lbs. 8½ oz. 7 days, A.R.
MARIE, 373 Neth.   Imp.   Milk 82 lbs. 5 oz. 1 day, P.
MARIE 2D, 494 D. F.   Imp.   Milk 83 lbs. 8 oz. 1 day, P.
MARIE 3D, 1659 H.   Janp, 452 H ; Marie 2d, 728 H.   Milk 51 lbs. 1 day, P.
MARIE DUTCHER, 743 H. F.   Bismarck, 224 Neth.; Marie II, 4248 Neth.   Milk 60 lbs. 11 oz. 1 day, 13,361 lbs. 6 oz. 10 months, A.R.
MARIE M 2D, 4720 H.   Imp.   Milk 63 lbs. 1 day, P.
MARIE NETHERLAND, 3802 H.   Netherland Prince, 716 H.; Marie Wortel 3d, 1808 H.   Milk 51 lbs. 1 day, 1304 lbs. 8 oz. 30 days, P.
MARIE STOMPSTAART, 5674 H.   Imp.   Milk 61 lbs. 1 day, P.
MARIE WORTEL, 1867 H.   Imp.   Milk 90 lbs. 10 oz. 1 day, P.   Butter 14 oz. 7 days, P.
MARIE WORTEL 3D, 1868 H.   Marie, 483 Neth.   Milk 78 lbs. 5 oz. 1 day, 2004 lbs. 10 oz. 30 days, P.
MARIE WORTEL 5TH, 6509 H. F.   Sir Henry of Anggie, 1450 H.; Marie Worzel, 1807 H.   Milk 50 lbs. 12 oz. 1 day, 1968 lbs. 30 days, P.   Butter 13 lbs. 6 oz. 7 days, P.
MARIGOLD, 207 Neth.   Imp.   Milk 35 lbs. 1 day, P.
MARIJTJE, 812 Neth.   Imp.   Milk 75 lbs. 3 oz. 1 day, P.
MARILLO, 6090 H.   Imp.   Milk 12,45- lbs. 1 year, P.
MARION, 891 H.   Imp   Milk 62 lbs. 1 day, 2712 lbs. 2 months, P.
MARION 2D, 3805 H.   Banjo, 564 H.; Marion, 891 H.   Milk 50 lbs. 1 day, P.
MARITZA, 7197 H.   Imp.   Milk 70 lbs. 2 oz. 1 day, 2015 lbs. 8 oz. 31 days, P.
MARJORIE, 2166 H.   Netherland Prince, 716 H.; Hortense, 1500 H.   Milk 68 lbs. 1 day, P.   Butter 14 lbs. 1 oz. 7 days, P.
MARJORIE DAW, 1839 H.   Imp.   Milk 66 lbs. 10 oz. 1 day, 11,821 lbs. 8 months 25 days, P.   Butter 8 lbs. 13½ oz. 7 days, P.
MARJORIE DAW 2D, 2111 H.   Imp.   Milk 57 lbs. 2 oz. 1 day, 13,052 lbs. 10 oz. 10 months, P.
MARJORIE DAW 3D, 5577 H.   Syracuse, 822 H.; Marjorie Daw, 1839 H.   Milk 58 lbs. 10 oz. 1 day, 12,348 lbs. 5 oz. 10 months 3 days, P.
MARJORIE DAW 4TH, 571 H. F.   Captain Daw, 2088 H.; Marjorie Daw, 1839 H.   Milk 42 lbs. 2 oz. 1 day, 7669 lbs. 13 oz. 10 months, P.
MARLETTE, 8254 H. F.   David, 492 F.; Bontbles, 1635 F.   Milk 50 lbs. 1 day, 569 lbs. 10 days, P.
MARTHA, 1005 H.   Imp.   Marchioness, 836 H.   Milk 76 lbs. 1 day, P.
MARTHA BEETS, 1002 D. F.   Victor Brimsma, 88 P. R.; Dora Beets 3d, 208 P. R.   Milk 77 lbs. 1 day, P.   Butter 22 lbs. 7 days, A.R.
MARTHA DEWDROP, 4275 H.   Imp.   Milk 50 lbs. 1 day, P.
MARTHA WASHINGTON, 1304 H.   Imp.   Milk 10,720 lbs. 11 months 20 days, A.R.
MARTINA, 9362 H F.   Archibald, 843 D. F.; Coba 2d, 1358 D. F.   Milk 10,498 lbs. 14 oz. 1 year, A.R.
MARTJE 2D, 5003 H.   Imp.   Milk 45 lbs. 14 oz. 1 day, P.
MARTTJE, 570 Neth.   Imp.   Milk 68 lbs. 4 oz. 1 day, P.
MARY, 187 H.   Imp.   Milk 70 lbs. 1C oz. 1 day, P.
MARY ANDERSON, 589 H.   Imp.   Milk 6299 lbs. 12 oz. 332 days, P.
MARY ANN, 6111 H.   Imp.   Milk 40 lbs. 9 oz. 1 day, 7285 lbs. 4 oz. 1 year, P.   Butter 14 lbs. 7 days, P.
MARY B, 3928 H. F.   Wing's Lad, 2015 H.; Moriana of Marshall, 8129 H.   Milk 80 lbs. 1 day, P.
MARY BELLE, 2904 H.   Imp.   Milk "1 lbs. 5½ oz. 7 days, P.
MARYKE, 5559 H.   Imp.   Milk 72 lbs. 6 oz. 1 day, 660 lbs. 10 days, P.
MARYKE 3D'S GERBEN, 23957 H. F.   Consul Gerben, 4304 H. F.; Maryke 3d, 31718 H. F.   Milk 58 lbs. 12 oz. 1 day, P.
MARY'S CHARM, 5051 H.   Imp.   Milk 15,112 lbs. 7 months 18 days, A.R.   Butter 16 lbs. 6 oz. 7 days, A.R.
MATADOR, 1533 D. F.   Karl, 269 F. II.; Afke 2d, 2288 F. H.   Butter 10 lbs. 9 oz. 7 days, A.R.
MATCHLESS, 898 H.   Imp.   Milk 5886 lbs. 6 months, P.
MATEO, 10365 H.   Imp.   Milk 49 lbs. 1 day, P.
MATERNA, 2195 H.   Banjo, 564 H.; Marion, 891 H.   Milk 64 lbs. 1 day, P.
MATHILDE, 1309 H.   Imp.   Milk 8320 lbs. 1 year, P.
MATRON, 857 H.   Imp.   Milk 87 lbs. 1 day, 10,007 lbs. 1 year, P.

MATTIE A, 5427 H. Imp. Milk 58 lbs. 8 oz. 1 day. P.
MATTIE DELL, 3999 H. F. Billy Bawn, 3087 H.; Dingle Dell 2d, 5576 H. Milk 5562 lbs. 15 oz. 10 months 8 days, P.
MATTIE DEWDROP, 5384 H. Imp. Milk 50 lbs. 8 oz. 1 day, P.
MAUD ARTIS, 5568 H. F. Artis Jr., 2723 H.; Duchess of Beemster, 4621 H. Milk 58 lbs. 1 day, 374 lbs. 8 oz. 7 days, P. Butter 2 lbs. 8 oz. 1 day, 12 lbs. 13 oz. 7 days, P.
MAUD CLAY, 390 H. Dictator, 82 H.; Lady Clay, 158 H. Milk 78 lbs. 1 day, P.
MAUD CLIFDEN 2D, 1785 H. F. Jan Wit, 2524 H.; Maud Clifden, 5263 H. Milk 30 lbs. 1 day, P.
MAUD D, 15268 H. F. Nye, 7629 H. F.; Bennett, 9015 H. F. Milk 420 lbs. 3 oz. 7 days, P. Butter 18 lbs. 10 oz. 7 days, P.
MAUDE OF ASHLEY, 4394 H. F. Mooie, 26 D. F.; Neiskje, 1204 H. Milk 60 lbs. 8 oz. 1 day, P.
MAUDE OF SEASIDE, 4396 H. F. Hulda's Empire, 3449 H.; Maude of Ashley, 4394 H. F. Milk 36 lbs. 1 day, P.
MAUD ETHELBERTA, 4505 H. F. Mozart, 4222 H.; Grace Ethelberta, 9542 H. Butter 18 lbs. 12½ oz. 7 days, A.R.
MAUDINA, 6349 H. Imp. Milk 63 lbs. 5 oz. 1 day, A.R.; 10,278 lbs. 11 oz. 10 months, P. Butter 16 lbs. 9½ oz. 7 days, A.R.
MAUD OF SHADELAND 3D, 2424 H. Imp. Milk 7945 lbs. 4 oz. 9 months A.R.
MAUD MULLER, 1850 H. Imp. Milk 4741 lbs. 12 oz. 4 months, 16 days, P.
MAUD OF SHADELAND, 2424 H. F. Imp. Milk 91 lbs. 13 oz. 1 day, 12,675 lbs. 10 months, A.R.
MAUD OF SHADELAND 4TH, 10765 H. F. Netherland Conqueror, 2476 H.; Maud of Shadeland, 2424 H. Milk 43 lbs. 1 day, 7327 lbs. 8 oz. 8 months, A.R.
MAUD SLOOVES, 1010 H. F. Lord of Cornwall, 3429 H.; Lady Sloooves, 6808 H. Milk 59 lbs. 1 day, P.
MAUD TENSON, 11011 H. F. Duke of Edgely, 552 H. F.; Cornelia Tenson, 1817 H. F. Milk 63 lbs. 1 day, P. Butter 18 lbs. 12 oz. 7 days, P.
MAY, 188 H. Rip Van Winkle, 35 H.; Dowager, 7 H. Milk 45 lbs. 1 day, 1320 lbs. 30 days, P.
MAY ARTIS, 10608 H. F. Netherland Alban, 4584 H.; Jessie Barnum, 10262 H. F. Butter 13 lbs. 15 oz. 7 days, A.R.
MAYFLOWER, 1505 D. F. Imp. Milk 10,688 lbs. 14 oz. 8 months 11 days, P. Butter 10 lbs. 7 oz. 7 days, A.R.
MAYO, 3966 H. F. Duke of Schagen, 141 H. F.; Mayblom, 42 H. F. Milk 60 lbs. 1 day, P.
MAY OVERTON, 2810 H. Imp. Milk 89 lbs. 6 oz. 1 day, 13,759 lbs. 4 oz. 220 days, A.R. Butter 2.26 lbs. 1 day, P.
MAZIE, 4309 H. Imp. Milk 45 lbs. 1 day, P.
MAZIE MERCEDES, 34753 H. F. Dotty 2d's Almee, 16152 H. F.; Hortensia's Second Mercedes, 11240 H. F. Milk 33 lbs. 1 day, P.
MEADOWBROOK FAIRY, 3896 H. F. Viking, 2062 H.; Tettje, 7093 H. Milk 36 lbs. 8 oz. 1 day, 7000 lbs. 11 months, P.
MEADOW LILY, 6863 H. Imp. Milk 53 lbs. 8 oz. 1 day, 1174 lbs. 14 oz. 30 days, P. Butter 12 lbs. 10 oz. 7 days, P.
MEADOW LILY 5TH, 10383 H. Netherland King, 1924 H.; Meadow Lily, 863 H. Milk 9017 lbs. 7 oz. 10 months, A.R.
MEADOW MAID, 1793 H. Imp. Milk 85 lbs. 3 oz. 1 day, 399 lbs. 13 oz. 5 days, P. Butter 9 lbs. 4½ oz. 7 days, P.
MECHTHILDE, 6718 H. Imp. Milk 112 lbs. 4 oz. 1 day, 14,786 lbs. 10 months, P. Butter 39 lbs. 10½ oz. 7 days, 150 lbs. 8 oz. 30 days, 292 lbs. 5½ oz. 60 days, P.
MECHTHILDE 6TH, 39002 H. F. Paul Zozo Prince, 16834 H. F.; Mechthilde, 6718 H. Milk 52 lbs. 4 oz. 1 day, 1408 lbs. 10 oz. 30 days, P. Butter 2 lbs. 8 oz. 1 day, 16 lbs. 9 oz. 7 days, 31 lbs. 12 oz. 14 days, P.
MEDDO, 2013 H. F. Willem 3d, 375 Neth.; Maria, 3004 Neth. Milk 8157 lbs. 1 year, P.
MEDINA, 9785 H. Panic, 871 H.; Memento 4th, 2078 H. Milk 60 lbs. 1 day, 11,374 lbs. 4 oz. 1 year, A.R. Butter 14 lbs. 13¼ oz. 7 days, A.R.
MEDORA, 1033 H. Stentor, 346 H.; Gipsey, 318 H. Milk 14,481 lbs. 1 oz. 10 months, A.R.
MEENIE, 24 H. Amsterdam, 1 H.; Texelaar 8th, 55 H. Milk 76 lbs. 1 day, P.
MEENIE 2D, 189 H. William, 56 H.; Meenie, 24 H. Milk 74 lbs. 1 day, P.
MEENIE 2D'S TEXALAAR, 4331 H. F. Walter Scott, 606 H.; Meenie 2d, 189 H. Milk 40 lbs. 1 day, P.
MEENIE 3D, 394 H. William, 56 H.; Meenie, 24 H. Milk 75 lbs. 8 oz. 1 day, P.
MEENIE 4TH, 1509 H. Karl, 278 H.; Meenie 3d, 394 H. Milk 60 lbs. 1 day, P.
MEG MERRILLES, 1288 H. Imp. Milk 68 lbs. 1 day, P.
MEG MERRILLES 2D, 1485 H. Imp. Milk 48 lbs. 1 day, P.
MEITJE, 1392 Neth. Imp. Milk 77 lbs. 1 day, P.
MEITJE 2D, 4618 H. Imp. Milk 44 lbs. 5 oz. 1 day, P.
MELINA, 5351 H. Imp. Milk 68 lbs. 1 day, P.
MELINA 2D, 3356 H. F. Billy Boelyn, 189 H.; Melina, 5351 H. Milk 52 lbs. 1 day, P.
MELINA'S VIOLET, 20686 H. F. Violet Prince, 4209 H.; Melina, 5351 H. Milk 56 lbs. 1 day, P.
MELROSE, 1733 H. Imp. Milk 60 lbs. 1 day, P.
MEMENTO, 397 H. Imp. Milk 76 lbs. 1 day, P.
MEMENTO QUEEN, 8542 H. Panic, 871 H.; Memento 4th, 2078 H. Milk 12,002 lbs. 11 months 8 days, A.R.
MEMORIA, 6882 H. Imp. Milk 71 lbs. 1 day, P.
MEMORIA 2D, 9265 H. F. Mercedes' Mahomet, 2943 H.; Memoria, 6882 H. Milk 1227 lbs. 90 days, P.
MENIE, 9333 H. Milk 40 lbs. 1 day, P.
MERCEDES, 723 H. Imp. Milk 88 lbs. 1 day, 2534 lbs. 31 days, P. Butter 3 lbs. 10 oz. 1 day, 24 lbs. 6 oz. 7 days, 99 lbs. 8½ oz., A.R.
MERCEDES 2D, 1658 H. Jaap, 452 H.; Mercedes 723 H. Milk 75 lbs. 8 oz. 1 day, 17,658 lbs. 14 oz. 6 months, P. Butter 3 lbs. 4 oz. 1 day, 26 lbs. 13 oz. 7 days, 37 lbs. 8 oz. 2 weeks, A.R.
MERCEDES JAANTJE MINK, 17106 H. F. Mink Prize, 5050 H. F.; Annele's Mercedes Jaantje, 6916 H. F. Milk 204 lbs. 8 oz. 7 days, P. Butter 17 lbs. 15 oz. 7 days, A.R.
MERCIE MERCEDES, 31912 H. F. Dotty 2d's Almee, 16152 H. F.; Hortensia's Second Mercedes, 11240 H. F. Milk 10,000 lbs. 1 year, P.
MERLO, 2014 H. F. Frans, 261 Neth.; Marie 6th, 4493 Neth. Milk 9596 lbs. 10 months 20 days, P.
MERMAID, 852 H. Imp. Milk 60 lbs. 12 oz. 1 day, 8089 lbs. 3 oz. 1 year, P. Butter 2 lbs. 4½ oz. 1 day, P.
MERTJE HARTOG, 6434 H. Imp. Milk 1578 lbs. 30 days, P.
MERZA W, 5230 H. Lord Le Baron, 528 H.; Alvia, 773 H. Milk 1211 lbs. 30 days, 2143 lbs. 60 days, P.
METAMORA, 8433 H. Imp. Milk 8978 lbs. 9 oz. 1 year, P.

MILK AND BUTTER RECORDS. 351

METEA, 9702 H. Imp. Butter 78 lbs. 10 oz. 30 days, P.
METZ, 9676 H. Imp. Milk 69 lbs 5 oz. 1 day, P.
MIDDY MORGAN, 1207 H. Imp. Milk 41 lbs. 1 day, 8000 lbs. 10 months 20 days, P.
MIDGET, 1518 H. Uncle Tom, 163 H.; Marion, 891 H. Milk 60 lbs. 1 day, P.
MIDLUMMER, 9860 H. Imp. Milk 41 lbs. 1 day, P.
MIGNONE, 1937 D. F. Theodore, 243 Neth.; Dieuwertje, 1132 Neth. Butter 11 lbs. 7 days, A.R.
MIGNONE 2D, 10635 H. F. Mooie Twisk 4th, 706 D. F.; Mignone, 1937 D. F. Milk 270 lbs. 3 oz. 7 days, P. Butter 20 lbs. 11 oz. 7 days, A.R.
MIGNONETTE, 2826 H. Imp. Milk 60 lbs. 1 day, 7342 lbs. 9 oz. 1 year, P.
MIGNONETTE 2D, 2827 H. Imp. Milk 46 lbs. 1 day, P.
MIGNONETTE 4TH, 8408 H. Netherland Prince, 716 H.; Mignonette, 2826 H. Butter 9 lbs. 7 days, P.
MIJNKE VON HOLINGEN, 17208 H. F. Peter. 103 Neth.; Mijnke, 697 Neth. Milk 92 lbs. 14 oz. 1 day, P.
MILD EYES, 1496 H. F. Cossack, 2001 H.; Hiatoga, 3308 H Milk 10,102 lbs. 9 oz. 1 year, P.
MILDRED OF SEA SIDE, 8561 H. F. Hulda's Empire, 8449 H.; First Duchess of Ashley, 2385 H. Milk 38 lbs. 1 day, P.
MILICENT, 148 H. F. Thorbecke, 349 F.; Emma, 3258 H. Milk 453 lbs. 4 oz. 10 days, 4712 lbs. 11 oz. 10 months, P. Butter 13 lbs. 12 oz. 7 days, A.R.
MILK MAID, 1894 D. F. Augusta Goudgeld 2d, 298 P. R.; Strabo, 134 P. R. M lk 15,400 lbs. 1 year, P.
MILKY WAY, 10144 H. Imp. Milk 50 lbs. 12 oz. 1 day, 10,516 lbs. 6 oz. 1 year, P. Butter 10 lbs. 8 oz. 7 days, A.R.
MILKY WAY 2D, 4080 H. F. Prince of Wayne 5th, 1910 H.; Milky Way, 10144 H. Milk 7883 lbs. 10 oz. 9 months, P.
MILLA (PIETERTJE 3D), 6408 H. Keyes 6th, 1692 H.; Pietertje 2d, 3273 H. Milk 80 lbs. 7 oz. 1 day, 17,927 lbs. 1 oz. 1 year, P.
MILLIE, 867 H. Imp. Milk 1517 lbs. 30 days, P.
MILLIE D, 4885 H. Neptune, 711 H.; Lady Marion, 1824 H. Milk 45 lbs. 1 day, P. Butter 15 lbs. 7 oz. 7 days, A.R.
MILLIE LINCOLN, 10022 H. Lincoln, 120 Neth. Milk 58 lbs. 15 oz. 1 day, P.
MINA, 678 H. Imp. Milk 71 lbs. 8 oz. 1 day, P.
MINA ROOKER, 9803 H. Pieter, 209 Neth. Imp. Milk 52 lbs. 1 oz. 1 day, P.
MINA SPAANZ 2D, 8753 H. Panic, 871 H.; Mina Spaanz, 1104 H. Milk 12,415 lbs 4 oz. 10 months, A.R.
MINDERTJE, 2249 H. Imp. Milk 60 lbs. 1 day, P.
MINERVA LINCOLN, 10023 H. Lincoln, 120 Neth. Imp. Milk 52 lbs. 1 day, P.
MINI SPAANZ, 5663 H. F. Lord Spaanz, 4012 H.; Melisse, 3592 H. Milk 60 lbs. 1 day, 12,004 lbs. 8 oz. 1 year, A.R. Butter 17 lbs. 6 oz. 7 days, A.R.
MINK, 402 H. Imp. Milk 96 lbs. 1 day, P.; 16,024 lbs. 8 oz. 1 year A.R. Butter 3 lbs. 9 oz. 1 day, 20 lbs. 7 oz. 7 days, 29 lbs. 6 oz. 10 days, A.R.
MINK 3D, 1924 H. Bismarck 6th, 500 H.; Mink, 402 H. Butter 2 lbs. 8 oz. 1 day, P.
MINKIE DE VRIES, 5037 H. F. Major Pel, 2763 H.; Jantje De Vries, 432 D. F. Milk 60 lbs. 1 day, P.
MINNA, 404 H. Roland, 144 H.; Dora, 117 H. Milk 7677 lbs. 153 days, P.
MINNESOTA, 1441H. Grueno, 431 H.; Wild Zwaan, 419 H. Milk 64 lbs. 1 day, P.
MINNETONKA, 6242 H. Imp. Milk 83 lbs. 8 oz. 1 day, P.
MINNIE, 1809 H. Silas, 522 H.; Poppe, 992 H. Milk 86 lbs. 1 day, P.; 18 lbs. 9 oz. 7 days, P.
MINNIE EDGE, 5413 H. Imp. Milk 63 lbs. 14 oz. 1 day, P. Butter 14 lbs. 11 oz. 7 days, P.
MINNIE HOMET, 3018 H. F. Mahomet, 280 H.; Minnetonka, 6242 H. Milk 48 lbs. 1 day, P.
MINNIE VERMAN, 371 D. F. Imp. M l < 71 lbs. 1 day, 2051 lbs. 30 days, P.
MINNIE WINKLE'S MINK, 13165 H. F. Mink Prince, 2865 H.; Minnie Winkle, 405 H. Butter 21 lbs. 7 oz. 7 days, P.
MINNIE Y, 10836 H. Imp. Milk 70 lbs. 1 day, P.
MIRA, 1534 H. Imp. Milk 71 lbs. 8 oz. 1 day, P.
MIRA 2D, 3619 H. Cresco, 730 H.; Mira, 1534 H. Butter 2 lbs. 1 oz. 1 day, 14 lbs. 8 oz. 7 days, P.
MIRANDA, 1227 H. Imp. Milk 45 lbs. 8 oz. 1 day, P.
MIRTILLA, 4169 H. F. Netherland Hero, 2342 H.; Shadeland Adele, 8377 H. Milk 189 lbs. 13 oz. 7 days, P. Butter 8 lbs. 12 oz. 7 days, P.
MIRTH, 6991 H. Imp. Milk 53 lbs. 12 oz. 1 day, 12,363 lbs. 1 year, P.
MISS ABRAHAM, 1903 H. F. Honest Abe, 749 H.; Lizzie D, 3313 H. Milk 54 lbs. 12 oz. 1 day, P. Butter 10 lbs. 12 oz. 7 days, P.
MISS DICK SPAANZ, 3955 H. Dick Spaanz, 778 H.; Holland Belle, 2160 H. Milk 51 lbs. 1 day, 10,398 lbs. 9 months 6 days, P.
MISS KWANTES, 7720 H. Imp. Milk 42 lbs. 8 oz. 1 day, P.
MISS LINCOLN, 6853 H. Imp. Milk 43 lbs. 4 oz. 1 day, 10,763 lbs. 8 oz. 1 year, P.
MISS MIGOS, 1200 H. Imp. Milk 8950 lbs. 7 months 2½ days, P.
MISS MORRIS, 6892 H. Alexander 2d 1552 H. Imp Milk 1548 lbs. 30 days, A. R.
MISS MORRIS 2D, 6074 H. F. Netherland Convoy, 2034 H.; Miss Morris, 6892 H. Milk 54 lbs. 1 day, 1548 lbs. 30 days, P. Butter 12 lbs. 8 oz. 7 days, A.R.
MISS NANNA, 2824 H. Imp. Milk 35 lbs. 7 oz. 1 day, 7022 lbs. 1 oz. 10 months, P. Butter 7 lbs. 13½ oz. 7 days, P.
MISS PARMA, 5151 H. Imp. Milk 59 lbs. 1 day, P.
MISS RACKETT, 2822 H. Imp. Milk 44 lbs. 12 oz. 1 day, P.
MISS SMYLIE, 6973 H. Imp. Milk 949 lbs. 1 month, P.
MISS SNOOKS, 3058 H. Lord Bantam, 1011 H.; Lady Helen. 1829 H. Milk 47 lbs. 1 day, P.
MITRA, 1420 H. F. Oswald, 3331 H.; Vabusca, 7226 H. Milk 8397 lbs. 13 oz. 10 months, P.
MOBUTA, 1135 H. Monitor, 299 H.; Boxer Kop, 777 H. Butter 2 lbs. 5 oz. 1 day, 16 lbs. 5 oz. 7 days, P.
MODEST GIRL, 10184 H. Imp. Milk 58 lbs. 10 oz. 1 day, P.; 10,229 lbs. 15 oz. 1 year, A.R. Butter 9 lbs. 8½ oz. 7 days, P.
MODEST GIRL 3D, 10515 H. F. Prince Aaggie Wayne, 1627 H. F.; Modest Girl, 10184 H. Milk 41 lbs. 1 day, 1126 lbs. 8 oz. 30 days, P.
MODESTY OF LYNWOOD, 6703 H. Imp. Milk 51 lbs. 6 oz. 1 day, 6794 lbs. 4 oz. 7 months, 15 days, P.
MODJESKA, 407 H. Imp. Milk 43 lbs. 1 day, 12,523 lbs. 1 year, P.
MOEDER, 720 H. Imp. Milk 87 lbs. 7 oz. 1 day, 17,197 lbs. 1 year, P.
MOEDER 2D, 3880 H. Napoleon, 706 H.; Moeder, 720 H Milk 40 lbs. 1 day, P.
MOEDER'S MAHOMET, 2784 H. F. Mercedes' Mahomet, 2943 H.; Moeder 2d, 3880 H. Milk 49 lbs. 1 day, P.
MOJESKA 2D, 5117 H. F. Smith's Conqueror, 3008 H.; Mojeska, 1615 D. F. Milk 54 lbs. 1 day, P. Butter 1 lb. 10 oz. 1 day, P.
MOLLIE 2D 4737 H. Lord Beemster, 285 H.; Mollie, 1137 H. Milk 9757 lbs. 1 year, P.

MOLLIE ANDERSON, 4273 H. Imp. Milk 80 lbs. 1 day, P. Butter 3 lbs. 8 oz. 1 day, 18 lbs. 12 oz. days, P.
MOLLIE DEWDROP, 5419 H. Imp. Milk 64 lbs. 4 oz. 1 day. P. Butter 2 lbs. 9 oz. 1 day, P.
MOLLIE EDGE, 4274 H. Imp. Milk 61 lbs. 8 oz. 1 day, P. Butter 11 lbs. 4 oz. 7 days, P.
MOLLIE GATES, 5424 H. Imp. Milk 60 lbs. 1 day, P.
MOLLIE OF ST. ANNE, 1996 H. F. Major Pel, 2763 H.; Lady of St. Anna, 431 D. F. Milk 80 lbs. 1 day, P.
MOLLIE PARAGON, 6842 H. F. Paragon, 1175 H.; Fokje 2d, 3285 H. Milk 55 lbs. 1 day, P.
MOLLY BAWN, 1298 H. Imp. Milk 76 lbs. 7 oz. 1 day, P.; 16,389 lbs. 1 oz. 1 year, A.R.
MOLLY BAWN 2D, 3777 H. Syracuse, 822 H.; Molly Bawn, 1298 H. Milk 70 lbs. 6 oz. 1 day, P.; 7761 lbs. 15 oz. 9 months 28 days, A.R.
MOLLY MIDDLETON, 4454 H. Imp. Milk 48 lbs. 1 day. P.
MOLLY S, 3055 H. Prince 3d, 625 H.; Grietje 2d, 516 H. Milk 13,151 lbs. 1 year, P.
MOLLY VISSER, 242 D. F. Paul Hartog, 6 M. R.; Trijn Visser, 36 M. R. Milk 83 lbs. 8 oz. 1 day, P.; 2217 lbs. 8 oz. 30 days, A.R. Butter 24 lbs. 1 oz. 7 days, A.R.
MONCASSEL, 2022 H. F. De Prins, 310 Neth.; Martha, 2383 Neth. Milk 11,717 lbs. 1 year, P.
MONEY BOX, 2785 H. F. 1st Duke of Oneida, 180 D. F.; Lady Seffinga 2d, 554 D. F. Milk 50 lbs. 4 oz. 1 day, P.
MOOIE BOUTE, 4108 H. Imp. Milk 40 lbs. 1 day, P.
MOOIKE, 689 H. Imp. Milk 72 lbs. 1 day, P.; 11,650 lbs. 10 months, A.R. Butter 19 lbs. 5 oz. 7 days, P.
MOOIKE 2D, 803 H. Taurus, 349 H.; Mooike, 689 H. Milk 7063 lbs. 1 year, P.
MOOIKE 2D B's 1ST, 14242 H. F. Robert S, 3210 H.; Mooike 2d B, 8477 H. Milk 43 lbs. 1 day, 5486 lbs. 10 months 24 days, P.
MOOIKE 2D B's 2D, 15217 H. F. Copia's Empire, 3559 H.; Mooike 2d B, 8477 H. Milk 4862 lbs. 10 months 6 days, P.
MOOIKE 3D, 1540 H. Johannis, 428 H.; Mooike, 689 H. Milk 11,108 lbs. 8 oz. 10 months, A.R. Butter 19 lbs. 5 oz. 7 days, A.R.
MOOIKE 3D A, 4749 H. Clarion, 870 H.; Mooike 3d, 1540 H. Milk 48 lbs. 1 day, 7160 lbs. 10 months, P.
MOOIKE 3D A's 1ST, 15218 H. F. Hilda's Empire, 3562 H.; Mooike 3d A, 4749 H. Milk 4601 lbs. 11 months, P.
MOOIKE 3D B's 1ST, 20590 H. F. Copia's Empire, 3559 H.; Mooike 3d B, 2443 H. F. Milk 27 lbs. 1 day, P.
MOOIKE 3D C, 14246 H. F. Copia's Empire, 3559 H.; Mooike 3d, 1540 H. Milk 4081 lbs. 1 year, P.
MOOIKE 7TH, 2434 H. F. Johannis, 428 H.; Mooike, 689 H. Milk 7356 lbs. 10 months, P.
MOOIKE 7TH A, 9127 H. F. Copia's Empire, 3559 H.; Mooike 7th, 2434 H. F. Milk 3550 lbs. 4 months, 5 days, P.
MOOIKE 8TE, 5271 H. F. Clarion, 870 H.; Mooike, 689 H. Milk 2581 lbs. 2 months, 26 days, P.
MOOIKE OF KENTUCKY, 1985 H. Imp. Milk 48 lbs. 12 oz. 1 day, P. Butter 27 lbs. 4 oz. 7 days, P.
MOOYE ARTIS, 7622 H. F. Artis, 127 Neth.; Nelly, 4452 Neth. Milk 2750 lbs. 5 oz. 4 months, P.
MOPPLE, 8739 H. Fifth Consul, 574 H.; Clarinda, 1042 H. Milk 62 lbs. 1 day, P.
MORAN, 1408 H. Imp. Milk 70 lbs. 1 day, 6217 lbs. 8 oz. 120 days, P.
MORAN 2D, 1436 H. Imp. Moran, 1408 H. Milk 55 lbs. 1 day, P.
MORAN 2D's PRINCESS, 6334 H. F. Admiration, 3843 H.; Moran 2d, 1436 H. Milk 23,016 lbs. 4 oz. 1 year, P.
MORNING DEW, 6531 H. F. Arian, 3525 H.; Wever, 10528 H. Milk 42 lbs. 12 oz. 1 day, P.; 4574 lbs. 4 months, A.R. Butter 12 lbs. 3 oz. 7 days, A.R.
MOSELLE, 27 D. F. Imp. Milk 2919 lbs. 8 oz. 90 days, P.
MOTTLED BEAUTY, 2828 H. Imp. Milk 54 lbs. 10 oz. 1 day, P.; 16,289 lbs. 15 oz. 1 year, A.R. Butter 21 lbs. 11 oz. 7 days, A.R.
MOTTLED BEAUTY 2D, 2829 H. Imp. Milk 49 lbs. 7 oz. 1 day, 11,249 lbs. 8 oz. 1 year, P. Butter 20 lbs. 13 oz. 7 days, A.R.
MOTTLED BEAUTY 5TH, 9077 H. F. Aegis Netherland Prince, 4585 H.; Mottled Beauty, 2828 H. Butter 9 lbs. 6¼ oz. 7 days, A.R.
MOUSIE, 6975 H. Imp. Milk 46 lbs. 1 oz. 1 day, P.; 11,093 lbs. 5 oz. 1 year, A.R. Butter 11 lbs. 4 oz. 7 days, P.
MOUSIE 2D, 9813 H. Clovis, 3303 H.; Mousie, 6975 H. Milk 49 lbs. 1 day, P.
MRS. GRUNDY, 9225 H. Venture, 1315 H.; Lady Neal, 2761 H. Butter 15 lbs. 6½ oz. 7 days, A.R.
MRS. LANGTRY 2D, 3771 H. Jaap, 452 H.; Mrs. Langtry, 1644 H. Milk 11,819 lbs. 2 oz. 1 year, P. Butter 15 lbs. 11 oz. 7 days, P.
MRS. LANGTRY'S TRITOMIA, 6068 H. F. Tritomia's Mercedes Prince, 3542 H.; Mrs. Langtry, 1644 H. Milk 30 lbs. 1 day, P. Butter 9 lbs. 15 oz. 7 days, A.R.
MUCHACHA, 8018 H. Imp. Milk 38 lbs. 15 oz. 1 day, 6157 lbs. 10 oz. 11 months 2 days, P.
MUFFIN 2D, 133 H. F. Oscar K, 2237 H.; Muffin, 7283 H. Milk 49 lbs. 1 day, P. Butter 1 lb. 13 oz. 1 day, 58 lbs. 13 oz. 30 days, P.
MULBERRY, 1504 D, F. Ype, 283 F.; Roosje, 1220 F. Butter 10 lbs. 7 oz. 7 days, A.R.
MURILLO, 5053 H. Imp. Milk 82 lbs. 1 day, 10,080 lbs. 1 year, P. Butter 2 lbs. 8 oz. 1 day, P.
MUSCILAGE, 18033 H. F. Mahomet, 280 H.; Oriana 4th, 7985 H. Milk 47 lbs. 1 day, P.
MUSEY, 12031 H. F. De Hoop, 718 F.; Klaasje, 846 F. Milk 57 lbs. 1 day, 1683 lbs. 30 days, P.
MUSIC, 565 H. Uncle Tom, 103 H.; Maid of Purmer, 382 H. Milk 40 lbs. 8 oz. 1 day, P.
MUSIC 2D, 2477 H. Neptune, 711 H.; Music, 565 H. Milk 44 lbs. 1 day, P.
MUSIQUE, 6002 H. Imp. Milk 8143 lbs. 5 oz. 9 months 5 days, P.
MUTUAL FRIEND, 10130 H. Imp. Milk 82 lbs. 5 oz. 1 day, P.; 16,281 lbs. 15 oz. 1 year, A.R. Butter 20 lbs. 13 oz. 7 days A.R.
MUTUAL FRIEND 2D. 10513 H. F. Young America, 1 H. F.; Mutual Friend, 10139 H. Milk 76 lbs. 15 oz. 1 day, 12,997 lbs. 3 oz. 1 year, P. Butter 25 lbs. 12½ oz. 7 days, A.R.
MUTUAL FRIEND 2D's WAYNE, 18456 H F. Aaggie Prince of Wayne, 8781 H. F.; Mutual Friend 2d, 10513 H. F. Milk 48 lbs 1 day, P.; 11,664 lbs. 6 oz. 1 year, A.R. Butter 22 lbs. 5¾ oz. 7 days, P.
MUTUAL FRIEND 3D, 28389 H. F. Duke Netherland, 1271 H. F.; Mutual Friend, 10139 H. Milk 66 lbs. 3 oz. 1 day, 5907 lbs. 3 oz. 100 days, P. Butter 21 lbs. 13½ oz. 7 days, A.R.
MYCALE, 6898 H. Imp. Milk 40 lbs. 1 day, 1420 lbs. 30 days, P.
MYDIA RANDOLPH, 6022 H. Imp. Milk 77 lbs. 8 oz. 1 day, 5584 lbs. 8 oz. 90 days, P. Butter 21 lbs. 8 oz. 7 days, A.R.
MYETTE, 1418 H. F. Cossack, 2008 H.; Wavelet, 3369 H. Milk 10,120 lbs. 12 oz. 1 year, P.
MY FAVORITE, 6361 H. Imp. Milk 517 lbs. 3 oz. 13 days, A.R. Butter 15 lbs. 7½ oz. 7 days, A.R.; 22 lbs. 2 oz. 10 days, P.
MYRETTA, 1507 D. F. Roel, 330 F.; Reinschje, 1636 F. Butter 10 lbs. 3 oz. 7 days, A.R.

MILK AND BUTTER RECORDS. 353

MYRICA, 1406 H. F. Constantyn, 2040 H.; Imrah, 6704 H. Butter 15 lbs. 1½ oz. 7 days, A.R.
MYRITTA, 6502 H. F. Duke of Oneida, 189 D. F.; Lady Retsummer, 550 D. F. Milk 46 lbs. 1 day, P.
MYRRHA, 6713 H. Imp. Butter 19 lbs. 14 oz. 7 days, P.
MYRRHNA, 9334 H. Imp. Milk 37 lbs. 1 day, P. Butter 22 lbs. 8 oz. 10 days, P.
MYRTLE, 1311 D. F. Imp. Butter 11 lbs. 12 oz. 7 days, A R.
MYRTLE HEEG, 15002 H. F. Hartog Twisk 2d, 713 D. F.; Myrtle, 1311 D. F. Milk 241 lbs. 2 oz. 7 days, P. Butter 13 lbs. 2 oz. 7 days, A.R.
MYSIE, 1495 H. F. Empyrean, 1006 H.; Agate, 236 H. Milk 8078 lbs. 6 oz. 1 year, P.
MYSSA, 5890 H. Imp. Milk 52 lbs. 1 day, 9204 lbs. 12 oz. 1 year, P. Butter 18 lbs. 3 oz. 7 days, P.
MYTH, 8096 H. Imp. Milk 71 lbs. 4 oz. 1 day, P. Butter 3 lbs. 2 oz. 1 day, P.

NAATJE, 3004 H. Imp. Milk 84 lbs. 1 day, P.
NADINE, 5540 H. Nero of California, 2209 H.; Maid of Goshen, 182 H. Milk 1000 lbs. 30 days, P.
NADINE ABBEKERK, 5592 H. Imp. Milk 75 lbs. 1 day, P. Butter 3 lbs. 8 oz. 1 day, P.
NAGELHOUT 2D, 3203 H. Imp. Milk 48 lbs. 1 day, P.
NAHE 2D, 6643 II. F. Klaas Dekker, 1311 H.; Nalie, 10112 H. Milk 43 lbs. 1 day, P. Butter 12 lbs. 4 oz. 7 days, P.
NANJKE 2D, 701 D. F. Mooie, 26 M. R.; Nanijke. 121 M. R. Milk 63 lbs. 1 day, P. Butter 17 lbs. 7 days, P.
NAMUR, 7173 H. Imp. Milk 15,221 lbs. 10 oz. 1 year, P.
NANA ABBEKERK, 9008 H. Imp. Milk 84 lbs. 1 day, P. Butter 3 lbs. 8 oz. 1 day, P.
NANNETTE, 4163 H. Empire, 588 H.; Nannie Smit, 548 H. Milk 50 lbs. 1 day, P.
NANNETTE 3D'S PLEDGE, 22281 H. F. Pledge's Joe, 7418 H. F.; Nannette 3d, 10539 H. F. Milk 361 lbs. 7 days, A.R. Butter 21 H3 lbs. 7 days, A.R.
NANNIE, 1403 H. Hepburn, 437 H.; Belle of the Grove, 695 H. Milk 11,400 lbs. 11 months 24 days, A.R.
NANNIE SMIT, 548 H. Imp. Milk 82 lbs. 1 day, P.
NANNIE SPOFFORD, 1785 H. Imp. Milk 80 lbs. 4 oz. 7 days, P.; 10,000 lbs. 10 oz. 6 months, A.R. Butter 16 lbs. 10 oz. 7 days, A.R.
NANN STONE, 9065 H. Imp. Milk 58 lbs. 8 oz. 1 day, 3270 lbs. 60 days, P. Butter 17 lbs. 8 oz. 7 days, P.
NAOMI 2D, 2038 H. Jaap, 452 H.; Nazmi, 725 H. Milk 44 lbs. 10 oz. 1 day, P.
NAOMIE, 1559 D. F. De Graaf II, 505 P. R.; Anna, 527 Neth. Butter 9 lbs. 10 oz. 7 days, A.R.
NAOMIE 3D, 15320 II. F. Dillon, 3680 H. F.; Naomie, 1559 D. F. Butter 19 lbs. 15 oz. 7 days, A.R.
NAPPIE, 7124 H. Imp Milk 70 lbs. 1 day, P.
NAREA OF DAKOTA, 11596 H. F. Jewel's Prince of Wayne, 32 H. F.; Geraldrada, 9550 H. Milk 11,311 lbs. 1 year, P.
NAREA STAR, 34752 H. F. Dotty 2d's Ahnee, 16152 H. F.; Narka of Dakota, 11596 H. F. Milk 35 lbs. 1 day, P.
NASHTJE, 8230 H. F. Wilhelm, 580 F. Cornelia, 2219 F. Milk 54 lbs. 1 day, P.; 504 lbs. 10 days, A.R.
NASHTJE 2D, 11883 H. F. Ademus, 6776 H. F.; Nashtje, 8359 H. F. Milk 42 lbs. 1 day, P.; 390 lbs. 10 days, P.
NATSEY, 2365 H. Imp. Milk 70 lbs. 1 oz. 1 day, P. Butter 34 lbs. 9 oz. 7 days, A.R.
NAZLI, 7103 H. Imp. Milk 59 lbs. 10 oz. 1 day, P.
NEAH, 8378 H. F. Friso, 11 F.; Grietje, 319 F. Milk 102 lbs. 1 day, 2786 lbs. 31 days, P. Butter 24 lbs. 15 oz. 7 days, P.
NEELTJE, 727 H. Imp. Milk 80 lbs. 1 day, P.
NEELTJE 2D, 2200 H. Jaap, 452 H.; Neeltje, 727 H. Milk 75 lbs. 1 day, P.
NEELTJE BEETS, 6421 H. Imp. Milk 52 lbs. 1 day, P.
NEELTJE LEE 2D, 3231 H. Imp. Milk 50 lbs. 1 day, P. Butter 17 lbs. 4 oz. 7 days, P.
NEELTJE WIT, 2075 H. F. Jacob Wit 2062 H.; Neeltje, 2614 H. Butter 2 lbs. 4 oz. 1 day. P.
NEENA CRUICKSHANK 2D, 5140 H. F. Jay-Eye-See, 3067 H.; Neena Cruickshank, 8560 H. Milk 45 lbs. 1 day, P. Butter 10 lbs. 12 oz. 7 days, P.
NEFTA NETHERLAND 2D, 5773 H. F. Duke of Niagara, 2030 H.; Neeta Netherland. Milk 30 lbs. 1 day, P.
NEILSON, 411 H. Imp. Milk 74 lbs. 22 oz. 1 day, 12,335 lbs. 12 oz. 10 months, P.
NEILTJI KORNDYKE, 9 D. F. Imp. Milk 13,092 lbs. 8 oz. 10 months, A R. Butter 23 lbs. 2 oz 7 days, 93 lbs. 12 oz. 30 days, A.R.
NEILTJI TWISK, 171 D. F. Lad of Twisk, 9 D. F.; Neiltji Korndyke, 9 D. F. Milk 12,666 lbs. 1 year, A.R.
NELLACE, 14010 H. F. Nannette's Credit, 830 H. F.; Janina, 7172 H. Milk 1600 lbs. 30 days, P.
NELLIE, 756 H. Kartanaer, 116 H.; Snowball, 449 H. Milk 68 lbs, 1 day, P.
NELLIE BURKE, 2840 H. Imp. Milk 74 lbs. 4 oz. 1 day, 2079 lbs. 30 days, P.
NELLIE BURKE 2D, 3746 H. F. Burr 1460 H.; Nellie Burke, 2840 H. Milk 70 lbs. 1 day, P. Butter 23 lbs. 4 oz. 7 days, P.
NELLIE GRANT, 943 H. Imp. Milk 64 lbs. 12 oz. 1 day, 10,476 lbs. 4 oz. 1 year, P. Butter 19 lbs. 3½ oz. 7 days, A.R.
NELLIE GRANT 4TH, 6624 H. Gold Foil, 1237 H.; Nellie Grant, 943 H. Milk 62 lbs. 4 oz. 1 day, P.; 16,752 lbs. 12 oz. 1 year, A.R. Butter 13 lbs. 13 oz. 7 days, A. R.
NELLIE RENSKE, 27163 H. F. Hamilton 2d, 5008 H. F.; Renske 2d, 231 D. F. Milk 50 lbs. 4 oz. 1 day, P.
NELLY, 5740 H. Imp. Milk 79 lbs. 3 oz. 1 day, P.
NELLY ROOKER, 9958 H. Jacob Wit, 2602 H.; Nelly, 2031 Neth. Milk 48 lbs. 3 oz. 1 day, 10,946 lbs. 4 oz. 11 months 22 days, P. Butter 22 lbs. 6½ oz. 7 days, P.
NELLY WAYNE, 4870 H. F. Prince of Wayne 5th, 1910 H.; Nellie Grant, 943 H. Milk 9,024 lbs. 10 months, P.
NENETZIN, 15463 H. Porcelain Prince, 4482 H.; Idaard, 4083 H. Milk 75 lbs. 12 oz. 1 day, 18,000 lbs. 10 months, P.
NERRA SPOFFORD, 5015 H. F. Glendale, 3417 H.; Niobe Spofford, 2073 H Butter 19 lbs. 2 oz. 7 days, P.
NETA PAUL, 5522 H. Climax, 204 H.; Johanna Paul, 677 H. Milk 58 lbs. 1 day, P.
NETHERLAND AAGGIE, 3948 H. Neptune. 711 H.; Lady Netherland, 1263 H. Milk 61 lbs. 1 day, 11,798 lbs. 2 oz. 1 year, P. Butter 13 lbs. 11 oz. 7 days, P.
NETHERLAND ADELA, 7424 H. F. Netherland Statesman, 3280 H.; Lakeside Adela, 9047 H. Butter 16 lbs. 8 oz. 7 days, A.R.
NETHERLAND BARONESS, 2635 H. Imp. Milk 72 lbs. 1 day, P.; 11,249 lbs. 7 oz. 10 months, A.R. Butter 21 lbs. 12 oz. 7 days, A.R.
NETHERLAND BARONESS 2D, 2636 H. Imp. Milk 13,087 lbs. 8 oz, 1 year, P. Butter 8 lbs. 3 oz. 7 days, P.

25

Netherland Baroness 2d's Princess, 6466 H. Netherland Prince, 716 H.; Netherland Baroness 2d, 2636 H. Milk 42 lbs. 14 oz. 1 day, 9,686 lbs. 8 oz. 1 year, P.
Netherland Baroness 3d, 2637 H. Imp. Milk 3,271 lbs. 4 oz. 4 months 17 days, P.
Netherland Baroness 4th, 2638 H. Imp. Milk 46 lbs. 11 oz. 1 day, 13,922 lbs. 11 oz. 1 year, P. Butter 22 lbs. 13¼ oz. 7 days, 90 lbs. 1¼ oz. 30 days, P.
Netherland Baroness 4th's Artis, 5767 H. F. Prince of Artis, 2479 H.; Netherland Baroness 4th, 2638 H. Milk 489 lbs. 5 oz. 10 days, P. Butter 13 lbs. 14 oz. 7 days, A.R.
Netherland Baroness 5th, 3483 H. Imp. Milk 41 lbs. 6 oz. 1 day, 10,292 lbs. 7 oz. 1 year. Butter 17 lbs. 1 oz. 7 days, A.R.
Netherland Beauty, 968 H. Imp. Milk 76 lbs. 10 oz. 1 day, 13,000 lbs. 1 year, P. Butter 16 lbs. 4 oz. 7 days, P.
Netherland Belle, 1876 H. Imp. Milk 77 lbs. 4 oz. 1 day, P.; 19,516 lbs. 8 oz. 1 year, A.R. Butter 16 lbs. 7 oz, 7 days, A.R.
Netherland Belle 2d, 1595 H. F. Netherland Prince, 716 H.; Netherland Belle, 1876 H. Butter 10 lbs. 10¼ oz. 7 days, A.R.
Netherland Belva, 2979 H. F. Netherland King, 1924 H.; Jacob Wit's Belva, 7791 H. Butter 10 lbs. 4 oz 7 days, P.
Netherland Bongilla, 13694 H. F. Netherland Convoy, 2934 H.; Bonzilla, 6936 H. Milk 37 lbs. 8 oz. 1 day, P.
Netherland Chaperone, 6995 H. Imp. Milk 63 lbs. 11 oz. 1 day, P.; 15,414 lbs. 8 oz. 1 year, A.R. Butter 19 lbs. 8¼ oz. 7 days, P.
Netherland Chaperone 3d, 6933 H. F. Netherland Monk, 4424 H.; Netherland Chaperone, 6895 H. Milk 8733 lbs. 2 oz. 10 months, A.R. Butter 14 lbs. 2¼ oz. 7 days, A.R.
Netherland Clara, 10006 H. Imp. Milk 10,199 lbs. 12 oz. 1 year, P. Butter 16 lbs. 5¼ oz. 7 days, P.
Netherland Consort, 2639 H. Imp. Milk 71 lbs. 12 oz. 1 day, P.; 17,873 lbs. 9 oz. 1 year, A.R. Butter 20 lbs. 4¼ oz. 7 days, A.R.
Netherland Corrinne, 13695 H. F. Netherland Convoy, 2934 H.; Corrinne of Oakhurst, 2773 H. Milk 38 lbs. 1 day, P.
Netherland Countess, 2634 H. Imp. Milk 50 lbs. 1 day, 11,472 lbs. 3 oz. 11 months, P. Butter 17 lbs. 4¼ oz. 7 days, P.
Netherland Countess 3d, 6068 H. Netherland Prince, 716 H.; Netherland Countess, 2634 H. Milk 35 lbs. 7 oz. 1 day, 4532 lbs. 5 months 30 days, P. Butter 10 lbs. 7 days, 80 lbs. 6 oz. 30 days, P.
Netherland Countess 4th, 2965 H. F. Prince of Artis, 2479 H.; Netherland Countess, 2634 H. Butter 10 lbs. 4 oz. 7 days, A.R.
Netherland Curran, 5338 H. F. Netherland Convoy, 2934 H.; Lampasas, 7008 H. Milk 64 lbs. 1 day, P.; 1727 lbs. 30 days, A.R. Butter 19 lbs. 7 days, A.R.
Netherland De Kol, 10605 H. Netherland Alban, 4584 H.; De Kol 2d, 734 H. Butter 20 lbs. 5 oz. 7 days, 82 lbs. 15 oz. 30 days, A.R.
Netherland Dora, 13697 H. F. Netherland Convoy, 2934 H.; Philidora, 6926 H. Milk 34 lbs. 8 oz. 1 day, P.
Netherland Dorinda, 6894 H. Imp. Milk 13,656 lbs. 7 oz. 1 year, A.R. Butter 24 lbs. 9¼ oz. 7 days, 96 lbs. 4¼ oz. 30 days, A.R.
Netherland Dorinda 2d, 2604 H. F. Sir Henry 2d of Aaggie, 1451 H.; Netherland Dorinda, 6894 H. Butter 13 lbs. 10½ oz. 7 days, A.R.
Netherland Dorinda 3d, 4560 H. F. Netherland Prince, 716 H.; Netherland Dorinda, 6894 H. Butter 11 lbs. 12¼ oz. 7 days, P.
Netherland Dowager, 2632 H. Imp. Milk 73 lbs. 1 day, P.; 17,160 lbs. 11 oz. 1 year, A.R. Butter 17 lbs. 3 oz. 1 day, P.
Netherland Dowager 2d, 2633 H. Imp. Milk 55 lbs. 1 oz. 1 day, 11,194 lbs. 4 oz. 1 year, P.
Netherland Dowager 2d's Princess, 6404 H. Netherland Prince, 716 H.; Netherland Dowager, 2633 H. Milk 8313 lbs. 7 oz. 1 year, P. Butter 11 lbs. 1 oz. 7 days, P.
Netherland Dowager 2d's Queen, 1568 H. F. Netherland Prince, 716 H.; Netherland Dowager 2d, 2633 H. Milk 4448 lbs. 8 oz. 9 months, P.
Netherland Duchess, 2498 H. Imp. Milk 61 lbs. 1 day, 16,520 lbs. 7 oz. 1 year, P. Butter 16 lbs. 15¼ oz. 7 days, A.R.
Netherland Duchess 2d, 7890 H. F. Clothilde 4th's Imperial, 1281 H. F.; Netherland Duchess, 2498 H. Milk 15,585 lbs. 1 year, P.
Netherland Duke's Nierop, 3649 H. F. Netherland Duke, 1571 H.; Nierop, 2519 H. Milk 8437 lbs. 8 oz. 9 months, 1 day, P. Butter 15 lbs. 2¼ oz. 7 days, A.R.
Netherland Gem, 1875 H. Imp. Milk 7695 lbs. 11 oz. 8 months 20 days, P.
Netherland Gem 2d, 2115 H. Imp. Milk 12,120 lbs. 1 oz. 1 year, P. Butter 14 lbs. 4 oz. 7 days, A.R.
Netherland Grace, 17052 H. F. Netherland Prince, 716 H.; Aaggie Cornelia 3d, 4342 H. Butter 13 lbs. 4 oz. 7 days, P.
Netherland Hengerveld, 13106 H. F. Aaggie Leila's Prince, 4410 H.; Dora Hengerveld 2d, 886 D. F. Milk 50 lbs. 1 day, 465 lbs. 7 days, A.R. Butter 20 lbs. 4 oz 7 days, A.R.
Netherland Hero's Elsie, 4531 H. F. Netherland Hero, 2342 H.; Queen Elsie, 2081 H. Milk 38 lbs. 3 oz. 1 day, 1060 lbs. 14 oz. 1 month, P.
Netherland Jewel, 2642 H. Imp. Milk 60 lbs. 12 oz. 1 day, 14,294 lbs. 10 oz. 1 year, P. Butter 18 lbs. 12 oz. 7 days, P.; 29 lbs. 4½ oz. 14 days, A.R.
Netherland Jewel 2d, 3492 H. Imp. Milk 11,596 lbs. 10 oz. 10 months 7 days, P. Butter 10 lbs. 8 oz. 7 days, P.
Netherland Jewel 3d, 6066 H. Prince Imperial, 1164 H.; Netherland Jewel, 2642 H. Milk 70 lbs. 3 oz. 1 day, 12,603 lbs. 4 oz. 1 year, P. Butter 14 lbs. 8 oz. 7 days, P.
Netherland Lady, 1316 H. F. Netherland Baron, 1573 H.; Zazel 5027 H. Butter 21 lbs. 3 oz. 7 days, 88 lbs. 6 oz. 30 days, P.
Netherland Maid, 6737 H. Imp. Milk 7010 lbs. 15 oz. 7 months, 23 days, P.
Netherland May, 33898 H. F. Dowager May's Pietertje Netherland, 16261 H. F.; Orpha, 19143 H. F. Milk 33 lbs. 8 oz. 1 day, P.
Netherland Mercedes, 1575 H. F. Netherland Prince, 716 H.; Mercedes 3d, 3760 H. Butter 11 lbs. 10¼ oz. 7 days, A.R.
Netherland Monk's Aaggie Constance, 20556 H. F. Netherland Monk, 4424 H.; Aaggie Constance, 2629 H. Milk 439 lbs. 9 oz. 7 days, A.R. Butter 17 lbs. 4 oz. 7 days, A.R.
Netherland Myrrhna, 4033 H. F. Netherland Knight, 1852 H.; Myrrhna, 9834 H. Milk 7283 lbs. 12 oz. 7 months, 16 days, P. Butter 14 lbs. 14 oz. 7 days, A.R.

NETHERLAND NORA, 13693 H. F. Netherland Convoy, 2934 H.; Lady Stanley, 4377 H. Milk 35 lbs. 1 day, P.
NETHERLAND ORPHAN, 5643 H. F. Netherland Elector, 3115 H.; Aaggie of Hoorn 2d, 6511 H. Butter 20 lbs. 5½ oz. 7 days, A.R.
NETHERLAND ORPHAN 2D, 14591 H. F. Netherland Mordant, 4521 H. F.; Netherland Orphan, 5643 H. F. Butter 14 lbs. 8½ oz. 7 days, A.R.
NETHERLAND PAMELA, 6893 H. Imp. Butter 16 lbs. 7 oz. 7 days, P.
NETHERLAND PEERESS, 2640 H. Imp. Milk 52 lbs. 7 oz. 1 day, 15,325 lbs. 13 oz. 1 year, P. Butter 25 lbs. 4 oz. 7 days, 45 lbs. 7 cz. 14 days, A.R.
NETHERLAND PEERESS 2D, 6059 H. Prince Imperial, 1104 H.; Netherland Peeress, 2640 H. Milk 38 lbs. 8 oz. 1 day, 7198 lbs. 9 oz. 9 months, 11 days, P.
NETHERLAND PEERESS 3D, 1571 H. F. Netherland King, 1924 H.; Netherland Peeress, 2640 H. Butter 19 lbs. 12 oz. 7 days, P.
NETHERLAND PET, 3468 H. Netherland Prince, 716 H.; Tritle, 1883 H. Milk 50 lbs. 1 day, P.; 12,525 lbs. 3 oz. 1 year, A.R.
NETHERLAND PET 2D, 1885 H. F. Falstaff, 1358 H.; Netherland Pet, 3468 H. Milk 5016 lbs. 6 oz. 6 months, 23 days, P.
NETHERLAND PIETERTJE PRINCESS, 23903 H. F. Milla's Pietertje Netherland, 7825 H. F.; Witkop 2d's Beauty's Netherland, 15372 H. F. Milk 361 lbs., A.R. Butter 18 lbs. 2 oz. 7 days, A.R.
NETHERLAND PRIDE, 2641 H. Imp. Milk 49 lbs. 4 oz. 1 day, 15,598 lbs. 12 oz. 1 year, P. Butter 16 lbs. 7 days, A.R.
NETHERLAND PRINCESS, 862 H. Imp. Milk 64 lbs. 3 oz. 1 day, P.; 16,766 lbs. 13 oz. 1 year, A.R. Butter 17 lbs. 11 oz. 7 days, A.R.
NETHERLAND PRINCESS 3D, 3481 H. Neptune, 711 H.; Netherland Princess, 862 H. Milk 42 lbs. 15 oz. 1 day, P.; 11,978 lbs. 3 oz. 1 year, A.R.
NETHERLAND PRINCESS 4TH, 6475 H. Netherland Prince, 716 H.; Netherland Princess, 862 H. Milk 42 lbs. 10 oz. 1 day, 11,478 lbs. 2 oz. 1 year, P. Butter 23 lbs. 10¼ oz. 7 days, 80 lbs. 4 oz. 30 days, P.
NETHERLAND PRINCESS 5TH, 1598 H. F. Netherland Prince, 716 H.; Netherland Princess, 862 H. Milk 14,153 lbs. 1 oz. 1 year, P. Butter 19 lbs. 6 oz 7 days, 60 lbs. 7¾ oz. 30 days, P.
NETHERLAND QUEEN, 414 H. Imp. Milk 83 lbs. 1 day, P.; 15,514 lbs. 9 oz. 1 year, A. R. Butter 20 lbs. 7 days, A.R.
NETHERLAND QUEEN 2D, 560 H. Uncle Tom, 163 H.; Netherland Queen, 414 H. Milk 12,622 lbs. 7 oz. 1 year, P. Butter 15 lbs. 7¾ oz. 7 days, P.
NETHERLAND QUEEN 2D'S HEIRESS, 6478 H. Netherland Prince, 716 H.; Netherland Queen 2d, 560 H. Milk 1,124 lbs. 12 oz. 30 days, P.
NETHERLAND QUEEN 3D, 1406 H. Uncle Tom, 163 H.; Netherland Queen, 414 H. Milk 65 lbs. 3 oz. 1 day, 12,770 lbs. 6 oz. 1 year, P. Butter 17 lbs. 7½ oz. 7 days, A.R.
NETHERLAND SADA, 13381 H. F. Aaggie Leila's Prince, 4419 H.; Crary Hengerveld, 807 H. F. Milk 387 lbs. 2 oz. 7 days, A.R Butter 18 lbs. 2 oz. 7 days, A.R.
NETHERLAND SIMPLICITY, 4558 H. F. Netherland Prince, 716 H.; Simplicity, 6995 H. Butter 10 lbs. 1 oz. 7 days, P.
NETHERLAND STATESMAN'S BENOLA, 11040 H. F. Netherland Statesman, 3280 H.; Benola Fletcher 2d, 9817 H. Milk 5,990 lbs. 8 oz. 181 days, P.
NETHERLAND STATESMAN CLARA, 8472 H. F. Netherland Statesman, 3280 H.; Netherland Clara, 10006 H. Butter 15 lbs. 8 oz. 7 days, P.
NETHERLAND TRIFLE, 6169 H. Netherland Prince, 716 H.; Trifle 2d, 2114 H. Milk 10,044 lbs. 7 oz. 8 months 10 days, P.
NETHERLAND TRIUMPH, 10013 H. Netherland Marquis, 2484 H.; Trijntje, 611 Neth. Milk 45 lbs. 15 oz. 1 day, P.; 13,139 lbs. 4 oz. 1 year, A.R. Butter 3 lbs. 1 oz. 1 day, 17 lbs. 4 oz. 7 days, P.
NETHERLAND WAUKESHA, 7007 H. Imp. Milk 12,141 lbs. 10 months 1 day, P.
NETHERLAND WAUPACA, 7011 H. Imp. Milk 8405 lbs. 3 oz. 11 months 12 days, P.
NETHERLAND WAUPACA 2D, 1509 H. F. Netherland Prince, 716 H.; Netherland Waupaca, 7011 H. Milk 6283 lbs. 5 oz. 7 months 16 days, P. Butter 21 lbs. 3¼ oz. 7 days, P.
NETHERLAND WAYNE, 13752 H. F. Duke Netherland, 1271 H. F.; Princess of Wayne 4th, 2339 H. Milk 55 lbs. 11 oz. 1 day, 11,269 lbs. 10 oz. 10 months, A.R. Butter 15 lbs. 15½ oz. 7 days, P.
NETHERLAND YSDELL, 7191 H. F. Teth Netherland, 3788 H.; Ysdelim, 928 H. Milk 71 lbs. 1 day, P.
NETTIE SCHOLTON, 6584 H. F. Flying Dutchman, 3881 H.; Lady Scholton 2d, 1055 H. Butter 30 lbs. 14 oz. 7 days, P.
NETTJE, 7287 H. Imp. Milk 84 lbs. 1 day, P.
NETTY, 850 H. Imp. Milk 52 lbs. 2 oz. 1 day, P.
NEVADA, 5185 H. Imp. Butter 9 lbs 3 oz. 7 days, A.R.
NIANIA, 3631 H. Damon, 831 H.; Florida, 1335 H. Milk 65 lbs. 1 day, P.
NICOLA, 8081 H. Nicolaas 2d, 451 H. Lalla Rookh, 1295 H. Milk 65 lbs. 1 day, P.
NICOLO, 5908 H. F. Parole, 391 H.; Teikje, 2918 H. Milk 54 lbs. 8 oz. 1 day, P.
NICOLO 2D, 14500 H. F. Thistle, 1829 H. F.; Nicolo, 5908 H. F. Milk 40 lbs. 1 day, P.
NIERDA, 2007 H. F. Lincoln, 120 Neth.; Cornelia, 4331 Neth. Milk 11,801 lbs. 11 months, 22 days, P.
NIEROP, 2519 H. Imp. Milk 116 lbs. 1 day, P.; 3129 lbs. 1 oz. 30 days, A.R.
NIESJE, 750 H. F. Willem II, 190 Neth.; Niesje, 103 Neth. Milk 82 lbs. 1 day, P.; 11,454 lbs. 14 oz. 8 months, A.R. Butter 20 lbs. 2¼ oz. 7 days, A.R.
NIETA, 18467 H. F. Bob Lockhart, 8406 H. F.; Hilton Maid 2d, 4936 H. Milk 46 lbs. 1 day, P.
NIG, 23040 H. F. Sieberen Pride, 7022 H. F.; Bregje, 1728 H. Milk 38 lbs. 1 day, P.
NILLETTE, 3097 H. Imp. Milk 8450 lbs. 1 oz. 7 months 7 days, P. Butter 15 lbs. 15 oz. 7 days, P.
NINA S, 2128 H. Roeloff, 989 H.; Akke, 1643 H. Milk 42 lbs. 1 day, P.
NINA SPOFFORD, 476 H. F. Sullivan 1058 H. F.; Nannie Spofford, 1785 N. Milk 8431 lbs. 1 oz. 8 months 29 days, P.
NINA SPOFFORD 2D, 6937 H. F. Furness, 4270 H.; Nina Spofford, 476 H. F. Milk 9206 lbs. 10 months, A.R. Butter 14 lbs. 4½ oz. 7 days, A.R.
NIOBA BEETS, 7964 H. F. Inka's Duke, 1161 H. F.; Dora Beets 2d, 265 D. F. Milk 8259 lbs. 6 oz. 9 months, A.R.
NIOBE, 816 H. Fourth Prince of Orange, 246 H.; Rachel, 432 H. Milk 70 lbs. 1 day, P.
NIOBE D, 1573 H. Rubenstein, 450 H.; Niobe, 816 H. Milk 70 lbs. 1 day, P.
NIOBE SPOFFORD, 2073 H. Imp. Nannie Spofford, 1785 H. Milk 15,092 lbs. 8 oz. 11 months, 9 days, A.R.
NITALIA, 7028 H. Imp. Milk 33 lbs. 1 day, P.
NIXIE L, 5155 H. Imp. Milk 80 lbs. 1 day, P.

NIXY, 6209 H. Prince Opperdoes, 387 H.; Fansta, 125 H. Milk 55 lbs. 1 day, P.
NOCO, 14166 H. F. Grimes, 4890 H. F.; Latuna, 8161 H. Milk 6192 lbs. 6 oz. 10 months, P.
NOLTJE, 8926 H. Imp. Milk 41 lbs. 3 oz. 1 day, 6810 lbs. 11 months, 8 days, P.
NONOTUCK, 5384 H. Imp. Milk 8169 lbs. 18 oz. 8 months, 15 days, P.
NONPAREIL, 2056 H. Nicolaas, 50 Neth.; Maike, 120 Neth. Milk 44 lbs. 8 oz. 1 day, P.; 7228 lbs. 3 oz. 8 months 1 day. A.R. Butter 11 lbs. 7 days, P.
NOONTIDE, 2843 H. Imp. Milk 31 lbs. 1 day, 3396 lbs. 1 oz. 4 months 28 days, P.
NORA B, 512 D. F. 2d Lad of Twisk, 9 M. R.; Boutje Kouing, 55 M. R. Milk 8720 lbs. 9 months 25 days, A.R.
NORA CORNELIA, 1361 H. F. Jacob Wit, 2662 H.; Nora, 1719 H. Milk 44 lbs. 1 day, P.
NORA JACOBA, 1360 H. F. Jacob Wit, 2062 H.: Nora, 1719 Neth. 56 lbs. 1 day, P.
NORNA, 418 H. Imp. Milk 60 lbs. 1 day, P.
NORRINNE, 7753 H. Imp. Milk 40 lbs. 1 day, P.
NORRISSA, 1842 D. F. Wittema, 125 F. H.; Vellinga. 362 P. R. Milk 10,171 lbs. 15 oz. 1 year, P.
NORTHERN QUEEN, 2933 H. F. Imp. Milk 10,000 lbs. 5 months. 1 day, P. Butter 9 lbs. 2 oz. 7 days, P.
NOVEKA PEL, 1645 D. F. Prince of Altijdwerk, 178 P. R ; Pel 4th. 194 M. R. Milk 54 lbs. 1 day, P. Butter 26 lbs. 14 days, P.
NOVELTY, 5348 H. F. Pel 2d. 327 D, F.; Belle of Woodside, 1676 D. F. Milk 13,624 lbs. 4 oz. 1 year, P.
NOWALINE, 2951 H. Imp. Milk 67 lbs. 1 day, A.R.; 16,135 lbs. 4 oz. 1 year, P.
NOVEKA PEL, 1645 D. F. Prince of Altijdwerk, 178 P. R.; Pel 4th, 525 P. R. Milk 54 lbs. 1 day, P. Butter 26 lbs. 14 days, P.
NUDINE, 2845 H. Imp. Milk 79 lbs, 1 day, 14,953 lbs. 11 oz. 1 year, A.R.
NUDINE 2D, 6413 H. Neptune, 711 H.; Nudine, 2845 H. Milk 64 lbs. 3 oz. 1 day, P.; 8021 lbs. 2 oz. 8 months, 4 days, A.R.
NUDINE 3D, 373 H. F. Captain Daw, 2088 H.; Nudine, 2845 H. Milk 35 lbs. 14 oz. 1 day, P.; 7542 lbs. 14 oz. 9 months, 23 days, A.R.
NUDINE 4TH, 3997 H. F. Billy Bawn, 3087 H. Nudine, 2845 H. Milk 42 lbs. 2 oz. 1 day, P.; 8051 lbs. 2 oz. 9 months, 16 days, A.R.
NUDINE 5TH, 8730 H. F. Billy Bawn, 3087 H.; Dusty, 6536 H. Milk 8990 lbs, 1 oz. 10 months, A.R.
NUMA, 5891 H. Imp. Milk 58 lbs. 1 day, P.; 11,339 lbs. 8 oz. 1 year, P. Butter 12 lbs. 11 oz. 7 days, P.
NUTMEG, 8865 H. Imp. Milk 50 lbs. 1 day, P.; 1059 lbs. 12 oz. 30 days, A.R.
NUTMEG 2D, 9680 H. F. Flora Clifden's Mercedes Prince, 3545 H.; Nutmeg, 8865 H. Butter 11 lbs. 15 oz. 7 days, A.R.
NYLEPTEA, 7708 H. F. Jonge Care, 2305 H.; Pietje Melkmeid, 4113 H. Milk 1019 lbs. 6 oz. 1 month, 4 days, P.
NYMPH, 2844 H. Imp. Milk 56 lbs. 1 day, P.
NYSSA, 5890 H. Imp. Milk 52 lbs. 1 day, 9294 lbs. 12 oz. 1 year, P. Butter 13 lbs. 3 oz. 7 days, P.

OASIS, 1505 H. Billy Bawn, 189 H.; Ondine, 828 H. Milk 58 lbs. 1 day, P.
OATKA, 945 H. Imp. Milk 87 lbs. 7 oz. 1 day, A.R.; 15.688 lbs. 1 oz. 1 year, P. Butter 22 lbs. 8½ oz. 7 days, 85 lbs. 7 oz. 30 days, A.R.
OBBE, 5759 H. Imp. Milk 71 lbs. 1 day, P.
OCCIDENT, 2846 H. Imp. Milk 82 lbs. 8 oz. 1 day, P.
OCTOROON, 916 H. Imp. Milk 79 lbs. 12 oz. 1 day, P.; 11,071 lbs. 8 oz. 7 months 27 days, A.R.
OEBELE, 5722 H. Imp. Milk 65 lbs. 1 day, P.
OHIO STATE TEST, 7240 H. F. Goldstone 2d, 949 H.; Jumbo Maid, 1187 H. Milk 43 lbs. 1 day, P.; 8,097 lbs. 12 oz. 8 months 17 days, A.R. Butter 13 lbs. 4½ oz. 7 days. A.R.
OHIO VALLEY, 4494 H. F. Commodore Preble, 3191 H.; Savina of Shadeland, 8611 H. Milk 35 lbs. 8 oz. 1 day, 945 lbs. 30 days, P.
OLA, 3375 H. Alkmaar, 459 H.; Saapke, 736 H. Milk 48 lbs. 1 day, P.
OLANY, 8987 H. Netherland Prince, 716 H.; Theta, 2902 H. Butter 13 lbs. 1 oz. 7 days, P.
OLGA CHICO, 5254 H. Imp. Milk 55 lbs. 1 day, 12,418 lbs. 1 year, P. Butter 15 lbs. 1 oz. 7 days, A.R.
OLLIE FLETCHER, 6170 H. F. Nimbus 2d, 2361 H.; Riuske, 5868 H. Butter 18 lbs. 1½ oz. 7 days, A.R.
OLLIVETTE, 3118 H. Imp. Milk 65 lbs. 1 day, P.
OMAHA'S ARTIS CARISA, 13673 H. F. Omaha, 3231 H. F.; Artis Carisa, 7798 H. Milk 11,498 lbs. 8 oz. 1 year, A.R.
OMAHA'S CHRYSTENAH, 13672 H. F. Omaha, 3231 H. F.; Chrystenah, 4024 H. F. Milk 11,363 lbs. 1 year, A.R.
OMAHA'S DOMINGO S' MABEL, 16890 H. F. Omaha, 3231 H.; Domingo S. Mabel of Pacofoc, 13668 H. F. Milk 12,275 lbs. 8 oz. 1 year, A.R.
OMAHA'S LUCY OF PACIFIC, 13674 H. F. Omaha, 3231 H. F.; Lucy of Pacific, 623 H. F. Milk 10,716 lbs. 1 year, A.R.
ONDINE, 828 H. Imp. Milk 90 lbs. 8 oz. 1 day, 2545 lbs. 30 days, P.
ONDINE'S MODEL, 4167 H. Empire, 588 H.; Onyx, 1066 H. Milk 70 lbs. 1 day, P.
ONDIT LASS, 2592 H. F. Ondit, 2292 H.; Huzzetta, 4164 H. Milk 35 lbs. 1 day, P. Butter 17 lbs. 13 oz. 7 days, P.
ONETTA, 1816 D. F. Ykema, 322 D. F.; Antje Santema, 948 D. F. Milk 10,607 lbs. 10 months, P. Butter 14 lbs. 4 oz. 7 days, P.
ONONDAGA PRINCESS 2D, 1450 H. Imp. Milk 65 lbs. 1 day, P. Butter 12 lbs. 4 oz. 7 days, P.
ONONDAGA PRINCESS 3D, 3367 H. Nabob, 719 H.; Onondaga Princess 2d, 1450 H. Milk 68 lbs. 1 day, P.
ONONIS, 2366 H. Empire, 586 H.; Onyx, 1066 H. Milk 68 lbs. 12 oz. 1 day, 11,001 lbs. 10 months, P.
ONONIS 3D, 12705 H. F. Constantyn, 2040 H.; Ononis, 2366 H. Milk 46 lbs. 1 day, P.
OOLOOLOO, 10719 H. F. Mink Prince, 2805 H.; Pearle Winkle, 3587 H. F. Butter 18 lbs. 7 days, P.
OPAL, 1376 H. Ashland Prince, 409 H.; Madge, 374 H. Milk 65 lbs. 1 day, P.
OPBELIA, 965 H. Imp. Milk 57 lbs. 1 oz. 1 day, 6291 lbs. 8 oz. 143 days, P. Butter 13 lbs. 5 oz. 7 days, P.
OPPERDOES 16TH, 44 H. Van Tromp, 50 H.; Maid of Opperdoes, 22 H. Milk 82 lbs. 1 oz. 1 day, 2545 lbs. 4 oz. 31 days, P.
OPPERDOES 17TH, 196 H. Third Dutchman, 46 H.; Opperdoes 16th, 44 H. Milk 10,254 lbs. 1 year, P.
ORANGE GIRL, 860 H. Imp. Milk 11,349 lbs. 10 months, A.R.
ORBONA, 7203 H. Imp. Milk 91 lbs. 1 day, 15,071 lbs. 1 year, P.
ORCA, 9339 H. Imp. Milk 52 lbs. 1 day, P.
ORELIA, 1799 H. Imp. Milk 57 lbs. 7 oz. 1 day, 8000 lbs. 6 months, P.

MILK AND BUTTER RECORDS. 357

ORETTA, 27690 H. F. Ophelia's Champion, 10547 H. F.; Ophelia Netherland, 9490 H. F. Milk 20,097 lbs. 10 months, P. Butter 14 lbs. 4 oz. 7 days, P.
ORIAN, 9467 H. Imp. Milk 41 lbs. 1 day, P.
ORIANA, 1209 H. Imp. Milk 60 lbs. 4 oz. 1 day, 12,300 lbs. 1 year, P. Butter 13 lbs. 8½ oz. 7 days, P.
ORIANA 4TH, 7985 H. Iroquois, 1074 H.; Oriana, 1209 H. Milk 60 lbs. 4 oz. 1 day, 12,300 lbs. 1 year, P. Butter 13 lbs. 3½ oz. 7 days, P.
ORIENT, 963 H. Imp. Milk 43 lbs. 6 oz. 1 day, 9225 lbs. 1 oz. 1 year, P. Butter 19 lbs. 11½ oz. 7 days, P.
ORIENT MAID, 12050 H. F. Imp. Milk 79 lbs. 1 day, P. Butter 16 lbs. 7 days, P.
ORIENT'S GRACIA, 6078 H. F. Orient, 1600 H.: Gracia 2d, 1442 H. Butter 14 lbs. 3 oz. 7 days, P.
ORPHE, 6237 H. Imp. Milk 67 lbs. 1 day, P. Butter 18 lbs. 3 oz. 7 days, P.
ORPHIA, 2851 H. Imp. Milk 33 lbs. 8 oz. 1 day, 13,000 lbs. 1 year, P.
ORPHIA 2D, 18402 H. F. Fairmount Tom, 2448 H.; Orphia, 2851 H. Milk 44 lbs. 1 day, P.
ORSINGA, 1539 D. F. De Nette, 281 F.; Wagenaar, 1240 F. Butter 11 lbs. 10 oz. 7 days, A.R.
OSAIRA, 3834 H. F. Graaf Jan, 366 Neth.; Mantel, 2697 Neth. Butter 10 lbs. 9 oz. 7 days, P.
OSWEGO COUNTY QUEEN, 14352 H. F. Anialga, 702 H. F.; Iona C, 3946 H. F. Milk 50 lbs. 1 day, P. Butter 17 lbs. 7 days, P.
OTA, 1847 D. F. Tell. 128 D. F.; Anke, 363 D. F. Milk 56 lbs. 1 day. 10,702 lbs. 5 oz. 1 year, P.
OTELIA, 2367 H. F. Dennis, 1344 H.; Zadee. 4726 H. Milk 31 lbs. 8 oz. 1 day, P.
OTTIE 2D, 2118 H. Imp. Milk 54 lbs. 8 oz. 1 day, P. Butter 12 lbs. 4 oz. 7 days, P.
OTTIE 3D, 3021 H. Promoter, 1518 H.; Ottie, 2010 H. Milk 50 lbs 1 day, P.
OTTILLIE, 5383 H. Imp. Milk 54 lbs. 1 day, P.
OUIRANA, 3970 H. F. Van Duren, 142 H. F.; Harrisette, 28 H. F. Milk 1000 lbs. 30 days, P.
OVERLOOPER, 1626 H. Imp. Milk 89 lbs. 1 day, P.; 480 lbs. 7 days, A.R. Butter 3 lbs. 2 oz. 1 day, 21 lbs. 10 oz. 7 days, P.
OVERLOOPER'S MERCEDES, 4517 H. F. Mercedes Prince, 2150 H.; Overlooper, 1626 H. Milk 45 lbs. 2 oz. 1 day P. Butter 15 lbs. 13 oz. 7 days, P.
OWANDAH, 8771 H. Imp. Milk 11,320 lbs. 10 months, P.

PADONIA, 7234 H. Imp. Milk 68 lbs. 1 day, 1996 lbs. 10 oz. 30 days, P.
PALADIN, 9028 H. Imp. Milk 75 lbs. 6 oz. 1 day, 13,117 lbs. 12 oz. 10 months, P. Butter 22 lbs. 13 oz. 7 days, P.
PALME, 1726 H. Imp. Milk 60 lbs. 1 day, P.
PALSKE, 2020 H. F. De Prins, 310 Neth.; Palski, 863 Neth. Milk 52 lbs. 1 day. P.
PANCHA, 7459 H. Imp. Milk 9420 lbs. 8 oz. 10 months, P.
PANHARINO, 9165 H. Imp. Milk 40 lbs. 1 day, P.
PANSYNE, 6923 H. Imp. Milk 1113 lbs 30 days, P.
PARANA ABBEKERK, 9594 H. Imp. Milk 91 lbs. 8 oz. 1 day, 11,546 lbs. 12 oz. 10 months, P. Butter 30 lbs. 8 oz. 7 days, P.
PARANA ABBEKERK 2D, 4500 H. F. Sir Henry of Maplewood, 2033 H.; Parana Abbekerk, 9594 H. Milk 71 lbs. 8 oz. 1 day, 2013 lbs. 12 oz. 30 days, P. Butter 18 lbs. 7 days, P.
PARANA ABBEKERK 5TH, 4590 H. F. Sir Henry of Maplewood, 2033 H.; Parana Abbekerk, 9594 H. Milk 77 lbs. 3 oz. 1 day, P. Butter 30 lbs. 7 days, P.
PARANA ABBEKERK MECHTHILDE, 12599 H. F. Sir Mechthilde, 2224 H. F. Parana Abbekerk 2d, 4500 H. F. Milk 43 lbs. 9 oz. 1 day, P.
PAREPA ROSA, 1294 H. Imp. Milk 56 lbs. 1 day, P.
PARMA GIRL, 1339 H. F. Burley, 394 H.; Leentje 2d, 2784 H. Butter 18 lbs. 13¾ oz. 7 days, P.
PARTELLA, 5981 H. Imp. Milk 37 lbs. 1 day, 1000 lbs. 30 days, P.
PARTHENIA, 1303 H. Imp. Milk 66 lbs. 1 day, 10,732 lbs. 10 oz. 9 months 10 days, P. Butter 38 lbs. 8½ oz. 7 days, P.
PARTHENIA 2D, 3494 H. F. Netherland Prince, 716 H.; Parthenia, 1303 H. Milk 81 lbs. 5 oz. 1 day, 7357 lbs. 8 oz. 9 months, P. Butter 15 lbs. 6 oz. 7 days, P.
PASTELEIN, 2011 H. F. Lincoln 120 Neth.; Pastijn, 4321 Neth. Milk 70 lbs. 1 day, P.
PASTELEINTJE 2D, 977 H. Imp. Milk 87 lbs. 8 oz. 1 day, P.
PASTELIJNTJE GALIS, 737 H. F. Harrington, 2103 H.: Pastelijntje I, 679 Neth. Milk 52 lbs. 15 oz. 1 day, 10,619 lbs. 10 oz. 9 months, A.R. Butter 15 lbs. 4½ oz. 7 days, A.R.
PATIENCE K, 3116 H. Imp. Milk 70 lbs. 1 day, P.
PATRICE ABBEKERK, 9600 H. Imp. Milk 54 lbs. 4 oz. 1 day, 8063 lbs. 8 oz. 10 months, P.
PATSY, 970 H. Imp. Milk 60 lbs. 1 day, 9040 lbs. 2 oz. 1 year, P. Butter 19 lbs. 10 oz. 7 days, A.R
PATSY 3D, 6146 H. F. Prince of Wayne 5th, 1910 H.; Patsy, 970 H. Milk 299 lbs. 8 oz. 7 days, P. Butter 21 lbs. 7 days, A.R.
PAULA, 200 H. Imp. Milk 82 lbs. 8 oz. 1 day, P. Butter 16 lbs. 12 oz. 7 days, P.
PAULA 2D, 421 H. Sir William, 155 H.; Paula, 200 H. Milk 68 lbs. 1 day, P.
PAULA 3D, 1030 H. Sir William, 155 H.; Paula, 200 H. Milk 57 lbs. 8 oz. 1 day, P. Butter 24 lbs. 12 oz. 7 days, P.
PAULA BOONSTRA, 12169 H. F. Prince of Paula, 1517 H. F.; Boonstra 3d, 3617 H. Milk 84 lbs. 8 oz. 1 day, P.
PAULINA, 1016 D. F. Willem, 204 F. H.; Emma, 864 F. H. Milk 80 lbs. 2 oz. 1 day, P.
PAULINE, 422 H. Heidelberg, 110 H.; Dorothea, 118 H. Milk 58 lbs. 8 oz. 1 day, P.
PAULINE 3D, 425 D. F. Nicolaas 2d, 29 M. R.; Pauline 2d, 18 A. R. Milk 48 lbs. 1 day, P.
PAULINE PAUL, 2109 H. Climax, 204 H.; Johanna Paul, 677 H. Milk 70 lbs. 1 day, P.; 18,649 lbs. 9 oz. 1 year, A.R. Butter 128 lbs. 13 oz. 30 days, 1,153 lbs. 5½, oz. 1 year, A.R.
PAULINE PAUL AMERICA, 28302 H. F. Paul De Kol, 14634 H. F.; America 2d, 10509 H. F Milk 45 lbs. 6 oz. 1 day, P.; 9,076 lbs. 1 oz. 1 year, A.R. Butter 13 lbs. 5 4-5 oz. 7 days, A.R.
PAULINE PAUL GRANT, 35053 H. F. Paul De Kol, 14634 H. F.; Nellie Grant 4th, 6624 H. Milk 52 lbs. 12 oz. 1 day, 5,149 lbs, 14 oz. 4 months, P. Butter 13 lbs. 1¾ oz. 7 days, P.
PAVIA, 7102 H. Imp. Milk 10,510 lbs. 12 oz. 10 months, A.R.
PAYNE'S LADY DE VRIES, 5895 H. Imp. Milk 91 lbs. 12 oz. 1 day, 18,848 lbs. 4 oz. 1 year, P.
PAYNE'S LADY DE VRIES 2D, 9034 H Commodore Perry, 2967 H.; Payne's Lady De Vries, 5895 H. Milk 72 lbs. 1 day, P.
PEARL ROOKER, 6405 H. F. Kenmore Boy. 4576 H.; Eliza Rocker, 9884 H. Milk 40 lbs. 1 day, 7485 lbs. 14 oz. 9 months, P.
PEEP, 8707 H. F. Billy Bawn, 3087 H.; Rustic Lass 2d, 2101 H. Milk 8055 lbs. 2 oz. 9 months, A.R.
PEL 4TH, 525 D. F. Wiersma, 10 F. Pel 2d. Milk 68 lbs. 8 oz. 1 day, P.
PENINGA, 5211 H. Imp. Milk 86 lbs. 12 oz. 1 day, 18,077 lbs. 4 oz. 1 year, P. Butter 19 lbs. 9 oz. 7 days, P.

PENOPA, 10391 H. Imp. Milk 70 lbs. 1 day, 7859 lbs. 5 oz. 10 months, 18 days, P.
PENSEROSA, 9562 H. Imp. Milk 43 lbs. 12 oz. 1 day, 1120 lbs. 1 month, P.
PERFECTION, 572 H. Imp. Milk 70 lbs. 1 day, 9189 lbs. 1 year, P.
PERFECTION 2D, 6843 H.; Lord Asnley, 2556 H.; Perfection, 572 H. Milk 74 lbs. 1 day, P.
PERRINE, 9343 H. Imp. Milk 48 lbs. 8 oz. 1 day, P.
PERSUA, 2961 H. Milk 7529 lbs. 12 oz. 10 months, P.
PESCE, 2011 F. H. Imp. Milk 50 lbs. 1 day, P.
PET, 900 H. Imp. Milk 70 lbs. 13 oz. 1 day, P.
PETERINA, 2960 H. Imp. Milk 75 lbs. 1 day, P.
PETERINA 2D, 12177 H. F. Billy Boelyn, 189 H.; Peterina, 2960 H. Milk 75 lbs. 1 day, 13,666 lbs. 4 oz. 1 year, P. Butter 15 lbs. 8 oz. 7 days, P.
PETERNELLA, 540 H. Imp. Milk 82 lbs. 5 oz. 1 day, P.
PET LEE, 2506 H. Imp. Milk 60 lbs. 1 day, P.
PETQUI, 7401 H. Imp. Milk 60 lbs. 1 day, P.
PETREA 2D, 10160 H. Jaap, 452 H.; Petrea, 5362 H. Milk 295 lbs. 11 oz. 10 days, A.R. Butter 14 lbs. 12 oz. 7 days, A.R.
PET TEXELAAR 2D, 7429 H. Wilde Oscar, 1322 H.; Pet Texelaar, 2307 H. Butter 2.37 lbs. 1 day, P.
PETTIE, 624 D. F. Imp. Milk 73 lbs. 12 oz. 1 day, P.
PETULA, 2855 H. Wouter 3d, 80 Neth.; Jannek, 30 Neth. Milk 32 lbs. 6 oz. 1 day, 7793 lbs. 7 oz. 10 months, 4 days, P.
PETUNIA, 2859 H. Imp. Milk 64 lbs. 5 oz. 1 day, 11,505 lbs. 2 oz. 10 months, P.
PHEBE LINCOLN, 10030 H. Imp. Milk 10,058 lbs. 1 year, P. Butter 11 lbs. 2 oz. 7 days, P.
PHEBE S, 4047 H. Imp. Milk 70 lbs. 2 oz. 1 day, 2703 lbs. 2 oz. 60 days, P. Butter 13 lbs. 11½ oz. 7 days, P.
PHILENE, 2194 H. Banjo, 504 H.; Prudence, 883 H. Milk 52 lbs. 1 day, P.
PHILIDORA, 6926 H. Imp. Milk 70 lbs. 8 oz. 1 day, A.R.; 668 lbs. 8 oz. 10 days, A.R. Butter 17 lbs. 3 oz. 7 days, A.R.
PHILPAIL, 10406 H. Imp. Milk 70 lbs. 1 day, P. Butter 18 lbs. 2 oz. 7 days, P.
PHOEBA ZEEMAN, 919 H. F. Imp. Milk 43 lbs. 10 oz. 1 day, P.
PHOEBA ZEEMAN 2D, 9169 H. F. Prairie Aaggie Prince, 2 H. F.; Phoeba Zeeman, 919 H. F. Milk 41 lbs. 12 oz. 1 day, P.
PICKANINNY, 8844 H. Imp. Butter 22 lbs. 7 days, P.
PIERKJE, 2222 H. Imp. Milk 76 lbs. 1 day, P.
PIERKJE 2D, 6671 H. F. Sir Edwin of Aaggie, 1801 H.; Pierkje, 2222 H. Milk 34 lbs. 12 oz. 1 day, P.
PIERSMA, 5730 H. Imp. Milk 91 lbs. 12 oz. 1 day, 12,507 lbs. 12 oz., P. Butter 14 lbs. 7 oz. 7 days, P.
PIETERTJE 2D, 3273 H. Imp. Milk 112 lbs. 7 oz. 1 day, 30,318 lbs. 8 oz. 1 year, A.R.
PIETERTJE 3D, 11244 H. F. Keyes 6th, 1692 H.; Pietertje 2d, 3273 H. Milk 60 lbs. 14 oz. 1 day, A.R.; 24,126 lbs. 2 oz. 1 year, P. Butter 27 lbs. 8½ oz. 7 days, P.; 110 lbs. 6½ oz. 30 days, A.R.
PIETERTJE 4TH, 11245 H. F. Netherland Duke, 1571 H.; Pietertje 2d, 3273 H. Milk 54 lbs. 4 oz. 1 day, 15,034 lbs. 2 oz. 1 year, A.R. Butter 22 lbs. 1½ oz. 7 days, P.
PIETERTJE 5TH, 11246 H. F. Netherland Duke, 1571 H.; Pietertje 2d, 3273 H. Butter 13 lbs. 3 oz. 7 days, P.
PIETERTJE HENGERVELD, 24137 H. F. Milla's Pietertje Netherland, 7825 H. F.; Netherland Hengerveld, 13106 H. F. Milk 492 lbs. 2 oz. 7 days, A.R. Butter 21 lbs. 12 oz. 7 days, A.R.
PIETERTJE KEKKE, 28352 H. F. Milla's Pietertje Netherland, 7825 H. F.; Kekke 3d, 887 D. F. Milk 207 lbs. 7 days, A.R. Butter 12 lbs. 6 oz. 7 days, A.R.
PIETJE, 253 D. F. Gerritt; Tietje. Milk 89 lbs. 1 day, P.
PIETJE 2D, 3271 H. Imp. Milk 53 lbs. 1 day, P.
PIETJE PIERSMA, 5478 H. Imp. Milk 44 lbs. 1 day, 1227 lbs. 1 month, P.
PINAFORE, 557 H. Uncle Tom, 163 H.; Lady Jane, 356 H. Milk 31 lbs. 1 day, P.
PINK, 555 H. Imp. Milk 40 lbs. 1 day, P.
PINK DE LAAG, 5704 H. Imp. Milk 80 lbs. 1 day, P.
PLEASANT VALLEY MAID, 9431 H. Imp. Milk 744 lbs. 10 days, A.R. Butter 29 lbs. 7 days, P.
PLEASANT VALLEY MAID 2D, 2860 H. F. Sir Duke, 4458 H.; Pleasant Valley Maid, 9431 H. Milk 8050 lbs. 14 oz. 10 months, A.R.
PLEDGE, 1506 H. Billy Boelyn, 189 H.; Plenty, 542 H. Milk 110 lbs. 8 oz. 1 day, P. Butter 19 lbs. 9 oz. 7 days, P.
PLUM, 4161 H. Empire, 588 H.; Plenty, 542 H. Milk 70 lbs. 1 day, P.
POEM, 1430 H. Uncle Tom, 163 H.; Prudence, 883 H. Milk 70 lbs. 1 day, P.
POLARIA, 7911 H. Imp. Milk 75 lbs. 1 day, P.
POLIANTHUS, 0921 H. Imp. Milk 57 lbs. 1 day, 13,100 lbs. 2 oz. 1 year, P.
POLINDA, 9281 H. F. Billy Draper, 479 H. F.; Durkette, 1916 H. F. Milk 44 lbs. 1 day, P.
POLLY JEFFERSON, 11112 H. F. Jan Wit 13th, 633 H. F.; Memento 4th, 2078 H. Milk 43 lbs. 1 day, 8746 lbs. 4 oz. 10 months, A.R. Butter 12 lbs. 1 oz. 7 days, A.R.
POND LILY, 10220 H. Keyes 6th, 1692 H.; Sietske S, 4892 H. Milk 45 lbs. 1 day, 280 lbs. 7 days, P. Butter 13 lbs. 4 oz. 7 days, P.
POND LILY, 2D, 10562 H. F. Balsam Prince, 1493 H. F.; Pond Lily, 10220 H. Milk 55 lbs. 1 day, P. Butter 12 lbs. 7 days P.
POPPY, 1745 H. Imp. Milk 65 lbs. 1 day, P.
POPPY 2D, 5913 H. Napoleon, 706 H.; Poppy, 1745 H. Milk 58 lbs. 1 day, P.
POPPY 4TH, 9266 H. F. Mercedes' Mahomet, 2943 H.; Poppy, 1745 H. Milk 1022 lbs. 90 days, P.
PORCELAIN, 201 H. Imp. Milk 80 lbs. 8. oz. 1 day, P.
PORCELEIN, 6071 H. Gerritt, 31 Neth.; Porcelein, 147 Neth. Milk 85 lbs. 1 day, P. Butter 21 lbs. 8 oz. 7 days, P.
PORCELEINTJE, 568 H. Imp. Milk 64 lbs. 9 oz. 1 day, 10,586 lbs. 3 oz. 9 months, P.
PORSELEINTJE 3D, 547 D. F. Imp. Milk 72 lbs. 6 oz. 1 day, P.
PORTER LOWRY, 10547 H. F. Netherland Convoy, 2934 H.; Elsie Chester, 4370 H. Milk 31 lbs. 8 oz. 1 day, P.
POSMA, 3061 H. F. Imp. Milk 65 lbs. 1 day, P.
POYNERITJE, 8264 H. F. Albert 493 F.; Zwarthak, 1647 F. Milk 79 lbs. 1 day, 2005 lbs. 30 days, P. Butter 23 lbs. 13 oz. 7 days, P.
PRAIRIE BELLE, 1800 H. Imp. Milk 70 lbs. 6 oz. 1 day, P. Butter 713 lbs. 4 oz. 7 days, P.
PRAIRIE FLOWER, 902 H. Imp. Milk 65 lbs. 12 oz. 1 day, 13,012 lbs. 3 oz. 1 year, P. Butter 20 lbs. 1 oz. 7 days, 81 lbs. 10½ oz. 30 days, A.R.

PRAIRIE FLOWER'S PAULINE PAUL, 32257 H. F. Paul De Kol, 14634 H. F.; Prairie Flower, 462 H. Milk 42 lbs. 6 oz. 1 day, P.; 8096 lbs. 8 oz. 8 months, 25 days, A.R. Butter 10 lbs. 12 oz. 7 days, A.R.
PRICELESS, 959 H. Imp. Milk 62 lbs. 10 oz. 1 day, 8250 lbs. 1 year, P. Butter 14 lbs. 8 oz. 7 days, P.
PRIDE, 5376 H. Imp. Milk 48 lbs. 1 day, 10.097 lbs. 12 oz. 1 year, P.
PRIDE O'DEE, 4993 H. Panic, 871 H.; Cora Belle Spaanz, 2077 H. Butter 16 lbs. 7 days, A.R.
PRIDE OF BEEMSTER, 424 H. Imp. Milk 55 lbs. 4 oz. 1 day, 12,750 lbs. 1 year, P.
PRIDE OF HERKIMER, 623 H. Chieftan 4th, 946 H.; Maid of Herkimer, 3331 H. Milk 58 lbs. 4 oz. 1 day, 15,439 lbs. 1 year, A.R. Butter 16 lbs. 2 oz. 7 days, A.R.
PRIDE OF LANCASTER, 2540 H. F. Mooie Twisk, 85 D. F.; Bakker 2d, 215 D. F. Milk 60 lbs. 1 day, P.
PRIDE OF TWISK, 920 H. Imp. Milk 88 lbs. 1 day, P. Butter 3 lbs. 8 oz 1 day, 30 lbs. 8 oz. 7 days, P.
PRIMA DONNA, 889 H. Imp. Milk 38 lbs. 9 oz. 1 day, 7,494 lbs. 7 oz. 361 days, P.
PRIMROSE, 202 H. Imp. Hedwig, 189 H. Milk 6,881 lbs. 6 oz. 11 months, P.
PRIMROSE 2D, 2935 H. Col. Fox, 206 H.; Primrose 202 H. Milk 60 lbs. 1 day, 408 lbs. 6 oz. 7 days, P. Butter 18 lbs. 9 oz. 7 days, A.R.
PRIMROSE LINCOLN, 10028 H. Lincoln, 120 Neth. Milk 6,881 lbs. 6 oz. 11 months, P. Butter 21 lbs. 7 days, P.
PRINCE OF TWISK'S ANTRIM, 7564 H. F. Prince of Twisk, 1055 H.; Antrim 2d, 246 H. Butter 14 lbs. 1½ oz. 7 days, A.R.
PRINCESS, 203 H. Hollander, 112 H.; Lady Tolsma, 167 H. Milk 80 lbs. 1 day, P.
PRINCESS AAGGIE, 3548 H. Neptune. 711 H.; Princess of Wayne 3d, 1315 H. Milk 54 lbs. 12 oz. 1 day, P.; 10,802 lbs. 15 oz. 1 year, P. Butter 16 lbs. 3½ oz. 7 days, P.
PRINCESS AAGGIE'S PAULINE DE KOL, 35056 H. F. Paul De Kol, 14634 H. F.; Princess Aaggie, 3548 H. Butter 9 lbs. 13½ oz. 7 days, P.
PRINCESS BESS, 2211 H. Billy Boelyn, 180 H.; Queen Bess, 429 H. Milk 51 lbs. 8 oz. 1 day, P. Butter 10 lbs. 7 days, P.
PRINCESS DE BRAVE HENDRIK, 3826 H. F. De Brave Hendrik, 230 H. F.; Eefje, 5085 Neth. Milk 261 lbs. 8 oz. 7 days, P. Butter 10 lbs. 8 oz. 7 days, P.
PRINCESS GALATIA, 27808 H. F. Sir Henry of Maplewood, 2033 H.; Galatia 2d, 4588 H. F. Milk 30 lbs. 8 oz. 1 day, P.
PRINCESS HOLLANDER, 9595 H. F. Sir Henry of Maplewood, 2033 H.; Hollander 2d, 5782 H. Milk 60 lbs. 14 oz. 1 day, P. Butter 2 lbs. 3 oz. 1 day, P.
PRINCESS IDALINE, 4996 H. Netherland Prince, 716 H.; Idalina, 2751 H. Milk 58 lbs. 8 oz. 1 day, 1,487 lbs. 8 oz. 30 days, P. Butter 10 lbs. 5½ oz. 7 days, P.
PRINCESS IDALINE'S CLOTHILDE, 16528 H. F. Clothilde 4th's Imperial, 1281 H. F.; Princess Idaline, 4996 H. Milk 9893 lbs. 2 oz. 10 months, 20 days, P.
PRINCESS IDLEWILD, 457 H. F. Idlewild, 1598 H.; Lady Ashley, 4374 H. Milk 40 lbs. 1 day, P.
PRINCESS MARGARET, 5256 H. Prince of Edom, 1076 H.; Prima Donna, 889 H. Milk 60 lbs. 1 day, P. Butter 20 lbs. 1½ oz. 7 days, P.
PRINCESS MARGARET 3D, 9558 H. F. Windsor, 1316 H.; Princess Margaret, 5256 H. Milk 363 lbs. 10 days, P.
PRINCESS NAPRAXINE, 6167 H. F. Kremlin, 1145 H.; Pascalina, 4072 H. Butter 12 lbs. 12½ oz. 7 days, A.R.
PRINCESS NICOLINA 3D, 2125 H. F. Sphinx, 1956 H.: Princess Nicolina, 3087 H. Milk 42 lbs. 1 day, P.
PRINCESS NICOLINA 4TH, 5414 H. F. Oakland Chief, 3259 H.; Princess Nicolina, 3087 H. Milk 42 lbs. 1 oz. 1 day; 285 lbs. 11 oz. 7 days, P. Butter 15 lbs. 2 oz. 7 days, P.
PRINCESS OF FRIESLAND, 10305 H. Imp. Milk 78 lbs. 8 oz. 1 day, P. Butter 21 lbs. 7 days, P.
PRIDE OF LANCASTER, 2549 H. F. Mooie Twisk, 85 D. F.; Bakker 2d, 215 D. F. Milk 60 lbs. 1 day, P.
PRINCESS OF VERONA, 8217 H. F. Neptune Fairview, 3886 H.; Mantel 3d, 2148 H. Milk 64½ lbs. 8 oz. 9 months, 20 days, P.
PRINCESS OF WAYNE, 954 H. Imp. Milk 113 lbs. 1 oz. 1 day, 29,008 lbs. 11 oz. 1 year, A.R. Butter 24 lbs. 14 oz. 7 days, 91 lbs. 8 oz. 30 days, A.R.
PRINCESS OF WAYNE 3D, 1315 H. Burly, 304 H.; Princess of Wayne, 954 H. Milk 83 lbs. 15 oz. 1 day, 19,122 lbs. 8 oz. 1 year, A.R. Butter 18 lbs. 12 oz. 7 days, 76 lbs. 12½ oz. 30 days, A.R.
PRINCESS OF WAYNE 4TH, 2339 H. Burly. 304 H.; Princess of Wayne, 954 H. Milk 71 lbs. 8 oz. 1 day, 14,010 lbs. 11 oz. 1 year, A.R. Butter 19 lbs. 8 oz. 7 days, A.R.
PRINCESS OF WAYNE 5TH, 5912 H. Lad of Walworth, 729 H.; Princess of Wayne, 954 H. Milk 68 lbs. 1 day, 11,765 lbs. 8 oz. 10 months, A.R. Butter 21 lbs. 15 oz. 7 days, A.R.
PRINCESS OF WAYNE 5TH'S AAGGIE, 4974 H. F. Royal Aaggie, 3463 H.; Princess of Wayne 5th, 5912 H. Milk 51 lbs. 6 oz. 1 day, 12,458 lbs. 1 year, P. Butter 14 lbs. 12 oz. 7 days, P.
PRINCESS OF WAYNE 7TH, 29690 H. F. Paul De Kol, 14634 H. F.; Princess of Wayne, 954 H. Milk 65 lbs. 1 oz. 1 day, 10,988 lbs. 14 oz. 9 months 15 days, P. Butter 9 lbs. 6 oz. 7 days, A.R.
PRINCESS PARTHENEA, 12091 H. F. Prince Wayne Mercedes' Echo, 2328 H.; Parthenea 2d, 4589 H. F. Milk 46 lbs. 1 day, P. Butter 2 lbs. 7 oz. 1 day, P.
PRINCESS PARTHENEA'S COLANTHA, 21388 H. F. Colantha's Sir Henry, 3733 H. F.; Princess Parthenea, 12091 H. F. Milk 52 lbs. 1 day, P.
PRINCESS ROSAMOND, 2868 H. Imp. Milk 50 lbs. 1 day, 6501 lbs. 11 months 19 days, P.
PRINCESS ROSAMOND 2D, 3506 H. Imp. Milk 50 lbs. 7 days, P.
PROMOTER'S NORTHERN STAR, 12392 H. F. Promoter, 1518 H.; Northern Star, 2935 H. Milk 403 lbs. 12 oz. 10 days, A.R.
PROSPERINE, 1475 D. F. Jacob, 207 F.; Pietje, 1367 H. Milk 56 lbs. 1 day, P.
PRUDENCE 2D, 8863 H. Kane, 564 H.; Prudence, 883 H. Milk 50 lbs. 1 day, P.
PRUNELLA, 2871 H. Imp. Milk 31 lbs. 13 oz. 1 day, 5440 lbs. 13 oz. 6 months 28 days, P.
PUSSY TIP TOES, 1497 H. F. Empyrean, 1006 H.; Hetty, 927 H. Milk 7009 lbs. 11 oz. 1 year, P.
PYPER, 10308 H. Imp. Milk 88 lbs. 1 day, 16,600 lbs. 10 months, P. Butter 19 lbs. 4 oz. 7 days, P.

QUALITY 2D. 12188 H. F. De Brave Hendrik, 230 H. F.; Quality, 8842 H. Milk 38 lbs. 1 day, P.
QUANTOCK, 7182 H. Imp. Milk 12,250 lbs. 4 oz. 1 year, A.R.
QUEEN ANNE, 1256 H. Imp. Milk 50 lbs. 1 day, 1306 lbs. 30 days, P.
QUEEN BELLE, 7769 H. F. Jacob W't 2662 H.; Juanita, 5025 H. Milk 42 lbs. 1 day, 408 lbs. 10 days, P.
QUEEN BESS, 429 H. Imp. Milk 84 lbs. 1 day, 11,000 lbs. 1 year, P. Butter 19 lbs. 7 days, P.
QUEEN ELSIE, 2081 H. Geneva Duke, 254 H.; Almina, 699 H. Milk 45 lbs. 8 oz. 1 day, 2535 lbs. 60 days, P.

QUEEN OF ASHLEY, 1509 H. Leander, 520 H.; Perfection, 572 H. Milk 2108 lbs. 30 days, P. Butter 20 lbs. 13 oz. 7 days, P.
QUEEN OF BUCHANAN, 6183 H. Chieftan 4th, 946 H.; Saunell, 683 H. Butter 19 lbs. 1 oz. 7 days, A.R.
QUEEN OF KENNETT, 6028 H. Imp. Milk 71 lbs, 8 oz. 1 day, 1858 lbs. 8 oz. 30 days, A.R. Butter 3 lbs. 8 oz. 1 day, P ; 20 lbs. 8 oz. 7 days, A.R.
QUEEN OF LAKEVIEW, 7254 H. Imp. Milk 79 lbs. 1 day, P.
QUEEN OF PACIFIC, 626 H. F. Imp. Milk 765 lbs. 10 days, A.R.; 13,341 lbs. 10 months, A.R.
QUEEN OF SYRACUSE, 1258 H. Imp. Milk 65 lbs. 1 day, P.
QUEEN OF THE HILL, 1244 H. Imp. Milk 76 lbs. 1 day, P; Butter 21 lbs. 4 oz. 8 days, A.R.
QUEEN OF THE HILL 2D, 2391 H. Imp. Milk 70 lbs. 1 day, 1002 lbs. 30 days, P. Butter 2 lbs. 8 oz. 1 day, P.
QUEEN OF THE HILL 3D, 2149 H. Ranger, 635 H.; Queen of the Hill, 1244 H. Butter 2 lbs. 1 day, P.
QUEEN OF THE HILL 4TH, 3793 H. Malcolm, 006 H.; Queen of the Hill, 1244 H. Milk 75 lbs. 1 day, 5341 lbs. 90 days, P. Butter 3 lbs. 9 oz 1 day. 23 lbs. 7 days, 91 lbs. 8 oz. 31 days, P.
QUEEN OF THE VALLEY 4TH 1284 H. F. Lad of Prescott, 2389 H.; Queen of the Valley, 430½ H. Milk 7942 lbs, 12 oz. 10 months, A. R.
QUEEN OF WAYNE, 955 H. Imp. Milk 75 lbs. 8 oz. 1 day, 14,506 lbs, 2 oz. 1 year, P. Butter 17 lbs. 4 oz. 7 days, A.R.
QUEEN OF WAYNE 2D, 6682 H. Burly, 894 H ; Queen of Wayne 955, H. Milk 62 lbs. 9 oz. 1 day, 11,567 lbs. 11 oz. 1 year, P. Butter 16 lbs. 6½ oz. 7 days, P.
QUEEN SKUNK, 431 H. Oost Dyke, 130 H.; Holland Queen, 144 H. Milk 9351 lbs. 3 oz. 1 year, P.
QUETTA, 7382 H. Imp. Milk 58 lbs. 1 day, P.
QUIZ, 7168 H. Imp. Milk 64 lbs. 1 day, 10,859 lbs. 11 months 10 days, P.

RACHEL ADINE B, 16356 H. F. Promoter, 1518 H.; Rachel Adine, 5611 H. Milk 45 lbs. 14 oz. 1 day, 425 lbs. 1 oz. 10 days, P.
RAG APPLE, 1286 H. F. Lad of Prescott, 2389 H.; Fiirstinn, 1596 H. Milk 9652 lbs. 4 oz. 10 months, A.R.
RALMER, 9554 H. Lincoln, 120 Neth.; Imp. Milk 15,000 lbs. 1 year, P.
RAMONA, 265 H. F. Constantyn, 2040 H.; Louisiana, 6609 H. Milk 63 lbs. 10 oz. 1 day, 359 lbs. 10 days, P. Butter 2 lbs. 6 oz. 1 day, P.
RANGELEY, 19032 H. F. Jonge Bloemhof, 751 F.; Johanna, 1270 F. Milk 49 lbs. 1 day, 1127 lbs. 30 days, P.
RAPHAELLA 3D, 22940 H. F. Aaggie Grace's Boy, 7008 H. F.; Raphaella, 6279 H. F. Milk 6987 lbs. 10 months, A.R.
RARA, 142 H. F. Bloemhof, 371 F.; Jan, 2474 F. Milk 387 lbs. 11 oz. 10 days, A.R. Butter 11 lbs. 9 oz. 7 days, A.R.
RARA TRITOMIA MERCEDES, 6913 H. F. Tritomia's Mercedes Prince, 3543 H.; Rara, 142 H. Milk 54 lbs. 8 oz. 1 day, 1596 lbs. 1 month, P. Butter 11 lbs. 9 oz. 7 days, P.
RAVENWOOD, 1373 H. Uncle Tom, 163 H.; Coquette, 000 H. Milk 85 lbs. 1 day, P. Butter 21 lbs. 6 oz. 7 days, P.
REBECCA, 433 H. Imp. Milk 7899 lbs 272 days, P.
REBECCA EGMOND, 6457 H. Imp. Milk 69 lbs. 12 oz. 1 day, P.; 12,038 lbs. 2½ oz. 10 months, A.R.
REESMON 3D, 4745 H. Johannis, 428 H.; Reesmow 2d, 1238 H. Milk 71 lbs. 1 day, 10,332 lbs. 10 months, P.
REESMON 3D A, 2444 H. F. Copia's Empire, 3559 H.; Reesmow 3d, 4745 H. Milk 71 lbs. 1 day, 11,818 lbs. 10 months, P.
REESMON 3D B, 9119 H. F. Copia's Empire, 3559 H ; Reesmow 3d, 4745 H. Milk 38 lbs. 1 day, 6637 lbs. 9 months 15 days, P.
REESMON 3D C, 14248 H. F. Hilda's Empire, 3562 H.; Reesmow 3d, 4745 H. Milk 2163 lbs. 6 months 14 days, P.
REESMON 3D D, 18030 H. F. Hilda's Empire, 3562 H.; Reesmow 3d, 4745 H. Milk 1673 lbs. 6 months 17 days, P.
REESMON 4TH A, 18045 H. F. Copia's Empire, 3559 H.; Reesmon 4th, 8482 H. Milk 28 lbs. 1 day, P.
REGIS, 5764 H. Imp. Butter 17 lbs. 12 oz. 7 days, A.R.
REGOLA, 4501 H. Imp. Milk 66 lbs. 1 day, 7741 lbs. 6 months, P. Butter 11 lbs. 9 oz. 7 days, P.
REGOLA 4TH, 14993 H. F. Zymel's Barrington, 1841 H. F.; Regola, 4501 H. Milk 50 lbs. 8 oz. 1 day, 477 lbs. 10 oz. 10 days, P.
REINTJE, 5367 H. Imp. Milk 50 lbs. 1 day, P.
REISINGA, 6522 H. F. De Brave Hendrik, 230 H. F.; Blokker 2d, 6409 H. Milk 40 lbs. 8 oz. 1 day, 9103 lbs. 8 oz. 1 year, P.
REMMETJE, 2012 H. F. Eillem 3d, 375 Neth.; Remmetje, 3876 Neth. Milk 12,035 lbs. 10 months, 24 days, P.
RENELLA ABBEKERK, 9587 H. Abbekerk, 206 Neth. Imp. Milk 10,030 lbs. 8 oz. 10 months, P. Butter 11 lbs. 12 oz. 7 days, P.
RENIE, 9349 H. Imp. Milk 50 lbs. 1 day, P.
RENSKE, 77 D. F. Imp. Milk 50 lbs. 1 day, P.
RENSKE 2D, 231 D. F. Mooie, 26 M. R.; Renske, 77 M. R. Butter 49 lbs. 2 oz. 21 days, A.R.
REPITA, 6521 H. F. Imp. Milk 36 lbs. 1 day, 5000 lbs. 6 months, P.
RESERVE PRINCESS, 5250 H. F. Consolation, 2661 H.; Ottillie, 5383 H. Milk 54 lbs. 1 day, P.
RHEA, 5292 H. Herman; Dan Marie. Milk 70 lbs. 1 day, P.
RHODA, 434 H. Roland, 144 H ; Texelaar 8th, 55 H. Milk 96 lbs. 12 oz. 1 day, 21,309 lbs. 1 year, P. Butter 23 lbs. 7 days, P.
RHODA CLIFDEN, 1110 H. F. Lord Clifden, 572 H.; Vesta of Potsdam, 470 H Milk 961 lbs. 10 days, A.R. Butter 27 lbs. 4 oz. 7 days, A.R.
RHODA 3D, 8203 H. Constantyn, 2040 H.; Rhoda, 434 H. Milk 66 lbs. 2 oz. 1 day, 406 lbs. 12 oz. 10 days, P. Butter 28 lbs. 1 day, P.
RHODOPE, 5303 H. Imp. Milk 72 lbs. 1 day, P.
RHOEBE H, 5228 H. Imp. Milk 89 lbs. 8 oz. 1 day, 10,260 lbs. 1 year, P. Butter 17 lbs. 11 oz. 7 days, P.
RICA, 7312 H. Imp. Milk 64 lbs. 1 day, 13,506 lbs. 9 months 18 days, P.
RIJANETA, 1131 H. Pilgrim, 317 H.; Janet, 758 H Milk 706 lbs. 8 oz. 10 days, 2013 lbs. 6 oz. 30 days, A.R. Butter 2 lbs. 1 day, P.; 30 lbs. 7 oz. 10 days, A.R.
RIJANETA 2D, 8416 H. Don Quixote, 1324 H.; Rijaneta, 1131 H. Butter 19 lbs. 12½ oz. 7 days, A.R.
RINDERTJE, 1522 D. F. Groote Pier, 194 F. H.; Rintje, 1032 F. H. Milk 6,852 lbs. 7 oz. 8 months 10 days, A.R.

RINGWALDA, 8919 H. Imp. Milk 8,700 lbs. 11 months 6 days, P.
RINTJE, 5357 H. Imp. Milk 40 lbs. 1 day, P.
RISTORI, 1890 H. Imp. Milk 38 lbs. 12 oz. 1 day, 8,744 lbs. 9 months 28 days, P.
RIXA SILVA, 1524 H. F. Mazda, 2672 F.; Silva Flora, 3853 H. Milk 79 lbs. 12 oz. 1 day, 2,190 lbs. 30 days, P.
ROBERTA, 2401 H. Apollo, 402 H.; Jessie, 342 H. Milk 45 lbs. 1 day, P.
ROCHELLE, 2876 H. Imp. Milk 58 lbs. 1 day, P.
ROCHESTER PRINCESS, 2706 H. Imp. Milk 64 lbs. 12 oz. 1 day, 13,837 lbs. 11 oz. 10 months, A.R. Butter 20 lbs. 11½ oz. 7 days, A.R.
ROE, 6011 H. Imp. Milk 42 lbs. 8 oz. 1 day, 12,267 lbs. 5 oz. 11 months 28 days, P. Butter 21 lbs. 14 oz. 7 days, A.R.; 52 lbs. 8 oz. 30 days, P.
ROETTA, 10392 H. Imp. Milk 38 lbs. 8 oz. 1 day, 7,093 lbs 11 months 7 days, P.
ROLOWESTRA, 1734 D. F. Roelof, 12C F. H.; Westra 2d, 3390 F. H. Milk 597 lbs. 8 oz. 10 days, P.
ROMELDA, 9351 H. Imp. Milk 50 lbs. 1 day, P.
ROMKJE, 1503 D. F. Sije, 264 F.; Trijntje, 871 F. Milk 13,796 lbs. 8 oz. 11 months 13 days, P. Butter 9 lbs. 9 oz. 7 days, A.R.
ROORDA DE GROAT, 1613 D. F. Imp Milk 537 lbs. 10 days, A.R. Butter 18 lbs. 8 oz. 7 days, A.R.
ROSA, 207 H. Imp. Milk 80 lbs. 1 day, P.
ROSA 2D, 208 H. Imp. Milk 1,259 lbs. 30 days, 11,490 lbs. 383 days, P.
ROSA B ARUMMER, 5856 H. Imp. Milk 77 lbs. 1 day, 2008 lbs. 30 days, P. Butter 3 lbs. 1 day, P.
ROSA BEECHWOOD, 3392 H. Prince of Edam, Jr., 1733 H.; Eudora, 3349 H. Butter 25 lbs. 2½ oz. 7 days, P.
ROSABELLE S. 4050 H. Imp. Milk 42 lbs. 8 oz. 1 day, 1213 lbs. 30 days, P.
ROSA BONHEUR, 890 H. Imp. Milk 106 lbs. 12 oz. 1 day, A.R.; 13,411 lbs. 4 oz. 1 year, P. Butter 25 lbs. 6 oz. 7 days, A.R.
ROSA BONHEUR 2D, 1372 H. Uncle Tom, 163 H ; Rosa Bonheur, 890 H. Butter 18 lbs. 8 oz. 7 days, P.
ROSA DARTLE, 1310 H. Imp. Milk 77 lbs. 10 oz. 1 day, 15,000 lbs. 1 year, P.
ROSA HECTOR, 527 H. Hector, 107 H.; Rosa 2d, 208 H. Milk 37 lbs 1 day, P.
ROSA LEE OF SEASIDE, 8963 H. F. Leander, 520 H.; Second Queen of Ashley, 4171 H. Milk 38 lbs. 1 day, P.
ROSALIND, 577 H. Imp. Butter 17 lbs. 6 oz. 7 days, A.R.
ROSALINE, 591 D. F. Imp. Milk 40 lbs. 12 oz. 1 day, 1351 lbs. 30 days, P.
ROSEALTHA. 7041 H. Prince Opperdoes 8th, 847 H.; Melrose, 1733 H. Milk 40 lbs. 1 day, P.
ROSE FAIRFAX, 200 H. F. Lord Battels, 2429 H. F.; Flora Fairfax, 4733 H. Milk 55 lbs. 1 day, P.
ROSE OF DECORAH, 4209 H. Tramp, 878 H.; Lady of Scholtom 5th, 1926 H. Butter 19 lbs. 8 oz. 7 days, P.
ROSE OF LAKESIDE, 2877 H. Imp. Milk 49 lbs 3 oz. 1 day, P.
ROSE OF SHARON, 66 H. F. Decatur, 2034 H.; Idaline, 2751 H. Milk 50 lbs. 1 day, P.
ROSETTA, 2369 H. F. Dennis, 1844 H. Wakazoo, 4728 H. Milk 33 lbs. 1 day, P.
ROSETTA OF SHADELAND 2D, 11451 H. F. Netherland Conqueror, 2476 H.; Rosetta of Shadeland, 2409 H. Milk 6590 lbs. 8 oz. 7 months, A.R.
ROSJE, 5080 H. Imp. Milk 41 lbs. 1 day, P.
ROSY MORN, 1492 H. F. Empyrean, 1006 H.; Dawn, H. Milk 9964 lbs. 1 year, P.
ROWENA AAGGIE, 5512 H. F. Sir Newton of Aaggie, 1858 H.; Rowena B, 2592 H. Butter 18 lbs. 2 oz. 7 days, P.
ROWENA B, 2592 H. Walter Scott, 606 H.; Tattycoram, 1024 H Milk 85 lbs. 1 day, P.; 834 lbs. 10 days, A.R. Butter 24 lbs. 8 oz. 7 days, A.R.
ROXIE, 812 D. F. Imp. Milk 10,416 lbs. 1 year, A. R. Butter 16 lbs. 6 oz. 7 days, A.R.
ROXOBEL, 10220 H. F. Koster 3d's Keyes, 3568 H. F.; Murillo, 5163 H. Milk 46 lbs. 1 day, 451 lbs. 10 days, P. Butter 15 lbs. 11 oz. 7 days, P.
ROZALIA SOMERS, 6940 H. Imp. Milk 12,588 lbs. 13 oz. 1 year, P. Butter 16 lbs. 11½ oz. 7 days, 32 lbs. 14¼ oz. 14 days, A.R.
RULAND, 8424 H. F. Dirk, 33 F. H.; Sietske. 185 F. H. Milk 43 lbs. 1 day, P.
RULAND 2D, 11888 H. F. Koster 3d's Keyes, 3568 H. F.; Ruland, 8424 H. F. Milk 41 lbs. 1 day, 397 lbs. 10 days, P.
RURAL, 5268 H. Imp. Milk 80 lbs. 3 oz. 1 day, P.
RUSTIC LASS 2D, 2101 H. Imp. Milk 58 lbs. 6 oz. 1 day, P.; 11,511 lbs. 8 oz. 9 months, A.R.
RUTH ARTIS, 4517 H. Imp. Milk 38 lbs. 11 oz. 1 day, P.; 11,916 lbs, 11 oz. 1 year, A.R.
RUTH ARTIS 2D, 10385 H. Netherland Prince, 716 H.; Ruth Artis, 4517 H. Milk 5070 lbs. 8 oz. 4 months, 20 days, P. Butter 18 lbs. 9½ oz. 7 days, A.R.
RUTH GATES, 5460 H. Imp. Milk 67 lbs. 8 oz. 1 day, P.; Butter 17 lbs 10 oz. 7 days, A R.
RUTH GATES 2D, 503 H. F. Imp. Milk 40 lbs. 8 oz. 1 day, P. Butter 15 lbs. 4 oz. 7 days, P.
RUTH SEFFINGA, 540 D. F. Imp. Milk 9203 lbs. 11 oz. 10 months, A.R.
RUTHSEF, 4409 H. F. Twisker, 413 D. F.; Ruth Seffinga, 540 D. F. Milk 6788 lbs. 10 months, A.R.

SAAKJE, 2357 H. Galtjo, 1109 H.; Anna Hill, 1183 H. Milk 75 lbs. 1 day, 1972 lbs. 30 days, P.
SAAPKE, 736 H. Imp. Milk 97 lbs. 8 oz. 1 day, 2784 lbs. 13 oz. 30 days, P.
SAAPKE 2D, 6180 H. Tim Lynch, 541 H.; Saapke. 736 H. Milk 84 lbs. 1 day, P.
SAAR 2d, 9371 H. Imp. Milk 8561 lbs. 14 oz. 11 months 28 days, A.R. Butter 9 lbs. 4 oz. 7 days, A.R.
SAARA, 2921 H. Imp. Milk 42 lbs. 1 day, P.
SAARETTE, 11100 H. F. Gerrit, 4280 H.; Saar 2d, 9371 H. Milk 4292 lbs. 10 oz. 5 months 21 days, P.
SAARTJE, 2991 H. Imp. Milk 61 lbs. 1 day, P.
SABRA, 9450 H. Imp. Milk 47 lbs. 8 oz. 1 day, P.
SACHET 2D, 8003 H. F. Billy Boelyn, 189 H.; Sachet, 6110 H. Milk 60 lbs. 1 day, P.
SADIE F, 3308 H. Imp. Milk 50 lbs. 8 oz. 1 day, P.
SADIE PAULINE PAUL, 35054 H. F. Paul de Kol, 14634 H. F.; Sadie Vale 2d, 13449 H. F. Milk 43 lbs. 5 oz. 1 day, 3724 lbs. 2 oz. 3 months 15 days, P. Butter 11 lbs. 11½ oz. 7 days, P.
SADIE VALE, 958 H. Imp. Milk 78 lbs. 1 day, 15,670 lbs. 2 oz. 1 year, P. Butter 23 lbs. 11 oz. 7 days, 90 lbs. 5 oz. 30 days, P.
SADIE VALE 2D, 18449 H. F. Duke Netherland, 1271 H. F.; Sadie Vale, 958 H. Milk 38 lbs. 12 oz. 1 day, A.R.; 11,282 lbs. 6 oz. 1 year, P. Butter 9 lbs. 9 oz. 7 days, A.R.
SADIE VALE CONCORDIA, 32259 H. F. Concordia's American Wayne, 14222 H. F.; Sadie Vale 2d, 18449 H. F. Milk 47 lbs. 2 oz. 1 day, 10,258 lbs. 4 oz. 1 year, P. Butter 13 lbs. 14½ oz. 7 days, A.R.
SADY'S TEAKE, 1821 D. F. Brigham, 244 P. R.; Teake 2d, 388 P. R. Milk 672C lbs. 6 months, P.
ST. CATHERINE, 4488 H. Imp. Milk 55 lbs. 14 oz. 1 day, 4527 lbs. 13 oz. 6 months, P.

ST. LAWRENCE QUEEN, 2567 H. Imp. Milk 45 lbs. 1 day, P.
SALLIE, 2152 H. Pioneer, 319 H.; Belle of Stoesetbania, 1530 H. Milk 45 lbs. 1 day, P.
SALLIE KIRBY, 2879 H. Imp. Milk 78 lbs. 4 oz. 1 day, P.; 6937 lbs. 4 oz. 4 months, A.R. Butter 19 lbs. 7 oz. 7 days, A.R.
SALLY GRAY, 1889 H. Imp. Milk 424 lbs. 8 oz 7 days, P.
SALLY HOOD, 4489 H. Imp. Milk 29 lbs. 12 oz. 1 day, 5309 lbs. 15 oz. 6 months 28½ days, P.
SALVISSA, 7509 H. Imp. Milk 60 lbs. 1 day, P.
SAN, 6577 H. Imp. Milk 52 lbs. 1 day, P.
SANNELL, 683 H. Imp. Milk 3525 lbs. 60 days, P. Butter 18 lbs. 3½ oz. 7 days, A.R.
SANNELL'S PRIDE, 6247 H. F. Jaques, 765 H.; Sannellin, 683 H. Butter 14 lbs. 11 oz. 7 days, P.
SAPPHO, 442 H. Pluto, 133 H.; Juniata, 154 H. Milk 64 lbs. 1 day, 6401 lbs. 15 oz. 6 months, P.
SARA, 717 H. Imp. Milk 81 lbs. 1 day, P.
SARA ARTIS, 4865 H. F. Artis, 127 Neth.; Sara, 2031 Neth. Milk 10,132 lbs. 4 oz. 1 year, P. Butter 21 lbs. 2 oz. 7 days, P.
SARNIA, 8089 H. Imp. Milk 78 lbs. 1 day, 1504 lbs. 1 month, P.
SATELLA, 2882 H. Imp. Butter 1 lb. 7½ oz. 1 day, P.
SATINETTE, 2885 H. Imp. Milk 59 lbs. 1 day, P. Butter 3 lbs. 8 oz. 2 days, P.
SAXAFRAGIA, 6974 H. Imp. Milk 50 lbs. 11 oz. 1 day, P.; 12,536 lbs. 1 year, A.R. Butter 9 lbs. 14 oz. 7 days, A.R.
SCHANK 2D, 5024 H. Imp. Milk 68 lbs. 1 day, 1959 lbs. 30 days, P.
SCHENK, 1405 H. Imp. Milk 77 lbs. 13 oz. 1 day, P.
SCHERMEER, 9357 H. Imp. Milk 72 lbs. 1 day, P. Butter 3 lbs. 1 day, P.
SCHERMER MAID, 4071 H. Imp. Milk 10,811 lbs. 9 months, P.
SCHOONE, 5995 H. Imp Milk 452 lbs. 11 oz. 7 days, A.R. Butter 18 lbs. 14 oz. 7 days, A.R.
SCHUILING, 3350 H. F. Imp. Milk 88 lbs. 1 day, 7000 lbs. 100 days, P.
SCHUILING 4TH, 14995 H. F. Zymel's Barrington, 1841 H. F.; Schuiling, 3350 H. F. Milk 45 lbs. 1 day, P.
SCIOTO GIRL, 8208 H. Netherland Prince, 716 H.; Adelaide, 1257 H. Milk 74 lbs. 4 oz. 1 day, 2521 lbs. 30 days, P.
SEALAMORE, 8427 H. F. Karel, 583 F.; Sibbeltje, 2003 F. Milk 45 lbs. 1 day, 1275 lbs. 30 days, P.
SEALCHI, 3959 H. Bantam, 1011 H.; Rosabel, 89 H. Milk 40 lbs. 1 day, P.
SEATACK, 8426 H. F. Beijma, 428 F.; Grietje, 134 F. Milk 61 lbs. 1 day, 1151 lbs 30 days, P. Butter 19 lbs. 11 oz. 7 days, P.
SEBIA, 5397 H. Imp. Milk 28 lbs. 3½ oz. 7 days, A.R.
SECOND MAID OF TWISK, 3866 H. Elswout, 94 H.; Maid of Twisk, 3318 H. Milk 8432 lbs. 8 oz. 1 year, P.
SECOND MARIANNA BEETS, 16 D. F. Burgomaster of Beemster, 1 D. F.; Marianna Beets, 7 D. F. Milk 96 lbs. 1 day, 13,754 lbs. 8 oz. 10 months, P.
SECOND QUEEN OF ASHLEY, 4171 H. First Duke of Ashley, 627 H. Queen of Ashley, 1509 H. Butter 14 lbs. 2 oz. 7 days, P.
SECOND TRLINTJE KUPERUS, 332 D. F. Dick Swiveler, 35 M. R.; Trijntje Kuperus, 43 M. R. Milk 75 lbs. 4 oz. 1 day, 2009 lbs. 8 oz. 30 days, P.
SECOND UNADILLA TWISK, 32 D. F. Burgomaster of Beemster, 1 D. F.; Maid of Twisk, 1 D. F. Butter 18 lbs. 8 oz. 7 days, P.
SEBIA, 5397 H. Imp. Milk 60 lbs. 1 day, P.
SELIA, 3648 H. Dirk Hatterick, 219 H.; Sumach, 453 H. Milk 7182 lbs. 7 oz. 10 months, A.R.
SELIMA, 1900 H. Dirk Hatterick, 219 H.; Sultana, 1032 H. Milk 9442 lbs. 1 oz. 10 months, A.R.
SELINA, 921 H. F. Consolation, 2661 H.; Calamus, 7925 H. Milk 7116 lbs. 10 months, P.
SEMANTHA, 9215 H. Imp. Milk 65 lbs. 8 oz. 1 day, P. Butter 15 lbs. 4 oz. 7 days, P.
SENORITA, 2193 H. Imp. Milk 71 lbs. 1 day, P.
SEPTIMA, 5181 H. F. Empyrean, 1006 H.; Sumach. 453 H. Milk 6727 lbs. 12 oz. 6 months 9 days, P.
SERADANA, 20838 H. F. Seer, 5027 H. F. Ednab, 6104 H. F. Milk 7613 lbs. 1 year, P.
SETHJE VEEMAN, 930 D. F. Victor Brimsma, 88 P. R.; 2d Durkje Veeman, 226 M. R. Butter 12 lbs. 2 oz. 7 days, A.R.
SETHJE VEEMAN 2D, 9607 H. F. Hamilton, 686 D. F.; Sethje Veeman, 936 D. F. Milk 60 lbs. 8 oz. 1 day, P. Butter 15 lbs. 12 oz. 7 days, P.
SETSKE W, 6578 H. Imp. Milk 527 lbs. 10 days, P. Butter 19 lbs. 4 oz. 7 days, P.
7TH DURKJE VEEMAN'S RUBY, 13297 H. F. Hamilton, 686 D. F.; 7th Durkje Veeman, 1905 D. F. Milk 51 lbs. 1 day, 5579 lbs. 6 months, P.
SEVERINE, 10600 D. F. Billy Draper, 479 D. F.; Janke Hibema, 626 D. F. Milk 59 lbs. 1 day, P.
SHADELAND ALBA 3D, 6048 H. F. Netherland Conqueror, 2476 H.; Shadeland Alba, 8376 H. Milk 50 lbs. 1 day, 8317 lbs. 12 oz. 8 months, A.R.
SHADELAND ADEL, 8377 H. Imp. Milk 306 lbs. 4 oz. 7 days, P. Butter 15 lbs. 12 oz. 7 days, P.
SHADELAND ALBA, 8376 H. Imp. Milk 69 lbs. 7 oz. 1 day, 8784 lbs. 6 oz. 8 months, A.R.
SHADELAND ALMA, 4911 H. Imp. Milk 60 lbs. 1 day, P. Butter 1 lb. 9 oz. 1 day, P.
SHADELAND BELLE, 1421 H. Imp. Milk 10,440 lbs. 11 oz. 10 months, A.R.
SHADELAND BELLE 3D, 6036 H. F. Snadeland Duke, 1693 H.; Shadeland Belle, 1421 H. Milk 68 lbs. 12 oz. 1 day, 9812 lbs. 12 oz. 7 months A.R.
SHADELAND BLISS, 8875 H. Imp. Milk 85 lbs. 4 oz. 1 day, 8150 lbs. 11 oz. 8 months, A.R.
SHADELAND BLOOM, 4919 H. Imp. Milk 83 lbs. 10 oz. 1 day, 10,341 lbs. 10 oz. 6 months, A.R.
SHADELAND BLOOM 2D, 8609 H. Othello of Shadeland, 2376 H.; Shadeland Bloom, 4919 H. Milk 57 lbs. 9 oz. 1 day, 6040 lbs. 13 oz. 7 months, A.R.
SHADELAND BLOOM 4TH, 6067 H. F. Netherland Conqueror, 2476 H.; Shadeland Bloom, 4919 H. Milk 107 lbs. 4 oz. 1 day, 9461 lbs. 6 months, A.R.
SHADELAND BLOSSOM, 4013 H. Imp. Milk 67 lbs. 13 oz. 1 day, 11,092 lbs. 3 oz. 7 months, A.R.
SHADELAND BLOSSOM 2D, 8619 H. Othello of Shadeland, 2576 H.; Shadeland Blossom, 4013 H. Milk 44 lbs. 6 oz. 1 day, 6571 lbs. 9 oz. 7 months, A.R.
SHADELAND BOON, 8887 H. Imp. Milk 69 lbs. 5 oz. 1 day, 10,796 lbs. 5 oz. 9 months, A.R. Butter 31 lbs. 15½ oz. 7 days, 125 lbs. 12 oz. 31 days, A.R.
SHADELAND BOON 2D, 8802 H. Imp. Milk 122 lbs. 8 oz. 1 day, 14,120 lbs. 12 oz. 8 months, A.R.
SHADELAND BREEZE, 8871 H. Imp. Milk 6798 lbs. 5 oz. 10 months, A.R.
SHADELAND BREEZE 2D, 2938 H. F. Shadeland Monarch, 2570 H.; Shadeland Breeze, 8871 H. Milk 69 lbs. 1 day, 0629 lbs. 8 oz 8 months, A.R.
SHADELAND CHARM, 3186 H. Imp. Milk 10,423 lbs. 7 oz. 9 months, A.R.
SHADELAND CHARM 2D, 8621 H. Shadeland Duke, 1693 H.; Shadeland Charm, 3186 H. Milk 63 lbs. 1 day, 10,550 lbs. 12 oz. 8 months, A.R.

MILK AND BUTTER RECORDS. 363

SHADELAND CHARM 3D, 2006 H. F.   Shadeland Monarch, 2570 H.; Shadeland Charm, 3186 H.   Milk 8271 lbs. 1 oz. 7 months, 13 days, A.R.
SHADELAND DAISY, 3181 H.   Imp.   Milk 77 lbs. 11 oz. 1 day, 14,320 lbs. 11 oz. 9 months, A.R.
SHADELAND DAISY 3D, 2960 H. F.   Shadeland Duke, 1693 H.; Shadeland Daisy, 3181 H.   Milk 8408 lbs. 12 oz. 8 months, A.R.
SHADELAND DAMSEL, 3190 H.   Imp.   Milk 8675 lbs. 1 oz. 10 months, A.R.
SHADELAND EVA, 4922 H.   Imp.   Milk 65 lbs. 1 day, 9641 lbs. 8 months, P.
SHADELAND ELITE, 21700 H. F.   Aaggie Alban, 3690 H. F.; Victoria of Shadeland 3d, 10768 H. F.   Milk 293 lbs. 7 days, A.R.   Butter 11 lbs. 10 oz. 7 days, A.R.
SHADELAND FLOSS, 10781 H. F.   Netherland Conqueror, 2476 H.; Shadeland Daisy 3d, 2960 H. F.   Milk 6977 lbs. 8 months, A.R.
SHADELAND FRINGE, 8881 H.   Imp.   Milk 83 lbs. 1 day, 11,165 lbs. 3 oz. 7 months, A.R.
SHADELAND FRINGE 2D, 6055 H. F.   Netherland Conqueror, 2476 H.; Shadeland Fringe, 8881 H.   Milk 55 lbs. 8 oz. 1 day, 7592 lbs. 12 oz 7 months, A.R.
SHADELAND GLEAM, 10782 H. F.   Netherland Conqueror, 2476 H.; Shadeland Charm 2d, 8621 H.   Milk 45 lbs. 8 oz. 1 day, 6740 lbs. 4 oz. 8 months, A.R.
SHADELAND IDLEDENA, 7178 H. F.   Idlewild, 1598 H.; Lopa, 7129 H.   Milk 52 lbs. 1 day, 8184 lbs. 12 oz. 8 months, A.R.
SHADELAND IDLELENA, 7179 H. F.   Idlewild, 1598 H.; Robinette, 7101 H.   Milk 8184 lbs. 12 oz. 8 months, A.R.
SHADELAND JESSIE 2D, 8006 H.   Uranus of Shadeland, 2375 H.; Shadeland Jessie, 4027 H.   Milk 88 lbs. 8 oz. 1 day, 10,478 lbs. 4 oz. 6 months, A.R.
SHADELAND JESSIE 3D, 2080 H. F.   Shadeland Duke, 1693 H.; Shadeland Jessie, 4027 H.   Milk 92 lbs. 1 day, 9402 lbs. 6 months, A.R.
SHADELAND JEWEL, 2407 H.   Imp.   Milk 68 lbs. 8 oz. 1 day, 10,853 lbs. 2 oz. 8 months, A.R.
SHADELAND LASSIE 2D, 8018 H.   Othello of Shadeland, 2570 H.   Shadeland Lassie, 3323 H.   Milk 6892 lbs. 2 oz. 8 months, A.R.
SHADELAND MEMO 2D, 6061 H. F.   Netherland Conqueror, 2476 H.; Shadeland Mema, 8380 H.   Milk 61 lbs. 1 day, 8028 lbs. 8 months, A.R.
SHADELAND MERVA, 8868 H.   Imp.   Milk 558 lbs. 3 oz. 10 days, A.R.
SHADELAND MERVA 2D, 10771 H. F.   Netherland Conqueror, 2476 H.; Shadeland Merva, 8868 H.   Milk 6504 lbs. 8 oz. 8 months, A.R.
SHADELAND NELL, 3180 H.   Imp.   Milk 65 lbs. 2 oz. 1 day, 7213 lbs. 4 oz. 6 months, A.R.
SHADELAND NELL 4TH, 10796 H. F.   Netherland Conqueror, 2476 H.; Shadeland Nell, 3180 H.   Milk 6609 lbs. 12 oz. 7 months, A.R.
SHADELAND NETTENA, 6057 H. F.   Netherland Conqueror, 2476 H.; Shadeland Nettie 2d, 8612 H.   Milk 62 lbs. 8 oz. 1 day, 10,850 lbs. 4 oz. 9 months, A.R.
SHADELAND NETTIE, 3324 H.   Imp.   Milk 63 lbs. 2 oz. 1 day, 11,008 lbs. 6 oz. 9 months, A.R.
SHADELAND NETTIE 2D, 8612 H.   Shadeland Duke, 1693 H.; Shadeland Nettie, 3324 H.   Milk 60 lbs. 8 oz. 1 day, 10,785 lbs. 12 oz. 9 months, A.R.
SHADELAND NUBIA, 8885 H.   Imp.   Milk 77 lbs. 8 oz. 1 day, 11,793 lbs. 14 oz 7 months, A.R.
SHADELAND NUBIA 2D, 10761 H. F.   Netherland Conqueror, 2476 H.; Shadeland Nubia, 8885 H.   Milk 7020 lbs. 4 oz. 8 months, A.R.
SHADELAND OTLEY, 9066 H.   Imp.   Milk 84 lbs. 1 day, A.R.; 11,301 lbs. 7 months, P.
SHADELAND OTLEY 2D, 2904 H. F.   Shadeland Monarch, 2570 H.; Shadeland Otley, 9066 H.   Milk 7154 lbs. 9 oz 7 months, A.R.
SHADELAND OTLEY 3D, 6062 H. F.   Netherland Conqueror, 2476 L.; Shadeland Otley, 9066 H.   Milk 7292 lbs. 13 oz. 9 months, A.R.
SHADELAND PET, 1419 H.   Imp.   Milk 10,928 lbs. 12 oz. 10 months, A.R.
SHADELAND PRIDE 3D, 6046 H. F.   Netherland Conqueror, 2476 H.; Shadeland Echora, 9145 H.   Milk 7043 lbs. 4 oz. 9 months, A.R.
SHADELAND PRIDE 4TH, 10763 H. F.   Netherland Conqueror, 2476 H.; Shadeland Pride, 1428 H.   Milk 7080 lbs. 8 months, A.R.
SHADELAND RENA, 3325 H.   Milk 80 lbs. 4 oz. 1 day, 11,391 lbs. 12 oz. 7 months, A.R.
SHADELAND RENA 2D, 8610 H.   Shadeland Duke, 1693 H.; Shadeland Rena, 3325 H.   Milk 74 lbs. 8 oz. 1 day, 10,836 lbs. 4 oz. 8 months, A.R.
SHADELAND RUBY, 4920 H.   Imp.   Milk 80 lbs. 8 oz. 1 day, 11,764 lbs. 4 oz. 9 months, A.R.
SHADELAND RUBY 2D, 8894 H.   Sir Henry of Aaggie, 1450 H.; Shadeland Ruby, 4920 H.   Milk 55 lbs. 10 oz. 1 day, 11,764 lbs. 4 oz. 9 months, A.R.
SHADELAND RUBY 2D'S EMPRESS, 6051 H. F.   Netherland Conqueror, 2476 H ; Shadeland Ruby 2d, 8894 H.   Milk 67 lbs. 12 oz. 1 day, 8078 lbs. 4 oz. 8 months, A.R.
SHADELAND RUBY 2D'S QUEEN, 10774 H. F.   Netherland Conqueror, 2476 H.; Shadeland Ruby 2d, 8894 H.   Milk 6924 lbs. 6 oz. 8 months, A.R.
SHADELAND STENA, 9144 H.   Imp.   Milk 42 lbs. 9 oz. 1 day, 7240 lbs. 14 oz. 8 months, A.R.
SHADELAND STENA 3D, 10798 H. F.   Netherland Conqueror, 2476 H.; Shadeland Stena, 9144 H.   Milk 6026 lbs. 9 oz. 8 months, A.R.
SHADELAND TARA, 9146 H.   Imp.   Milk 91 lbs. 1 day, 8433 lbs. 12 oz. 7 months, A.R.
SHADELAND TARA 2D, 6052 H. F.   Carlos of Shadeland, 2778 H.   Shadeland Tara, 9146 H.   Milk 7878 lbs. 4 oz. 9 months, A.R.
SHADELAND THYME, 8883 H.   Imp.   Milk 10,762 lbs. 5 oz. 9 months, A.R.
SHADELAND THYME 4TH, 6030 H. F.   Netherland Conqueror, 2476 H.; Shadeland Thyme, 8883 H.   Milk 55 lbs. 1 day, 8821 lbs. 1 oz. 8 months, A.R.
SHADELAND TRIVA, 9153 H.   Imp.   Milk 8582 lbs. 2 oz. 6 months, A.R.
SHADELAND TRIVA 2D, 2995 H. F.   Shadeland Monarch, 2570 H.; Shadeland Triva, 9153 H.   Milk 79 lbs. 8 oz. 1 day, 9092 lbs. 8 oz. 7 months, A.R.
SHADELAND TUNA 2D, 6042 H. F.   Shadeland Monarch, 2570 H.   Shadeland Tuna, 8361 H.   Milk 40 lbs. 14 oz. 1 day, P.
SHADELAND UNA, 10795 H. F.   Netherland Conqueror, 2476 H.; Shadeland Charm 3d, 2996 H. F.   Milk 6614 lbs. 14 oz. 8 months, A.R.
SHADELAND VENIA, 8383 H.   Imp.   Milk 90 lbs. 1 day, 11,852 lbs. 12 oz. 9 months, A.R.
SHADELAND VENIA 2D, 2976 H. F.   Shadeland Monarch, 2570 H.; Shadeland Alba, 8370 H.   Milk 68 lbs. 8 oz. 1 day, 9697 lbs. 4 oz. 8 months, A.R.
SHADELAND WINNIE, 10760 H. F.   Carlos of Shadeland, 2778 H.; Shadeland Queen 2d, 2487 H.   Milk 84 lbs. 1 day, 7888 lbs. 8 oz. 7 months, A.R.
SHAHIS, 8430 H. F.   De Deugd, 150 F.; De Mooie, 1654 F.   Milk 71 lbs. 1 day, P.
SHASTA, 7008 H.   Imp.   Milk 68 lbs. 12½ oz. 1 day, P.

SHENA VIE, 8927 H. Imp. Milk 34 lbs. 9 oz. 1 day, 8000 lbs. 1 year, P.
SHIRLEY, 8247 H. Imp. Milk 39 lbs. 1 day, P.
SIBBELTJE, 147 D. F. Imp. Milk 66 lbs. 1 day, P.
SIBYL, 951 H. Imp. Milk 65 lbs. 6 oz. 1 day, 9616 lbs. 6 oz. 1 year, P. Butter 18 lbs. 3½ oz. 7 days, A.R.
SIBYL 2D, 1380 H. Burley, 394 H.; Sibyl, 951 H. Milk 65 lbs. 8 oz. 1 day, P.; 11,263 lbs. 1 year, A.R. Butter 18 lbs. 3½ oz. 7 days, P.
SIBYL 4TH, 2588 H. F. Prince of Wayne 5th, 1910 H.; Sibyl, 951 H. Milk 44 lbs. 9 oz. 1 day, P. Butter 17 lbs. 3 oz. 7 days, A.R.; 6 lbs. 10 oz. 3 days, P.
SICADO, 1563 D. F. Leeghwater, 279 Neth.; Grietje, 1706 Neth. Butter 9 lbs. 4 oz. 7 days, A.R.
SIEBA NIKO, 9622 H. Imp. Milk 50 lbs. 1 day, 9280 lbs. 10 months, P.
SIEBEREN, 702 H. Imp. Milk 1864 lbs. 30 days, P.
SIEBRIEGJE, 13 D. F. Imp. Milk 45 lbs. 1 day, P.
SIEBRIEGJE 2D, 707 D. F. Moole, 26 M. R.; Siebriegje, 113 M. R. Butter 13 lbs. 8 oz. 7 days, A.R.
SIEMKE, 3992 H. Imp. Milk 63 lbs. 1 day, P.
SIEMKE 2D, 1877 D. F. Rex Twisk, 245 P. R.; Siemke, 1332 P. R. Milk 61 lbs. 10 oz. 1 day, 1669 lbs. 2 oz. 30 days, P. Butter 2 lbs. 3 oz. 1 day, P.
SIEMKE 2D'S BEAUTY, 7797 H. F. Prince of Altijdwerk, 178 D. F.; Siemke 2d, 1877 D. F. Milk 61 lbs. 1 day, 552 lbs. 8 oz. 10 days, P.
SIEMONTJE, 6581 H. Imp. Milk 8581 lbs. 11 oz. 8 months 9 days, P. Butter 19 lbs. 15 oz. 7 days, P.
SIEMPJE, 635 H. Imp. Milk 69 lbs. 1 day, P. Butter 10 lbs. 2 oz. 7 days, P.
SIENTJE 3D, 1383 D. F. Imp. Milk 11,059 lbs. 14 oz. 1 year, A.R. Butter 17 lbs. 6 oz. 7 days, A.R.
SIEPKJE, 120 D. F. Imp. Milk 74 lbs. 1 day, 13,021 lbs. 1 year, P. Butter 12 lbs. 6 days, P.
SIEPKJE 3D, 2387 H. F. Rothmere, 326 D. F.; Siepkje, 120 D. F. Milk 11,109 lbs. 8 oz. 10 months, P. Butter 16 lbs. 7 days, P.
SIEPKJE 4TH, 10349 H. F. Rothmere, 326 D. F.; Siepkje, 120 D. F. Milk 41 lbs. 8 oz. 1 day, 7597 lbs. 188 days, P. Butter 13 lbs. 4 oz. 7 days, P.
SIETSCHE, 7805 H. F. De Deugd, 702 F.; Snitzer, 3726 F. Milk 45 lbs. 1 day, P; 378 lbs. 10 days, A.R.
SIETSKEWAAN 2D, 14085 H. F. Mooie Sjoerd, 235 D. F.; Sietskewaan, 1719 D. F. Milk 60 lbs. 1 day, P. Butter 22 lbs. 7 days, P.
SIEVIA KEYES, 1741 H. F. Keyes 6th, 1692 H.; Daisy A, 3450 H. Milk 65 lbs. 8 oz. 1 day, P.; 2015 lbs. 31 days, A.R.
SIGNET, 1817 H. Imp. Milk 5888 lbs. 2 oz. 349 days, P.
SIJBRANDIJ, 656 D. F. Imp. Milk 55 lbs. 1 day, 1501 lbs. 30 days, P.
SIJKE, 154 D. F. Imp. Milk 40 lbs. 1 day, P.
SIJTJI BLEEKER 2D, 168 D. F. Imp. Milk 50 lbs. 1 day, P.
SIJTJI BLEEKER, 4 D. F. Imp. Milk 81 lbs. 8 oz. 1 day, 14,508 lbs. 6 oz. 1 year, P.
SIJTJE BLEEKER 3D, 715 D. F. Mooie Twisk, 85 P. R; Sijtje Bleeker, 4 D. F. Milk 429 lbs. 10 days, A.R.
SIJ YPMA 2D, 855 D. F. Hendrik Freeks; Ypma. Milk 54 lbs. 1 day, P.
SILENE, 2890 H. Imp. Milk 13,763 lbs. 5 oz. 1 year, P.
SILENE 2D, 6054 H. Prince Imperial, 1164 H.; Silene, 2890 H. Milk 8258 lbs. 5 oz. 1 year, P.
SILHOUETTE, 1787 H. Imp. Milk 71 lbs. 1 day, P.
SILOA, 5579 H. F. Donker 3d, 2321 H.; Knultje 2d, 8342 H. Milk 7441 lbs. 8 oz. 254 days, P.
SILVER BELLE, 971 H. Imp. Milk 52 lbs. 1 day, 6616 lbs. 8 oz. 159 days, P.
SILVERONE, 4611 H. F. Endymion, 817 H.; Pastelijntje Galis, 737 H. Milk 380 lbs. 9 oz. 10 days, A.R.
SILVIO, 1424 H. F. Cossack, 2008 H.; Pavia, 7162 H. Milk 9723 lbs. 9 oz. 10 months, P.
SIMKJE, 5348 H. Imp. Milk 70 lbs. 1 day, P.
SIMPLICITY, 6995 H. Alexander, 83 Neth. Imp. Milk 4239 lbs. 11 oz. 5 months 13 days, P.
SINCERITY, 2892 H. Imp. Milk 40 lbs. 5 oz. 1 day, 12,312 lbs. 12 oz. 1 year, P. Butter 15 lbs. 2 1-2 oz. 7 days, A.R.
SINNEMA'S PEL 2D, 1755 D. F. Pel Koopmans, 301 P. R.; Sinnema, 340 P. R. Milk 8341 lbs. 4 oz 1 year, A.R.
SIR ARCHIBALD'S ORPHIE, 2603 H. F. Sir Archibald, 3045 H.; Orphie, 6257 H. Milk 66 lbs. 1 day, P.
SIRENA, 7450 H. Imp. Milk 06 lbs. 1 day, P. Butter 16 lbs. 7 oz. 7 days, P.
SIR HENRY OF AAGGIE'S ELLAND, 6896 H. Imp. Milk 56 lbs 12 oz. 1 day, 10,003 lbs. 7½ oz. 7 months 24 days, P. Butter 21 lbs. 10 oz. 7 days, A.R.; 91 lbs. 2¾ oz. 30 days, P.
SIR HENRY OF AAGGIE'S LUZELLA, 6886 H. Sir Henry of Aaggie, 1450 H.; Porcellen 2d, 392 Neth. Milk 8725 lbs. 9 months 9 days, P. Butter 18 lbs. 6½ oz. 7 days, P.
SIR HENRY OF AAGGIE'S NAVASTO, 7005 H. Imp. Milk 57 lbs. 1 day, 1412 lbs. 30 days, P.
SIR HENRY OF AAAGGIE'S PHLOX, 6943 H. Imp. Milk 10,024 lbs. 3 oz. 1 year, P.
SISSY, 6114 H. Imp. Milk 57 lbs. 1 day, 16965 lbs. 12 months 11 days, P.
SISSY BAKER, 25667 H. F. Judge Baker, 11884 H. F.; Sissy, 6114 H. Milk 46 lbs. 1 day, 1305 lbs. 30 days, P.
SJERPS, 4262 H. Imp. Milk 36 lbs. 1 day, P.
SJOERD, 71 D. F. Butter 20 lbs. 8 oz. 7 days, A.R.
SJOERD 2D, 161 D. F. Butter 19 lbs. 8 oz. 7 days, A.R.
SJOERD 3D, 229 D. F. Mooie, 26 M. R.; Sjoerd, 161 M. R. Butter 18 lbs. 5 oz. 7 days, P.
SJOERD 5TH, 698 D. F. Mooie, 26 M. R.; Sjoerd 2d, 161 M. R. Butter 15 lbs. 5 oz. 7 days, A.R.
SJOERD 6TH, 700 D. F. Mooie Twisk, 85 P. R.; Sjoerd 3d, 229 P. R. Milk 411 lbs 4 oz. 10 days, A.R.
SJOERD IJEEG, 1082 D. F. Groot Pier, 107 D. F.; Sjoerd, 71 D. F. Milk 75 lbs. 1 day, P.
SLINK 9311 H. Imp. Milk 11,044 lbs. 1 year, P.
SMALL HOPES, 3662 H. Prince of Twisk, 1055 H.; Posch, 2510 H. Milk 441 lbs. 8 oz, 10 days, A.R.; 7963 lbs. 9 oz. 9 months 18 days, A.R.
SMALL HOPES 2D, 5865 H. F. Admiral 2d, 3972 H.; Small Hopes, 3662 H. Milk 10,104 lbs. 4 oz. 1 year. Butter 17 lbs. 6 oz. 7 days, P.
SMIT, 717 Neth. Imp. Milk 73 lbs. 1 day, P.
SNITZER, 3726 F. H. R. Imp. Milk 5 lbs. 1 day, P.
SNOW DROP, 206 D. F Paul Hartog, 6 M. R.; Wilhelma Goudgeld, 41 M. R. Butter 10 lbs. 7 days, P.
SNOW FLAKE 5TH, H. Hamilcar, 17 H.; Agoo, 1 H. Butter 27 lbs. 14 oz. 10 days, P.
SODA, 8846 H. Imp. Butter 9 lbs. 12 oz. 1 day, P.
SODA 3D, 6434 H. F. Billy Boelyn, 189 H.; Soda, 8846 H. Milk 520 lbs. 10 days. A.R.
SOLDENE, 2896 H. Imp. Milk 57 lbs. 15 oz. 1 day, 14,617 lbs. 15 oz. 1 year, P. Butter 13 lbs. 7 days, P.
SOLDENE 2D, 9808 H. Prince Imperial, 1164 H.; Soldene, 2896 H. Milk, 13,808 lbs. 11 oz. 1 year, P. Butter 19 lbs. 7 days, A.R.

MILK AND BUTTER RECORDS. 365

SOLDENE 2D'S CLOTHILDE, 16540 H. F. Clothilde 4th's Imperial, 1281 H. F.; Soldene 2d, 9808 H. Milk 42 lbs. 4 oz. 1 day, 6150 lbs. 4 oz. 8 months, P. Butter 2 lbs. 5 oz. 1 day, P.
SONGSTRESS 1423 H. F. Empyrean, 1006 H.; Ulrica, 1192 H. Milk 7009 lbs. 11 oz. 1 year, P.
SOPHIA, 2974 H. Imp. Milk 84 lbs. 1 day. Butter 17 lbs. 8 oz. 1 day, P.
SOPHIE, 718 H. Imp. Milk 76 lbs. 1 day, P.
SOPHIE 4TH, 6515 H. Climax 204 H.; Sophie, 718 H. Milk 64 lbs. 8 oz. 1 day, P.
SOPHIE ARTIS 3D, 1673 H. F. Viking, 2062 H.; Sophie Artis, 4527 H. Milk 9085 lbs. 12 oz. 1 year, P.
SOPHIE OF TIMBER POINT, 1359 H. F. Imp. Milk 40 lbs. 1 day, P.
SOPHIE SPARKLE, 1172 D. F. Imp. Milk 7080 lbs. 11 oz. 7 months 15 days, P.
SOUTHERN BEAUTY, 860 H. Imp. Milk 68 lbs. 1 day, P.
SOZIE, 6411 H. F. Frank Rice, 2547 H.; Snorrine, 9192 H. Milk 33 lbs. 8 oz. 1 day, P.
SOZINA, 1342 H. Imp. Milk 13,770 lbs. 4 oz. 1 year, P.
SPILETTA, 5188 H. F. Empyrean, 1006 H.; Statira, 7891 H. Milk 8926 lbs. 2 oz. 1 year, P.
SPINAWAY 2D, 2606 H. F. Prince of Artis, 2479 H.; Spinaway, 6953 H. Milk 5307 lbs. 8 months 10 days, P.
SPIRAEA, 7020 H. Imp. Milk 78 lbs. 10 oz. 1 day, 511 lbs. 13 oz. 7 days P.
SPLENDID, 8699 H. Imp. Milk 43 lbs. 15 oz. 1 day, 9579 lbs. 3 oz. 1 year, P. Butter 13 lbs. 10 oz. 7 days, A.R.
SPLENDOR 2D, 2457 H. F. Consolation, 2861 H.; De Hippeld, 5797 H. Milk 60 lbs. 1 day, P.
SPOOK OF UPLANDS, 834 H. F. Lord Bantam, 1011 H.; Gladys, 3063 H. Milk 39 lbs. 12 oz. 1 day, P.
SPRING BELLE, 4596 H. Imp. Milk 45 lbs. 1 day, P.
SPRAT, 10031 H. F. Oatka 3d's Neptune Jr, 4531 H.; Silver Star's Beauty, 3683 H. F. Milk 6761 lbs. 7 months, A.R.
STAPEL 3D, 1226 H. Imp. Milk 60 lbs. 1 day, 10,759 lbs. 10 months, P.
STAPEL 3D C, 8741 H. Clarion, 870 H.; Stapel 3d, 1226 H. Milk 35 lbs. 1 day, 6281 lbs. 10 months, P.
STAPEL 4TH, 2987 H. Johannus, 424 H.; Stapel 3d, 1226 H. Milk 70 lbs. 4 oz. 1 day, P.; 8745 lbs. 8 oz. 8 months 19 days, A.R.
STAPLE, 704 Neth. Imp. Milk 72 lbs. 1 day, P.
STAR, 2345 H Burly, 394 H.; Jenny Lind, 960 H. Milk 74 lbs. 8 oz. 1 day, P.; 14,985 lbs. 6 oz. 1 year, A.R. Butter 20 lbs. 9 oz. 7 days, A.R.
STAR OF NETHERLAND, 3398 H. F. Netherland Duke, 1575 H.; Japonica, 3714 H. Milk 41 lbs. 1 day, P.
STARRETTA, 6113 H. General Grant, 497 H.; Amreal, 8041 R. Milk 56 lbs. 1 day, P.
STAR'S NETHERLAND, 13802 H. F. Duke Netherland, 1271 H. F.; Star, 2345 H. Milk 54 lbs. 5 oz. 1 day, 13,078 lbs. 11 oz. 1 year, P. Butter 20 lbs. 10 oz. 7 days, P.
STARUCCA, 5271 H. Imp. Milk 52 lbs. 8 oz. 1 day, P.
STATELY, 8154 H. Imp. Milk 99 lbs. 1 day, 2489 lbs. 7 oz. 31 days, P.
STEENBEEK, 6588 H. Imp. Milk 91 lbs. 14 oz. 9 months 11 days, P. Butter 10 lbs. 8 oz. 7 days, P.
STEENIE, 1378 H. Pilgrim, 317 H.; Spinola, 763 H. Butter 12 lbs. 2 oz. 7 days, P.
STEINER, 3719 H. F. Flora Clifden's Mercedes Prince 3545 IL.; Tjitske, 5477 Neth. Milk 50 lbs. 1 day, P.
STELLA, 451 H. Imp. Milk 51 lbs. 14 oz. 1 day, 12,984 lbs. 12 oz. 1 year, P. Butter 15 lbs. 8 oz. 7 days, P.
STELLA ARTIS, 4557 H. Artis, 127 Neth.; Princesje, 520 Neth. Milk 72 lbs. 1 day, P.; 12,984 lbs. 1 year, A.R.
STELLA ARTIS 4TH, 7569 H. F. Netherland Statesman, 3280 H.; Stella Artis, 4557 H. Milk 6700 lbs. 14 oz. 8 months, P.
STELLA BARNUM, 8098 H.F. Netherland Alban, 4584 H.; Lady Barnum, 6281 H. Butter 16 lbs. 13½ oz. 7 days, A.R.
STELLAPIA, 12250 H. F. Copia's Empire No. 2, 3914 H. F.; Aaggie Stella 2d, 574 H. F. Milk 7156 lbs. 2 oz. 10 months, P.
STELLETA, 6938 H. Imp. Milk 45 lbs. 11 oz. 1 day, 10,665 lbs. 3 oz. 1 year, P. Butter 15 lbs. 12 oz. 7 days, P.
STEPHANA, 5054 H. Nabob, 719 H.; Hortense, 1500 H. Milk 58 lbs. 1 day. Butter 10 lbs. 2 oz. 7 days, P.
STEVIA, 7921 H. Imp. Milk 900 lbs. 1 month, P.
STIENTJE, 2909 H. Imp. Milk 71 lbs. 1 day, P.
STINS, 4712 H. Imp. Milk 31 lbs. 1 day, P.
STRATTON, 8252 F. H. B. De Roos, 387 F. H. B.; Akke, 209? F. H. B. Milk 38 lbs. 1 day, P.
SUCCESS, 1316 H. Burly, 394 H.; Silver Belle, 971 H. Butter 14 lbs. 7½ oz. 7 days, P.
SUE PEL, 936 H. F. Pel, 122 F. H. B.; Teakje, 1084 F. H. B. Milk 288 lbs. 8 oz. 7 days. Butter 12 lbs. 4 oz. 7 days, P.
SULTANA, 1032 H. Stentor, 346 H.; Hetty, 327 H. Milk 101 lbs. 4 oz. 1 day, A.R.; 22,043 lbs. 8 oz. 1 year, A.R. Butter 9 lbs. 5 oz. 7 days, A.R.
SUMACH, 453 H. Imp. Milk 16,725 lbs. 11 oz. 11 months 19 days, A.R.
SUNBEAM, 864 H. Imp. Milk 67 lbs. 1 day, P.
SUNRISE, 8693 H. Imp. Milk 33 lbs. 7 oz. 1 day, 8348 lbs. 3 oz. 1 year, P. Butter 12 lbs. 4 oz. 7 days, A.R.
SUNSET, 8694 H. Imp. Milk 44 lbs. 1 day, P.; 10,927 lbs. 14 oz. 1 year, A.R Butter 12 lbs. 15 oz. 7 days, A.R.
SUPERB, 961 H. Imp. Milk 73 lbs. 3 oz. 1 day, 2066 lbs. 13 oz. 30 days, P. Butter 15 lbs. 10½ oz., P.
SUPERLATIVE, 7802 H. Imp. Milk 1,448 lbs. 1 year, P.
SURE, 9313 H. Imp. Milk 41 lbs. 1 day, P.
SURILDA, 4153 H. Benson, 1306 H. Jessie, 342 H. Milk 30 lbs. 1 day, P.
SUSANNA, 1523 D. F. Prins, 153 F. H. B.; De Zwarte, 946 F. H. B. Milk 71 lbs. 4 oz 1 day, 1909 lbs. 4 oz. 30 days, P.
SUSAN NIPPU, 1286 H. Imp. Milk 13,569 lbs. 3 oz. 10 months 30 days, P.
SUSIE, 1254 H. Imp. Milk 57 lbs. 12 oz. 1 day, P.
SUSIE LEE, 2900 H. Imp. Milk 15 233 lbs. 15 oz. 1 year, P.
SUSIE LEE 2D, 6468 H. Neptune, 71 H.; Susie Lee, 2900 H. Milk 10,119 lbs. 13 oz. 1 year, P.
SUSIE SPAANZ 2D, 10462 H. F. Jan Wit 13th, 633 H.; Susie Spranz, 2536 H. Milk 40 lbs. 1 day, P.; 9727 lbs. 12 oz. 1 year, A.R. Butter 10 lbs. 7 3-4 oz. 7 days, A.R.
SUSPENSION BRIDGET, 4844 H. F. Emperor William, 2861 H.; Gayanesha, 1928 D. F. Milk 35 lbs. 1 day, 9161 lbs. 1 year, P.
SWARTEAK, 8929 H. Imp. Milk 6100 lbs. 12 oz. 1 year, P.

HOLSTEIN-FRIESIAN CATTLE.

SWEET BOUGH, 7328 H. Lad of Prescott, 2389 H.; Fiirstinn, 1598 H. Milk 442 lbs. 12 oz. 10 days, 10,019 lbs. 10 months, A.R.
SWENODA, 7713 H. Imp. Milk 62 lbs. 1 day, P.
SWOPEJE, 7806 H. F. Garfield, 113 F. H. B.; Kwak, 1644 H. Milk 89 lbs. 1 day, 2135 lbs. 30 days, P.
SYBIL, 9123 H. Mercuries, 242 H.; Doll, 3696 H. Milk 67 lbs. 4 oz. 1 day, 9506 lbs. 6 oz. 1 year. Butter 18 lbs. 3 1-2 oz. 7 days, P.
SYENE, 7712 H. Imp. Milk 64 lbs. 1 day, P
SYKJE, 6347 H. Imp. Milk 80 lbs. 1 day. Butter 19 lbs. 8 oz. 7 days, P.
SYLEA, 1419 H. F. Oswald, 3331 H.; Janina, 7172 H. Milk 10,090 lbs. 1 year, P.
SYLVIA, 573 H. Imp. Milk 91 lbs. 1 day, P.
SYLVIA, 1541 D. F. Rembrandt, 172 F. H. B.; Baaye, 2030 F. H. B. Milk 75 lbs. 1 day, 544 lbs. 4 oz. 10 days, P. Butter 3 lbs. 4 oz. 1 day, P.
SYMPATHY, 3820 H. Imp. Milk 83 lbs. 4 oz. 1 day, P.
SYNER. Imp. Milk 472 lbs. 8 oz. 10 days, P. Butter 19 lbs. 10 days, P.
SYRIA, 6142 H. Imp. Butter 3 lbs. 8 oz. 1 day, P.
SYRIA 2D, 6439 H. F. Trijn Prince, 3184 H.; Syria, 6142 H. Milk 10,939 lbs. 1 year. Butter 448 lbs. 1 year, P.

TACONA, 8142 H. Paragon 1175 H.; Queen of the Hill 3d, 2149 H. Milk 72 lbs. 1 day, 8752 lbs. 10 oz. 11 months, P. Butter 30 lbs. 2 oz. 7 days, P.
TACONA 2D, 4167 H. F. Green Mountain Chief, 4148 H.; Tacona, 8142 H. Milk 48 lbs. 1 day. Butter 22 lbs. 6 oz. 7 days, P.
TAETSTE, 7807 H. F. Oneides, 317 F. H. B.; Saakje, 1502 F. H. B. Milk 66 lbs. 1 day, 1972 lbs. 30 days, P.
TAFFY, 6935 H. Imp. Milk 92 lbs. 1 day, A.R., 4529 lbs. 8 oz. 60 days, A.R. Butter 21 lbs. 4 oz. 7 days, A.R.
TAFFY'S FEDALANA, 5341 H. F. Netherland Convoy, 2934 H. F.; Taffy, 6935 H. Milk 58 lbs. 1 day, 1582 lbs. 8 oz. 30 days, P. Butter 17 lbs. 8 oz. 7 days, A.R.
TAFFY'S FEDALMA, 5341 H. F. Netherland Convoy, 2934 H.; Bonzilla, 6936 H. Milk 1582 lbs. 8 oz. 30 days, A.R.
TAFFY'S TULU OF OAKHURST, 2774 H. F. Prince Imperial, 1104 H.; Taffy, 6935 H. Milk 61 lbs. 1 day, P.; 3157 lbs. 60 days, A.R. Butter 13 lbs. 12 oz. 7 days, A.R.
TALEA, 1351 H. Imp. Milk 61 lbs. 8 oz. 1 day, 780 lbs. 15 oz. 13 days, P.
TALESFORD, 8367 H. Frisco, 480 F. H. B.; Vogel, 4093 F. H. B. Milk 40 lbs. 1 day, P.
TALSMA 2D, 2578 H. Imp. Milk 58 lbs. 8 oz. 1 day. Butter 2 lbs. 4 oz. 1 day, P.
TAN, 0502 H. F. Furst Heksl, 3899 H.; Janauschek 2d, 8297 H. Milk 9865 lbs. 13 oz. 10 months, A.R.
TASTREA, 525 H. Imp. Milk 77 lbs. 8 oz. 1 day, 641 lbs. 9 days, P.
TASTREA 2D, 2064 H. Piet Hein, 316 H.; Tastrea, 525 H. Milk 70 lbs. 1 day, P.
TATTYCORAM, 1024 H. Knickerbocker, 118 H.; Gretchen 3d, 310 H. Milk 68 lbs. 1 day, P.
TEAKJE, 1084 F. H. B. Imp. Milk 70 lbs. 1 day, P.
TEAKJE 3D, 1710 D. F. Oosterbaan, 185 P. R.; Teakje 2d, 355 P. R. Milk 458 lbs. 8 oz. 10 days, A.R.
TEIKJE, 2918 H Imp. Milk 87 lbs. 1 day, 2017 lbs. 30 days, P. Butter 3 lbs. 3 oz. 1 day, P.
TEITJE 2D, 726 H. Imp. Milk 60 lbs. 1 day. Butter 20 lbs. 7 days, P.
TEKLA, 7178 H. Imp. Milk 12,687 lbs. 15 oz. 1 year, P.
TELEGRAPH, 8697 H. De Dengd, 159 F. H. B.; Ruurd Aukes, 203 F. H. B. Milk 41 lbs. 11 oz. 1 day, 5810 lbs. 5 oz. 169 days, P. Butter 12 lbs. 4 oz. 7 days, P.
TELEPHONE, 8608 H. Imp. Milk 41 lbs. 3 oz. 1 day, P.; 9500 lbs. 10 oz. 1 year, A.R. Butter 12 lbs. 4 oz. 7 days, A.R.
TELEPHONE 3D, 10058 H. F. Burly, 304 H.; Telephone, 8608 H. Milk 47 lbs. 12 oz. 1 day, P. Butter 15 lbs. 15 oz. 7 days, A.R.
TELKA 2D, 2045 H. Fifth Consul, 574 H.; Zuyder Zee 17th, 485 H. Milk 60 lbs. 1 day, P.
TENA GOLDEN, 8264 H. Balderik 5th, 1417 H.; Dora Opperdoes, 2233 H. Milk 39 lbs. 1 day, 10,206 lbs. 1 year, P.
TENKE, 6594 H. Imp. Milk 47 lbs. 8 oz. 1 day, P.
TERKJE, 2918 H. Imp. Milk 48 lbs. 1 day, P.
TERPSTRA, 6595 H. Imp. Milk 76 lbs. 15 oz. 1 day, P.; 714 lbs. 13 oz. 10 days, A.R. Butter 23 lbs. 13 oz. 7 days, A.R.
TERPSTRA 2D, 8594 H. Pel, 122 F. H. B.; Terpstra, 6595 H. Milk 43 lbs. 5 oz. 1 day, 293 lbs. 2 oz. 7 days, P. Butter 12 lbs. 12 oz. 7 days, A.R.
TESSAMA, 139 H. F. Pel, 122 F. H. B.; Tiesema, 1461 F. H. B. Milk 487 lbs. 2 oz. 10 days, A.R. Butter 10 lbs. 7 days, A.R.
TET 2D, 4395 H. F. Imp. Milk 56 lbs. 10½ oz. 1 day, P.
TETH NETHERLAND'S GRIETJE, 4329 H. F. Teth Netherland, 3738 H.; Grietje W, 5718 H. Milk 55 lbs. 1 day, P.
TETH NETHERLAND'S OEBELE, 4330 H. F. Teth Netherland, 3738 H.; Oebele, 5722 H. Milk 65 lbs. 1 day, P.
TETTJE JANZEN, 627 D. F. Imp. Milk 70 lbs. 4 oz. 1 day, P.; 445 lbs. 6 oz. 7 days, P. Butter 4 lbs. 10 oz. 1 day, 30 lbs. 9 oz. 7 days, P.
TEXAL NETHERLAND, 3337 H. F. Netherland Duke, 1570 H.; Lady Texal 4th, 10 D. F. Milk 39 lbs. 1 day, P.
TEXELAAR, 51 H. Imp. Milk 76 lbs. 5 oz. 1 day, 4018 lbs. 14 oz. 63 days. Butter 17 lbs. 14 oz. 6 days, P.
TEXELAAR 8TH, 55 H. Zuider Zee 2d, 57 H.; Texelaar, 51 H. Milk 68 lbs. 1 day, P.
TEXELAAR 9TH, 56 H. Van Tromp, 50 H.; Texelaar 3d, 52 H. Butter 12 lbs. 12 oz. 7 days, P.
TEXELAAR 30TH, 1234 H. Benno, 192 H.; Texelaar 29th, 1050 H. Milk 9837 lbs. 1 year, P.
TEXELAAR 30TH'S A 2D, 15220 H. F. Copia's Empire, 3550 H.; Texelaar 30th A, 9479 H. Milk 7751 lbs. 10 months, P.
TEXELAAR 30TH B, 2439 H. F. Clarion, 870 H.; Texelaar 30th, 1234 H. Milk 7944 lbs. 10 months, P.
THEDA OF MAPLECROFT, 3697 H. F. Netherland Alban, 4584 H.; Maid of Maplecroft, 7499 H. But ter 16 lbs. 1 oz. 7 days, P.
THELIA 3D, 536 H. Prairie Duke, 134 H.; Thelia, 462 H. Milk 76 lbs. 1 day. Butter 3 lbs. 2 oz. 1 day, P.
THE MISSUS, 3475 H. F. Count Flanders, 3052 H.; Mira 2d, 3619 H. Butter 11 lbs. 5 oz. 7 days, P.
THEORA, 5527 H. Snowboy, 2046 H.; Camilla 2d, 3916 H. Milk 1224 lbs. 30 days, P.
THETA, 2902 H. Imp. Milk 8056 lbs. 1 oz. 1 year, P.
THETIS, 4012 H. Imp. Milk 52 lbs. 12 oz. 1 day. Butter 20 lbs. 7 days, P.

MILK AND BUTTER RECORDS. 367

THIRD MAARTJE KORNDYKE, 17 D. F. Burgomaster, 1 D. F.; Maartje Korndyke, 8 D. F. Milk 68 lbs. 1 day, P.
THISBE V, 1816 H. Imp. Butter 16 lbs. 10 oz. 7 days, A.R.
THISTLEDOWN, 7980 H. Imp. Milk 58 lbs. 1 day, 10,625 lbs. 1 year, P.
THORA, 7918 H. Imp. Milk 64 lbs. 1 day, 14,937 lbs. 1 year, P. Butter 16 lbs. 12 oz. 7 days, P.
TIESMA, 1461 F. H. B. Imp. Milk 73 lbs. 1 day, P.
TIE-TIE, 10402 H. Imp. Milk 54 lbs. 1 day. Butter 11 lbs. 2 oz. 7 days, P.
TIETJE VON HOLINGEN, 17210 H. F. Imp. Milk 76 lbs. 1 day, P.
TIETJE 2D., 726 H. Imp. Milk 65 lbs. 1 day, P.; 410 lbs. 7 days, A.R. Butter 20 lbs. 7 days, A.R.
TIETJE 5TH. Jaap, 452 H.; Tietje 2d., 726 H. Butter 10 lbs. 10 oz. 7 days, A.R.
TIETJE 6TH, 642 H. F. Mercedes Prince, 2150 H.; Tietje 2d, 726 H. Milk 27 lbs. 11 oz. 1 day, 303 lbs. 5 oz. 10 days, P. Butter 24 lbs. 15 oz., P.
TIET KAASTRA, 982 D. F. Imp. Milk 59 lbs. 2 oz. 1 day, 11,587 lbs. 9 oz. 1 year, P.
TIET KAASTRA 2D, 2501 H. F. Pel 2d, 327 D. F.; Tiet Kaastra, 982 D. F. Milk 60 lbs. 6 oz. 1 day, 13,255 lbs. 14 oz. 1 year, P.
TIET KAASTRA 3D, 14163 H. F. Duke of Woodrid, 2401 H. F.; Tiet Kaastra, 982 D. F. Milk 5757 lbs. 9 oz. 9 months, P.
TIETTIE, 680 D. F. Butter 21 lbs. 13 oz. 7 days, P.
TILDA, 535 H. Imp. Milk 63 lbs. 1 day, P.
TILDA 2D, 1079 H. Prince Opperdoes 987 H.; Tilda, 535 H. Milk 364 lbs. 10 oz. 7 days, 10,080 lbs. 336 days. Butter 16 lbs. 13 oz. 7 days, P.
TIMBER POINT BEAUTY, 1362 H. F. Imp. Milk 48 lbs. 1 day. Butter 11 lbs. 12 oz. 7 days, P.
TINA CLIFDEN 2D, 6406 H. Hilt, 860 H.; Tina Clifden, 1584 H. Milk 69 lbs. 1 day. Butter 17 lbs. 7 days, P.
TINAJ, 512 H. Imp. Milk 45 lbs. 1 day, P.
TINTA PEL, 1706 D. F. Prince of Altjidwerk, 178 P. R.; Pel 4th, 194 P. R. Milk 55 lbs. 1 day. Butter 26 lbs. 4 oz. 14 days, P,
TIRA, 10030 H. F. Oatka 3d's Neptune Jr., 4531 H.; Marble, 8206 H. Milk 7511 lbs. 8 months 10 days, A.R.
TIRANIA, 6716 H. Imp. Milk 91 lbs. 1 day, 536 lbs. 12 oz. 10 days, P. Butter 3 lbs. 12 oz. 1 day, 36 lbs. 11 oz. 7 days, P.
TIRANIA 2D, 12605 H. F. Sir Henry of Maplewood, 2933 H.; Tirania 6716 H. Butter 22 lbs. 8 oz. 7 days, P.
TIRANIA 4TH, 29976 H. F. Artis Peer, 6048 H. F.; Tirania, 6716 H. Milk 48 lbs. 1 day. Butter 2 lbs. 8 oz. 1 day, P.
TITA, 2381 H. Burly, 393 H.; Crystal, 948 H. Milk 36 lbs. 6 oz. 1 day, 1008 lbs. 30 days, P. Butter 8 lbs. 6 oz. 7 days, P.
TJALKJE, 669 D. F. Imp. Milk 61 lbs. 11 oz. 1 day, 1735 lbs 5 oz. 30 days, I . Butter 17 lbs. 1 oz. 7 days, A.R.
TJALKJE 2D, 4510 H. F. Sportsman, 3480 H.; Tjalkje, 669 D. F. Milk 60 lbs. 1 day, P.
TJALMA, 1510 D. F. Imp. Milk 60 lbs. 15 oz. 1 day, P.
TJALMA 3D, 18604 H. F. Siemke's Prince, 1973 H. F.; Tjalma, 1510 D. F. Milk 60 lbs. 15 oz. 1 day, P.
TJALMA 3D'S LADY, 29209 H. F. Kroontje Champion, 10179 H. F.; Tjalma 3d. Milk 42 lbs. 2 oz. 1 day, 403 lbs. 13 oz. 10 days, P.
TJALTJE, 3738 H. Imp. Milk 61 lbs. 11 oz. 1 day. Butter 17 lbs. 1 oz. 7 days, P.
TJERK, 224 D. F. Mooie, 26 M. R.; Andrieske, 123 M. R. Butter 16 lbs. 14 oz. 7 days, A.R.
TJITSKE, 5477 H. Imp. Milk 60 lbs. 1 day, P.
TJITSKE SWART, 407 D. F. Imp. Milk 48 lbs. 4 oz. 1 day. Butter 2 lbs. 1 day.
TNSCH, 11824 H. F. Pieter, 10 Aux F. H. B.; Froukje, 1480 F. H. B. Milk 41 lbs. 1 day, 1061 lbs. 30 days, P.
TOBAGO, 8435 H. F. Imp. Milk 82 lbs. 1 day, 2141 lbs. 30 days, P. Butter 22 lbs. 13 oz. 7 days, P.
TOL, 7318 H. F. Garnet, 1576 H.; Annsie, 718 D. F. Milk 68 lbs. 1 day, P.
TOLBERT, 2306 F. H. B. Imp. Milk 64 lbs. 1 day, P.
TOLLA NIKO, 9615 H. Imp. Milk 8786 lbs. 12 oz. 1 year, P.
TOLONA, 7506 H. Imp. Milk 42 lbs. 4 oz. 1 day, P.
TOLSMA HARTOG, 7967 H. F. Mooie Hartog 4th, 418 D. F.; Aaltje Tolsma, 1110 D. F. Butter 17 lbs. 7 days, P.
TONQUIN, 8428 H. F. Imp. Milk 93 lbs. 1 day, 2215 lbs. 30 days, P. Butter 23 lbs. 11 oz. 7 days, P.
TONY, 1766 H. Compeer 200 H.; Lady Delight, 1766 H. Milk 11,680 lbs. 1 year. Butter 2 lbs. 9 oz. 1 day, P.; 18 lbs. 1 oz. 7 days, P
TONY'S LADY DELIGHT, 2952 H. F. Count Flanders, 3152 H.; Tony, 1766 H. Butter 11 lbs. 12 oz. 7 days, P.
TOPAZ, 870 H. Kees, 51 Neth.; Jacoba, 263 Neth. Milk 37 lbs. 13 oz. 1 day, 14,630 lbs. 2 oz. 1 year, P. Butter 13 lbs. 3 oz. 7 days, P.
TOPAZ 3D, 2106 H. Netherland Prince, 716 H.; Topaz, 807 H. Milk 3325 lbs. 2 oz. 4 months, 23 days, P.
TOPAZ 3D'S HENRIETTA, 1580 H. F. Sir Henry 2d of Aaggie, 1451 H.; Topaz 3d, 2106 H. Milk 52 lbs. 1 day, P. Butter 19 lbs. 13½ oz. 7 days, A.R.
TOPAZ 4TH, 3577 H. Neptune, 711 H.; Topaz, 870 H. Milk 42 lbs. 3 oz. 1 day; 11,480 lbs. 12 oz. 1 year, A.R. Butter 13 lbs. 13½ oz. 7 days, P.
TOPSEY, 61 H. Hollander, 20 H.; Dowager, 7 H. Milk 70 lbs 1 day, 6005 lbs. 5 months, P.
TOSTEE 2D, 4334 H. Gortus, 642 H.; Tostee, 465 H. Milk 40 lbs. 1 day, P.
TOURMALINE, 7020 H. Milk 20 lbs. 4 oz. 1 day. Butter 13½ oz. 7 days, A.B.
TOURMALINE'S MERCEDES, 10556 H. F. Mercedes Prince, 2150 H.; Tourmaline, 7020 H. Milk 413 lbs. 8 oz. 10 days, 9381 lbs. 10 months, A.R. Butter 13 lbs. 9 oz. 7 days, A.R.
TRANQUILITY, 6978 H. Imp. Milk 58 lbs. 12 oz. 1 day, 10,302 lbs. 1 year. Butter 2 lbs. 8 oz. 1 day, P.
TREASURE, 8689 H. Imp. Milk 41 lbs. 11 oz. 1 day, 9984 lbs. 14 oz. 1 year, P. Butter 12 lbs. 12 oz. 7 days, A.R.
TREASURE 2D, 85 H. F. Jacob 2d, 463 Neth.; Treasure, 8689 H. Milk 39 lbs. 10 oz. 1 day, 11,045 lbs. 3 oz. 1 year. Butter 11 lbs. 12 oz. 7 days, P.
TREASURE 2D'S TREASURE, 10949 H. F. Young America, 1 H. F.; Treasure 2d, 85 H. F. Milk 310 lbs. 6 oz. 7 days, P. Butter 15 lbs. 4 oz. 7 days, P.
TREUITJE, 1919 N. H. B. Imp. Milk 34 lbs. 1 day, P.
TRIEN, 6596 H. Imp. Milk 40 lbs. 1 day, P.
TRIFLE, 1888 H. Imp. Milk 70 lbs. 1 day, 1878 lbs. 30 days, P.
TRIJN, 3025 H. Imp. Milk 61 lbs. 3 oz. 1 day, 13,349 lbs 12 oz. 1 year, P. Butter 15 lbs. 8 oz. 7 days, P.

TRIJNTJE, 2043 H. Imp. Milk 95 lbs. 1 day, 8204 lbs. 10 months. Butter 18 lbs. 9 oz. 7 days.
TRIJNTJE KUPERUS, 43 D. F. Imp. Milk 9134 lbs. 8 oz. 7 months 11 days, A R.
TRILIUM, 8849 H. Imp. Milk 40 lbs. 8 oz. 1 day, 8092 lbs. 8 oz. 1 year, P.
TRINTJEAN, 6775 H. Imp. Milk 53 lbs. 6 oz. 1 day. P.
TRIPPIF, 5180 H. F. Empyrean, 1006 H.; Dawn, 277 H. Milk 4793 lbs. 1 year, P.
TRITOMIA, 4004 H. Imp. Milk 82 lbs. 10 oz. 1 day, P.; 2962 lbs. 8 oz. 30 days, A.R. Butter 25 lbs. 8½ oz. 7 days, A.R.
TRITOMIA 2D, 4567 H. F. Netherland Prince, 716 H.; Tritomia, 4004 H. Butter 22 lbs. 4 oz. 7 days, P.
TROOSTJE 2D, 979 H. Imp. Milk 49 lbs. 12 oz. 1 day, 1365 lbs. 30 days, P.
TROZINES PANZY, 5447 H. Imp. Milk 40 lbs. 8 oz. 1 day, P.
TRUMPETTA 2D, 10829 H. F. Barrington, 2103 H.; Trumpetta, 5168 H. Milk 49 lbs. 1 day, P.; 5010 lbs. 4 months, P.
TRUNDY, 19084 H. Kees, 701 F. H. B.; Trijntje, 3721 F. H. B.. Milk 56 lbs. 1 day, P.
TRUTH, 5024 H. Imp. Milk 89 lbs. 1 day, 2089 lbs. 30 days. Butter 24 lbs. 7 oz. 7 days, P.
TRYNIE, 2015 H. F. Willem 2d, 183 Neth.: Trijntje, 1643 Netb. Milk 51 lbs. 1 day, 9050 lbs. 1 year, P.
TRYNTJE, 35 Neth. Imp. Milk 80 lbs. 10½ oz. 1 day, P.
TRYNTJEAN, 6775 H. Imp. Milk 53 lbs. 6 oz. 1 day, P.
TRYNTJE BLAAR, 5673 H. Imp. Milk 200 lbs. 4 days, P.
TRYNTJE BRANTJES, 6010 H. Imp. Milk 12,780 lbs. 1 year, A.R.
TRYNTJE DE YONG, 17212 H. F. Imp. Milk 64 lbs. 1 day, P.
TRYNTJE KLENE, 6446 H. Imp. Milk 12,521 lbs. 4 1-2 oz. 10 months, A.R.
TRYNTJE LINCOLN, 6450 H. Imp. Milk 55 lbs. 1 oz. 1 day, 5388 lbs. 4 months, P.
TRYNTJE OF ACHLUM, 6597 H. Imp. Milk 56 lbs. 1 day, P.
TRYNTJE VON HOLINGEN. 17207 H. F. Imp. Milk 76 lbs. 1 day, P.
TRYNTJE VELTHUS, 5467 H. Imp. Milk 52 lbs. 8 oz. 1 day, P.
TRYPHOSA, 7761 H. Imp. Milk 37 lbs. 1 day, P.
TULIP KONING, 156 D. F. Imp. Milk 40 lbs. 1 day, P.
TULLIA, 8094 H. Imp. Milk 63 lbs. 1 day, 5343 lbs. 5 months, 10 days, P.
TULLIA'S AAGGIE ROSA PRINCESS, 9038 H. F. Aaggie Rosa Prince, 3132 H.; Tullia, 8094 H. Milk 63 lbs. 1 day, P.
TWEEDLEDUM, 6951 H. Imp. Milk 10,604 lbs. 4 oz. 1 year, P.
TWILINE, 467 H. Imp. Milk 77 lbs. 8 oz. 1 day, P.
TWILINE 3D, 1154 H. Fifth Prince of Orange, 243 H.; Twiline, 467 H. Milk 60 lbs. 1 day. Butter 20 lbs 7 days, P.
TWINKLE, 652 H. Fifth Prince of Orange, 243 H.; Twiline, 467 H.; Milk 39 lbs. 4 oz. 1 day, P.
TYGERIN PYZN 2D, 15004 H. F. Pierre, 1348 H.; Tygerin Pyzn, 5693 H. Milk 46 lbs. 1 day, P.

UBE, 92 Aux F. H. B. Imp. Milk 84 lbs. 1 day, P.
ULA SILVA, 1528 H. F. Mazda, 2672 H.; Silva Flora, 3853 H. Milk 68 lbs. 1 day, 1959 lbs. 30 days, P.
ULA SILVA 3D, 20471 H. F. Jack Spaanz, 8311 H. F.; Ula Silva, 1528 H. F. Milk 5781 lbs. 6 months, P.
ULEJE S, 5476 H. Imp. Milk 59 lbs. 9 oz. 1 day, 285 lbs. 1 1-2 oz. 5 days, P. Butter 17 lbs. 7 days, P.
ULRICA, 1192 H. Poke, 320 H.; Wytske, 483 H. Milk 10,146 lbs. 15 oz. 10 months, A.R.
UMATILLA, 7187 H. Imp. Milk 595 lbs. 4 oz. 10 days, A.R.
UNAWEEP, 7191 H. Imp. Milk 15,147 lbs. 1 year, P.
UNDINE, 2D, 3853 H. Uncle Tom, 163 H.; Undine, 913 H. Milk 10,942 lbs. 8 oz. 8 months 29 days, A.R.
UNDINE 3D, 4190 H. Baron, 2133 H.; Undine 2d, 3868 H. Milk 6795 lbs. 9 months, 12 days, A.R.
URSINA, 7214 H. Imp. Milk 8885 lbs. 9 oz. 1 year, P.
URSULA, 1189 H. Poke, 320 H.; Agate, 263 H. Milk 6002 lbs. 1 year, P.
UTOPIA, 5299 H. Imp. Milk 75 lbs. 1 day, P.

VALENTINE, 10140 H. Imp. Milk 54 lbs. 10 oz. 1 day, 1638 lbs. 37 days, P.
VALLEY BEAUTY, 4562 H. Imp. Milk 62 lbs. 7 oz. 1 day, 17,009 lbs. 8 oz. 1 year, P.
VALLEY BEAUTY 2D, 4532 H. De Valk, 160 Neth.; Valley Beauty, 4562 H. Milk 54 lbs. 13 oz. 1 day, 12137 lbs. 13 oz. 1 year, P.
VALLEY BEAUTY 3D, 4533 H. De Valk, 160 Neth.; Valley Beauty, 4562 H. Milk 9096 lbs. 1 year, P. Butter 13 lbs. 8½ oz. 7 days, P.
VALLEY BEAUTY 4TH, 6477 H. Netherland Prince, 716 H.; Valley Beauty, 4562 H. Milk 5633 lbs. 7 months. Butter 16 lbs. 8½ oz. 7 days, P.
VALLEY QUEEN, 851 H. Imp. Milk 38 lbs. 11 oz. 1 day, 1085 lbs. 9 oz. 30 days, P.
VAN DER GOOT, 4456 F. H. B. Imp. Milk 75 lbs. 1 day, P.
VAN DER LEI 2D, 4496 F. H. B. Imp. Milk 68 lbs. 1 day, P.
VAN DER LEI 3D, 1722 D. F. Imp. Milk 77 lbs. 2 oz. 1 day, P.; 18,803 lbs. 5 oz. 1 year, A.R.. Butter 17 lbs, 13 oz. 7 days, A.R.
VAN DER LESSIJE, 5147 F. H. Lincoln, 120 Neth.; Paulina, 4288 Neth. Milk 11,536 lbs. 1 year, P.
VAN DER VALK, 11827 H. F. Alva, 415 F. H. B.; Van der Valk, 3229 F. H. B. Milk 74 lbs. 1 day, P., 441 lbs. 10 days, P.
VAN DER VALK, 3229 F. H. B. Imp. Milk 74 lbs. 1 day, P.
VAN FRIESLAND, 4986 H. Imp. Milk 60 lbs. 1 day, P.
VANITY, 4824 H. Imp. Milk 597 lbs. 8 oz. 10 days, A.R.
VASALINE, 15023 H. F. Fairmont Tom, 2448 H.; Nancy Dewdrop, 5465 H. Milk 50 lbs. 1 day, 298 lbs. 12 oz. 6 days, P.
VEEDER, 8429 H. F. Oscar, 564 F. H. B.; Bleske, 1500 F. H. B. Milk 51 lbs. 1 day, 1405 lbs. 30 days, P. Butter 19 lbs. 7 oz. 7 days, P.
VEEDERZAAM, 8257 H. F. Groote Jan, 534 F. H. B.; Jeltje, 2230 F. H. B. Milk 54 lbs. 1 day, P.; 390 lbs. 10 days, A.R.
VELLINGA, 362 D. F. Imp. Milk 67 lbs 4 oz. 1 day, 12,459 lbs. 2 oz. 1 year, P.
VENETIA, 7984 H. Imp. Milk 1106 lbs. 5 oz. 30 days, P.
VENEZUELA, 6674 H. F. Wilfred, 506 D. F.; Nikosla, 1679 D. F. Butter 18 lbs. 6½ oz. 7 days, A.R.
VENIE, 1515 D. F. Geertje, 2330 F. H. B.; Phillippus, 156 F. H. B. Butter 9 lbs. 7 oz. 7 days, A.R.
VENLOE 4TH, 5121 H. F. Pentaur, 3849 H.; Venloe, 600 H. Butter 16 lbs. 12½ oz. 7 days, A.R.
VENUS, 875 H. Imp. Milk 51 lbs. 2 oz. 1 day, 1209 lbs. 12 oz. 30 days, P.
VENUS 3D, 2308 H. Storm King, 626 H.; Venus, 875 H. Milk 58 lbs. 1 day, P.
VENUS 4TH, 3753 H. Iroquois, 1074 H.; Venus, 875 H. Milk 38 lbs. 1 day, 9108 lbs. 8 oz. 270 days, P.

MILK AND BUTTER RECORDS. 369

VENUS 5TH, 5095 H. F. Viking, 2062 ℍ.; Venus, 875 H. Milk 8227 lbs. 2 oz. 10 months 19 days, P. Butter 14 lbs. 9¼ oz. 7 days, A.R.
VERA L, 2936 H. Imp. Milk 72 lbs. 1 day, P.
VERBENA, 1600 H. Anton, 642 H.; Violet, 743 H. Milk 61 lbs. 1 day, P.
VERDA, 966 H. F. Bouwke 2d, 262 Neth.; Grietje, 723 H. Milk 46 lbs. 1 day, P.
VERONA NETHERLAND, 9160 H. F. Netherland Duke, 1571 H.; Leila Promoter, 1744 H. F. Milk 40 lbs. 1 day, P.
VERO NIKO 0621 H. Imp. Milk 70 lbs. 1 day, 9833 lbs. 12 oz. 1 year, P. Butter 2 lbs. 6 oz. 1 day, 12 lbs. 13 oz. 7 days, P.
VERVAIN, 9049 H. Imp. Milk 78 lbs. 1 day. Butter 19 lbs. 7 oz. 7 days.
VERVAIN 2D, 759 H. F. Imp. Milk 42 lbs, 1 day, P.
VESTA, 1429 D. F. Rauward, 25 M. R.; Rienks, 452 P. R. Butter 15 lbs. 7 days. P.
VEVIE, 666 H. Imp. Milk 9071 lbs. 4 oz. 1 year, P.
VIANNA, 5195 H. F. Sancho, 3002 H.; Quantock, 7182 H. Milk 8040 lbs. 2 oz. 1 year, P.
VICTORIA OF SHADELAND, 2421 H. Imp. Milk 8099 lbs. 12 oz. 10 months, A.R.
VICTORIA OF SHADELAND, 10768 H. F. Netherland Conqueror, 2476 H.; Victor a of Shadeland, 2421 H. Milk 7132 lbs. 4 oz. 8 months, A.R.
VIDETTE, 4268 H. Imp. Milk 78 lbs. 8 oz. 1 day, P.
VILLONIA, 8527 H. Pierpont, 1352 H.; Veres, 4722 H. Milk 35 lbs. 8 oz. 1 day, P.
VINCA, 6985 H. Imp. Milk 40 lbs. 4 oz. 1 day, P.
VINETA, 473 H. Hector, 107 H.; Adele, 68 H. Milk 63 lbs. 1 day. 8261 lbs. 0 months, P.
VINNIE, 1637 H. Imp. Milk 92 lbs. 1 day. Butter 24 lbs. 9 oz. 7 lays, P.
VIOLET, 743 H. Imp. Milk 86 lbs. 12 oz. 1 day, 18,677 lbs. 4 oz. 1 year, P. Butter 19 lbs. 9 oz. 7 days, P.
VIOLETA, 7306 H. Billy Boelyn, 180 H.; Violet, 743 H. Milk 45 lbs. 1 day, 9213 lbs. 8 oz. 1 year, P. Butter 15 lbs. 4 oz. 7 days, P.
VIOLET BELLADONNA, 9380 H. Wouter, 400 H.; Violet, 743 H. Milk 70 lbs. 8 oz. 1 day, 14, 504 lbs. 1 year, P. Butter 15 lbs. 2 oz. 7 days, P.
VIOLET BELLADONNA 3D, 8013 H. F. Billy Boelyn, 180 H.; Violet Belladonna, 9380 H. Milk 47 lbs. 8 oz. 1 day. Butter 11 lbs. 1 oz. 7 days, P.
VIOLET CYBELE, 770 H. F. Violet King, 4210 H.; Cybele, 5291 H. Milk 75 lbs. 1 day, P.
VIOLET MUGGINS, 1265 H. F. Violet King, 4210 H.; Muggins, 609? H. Milk 50 lbs. 1 day, P.
VIOLET NIN, 8017 H. F. Violet King, 4210 H.; Nin, 8839 H. Milk 44 lbs. 1 day, P.
VIOLET VERBENA, 9388 H. Anton, 402 H.; Violet, 743 H. Milk 69 lbs. 8 oz. 1 day. Butter 12 lbs. 5 oz. 7 days, P.
VITA, 6149 H. Imp. Milk 86 lbs. 8 oz. 1 day, P.
VLEEL, 2947 H. F. Leip 2d, 2557 H.; Vleelgeefster 7th, 3223 H. Milk 12,544 lbs. 10 months. A.R. Butter 22 lbs. ¼ oz. 7 days, A.R.
VLEEL 2D, 9753 H. F. Van Kon Friesland, 1949 H. F.; Vleel, 2947 H. F. Butter 15 lbs. 14½ oz. 7 days, A.R.
VLEEL GEEFSTER 7TH, 3223 H. Imp. Milk 40 lbs. 1 day, P.
VOGEL, 4093 F. H. B. Imp. Milk 68 lbs. 1 day, P.
VOGEL 2D, 814 D. F. Imp. Milk 15,130 lbs. 1 year, P. Butter 18 lbs. 4 oz. 7 days, A.R.
VOGELTJE, 800 D. F. Imp. Milk 77 lbs. 5½ oz. 1 day, P.
VOLINIA, 5603 H. Imp. Milk 50 lbs. 8 oz. 1 day. Butter 13 lbs. 4 oz. 7 days, P.
VOLINIA 2D, 5102 H. F. Herder, 2331 H.; Volinia, 5603 H. Milk 5283 lbs. 4 oz. 9 months 25 days, P. Butter 11 lbs. 9 oz. 7 days, A.R.
VORA, 14011 H. F. Sultano, 3496 H. F.; Medora, 1038 H. Milk 3099 lbs. 0 oz. 3 months, P.
VREDA, 2250 H. Imp. Milk 67 lbs. 1 day, 1878 lbs. 31 days, P.
VROUKJE, 2585 H. Imp. Milk 75 lbs. 1 day, P.
VROUWKJE, 129 D. F. Imp. Milk 45 lbs. 1 day, P.

WABUSCA, 7226 H. Imp. Milk 10,740 lbs. 1 oz. 10 months, P.
WACONETA 2D, 5603 H. F. Armory, 3345 H.; Waconeta, 7235 H. Butter 13 lbs. 4 oz. 7 days, 1.
WACONSTA, 4267 H. Imp. Milk 81 lbs. 2 oz. 1 day, P.
WADMANTJE 7TH. 1308 D. F. Imp. Milk 71 lbs. 8 oz. 1 day, P.
WAIBOER'S ANTJE 3D, 813 D. F. Cornelius, 195 Neth.; Antje 2d, 1516 H. F. Milk 13,617 lbs. 10 oz. 10 months 25 days, A.R.
WAKALEE, 7239 H. Imp. Milk 10,579 lbs. 1 oz. 10 months, P.
WAKAZOO, 4723 H. Arlington, 477 H.; Altje, 2566 H. Milk 56 lbs. 1 day, P.
WALMA, 1504 F. H. B. Imp. Milk 68 lbs. 1 day, P.
WALTHAM MAID, 1987 H. Imp. Milk 45 lbs. 2 oz. 1 day, P.
WANDA, 2243 H. Imp. Milk 304 lbs. 8 oz. 7 days, A.R. Butter 6 lbs. 15 oz. 7 days, A.R.
WAPSIE PRINCESS, 9240 H. F. Wapsie Prince, 2990 H. F.; Index, 987 H. Butter 14 lbs. 7½ oz. 7 days, P.
WARDELL, 12083 H. F. Simson, 30 Aux F. H. B.; Pietje, 268 Aux F. H. B. Milk 61 lbs. 1 day, 1170 lbs. 30 days, P.
WARGA, 5753 H. Imp. Milk 62 lbs, 1 day, P.
WARGA BEAUTY, 6362 H. Imp. Milk 41 lbs. 1 oz. 1 day. Butter 1 lb. 12 oz. 1 day, P.
WASSENAAR, 3998 F. H. B. Imp. Milk 77 lbs. 1 day, 11,679 lbs. 8 oz. 10 months, A.R.
WAUSAU, 7701 H. Imp. Milk 40 lbs. 4 oz. 1 day, P.
WAVELET, 3369 H. Dirk Hatterick. 219 H.; Wytske, 483 H. Milk 7502 lbs. 6 oz. 10 months, A.R.
WAVERLY, 5284 H. Imp. Milk 62 lbs. 1 day, P.
WAWONA RAY, 7692 H. Imp. Milk 338 lbs. 10 days. Butter 1 lb. 12 oz. 1 day, P.
WEA, 1348 H. Imp. Milk 71 lbs. 1 day, P.
WEGDAL RAY, 7085 H. Imp. Milk 11 690 lbs. 10 months, A.R. Butter 15 lbs 7½ oz. 7 days, A.R.
WEIBJE, 11828 H. F. Alva, 415 F. H. B.; Ketelaar, 3231 F. H. B. Milk 41 lbs. 1 day, 1194 lbs. 30 days, P.
WEIGER, 232 D. F. Oosterzee, 15 M.R.; Jantje, 5 A.R. Milk 63 lbs. 8 oz. 1 day, 1240 lbs. 30 days, P.
WEIJER, 2311 F. H. B. Imp. Milk 61 lbs. 8 oz. 1 day P.
WELCOME, 1620 D. F. Hjerre, 225 F. H. E. Milk 60 lbs. 1 day, P.
WELLFLEET, 12035 H. F. Johannes, 085 F. H. B.; Bonte Tweeling, 4332 F. H. B. Milk 60 lbs 1 day, 1593 lbs. 30 days, P. Butter 18 lbs. 5 oz. 7 days, P.
WERRA, 3150 H. Imp. Milk 65 lbs. 1 day, P.
WESSELINA, 1022 H. Imp. Milk 68 lbs. 1 day, P.
WHISPER, 10137 H. Imp. Milk 55 lbs. 1 day, P.

WHISPER 3D, 6685 H. F. Gold Foil, 1237 H.; Whisper, 10137 H. Milk 40 lbs. 1 day, P.
WHITE TAIL. 1862 H. F. Lubbert, 3384 H.; Maartqui, 8624 H. Milk 431 lbs. 8 oz. 10 days, A.R.
WIBBINA, 5170 H. Imp. Milk 50 lbs. 1 day, P.
WICHITA, 4941 H. Dirk Hatterick, 219 H.; Dawn, 277 H. Milk 8142 lbs. 3 oz. 1 year.
WIDE AWAKE, 6875 H. Imp. Milk 77 lbs. 12½ oz. 1 day, P.
WIDGEON, 5629 H. Imp. Milk 91 lbs. 4 oz. 1 day, P.; 10,409 lbs. 2 oz. 9 months 18 days, A.R. Butter 19 lbs. 9 oz. 7 days, A.R.
WIEBE 2D, 3277 H. Imp. Milk 60 lbs. 1 day, P.
WIEBKJE, 11828 H. F. Alva, 415 F. H. B.; Ketelaar, 3231 F. H. B. Milk 41 lbs. 1 day, 1194 lbs. 30 days, P.
WIEDMAN'S TINETTE, 5670 H. Imp. Milk 64 lbs. 6½ oz. 10 days, A.R.
WIEPJE, 143 D. F. Imp. Milk 50 lbs. 1 day, P.
WIERSMA, 5622 H. Imp. Milk 73 lbs. 3½ oz. 1 day. P.
WIETSKE's PAPOOSE, 28810 H. F. Mondamin's Barrington, 2433 H. F.; Wietske, 2573 H. Milk 353 lbs. 6 oz. 7 days, A.R. Butter 15.6 lbs. 7 days, A.R.
WILD ROSE, 987 H. Imp. Milk 35 lbs. 4 oz. 1 day, 1007 lbs. 12 oz. 30 days, P.
WILD ZWAAN, 478 H. Imp. Milk 81 lbs. 1 day, P.
WILHELMA GOUDGELD, 41 D. F. Imp. Milk 9184 lbs. 9 months, 5 days, A.R.
WILHELMINA, 739 H. Imp. Milk 45 lbs. 1 day, P.
WILLEMENKE, 7171 F. H. B. Imp. Milk 44 lbs. 1 day, 426 lbs. 10 days, P.
WINANA, 4697 H. Imp. Butter 17 lbs. 14 oz. 7 days, A.R.
WINKLE, 667 H. Imp. Milk 64 lbs. 1 day, P.
WINNABOWKEY, 7566 H. Imp. Milk 60 lbs. 1 day, P.
WINNEMISSITT, 7664 H. Imp. Milk 56 lbs. 8 oz. 1 day, P.
WINNEMUCCA, 790 H. Imp. Milk 12,228 lbs. 10 months 17 days, P.
WINNIE HOMET, #217 H. F. Mahomet, 289 H.; Wibbina, 5170 H. Milk 46 lbs. 1 day, P.
WINSOME, 480 H. Fifth Prince of Orange, 243 H.; Berenice, 97 H. Milk 45 lbs. 12 oz. 1 day, 7822 lbs. 8 oz. 333 days, P.
WINSOME MAID, 4575 H. Imp. Milk 55 lbs. 1 day, 1504 lbs. 30 days, P.
WINSUM, 2261 H. Imp. Milk 9602 lbs. 9 months 5 days, P.
WIRDUM, 9656 H. Imp. Milk 487 lbs. 8 oz. 10 days, A.R. Butter 13 lbs. 7 days, A.R.
WISSAHICKON, 4016 H. F. Netherland King, 1924 H.; Lakeside Edella, 10009 H. Milk 12,009 lbs. 8 oz. 1 year, A.R.
WISTERIA, 5343 H. Imp. Milk 75 lbs. 1 day, P.
WISTERIA 2D, 6440 H. Billy Boelyn, 189 H.; Wisteria, 5343 H. Milk 45 lbs. 1 day, P.
WITCH OF BROOKLAWN, 5948 H. Meadow Prince, 1154 H.; Madame Augusta, 2806 H. Milk 62 lbs. 1 day, P.
WITHOOFD 2D, 1439 D. F. Withoofd, District Bull of Twisk. Milk 75 lbs. 1 day, P.
WITKOP 2D, 266 D. F. Burg Hartog, 3 M. R.; Witkop, 75 M. R. Milk 50 lbs. 1 day. Butter 14 lbs. 8 oz. 7 days, P.
WITKOP 2D's BEAUTY, 4287 H. F. Prince of Monroe, 1630 H.; Witkop 2d, 266 D. F. Milk 56 lbs. 3 oz. 1 day, 10,057 lbs. 9 months 25 days, P. Butter 26 lbs. 7 oz. 7 days, P.
WITSMUT, 91 F. H. B. Imp. Milk 77 lbs. 1 day, P.
WITTEVEEN, 1557 D. F. Excelsior, 266 Neth.; Aaltje, 1095 Neth. Butter 9 lbs. 8 oz. 7 days, A.R.
WITTOF, 675 H. Imp. Milk 56 lbs. 1 day, 382 lbs. 8 oz. 7 days, P. Butter 19 lbs. 5½ oz. days, A.R.
WITTOF 2D, 1446 H. F. Don Quixote. 1324 H.; Wittof, 675 H. Milk 56 lbs. 10 oz. 1 day, 363 lbs. 2 oz. 7 days. Butter 21 lbs. 1 oz. 7 days, A.R.
WITZYDE SJOT, 18815 H. F. Tecumseh Witzyde, 5967 H. F.; Sjut, 1009 D. F. Milk 60 lbs. 1 day. Butter 15 lbs. 7 days, P.
WONDER, 952 H. Imp. Milk 60 lbs. 3 1-5 oz. 1 day, P.; 7096 lbs. 7 oz. 10 months, A R. Butter 13 lbs. 12 ½ oz. 7 days, P.
WOODBINE, 8686 H. Imp. Milk 45 lbs. 13 oz. 1 day, 10,717 lbs. 13 oz. 1 year, P. Butter 12 lbs. 15 oz. 7 days, A.R.
WOODLAND QUEEN, 7953 H. F. Inka's Duke, 2580 H. Milk 62 lbs. 5 oz. 1 day, P.; 343 lbs. 4 oz. 7 days, A.R. Butter 15.4 lbs. 7 days, A.R.
WOPKE 2D, 3279 H. F. Imp. Milk 59 lbs. 1 day, P.
WOUTER, 6567 H. Imp. Milk 56 lbs. 8 oz. 1 day, P.
WYDAAR, 8827 H. Imp. Milk 10,480 lbs. 10 months. 24 days, P.
WYNTJE, 481 H. Imp. Milk 9534 lbs. 324 days, P.
WYTHE KEY, 7641 H. Imp. Milk 50 lbs. 1 day, 516 lbs. 10 days, P.
WYTSE LEE, 1632 D. F. Imp. Milk 22 lbs. 1 day, P.
WYTSKE, 483 H. Imp. Milk 11,907 lbs. 13 oz. 9 months 19 days, A.R.

XALPHA, 9168 H. Imp. Milk 81 lbs. 1 day, P.

YAMPA KEY, 7632 H. Imp. Milk 426 lbs. 10 days, P.
YANKEE GIRL, 7522 H. Imp. Milk 71 lbs. 4 oz. 1 day, 1692 lbs. 12 oz. 27 days, P.
YAPHANK, 7629 H. Imp. Milk 45 lbs. 4 oz. 1 day, P.
YARLAND, 8098 H. Imp. Milk 80 lbs. 8 oz. 1 day, 2157 lbs. 30 days, P.
YENTJE 2D, 1446 D. F. De Watergeus, 239 P. R.; Yentje, 662 P. R. Milk 386 lbs. 12 oz. 7 days, 10,848 lbs. 10 months, A.R. Butter 16 lbs. 7 days. A.R.
YEREA MAYO, 7570 H. Imp. Milk 57 lbs. 8 oz. 1 day, P.
YETENNE, 7128 H. Imp. Milk 274 lbs. 12 oz. 7 days. Butter 11 lbs. 4 oz. 7 days, P.
YINGST KEY. 7610 H. Imp. Milk 61 lbs. 1 day, 1696 lbs. 4 oz. 30 days, A.R. Butter 20 lbs. 2 oz. 7 days, P.
YLSTRA'S HINKE 3D, 1357 D. F. Imp. Milk 71 lbs. 1 day, P.; 10,401 lbs. 8 oz. 11 months 4 days, A.R.
YODH, 8168 H. F.; Simon 3d, 1477 H.; Dinah, 1892 H. Milk 80 lbs. 1 day, P.
YONGE GALIS, 8226 H. Imp. Milk 78 lbs. 1 day, P.
YOPHANK, 7629 H. Imp. Milk 45 lbs. 4 oz. 1 day, P.
YOTA MAYO, 7572 H. Imp. Milk 39 lbs. 12 oz. 1 day, P.
YOUNG KEILWIER, 4982 H. Imp. Milk 61 lbs. 1 day, P.
YOUNG NIEROP, 2514 H. Imp. Milk 78 lbs. 10½ oz. 1 day, P.
YPSILANTE, 7597 H. Imp. Milk 50 lbs. 1 day, 1550 lbs. 1 month, P. Butter 18 lbs. 3½ oz. 7 days, A.R.
YPSILANTE 2D, 4582 H. F. Jacob, 608 H.; Ypsilante, 7597 H. Milk 56 lbs. 1 day, P.; 9710 lbs. 12 oz. 10 months, A.R. Butter 14 lbs. 7¾ oz. 7 days, A.R.
YREKA MAYO, 7570 H. Imp. Milk 57 lbs. 8 oz. 1 day, P.

YSDELL, 928 H. Imp. Milk 71 lbs. 1 day, P.
YTJE, 1628 H. Imp. Milk 78 lbs. 1 day, P.
YTJE 2D, 2272 H. Claudius Civilus, 6 F. H. B.; Ytje, 1628 H. Milk 50 lbs. 1 day, P.

ZALEDA, 6105 H. F. Promoter, 1518 H.; Owandah, 8771 H. Milk 10,742 lbs. 1 year, P.
ZAPATO MAYO, 7537 H. Imp. Milk 43 lbs. 8 oz. 1 day, P.
ZAPP LIDA, 6365 H. Lunter, 2664 H.; Zapp Mayo, 7528 H. Milk 48 lbs. 1 day. 1234 lbs. 1 month, P. Butter 64 lbs. 8 oz. 31 days, P.
ZARA, 7380 H. Milk 3263 lbs. 6 oz. 2 months, A.R. Butter 20 lbs. 9 oz. 7 days, A.R.
ZARD MAYO, 7527 H. Imp. Milk 57 lbs. 12 oz. 1 day. Butter 15 lbs. 12 oz. 7 days, P.
ZAZETTE, 6950 H. Imp. Milk 76 lbs. 1 oz. 1 day, P.
ZEDLAR MAYO, 7530 H. Imp. Milk 43 lbs. 12 oz. 1 day, P.
ZELIE, 3957 H. Netherland Prince, 756 H.; Czarina, 1837 H. Milk 40 lbs. 13 oz. 1 day, P.
ZELL MAYO, 7524 H. Imp. Milk 40 lbs. 1 day, P.
ZENNIA, 7171 H. F. McCullough, 3095 H.; Corretta, 5111 H. Milk 81 lbs. 1 day, 2350 lbs. 31 days, P.
ZEPHYR, 949 H. Imp. Milk 42 lbs. 1 day, 8130 lbs. 6 oz. 1 year, P.
ZERLINA, 494 H. Eighth Highland Chief, 90 H.; Zuider Zee 5th 64 H. Milk 64 lbs. 1 day, P.
ZETTA, 2353 H. F. Klaas Dekker, 4411 H.: Bariah, 10065 H. Milk 32 lbs. 1 day, P.
ZIBIAH, 10643 H. Hamilton, 686 D. F.; 2d Sethje Veeman, 1006 D. F. Milk 54 lbs. 1 day, 1438 lbs. 30 days, P.
ZIDDA, 2165 H. Duplicate, 2326 H.; Kerkineer 2d, 3238 H. Milk 404 lbs. 10 days, A.R. Butter 10 lbs. 14 oz. 7 days, A.R.
ZIEWIE, 1406 H. Imp. Milk 60 lbs. 1 day, P.
ZILLIE, 2166 H. Duplicate, 2326 H.; Grietje Rauwerd, 5728 H. Milk 400 lbs. 8 oz. 10 days, A.R. Butter 9 lbs. 12 oz. 7 days, A.R.
ZILLIE'S KONINGIN, 13501 H. F. Zillie, 2166 H. F. Butter 27 lbs. 14 oz. 15 days, A.R.
ZINA B, 5872 H. F. Major J, 2442 H.: Zora 2d, 1412 H. Butter 0 lbs. 14 oz. 7 days, A.R.
ZINKA, 3042 H. Imp. Milk 84 lbs. 1 day, P.
ZOBEIDEY, 3813 H. F. Groot 3d, 393 Neth.; De Jong, 4100 Neth. Milk 42 lbs. 1 day. Butter 1 lbs. 3 oz. 7 days, P.
ZOPHA, 1176 H. Imp. Milk 54 lbs. 1 day, 1437 lbs. 30 days, P.
ZORA 2D, 1412 H. Imp. Milk 50 lbs. 1 day, P.
ZORAYDA, 5705 H. F. Gilroy, 3079 H.; Afke Lee, 5714 H. Milk 474 lbs. 12 oz. 10 days, P.; 10,686 lbs. 10 months 14 days, A.R.
ZOZO, 10260 H. Endymion, 817 H.; Pauline Paul, 2199 H. Milk 83 lbs. 1 oz. 1 day, P. Butter 25 lbs. 10½ oz. 7 days, 104 lbs. 12 oz. 1 year, A.R.
ZOZO'S PRINCESS, 6320 H. F. Forster, 2771 H.; Zozo, 10260 H. Butter 18 lbs. 12 oz. 7 days, P
ZUCK MAYO, 7549 H. Imp. Milk 40 lbs. 1 day, P.
ZUIDHOCKSTER, 546 B. F. Milk 9820 lbs. 10 months, A.R.
ZUIDHOCKSTER 2D, 7144 H. Imp. Milk 6742 lbs. 10 months, A.R.
ZULU ZONG, 3097 H. St. Elmo, 714 H. Albarda, 1175 H. Milk 837 lbs. 10 days. Butter, 28 lbs. 5 oz. 7 days, A.R.
ZUR 2D, 10437 H. F. Clink, 3481 H.; Zur, 9393 H. Milk 394 lbs. 4 oz. 7 days, A.R. Butter 16 12 lbs. 7 days, A.R.
ZUURBIER LASS, 3812 H. F. Groot 3d, 393 Neth.; Zuurbier, 4107 Neth. Milk 41 lbs. 1 day, P.
ZWAAN, 234 H. Imp. Milk 71 lbs. 4 oz. 1 day, 13,403 lbs. 1 year, P.
ZWANTJE, 3743 H. Imp. Milk 89 lbs. 1 day, 2110 lbs. 30 days, P. Butter 10 lbs. 2 oz. 7 days, P.
ZWART BELSUMER, 7808 H. F. Doede, 563 F. H. B.; Belsumer, 2015 F. H. B. Milk 55 lbs. 1 day, 1427 lbs. 30 days, P.
ZWARTE, 2034 H. Imp. Milk 70 lbs. 1 day, 500 lbs. 250 days, P. Butter 19 lbs. 4 oz. 7 days, P.; 38 lbs. 8 oz. 14 days, P.
ZWARTHAK, 5534 H. F. Imp. Milk 72 lbs. 1 day, P.
ZWARTHAH, 1647 F. H. B. Imp. Milk 76 lbs. 1 day, P.
ZWARTJE, 4699 H. Imp. Milk 79 lbs. 1 day, P.
ZWARTKOP, 600 H. Imp. Milk 12.379 lbs. 10 months, P.
ZWARTSY, 2503 H. Imp. Milk 70 lbs. 1 day, 2483 lbs. 2 oz. 30 days, A.R.
ZWARTSY'S NETHERLAND, 9340 H. F. Duke Netherland, 1271 H.; Zwartsy, 2503 H. Milk 42 lbs. 8 oz. 1 day, P.
ZWATKOF, 2925 H. F. Jacob, 215 Neth.; De Zwartkop, 4265 Neth. Milk 10.289 lbs. 11 months 21 days, P.
ZWELLE, 10852 H. Tell, 128 D. F.: Auke, 364 D. F. Milk 11,474 lbs. 13 oz. 1 year, P.
ZWELLO, 10853 H. F. Tell, 128 D. F. Auke, 364 D. F. Milk 7481 lbs. 15 oz. 10 months, P.
ZWEN, 10854 H. F. Tell, 128 D. F.; Vellinga, 362 D. F. Milk 10,701 lbs. 10 oz. 1 year, P.
ZWIGU'S BEAUTY, 6372 H. Imp. Milk 55 lbs. 8 oz. 1 day. Butter 14 lbs. 9½ oz. 7 days, P.
ZWOBKJE, 135 D. F. Imp. Milk 49 lbs. 1 day, P.
ZYP 3D, 4740 H. Johannus, 428 H.; Zyp 2d, 1231 H. Milk 49 lbs. 1 day, 7205 lbs. 9 months, P.
ZYP 3D A, 9117 H. F. Hilda's Empire, 3562 H.; Zyp 3d, 4740 H. Milk 6210 lbs. 9 months, P.
ZYP 3D B. Mooike 2d's Clarion, 1905 H.; Zyp 3d, 4740 H. Milk 6588 lbs. 96 days, P.